AF605787

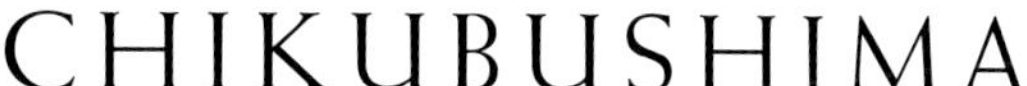

CHIKUBUSHIMA

Deploying the Sacred Arts in Momoyama Japan

CHIKUBUSHIMA

ANDREW M. WATSKY

UNIVERSITY OF WASHINGTON PRESS

SEATTLE • LONDON

Chikubushima was published with the assistance of the Getty Grant Program.

This book also received generous support from the Publications Committee, Department of Art and Archaeology, Princeton University, and from the Blakemore Foundation.

Photo acquisition and publication rights were supported by a grant from The Metropolitan Center for Far Eastern Art Studies.

Printed in China
Design by Sigrid Albert

10 09 08 07 06 05 04 5 4 3 2 1

University of Washington Press
PO Box 50096
Seattle, WA 98145
www.washington.edu/uwpress

Library of Congress Cataloging-in-Publication Data

Watsky, Andrew Mark, 1957–
Chikubushima : deploying the sacred arts in Momoyama Japan / Andrew M. Watsky.
p. cm.
Includes bibliographical references and index.
ISBN 0-295-98327-2 (alk. paper)
1. Art, Japanese—Japan—Chikubu Island. 2. Art and religion—Japan—Chikubu Island. 3. Art, Japanese—Kamakura–Momoyama periods, 1185–1600. I. Title.

N7356.C48W38 2003
709'.52185—dc21 2003046764

The paper used used in this publication meets the minimum requirements of American National Standard for Information Sciences—Permanence of Paper for Printed Library Materials, ANSI Z39.48-1984.

In memory of

Ueda Akira (1926–1997)

He opened my eyes to the Momoyama

Contents

List of Abbreviations / VIII

Note to Readers / IX

PREFACE *Considering Chikubushima* / XI

Acknowledgments / XIII

INTRODUCTION *The Sacred and Momoyama Japan* / 3

1 *Chikubushima, from Its Origins to the Ascendancy of Hideyoshi* / 39

2 *Hideyoshi and the Sacred: Manipulating Convention* / 69

3 *Encoding the Sacred* / 101

4 *The Material of the Sacred* / 143

5 *After Hideyoshi: Hideyori's Enlistment of the Sacred* / 197

6 *Hideyori and Chikubushima's New Ensemble* / 231

EPILOGUE *Chikubushima in Post-Toyotomi Japan* / 267

Notes / 275

Appendix / 309

Bibliography / 323

Illustration Credits / 337

Index / 339

List of Abbreviations

CM	*Chikubushima monjo*
DNS	*Dai Nihon shiryō*
GJN	*Gien Jugō nikki*
HAGS	*Higashi Asai Gun shi*
JEKK	*Jōe Enmyō Kokushi kyohakuroku*
KTJHSKH	Kokuhō Tsukubusuma Jinja Keidai Shuppansho, ed., *Kokuhō Tsukubusuma Jinja Honden shūri kōji hōkokusho*
RN	*Rokuon nichiroku*
SK	*Shunkyū ki*
T	*Taishō shinshū Daizōkyō*
TCH	Nagahama Castle Historical Museum, *Tokubetsuten: Chikubushima Hōgonji*
TN	*Tamon'in nikki*

Note to Readers

All Japanese names are listed in the traditional Japanese manner, family name followed by given name. Months and days are given according to the lunar calendar, which was used in Japan during the period covered in this book, although years are rounded to the closest equivalent according to the Western calendar: for example, Tenshō 19.8.4 refers to the fourth day of the eighth month of 1591.

Revised portions of my articles, "Floral Motifs and Mortality: Restoring Numinous Meaning to a Momoyama Building," *Archives of Asian Art* 50 (1997–1998), pp. 62–92, and "Sutemaru no gen'ei: Tsukubusuma Jinja Honden moya o megutte," *Bijutsu kenkyū,* no. 366 (February 1997), pp. 51–76, appear with permission in Chapter 3.

Below is a list of the English translations of the names of the Japanese museums and collections used in this book, followed by their Japanese names:

Gotoh Museum	Gotō Bijutsukan
Ishikawa Prefectural Museum of Art	Ishikawa Kenritsu Bijutsukan
Itabashi Art Museum	Itabashi Kuritsu Bijutsukan
Itsuō Art Museum	Itsuō Bijutsukan
Kanagawa Prefectural Museum	Kanagawa Kenritsu Hakubutsukan
Kyoto National Museum	Kyōto Kokuritsu Hakubutsukan
Masaki Museum of Art	Masaki Bijutsukan
Mitsui Bunko Foundation	Mitsui Bunko
MOA Museum of Art	MOA Bijutsukan
Museum of Modern Art, Shiga	Shiga Kenritsu Kindai Bijutsukan
Museum Yamato Bunkakan	Yamato Bunkakan
Nagahama Castle Historical Museum	Shiritsu Nagahamajō Rekishi Hakubutsukan
Nagoya City Museum	Nagoya Shi Hakubutsukan
Nara National Cultural Properties Research Institute	Nara Bunkazai Kenkyūjo
Nara Prefectural Museum of Art	Nara Kenritsu Bijutsukan
National Museum of Japanese History	Kokuritsu Rekishi Minzoku Hakubutsukan
Nezu Institute of Fine Arts	Nezu Bijutsukan
Osaka Castle	Ōsakajō Tenshukaku
Osaka City Museum	Ōsaka Shiritsu Hakubutsukan
Sakai City Museum	Sakai Shi Hakubutsukan

Sezon Museum of Art	Sezon Bijutsukan
Shizuoka Prefectural Museum of Art	Shizuoka Kenritsu Bijutsukan
Sunritz Hattori Museum of Arts	Sanritsu Hattori Bijutsukan
Suntory Museum of Art	Santorii Bijutsukan
Tokugawa Art Museum	Tokugawa Bijutsukan
Tokugawa Museum	Tokugawa Hakubutsukan
Tokyo Metropolitan Central Library	Tōkyō Toritsu Chūō Toshokan
Tokyo Metropolitan Edo-Tokyo Museum	Tōkyō To Edo Tōkyō Hakubutsukan
Tokyo National Museum	Tōkyō Kokuritsu Hakubutsukan
Tokyo National University of Fine Arts & Music	Tōkyō Geijutsu Daigaku
Wakayama Prefectural Museum	Wakayama Kenritsu Hakubutsukan
Yokohama History Museum	Yokohama Shi Rekishi Hakubutsukan

PREFACE

Considering Chikubushima

Today most people consider the island of Chikubushima, if they consider it at all, to be a remote and peripheral place. The northern tip of Lake Biwa in Shiga Prefecture, where it is located, is almost off the modern map of urbanized Japan, on the fringe of commuting distance to the nearest city of size, Kyoto. The quickest route to the island from Kyoto requires an hour's express-train ride, followed by a healthy walk or a taxi to the shores of the lake, and then a forty-minute trip by high-speed boat. Chikubushima is now best known as the thirtieth of thirty-three stops on the centuries-old Western Japan pilgrimage route dedicated to the popular Buddhist deity Kannon, and visiting devotees hurry up a long, steep flight of stairs to a booth where they receive the stamps and inscriptions that verify they made the holy journey. For non-pilgrims, and there are many of them today, the island is a scenic destination for an afternoon outing; the row of souvenir stands at the boat landing is crowded with people buying the customary tourist trinkets or beer to enjoy in the arcadian setting. Few of these modern visitors, pilgrim or tourist, spend much more than one hour on the island before they are herded back onto the boats for the return trip to the mainland.

More than twenty years ago I was one of the latter types of visitors. I lived in the nearby town of Hikone, and I found myself drawn to the island several times just to enjoy its unfamiliar beauty. At the time I had no sense of what it preserved in its architecture and art, though I admit to enjoying a beer or two. The grandson, son, and brother of roofing professionals, I have only one photograph of any building on the island from that time, a picture looking down onto a dramatically curved roof. In 1989, when I was a graduate student at Princeton University, I came upon a book that reproduced a set of refined paintings whose caption indicated that they were located in a building on

Chikubushima. With my memory of the place awakened, I chose those paintings as the subject of my seminar paper. As I worked, the subject broadened into an examination of the larger context of the paintings, including the architecture, lacquer, woodcarvings, and other ornament that together created an entire ensemble of decoration. That paper developed, in turn, into a Ph.D. dissertation topic. Now, a decade later, I am still studying that ensemble, as well as the island where it is located, and many of the historical events and religious practices that shaped and are reflected in them. I have visited the island countless times over the past decade, and I continue to be drawn by its remarkable appeal. The beer still tastes good, too.

Acknowledgments

I am indebted to countless people, in Japan, in Europe, and in the United States, for their help in completing this book. My deepest gratitude goes to Mr. Ikushima Itsuo, Head Priest of the Tsukubusuma Jinja, who during my numerous research trips allowed me virtually unlimited access to the main focuses of the book, Chikubushima and the building he ministers there. Portions of the book derive from my doctoral dissertation, in the writing of which I received the steadfast support of Professors Yoshiaki Shimizu and Martin Collcutt of Princeton University, and Professors Tsuji Nobuo and Sasaki Jōhei, who sponsored my studies, respectively, at the University of Tokyo and Kyoto University.

Numerous friends, colleagues, and teachers have assisted me at every step along the way, and—more than this simple list might suggest—I am deeply grateful to them all: Asao Naohiro, Robert Bagley, John Boorsch, Chino Kaori, Annalisa Clink, Bruce Coats, Michael Cooper, Doi Michihiro, Patricia Fister, Barbara Ford, Sherry Fowler, Fujii Keisuke, Christine Guth, Haino Akio, Dax Kajiwara, Sinéad Kehoe, Anne Rose Kitagawa, Konno Toshifumi, Kōno Motoaki, Kumamoto Hideto, Irving Lavin, Gregory Levine, Yukio Lippit, Melissa McCormick, Murata Gen, Murose Kazumi, Nagaoka Yumiko, Richard Peterson, Joseph Richard, Sakurai Toshio, Satō Yoshio, Jacqueline Stone, Takeuchi Jun'ichi, Melanie Trede, Takeda Tsuneo, Richard Watsky, Mary Yakush, and Mimi Yiengpruksawan. Each according to his or her individual expertise has helped me in important ways.

And there are many others. Itō Futoshi, Katō Hiroshi, Kitagawa Hiroshi, Ōta Hiroshi, and Suzuki Hiroyuki have been especially and continually helpful over the long course of my research. Kanai Morio extended himself greatly to help me acquire many photographs both in and out of the Kyoto National Museum. I am grateful, too, for the support of my colleagues at Vassar, and also of my students, historians of Japanese art who have gone on to careers as artists, lawyers, and veterinarians—and even art historians and whose enthusiasm for Japanese art has been an inspiration. I offer an overdue note of appreciation to my first art history teacher and a most cherished mentor, William Hood of Oberlin College, who, for perhaps the first and only time in his life, turned a student onto a path that led to Japan. Special thanks are reserved for Dr. Tsujimura Ryūzō and his family, and my many friends in Hikone. I am indebted to the University of Washington Press, and especially Michael Duckworth, for embracing this project and realizing it in its final form. Naomi Noble Richard, editor extraordinaire, has kept me on my toes—and revising at the computer—for the last several years. The mistakes that remain, despite the best efforts of these many supporters (and of many others whose names could also grace this page), are my own.

I have been the fortunate recipient of many research grants, without which I could not have completed the book. In its early stages my research was generously supported by a Japan Foundation Dissertation Fellowship; a Fulbright-Hays Doctoral Dissertation Research Abroad Fellowship; a Metropolitan Center for Far Eastern Art Studies Doctoral Grant; a Mellon Fellowship in the Humanities; and a grant from the Joint Committee on Japanese Studies of the Social Science Research Council and the American Council of Learned Societies. More recently I have received generous grants from the National Research Institute for Cultural Properties, Tokyo, the Northeast Asia Council of the Association for Asian Studies and, especially, Vassar College.

I am grateful to my families, both in the United States and in Japan, for their encouragement throughout my work on this book. My wife, Chiharu, has sustained me always; Amy and Cy have kept it all in perspective.

Poughkeepsie, N.Y.
2003

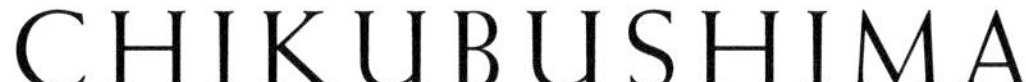

CHIKUBUSHIMA

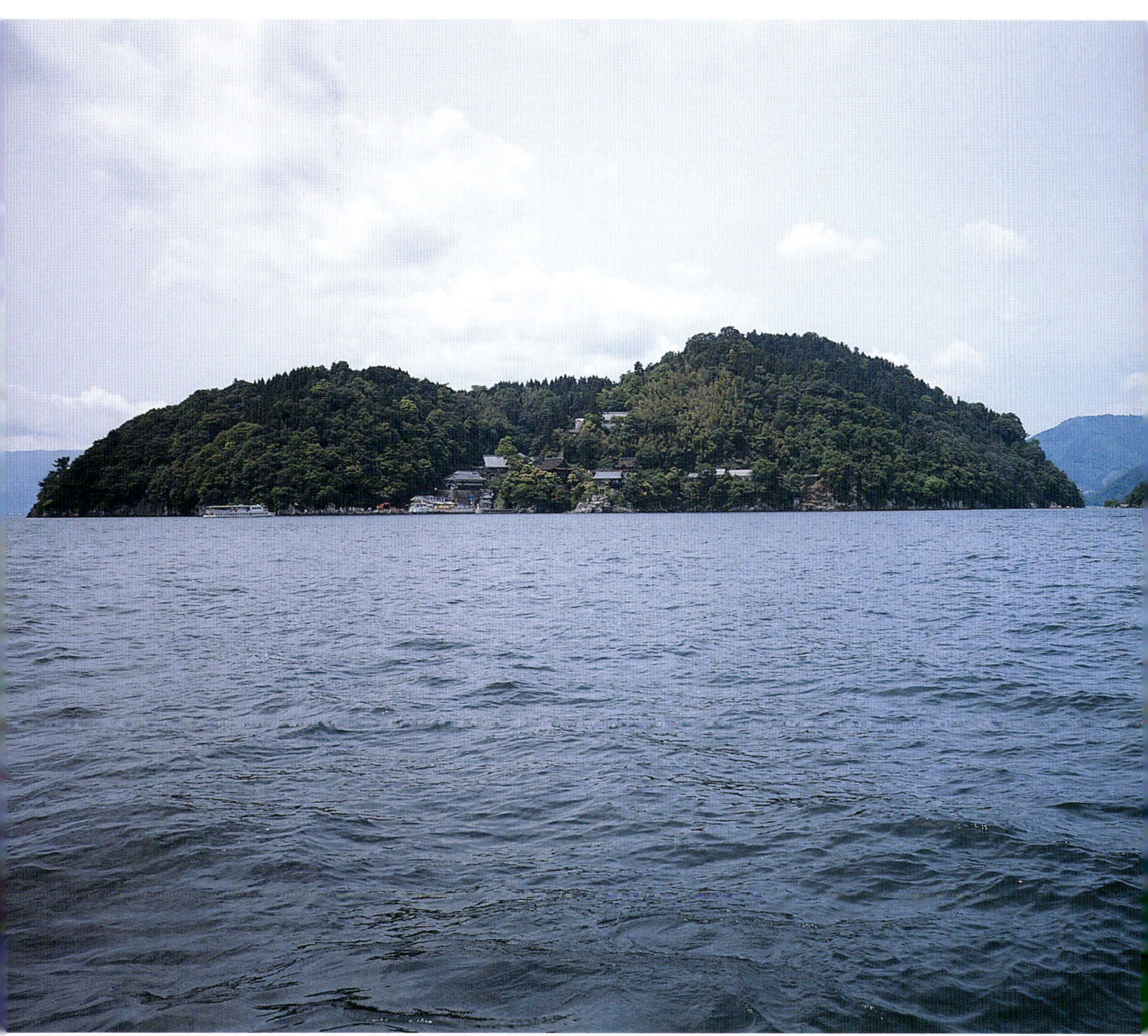

FIG. 1 Chikubushima, Shiga Prefecture.

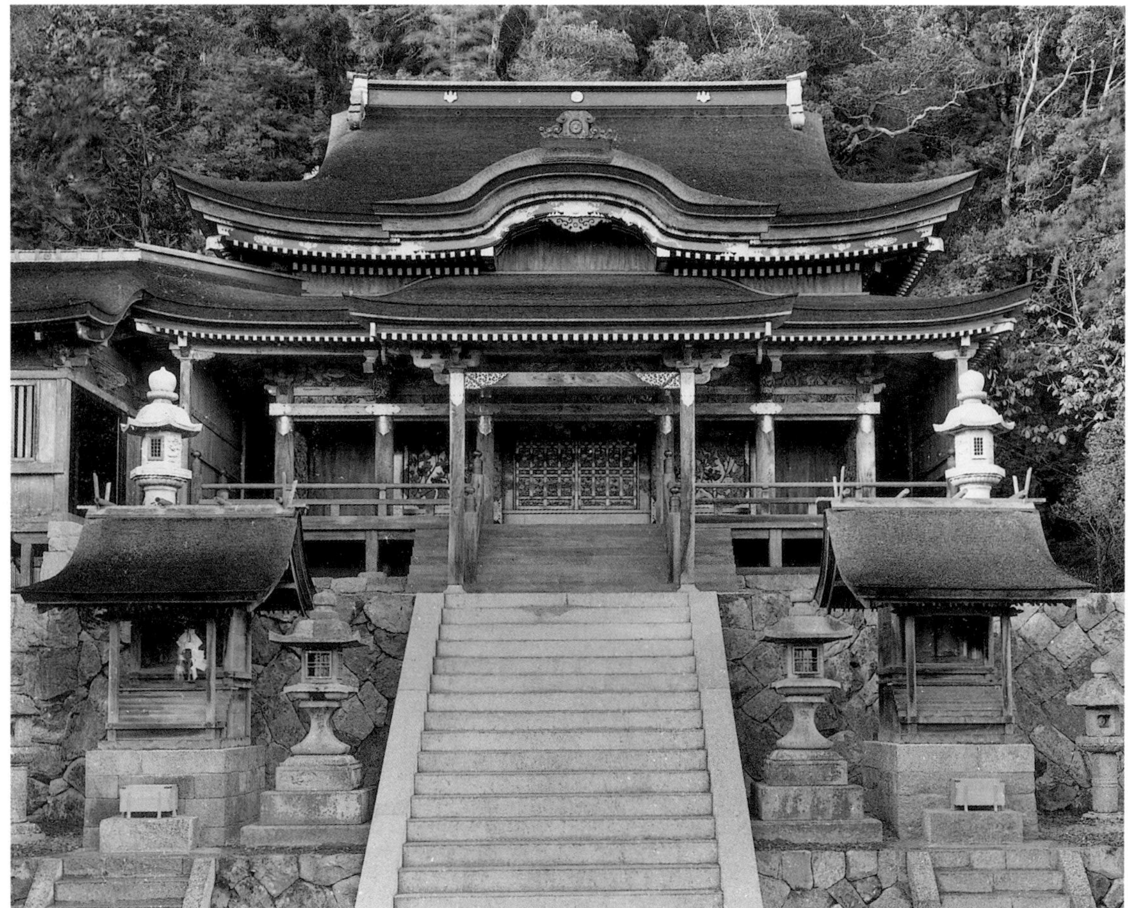

FIG. 2 Tsukubusuma Main Hall. Exterior, south side (front). Chikubushima, Shiga Prefecture. Photograph by Nara National Cultural Properties Research Institute.

FIG. 3 (right) Tsukubusuma Main Hall. View of exterior, south side, looking east from west corner. Chikubushima, Shiga Prefecture.

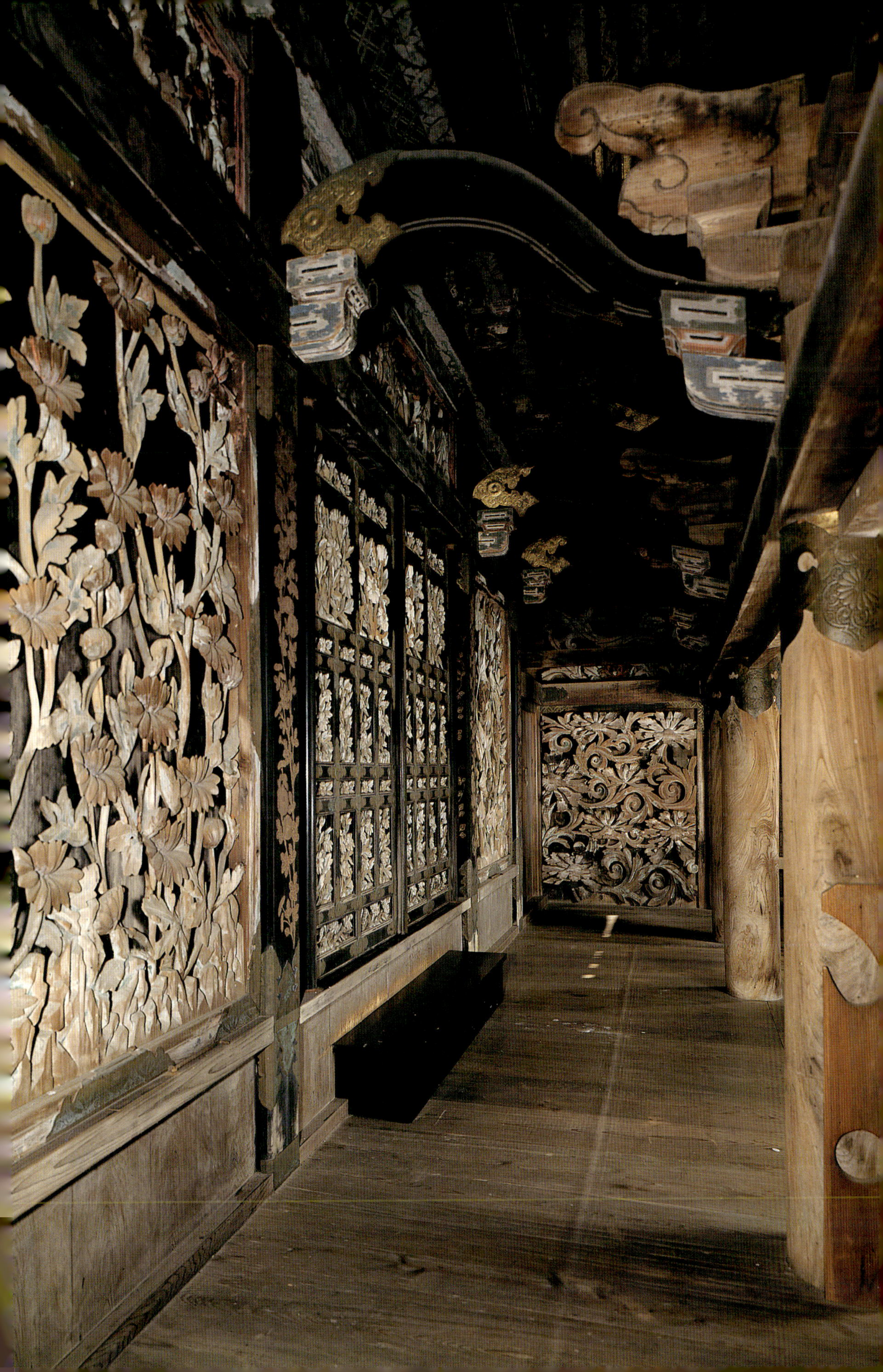

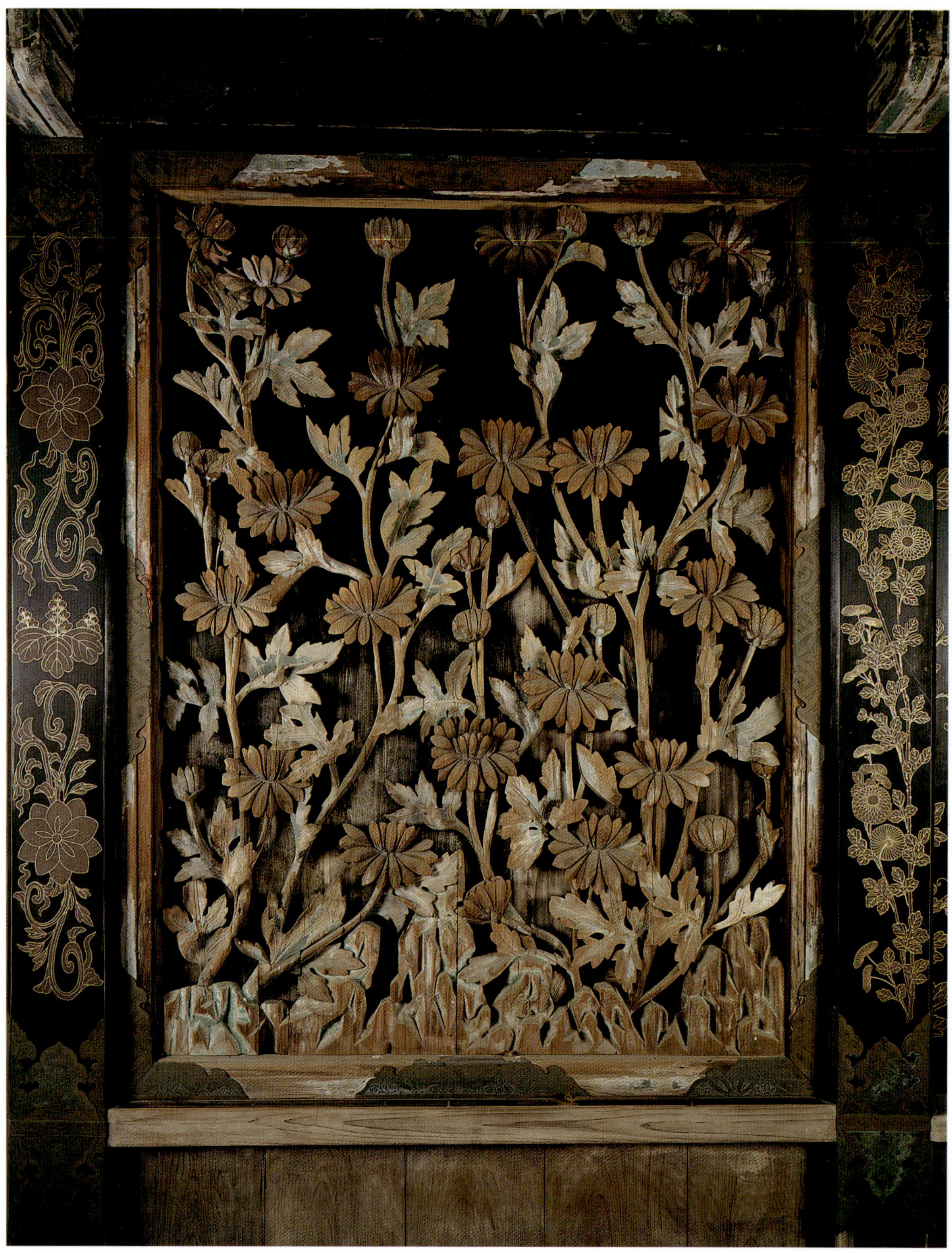

FIG. 4 Tsukubusuma Main Hall. Wood carving of chrysanthemums. Moya exterior, south side, west bay. Chikubushima, Shiga Prefecture.

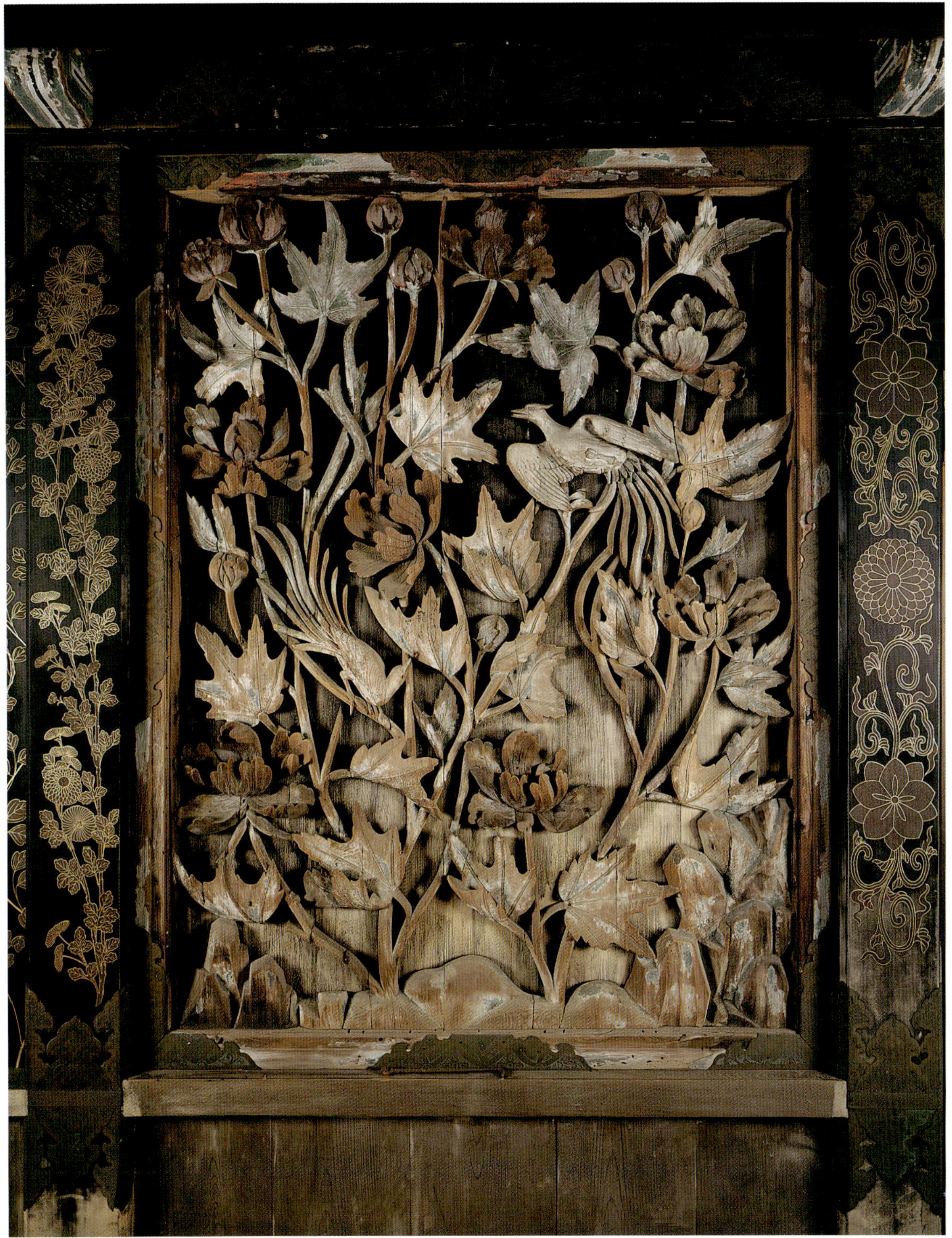

FIG. 5 Tsukubusuma Main Hall. Woodcarving of fuyō. Moya exterior, south side, east bay. Chikubushima, Shiga Prefecture.

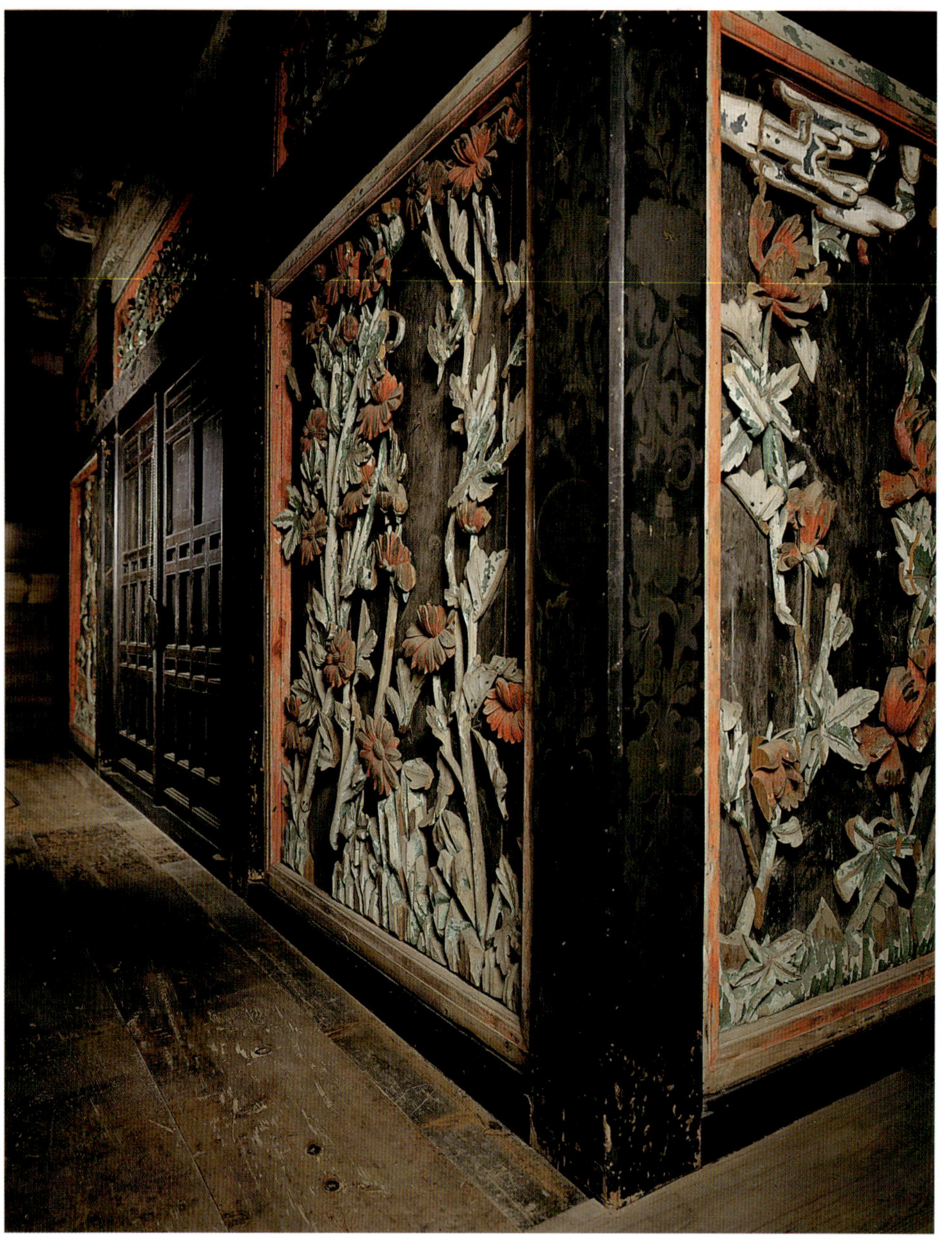

FIG. 6 Tsukubusuma Main Hall. View of moya exterior, north side, looking east from northwest corner. Chikubushima, Shiga Prefecture.

FIG. 7 (opposite) Tsukubusuma Main Hall. View of moya exterior, west side, looking south from northwest corner. Chikubushima, Shiga Prefecture.

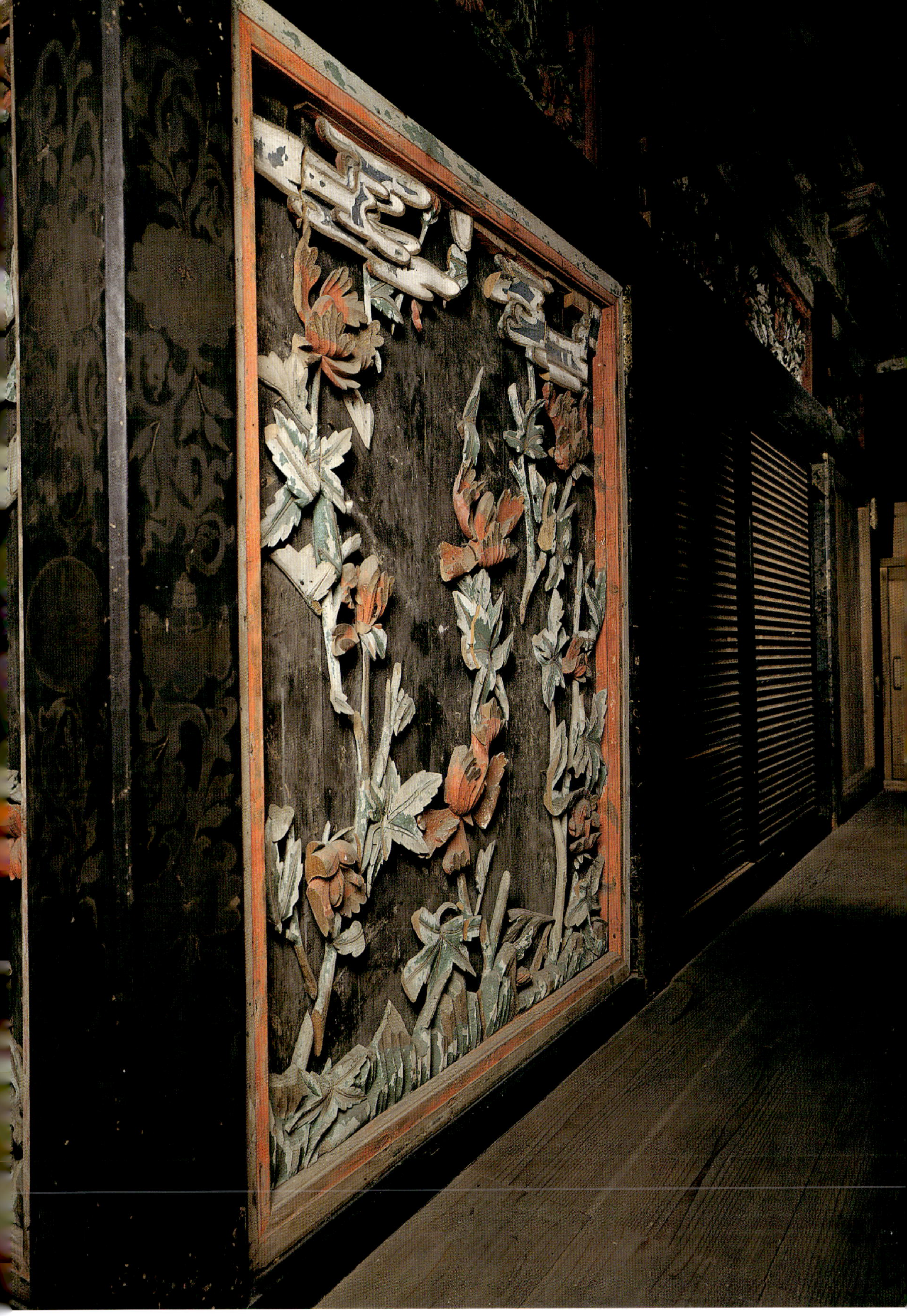

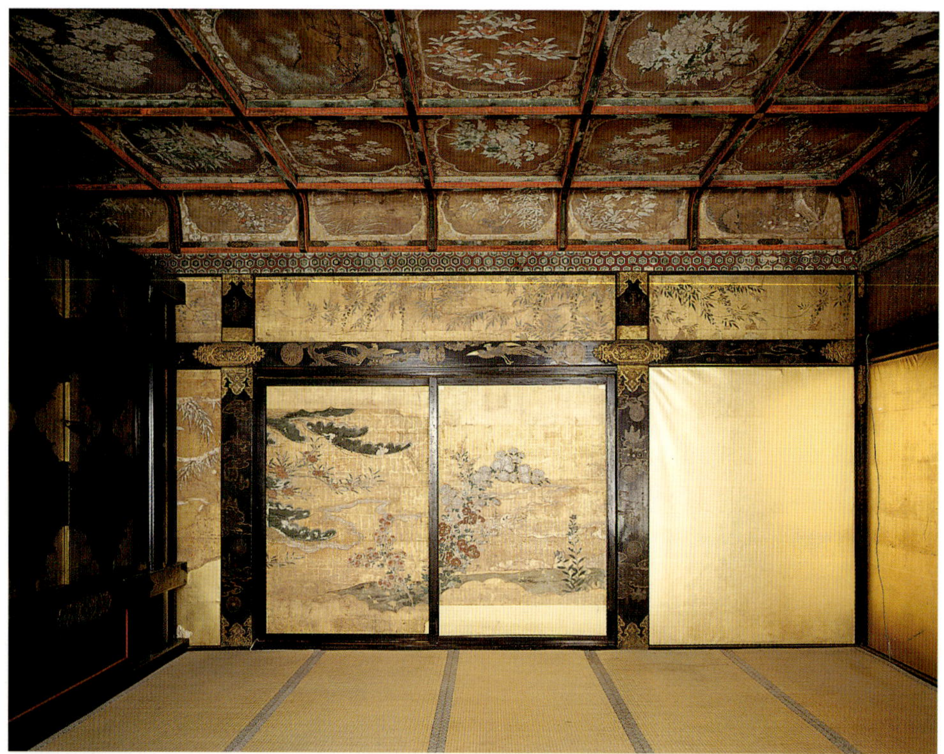

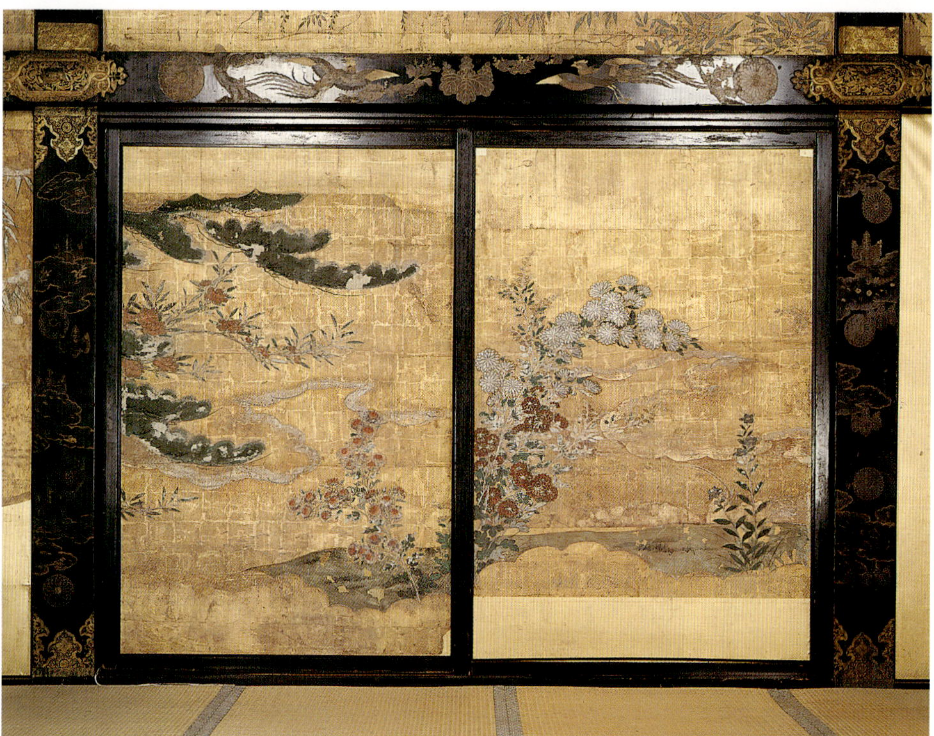

FIG. 8 (top) Tsukubusuma Main Hall. Moya interior, east side. Chikubushima, Shiga Prefecture.

FIG. 9 (bottom) Tsukubusuma Main Hall. Moya interior, east side, central bay. Chikubushima, Shiga Prefecture.

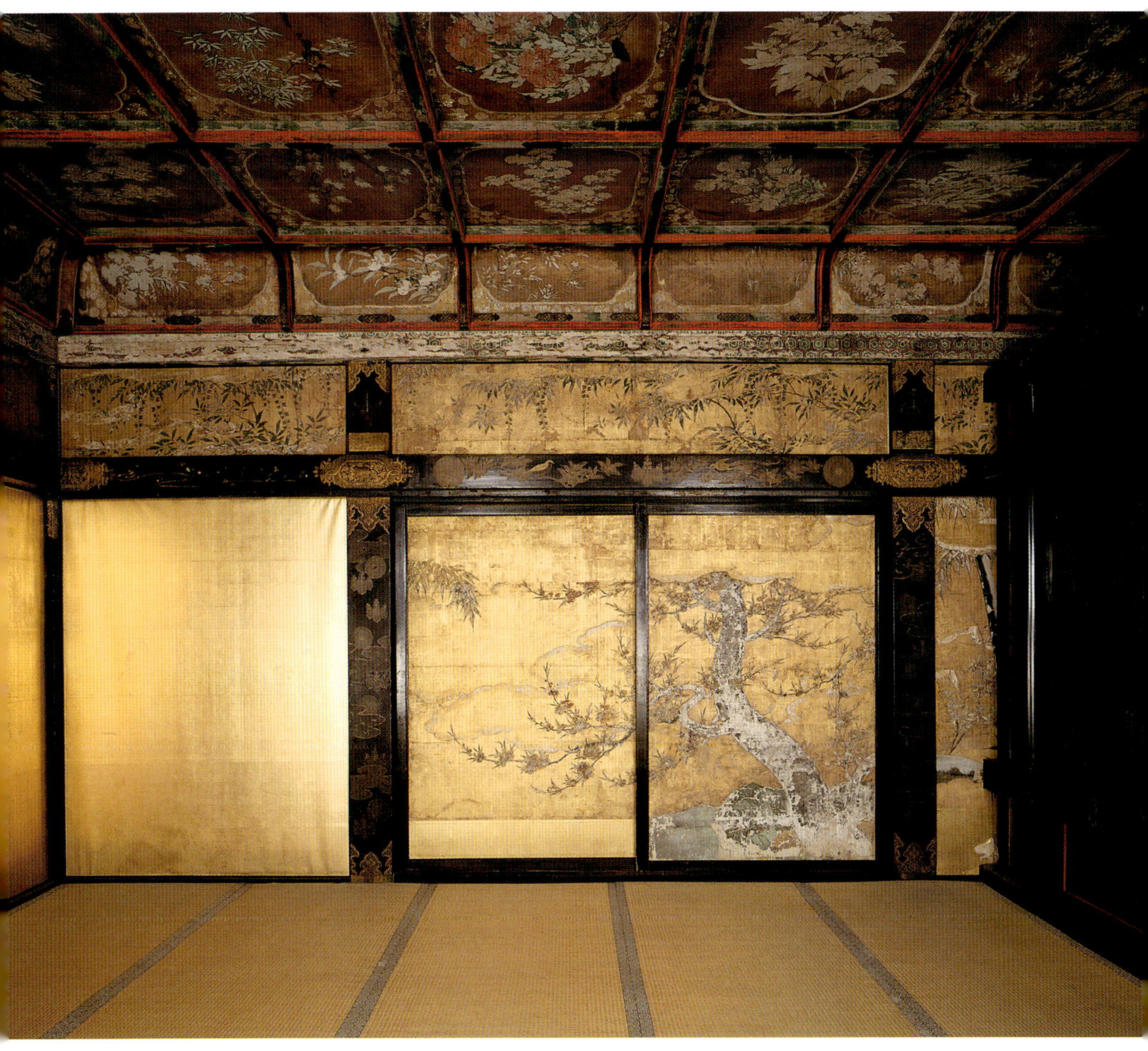

FIG. 10 Tsukubusuma Main Hall. Moya interior, west side. Chikubushima, Shiga Prefecture.

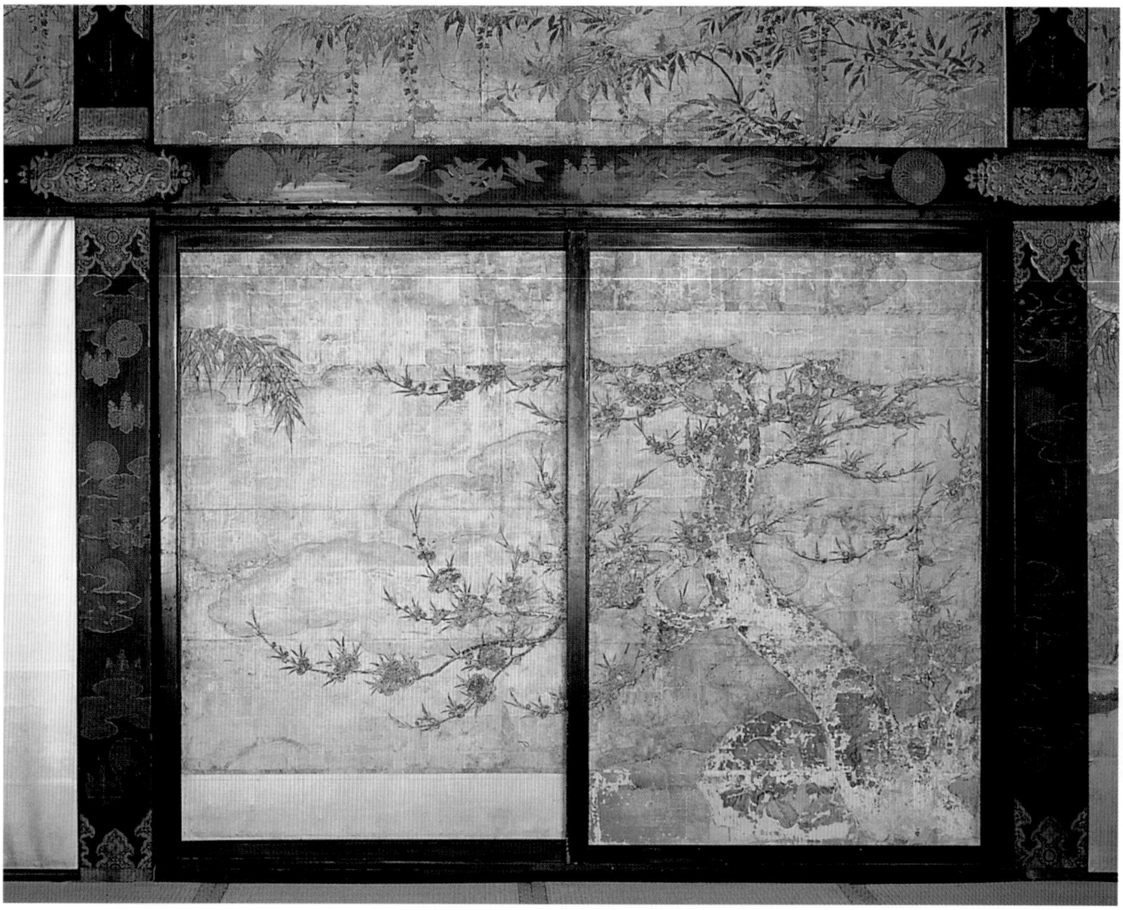

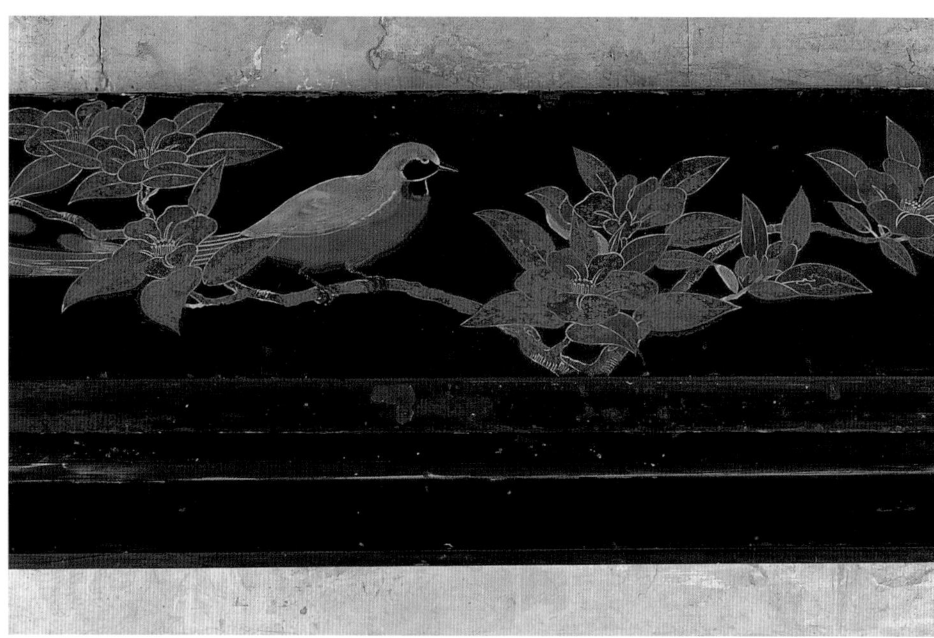

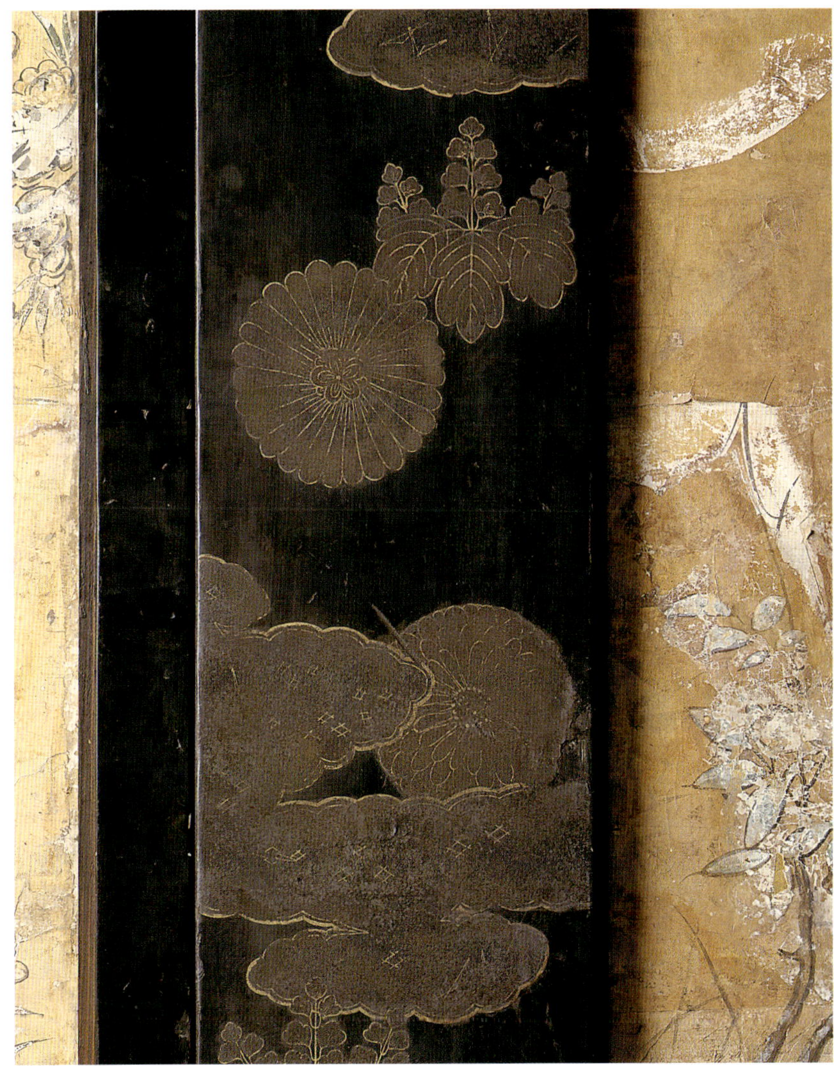

FIG. 13 Tsukubusuma Main Hall. Chrysanthemum and paulownia crests. Makie lacquer. Moya interior, west side, north pillar of central bay. Chikubushima, Shiga Prefecture.

FIG. 11 (opposite top) Tsukubusuma Main Hall. Moya interior, west side, central bay. Chikubushima, Shiga Prefecture.

FIG. 12 (opposite bottom) Tsukubusuma Main Hall. Long-tailed bird on peony branch. Makie lacquer. Moya interior, west side, lintel-beam of central bay. Chikubushima, Shiga Prefecture.

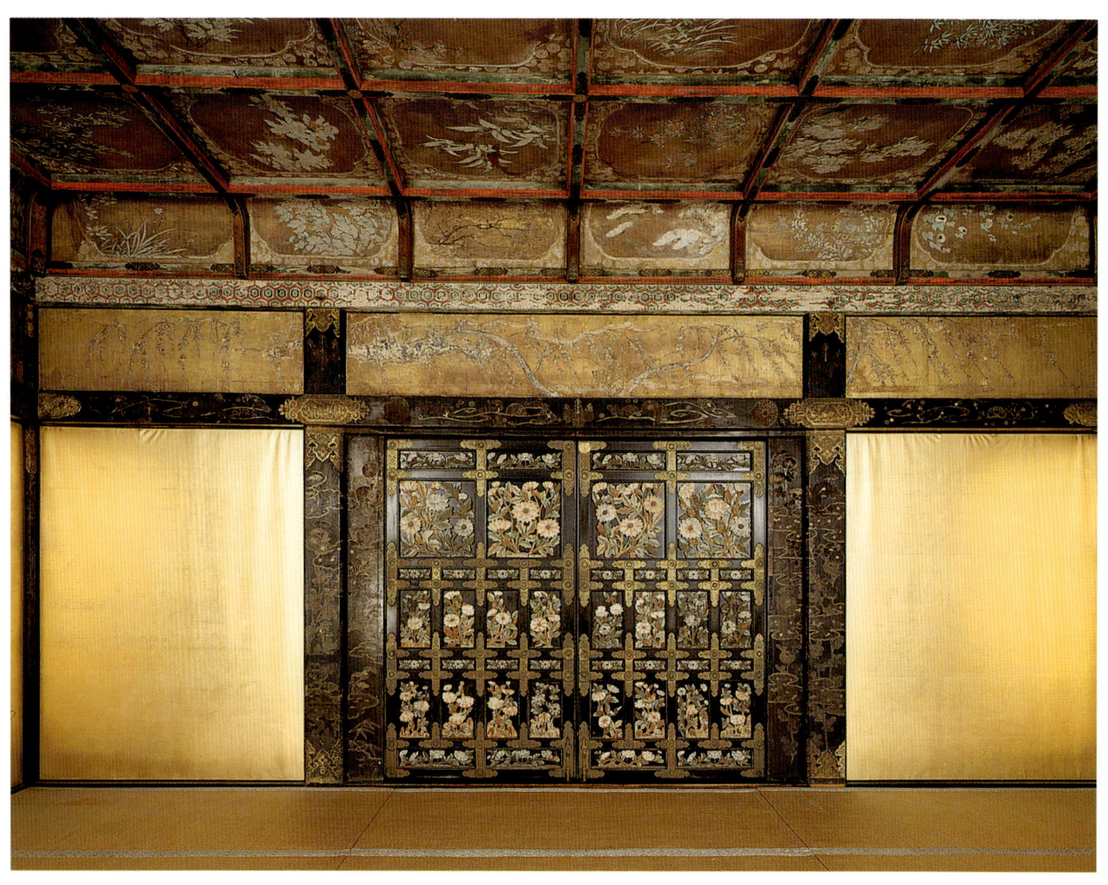

FIG. 14 Tsukubusuma Main Hall. Moya interior, south side. Chikubushima, Shiga Prefecture.

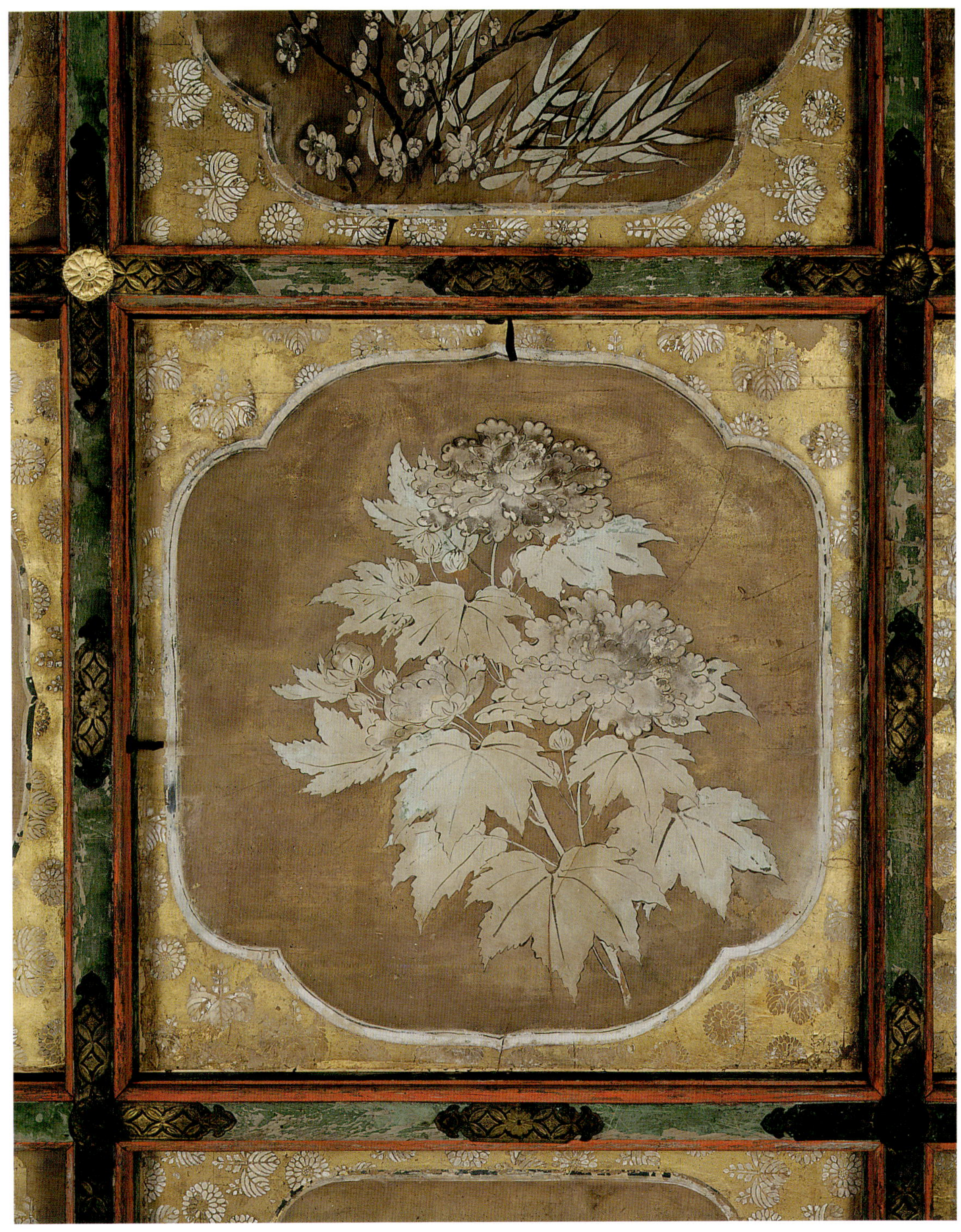

FIG. 15 Tsukubusuma Main Hall. Ceiling painting of fuyō. Moya interior. Chikubushima, Shiga Prefecture.

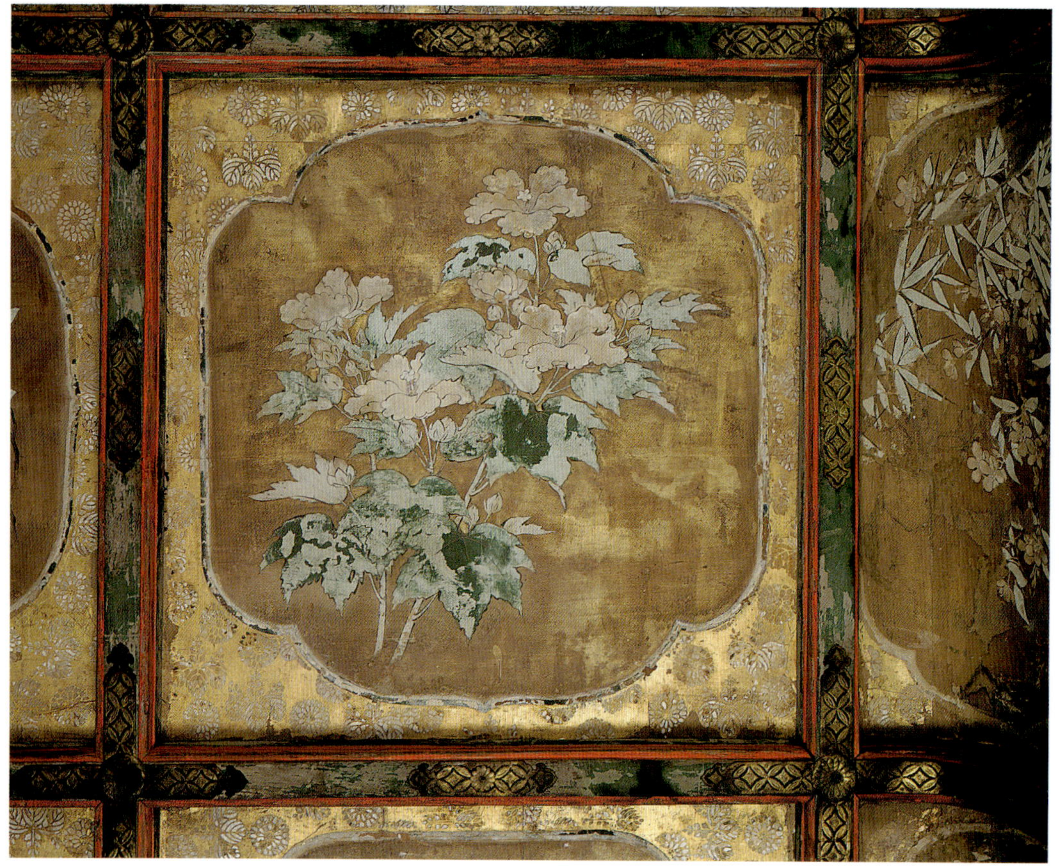

FIG. 16 Tsukubusuma Main Hall. Ceiling painting of fuyō. Moya interior. Chikubushima, Shiga Prefecture.

FIG. 17 (right) Tsukubusuma Main Hall. Moya exterior, north side. Chikubushima, Shiga Prefecture.

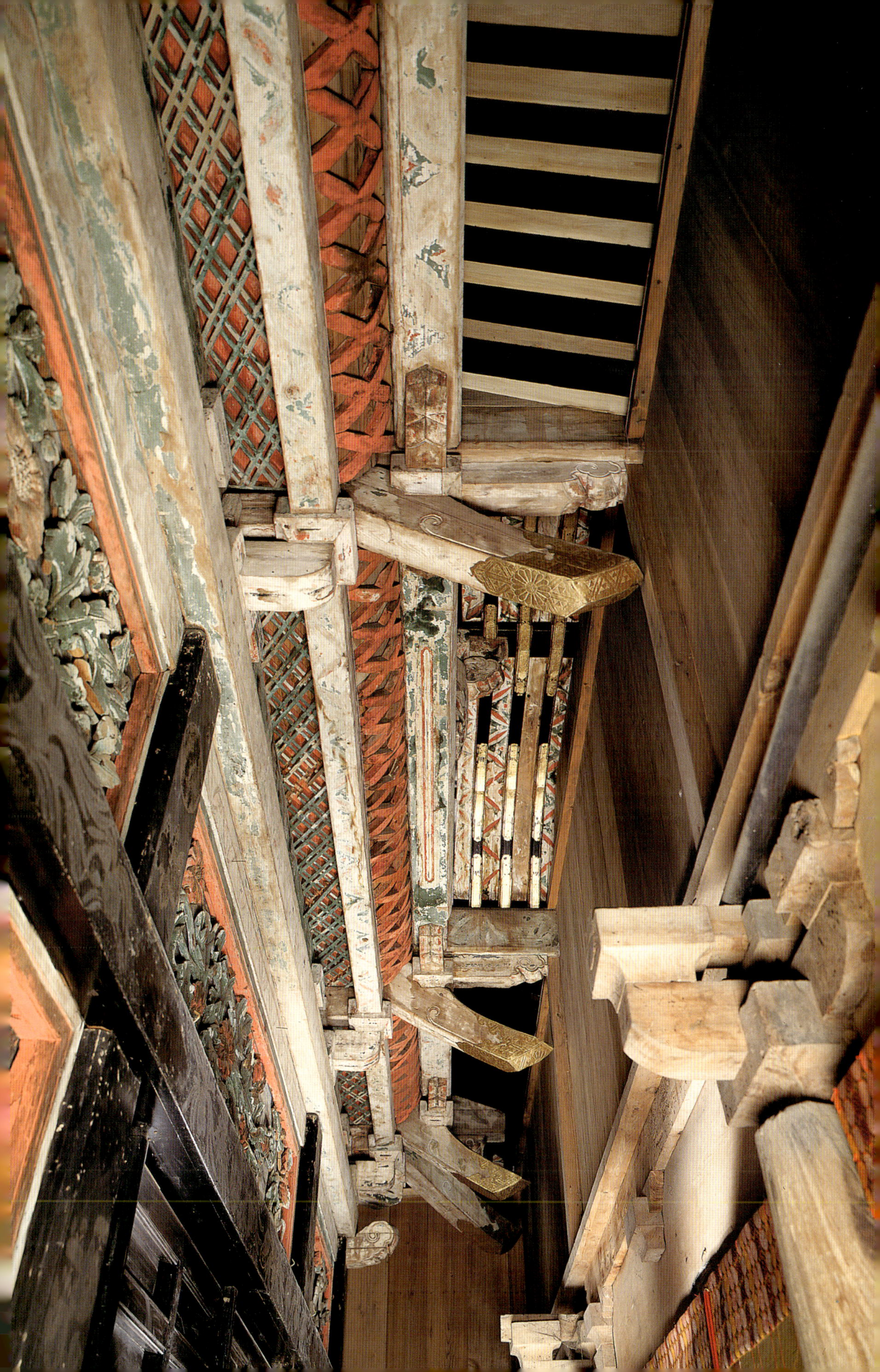

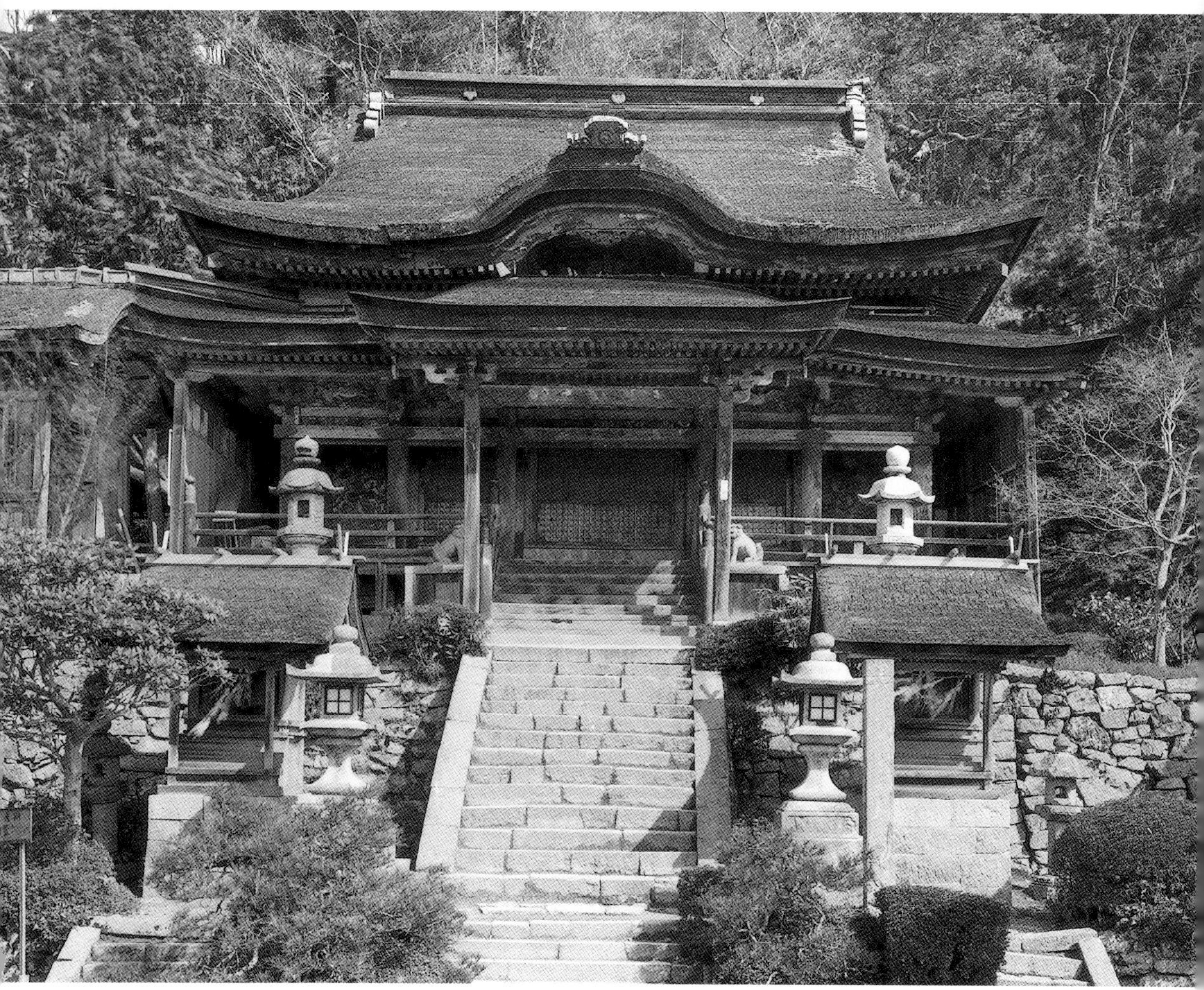

FIG. 18 Tsukubusuma Main Hall before 1936–1937 repairs. Exterior, south side (front). Chikubushima, Shiga Prefecture. Photograph by Nara National Cultural Properties Research Institute.

FIG. 19 (opposite) Tsukubusuma Main Hall before 1936–1937 repairs. View of Main Hall exterior, south side, looking west from east corner. Chikubushima, Shiga Prefecture. Photograph after *KTJHSKH,* pl. 32.

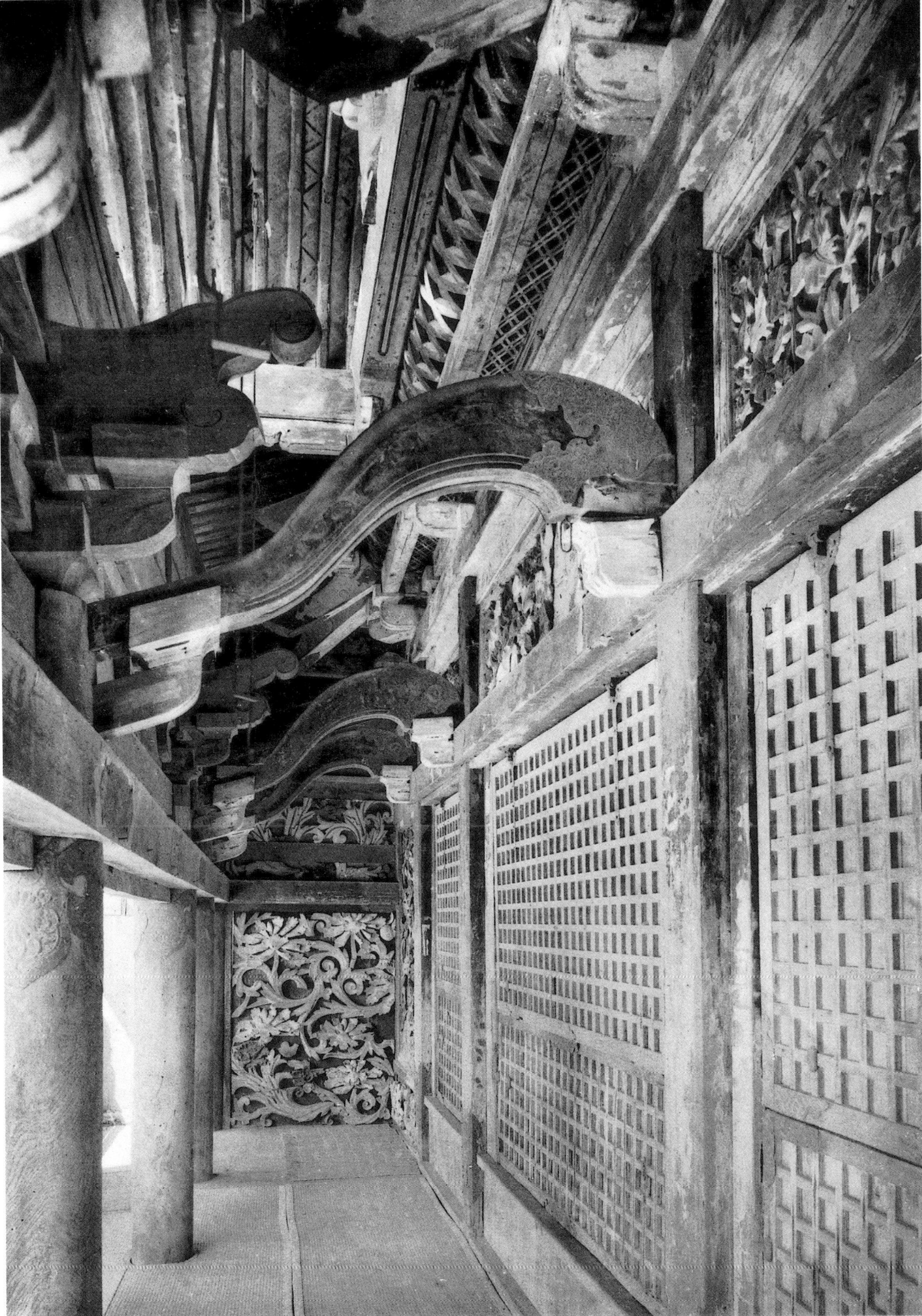

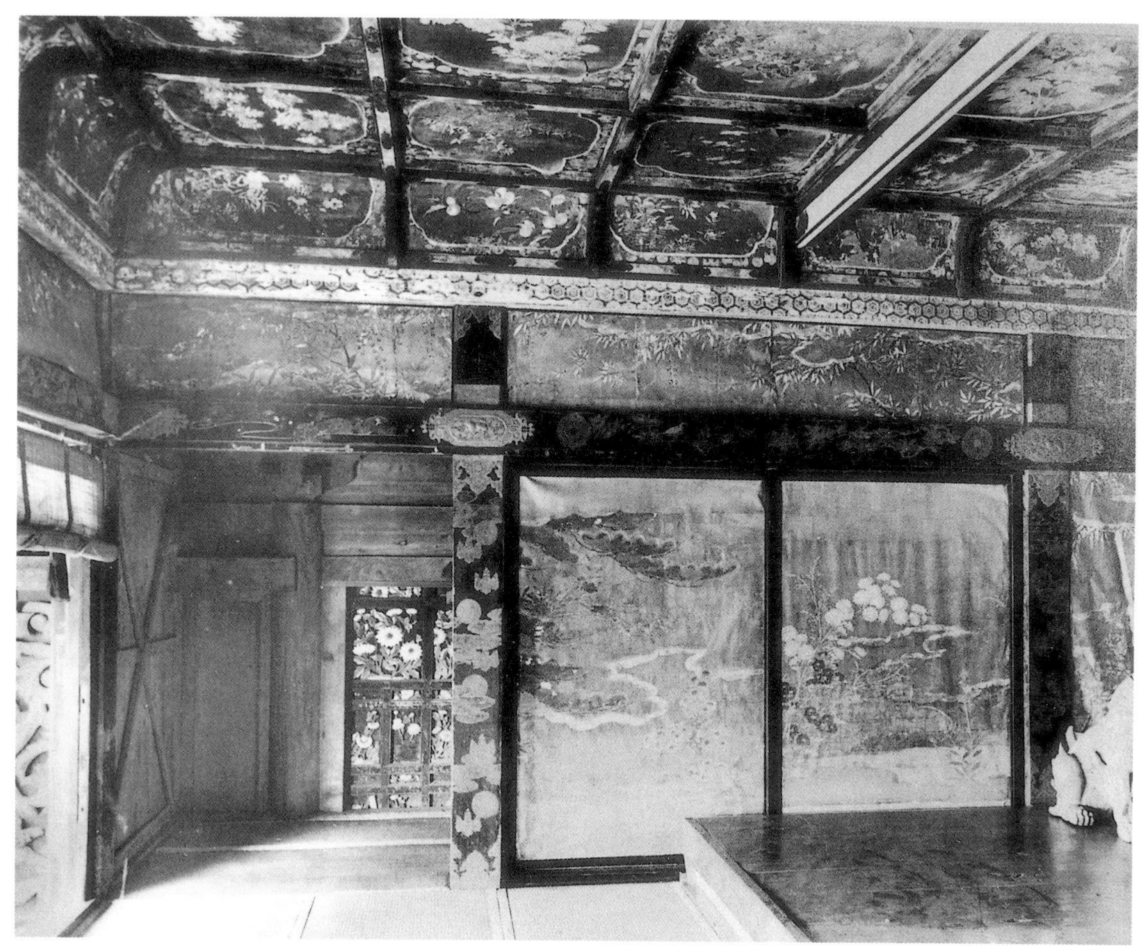

FIG. 20 Tsukubusuma Main Hall before 1936–1937 repairs. Moya interior, west side. Chikubushima, Shiga Prefecture.

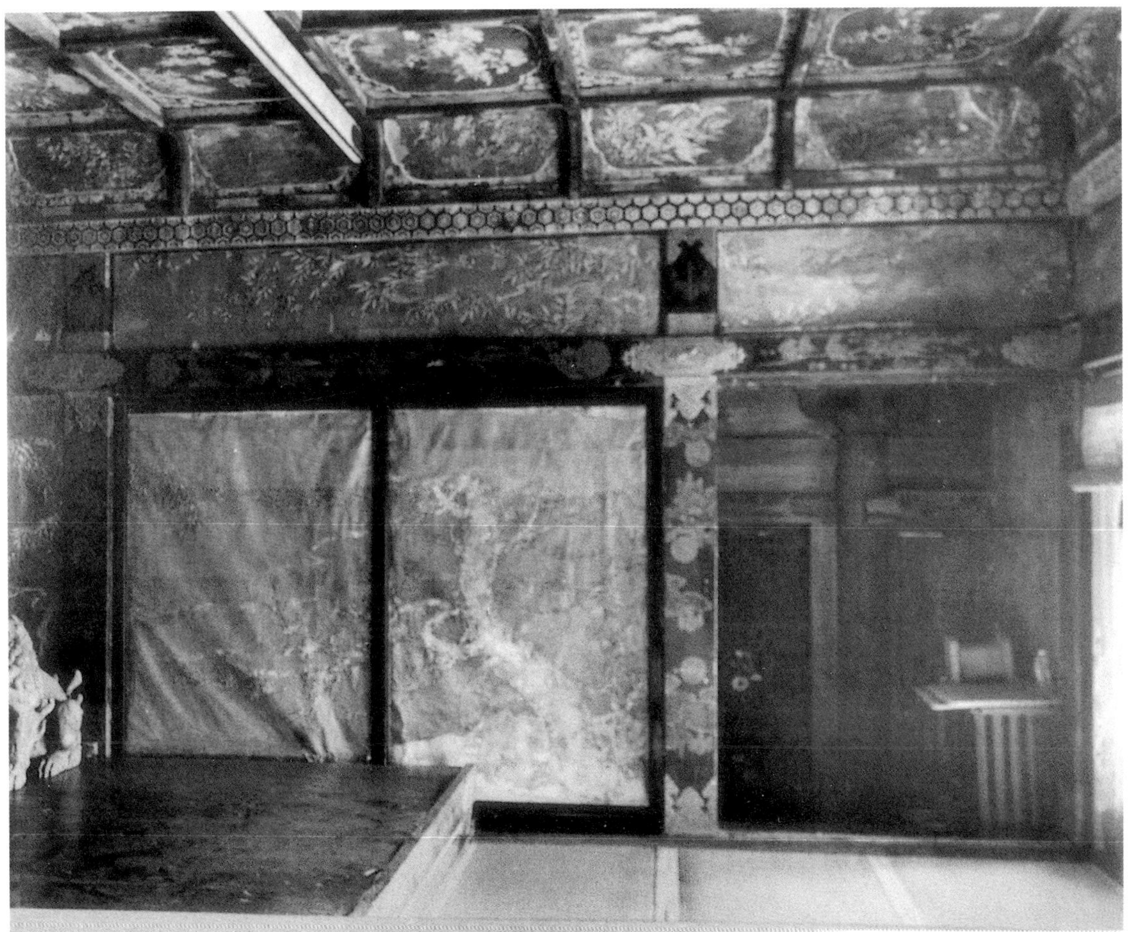

FIG. 21 Tsukubusuma Main Hall before 1936–1937 repairs. Moya interior, east side. Chikubushima, Shiga Prefecture. Photograph by Nara National Cultural Properties Research Institute.

INTRODUCTION

The Sacred and Momoyama Japan

> Among all the people of this Orient, they are the most inclined to religion and the worship of divine things. This is not only to obtain temporal benefits such as long life, health, wealth, prosperity, children, and other such things for which they ask their false gods, but also even more to obtain with all their hearts salvation in the next life. This they do in their false and erroneous ways. Proof of this may be seen in this kingdom's sumptuous temples, the great respect and reverence shown towards the priests of their idols and teachers of salvation, the incredibly severe penances that they undertake, fasting and abstinence from meat and living things, the various vows and alms paid to the idols.

So observed the Portuguese Jesuit missionary João Rodrigues (1561–1633) in his book *The History of the Church of Japan*, which he wrote after living in Japan for more than thirty years, from 1577 to 1610.[1] Contempt for Japanese deities is to be expected from this man of the Christian cloth, yet mixed with his censure is also a measure of objective observation, an attempt to catalogue the substance of the heterodox convictions Rodrigues' Order hoped to displace. Japanese religious belief was more complicated, of course, than his brief assessment allows, but he was a perceptive enough observer to note several distinctive traits of Japanese piety that will reappear throughout our own examination of this period: reliance on the divine for benefits in this life; desire for rebirth after death in a paradisal realm (the Buddhist Pure Land); zeal for the construction of admirable buildings, in which the believers performed—with dedication and reverence—

religious rituals. In one short paragraph Rodrigues condemns the Japanese conception of the sacred and acknowledges the seriousness with which the Japanese engaged it during his term of observation.

The "sacred," as I employ it in this book, takes account of Rodrigues' insights into Japanese religious practice and refers more generally to the deities of Japan and all that was ascribed to their realm of divine existence in the late sixteenth and early seventeenth century. As we shall explore, the deities were capable of marvelous behavior, much of which benefitted attentive human patrons. These sacred beings were active in the mundane world at recognized places and were known, too, to preside over worlds unavailable to human vision. All sacred realms—both seen and unseen—were characterized by the utmost numinous beauty, a beauty that was described in the sutras and was represented in our world with splendid combinations of architecture and ornament. This beauty—whether depicted in writing or in the visual arts—was inescapably a human construction (as was, of course, the very conception of the sacred itself), and its elements were drawn from the world of human experience: pavilions, ponds, musicians, dancers and, especially, flora and fauna. In the Momoyama period these elements were glorified to the limit of human conception in constructions that employed the mediums held in greatest esteem, particularly ink, polychrome, and gold paintings, black-and-gold lacquer, gilt metalwork, and sculpture in relief and in the round; wood architecture provided the skeleton upon which all joined in fruitful combination. It is these ornamented constructions that form the core of this study.

My understanding of what constituted the sacred derives from texts authored by the Japanese and by Europeans visiting during this, the first era of direct contact between Japan and the West, and from the "ornamented constructions" as well as other Japanese paintings and sculptures.[2] Evidence from all these sources is most abundant and informative as regards beliefs and attitudes among Japan's privileged social groups, principally the warrior elites and the clergy with whom they interacted, though it will be clear that at least some aspects of the sacred that I discuss were embraced also by other parts of the Japanese populace. In brief, this evidence tells us that the sacred was an amply articulated and often tangible aspect of life in Japan at this time. *Vocabvlario da Lingoa de Iapam,* for example, an invaluable Japanese-Portuguese dictionary published by resident Jesuit missionaries in 1603, defines numerous religious terms and thereby records the profusion and wide currency of sacred conceptions.[3] In the capital, Kyoto, the dominant building—the largest and most visible, and a major focus of paintings and written descriptions of the city—was the Great Buddha Hall, which housed a suitably monumental sculpture of the omnipotent Vairocana Buddha; begun in 1586, the building and its Buddha were repeatedly damaged or destroyed and, reaffirming their crucial roles in Kyoto's sacred fabric, repeatedly reconstructed over the next thirty years.

The sacred was thus omnipresent, the continuing fruit of long and constant Japanese devotion to the work of sacralization.[4] People knew the gods to be, variously, givers of good fortune or of harsh punishment, healers of the ill, munificent providers of bountiful harvests, and wielders of many other awesome powers that will be discussed below.

(The Japanese accepted as a matter of course the interconnectedness of what we now refer to as Shinto and Buddhism.[5]) The rulers in these decades sought to bolster their fortunes by linking them to traditionally ascribed capabilities of the sacred: to protect Japan—for the deities were understood to shield against unseen yet horrible enemies; to confer legitimacy—because the sacred was traditionally a source of sanction for secular authority; and to assure dynastic longevity—a function especially meaningful to the powerful warrior leaders of the time, all of whom sought (but few of whom secured) this last aim.[6] That each of the three warrior families who ruled during Rodrigues' tenure claimed divine status and, by virtue of that status, an incontrovertible right to govern, is perhaps the most compelling indication of how Japanese then viewed the power of the sacred.

The sacred realm overlay and intersected with the world of humans, and the boundaries between the two often were crossed. Deities manifested themselves in known places throughout the Japanese archipelago—numerous tales record human perception of their traces—and many of these places were designated off-limits for mortal habitation (though mortals could visit as pilgrims). Priests were the human intercessors between the two realms. They directed myriad rituals to the deities, frequently with the financial support of lay patrons, in renowned buildings decorated to conjure up the ethereal environments described in religious texts and in which the deities dwelled. The sacred, in sum, was an otherworldly reality that formed, with the mundane world, the single whole of human experience, in the here and now as well as the hereafter.

The sacred was ubiquitous, but it was not everything. Rodrigues and other Europeans observed eagerly and wrote home at length (if often in bewilderment) about all that caught their attention. Rodrigues, in particular, acquired an encyclopedic knowledge of the Japan of his time, imparted in the *History* in learned discourses on a wide range of topics, including others less controversial than religion; we shall turn periodically to his astute assessments, especially of what he called the "mechanical arts." The Europeans provide for us basic information that the Japanese took for granted and therefore omitted from their own writings. Their chronicles afford a glimpse of Japan as brief as it was precious, however, for not long after Rodrigues' Japanese sojourn ended, European access to Japan was greatly limited—a restriction lasting until the mid-nineteenth century—and such writing significantly decreases.[7]

Japanese diaries, letters, and official documents are enlightening in different ways, contributing a level of detail and insight that even the most perceptive visitor could not attain. Gien (1558–1626), for example, a confidant of political leaders and the head priest of Daigoji, a massive Buddhist temple complex that covers an entire mountain just south of Kyoto, was one of the most alert observers and eloquent writers of his time. He wrote illuminating descriptions of the religious buildings going up in Kyoto, learned historical accounts of his own ancient temple precincts, and detailed chronicles of the life he lived at the highest level of privileged access. With an attentive eye to the political intrigues and natural cataclysms that helped define the period, and from the vantage of his high position in the Buddhist hierarchy, Gien sheds light on aspects of Kyoto that were erased or altered by later rulers.

RECONFIGURING RELIGION

In the Japan that Rodrigues, Gien, and their contemporaries wrote about, the role of the religious establishment was being reconfigured, a revolutionary occurrence that developed out of violent convulsions that were sweeping the country. Until this time some of the great Buddhist temples had wielded not only spiritual authority but also political and military clout, so much so that they were as significant a force in local and even wider secular affairs as the warrior-class men who principally dominated Japanese governance. For about a century beginning in the mid-1460s, civil war engulfed and fractured Japan; armies—secular and religious alike—battled for local control as central authority ebbed almost to vanishing and the sense of a unified realm disappeared.[8] From the 1560s, however, the more successful warrior leaders engrossed ever wider swathes of territory, and the fractured country began to consolidate once again. As part of this consolidation—or, more bluntly, this elimination of rivals—some warriors fought pitched battles against the militarized temples and defeated them utterly. Stripped of its war-making capability, the one undeniably compelling means of contesting warrior-class ambition, the religious community could no longer forcefully assert itself in fundamentally worldly matters.

The disarming of the great temples—and of the sacred—changed the role of religion in Japan. As they had for centuries, the Japanese continued to engage the numinous in response to the exigencies of life and death, the everyday and the extraordinary, and so religion endured as an important force in Japan. The warrior-class leaders who emerged from the conflicts of the sixteenth century, however, made new demands on the religious establishment that deeply altered its character and relevance. Temples were forced to choose sides in the increasingly decisive campaigns waged by the great warriors and to suffer the consequences of backing the losers. Shinto and Buddhism both admitted deified warrior-class rulers into their respective pantheons, gods whose cults immediately became dominant focuses of Japanese worship and who first and foremost promoted warrior rule. Normally uncooperative Buddhist sects reluctantly collaborated in massive communal ceremonies, on the order of a warrior ruler who sought to make Buddhism serve his will. The sacred was still profoundly important in the late sixteenth through early seventeenth century, but it was also profoundly transformed.

THE TOYOTOMI AND THE MOMOYAMA PERIOD

More instrumental than most in shaping this transformation was one warrior-class house, the Toyotomi. Four Toyotomi family members dominate the narrative:

> Hideyoshi (1537–1598), the clan progenitor, who rose from obscure origins to serve the period's first great leader, Oda Nobunaga (1534–1582), and then to rule Japan himself from 1582 until his death in 1598 *(Fig. 22);*

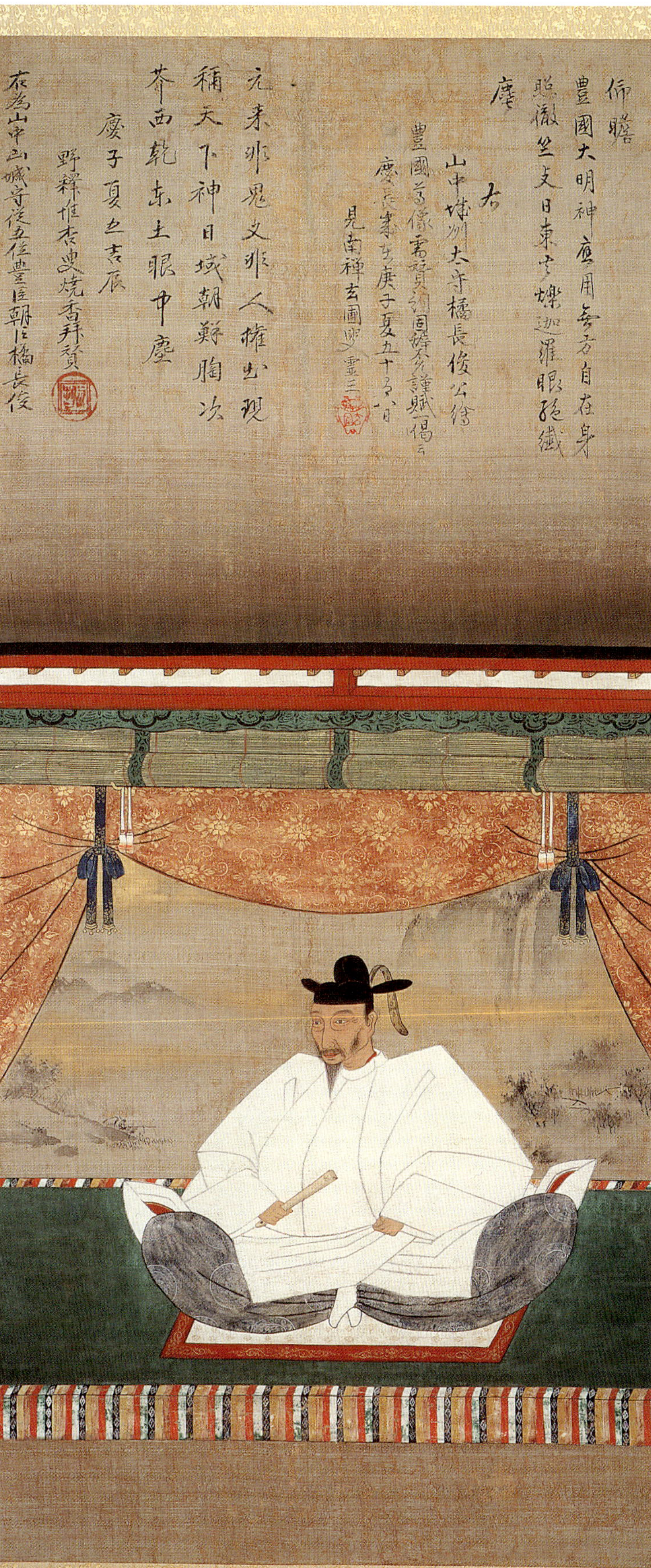

FIG. 22 *Portrait of Toyotomi Hideyoshi.* Early seventeenth century. Hanging scroll; ink and color on silk. Saikyōji, Shiga Prefecture. Photograph by Kyoto National Museum.

Sutemaru (1589–1591), Hideyoshi's first-born son and intended heir, whose early death provoked Hideyoshi to acts of madness (according to contemporary observers) as well as to spectacular commemorative constructions *(Fig. 23);*

Hideyori (1593–1615), Hideyoshi's second son and actual heir, the young figurehead in the Toyotomi attempt to remain politically relevant after Hideyoshi's death *(Fig. 24);* and, finally,

Yododono (d. 1615), Hideyori's mother (and, not coincidentally, Hideyoshi's favored consort), the true power behind the young Hideyori *(Fig. 25).*

Most of the structures and objects that are the focus of this study were inspired or commanded by these individuals in response to their circumstances within the context of political competition and societal transformation.

The Toyotomi house's period of activity coincides with what today is most often referred to as the Momoyama period. Although this name for the period is a relatively recent invention—shorter eras, with auspicious names like Tenshō (Heavenly Virtue, 1573–1592), Bunroku (Enlightened Benevolence, 1592–1596), and Keichō (Eternal Jubilance, 1596–1615), were the original units of periodization—it conveniently encompasses a distinct and pivotal, if brief and only retrospectively recognized, epoch in Japanese history.[9] The name Momoyama (Peach Mountain), which refers to the site of Hideyoshi's Fushimi Castle, just south of Kyoto, is itself a hindsight coinage: the area, earlier known as Fushimi, became noted for its abundance of blossoming peach trees only well after Fushimi Castle had disappeared. A fuller version of the period name, Azuchi-Momoyama, includes the location of Nobunaga's famed castle just northeast of Kyoto. The period's dates are a matter of debate.[10] Its beginning is variously ascribed to 1568 (the year I favor, when the warrior and imminent ruler Oda Nobunga first entered the capital, Kyoto), to 1573 (when Nobunaga deposed the incumbent Ashikaga shogun), or to 1576 (when Nobunaga built Azuchi Castle). Its end is dated either to 1603 (when Tokugawa Ieyasu [1542–1616] assumed the post of shogun) or to 1615 (my strong preference, when Ieyasu utterly obliterated the Toyotomi house in the battles at Osaka Castle). The activity of the Toyotomi, who emerged on Japan's stage in the late 1560s and disappeared from it in 1615, exactly corresponds with the period known as Momoyama.

In its sequence of roles—as Nobunaga's vassal, as acknowledged hegemon, and as contender for disputed leadership—the Toyotomi house laid claim, with increasing intensity, to the sacred as a means of personal salvation, an instrument of political success, and a source of identity. After Hideyoshi's death, indeed, it was primarily by engaging this realm that the Toyotomi sought to affirm their continued relevance in Japan. At all times they asserted their affinity to the sacred most concretely through their massive sponsorship of religious architecture, much of it decorated by the most famous artists of the day. Although they also commissioned prodigious amounts of secular construction, their patronage of temples and shrines virtually rebuilt the architectural framework of Japan's sacred realm; indeed, some of the most famous religious buildings of

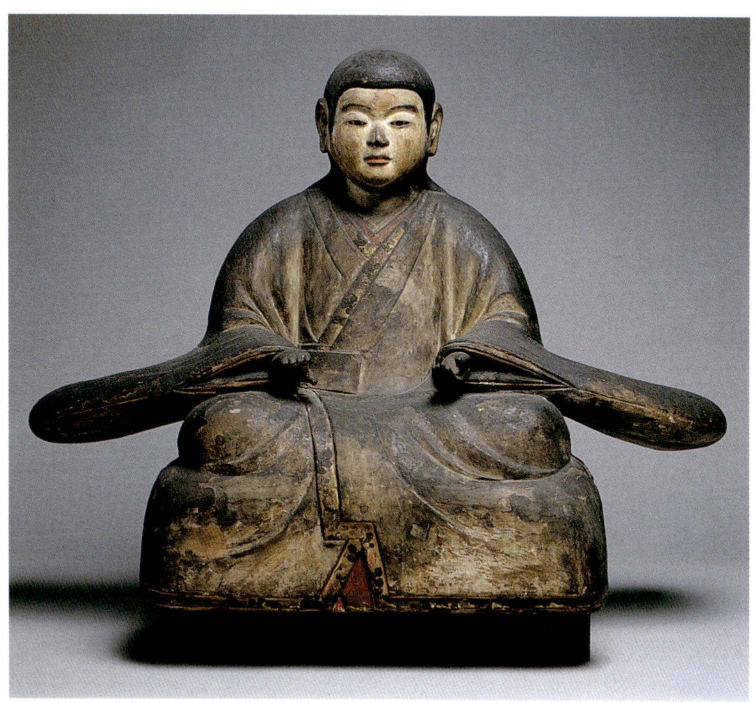

FIG. 23 *Portrait of Sutemaru.* Late sixteenth century. Polychromed wood. Rinkain, Kyoto. Photograph by Kyoto National Museum.

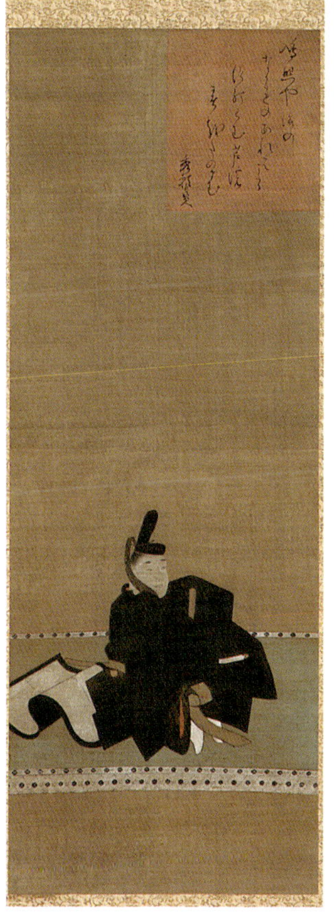

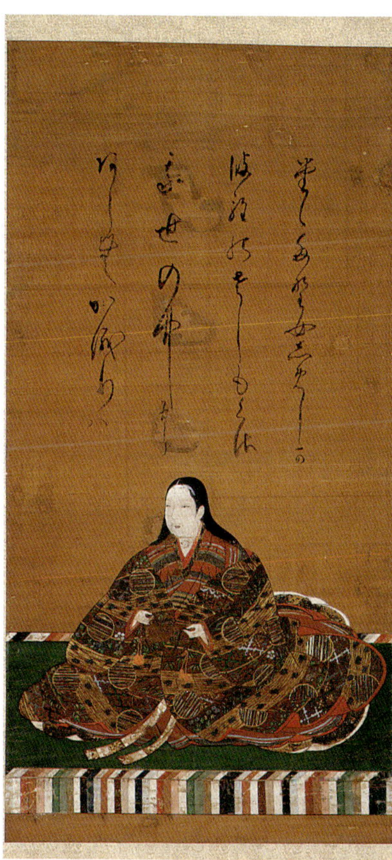

FIG. 24 (left) *Portrait of Toyotomi Hideyori.* Early seventeenth century. Hanging scroll; ink and color on silk. Tokyo National University of Fine Arts and Music.

FIG. 25 (right) *Reputed Portrait of Yododono.* Early seventeenth century. Hanging scroll; ink and color on silk. Nara Perfectual Museum of Art. Photograph by Kyoto National Museum.

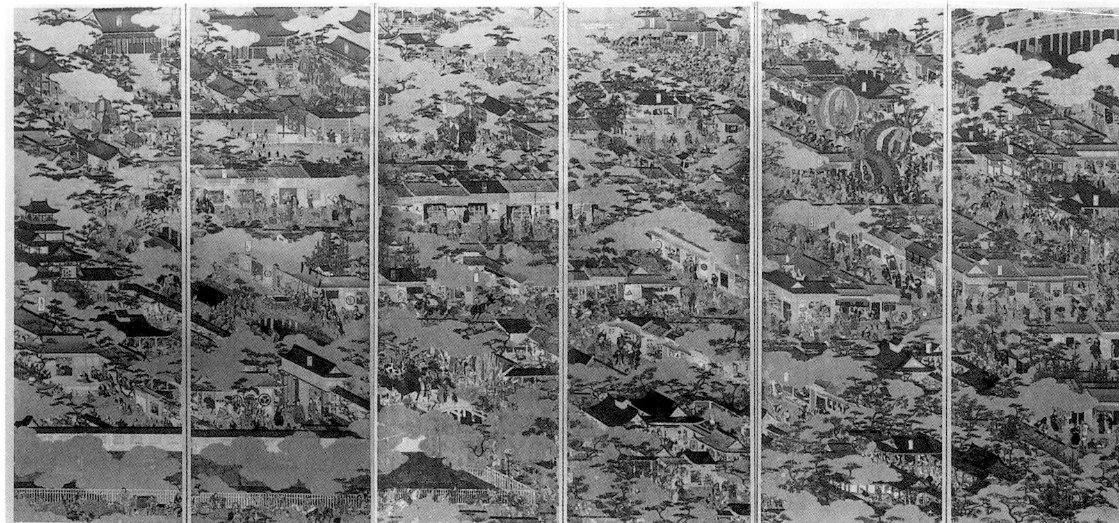

even ancient times—the seventh-century Hōryūji and the tenth-century pagoda at Daigoji, for example—exist today, arguably, because of the Toyotomi's attentions. Religious architecture and its decoration were the most enduring forms in which the Toyotomi asserted their authority.

KYOTO, THE CAPITAL

Nowhere was the Toyotomi patronage of religious construction more pronounced than in the longtime capital of Kyoto, whose building boom was reflected in a new type of painting that emerged in the early sixteenth century and grew in popularity throughout the Momoyama period: *Sights in and around the Capital (Rakuchū rakugai zu),* a format of paired folding screens that took as their subject matter Kyoto and all that it contained: geography, buildings, people, and events.[11] These paintings were not neutral renderings of urban reality (if such a thing is possible), but complex interpretations of place and constructions of their own realities, as demonstrated in one pair formerly in the Funaki collection and now in the Tokyo National Museum *(Fig. 26).* On one level the Funaki screens depict the routine life cycle of the bustling city: commoners conduct their daily business, selling, transporting, or buying goods, tending their fields, or fishing in the Kamo River; the aristocrats of the Imperial Court soberly perform their ancient ceremonies; numerous warriors pass through the streets on foot or on horseback, or loll about in the pleasure quarters; in the many temples and shrines clergy perform rituals or interact with lay worshippers. Amidst it all, the annual Gion Festival, a venerable event rooted in ancient anti-pestilence rites, enlivens the city with its exuberant parade of elaborate floats, fantastically costumed figures, and hordes of participants. In this self-contained cosmopolis, all sectors of society properly engage their roles, and often intermingle, as befits Kyoto's status as capital.

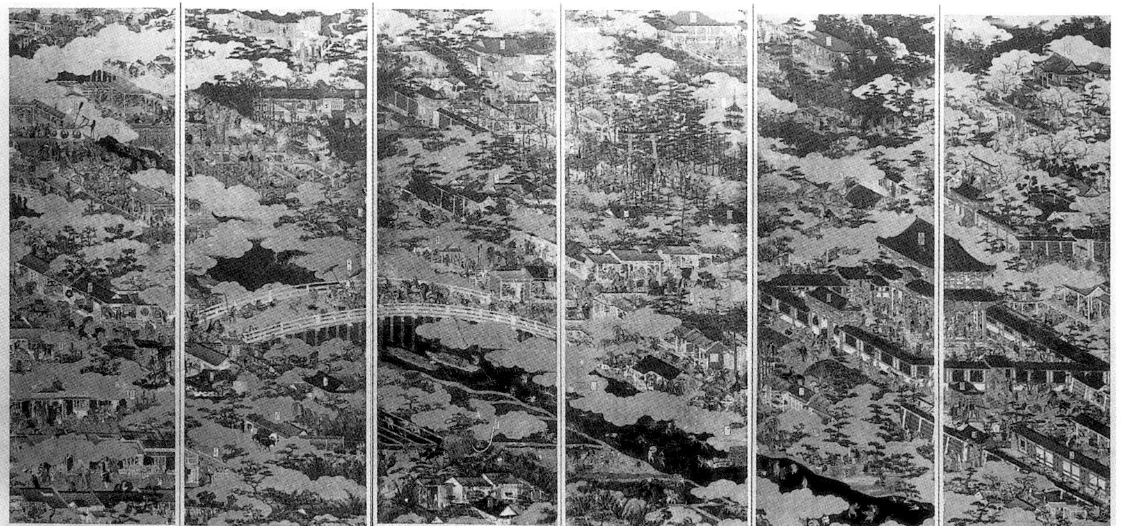

FIG. 26 (this page and opposite) *Sights in and around the Capital (Rakuchū rakugai).* Late sixteenth–early seventeenth century. Pair of six-panel folding screens; ink, color, and gold leaf on paper. Tokyo National Museum. Ex-Funaki collection.

Other aspects of the Funaki screens reveal the political fissures that destabilized late Momoyama Japan. The horizontal breadth of the paired screens depicts a roughly diagonal swathe of Kyoto, from the southeast to the central west, framed at its far edges by two eminent architectural complexes: on the far right of the southeastern screen is a lofty hall easily recognized as the Toyotomi's Great Buddha Hall—then the largest building in all Japan, whose construction occupied the Toyotomi from 1586 through the end of the period; on the extreme bottom left of the western screen is a large walled compound that can be identified, because of the stylized hollyhock family crests on the cloth festoons, as Nijō Castle, the Kyoto residence of the Tokugawa family. The placement of these complexes, facing each other and anchoring their respective sides of the painting, symbolizes the standoff that persisted between these two rival clans from Hideyoshi's death in 1598 until the Tokugawa's final military assault and bloody victory over the Toyotomi in 1615. Period viewers, whether anticipating or looking back on the dénouement, may well have recognized the implied tension, which is heightened and pointed up by the vignette (just below the most conspicuous marchers of the Gion Festival) of a group of monks soliciting funds under the banner of a great bell *(Fig. 27).* This is an unsubtle reference to the bronze bell that the Toyotomi cast for the Great Buddha Hall, bearing an inscription that offended the Tokugawa and afforded them the pretext for attacking the Toyotomi.[12]

The painting purports to represent a moment shortly before the violent conclusion, when both powerful contenders coexisted and the built environment of Kyoto was at its most splendid. The very existence of this type of painting, predicated on the belief that the capital city and its buildings were a suitable subject for monumental screens, suggests architecture's prominence in this period as emblem of stability, authority, and rebirth—an antidote and antithesis to the ravage of Kyoto in the previous century.[13] In the Funaki screens the architectural assertion of Toyotomi presence receives great emphasis: above the Great Buddha Hall unfold the sprawling precincts of Toyokuni Shrine (at the top of the first panel), built by the Toyotomi for the worship of the deified Hideyoshi; in between them is the Zen complex of Shōunji, constructed by Hideyoshi for memorial worship for his dead son Sutemaru.[14] All three of these structures—the Great Buddha Hall, the Toyokuni Shrine, and Shōunji—will figure prominently in our discussions. By their number, size, and splendor, these and other religious establishments accurately reflect how diligently the Toyotomi tended the sacred realm.

BEYOND KYOTO: CHIKUBUSHIMA

Kyoto was not the only locus of Japanese authority in this period: the new men of Momoyama who reunited the country under their own rule after a century of strife and disjunction actively explored the geomantic power of other places as well. This interest in geography is reflected in maps made of Japan in the early seventeenth century, such as one of a pair of six-fold screens in the Fukui Prefecture temple Jōtokuji (*Fig. 28; Fig. 29* is a map based on this painting).[15] Some still-famous geologic features of Japan are emphasized through graphic means, such as the familiar conical form of Mount Fuji and the massif of the Japan Alps which runs down the spine of the main island. Differentiated by a lighter shade of brown from other parts of the Japanese landmass is an oval area on the southern coast of Honshu, the main island of Japan: this is Osaka, which the Toyotomi chose as their primary urban seat of power. Although they maintained a prominent presence in Kyoto throughout the period, through their architecture and occasional residency, the Toyotomi also sought distance from Kyoto, and found in this historied and economically vibrant port city the ideal place to be both near the capital and comfortably removed from it.[16]

Also highlighted on this map is another place of exceptional countrywide significance in this period, especially for the Toyotomi. Just above Osaka is pictured the largest body of fresh water in Japan, Lake Biwa, and in the northern part of the lake an island whose location identifies it unquestionably as Chikubushima, literally, "Bamboo Grove Island." On such maps Chikubushima is typically the only island depicted in Lake Biwa, even though it is not the biggest (in the southern part of the lake is a larger island, Okishima, home to fishing communities from early times until today). Moreover, Chikubushima is represented on the map proportionally far larger than its true small size *(Fig. 1)*. This peculiarity stems from the island's special character at this time as a sacred place: it was one of the three chief abodes in Japan of the powerful protector-goddess Benzaiten and, as such, possessed a conceptual largeness that belied its actual physical size. This prominence was particularly concentrated in one building on the island, a hall dedicated to the worship of Benzaiten *(Fig. 2)*.

The Benzaiten Hall (now called by another name, the Tsukubusuma Jinja Honden,

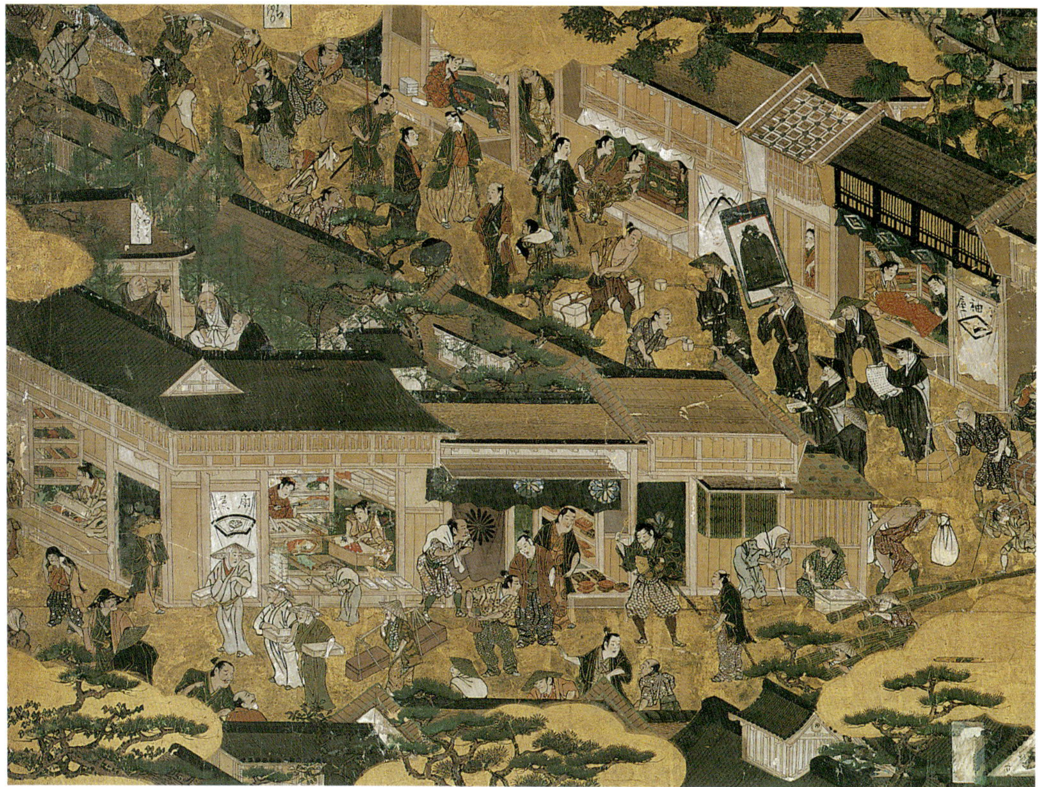

FIG. 27 Detail of Fig. 26.

for reasons we will consider later) has one of the most unusual histories of any building in Japan. It is a composite structure, whose two main parts were at one time independent of each other; in the early seventeenth century they were combined to form what in essence still stands today. One of these parts, the *hisashi*—the outer portion of the building that surrounds the central core—dates to a rebuilding project on the island in the 1560s, after a destructive fire in 1558. Even more notable is the other part, the central core, known in Japanese as the *moya.* It is, on its own, the most fully decorated Momoyama structure extant, adorned with a glorious ensemble of polychrome paintings, relief wood carvings, gilt metalwork, architectural coloring, and—of special note—black-and-gold lacquer, which is applied here more abundantly than on any building from any time in the history of Japan. This core, before it was incorporated into the present building, stood in late-sixteenth-century Kyoto as—I shall argue—a most noteworthy commission by the ruler Hideyoshi, a Buddhist memorial to his prematurely lost son, Sutemaru. The Benzaiten Hall, benefitting from the visual magnificence of this marvelous transplanted structure and sited on the sacred island, remains one of the most important, though least well understood, Momoyama buildings.[17] Chikubushima and this building (in its—and its parts'—various reincarnations) will appear and reappear throughout this study, as their links with all four Toyotomi family members chronologically unfold.

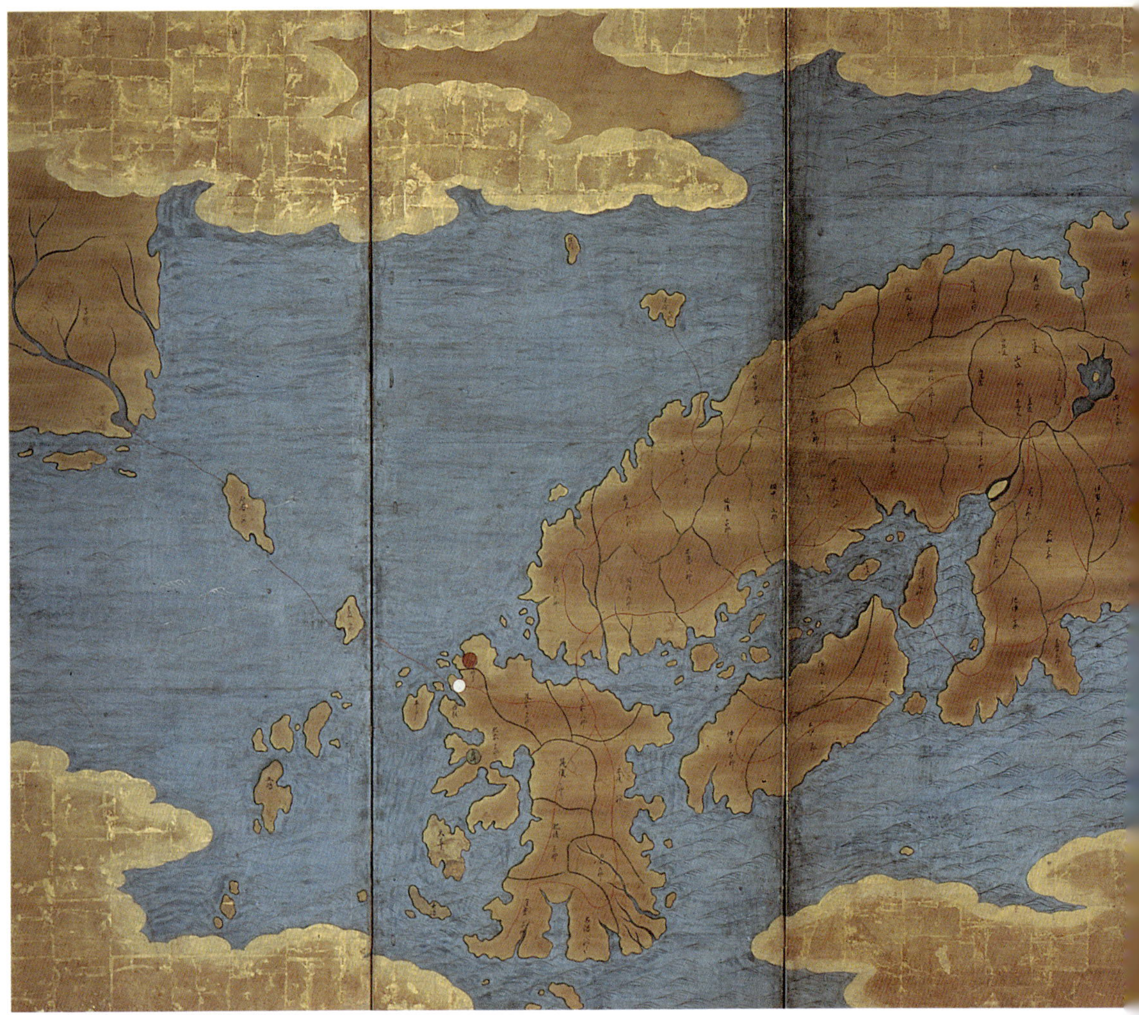

ART HISTORIANS AND THE MOMOYAMA PERIOD

Although the sacred was an explicit presence in Momoyama Japan, art historians until recently have characterized this period as predominantly secular, and they have overlooked tinctures of religious motive and meaning in works of art that are not overtly religious in subject matter. Inevitably, that perspective has limited, if not distorted, analysis of Momoyama art. Scholars have begun to amend this restricted approach, finally, with liberating effect. Reinterpretation of Kano Hideyori's celebrated folding-screen painting, *Maple Viewing at Mount Takao,* for example, newly emphasizes the critical presence of the sacred realm in what was formerly taken to be an uncomplicated genre depiction of leisure activities *(Fig. 30).*[18] True, the painting depicts a group of men and another of women and children, all in fine secular dress, dancing, conversing, and drinking in seasonal celebration under the famous colorful autumn foliage of Takao in northwest Kyoto. The sacred context of this festivity, though, is clearly indicated by the presence

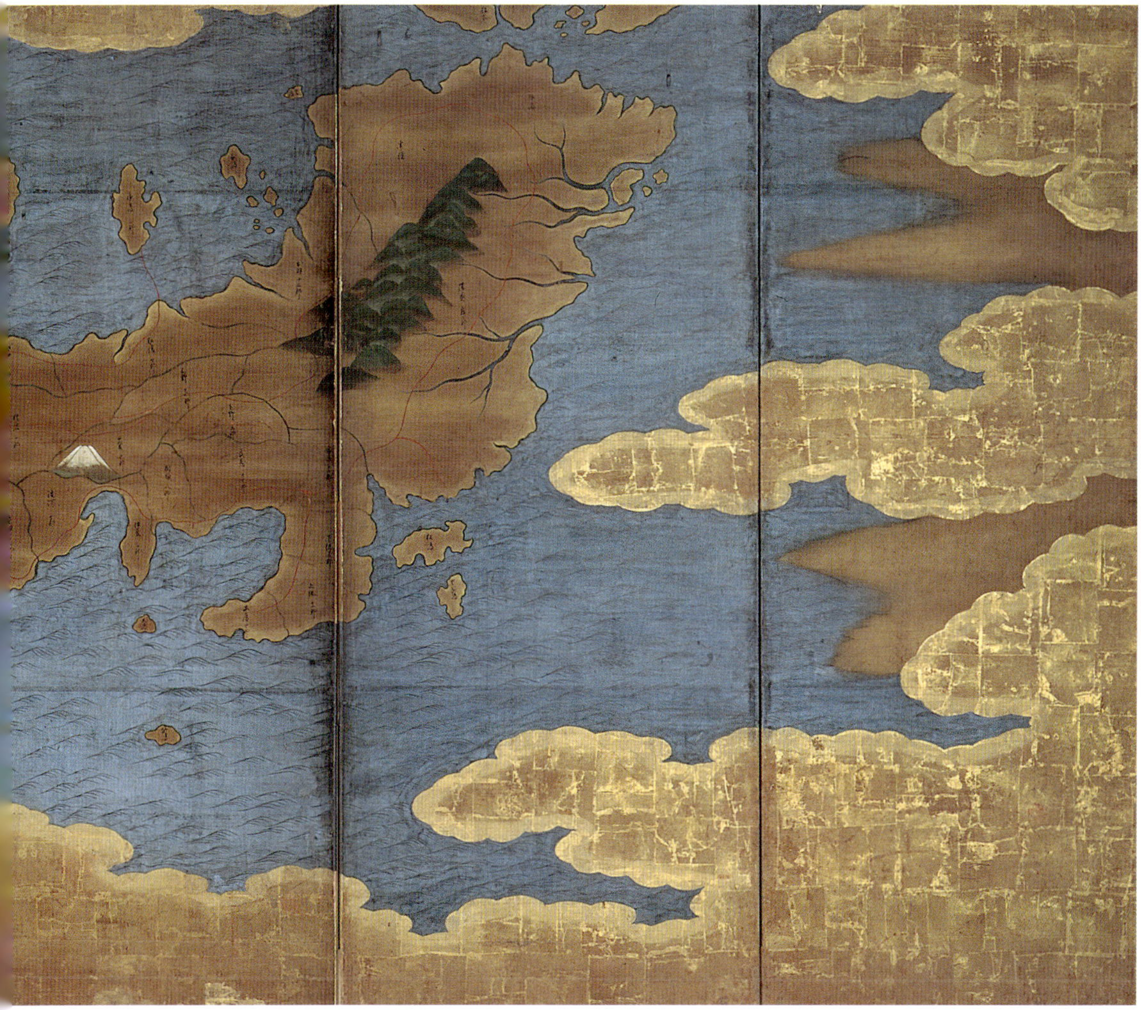

FIG. 28 *Map of Japan.* Late sixteenth–early seventeenth century. Six-fold screen; ink, color, and gold leaf on paper. Jōtokuji, Fukui Prefecture.

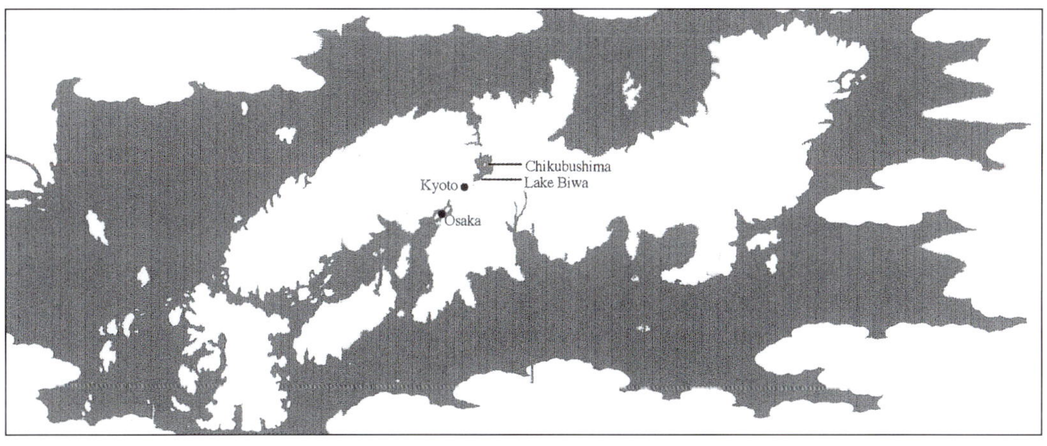

FIG. 29 Map based on Fig. 28. Prepared with the aid of Dax Kajiwara.

of two ancient and famous religious precincts in the upper half of the painting, on the far shore of the Kiyotaki River: the Shinto torii gate of Atago Shrine at the left, and the Buddhist temple halls and pagoda of Jingoji at the right. Linking the revellers to this realm is a bridge, a motif commonly used to unite the sacred and mundane, before which Buddhist monks stand. A turtle reposes in the river and flocks of herons and geese traverse it; these are all auspicious creatures, and here they are emblematic of the essential tie between the two realms.

So, too, fresh attention to previously undervalued types of painting and sculpture, notably mortuary portraiture, has pointed up the centrality of non-secular Momoyama art.[19] The portraits of the Toyotomi family members illustrated above are posthumous representations of the sitters that were used in a religious context, either as a focus for memorial worship or, in the case of Hideyoshi, for veneration of his deified posthumous manifestation. These representations, carefully rendered to give a sense of physiognomic individuality (their accuracy, of course, is another question), with the subjects' status indicated by their fine clothing and hieratic settings, were indispensable to communication—by way of ritual performance—between the living and those deceased and residing, it was hoped, in the numinous realm. Often painted or sculpted by the most esteemed artists of the day, such portraits are a quintessential Momoyama production.

Research of late into the role of ornament in Japanese culture and its connection with religious activity has also broadened and deepened our study of the sacred in art.[20] Fundamental in this regard is the concept of *shōgon,* which denotes adornment that proclaims and celebrates the divine.[21] Deriving from Indian concepts and appearing frequently in sutra passages describing the holy, the term arrived in Japan with Buddhism. Its currency in the Momoyama vocabulary is indicated by its inclusion in *Vocabvlario da Lingoa de Iapam,* the 1603 Japanese-Portuguese dictionary, which defines shōgon as "resplendence, or decoration."[22] This definition suggests that the Jesuits either did not perceive or chose not to emphasize the religious aspect of the term, but rather understood it in its broader meaning of impressive ornament. Shōgon certainly had this more general connotation, but in Japan the term was principally used to specify ornament in a sacred context, ornament whose purpose was the adornment of the divine. As we will see, Momoyama patrons often enhanced their religious buildings with the powerfully charged resplendence indicated by the word shōgon.

Exhilarating new forms of architecture, both secular and religious, emerged during this period. Castles of unprecedented vastness and elevation were built, the most important with interior decoration by leading artists; the towers dominated their surrounding towns in a manner previously unseen in Japan. *Chanoyu,* the ritualized drinking of tea, began to be practiced within buildings specially constructed to facilitate the aesthetic discourse that was at its heart. Hideyoshi's enthusiasm for tea and his patronage of the leading tea master Sen no Rikyū (1522–1591) spurred the invention of remarkably diverse chanoyu buildings: almost simultaneously, in the 1580s, were created Hideyoshi's portable chanoyu structure covered almost entirely with gold (as were its requisite tea paraphernalia), within which Hideyoshi received the emperor in lucent brilliance

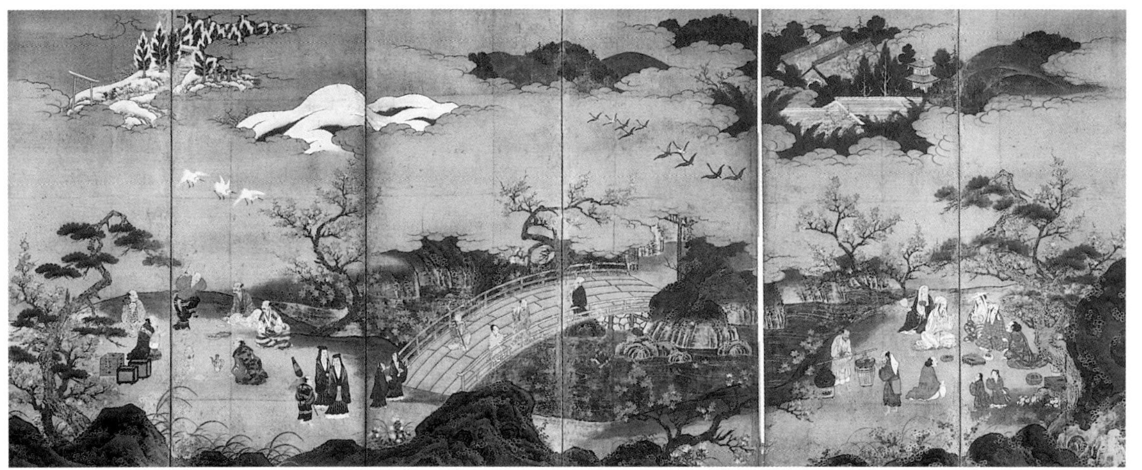

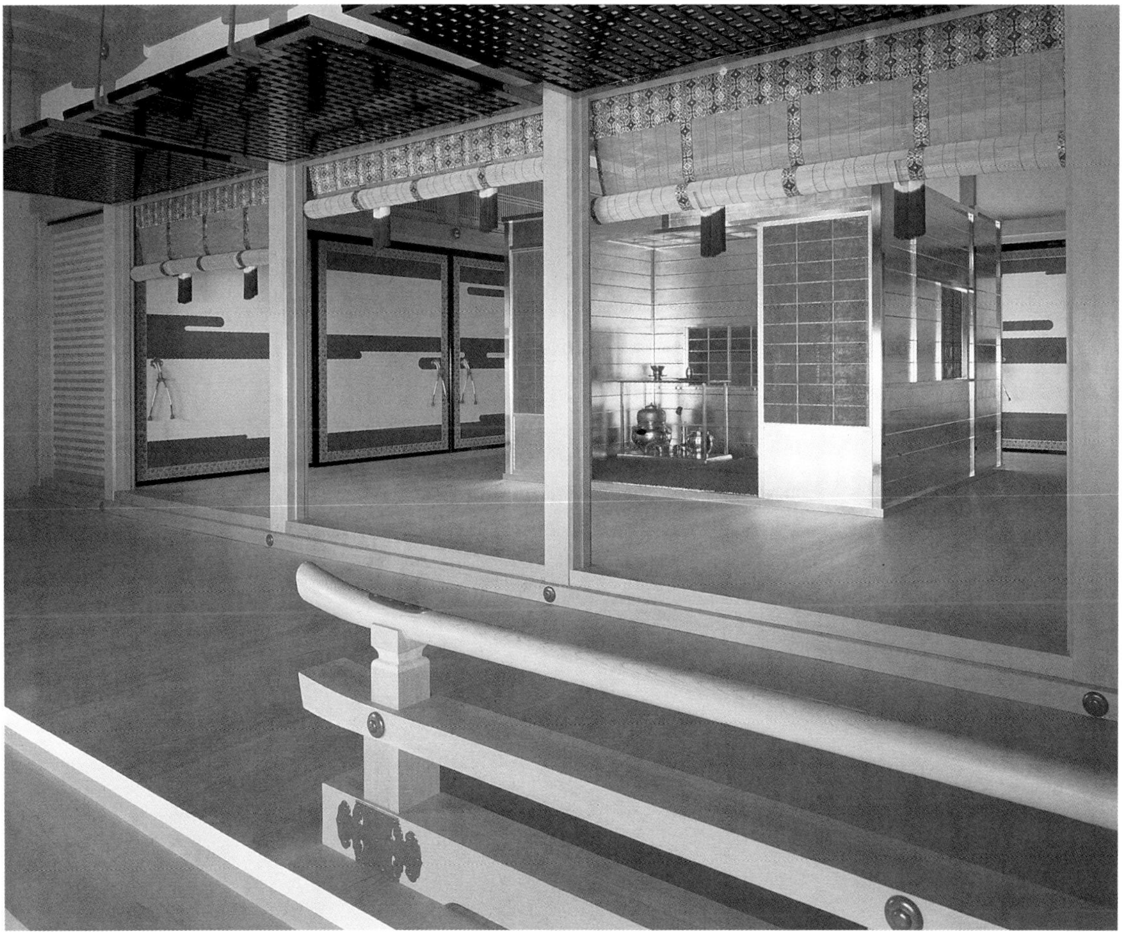

FIG. 30 (top) Kano Hideyori (d. ca. 1576 / 1577). *Maple Viewing at Mount Takao.* Late sixteenth century. Six-fold screen; ink and color on paper. Tokyo National Museum.

FIG. 31 (bottom) Reconstruction of Gold Tea Room. MOA Museum of Art, Shizuoka Prefecture.

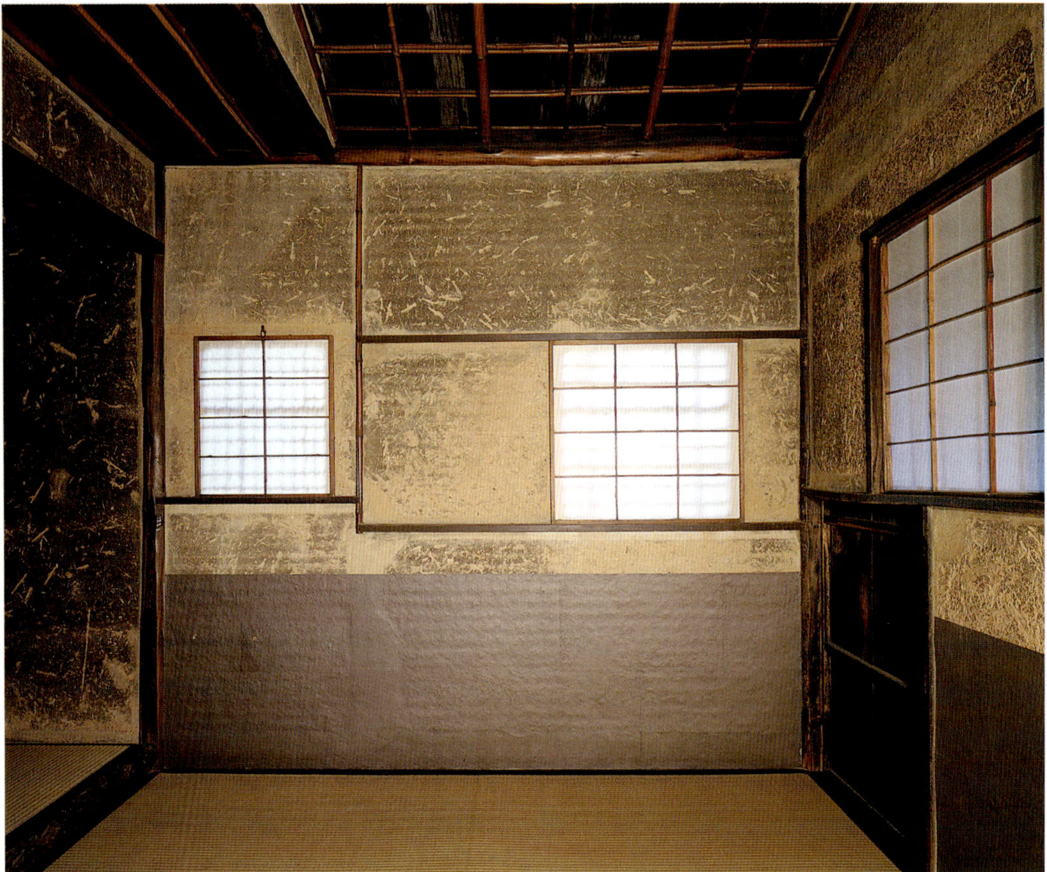

FIG. 32 Taian. Late sixteenth century. Myōkian, Kyoto. Photograph by Tankōsha.

(Fig. 31),[23] and Taian, a radically condensed chanoyu space, only nine feet square, that focused the participants' attentions on the tea objects, on the ritual itself, and on the masterly use of the commonplace materials from which it was made—earth, paper, bamboo, and raw wood *(Fig. 32)*. The spirit of architectural innovation led also to the creation of remarkable religious structures, including the Benzaiten Hall on Chikubushima, which announces its importance with an extraordinary application of resplendent ornament (as its core did when it originally stood in Kyoto).

The Momoyama warrior-rulers, their ornamented architecture, and the sacred most compellingly intersect within a geographic matrix formed of Osaka and Chikubushima and the places in between, foremost Kyoto and Ōmi Province (the old name of Shiga Prefecture). That intricate intersection is the story this book attempts to tell.

1

Chikubushima, from Its Origins to the Ascendancy of Hideyoshi

CHIKUBUSHIMA AS SACRED REALM

The sacred character of a place is often born of distinctive geographic and topographic features, peculiarities that distinguish it by appearance and location from sites that people normally inhabit: a place *looks* different, and so it must *be* different. (A place may also be designated as sacred because, and only after, something sacred happened there: Bodhgaya achieved its status because the Buddha reached enlightenment there, Bethlehem because Jesus was born there. This, however, is a quite different origin of sacred status.) Lofty mountains are invested with the divine worldwide; in Japan, the distinctive Mount Fuji, its conical form rising abruptly from the flatness of the surrounding Kantō plains, was long recognized to be an abode of the gods, but so are a great many others: Kōya, Kumano, Hiei, Mikasa, Futara, and on and on.[1] Caves are conduits to supernatural space, as at Mount Murō in Nara Prefecture, where they are lairs of the Dragon King.[2] Waterfalls—thunderous shafts of cascading energy, simultaneously fluid and impenetrable—harbor deities, as at Nachi, where the bodhisattva Kannon dwells.[3] Although ill suited for human habitation, unusual landscape befits the divine.

Likewise, people sometimes have perceived the sacred in the small solitary island, the land fragment that emerges from and is animated by ever-flowing waters. Its water-defined separateness makes the island seem a world unto itself and therefore possibly of numinous character. The sense of sacredness is even more pronounced when the island is visible from the mainland, making it part of people's daily visual environment, but distant enough to seem a place apart, an otherworldly place to which access from our world is possible, but requires special effort. Again, the Japanese inventory is long: Miyajima and Enoshima, sited just off Japan's ocean coast, are but two of the best-known island abodes of deity.

Especially arresting is the sight of Chikubushima, a jot of land (a bit less than a mile in circumference) in the northernmost reaches of Lake Biwa, Japan's largest lake *(Fig.1)*. Chikubushima's distinctive asymmetric double mound is crisply framed in clear weather by a wall of undulating mountains along the lake's northern rim; on hazy days, it appears to float in the mists. Visually equidistant from the east and west shores of the lake, the island looks perfectly positioned, as if intentionally placed. This improbably well composed setting—the sense of an ideal arrangement not typically found in nature—combines with a luxuriant, elysian environment. The island's steep, rocky shores rise precipitously from deep crystalline waters, and its body is leafy green with dense bamboo and trees.[4] In Chikubushima, disengaged from the bustle of modern Japan, nature is still profoundly present: birds flock in the forest canopy, snakes abound in the creviced terrain, and fish teem in the surrounding waters.

On the wide southern exposure of the island, facing the expanse of the lake, clusters of buildings occupy the few flat areas or cling to the rocks. Grand, sweeping roofs, several of them tiled or wood-shingled, are the first clues to the high status of many of these buildings, and a torii gate verifies that they are religious. This is our first confirmation that people have indeed found the sacred here and, in the long-sanctioned way, have constructed buildings to honor and minister to it. Modern awe at the natural wonder and sacred atmosphere of Chikubushima, however, was not the inspiration for this architectural efflorescence (though some of the buildings are recent).

In pre-modern times, and especially in the Momoyama period (1568–1615), Chikubushima was a critical place in the Japanese consciousness. Ōmi Province (present-day Shiga Prefecture), where it is located, was geographically principal and economically vital to the whole country. Lake Biwa was a major trade and transportation route, linking the capital district of Kyoto and the northern parts of Japan. The fertile Ōmi plains, abutting the eastern shore of the lake, were historically an area of abundant agricultural production.[5] Northern Ōmi was a frequent battleground in the warfare of the period: Sekigahara, located nearby, was the site in 1600 of one of the most famous battles in Japanese history, whose outcome incidentally elevated Chikubushima into even greater prominence.

CHIKUBUSHIMA AND BENZAITEN

Most importantly, Chikubushima was celebrated within Japan's sacred geography as a primary locus for the worship of Benzaiten, a female Buddhist deity and often, in Japan, an island dweller. Other deities also figured prominently within the Shinto-Buddhist complex that covered the island, including the goddess Azaihime no Mikoto (who was viewed as the Shinto manifestation of Benzaiten) and the bodhisattva Kannon; from at least the twelfth century, however, Benzaiten was the primary ritual focus.[6] Her chief

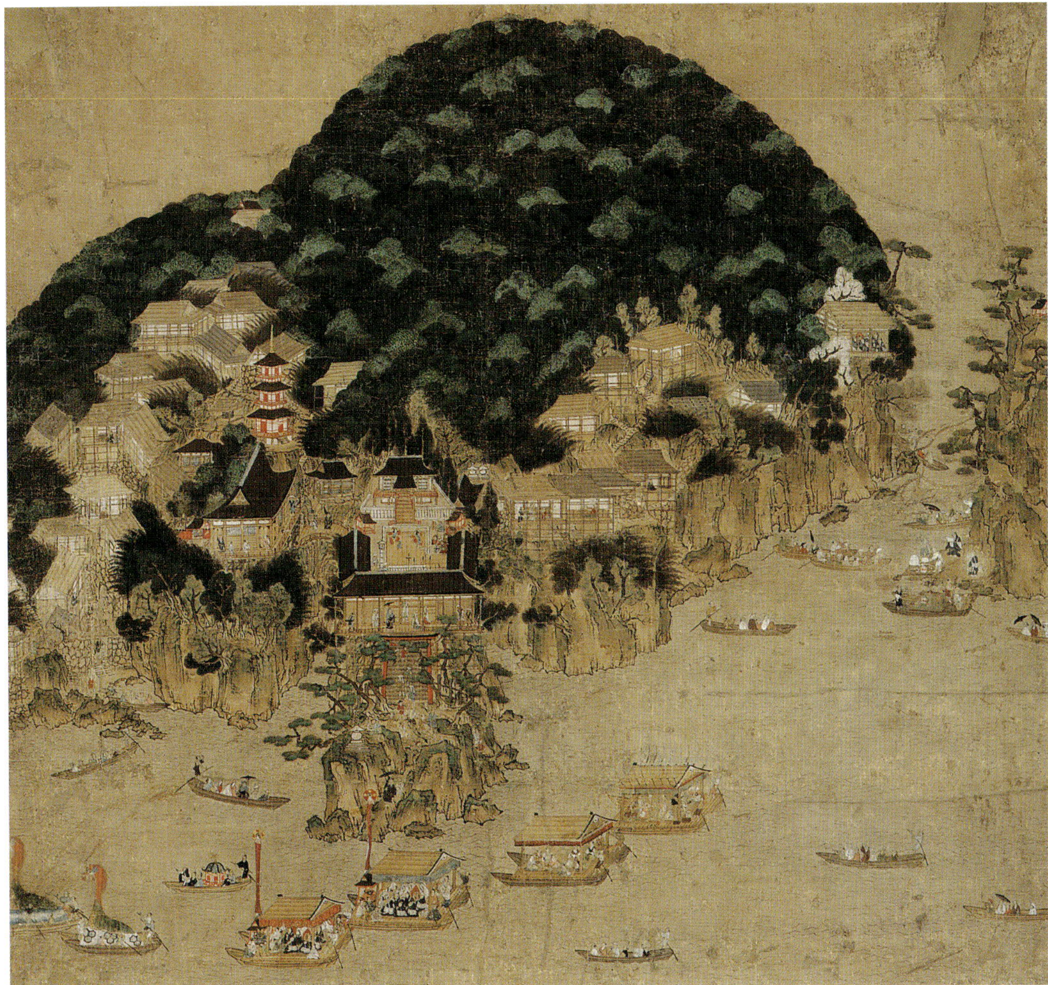

FIG. 33 *Chikubushima Lotus Festival.* Sixteenth century. Hanging scroll; ink and color on paper. Tokyo National Museum.

manifestation there was as a powerful and fierce protector, a persona that attracted many elite warrior devotees, especially in the Momoyama period.

This significance of Benzaiten we know from extensive documentary evidence as well as from a sixteenth-century painting in the Tokyo National Museum *(Fig. 33)* that chronicles the Lotus Festival (Rengee).[7] The Lotus Festival was the chief event in the liturgical calendar of the island, a splendid annual affair that took place over several days and celebrated the powers of Benzaiten. Each year, elite lay constituents from the surrounding area in Ōmi competed to be selected as the secular sponsor of the festival, a role that conferred tremendous prestige. The festival required each sponsor to commission a new sculpture of Benzaiten, which was carried to the island in a grand boat procession, as depicted in the painting, and then donated to the island. Dozens of the sculptures still exist, lined up in no particular order within the interior corridors of the main hall of the Chikubushima temple Hōgonji, a structure built in 1942.

The painter took care to render the island's distinctive shape, lush greenery, and craggy shoreline (as well as the tiny islet of Kojima, just east of Chikubushima), but the focus of the composition, reflecting the scale of the religious enterprise on Chikubushima, is the array of buildings that covers the lower part of the island. Most of the buildings, depicted in brown monochrome with thatch roofs, are subsidiary structures and the living quarters of the monks. Several buildings, however, including a three-story pagoda, are described in darker browns and bright red, thereby distinguishing them as especially important. At the center of this cluster is a building shown head-on; it is fronted by a square courtyard that is surrounded by a roofed corridor. Numerous figures ascend the rocky path from the boats to the corridor, and in the courtyard in front of the building two figures perform ritual dance as part of the festival proceedings. This is the chief building on the island, the hall enshrining Benzaiten.

THE TSUKUBUSUMA MAIN HALL

In 1558 a great fire swept over the island, consuming most if not all of the buildings pictured in the Tokyo National Museum painting.[8] It was left to later believers and patrons to rebuild Chikubushima and so permit the religious activities to continue. Fortuitously, this disaster occurred just as immense political transformations were shaking Japan, with enormous implications for the sacred realm; coincidentally, Chikubushima was well positioned to benefit from those transformations. Throughout the late sixteenth and early seventeenth century newly ascendant warrior leaders—especially Toyotomi Hideyoshi (1537–1598) and his descendants—retooled the traditional conception of Chikubushima into something of deepened contemporary relevance and heightened sacredness. The tangible expression of their reverence was a multistage building campaign that created the pre-modern buildings extant on the island today, including the hall used at that time for the worship of Benzaiten *(Fig. 2).* As the ritual heart of the island, the Benzaiten Hall was the special focus of secular attention, though what that attention comprised, and many other fundamental aspects of the building, have been obscured over the intervening centuries.

Even its present name—formally, the Tsukubusuma Jinja Honden (Tsukubusuma Shrine Main Hall)—is a nineteenth-century fabrication. It was conferred in 1871 as part of the new national policy to separate Shinto and Buddhism: the Shiga prefectural government declared the building to be Shinto and ordered that it be called by the Shinto name Tsukubusuma Jinja in place of the one then used, Benzaitensha.[9] Objects associated with Benzaiten were replaced with Shinto ceremonial implements, and the *kami* Azaihime no Mikoto was made the new focus of worship.[10] The building's new name had an impressive ancient pedigree: it was taken from a tenth-century list of Shinto shrines in the general area around Chikubushima, known as Asai County.[11] Applying the name to the Benzaiten Hall on Chikubushima, however, was at best of dubious historical validity, for there is no firm evidence that it had ever been used for this building. It surely was not the name of the building in the Momoyama period, when it was, as it had been from much earlier, referred to by several names that reflected its function as a hall dedicated to the worship of Benzaiten.[12] The invented name is still used today, and Benzaiten's ritual objects remain exiled from their historical home, obscuring the pre-Meiji character of the building (and also of the thoroughly interwoven Shinto and Buddhist ritual activities of the island). In light of these circumstances, I refer to the building as the Tsukubusuma Main Hall: this designation acknowledges the name by which the building is today officially and familiarly known, but by avoiding the term *jinja* (which refers to a Shinto shrine), it de-emphasizes one aspect of the present name that is particularly anachronic in the context of the Momoyama period.[13]

The building is, in many ways, a typical example of Japanese Buddhist architecture: it is made of wood, employs post-and-lintel construction, sits on a raised foundation, and has an impressive roof. Its modest size—only a few worshippers can gather at the front porch—is well proportioned to the constrictive site: the building backs hard against the island's steep mountain and is fronted by a small clearing that drops off sharply into the lake. Its most striking feature is the grand cypress-bark roof, with graceful cusped gables front and back in the upper portion, its edges trimmed with metalwork; below that is a lower tier of narrow eaves and a protruding central porch at the front.[14] When viewed from the usual southern approach to the island, the roof's elegant curves stand out against the vertical mountainside and announce the building's place of importance among the many structures on the island. Finally, a long horizontal corridor snakes against the mountain from the west side (just visible at the left of *Fig. 2*), linking the Main Hall to the neighboring Kannondō (Kannon Hall) and further fusing it into the precipitous geology of the island.

COMPOSITE ARCHITECTURE

Initially, then, the Main Hall—the former Benzaitan Hall—gives the impression that it is, like countless other old structures, a building weathered over time but essentially preserving a singular, original state. This impression is deceiving, for the building was an improbable composite from its inception in the early seventeenth century, a combination of two then-recent though formerly unrelated buildings and other stray architectural elements. It seems so whole, though, and so successfully wedded to its site, that to the unsuspecting eye the disjunctures among its hybrid parts are rendered almost invisible. That was the intent of its makers, of course, to create not an awkward amalgam, but a suitably polished architectural setting for the worship of Benzaiten. The composite building succeeded in this regard, and so became an "original" architectural state.

But each of the constituent parts had its own previous and compelling original form that, as we will see, prompted its inclusion in Benzaiten's refurbished hall. The building principally comprises a three-bay-square *moya* (core) surrounded by a *hisashi* (the outer portion of the building that envelops much of the core) that is five bays by four

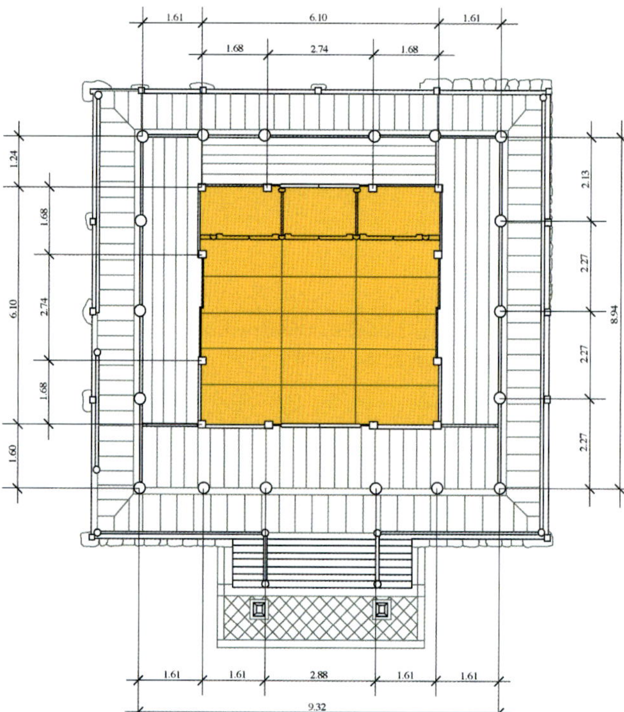

FIG. 34 Tsukubusuma Main Hall. Plan, with moya marked in yellow. Prepared with the aid of Dax Kajiwara, adapted from *KTJHSKH*, pl. 37.

bays (see plan, *Fig. 34;* the moya is indicated in yellow), and it is these parts that were once independent buildings with separate origins. The two are distinguished, first, by their differently shaped pillars—those of the moya are square and those of the hisashi are round—and even more distinctly by the finish of their structural elements: the pillars and lintel-beams of the moya are coated with black-and-gold *makie* lacquer, while those of the hisashi are plain wood *(Fig. 3).* By this description it seems a clumsy and therefore easily detected mix.

The potentially jarring effect of these differences is minimized, however, by the way the two parts combine. Only the front of the moya is visible from the outside, and it is deeply and darkly recessed by the protruding roof and porch *(Fig. 35).* Its other three sides are surrounded by the hisashi; on these sides, between the moya and hisashi walls, is thereby formed a narrow U-shaped corridor (the corridor is indicated in gray in *Fig. 36*). The two ends of the corridor, on the south side of the building, are sealed by walls linking the moya pillars with the hisashi walls (marked "A" and "B" in *Fig. 36*), with the result that the corridor is virtually undetectable. The corridor thus masks much of the moya's exterior, thereby deemphasizing its lacquered state *(Figs. 6, 7).* Most of the visible outer faces of the walls of the composite building are covered with relief carvings, which serve to further solidify the visual link between the moya and the hisashi *(Figs. 3, 37–39).* Only close inspection—difficult to do in the shadow of the overhang—reveals stylistic differences between the carvings on the moya and those on the hisashi, and even once observed, the differences do not automatically appear meaningful. Moreover,

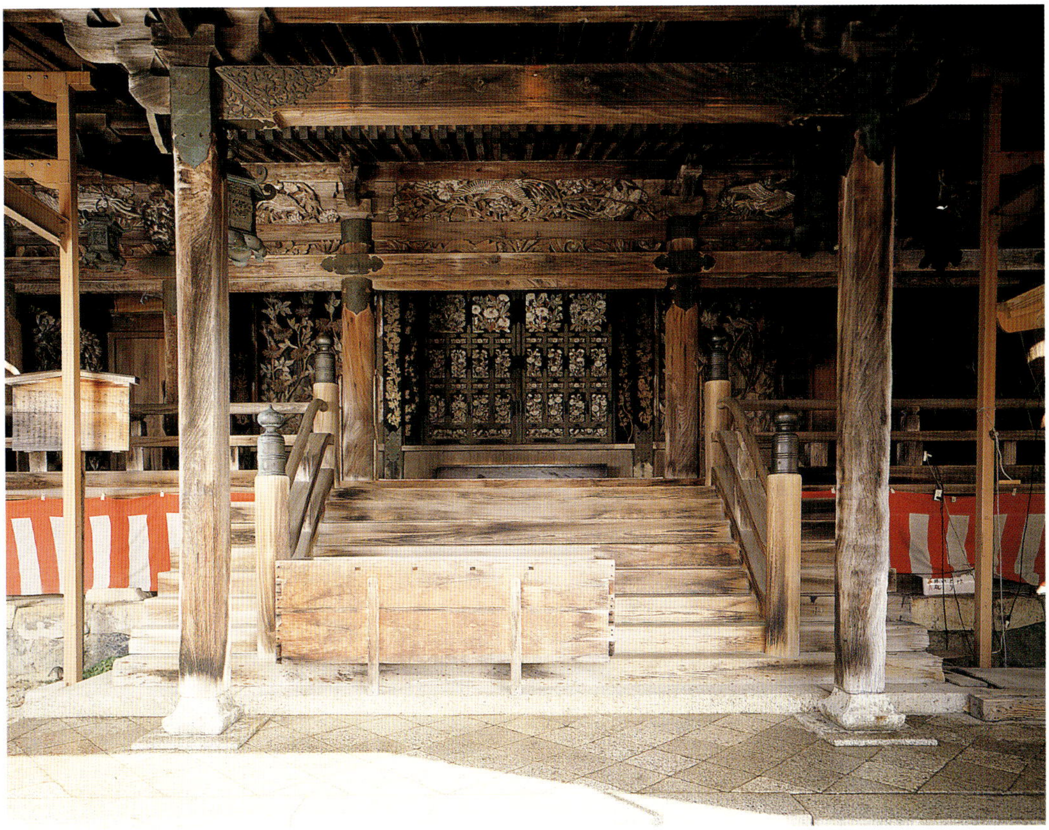

FIG. 35 Tsukubusuma Main Hall. View of exterior, south side. Chikubushima, Shiga Prefecture.

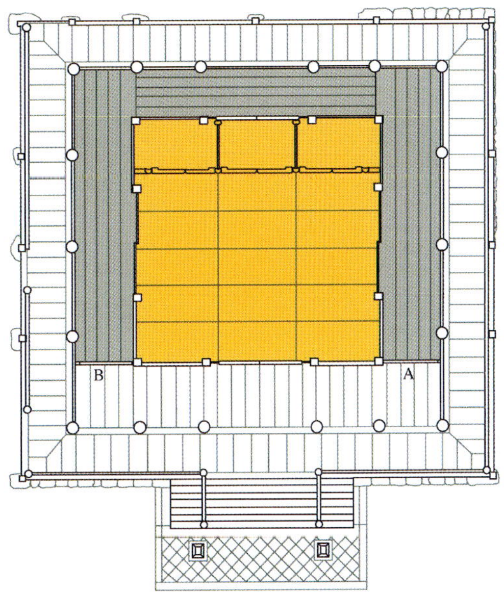

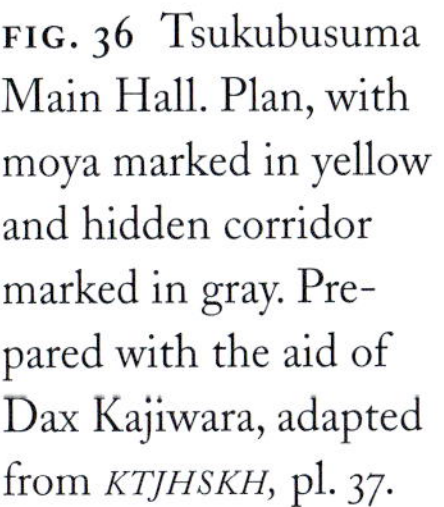

FIG. 36 Tsukubusuma Main Hall. Plan, with moya marked in yellow and hidden corridor marked in gray. Prepared with the aid of Dax Kajiwara, adapted from *KTJHSKH*, pl. 37.

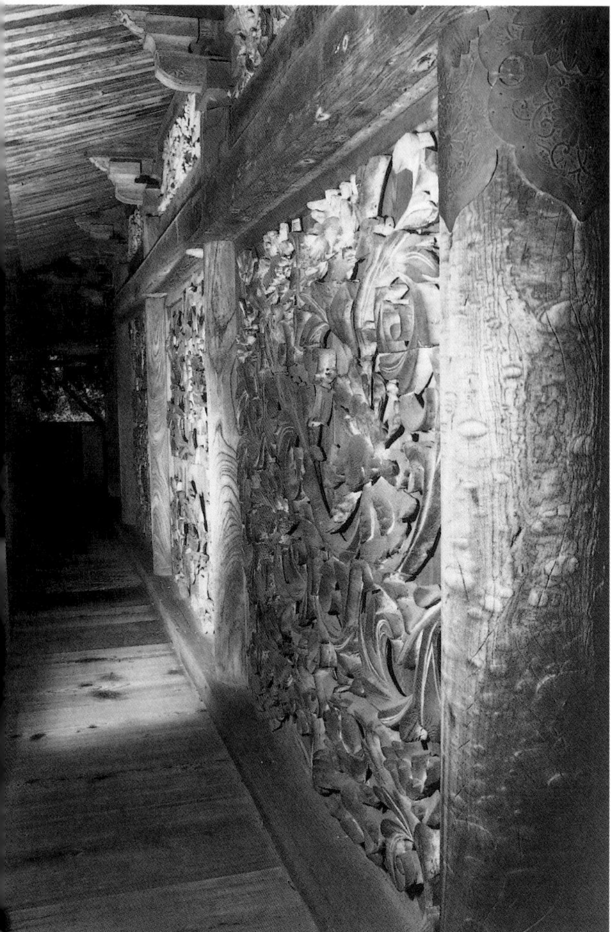

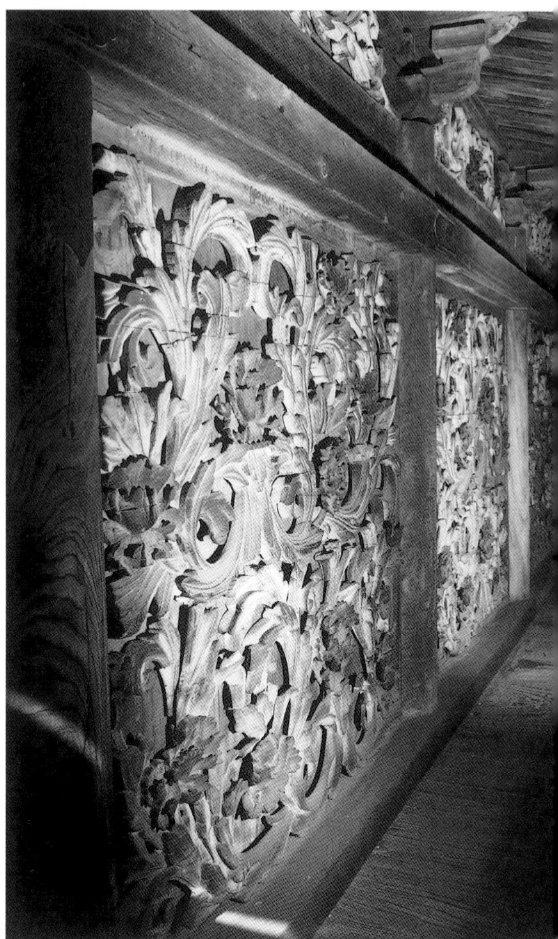

one glance at the luxurious decoration of the moya's interior—its paintings, makie lacquer, and gilt metalwork—helps seduce one into accepting this as a marvelously unified building *(Figs. 8–14)*.

The most surprising architectural discrepancies were revealed only during a major conservation project in 1936–1937.[15] During this, the first attempt at a thorough examination of the building, it was found that the moya and hisashi attach to each other in an unexpectedly limited fashion. At the front of the building, for example, the four moya pillars are connected with the four corresponding pillars of the hisashi by *ebikōryō* ("shrimp-shaped rainbow beams"), commonly used in Japanese architecture as linking elements *(Fig. 3)*. But at two of these points—the central pairs of pillars at either side of the entrance—the moya and hisashi pillars are not perfectly aligned, and so the ebikōryō extend between them at a slightly oblique angle. No ebikōryō at all tie the moya and hisashi pillars along the other three sides (which lie within the hidden corridor), not even at the rear, which mirrors the layout of the front *(Fig. 6)*. So misaligned are the pillars on the east and west sides that no ebikōryō could possibly be used to connect them (at present only rough lengths of wood awkwardly connect the moya and hisashi at these points, *Fig. 7*). In this regard, the moya and hisashi are linked primarily by physical proximity, rather than by structural parallelism.

A more unusual discovery still was the configuration of the double-layered roof (for sections of the building, see *Figs. 40, 41*).[16] The lower roof issues from a wall of wood planks that rises vertically from the top of the hisashi pillars to the lower rafters of the upper roof. It is supported by hip rafters, composed of two partly overlapped lengths of wood; such two-part construction would not be unusual if the hip rafters spanned a substantial length. Their shortness, however, indicates that something is amiss, most likely that the lower pieces had been at one time considerably longer and extended inward beyond the wall to connect with, and receive the support of, the interior pillars. That the lower pieces are so short strongly suggests that they have been cropped and that the weight of the lower roof was at one time differently borne than at present.[17] The lower roof, in other words, has undergone a dramatic change that altered its structural relationship to the building; now it is an oddly appended decorative complement to the sweeping arc of the upper roof, which is supported only by the moya pillars.

Apparently, the hisashi too has been markedly altered since it was first built. All of its bays on the east and west sides are of a consistent width—2.27 meters—except for

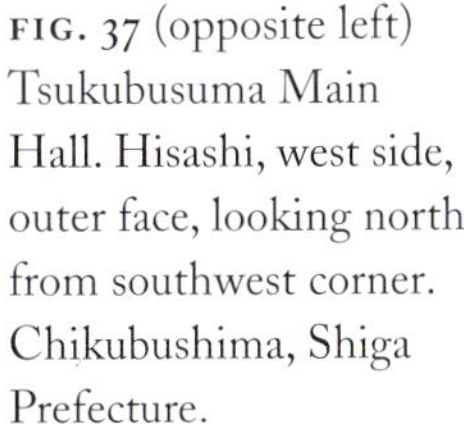

FIG. 37 (opposite left) Tsukubusuma Main Hall. Hisashi, west side, outer face, looking north from southwest corner. Chikubushima, Shiga Prefecture.

FIG. 38 (opposite right) Tsukubusuma Main Hall. Hisashi, east side, outer face, looking north from southeast corner. Chikubushima, Shiga Prefecture.

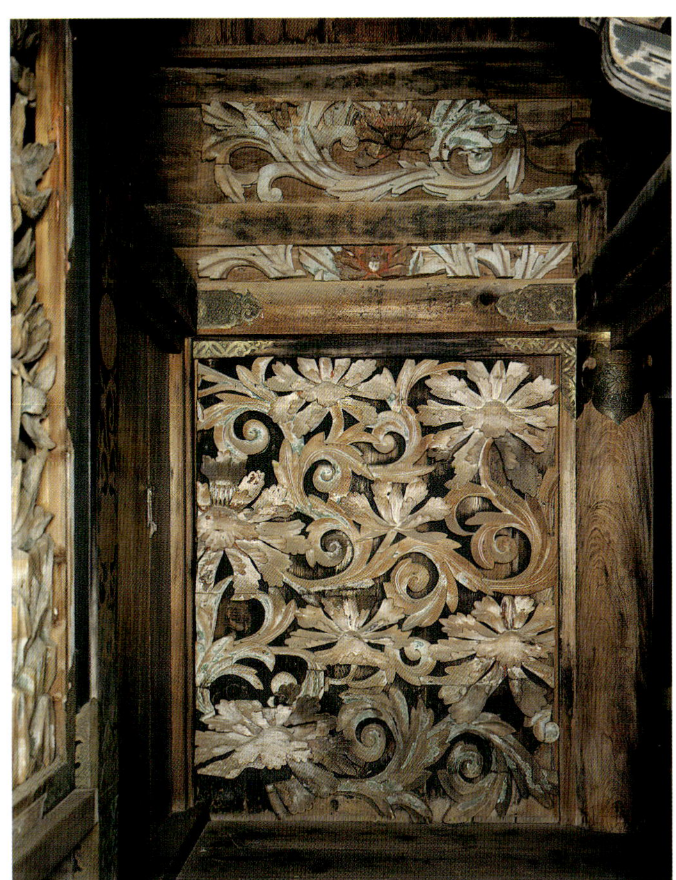

FIG. 39 (right) Tsukubusuma Main Hall. Wood carvings of peonies. Hisashi, east side, inner face. Chikubushima, Shiga Prefecture.

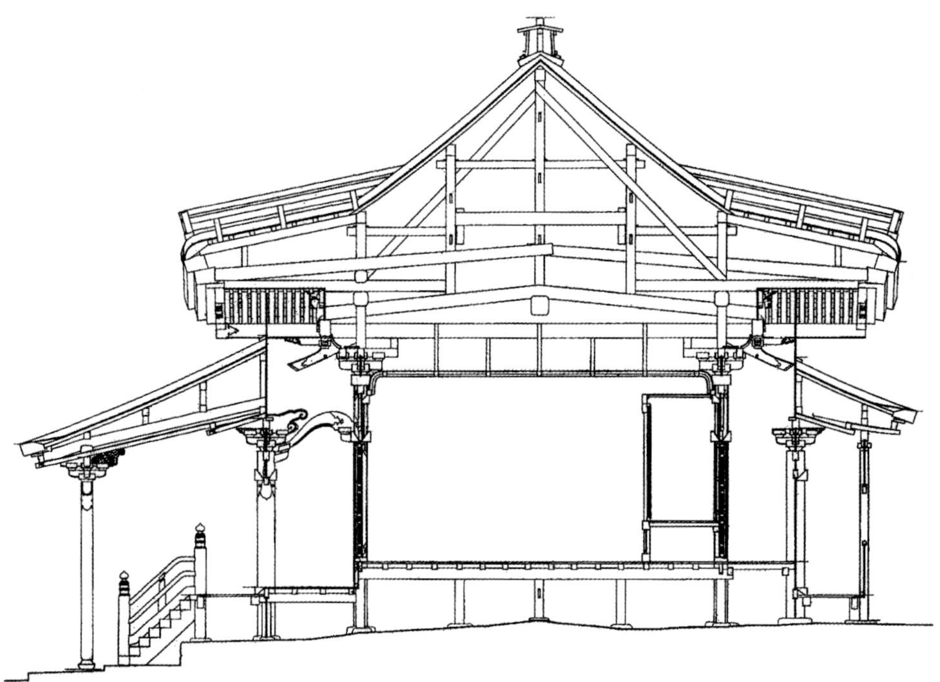

FIG. 40 Tsukubusuma Main Hall. North-south section. Prepared with the aid of Dax Kajiwara, adapted from *KTJHSKH*, pl. 42.

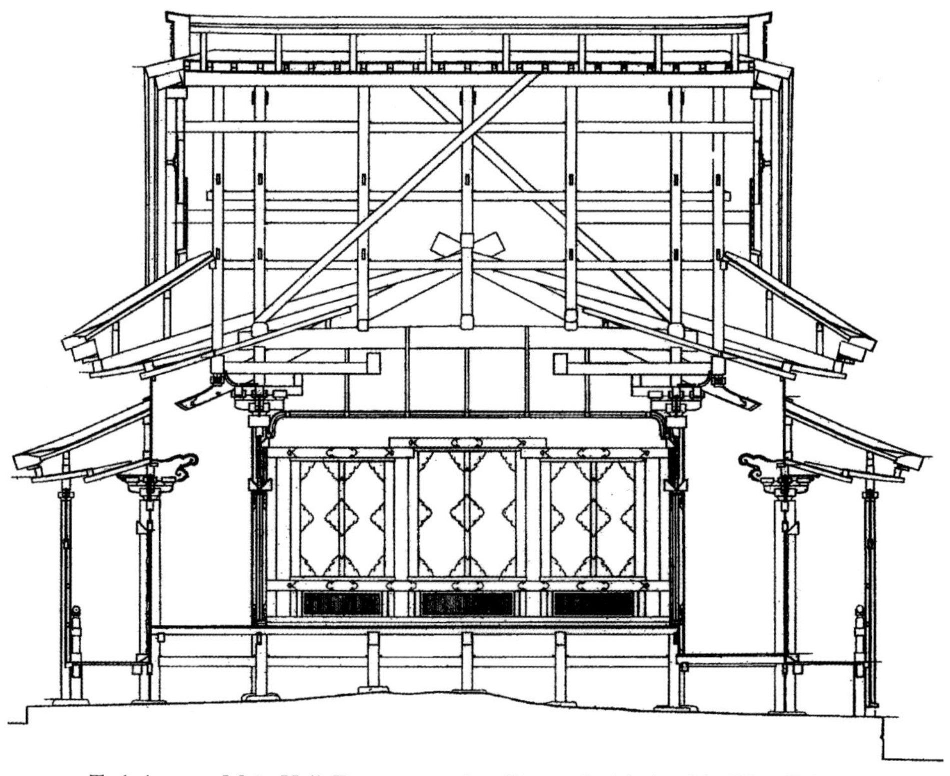

FIG. 41 Tsukubusuma Main Hall. East-west section. Prepared with the aid of Dax Kajiwara, adapted from *KTJHSKH*, pl. 41.

the rear, or northernmost, bays, which are smaller by 14 centimeters *(Fig. 34)*. The repairers also found that the hisashi was constructed primarily of zelkova *(keyaki)* wood, except for the smaller bays, where Japanese cedar *(sugi)* was employed.[18] At some time, it would appear, the north-south dimension of the hisashi either was decreased slightly or, alternatively, enlarged by one bay; that the odd-sized bay is smaller than the others indicates that the change was made to effect a particular size. Evidence suggests that this modification occurred to accommodate the building that is now the moya.

The history of the hisashi before this transformation is still somewhat sketchy in detail. If it was built on the island (and there is no evidence to suggest otherwise), then it certainly postdates the 1558 conflagration, which reduced to ashes most, if not all, structures on Chikubushima; no subsequent blaze has so ravaged the island. A major reconstruction campaign, begun soon after the disaster, certainly included rebuilding the hall dedicated to the chief deity of Chikubushima, Benzaiten.[19] Scholars presume that it is this mid-sixteenth century building that was the original form of the present Main Hall and that is partly preserved as the hisashi.[20] It is thought, in other words, that what is now the hisashi was originally the Benzaiten Hall reconstructed on Chikubushima after the 1558 fire and later modified to encompass the lacquered moya.

The early history of the moya can be traced with greater certainty. An inscription on a moya rafter, discovered during the conservation project, provides one key clue; it states, "This lacquered thing was coated at the Daibutsu," and includes the names Seiami and Fusai, identified as lacquerers *(nushi)*.[21] "Daibutsu" refers to the celebrated Daibutsuden (Great Buddha Hall) of the Hōkōji temple complex in Kyoto, begun by Toyotomi Hideyoshi in the mid-1580s and completed in the mid-1590s. The inscription indicates that the moya was originally made at this location, at a lacquer workshop near the Great Buddha Hall. It is well documented that at the time of this project, hundreds of artisans gathered in Kyoto from the surrounding provinces and settled in residences specially built for them near the construction site. Many of the craftsmen stayed on in the area even after the completion of the Great Buddha Hall and continued to practice their trades at other projects in Kyoto.[22]

The lacquer, moreover, confirms that the moya was once an independent building. Even though the outer faces of the north, east, and west walls of the moya are now hidden behind the hisashi walls of the Main Hall, the fading and damage to all of the exterior lacquer indicates that at one time the moya was not enclosed, but was subject to the effects of weather; when first created, what is now the Tsukubusuma Main Hall's moya stood open to the elements, independent of other buildings. The inscription on a ridgepole placard *(munafuda)* suggests that this structure was moved to Chikubushima about 1602.[23] Dated to 1602.9.6, the brief text of the placard states, "Construction of Benzaiten," specifies Katagiri Katsumoto (1556–1615) as the administrator, and gives the names of four other men involved in the project. Ridgepole placards were generally written to commemorate the completion of a construction project, so this placard indicates that work on the newly configured Benzaiten Hall was brought to a successful conclusion by the ninth month of that year. Katagiri Katsumoto was the administrator of many of the Toyotomi family's construction projects in the early 1600s, indicating that it was Hideyoshi's descendants who sent the structure to the island.

This diverse evidence all indicates that the extant Tsukubusuma Main Hall is a composite structure, consisting of an originally unrelated moya and hisashi. When the unusual structural relationship between the moya and the hisashi is considered in light of the moya and placard inscriptions, it would appear that the Toyotomi removed a building from its original site in Kyoto and transported it to Chikubushima. On the island it was likely rotated from its initial orientation[24] and installed into a pre-existing building, requiring modification of that building's size and removal of its smaller interior. In addition, large relief carvings were added to the exterior of the building-turned-hisashi (as we will see, the moya already had its own carvings before the move), and so was completed a most unusual—and complicated—refurbishing.

What is now the moya of the Tsukubusuma Main Hall on Chikubushima, in short, was first built in the capital city of Kyoto sometime after 1586, and there it stood as an independent building until 1602. In 1602 it was removed from Kyoto by the Toyotomi and placed in an entirely new context—as the moya of the Main Hall—on the island of Chikubushima. Thereby was formed a new hall within which the worship of Benzaiten was conducted until the mid-nineteenth century. To explain the scenario behind this synopsis of physical transformation, we must inquire how the secular sought to transform the sacred in the Momoyama period: how ornamented architecture served the purposes of assertive warriors and of Buddhist monks, throughout Japan and at Chikubushima.

CHIKUBUSHIMA'S PRE-MOMOYAMA IMAGE

From long ago, Chikubushima's otherworldly image was particularized and disseminated through exegetic texts. They are as varied as the *Chikubushima engi,* an account of the island's legendary past; the *Tale of the Heike,* the classic narrative of twelfth-century battles between the Taira (Heike) and Minamoto warrior clans; the *Keiran shūyōshū,* a fourteenth-century encyclopedic assemblage of religious information, including that relating to Chikubushima; and a Nō drama entitled *Chikubushima* (to be considered in a later chapter). All present vivid characterizations of Chikubushima and contributed to the island's important position in the Japanese consciousness of sacred place.

The *Chikubushima Engi*

An early and detailed account of the island is provided in two often concordant versions of the island's official history, or *engi,* dating respectively from 931 and 1415; the kami-centered Chikubushima of the earlier engi becomes, in the later one, a place where Buddhism is especially strongly manifested.[25] The engi was a common ecclesiastical genre, a chronicle whereby a temple purported to record its origins and development over time, and it was an important tool by which a temple asserted its desired secular and sacred affiliations. As such, the veracity of any engi is deeply suspect: many of the happenings occur in the unobserved divine realm, and those occurring in our world are often unverifiable. Accuracy, however, was not the major goal of the engi; more important, rather, was the construction of a commendable temple history and, as well, the willingness of the audience to appreciate (if not necessarily to believe) the engi's claims.

Precisely who constituted this audience is often uncertain, though the author of Chikubushima's 1415 version, an otherwise unknown monk from Mount Hiei named Fumon, provides a clue: he notes in a postscript that he visited the island in 1414 and was instructed in a dream to write the engi since people did not know of the origins of the sacred character of the island. He returned to Hiei, assembled twenty-three other monks to assist him, and on the basis of earlier records (including, presumably, the 931 engi) composed his text, which he then deposited in the island's treasure hall. The intended audience here thus included pilgrims who, like Fumon, journeyed to the island and examined its buildings and their contents, and needed to be informed about their history and sacredness.[26] What this audience needed to hear, and what Fumon's rendering provided, was an account that analyzed the island and its monuments in light of intertwined Shinto and Buddhist beliefs.

Both versions begin with the same engaging and impressive story of the genesis of the island's sacral character. Chikubushima was created in ancient times, during the reign of the Kōrei emperor (in the third century B.C.E., according to the Western calendar), when there occurred a contest of strength between the brother and sister deities Ibukio no Mikoto and Azaihime no Mikoto (the Shinto deity now enshrined in the Tsukubusuma Main Hall). Azaihime no Mikoto lowered herself in the northern part of Lake Biwa: she solidified the water's spray to form a rocky shore and piled the wind-borne dust to create an island; she commanded fish to pile stones at the island to form a spit of land and called on birds to scatter the seeds of various trees. Bamboo, we are told, was the first thing to take root there, and so the name of the island came to be written with the characters for "bamboo" and "grow" (*chiku* 竹 and *bu* 生), and to be read as Chikubushima.

Fumon adds to this a long discussion centered on events that purportedly occurred during a visit by Gyōki (668–749), the saintly Nara-period monk whose compassionate works for the poor earned him the title of living bodhisattva and who also was summoned to serve the emperor on such exceptionally important projects as the construction of Tōdaiji, the greatest temple of eighth-century Japan. In Gyōki's presence, we are told, "a deity *(myōjin)* appeared, pointed to the ground, and stated that the island emerged from the Konrinzai," that is, the Gold Layer, a Buddhist term that refers to the uppermost of the three layers that exist beneath the ground, the one that supports the world (the other two, consecutively beneath the Gold Layer, are the Water Layer and the Wind Layer). The deity also described the island as "a Diamond-Treasure Seat Rock," a place, that is, where enlightenment may be reached. Thus begins Fumon's layering of Buddhist interpretations on the sacred site.

Fumon continues with a second, Buddhist, explanation for the name of the island.

Gyōki stuck a bamboo staff into the ground and made an oath: "If this is a place that upholds the Three Treasures"—the three basic elements of Buddhism: the Buddha, the Buddhist law, and the priesthood—"then this bamboo will grow tall." Immediately, the staff took root and grew like living bamboo. And so the island came to be called Chikubushima—Bamboo Grove Island.[27]

He next reports a legend told by an old man: "This island appears in an explanation of the *Kegon Sutra.*" The engi then reiterates that the island emerged from the Konrinzai and adds that the Diamond-Treasure Seat Rock had been in existence from the time of the kami, that is, prior to Buddhism's arrival in Japan (and so interweaves indigenous and Buddhist histories). This tantalizing mention of the *Kegon Sutra,* one of the principal scriptures of the Buddhist canon, is less than absolutely credible to the careful reader: the word "explanation," *setsu* 説, probably connotes an informal explication of the sutra (in contrast to an official, doctrinally weighty commentary, which more likely would be indicated by the term *sho* 疏), and no such explanatory text with such a passage is known; moreover, the source of this information is pointedly vague, the unconfirmed report of an anonymous old man. Whether or not such a text or tale existed, however, the engi, by insinuating a link between Chikubushima and the revered sutra, enhances the island's reputation for sanctity.

Fumon then submits a variant on the first account of the island's origins: Azaihime no Mikoto sat on the Treasure Rock (referring, literally, to a physical Buddhist core beneath the visible surface of the island) and commanded fish to pile stones to conceal it. Thus he recasts the origins of the island in a distinctly Buddhist light, while declaring that there is no discrepancy between this version of events and the one related earlier. He then glosses that claim with the resounding assertion that Azaihime no Mikoto is a manifestation of Shaka Nyorai, the Historical Buddha. With this extended explanation, the island's character as a site of fully unified Shinto-Buddhist sanctity is confirmed (a character that continued uninterrupted until the government directives of 1871). Both engi then recount other miraculous events concerning gigantic catfish and improbably long snakes, related to the water-aspect of the island's divinities.

The lengthy remainder of both versions mostly comprises a chronological narration of other notable events on the island, and includes a remarkable cast of secular and religious elites from throughout Japanese history, all of whom realized the sanctity of the place and most of whom honored it by building appropriate structures. The first construction on the island, in 738, is credited to Gyōki: he visited the island, and sensing there a "miraculous spirit *[reii],*" built a simple thatch structure and performed rituals for "tranquility in the realm, and protection of the state."[28] Gyōki also made statues of the Four Heavenly Guardian Kings and built a small hall for them. In 752 a local resident replaced Gyōki's small hall with a larger three-bay Buddha Hall, presumably quite sturdy, since both versions claim it was extant at the time of their writing. In 753 a regional powerholder sensed Gyōki's aura and made a gold-colored Kannon that was remarkably effective in answering supplications (the engi claim that this statue was the very same Thousand-armed Kannon then extant). In 764, Fumon's version tells us, renegade forces rebelled against the emperor and, after losing a battle, attempted to escape by boat; the head of the imperial forces faced the island and offered prayers. Suddenly a great wind blew the rebels' boat back, their leader was apprehended, and peace was restored to the realm. On behalf of Emperor Kanmu in 788 (again according to the later text), Saichō (767–822, the founder of the Tendai sect in Japan and of its head temple, Enryakuji) established a subtemple on the island (again, then surviving), installed a statue of Yakushi Nyorai, and performed rituals for peace and tranquillity in the realm; thereupon Benzaiten suddenly and miraculously manifested herself. And these are just some of the eighth-century high points.

Subsequent centuries brought equally notable events. In 860 En'nin (794–864), chief priest of Enryakuji, consummated Saichō's last wishes and built the Monju Rōin (probably the subtemple of that name on Mount Hiei). At that time protection was needed against dangers issuing from the northeast—it is from the northeast (also called the *kimon,* or demon's gate) that the most dangerous enemies of Buddhism, and therefore of Japan, were believed to come—and so vows were made to Benzaiten, and a novice was sent to Chikubushima to rebuild a shrine, within which was installed an image En'nin had made with his own hands. In 871 a member of the locally influential Asai family dismantled one of his own buildings, brought it to the island, and rebuilt it as the refectory. In 890 a group of Tendai monks, who had heard that Benzaiten took the appearance of a human, travelled to the island and built, among other structures, the Middle Gate and a stone bridge. The chronicle of construction and donations continues in the tenth century: in 900, on the occasion of a visit to the island by the retired emperor Uda (867–931), the imperial Wood Construction Department was summoned, and a three-bay building there was expanded to seven bays; in 906 several Tendai monks brought items of sacred adornment *(shōgon);* in 913 several monks sponsored the casting of a great bronze bell; in 916 a pagoda was built for peace and tranquillity in the realm; in 930 a Hokke Zanmaidō, a building for Hokke meditation, was constructed, in which was installed a gold-colored statue of Shaka Nyorai and Four Heavenly Guardian Kings; many illustrious visitors came; and so on. The engi ends with an extended eulogy of Benzaiten's presence on the island and the benefits thus accrued for Japan.[29]

The basic engi pattern is followed: after a place acquires its sacred character, the sensitive visitor—pious monk, munificent ruler, or generous local—recognizes and celebrates it by constructing or reconstructing a religious building and, often, by installing the image of a deity. The quality of the place is measured by the status of those visitors and by the accumulation of the buildings they donate or refurbish. Chikubushima's benefactors could not be more diverse or more illustrious: they begin with Gyōki, the consummate compassionate Buddhist monk, and include an emperor, a former emperor, the founder of the Tendai sect and of Enryakuji, countless monks, and local elites. By the time of the later engi Chikubushima was a branch temple of Enryakuji, the head Tendai temple, located on Mount Hiei overlooking the capital of Kyoto, so the many links traced by the Tendai author of the engi are only to be expected. Some of the visitors recognized the site as a potent source of protection for the nation, and so performed appropriate rituals to that end: the island is located to the northeast of Kyoto, so it was Benzaiten's awesome responsibility to protect the capital and thus Japan from the many evils that emanated from this most fearful direction.

The buildings are as impressive as the visitors—or put another way, the buildings are impressive in the text by virtue of the visitors responsible for them. They endure as the lasting and tangible traces left behind by eminent though ephemeral pilgrim-patrons. They are, too, the visible loci of deities: some of the distinguished patrons encountered or sensed a deity manifesting itself, an experience not granted to most people, and the monuments they left attest to those miraculous events. The engi text links the concrete present—the buildings and their enshrined contents—with a partly legendary past of remarkable personages. It guides the visitor to the right way of looking and perceiving, and conveys to its audience a most exalted impression of the place.

For an engi's claims to be received by more than just the local constituency and the occasional distant visitor, the place celebrated in the engi had to exert a widespread presence. For Chikubushima, this was accomplished in several ways. First, it became a stop on the Kannon pilgrimage route of western Japan, a distinction that linked it to other notable religious sites in Japan and brought to the island pilgrims who might not have made the arduous journey if Kannon, one of the most widely popular of all Buddhist deities in Japan, had not been enshrined there.[30] Although Benzaiten was the primary deity on Chikubushima, in other words, it was Kannon's presence that would attract to the island many worshippers, who then would be in a position to learn of Benzaiten's marvelous attributes first-hand. That is not to say that visitors did not come specifically because of Benzaiten, as evidenced by the many examples offered by Fumon in his engi as well as by the diary in which a Shōkokuji monk records his attendance in 1536 at the Lotus Festival and his offering to Benzaiten.[31]

Chikubushima and the *Tale of the Heike*

Chikubushima also appeared in literature which reached a vast audience, most importantly in the *Tale of the Heike,* the time-honored account of the twelfth-century conflict between the Taira (Heike) and Minamoto warrior clans. Almost midway in the narrative, in 1183, Chikubushima is the site of a prominent episode that centers on the sanctity and scenic appeal of the place.[32] The high-ranking Taira warrior Tsunemasa, also a distinguished poet and musician, passes along the shores of Lake Biwa and asks an attendant the name of the island he sees in the distance. "It is the famous Chikubushima," is the answer, to which Tsunemasa replies, "Oh, yes, of course I know the name. Let's go there." Accompanied by several other warriors, he travels to the island in a small boat and is deeply moved by its natural beauty. The narrator remarks that "even thus must have been the appearance of Mount Hōrai," likening Chikubushima to the mythical Chinese island of immortality, Peng Lai, one of the preeminent otherworldly islands in all East Asia. He then imparts the specific source of Chikubushima's sacredness: "A sutra says, 'In the world of humans, there is a lake, and in that lake, emerging from the

Gold Layer, there is a crystal mountain. There the Tennyo dwells.' This was that very island."[33] Although the sutra remains unnamed and the supposed quotation unverified—could this be another oblique reference to the *Kegon Sutra* mentioned in the 1415 engi?—there was no more convincing assertion of the holiness of a place than to claim that it is described in the Buddhist tripitaka as the home of the Tennyo, literally, the Celestial Woman, another name for Benzaiten. The Gold Layer refers to the Buddhist cosmological feature also noted in the 1415 engi, suggesting either that the engi was based on this *Heike* account, or, more likely, that both texts were based on the same now-lost source. The narrator emphasizes that Chikubushima is indeed the jewel-island mentioned in the putative sutra.

Tsunemasa then kneels at the building that enshrined Benzaiten, praising her divine attributes and reciting sacred texts. Evening falls, and the expansive lake and the shrine are bathed in a moonlit glow, creating a poignant nocturnal scene that moves the resident monks to bring their famous musical guest a biwa lute. Tsunemasa plays several "secret compositions," which "resounding inside the shrine, moved the goddess to manifest herself above his sleeve in the guise of the White Dragon," one of Benzaiten's standard aspects. Tsunemasa is inspired to compose a poem reflecting on the auspiciousness of her appearance and how it augurs well for his success in battle. He reboards his boat and heads back to the mainland and the world of warfare. In the following year, 1184, Tsunemasa was one of over two thousand Heike troops who were killed in the great battle of Ichinotani and whose decapitated heads were paraded through the avenues of Kyoto.[34]

The *Tale of the Heike* flourished over the centuries, perennially reaching a vast audience as a work of literature in various recensions and, notably, as an oral text recited by itinerant *biwa hōshi,* "lute priests," some of whom specialized exclusively in the *Heike.*[35] We can imagine that they performed the Chikubushima episode with special interest because it includes a biwa recital (the very activity the biwa hōshi themselves engaged in), and so the image of Benzaiten's ethereal site was disseminated widely.

Chikubushima and the *Keiran shūyōshū*

Other texts defined Chikubushima's exact position within the sacred hierarchy of Japan, among them the *Keiran shūyōshū,* a fourteenth-century compilation of religious knowledge assembled by the Mount Hiei monk Kōshū (1276–1350). An entry on Benzaiten discusses this point, in a question-and-answer format:

> Within Japan, how many places are there that are Pure Lands of Benzaiten? The answer, according to legend, is Tennokawa, which is deep in Yoshino [in present-day Nara Prefecture], Itsukushima in Aki [Hiroshima Prefecture], and Chikubushima in Gōshū [Ōmi Province, present-day Shiga Prefecture]. These three places, like the three jewels of eloquence, are linked together by an underground tunnel.[36]

In subsequent entries in the *Keiran shūyōshū* the island figures as well in other, more inclusive listings of Benzaiten sites in Japan: noted are the "Six Benzaitens," adding to the more exclusive list Enoshima (in present-day Kanagawa Prefecture), Minoo (in Osaka Prefecture), and Sefurisan (in Saga Prefecture).[37] Chikubushima is thus designated as one of the major Benzaiten cult centers in the country, a distinction the island retained over the centuries. Overlying—or underlying—the seeable landscape is an invisible realm, a web of sacred connections that the *Keiran shūyōshū* makes discernible with precise description.[38]

The longest set of entries devoted to Chikubushima in the *Keiran shūiyōshū* provides a wealth of information about the history of the place, beginning with a most tantalizing and potent claim to sacredness:

> The *Kegon Sutra* states, "In the northeast, there is a small country, and in it there is a large lake, and in this lake there is a small island; there the living Benzaiten resides."[39]

In this remarkable passage the *Keiran shūyōshū* purportedly cites the *Kegon Sutra* directly and suggests a consonance between the sacred text and Japan's actual geography: since the *Kegon Sutra* originated in India, the small country in the northeast could plausibly be Japan and the large lake, Lake Biwa. In fact, neither of the two major Chinese translations of the *Kegon Sutra* transmitted to Japan includes the above section, nor—even if a translation of the sutra containing such a passage did exist—would the original Indian authors of the sutra have known of Chikubushima in distant Japan.[40] More likely, the *Keiran shūyōshū* refers to a commentary on the sutra—such as the unofficial explanation conveyed orally by an old man and alluded to by Fumon in the 1415 engi cited above (or the engi might, indeed, be hinting at the reference in the *Keiran shūyōshū*); perhaps it refers to a more formal commentary that was written only after the sutra arrived in Japan and is presently unknown. Japanese clerics, in short, attributed to the sutra a fabricated description of a place that closely matched the characteristics of Chikubushima. The remarkable similarity between the actual island and the description, contrived as it was, contributed to the island's reputation as a sacred place and reinforced its association with Benzaiten.

The *Keiran shūyōshū* was not the only early text to claim such a direct link between the *Kegon Sutra* and Chikubushima. More than a century later a similar passage appeared in a 1455 *kanjinchō,* or temple solicitation register, for a large-scale construction project on Chikubushima. The long kanjinchō text sings the praises of the island as an abode of Benzaiten, and the embedded "*Kegon Sutra*" passage bolsters this claim:

> The *Kegon Sutra,* in the *Jūji Bosatsubon,* states, "East of here, there is one small country, and in the country is a large lake, and in the lake there is a lone island, and there Benzai Tennyo has gained her living body and endured; she lives at this place."[41]

Differing slightly in wording from the geographical description cited in the fourteenth-century *Keiran shūyōshū* (but still fitting Japan's coordinates), this text situates the *Kegon Sutra* passage specifically in Book Twenty-six, the Ten Stages. It is also prefaced by an indication that the impressive citation is one that had been heard, rather than read firsthand by the kanjinchō's author. This apparently specious citation gains conviction from its very specificity, however, as was surely intended, and probably went unquestioned by most of its readers. The kanjinchō passage indeed might have been based on the reference in the *Keiran shūyōshū,* or both could have derived from a now-lost common source. Whatever its origins, this marvelous tale surely enhanced the awesomeness of the island's aura, and its repetition could only have increased the sense of its authenticity.

By the time of the great fire in 1558, therefore, Chikubushima had attained an admirable level of prominence as a sacred island that was one of Benzaiten's principal homes in Japan. All these texts had a part in transforming this island, part of the natural, earthly environment of Japan, into something of supramundane relevance: through these acts of description Chikubushima became something more than simply a small island in a large lake. Soon this prominence was to be elevated further by political events that were beyond the control of the island, many of which the Chikubushima monks certainly viewed, at least initially, with great trepidation.

RELIGIOUS INSTITUTIONS IN THE WAR-TORN REALM

A temple or shrine's conduct of ritual affairs—what we might consider the most obvious business of a religious establishment—always has been dependent upon its ability to maintain an independence achieved, to some degree, through worldly activity. Like any institution that forms part of a larger society, it must coexist with its neighbors, religious and secular alike, and maintain security and economic stability. By the mid-sixteenth century, fulfillment of these needs rendered some Buddhist temples very powerful in extra-religious ways. The largest and best-established wielded enormous economic power: they managed vast landholdings, and the income derived from those lands, and monopolistic commercial ventures within and near their precincts. Among these heavyweights were Enryakuji, the head Tendai-sect complex on Mount Hiei overlooking Kyoto (and Chikubushima's superior), and, in Wakayama Prefecture, the Shingon centers of Kongōbuji on Mount Kōya and Negoroji, each of which controlled commercial centers and networks of towns in its environs.[42] To defend such temporal as well as sectarian interests, these temples (despite Buddhist prohibitions against killing) also fielded hordes of armed monks, *sōhei,* and there are numerous instances of temples being a party to violent conflict: one of the fiercest was the Tenbun Hokke Disturbance of 1536, which pitted the Tendai-sect temple Enryakuji against the Nichiren sect (popularly referred to as Hokke). According to contemporary diaries, the Enryakuji sōhei swept down from their mountain into Kyoto leading "a force of some tens of thousands" (including Buddhist troops from the provinces), torched the twenty-one Nichiren temples there, killed numerous Hokke sectarians, and burned, as well, all of southern Kyoto and half of northern Kyoto.[43] Honganji, the head temple of the Jōdo Shin sect in Ishiyama (in the city of Osaka), had grown into perhaps the most formidable Buddhist institution of all, an enormous walled temple-fortress as well as commercial center and port. It counted untold numbers of ardent adherents in communities across Japan who could rise against enemies of the sect.

The temporal influence of these temples—their economic clout and the military power of their hordes of soldier-monks—was strongly felt in the century preceding the Momoyama period, when political authority throughout Japan was enormously fragmented and unstable.[44] In this, the era of Warring States (Sengoku, 1467–1568), the Ashikaga shoguns were the nominal but mostly ineffective warrior-class rulers based in Kyoto, and the provinces were controlled by military men who dominated the often titular local authorities. In short, the old order of Japan, in which jurisdiction over political and economic matters emanated from the traditional elites based in Kyoto (the Imperial Court and shogunate), was attacked and gradually transformed. It was a chaotic process of unstable coalitions and continual usurpations at all levels of power. Violence was a common feature of daily life for over a century (the Tenbun Hokke Disturbance was but one of many), making Japan less a unified country than an unstable assemblage of independent and belligerent states and Kyoto less a center of government than an embattled target of competing warlords.

NOBUNAGA AND THE SACRED

From the mid-sixteenth century, however, the generalized disorder began to consolidate into fewer but larger-scale conflicts among more powerful competitors. Several warriors amassed ever larger spheres of power, extending far beyond their home domains, and began, apparently, to entertain ideas of replacing the prevailing disorder with their own hegemony. They prosecuted their campaigns in and around the capital of Kyoto and then expanded them to neighboring areas. The list of the most powerful challengers to the inconstant norm was, in the mid-sixteenth century, quite long: Takeda Shingen (1521–1573), Uesugi Kenshin (1530–1578), the Miyoshi family, the Rokkaku, the Shimazu, and Oda Nobunaga (1534–1582) were all viable contenders. Inevitably the large temples, seeking to protect their long-held autonomous interests, became embroiled in the brutal warfare, a development whose outcome fundamentally transformed Buddhism's role in Japan.

Ultimately, it was Nobunaga who battled his way to decisive superiority over his secular competitors and who, in fierce campaigns, not merely neutralized but destroyed the most belligerent militarized temples near Kyoto. It is this all-out antagonism that set the tone for the young and ascendant Hideyoshi in his dealings with the Buddhist temples in his own domain. Nobunaga's war against Ishiyama Honganji occupied almost the entire period of his rule, unfolding over the decade from 1570 through 1580, ending with the sectarians burning their city-temple before relinquishing the ruins to Nobunaga's forces.[45] Honganji was far and away the most recalcitrant of Nobunaga's Buddhist enemies, and came perhaps closer than any other foe, warrior or temple, to defeating Nobunaga on the battlefield.

Nobunaga's most infamous action against a temple was his destruction in 1571 of Enryakuji and its numerous subtemples on Mount Hiei, along with thousands of their inhabitants.[46] The collision was inevitable: not only did Mount Hiei overlook Kyoto, the center of contested territory, it was also allied with a confederation of anti-Nobunaga warrior houses, primarily the powerful Asai and Asakura. It provided them safe haven after their defeat by Nobunaga in a battle, refusing the opportunity to switch allegiance to the Nobunaga camp.

In the ninth month of 1571 Nobunaga's forces gathered at the foot of Mount Hiei and, as ordered, marched up the mountain, destroying everything along the way. Oze Hoan (1564–1640), Nobunaga's own biographer, retrospectively described the scene as follows:

> [Nobunaga's] men launched the assault from all sides with a fierce battle cry. Although the troops of the monastery contested every inch of the hill, they were not equal to the occasion. Everything, everywhere, from the central cathedral to the twenty-one shrines of the Mountain King, the bell tower and the library, were burned to the ground. Moreover, the holy scriptures—both esoteric and exoteric—and the records of the imperial capital under generations of emperors were destroyed at once. Great scholars, men of rare talents, aged priests and young boys—still with their innocent, delicate features—were either beheaded or taken captive. . . . The roar of the huge burning monastery, magnified by the cries of countless numbers of the old and the young, sounded and resounded to the ends of heaven and earth.[47]

The essence of this account is confirmed in the courtier Yamashina Tokitsugu's contemporary diary entry: "On the mountain top, he set fire [to all the buildings] and massacred three to four thousand priests and laity (both men and women),"[48] a figure repeated even in the rumors heard by Luis Frois (1532–1597), who reported that "there had perished about 1,500 bonzes and the same number of layfolk, men, women and children."[49]

And yet, despite these enormities, it is a mistake to describe Nobunaga as fundamentally anti-Buddhist. Nobunaga treated Honganji and Enryakuji as he did other partisan groups with military potential: they were either allies or enemies, and he dealt with them accordingly. Allegiances also shifted, requiring quick and assertive responses: even Enryakuji initially viewed Nobunaga as a friendly party, who might assist them in securing compromised land rights, but when those expectations went unfulfilled it opposed him and allied with his warrior foes. When militarized temples stood in the way of

Nobunaga's geopolitical goals, he fought them. Some contemporaries ascribed these actions to anti-Buddhist hostility. The Honganji leaders referred to Nobunaga with the epithet Hōteki, "Enemy of the [Buddhist] Law."[50] These are the words of his enemies, however, interpreting aggression against the Buddhist military as an attack upon the Buddhist faith. But Nobunaga's policy did not require the suppression of a temple's religious functions, so long as they could be separated from its other, to him pernicious, activities. His most enduring impact on Japanese Buddhism was not the destruction he rained on some of the most influential temples, but rather the general circumscription of its role in Japanese society: Buddhism in Japan thenceforth was divested of its military capacity, and its economic condition was dictated by the secular ruler; its only autonomy, and even this not entirely unfettered, lay in activities concerning the sacred realm.

Nobunaga demonstrated, often, respectful care in his policies toward Buddhist institutions. He was attentive to many temples' legitimate security concerns in the dangerous times. Politically neutral and unmilitarized temples located within a war-torn territory escaped his most oppressive acts. To temples in embattled areas that did not hinder his campaigns, Nobunaga issued numerous letters of protection, documents that promised the receiver Nobunaga's protection against acts of aggression. Some temples he accorded tremendous respect, including Daitokuji, Myōshinji, and Hōryūji.[51]

Most important, Nobunaga found in the sacred a foundation for his own newly won authority, a means of buttressing that authority by removing it from the realm of continual military challenge and giving it ideological sanction. He incorporated the sacred into his most idealized visions of new Japan, especially Azuchi Castle, his spectacular residence begun in 1577 just outside Kyoto on a hill at the southeastern shore of Lake Biwa. It was admired by all who were received there, Japanese and foreign alike: "As regards architecture, strength, wealth and grandeur," Frois declared, Azuchi "may well be compared with the greatest buildings of Europe."[52] On the basement level of the seven-story residential donjon, where one entered, and reaching up to the third story was an enormous Buddhist stupa, and one entire upper level was filled with paintings of Buddhist deities; these inclusions proclaimed his dominance over the Buddhist realm, certainly, but also his wish not to eliminate but to include that realm within this microcosm of his domain.[53] He moved several Buddhist temples into the town built around the castle, and allowed the Jesuits to build a seminary there. Just below the castle was the temple Sōkenji, whose principal image was Kannon; also enshrined and venerated there was a Benzaiten, which Nobunaga had acquired from Chikubushima, visible in the distance from atop the castle hill.[54]

As Nobunaga gained military supremacy, he sometimes defined his power in sacred terms. After a battle in 1575 he demanded that his troops venerate him, promising them in return divine protection and long life; to a warrior Nobunaga wrote in 1579 that compliance would bring benefits not only in this life but also in the next; in the New Year celebrations of 1582 Nobunaga's son led a procession of daimyo who offered monetary gifts to Nobunaga "as to a living god."[55] There is also the controversial matter of Nobunaga's apotheosis: the Jesuit Luis Frois wrote in a letter that Nobunaga, less than three weeks before his unexpected death, declared himself a Buddhist deity, installed a symbol of his deified self in Sōkenji, and encouraged his vassals to offer appropriate veneration.[56] Though this astounding behavior is corroborated in no other source (and some scholars reject it), it is not uncharacteristic of Nobunaga's self-aggrandizing nature and it is consistent with his search for new ways to assert political authority.[57] If Frois' account is true, its most notable aspect is that Nobunaga apparently deified himself, without seeking the sanction of an accepted legitimator: as attested by the later deifications of Hideyoshi and Ieyasu (and scholars do not doubt that these deifications occurred), the apotheosis of a warrior ruler was not unacceptable in Momoyama Japan, but to carry validity, it needed conventional channels of legitimation. Had Nobunaga lived longer, perhaps he would have sought such sanction, though this of course cannot be known. Many earlier warrior rulers had patronized the sacred generously to bolster their authority, but none had presented themselves so unequivocally *as* the sacred; the Toyotomi, especially after Hideyoshi's death, explored even more successfully this new role of warrior as principal in both mundane and sacred realms.

NOBUNAGA THE OVERLORD, HIDEYOSHI HIS DEPUTY, AND CHIKUBUSHIMA

Nobunaga's Overture

Nobunaga circumscribed the role of Buddhism in Japan—and he inserted himself into that narrowed scope in a way that was surely unwelcome to many—but the Buddhist institution was allowed to survive, as practitioners of Buddhist ritual, as protectors of the sacred realm and, in turn, of Japan as a whole. Some temples even thrived. Chikubushima fared as well as any, especially with the attention of Nobunaga's representative Hideyoshi, though initial interactions were notably difficult.

In 1570 Hideyoshi was in his early thirties and a retainer of Nobunaga, who had himself only two years earlier entered Kyoto and emerged from Warring States battle to widespread influence. On the twenty-fifth day of the seventh month of 1570, the young warrior (who then called himself Kinoshita Tōkichirō Hideyoshi) sent a letter to the Chikubushima Administrative Council; the earliest of many extant documents either addressed to the island's religious establishment by Hideyoshi or invoking his name, it exemplifies the confrontational tone of those violent and unsettled times.[58]

> With regard to the 'Buddha fields,' various donations, dormitory lands, dormitory-related domains, and purchased land of this temple, the matter of unfair special taxes should be laid out as it has been up to now. Regarding the question of Hayasaki Village, as for [the market activities] in front of the gate the

> various matters should be carried out in accordance with the regulations of this temple. In addition, regarding such matters as the Tennyo rituals and transportation boats, they should be followed as before without deviation. It is so commanded.

Hideyoshi comments on a wide range of the island's most important interests, such as taxation on its various sources of income, market activities, transportation, and "the Tennyo rituals," that is, rites associated with Benzaiten. Ostensibly, the letter offers no interference with the affairs of the island; in all matters touched on, Hideyoshi instructs the island to continue as before: he confirms the status quo. In fact, as was surely understood by both parties, the intent of the letter was the opposite. To confirm a practice asserts by implication the authority to deny it, and so Hideyoshi's imprimatur actually claimed control over Chikubushima's affairs (on behalf, of course, of Hideyoshi's overlord, Nobunaga). This was the first of several volleys directed at the island, designed to test its position regarding independence or submissiveness.

Indirectly, Hideyoshi's letter also signals that Nobunaga is challenging the authority of the Asai house, the heretofore undisputed warrior rulers of northern Ōmi (and, at this time, also Enryakuji's ally and Nobunaga's recalcitrant foe). Asai Nagamasa (1545–1573), then head of the clan, was especially attentive to the temples and shrines in his domain, making frequent visits and donations.[59] The island temple had long maintained good relations with the Asai, as demonstrated in correspondence concerning economic and religious matters beginning in the 1530s.[60] In two of many letters addressed to Chikubushima, Nagamasa exempted it from decrees that cancelled debts, insuring that debts owed the temple would be paid and thus protecting the continuity of temple income.[61] The Asai also supported the annual Lotus Festival from as early as 1533, when they made a donation of rice fields; in 1566 the Asai daimyo's mother served as a chief secular sponsor of the festival (a role known as *tōnin*), as inscribed on an extant statue of Benzaiten she commissioned for the occasion, and Nagamasa also pledged support for the ritual during his tenure as daimyo.[62] Nagamasa was especially solicitous of the needs of the island: he ordered negligent donors to make their customary contributions, and he and his father Hisamasa (d. 1573) made financial grants to the island independent of the Lotus Festival.[63]

Not only the rituals but also buildings received support from the Asai. In the early 1540s they assisted in the collection of funds for the construction of a corridor-bridge and sutra hall.[64] After the devastating fire of 1558 Hisamasa, then daimyo, wrote to a Chikubushima monk: "Your temple went up in flames, and I am beyond words. I fear you suffered much. On that occasion, you made it your first priority to save my belongings. . . . Of the seven [objects that were] in the Goten, four have arrived."[65] Goten refers to the hall dedicated to the worship of Benzaiten, and it would appear that Hisamasa had dedicated a number of objects there which the monk had saved and returned to the warrior. Although there is no secure proof of Asai participation in the post-fire reconstruction, such participation would have been a natural outgrowth of the preexisting relationship. Perhaps it was for such a project that the Asai stored lumber on the island—lumber later requisitioned by Nobunaga.

Chikubushima's association with the Asai, however, could not but damage its ensuing relationship with Nobunaga. Hideyoshi's letter dates only two months before Nobunaga's attack on Mount Hiei; since Chikubushima was a branch temple of Enryakuji, and Enryakuji was allied with the Asai, Nobunaga would have reason to view the island as leagued against him. A second letter, almost identical in content to Hideyoshi's and dated to the same day, was launched at the island by Higuchi Naofusa, another ambitious warrior who had tied his fortunes to those of Nobunaga.[66] The wildfire conflicts of the earlier Warring States era were burning out. Nobunaga was poised to wrest total control of the area around the island from the Asai, and Chikubushima was inevitably caught between.

One month later, Higuchi Naofusa sent a second letter to Chikubushima regarding a more blatantly hostile act against the island.[67]

> Members of our naval forces took two transportation boats from Hayasaki Village. Accordingly, I have ordered that [the boats] be returned. You took the trouble of sending cask[s of *sake*] and 20 *hiki* [of money]. I am humbly [grateful] for your frequent kindnesses. The details [of these matters] will be discussed with Minbukyō Dono. Respectfully conveyed.

Nobunaga's naval forces had confiscated two boats from Chikubushima's mainland port of Hayasaki, and Naofusa promises their return. It is no coincidence that his order followed Chikubushima's gift of sake and twenty hiki of cash. Naofusa's expression of polite appreciation masks the real threat implicit in the confiscation: Hayasaki was Chikubushima's *monzenmachi,* literally, the "town before the [temple] gate," where markets and other commercial activities took place, and the boats (alluded to in the previous letter as well) provided the essential link between the island and the mainland; Nobunaga could sever the link and choke the island at will. Behind Naofusa's polite letters, as also Hideyoshi's, loomed that threat. Chikubushima's "gift" of sake and money was a prudent acknowledgement of Nobunaga's military power and its own jeopardy.

After the 1571 assault on Enryakuji, Nobunaga battled enemies on a number of fronts, and it was not until the eighth month of 1573 that he was finally able to turn his attention fully to northern Ōmi and the Asai.[68] Once engaged, Nobunaga's forces overwhelmed the Asai stronghold at Odani Castle, and Nagamasa and his father, Hisamasa, committed suicide. In northern Ōmi, Nobunaga was master at last.

Just before this battle got underway, Nobunaga initiated direct contact with Chikubushima. First, he issued confirmation of Chikubushima's holdings in a document over his own name and the seal whose menacing legend reads "Tenka fubu" ("Enveloping the Realm with Military Force"), which he had begun using a few years earlier.

> The buildings and temple holdings of this temple should [be treated] according to precedent. There should not be even the slightest transgression. With-

> out deviation, [precedent] should be followed energetically and with diligence. Isono Tanba no Kami will report this. It is so commanded.[69]

Like the earlier missives, this one concerns economic matters and, like them, it orders the island to continue to observe existing regulations. But rarely has a directive to carry on as before been made to sound so threatening, its curt reiterations capped by the warning that its contents also will be conveyed in person by Isono Kazumasa, one of Nobunaga's vassals. In the same year Chikubushima sent "courtesy money" to Nobunaga in recognition of the warlord's authority. Kazumasa acknowledged the money for Nobunaga, then explicitly demanded more.[70] Chikubushima must have realized that under the new regime they were navigating new and frightening waters.

NOBUNAGA AND CHIKUBUSHIMA'S TREASURES

Soon after the fighting ended, the island discovered another aspect of Nobunaga: his penchant for prized objects and for seeing himself in the role of connoisseur. A letter from Nobunaga to the island, bearing his vermilion seal, expresses courteous enthusiasm for two Nō flutes which the island had sent for his inspection. The polite tone of the letter, so different from his previous communiqués, shows Nobunaga's ability to modulate from fierce conqueror to civilized ruler.[71]

> The flute named Aoba has arrived. It is indeed a *meibutsu,* truly fine. I will keep it for a short while, and after inspecting it, have it returned. I wonder about the circumstances of the donation of this flute to the mountain [i.e., Chikubushima] and who previously owned it. The small flute accompanies it. Please write down what is reliably known of their lineages and send it to me. Also, regarding the small drum [said to have been] owned by Shizuka, the makie lacquer design on the body is of thunder. Please take a look at it. Isono will discuss this with you. Respectfully submitted.

Nobunaga was obsessed with these objects, much as he was, throughout his maturity, with utensils used in chanoyu, which Nobunaga practiced assiduously for its intertwined aesthetic and political purposes.[72] He renders his discerning evaluation of the one named flute, Aoba—he designates it a meibutsu ("famous object") of great quality, which is high praise—and is keen to learn its provenance.

On the same day that Nobunaga sent this letter to Chikubushima, he sent another to his vassal Isono Kazumasa, repeating his admiration for the two flutes and directing him to "inquire carefully and make a written note of the known things [about them], and have it sent to me."[73] Nobunaga wished to corroborate his assessment of their visual qualities with what he suspected was an equally impressive pedigree; as in chanoyu, the perceived quality of an old object was greatly affected by its provenance. Neither of these flutes is known today, on Chikubushima or elsewhere, suggesting that Nobunaga may have reneged on his pledge to return them, or that Chikubushima may have given them to the ruler as a gift in the hopes of some future benefaction.[74]

Nobunaga also inquires about a drum body he had heard about, and wants to see in person, with a thunder design in makie lacquer. Legend had it that the drum had been owned by Shizuka, consort of the tragic warrior-hero Minamoto no Yoshitsune (1159–1189), adding enormous historical significance to its aesthetic virtues.[75] Mochinobu, a retainer of the sixth Ashikaga shogun, Yoshinori (1394–1441), had offered the object to Benzaiten almost one hundred and fifty years prior to Nobunaga's time, an early example of a political figure paying his respects to the religious authority of Chikubushima, and specifically to Benzaiten. Nobunaga's interest in the drum was motivated less by piety than by his insatiable desire for famous objects; nonetheless, the island's ownership of such objects no doubt raised its profile in his mind.

HIDEYOSHI'S DEBUT

Nobunaga's personal involvement in Chikubushima's affairs is perhaps most succinctly, and certainly more characteristically, captured in a letter sent after a visit he made to the island. It begins by stating that the ruler (referred to as Tonosama) travelled to the island to pay his respects to Benzaiten (Tennyo):

> The other day Tonosama made a pilgrimage to the Tennyo, and when he left he sent a messenger to report to the effect that he saw there were people who sold the subtemple dormitories of your temple. This is not good. Previously, Chikushū was of the same opinion. Hereafter, for such sales, punishment will be administered. In addition, bamboo and trees in the island's forests are being felled too freely. This too is not good. Furthermore, with regard to the subtemple income donated from Hayasaki, people not in residence at the temple should not get a stipend. If there are people who say they should get [the stipend], stop the matter and report to me. In regard to all [of the above matters, Nobunaga] feels most strongly, which I report by way of this letter.[76]

The letter could hardly be more blunt: Nobunaga is disturbed by flagrant irregularities in the conduct of economic affairs—three types of abuses are described—and repercussions are unequivocally threatened if they are not corrected. The first and third abuses are financial improprieties within the island's various subtemples, where the monks lived. The second was a matter of special importance in this time of surging monumental construction: after centuries of unregulated exploitation, forests were a resource in need of protection in the sixteenth century; although it is unlikely that the small island supported massive stands, its trees as well as bamboo were still assets over which Nobunaga wished to assert control.[77] The letter ratchets up the immediacy of its threat by noting that the island had already received one warning from a certain Chikushū about at least one of the problems, but had apparently ignored him.

Chikushū, referring by title to none other than Toyotomi Hideyoshi, is here shown as Nobunaga's representative in Chikubushima's affairs; as further proof of Hideyoshi's role, Bokushinsai Nobusada, signer of the letter, was Hideyoshi's retainer. Soon after his victory over the Asai in the ninth month of 1573, Nobunaga installed Hideyoshi as daimyo of northern Ōmi. The following year Hideyoshi settled in Imahama on the northeast shore of Lake Biwa, renamed the place Nagahama, and began constructing a castle as his seat of power. It was Hideyoshi's first domain, and the ascendant warrior rapidly insinuated himself into the supervision of nearby Chikubushima. Hideyoshi was Nobunaga's primary agent who administered Nobunaga's policies at the local Ōmi level. His mandates were backed by the authority of Nobunaga, which could be invoked as needed (as here), for reinforcement.

Hideyoshi emerges in the correspondence as a figure fully capable of implementing Nobunaga's ruthlessness in policy and harshness in style. In a short letter dating in early 1574 Hideyoshi demands that Chikubushima deliver to him lumber that had been stored on the island by Asai Nagamasa, perhaps, as suggested above, material designated for an ongoing Asai reconstruction of the island's buildings. He ends with a threat: "If there are problems, serious repercussions will result."[78] A couple of months later Hideyoshi's deputy Ishikawa Mitsumasa forwarded the document to the island with his own, longer letter, which repeats Hideyoshi's demand (and invokes his name), and asks for a detailed accounting of the material, which he promises to report to Hideyoshi.[79] On both letters was later noted, "By these letters, all of the lumber was passed over. [The matter] is resolved." In all likelihood Hideyoshi wanted this lumber for use in Nagahama Castle, then under construction.[80] At the same time, demanding the lumber was a reiteration of Hideyoshi's authority over the Asai's former ally; Chikubushima, in relinquishing the lumber, signifies its acknowledgment and acceptance of the change in temporal power.

Later in 1574 Hideyoshi issued documents stating the annual income of religious establishments throughout his newly won realm, including Chikubushima.

> I donate 300 *koku* from within Hayasaki District of this county. It should absolutely be a temple contribution. Concerning the above, as before, there should be no negligence as regards the religious services.[81]

The wording of the document indicates that Hideyoshi did not simply confirm earlier precedent, but instead reevaluated the annual donation and bestowed it anew. An Edo-period document suggests, in fact, that the donation of 300 koku represented a reduction for Chikubushima.[82] The wording expresses Hideyoshi's successful attempt to dictate the purview of Chikubushima's activities: Chikubushima's guaranteed revenue is predicated on its dedication to sacred matters exclusively. This lessened range of permissible activity was typical of Nobunaga's warrior policy toward religious establishments, here administered by Nobunaga's representative, Hideyoshi.

On the other hand, Hideyoshi explicitly avoided interference in Chikubushima's religious affairs. Bokushinsai Nobusada and Kuwayama Shigekatsu, another Hideyoshi retainer, sent the following letter to Chikubushima during the mid-1570s:

> Regarding the matter of the *sairei,* we have learned of the details by way of your monk representative and letter. Chikushū [i.e., Hideyoshi] is in Gifu. On his return to the castle [in Nagahama], we will report this to him. Regarding the matters of Buddhist and Shinto sairei and other religious affairs, [Hideyoshi] generally accedes to precedent. Accordingly, we hear how things have been done until now, and follow that.[83]

Sairei is the term often used in documents to refer to Chikubushima's annual Lotus Festival. In purely religious matters Hideyoshi encouraged the island to continue its accustomed practices. Religious ritual was Chikubushima's business, the one area beyond secular control.

Hideyoshi also made private financial contributions, a practice independent of national policy and expressive of his personal concern for the welfare of the temple establishment. The *Chikubushima hōgachō,* a lengthy list of donations made to the island in the 1570s and 1580s, begins with Hideyoshi's generous 100 koku grant, followed by smaller amounts given by his family and well over one hundred of his retainers, many of which are promised annual contributions.[84] Bokushinsai Nobusada and Kuwayama Shigekatsu, for example, each gave rice in 1576, the former donation described as "every year." Although most of the donations took the form of rice or cash, one of the earlier offerings was a table to be placed before Benzaiten.[85]

While based in Nagahama, Hideyoshi was an active participant in the affairs of Chikubushima. As local agent of Nobunaga's authority, he invoked either directly or indirectly the warlord's name to enforce stern directives toward the island. At the same time, he ensured survival of the island as a center of religious activity, dedicated to the worship of Benzaiten. Although his earliest communications show him to have been only one of several temporal figures charged with carrying out Nobunaga's policies, Hideyoshi quickly became the key secular determinant of Chikubushima's day-to-day function within the social fabric of Ōmi. Although the island no doubt interpreted (correctly) many of Hideyoshi's actions in this period as inimical, it also grew to understand that, by offering no challenge to secular authority—which it had never done, save for accepting the munificence of the previous temporal ruler—and engaging the sacred as its sole concern, it could benefit. Interactions over more than a decade forged a close association between the sacred island and the new secular powerholder. It was a relationship that endured even after Hideyoshi rose to countrywide prominence.

On the first day of the sixth month of 1582 Oda Nobunaga was at Honnōji, a Nichiren temple in central Kyoto. That evening he hosted a tea gathering, for which he had brought many of his most treasured chanoyu utensils, including many famed objects previously owned by past shoguns and tea masters.[86] This cultured gathering was his last, however, for at dawn Akechi Mitsuhide (d. 1582), a general who for years had served Nobunaga faithfully, rose in rebellion and set Honnōji ablaze. Escape was impossible and capture dishonorable. Nobunaga took his own life. His heir, attempting to flee, was killed, and so ended Nobunaga's often harsh rule and his dynastic hopes. After a brief, futile attempt to assume authority, Akechi fled into the provinces, pursued by Hideyoshi, and was soon hunted down and killed.

Hideyoshi consolidated the support of major warrior rivals or, if they proved hostile, defeated them in battle (notably Shibata Katsuie in 1583), aggrandizing his own position of leadership and bringing increasing peace and political stability to Japan. By mid-1583 Hideyoshi controlled more territory than Nobunaga ever had. He transferred his base from Nagahama to the port city of Osaka, where he began construction on a castle of unprecedented scale that remained the Toyotomi stronghold until their extermination in 1615. At the end of 1584 Hideyoshi concluded a peace treaty with Tokugawa Ieyasu (1542–1616), his major rival. The Imperial Court awarded Hideyoshi successively higher honorary ranks within the court hierarchy,[87] and in mid-1585 appointed him to the high office of *kanpaku* (chancellor), an office by then bereft of power but replete with prestige; by accepting these titles Hideyoshi acknowledged the legitimating authority of the Court (and, like other warrior rulers before him, expertly choreographed the Court's awards to suit his needs). Within little more than a decade Hideyoshi had risen from his status as Nobunaga's subordinate, ruling a domain in northern Ōmi, to become the paramount civil authority, securely seated in the region of Japan's traditional capital.

2

Hideyoshi and the Sacred: Manipulating Convention

RESTORING KYOTO

Despite notable episodes of extreme violence—especially during Nobunaga's sovereignty and Hideyoshi's campaigns against outlying foes and his subsequent invasions of Korea—the Momoyama period saw Japan gradually emerge from widespread war-torn chaos and, forcefully guided by its military rulers, move toward stability. The capital city of Kyoto, repeatedly a devastated battleground during the previous century, was over time restored to order and to its position as Japan's center of effective political power. As peace increasingly took hold, Kyoto became the focus of an extraordinary construction campaign, begun by Hideyoshi in the 1580s, that repaired the ruined city and dramatically reshaped its built environment. Hideyoshi redrew the city boundaries, erected a city wall, laid new streets and bridges, and both he and his successors sponsored the building of temples, shrines, and spectacular residences, remaking the capital into a place that by the late sixteenth century deserved its reputation as "the greatest Citie of Japan," "noble and populous," and "justly famous throughout the world for the wonderful things told about it."[1] Natural disasters wreaked additional destruction on Kyoto during this time, but their effect was to stimulate further rebuilding, since the repair and rebuilding of damaged structures was generally understood to betoken the Toyotomi's benevolence and good rulership. Having achieved power by violence and destruction, the new regime claimed authority by virtue of its commitment to order and construction.

Hideyoshi sponsored several remarkable secular buildings in or near Kyoto. The Toyotomi castle in Osaka, Hideyoshi's headquarters city southeast of Kyoto, was begun in 1583 with legions of workers to speed its progress: by 1584 Hideyoshi held a tea gath-

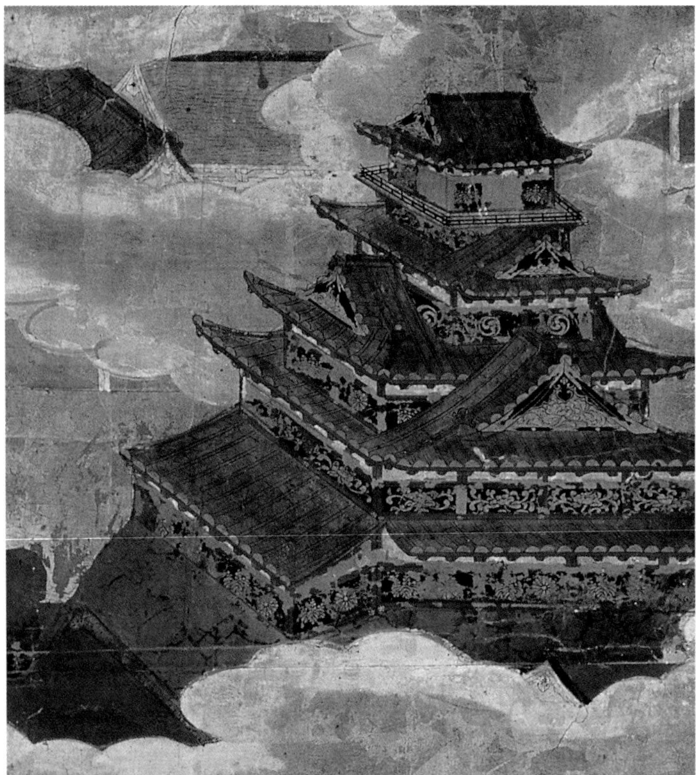

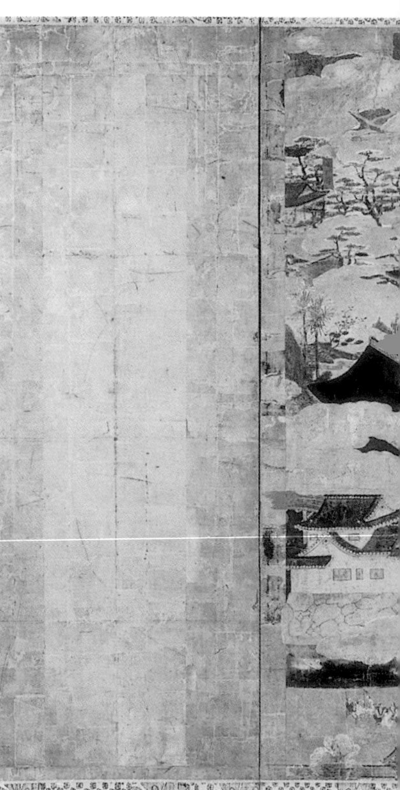

FIG. 42 (left) Detail from *Osaka Castle.* Seventeenth century. Six-fold screen; ink, color, and gold leaf on paper. Kawakami collection, Tokyo. Photograph by Osaka Castle.

FIG. 43 (right) *Jurakutei.* Late sixteenth century. Six-fold screen; ink, color, and gold leaf on paper. Mitsui Bunko Foundation, Tokyo. Photograph by Kyoto National Museum.

ering in a room there, and in the following year he guided elite clerical and warrior visitors around the unfinished donjon and other major portions; in 1586 tens of thousands (as Hideyoshi told Luis Frois) toiled night and day on the exceptionally wide and deep surrounding moat; this initial phase of construction concluded in early 1588 *(Fig. 42).*[2] Period accounts of Osaka Castle describe a building that equalled Nobunaga's Azuchi Castle in lavishness of decoration and surpassed it in size: Azuchi had been seven stories high, Osaka was eight. Built on the site of the former Ishiyama Honganji, it was a massive, towering symbol of Hideyoshi's expropriation—physical and conceptual—of that most recalcitrant foe. Improved and enlarged over the years, Osaka Castle remained the Toyotomi's central citadel even after Hideyoshi's death, until the family's annihilation in 1615.

Hideyoshi also built a celebrated residence for himself in Kyoto, Jurakutei *(Fig. 43).* Begun in 1586 and completed the following year on land that once had been part of the old Imperial Palace (once again asserting by location Toyotomi dominance, in this case over the once powerful Court), it was renowned for its great size, its numerous buildings, and its magnificence. The central five-storied keep with a tiled and gilt-edged roof

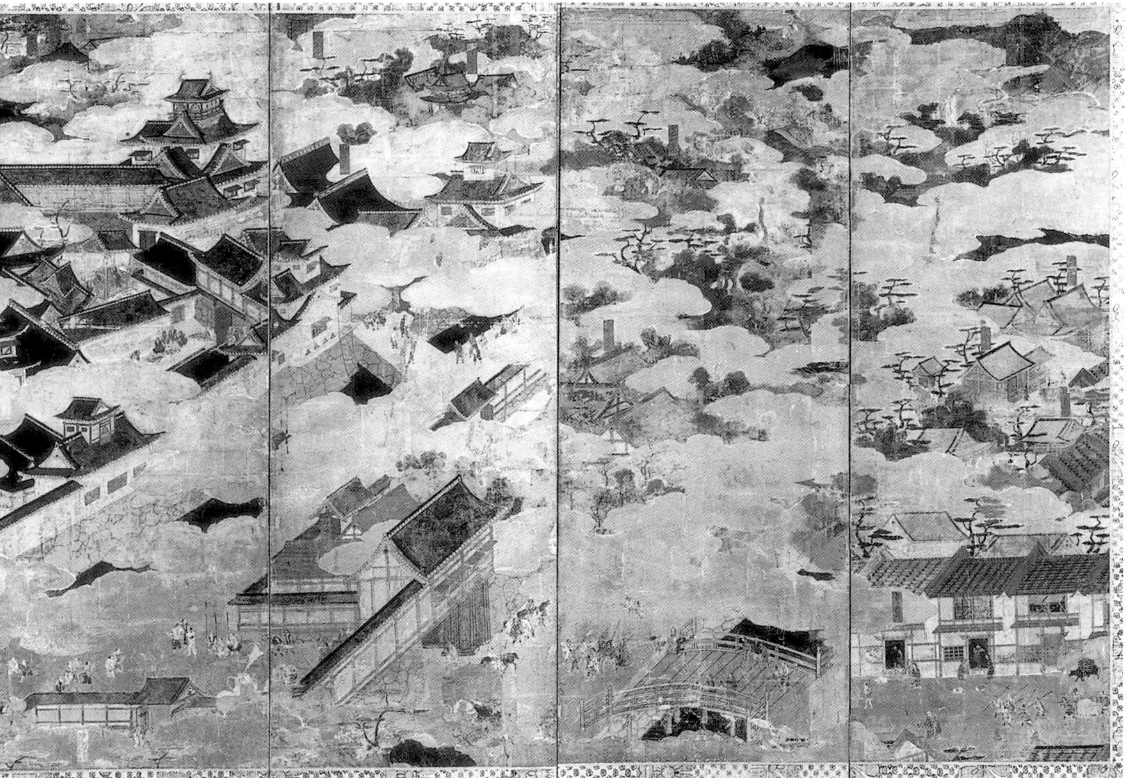

towered above all its surroundings; its interior boasted paintings by the famed Kano workshop artists Eitoku (1543–1590) and Sanraku (1559–1635). The walled compound had well-planted grounds—pines were transplanted from other parts of Japan—and gardens, for which Kyoto Buddhist temples donated treasured stones.[3] João Rodrigues (1561–1633) described it as "such a beautiful palace that people said that there had never been anything so splendid in Japan in the past nor would there be in the future, as indeed so far there has not."[4] Hideyoshi cleared the area surrounding Jurakutei and ordered his leading vassals to build their own residential compounds there, creating an entire district of new elite warrior architecture. During the several years that Hideyoshi lived there, Jurakutei was the political center of Japan, the place where foreign delegations were received and, in 1588, where Emperor Goyōzei (1571–1617) was entertained during an extravagant five-day visit, a rare instance of an emperor leaving his palace to travel to a warrior ruler's residence. Although the Court had lost its governing authority, it was still greatly important as protector of Japan's ancient traditions and as legitimator of present claimants to rule; as recipient of an imperial visit, and by feting the emperor in a manner that befit such a lofty (if dispossessed) personage, Hideyoshi demonstrated his own cultivation and aptness to rule.

HIDEYOSHI AND SACRED CONSTRUCTION

Much of Hideyoshi's construction campaign was devoted to religious institutions. He increased landholdings and built or repaired halls at numerous Buddhist sites, including the Zen monasteries Nanzenji, Tōfukuji, Shōkokuji, and Kenninji, the Shingon temples Tōji, Daigoji, and Rokuhara Mitsuji, and the Tendai temple of Myōhōin.[5] The rebuilding and rededication of the Ise Shrine every twenty years, a centuries-old hallowed tradition, had fallen into abeyance during the Warring States disorders; Hideyoshi donated funds for the rebuilding and the costly attendant ritual in 1585.[6] Hideyoshi rebuilt temples affiliated with the Jōdo Shin sect, only a decade earlier Nobunaga's dangerous opponent, and in 1591 allowed the sect to select a plot of land in Kyoto as the site for a new Honganji precinct. The gesture was perhaps less conciliatory than controlling—in Kyoto the temple could not escape his surveillance—but it is notable nonetheless that Hideyoshi did not simply refuse permission to rebuild. He moved as many as 180 individual temples, originally located within the most populous parts of Kyoto, to three areas on the periphery, thereby consolidating them and separating them from the long-fostered support of their surrounding communities and, once again, asserting his authority over them.[7]

Hideyoshi also founded new religious centers in Kyoto, intended to equal in spiritual power those of ancient times. The Great Buddha Hall at Hōkōji (discussed below), for example, was erected to rival the eighth-century one at Tōdaiji in Nara. These buildings became the sites of rituals that invoked Buddhist protection of the Toyotomi family and the state and thereby expressed Toyotomi power. Though in part politically motivated, such religious activity cannot be dismissed as purely cynical demonstrations of secular authority. Ample evidence for the earnest sponsorship of ceremonies to address dire family crises suggests, rather, that the sacred was not called upon sanctimoniously: political considerations might be present, but the piety was real. The passage to mostly peaceful rule, in short, was accompanied by a vigorous construction campaign in Kyoto, devoted in considerable part to religious monuments and to the ceremonies that took place at them.

The construction at these places embodied Hideyoshi's assertion of an exceptional relationship with the sacred, a claim that recalls that of his predecessor Nobunaga—in the sense that both invoked the sacred as a mechanism to affirm their own authority—though Hideyoshi's claim was more fully developed and, eventually, used to greater effect. Born to peasant parents and so without the inherited status expected of a Japanese ruler, Hideyoshi repeatedly professed that divine omens surrounded his birth. To S. Pedro Bautista Blanquez (d. 1597), a Franciscan who travelled to Japan in 1593 as ambassador of the Philippines, Hideyoshi explained, "When I was born, a sunbeam fell on my chest, and when the diviners were asked about this, they told me that I was to be the ruler of all that lies between east and west."[8] To other Europeans he asserted the superior divinity of the diversely manifested Japanese deities: Japan, he wrote, "is the land of the *kami*" (which he equated with the Buddhist deities of India and the Confucian sages of China), and these kami were "the root and source of all phenomena."[9] After his death Hideyoshi was apotheosized as a kami, venerated long and widely throughout Japan.

SCALING DOWN THE VIOLENCE

In his first years as ruler Hideyoshi continued Nobunaga's brutal campaign against militarized religious establishments; and yet, at the same time, he offered temples that forswore military action and political meddling the promise of survival. In the third month of 1585 Hideyoshi's forces poured into the Kii peninsula and laid waste to much of Negoroji, an enormously wealthy and well-armed Shingon temple. They then moved on to nearby Saiga, which held the last remaining pocket of Jodō Shin sectarians, and forced their capitulation.[10] In 1584, on the other hand, only two years after Nobunaga's death, Hideyoshi issued permission for the reconstruction of Enryakuji on Mount Hiei, allowing that most potent symbol of the old sacred order to regain its physical presence at its original site. As a condition for his sanction, Hideyoshi specified that the temple henceforth perform rituals for the protection of Japan: to survive, the temple that once had promoted its private interests with aggressive force was required to act as one of Hideyoshi's facilitators of divine protection.[11] As we shall see, this became a central theme of Hideyoshi's policies towards the sacred.

The consequences of defiance—and of compliance, too—were certainly well known, then, when Hideyoshi turned his attention in 1585 to Mount Kōya, another massive stronghold of the Shingon sect on the Kii peninsula. Hideyoshi issued an ultimatum to the temple: forsake your manufacture and ownership of arms or face the same fate as Mount Hiei and Negoroji.[12] With the Kōya monk Ōgo (1536–1608) mediating, Kōya accepted Hideyoshi's conditions. This proved to be the final major confrontation between the Oda-Toyotomi interests and the Buddhist establishment. Thenceforth Buddhist institutions acquiesced in the sphere of activity delimited by Hideyoshi. Many temples (such as Daigoji, discussed below) had not been militant or had been previously neutralized; these submitted to the Toyotomi regime without confrontation and reaped concomitant rewards.

HIDEYOSHI AND CHIKUBUSHIMA IN THE POST-NAGAHAMA PERIOD

Hideyoshi's relocation to the capital region pulled Chikubushima, too, more fully onto a larger stage, as the two parties continued to maintain the bonds they had formed over the previous decade. The documentary record of the mid-1580s shows a pattern of civil, constructive correspondence between Chikubushima and Hideyoshi. Chikubushima paid homage to the ruler with gifts, and Hideyoshi replied with letters of appreciation: in 1585 Chikubushima sent *shiitake* mushrooms and *konbu* seaweed, for which Hideyoshi duly dispatched a vermilion-seal letter of thanks.[13] On at least three other occasions in this period Hideyoshi similarly acknowledged Chikubushima's New Year's gifts of such things as *kanju* (records of rites conducted on Hideyoshi's behalf), money, and dried persimmons.[14] Hideyoshi also issued Chikubushima conventional affirmation of its existing rights. In the third month of 1584 he issued a three-item letter of protection regarding Hayasaki, the source of Chikubushima's 300 *koku* income,[15] and in 1591 Hideyoshi sent the island a vermilion-seal document confirming the amount of the income itself, which he had earlier established during his tenure in Nagahama.[16] Such exchanges describe a relationship between Japan's ruler and a religious establishment that was typical of the period.

In some respects, however, Hideyoshi's treatment of Chikubushima went beyond customary formalities and demonstrated his private commitment to the island and its religious activities. In 1585, for example, the island was assured by letter that Hideyoshi would continue, as had been his custom at Nagahama, to make a donation for "Benzaiten *mitarashi* reeds."[17] Certainly Hideyoshi had begun making such a donation—for reeds used in some way for the water basin where worshippers washed their hands—during his tenure in Nagahama; in his new position of authority he did not need to continue, but evidently he wished to.

And Chikubushima asked for, and received, more from its powerful patron. Connections established in the 1570s favorably positioned the island in the 1580s and 1590s vis à vis Hideyoshi's new regime: the island had longstanding ties not only with Hideyoshi, but also with administrators in his government who were able to facilitate Chikubushima's entreaties, acting as the island's advocates and offering advice available only to those close to the center of power. Two letters from this post-Nagahama period show the range of Chikubushima's expectations of assistance. The first, dated 7.20, was written by Bokushinsai Nobusada, whose letter had conveyed Oda-Toyotomi dictates to the island in the Nagahama period (see p. 67). The second, dated to the following day, was written by Itō Hidemori, another Hideyoshi retainer whose name appears as a donor in the *Chikubushima hōgachō* and who is also known to have dealt with Chikubushima during the 1570s.[18]

Both letters begin with thanks for a letter and gift of cash sent by Chikubushima. Although Chikubushima's letter is no longer extant, the responses suggest that the island had petitioned Hideyoshi for a judgment on its behalf. Itō Hidemori reports that he presented the letter to Hideyoshi, who "accepted it in a good mood," and Bokushinsai Nobusada adds that he believes Chikubushima "will be satisfied" with the results. Both men refer to a "series of official documents," perhaps Chikubushima's archive of notable historical records and claims to domain income, which the two men describe as "impressive" and promise to show to Hideyoshi. Hidemori adds that the Chikubushima *"hōmotsu"* ("treasures") and gifts should certainly be shown to Hideyoshi, as this would gratify the ruler's love of valuable objects. Hideyoshi's busy schedule—he has just returned from battle and will soon be leaving Osaka for Kyoto—makes the timing of presentation difficult. Hideyoshi will shortly return to Osaka, however, and Hidemori suggests that "at that time, send one more monk-messenger, and at Osaka, even if it takes some negotiations, approach him when he is in good spirits and make every effort to get the *onsho*," referring perhaps to a vermilion-seal document.

Several other significant matters are mentioned. Bokushinsai Nobusada promises to address the "disturbing" matter of water damage to Chikubushima holdings, a mischance that would seriously diminish the island's income. Chikubushima apparently also requested help of some sort with the annual Lotus Festival. Nobusada assures Chikubushima that their needs can be easily met, and adds in a familiar, concerned manner, "As I have said before, I have aged. I cannot perform my duties as I have in the past and am refraining from engaging myself in things. I will, however, exert myself [on your behalf]." Itō Hidemori tells Chikubushima that he will report to them on the Lotus Festival matter in a separate letter.

Hidemori's letter ends with a tantalizing mention of construction on Chikubushima of the "Hondō." Which building was so named is unclear, though it is unlikely to have been the structure dedicated to Benzaiten, now the Tsukubusuma Main Hall; none of the many historical references to the Benzaiten building refer to it as the Hondō. It may have been the Kannondō, neighboring the Tsukubusuma Main Hall, though this cannot be confirmed. In any case, it would appear that Hidemori is responding to Chikubushima's solicitation of Hideyoshi's support for a building project on the island. No earlier reference to such a project is known, but Hidemori's brief mention suggests an ongoing undertaking. When we consider below the construction that occurred on Chikubushima in the early seventeenth century, after Hideyoshi's death, we should keep in mind the possibility that Hideyoshi's heirs were honoring Hideyoshi's own inclinations and promises.

Even after Hideyoshi rose to undisputed hegemony of Japan and moved his headquarters from northern Ōmi to the capital district, the association between the ruler and Chikubushima thus continued. Hideyoshi favored the island with bureaucratic attention as well as funds for the worship of Benzaiten. He did so because he desired access to the spiritual power of this sacred place, for such power, he felt, was necessary to his success as ruler of Japan. As we shall see below, Hideyoshi's most substantial religious projects reflect his belief that secular authority emanated in part from the spiritual realm. Of first importance in this regard was the prevailing view that the sacred was a locus of safety for the country. From the beginning of its successful entry into Japan, Buddhism was presented as an effective safeguard for the country. In this regard the ruler's agency was critical: it was one of the uses of his authority to secure divine protection for the secular realm. And this role Hideyoshi endeavored to fill.

EMULATING EMPEROR SHŌMU: HIDEYOSHI'S GREAT BUDDHA HALL

Prelude: Tenshōji

While he was thus limiting the scope of activity of established temples, Hideyoshi made his first venture at creating new religious institutions.[19] Late in 1584, the twelfth year of

Tenshō, shortly after moving to the capital region, he issued an order to establish a large temple complex in Kyoto, donated land for it just to the southwest of Daitokuji, and engaged the Daitokuji monk Kokei Sōchin (1532–1597) to oversee its creation. Kokei formulated a name for the prospective temple, Taiheizan Tenshōji, which, by incorporating the eponymous era-name, signified Hideyoshi's intention to make this the representative architectural project of its time. Initially Hideyoshi envisioned Tenshōji as the repository of Nobunaga's mortuary tablet; previously he had founded the subtemple Sōken'in at Daitokuji, completed in 1583, as Nobunaga's memorial temple, but Tenshōji was to be even grander, as befit his predecessor's memory. Soon he amplified Tenshōji's scope, stating in his donation letter that Tenshōji should serve the civil function of offering rituals for "peace in the realm." From this temple, as from the reconstituted Enryakuji, Hideyoshi demanded institutionalized state devotional practice. Increasingly, he envisioned the sacred as a realm under his jurisdiction and with the duty of providing divine protection for the Toyotomi state, and the temples as conduits between the state and the sacred realm. In this grand economy, Tenshōji was to be the principal institution.

Construction commenced by the end of 1584 and continued into the following year. Seventy laborers carted large stones to the site, and one of Negoroji's surviving halls—Hideyoshi's plunder from that defeated temple—was to be relocated there. By the middle of 1585, however, documentary evidence for construction activity disappears and the temple is never again mentioned in any known record. Tenshōji was given up. The abandonment of so central and ambitious an enterprise reflects Hideyoshi's ever-expanding notion of his role in the sacred realm, for his subsequent projects dwarfed the Tenshōji plans. Tenshōji was abandoned because it was not grandiose enough.

Hōkōji and Its Great Buddha and Great Buddha Hall

Soon thereafter, in the southeastern part of Kyoto, Hideyoshi embarked on the largest building project of his career: the vast Tendai temple Hōkōji, incorporating a Daibutsuden, or Great Buddha Hall, and its massive sculpture of Buddha. Its size, location, and function marked it as the centerpiece of Hideyoshi's remaking of Kyoto's sacred cityscape. The first notice of this project comes on the first day of the fourth month of 1586, when the Toyotomi confidant Yoshida Kanemi (1535–1610) reports in his diary that Hideyoshi had inspected a site near Tōfukuji for the construction of a Great Buddha.[20] Ten days later Hideyoshi sent to the western Honshu daimyo Mōri Terumoto (1553–1625) a lengthy letter on many topics, including preparations for the upcoming invasion of Korea, and ending with an intriguing though unelaborated mention of "the matter of lumber for the Great Buddha Hall."[21] The preparations were underway.

A most informative comment regarding this earliest stage is provided by the Portuguese Jesuit missionary Luis Frois, who about five months after the above initial notices, wrote in a letter to the Society that Hideyoshi had commanded that a Great Buddha, like the one in Nara, be built near the Sanjūsangendō in Kyoto and that the scope of the construction, which had begun about a month and a half earlier, was enormous.[22] Frois, writing from Kyushu, had likely heard the news secondhand: from the beginning Hideyoshi's new project was a topic of rumor, so widely discussed that even the European community was well informed. The choice of site is the first clue to the ambitiousness of Hideyoshi's plans. Except for the Sanjūsangendō, the thirteenth-century Hall of Thirty-three Bays, the area was relatively free of prominent temples; Tenshōji, at its projected site, would have been in the shadow of the ancient, sprawling Daitokuji. No such vast and venerable institutions impinged on the site chosen for Hōkōji.

Tōdaiji as Precedent

The key point in Frois' account is his explicit coupling of Hideyoshi's Great Buddha with the eighth-century one in Nara, for in this association lies the significance of Hideyoshi's project. The Nara antecedent, familiarly known as Tōdaiji (the Great Eastern Temple), resonated strongly in the minds of Hideyoshi and his audience. Its history remained well enough known that another Portuguese Jesuit, Luis de Almeida (1525–1584), resident in Japan in the 1550s, recorded correctly that it "was founded 700 years ago and took 20 years to build; it was burnt down 400 years back and rebuilt in 15 years."[23] This information formed part of the collective memory in Japan, available even to the visiting Jesuits. Japanese reverence for Tōdaiji's ancient origins and its place within the sacred cosmography ran deep, and at the cusp of the Momoyama period the temple remained "a great centre of pilgrimage."[24] Tōdaiji was not a random choice for emulation: it was a site where Buddhism was first explicitly enlisted to protect the Japanese state, the ruler, and the people; its Great Buddha Hall was the largest building ever constructed in Japan, unsurpassed in the intervening centuries. Finally, Tōdaiji was remembered as having been built by Emperor Shōmu (701–756), often celebrated by the Toyotomi as the model ruler of Japan's golden past and their own revered precursor.

Eighth-Century Tōdaiji

Shōmu, with the assistance of his wife, Empress Kōmyō (701–760), created Tōdaiji as the center of a countrywide system of government-sponsored Buddhist worship. At this early stage of Buddhism's presence in Japan, Shōmu endorsed the faith in large part because it offered divine protection to a country led by a devout ruler, a state of affairs he wished for Japan, and which he could find described in one of the most influential sutras of the time, *Sutra of Golden Light (Konkōmyō saishōō kyō):*

> When, in some future time, this *Sūtra of the Golden Light* is transmitted to every part of a kingdom—to its cities, towns and villages, its mountains, forest and fields—if the king of the land listens with his whole heart to these writings, praises them, and make offerings on their behalf, and if moreover he supplies this sūtra to the four classes of believers, protects them and keeps

> all harm from them, we Deva Kings, in recognition of his deeds, will protect that king and his people, give them peace and freedom from suffering, prolong their lives and fill them with glory. . . . [Then the Buddha said] If any king upholds this sūtra and makes offerings in its behalf, I will purify him of suffering and illness, and bring him peace of mind. I will protect his cities, towns and villages, and scatter his enemies.[25]

In short, a ruler who follows the precepts of Buddhism will thrive, as will all his people; the entire land will be defended against misfortune by the Buddha and the Buddhist pantheon. Though far removed from the contemplative focus of early Buddhism, the concept of the protection of the nation as a benefit of the faith had developed well before Buddhism arrived in Japan in the sixth century. The idea had wide appeal throughout much of East Asia, as well as to the Japanese emperor. Shōmu enacted the sutra's dictate to the "king of the land," commanding each of the sixty-seven provinces to own ten copies of the sutra. He anchored the power of Buddhism in his capital, Nara, at his new temple, Tōdaiji, more formally (and informatively) known as the Temple for the Protection of the Nation by the Golden Radiant Four Divine Kings (Konkōmyō Shitennō Gokokuji). To transmit the faith and its protection to every part of his kingdom he chartered one monastery and one nunnery in every province for the "Protection of the Realm," a network of which Tōdaiji was headquarters.

To give impressive substance and focus to his project, Emperor Shōmu in 743 commissioned a Buddha sculpture of enormous size and a correspondingly immense hall to house it, respectively the Great Buddha (Daibutsu) and the Great Buddha Hall (Daibutsuden), and it was this aspect of Shōmu's creation which Hideyoshi most concretely and visibly sought to emulate. Shōmu's proclamation of the project echoes the *Sutra of Golden Light* regarding the secular ruler's importance; he begins by implying his divine right to rulership and his solicitude toward the people of Japan, and then explains how the project will unfold:

> We take this occasion to proclaim Our great vow of erecting an image of Lochana [Vairocana] Buddha in gold and copper. We wish to make the utmost use of the nation's resources of metal in the casting of this image, and also to level off the high hill on which the great edifice is to be raised, so that the entire land may be joined with Us in the fellowship of Buddhism and enjoy in common the advantages which this undertaking affords to the attainment of Buddhahood.[26]

The sculpture and its hall will require the country to consolidate its energies in this one grand effort, and all will benefit from its completion. Shōmu then states that it is he "who possess[es] the wealth of the land"; it is he "who possess[es] all power in the land," and it is he who has "resolved to create this venerable object of worship," and thereby induce the Buddha to protect Japan. He invites the whole country to take part in the great project, even those who "have no more to offer than a twig or handful of dirt." All in Japan were thereby enlisted in this colossal undertaking, no matter how slight their contribution might be, and all were promised the rewards of the Buddha's benevolence in the event of its successful completion. The enterprise engaged all of Japan—its lands, wealth, and people—for the common good. Shōmu was at its head, servant of the Buddha and ruler over the temporal world, the irreplaceable intermediary between the two realms.

This great project was the most costly and complex ever realized in Japan, requiring a vast commitment of manpower and resources.[27] A special government agency, the Office for the Construction of Tōdaiji, was created to execute it, and its various departments oversaw an army of workers in every conceivable craft. Numerous religious advisors assisted Shōmu, including the elderly monk Gyōki (668–749), who travelled the country raising funds for the project and eventually became the first senior high priest of Tōdaiji. (This is the very same Gyōki who is credited with first recognizing the sacredness of Chikubushima; as we shall see, he, like Shōmu, enjoys renewed consequence in the Momoyama period, another important figure in the Tōdaiji project whom the Toyotomi resurrected and linked to themselves.) The Great Buddha sculpture was cast in bronze in a process that lasted, from the creation of the mold to the final gilding, from 744 through 757. In 752, before it was actually completed, the sculpture was consecrated at a grand eye-opening ceremony, in which the pupils were painted in and the sculpture thereby "awakened"; this spectacular ceremony, heightened by dance and music, was attended by ten thousand monks, the elite Japanese laity, and guests from throughout Asia. The finished complex gave physical form to the ideal of a sanctified union between the protective sacred realm and the earthly ruler. And so the original Tōdaiji, and its Great Buddha and Great Buddha Hall, were born.

Tōdaiji over the Centuries

Tōdaiji was one of a handful of ancient monuments that became increasingly prestigious over time, its original significance augmented by continuing eminent patronage. (It remains today one of the canonical sites of elite Buddhist art, architecture, and culture of the eighth century.) Even as subsequent emperors moved the capital to Kyoto, Tōdaiji remained for many a symbol of Buddhism's beneficent engagement with Japan. Its remarkable sacred powers are celebrated, for instance, in an episode of the *Miraculous Origins of Mount Shigi,* in which a nun in search of her long-lost brother, the monk Myōren, spends a night before the Great Buddha and is vouchsafed the whereabouts of his remote mountain temple in a dream.[28]

Then, in the late twelfth century, Shōmu's Tōdaiji was destroyed. In 1180, a warrior commander of the Taira clan torched the great precincts during battles with the rival Minamoto, an event viewed as much more than the deplorable loss of a prominent temple during violent times. As famously described in the *Tale of the Heike,* composed in the early thirteenth century, this bloody conflagration augured the possible ruin of Japan:

> At the Tōdaiji, there had been a one-hundred-and-sixty-foot gilt bronze statue of Vairocana Buddha, erected by Emperor Shōmu (who had personally assisted with the polishing) and designed to serve as a representation of the eternal, indestructible, enlightened being whose physical body appears in the Land of Buddha-Reward in Reality and the Land of Eternally Tranquil Light. . . . But now the head of that holy image—that face resplendent as a full moon—melted and fell to earth, and the body fused into a mountainous heap. . . . Smoke permeated the heavens; flames filled the air below. Those present who witnessed the sight averted their eyes; those afar who heard the story trembled with fear. . . . It was impossible to imagine such a devastating blow to the Buddhist faith in India or China, to say nothing of our own country. . . .
>
> "If my temple prospers, the realm will also prosper; if my temple declines, the realm will also decline," Emperor Shōmu had said in a document written by his own hand. Thus it seemed that the realm was assuredly doomed to decline.[29]

And so fell what had been the largest building and Buddha statue in Japan; but it was not forever lost. The sense of the place as deeply spiritual and broadly significant endured. Over the following centuries the *Tale of the Heike* passage preserved and disseminated a powerful image of the revered site, articulating the memory of the original Tōdaiji, and warning of what might befall Japan by reason of its destruction. In the Momoyama period, as the diaries of the elite tell us, the *Heike* text was still frequently read, recited, illustrated, and discussed.[30] The Yamashina family, which for generations held appointment in the imperial treasury department and also served as doctors to the Court, played a major role in this dissemination as prominent patrons of the itinerant *biwa hōshi* reciters of *Heike* and as interpreters of the received text.[31] In 1582, for example, Yamashina Tokitsune (1543–1611) transcribed a *kana* version of *Heike*—more accessible than the original text in Chinese characters—for Oda Nobunaga's consort.[32]

While the readers and reciters of *Heike* preserved Tōdaiji's conceptual presence, others restored its physical state. The year after Tōdaiji's destruction, Retired Emperor Goshirakawa (1127–1192) issued an edict for its rebuilding.[33] The Tōdaiji monk Chōgen (1121–1206) tirelessly solicited funds throughout the country, gathered enormous timbers for the hall, and is said to have travelled to China to find a bronze caster to recreate the famous statue. Neither the Imperial Court nor the indomitable Chōgen, however, could supply the resources or the conditions necessary for reconstruction. The battles that destroyed Tōdaiji were part of a larger civil upheaval that culminated in the Imperial Court's loss of effective sovereignty; the Minamoto warrior clan, finally victorious over the Taira in 1185, was the first of the military houses to succeed to the supreme secular power.

The Minamoto had come to power through brute force, but as rulers of a Japan at peace sought to legitimize their authority through accepted courtly actions. To this end, the first Minamoto shogun, Yoritomo (1147–1199), helped finance the reconstruction of Tōdaiji: the Taira's act of vengeful destruction thus allowed the Minamoto to revive

Shōmu's goal of securing divine protection for Japan and to make that goal their own. The new Great Buddha Hall, as enormous as the original but in a style then popular in China, was completed in 1203 to house the recast Great Buddha, dedicated in 1185 in a ceremony attended by the newly empowered Yoritomo and Retired Emperor Go-shirakawa. The precedent set by the warrior ruler's assumption of what earlier had been the prerogative of the Imperial Court—the sponsorship of Buddhism in protection of Japan—was one of the most significant developments of this great transformation from court to warrior rule, with implications that reverberated strongly in the Momoyama period. (Hideyoshi was explicit about taking the first warrior ruler as his model, declaring in a 1584 letter that under him "the government of Japan will be superior to anything since Yoritomo."[34]) Yoritomo's rebuilt Tōdaiji remained the object of warrior-ruler responsibility: in the early fifteenth century the shogun Ashikaga Yoshimochi (1386–1428) sponsored a repair of the Great Buddha's faded surface by donating several hundred gold coins, which were pounded into sheets of gold leaf and then applied to the statue, making it spectacular once more.[35]

Allowing Tōdaiji to Decay

Again, though, the sacred precincts were devastated during warrior clashes: in 1567, at the onset of the Momoyama period, the Great Buddha Hall was completely destroyed and only a small portion of the lower parts of its immense statue survived; adding insult to injury, one of the combatants in that battle, Matsunaga Hisahide (1510–1577), looted Tōdaiji's surviving treasures and returned them only after receiving ransom.[36] Almost immediately repair to the shattered precincts began, though this time the process was considerably more discontinuous than before. In 1568 the emperor called for a reconstruction effort, enlisting the support of Oda Nobunaga and others, and over the following several years emergency repairs were made; major work was still required as late as 1580, when the entire right hand was refashioned.[37] In 1572 Nobunaga authorized a campaign to collect funds for reconstruction of the Great Buddha Hall, although only a temporary shelter was actually built.[38]

As this description suggests, Nara's Great Buddha and the building that contained it did not attract sufficient support in this period, even from Nobunaga, to return them to the impressive form they earlier possessed. In 1601 Abbot Gien (1558–1626) of Daigoji recorded his astonishment at the size of the Great Buddha Hall's "ruins" and, seeing Tōdaiji's Great South Gate, then and today still standing, recalled that it was first built by Emperor Shōmu.[39] Gien's diary reveals the new connotations of these precincts in the Momoyama period: no longer was the site a critical conduit for divine protection of the country, though it remained a historical reference point, an evocative reminder of an ancient Japanese past and of the transience of even the greatest monument. Hideyoshi chose not to restore Emperor Shōmu's Great Buddha and its grand building but instead to appropriate their form as well as tutelary powers for the capital in Kyoto. In so doing, he sought to succeed Shōmu as secular sponsor of the deity and of the foremost religious architecture in the realm. But even while attempting to supersede

Tōdaiji, Hideyoshi invoked its renown: his great temple in Kyoto, begun in 1586 and a subject of widespread interest, was called Hōkōji, in reference to the most important ceremony at Tōdaiji.[40]

REALIZING HIDEYOSHI'S GREAT BUDDHA HALL

In 1588 construction on Kyoto's Hōkōji was proceeding with speed and urgency, as reported in period diaries, and even the incomplete construction documents that still exist record a project of staggering ambitiousness. In a thirteen-month period in 1588 and 1589 Hideyoshi ordered daimyo throughout the country to supply lumber and over sixty thousand laborers. From 1591 thorough 1593 the pace of work increased, and Hideyoshi summoned additional laborers to the site from all over the country: over this period some two hundred thousand workers—carpenters, woodcutters, blacksmiths, and roofers—labored at the site each year, and seven hundred men were employed to oversee them.

The raising of Hōkōji, extending over almost a decade, was itself an event that captured the imagination of Kyoto's populace, and notations of its progress punctuate diaries of the period. In the fifth month of 1588 the Kōfukuji priest Tamon'in Eishun (1518–1596) reported that the Kyoto townspeople were celebrating at the site with sake and rice cakes on an altar of piled stones, indicating perhaps the ground-breaking ceremony.[41] A few years later, in 1591, a Shōkokuji monk travelled to inspect the site, saw that one great pillar had been raised, and was amazed by the enterprise.[42] In 1593 Eishun reported that the ridgepole had been raised, indicating that the framing of the grand structure was complete.[43] In 1596, when the temple's completion was near, the inveterate observer Gien reported the raising of the pillars of the Middle Gate.[44]

The completed complex was routinely compared—favorably—with its model. The longest Momoyama account of the Great Buddha Hall, in the *Taikōki,* frames much of its description in comparisons with the earlier project.[45] Whereas the eighth-century hall took twenty years, it states, ingenious techniques would allow Hideyoshi's to be completed in five. Nara's Great Buddha sculptor and his son, a certain Munesada and Munein (respectively holding the high honorary ranks bestowed upon artists, *hōin* and *hōgen*), along with the Great Buddha carpenter, were summoned and closely questioned about their work; an understanding of the myriad details was gained, and all of this knowledge was conveyed to those responsible for the Kyoto project. Lumber was obtained far and wide and transported in great boats to Osaka (and from there presumably upriver to Kyoto).

The center of the project was the image of the Great Buddha, which, unlike its Nara precedent, was made not of bronze but of wood. The *Taikōki* explains the difference of material as a sensible, time-saving choice, and implies that the result was no less impressive: the surface of the image was carefully primed, then painted in bright colors. In size, sixteen *jō* (over 48 meters), it equalled the earlier image. Kōshō (1534–1621), its sculptor, was the twenty-first-generation head of Kyoto's oldest and most prestigious workshop of Buddhist sculpture, the Seventh Avenue Atelier (Shichijō Bussho), and this, the period's largest commission, was his greatest work.[46] In one of his famous displays of absolute power Hideyoshi ordered farmers to surrender all weapons, the swords to be reworked into rivets and clamps for his Great Buddha image; in return, says Hideyoshi's edict, donors would receive the blessings of the Buddha.[47] Though the need for metal was a thinly disguised pretext for disarming the commoners, Hideyoshi's edict also echoed Shōmu's call to eighth-century common folk to donate even "a twig or handful of dirt" in order to participate in the great project. In all these ways, Hideyoshi endowed his Hōkōji with Tōdaiji's physical and conceptual aura.

SENSŌE: THE RITUAL OF ONE THOUSAND MONKS

For Hideyoshi, Hōkōji was the modern equal, if not the better, of Nara's ancient (and declined) Tōdaiji; its Great Buddha Hall dominated the landscape of the renewed capital and epitomized Toyotomi ascendancy. It was also a setting in which to demonstrate his greatness, as he did by frequent sponsorship of Buddhist rituals. The powerful political resonances of these rituals are nowhere better exemplified than in the Sensōe.

As its name suggests, the "Ritual of One Thousand Monks" convened an immense assemblage of Buddhist monks (not necessarily an exact thousand), who partook of a meal and conducted a service. Writing in early 1596, Gien indicates that monthly performance of the Sensōe had begun on the twenty-fifth day of the ninth month of the previous year, that its sponsor was Hideyoshi himself, and that its purpose was the salvation of his ancestors.[48] The Sensōe was performed in an appropriately magnificent hall, the enormous twenty-one-bay wide Sutra Hall that Hideyoshi commissioned in 1595 just to the east of the Great Buddha Hall.[49] That this ritual was performed here, not within the Great Buddha Hall, further differentiated it from the others that took place within the complex. Most if not all other rituals were performed in the Great Buddha Hall; performing the Sensōe in a different place lent it further distinction.

The sheer number of monks participating in the ritual insured an impressive spectacle, which was enhanced by well-coordinated ecclesiastic dress. On one occasion in 1596 the Tendai temple of Enryakuji, in preparation for an upcoming Sensōe, sent a letter to its branch temple on Chikubushima with instructions to send ten of its monks to the ceremony; the senior monks were to wear purple *kesa* and the younger ones dark gray.[50] Gien's careful records of his own garb when he attended indicate not only his own concern with sartorial display but also the importance of such display in the grand ritual. The central image of the hall housing the ceremony was a Shaka triad, which was certainly surrounded by the requisite ritual objects—jewelled canopies, brocade or bronze banners, gilt bronze pendants *(keman)* and censers, and so on. The whole would have created a magnificent display and a powerful sense of *shōgon,* sanctification through adornment.[51]

The Sensōe brought together a great diversity of Buddhist sects. At the Sensōe of the first month of 1596 Gien noted monks from eight different sects: Shingon, Tendai, Ritsu, Zen, Jōdo, Nichiren, Ji, and Ikkō.[52] Until the destruction of the Toyotomi in 1615, the Sensōe was conducted with nearly unbroken regularity: two major Sensōe observances annually, led by either Tendai or Shingon, with the same eight sects attending, took place on the twenty-fifth day of the fourth month and the twenty-ninth day of the sixth month—the death dates of Hideyoshi's maternal grandfather and grandmother, respectively.[53] In other months, on either the twenty-fifth or twenty-ninth day in honor of those ancestral anniversaries, the various sects alternated their participation.

Most sects perceived attendance as compulsory by virtue of the patron. Enryakuji, in the instance cited above, gave weight to its command to Chikubushima by noting that the directive originated "from above" and by warning that "although it is troublesome, on this occasion it is important that [the monks] attend without fail." The content of the ritual varied according to the sect officiating, undoubtedly generating doctrinal discomfort for the nonofficiating sects, but we can surmise that this discomfort was a part of Hideyoshi's intent—to remind the sectarians that his will outweighed their beliefs.[54]

Some sects complied reluctantly, however, and the Nichiren divided over whether or not to participate.[55] Two weeks before the first observance of the ritual in 1595, the Toyotomi's magistrate of Kyoto, Maeda Gen'i (1539–1602), wrote to the Nichiren, bidding them (and every other sect) to send one hundred monks to the monthly service for Hideyoshi's ancestors, the Sensōe.[56] The Nichiren temples convened in Kyoto to decide their response. The order compromised the sect's principle against cooperation with nonadherents, and was especially offensive because it required Nichiren not only to cooperate with sects which were doctrinally at odds with Nichiren, but to do so for the express purpose of venerating the ancestors of a man who was not a Nichiren adherent. Such was the authority of Hideyoshi, however, that the Nichiren sect bowed to his purpose: while Hideyoshi was alive, it participated as commanded. In the late sixteenth century Hideyoshi was the only man whose secular authority prevailed over even the most dogmatic segments of the Buddhist establishment.

Further letters from Maeda Gen'i stated that the Sensōe not only constituted veneration for the Toyotomi ancestors but also produced benefits for Japan,[57] which cast Hideyoshi in the historically resonant role of sponsor of Buddhism's protective powers. The Sensōe had an ancient presence in Japan, and when it was performed, it was often as an impressive bulwark against perceived threats to the country.[58] In the second month of 1099 it was convened in the Imperial Palace compound and at Enryakuji for the express purpose of calming unrest in the world, and in the fifth month the ceremony was held at Tōdaiji to combat an outbreak of disease. Several years later, in 1103, it was conducted at Enryakuji and Tōdaiji for the emperor Horikawa (1079–1107), then nearing the end of his life and probably in declining health. In the mid-twelfth century the ritual was held in the second month of four successive years—1142 through 1145—at Hosshōji, an imperially sponsored temple in Kyoto; although the records fail to state the purpose of these performances, they were attended by the highest elites of the time, including the two abdicated emperors, Toba (1103–1156) and Sutoku (1119–1164). In the fifth month of 1145 the ritual was performed at Hosshōji, Tōdaiji, and Enryakuji, in fearful response to the appearance of a comet.

In reviving the rite at his new Kyoto temple, Hideyoshi conflated ritual for his extended clan with traditional ritual for the protection of Japan. As patron of this activity, Hideyoshi called upon Buddhism not only to protect Japan directly but also to support himself, as Japan's secular leader, who claimed to control all realms, temporal and sacred. We know that this ritual and its message were received not only by the many participating monks, but also by an audience of spectators and, even more broadly, by the branch temples and lay members of the participating institutions.[59] All aspects of the Sensōe conjoined to imply Toyotomi hegemony over Japan's Buddhist institutions, and to convey that implication unmistakably to the Buddhist community.

APOTROPAIC RITUAL

Hideyoshi's exercise of rigorous authority over the diverse Buddhist sects—including his orchestration of the Sensōe and his calculated humbling of the ferociously sectarian Nichiren devotees—does not necessarily mean that Hideyoshi lacked faith in the efficacy of religious activities. Hideyoshi perceived the sacred to be, as it had been historically, a fount of private salvation.

In response to his mother Ōmandokoro's ill health, for instance, Hideyoshi always turned to ritual.[60] Her serious illness in 1588 prompted Hideyoshi to order ceremonies at important Shinto and Buddhist complexes (including Ise, Kasuga, Gion, Atago, and Kitano, and Kiyomizudera, Kōfukuji, and Kuramadera); for these he sent funds and promised additional payments upon her recovery. He also enlisted the Imperial Court to sponsor *kagura* dance and rites and to send imperial representatives beseeching intercession to various shrines. Fearing the worst, Hideyoshi initiated work at Daitokuji on his mother's memorial subtemple, Tenzuiji, and granted it an annual income of 300 koku.[61] She recovered, but another illness in 1592 again inspired massive sponsorship of ceremonies at major temples and shrines and also the promise of a Great Pagoda to be constructed at Mount Kōya in return for Buddist rituals. This time Ōmandokoro did not recuperate, and in her memory Hideyoshi sponsored a temple on Mount Kōya and the rebuilding of a Great Pagoda at Tōji (on the third death anniversary); he also promised construction of numerous buildings at Shitennōji in Osaka, which had been destroyed by Nobunaga in 1576, although this project was not realized in Hideyoshi's lifetime. This resort to ceremonial ritual in times of distress—and construction of religious architecture at life's end—was entirely typical behavior for Hideyoshi.

RITUALS FOR SUTEMARU

Hideyoshi's faith in the curative effect of ritual was never more evident than during the short life of his first son, Sutemaru (1589–1591), born to the ruler and his consort Chacha (d. 1615) on the twenty-eighth day of the fifth month of 1589.[62] To mark the great event "many lavish celebrations were held," for which the elites of Japan left Kyoto for Yodo Castle, where the infant was cloistered with his mother (hence her more common sobriquet, Yododono).[63] Hideyoshi was obsessed with the boy: though he still waged military campaigns in this period, Sutemaru was always foremost in his thoughts. In 1589 Hideyoshi requested his infant son be sent to him in Osaka.[64] In each letter home during his successful siege of the Hōjō stronghold in 1590, he inquired after Sutemaru; one ends with the command, "Please take ever greater care of the young prince." These letters show a general concern for the boy's health and a fervent desire to see him, as well as intensely specific anxieties—one letter asks if Sutemaru is growing and directs his mother to make sure the child is kept warm enough and to guard vigilantly against fire. This was more than ordinary parental love and concern; upon Sutemaru's well-being hung the Toyotomi prospects for dynastic continuity. Hideyoshi fathered no children with his wife, Kita no Mandokoro (1549–1624), making Sutemaru his sole hope that the Toyotomi regime would outlast that of Nobunaga.

Sutemaru was a frail child, however, often ill, to which Hideyoshi responded by sponsoring abundant ritual activity. Eishun, for example, several times notes in his diary that he was ordered to perform ceremonies for Sutemaru when the young heir was sick.[65] Hideyoshi paid generously for the ceremonies—300 koku on just one occasion[66]—and when they were concluded, records of the proceedings were sent to Hideyoshi, as talismanic documents. Apparently the ceremonies were efficacious, for Sutemaru recovered.

In the eighth month of 1591, however, the young heir fell ill again, this time more seriously. On the second day of the month the diary of Yoshida Kanemi reports that Wakagimi, the Young Lord, is ill and that Hideyoshi is travelling to Yodo Castle to be by his side; on the fourth, he reports that the boy is in such "terribly bad condition" that he and others would not make the normally expected convalescent visits.[67] The news quickly spread, and a massive campaign of rituals was begun. Monk Ōgo of Mount Kōya, a major recipient of Hideyoshi's largesse, sent a desperate letter on the fourth to Muryōjuin and Hōshōin, two temples in the Shingon complex on Mount Kōya.[68] In it he describes the vast program of frenzied ritual performance that the illness provoked—"various temples and various shrines are performing vows and rites on a large scale"—and he enjoins "special strict ceremonies before the altar of Yakushi," the Healing Buddha. Reflecting the gravity and sudden onset of the illness, the letter ends with an urgent warning to waste no time: "Quickly conduct prayer and send records [that register its performance]."

Chikubushima was enlisted in this sweeping effort, as revealed by a letter to the island dated to the third day of the month:

> If the Young Lord recovers, a donation of *goryūganmai* [rice for rituals] will be made. In addition, furthermore, [Hideyoshi] proclaimed that there will be a donation of fifty *koku.* Saving-prayers should be conducted before the deity. Without negligence there should be prayer. Respectfully conveyed. For the time being, three hundred *hiki* will be sent.[69]

The order was given great weight by the high status of its signers—Mashita Nagamori (1545–1615) and five other top-level Toyotomi administrators, including Ishikawa Mitsushige and Maeda Gen'i—and it is clear from the contents that Hideyoshi was directing the effort. Hideyoshi had recruited the island for earlier campaigns of ritual performance; this time he specified that the powers of Benzaiten be tapped. A similar request was directed to another nearby Ōmi temple, Jōshinji in Kinomoto, devoted to Jizō, a deity who particularly aids children.[70]

Larger complexes, such as Kōfukuji in Nara, were often profferred correspondingly greater financial incentives in return for their devotions, as described by Eishun in a diary entry dated to the fourth:

> Because the Young Lord is ill, Kanpaku Dono [Hideyoshi] has ordered, under the seal of Mashita and five others, that there be special prayer rituals. It was clearly stated that if he recovers, the 700 koku remaining from the previous stage and the 7,000 koku left from the time of Ōmandokoro, as well as an additional 1,000 koku, will be passed over.[71]

Through the same six administrators, who were apparently coordinating the entire countrywide effort, Hideyoshi offered substantial sums for rituals on behalf of Sutemaru's recovery, including as-yet-unpaid funds from earlier invocations for Sutemaru and for Hideyoshi's mother, and a generous bonus in the event of success.

The magnitude of these rewards reveals much about the function of curative ritual in popular belief and in the temple economy. Kōfukuji, like many religious institutions in this period, had lost much of its former economic security, and under Hideyoshi especially, its allotted annual income was repeatedly and drastically reduced.[72] In these circumstances the performance of rituals on demand became a necessary source of income. In 1590 Kōfukuji received 7,000 koku as compensation for rituals for Hideyoshi's sick stepbrother, and the following year it was confirmed in holdings in the amount of 15,000 koku, considerably less than formerly but still a partial restoration of the most recent cuts. The 8,700 koku promised in 1591 for rituals on behalf of Sutemaru thus represented a compelling sum for Kōfukuji. Hideyoshi wielded the power of the purse not only for political control of religious institutions but also for metaphysical benefits. Despite his legendary wealth and his attachment to Sutemaru as son and as heir, Hideyoshi would not have disbursed such funds unless he believed in the efficaciousness of rituals.

Notwithstanding, Sutemaru passed away the next day, the fifth day of the eighth month. On the sixth Eishun wrote in his diary, "It is said that yesterday the Young Lord died. The prayer rituals were insufficient."[73]

CONSTRUCTING SHŌUNJI

Hideyoshi's distress at the loss of his only son—Eishun described it as "such that one cannot even bear to look at [Hideyoshi]"—provoked a series of dramatic responses.[74] Diaries are filled with reiterations of an account given by Yoshida Kanemi, who on the sixth wrote: "Word arrived this morning that the Young Lord departed this world yesterday. Denka went to Tōfukuji, and it is said that he cut his topknot loose, but this is not confirmed. It is an inevitable result of his deep grief. . . . A messenger came and said that various officials and others loosened their topknots, and this is an unexpected turn of events."[75] Hideyoshi's anguish, expressed by undoing his warrior's topknot, a preeminent symbol of his status, impelled his entourage to the same act. A more frightening effect is suggested in the diary of the courtier Kajūji Haretoyo (1544–1602), which reports the rumor that Hideyoshi speaks "only about the invasion of China."[76] Although Hideyoshi had contemplated an assault on the Asian mainland from at least as early as 1586 and had many motives, Haretoyo's observation suggests that Hideyoshi's anguish catapulted him from deliberation into action.[77] The same interpretation is also supported by a letter that Hideyoshi's vassal Ishida Masazumi sent three weeks later to the Sagara warrior clan; it was understood at the time that Sutemaru's death had impacted Hideyoshi's policy.[78] The invasion commenced in early 1592.

Hideyoshi also pursued a more conventional, fittingly magnificent, response to Sutemaru's death: Buddhist ritual and the construction of appropriate buildings within which to conduct it. Preparations were soon made for the final rites: Eishun reported on the eighth that Sutemaru's remains had been moved to Tōfukuji, and Kanemi added that "already cleansing preparations are taking place."[79] Those close to Hideyoshi sent sutra scrolls. The funeral was organized by Ishikawa Mitsushige, the Toyotomi administrator who had been responsible for looking after Sutemaru's welfare, and took place at Myōshinji, and thereafter Hideyoshi sponsored Buddhist rites on several important death anniversaries.[80]

To accomodate these regular post-funeral observances, Hideyoshi soon embarked on the construction in Kyoto of a permanent site of worship, Shōunji, the young boy's memorial temple. The only informative contemporary mention of Shōunji is included in a eulogy for the third anniversary of Sutemaru's death, written in 1593 by the temple's chief abbot, Nanka Genkō (1538–1604): "At the end of the Tenshō era [1573–1592], the Kanpaku Sashōfu [Hideyoshi] ordered the construction of a temple building to the southeast of the Great Buddha Hall for Tairei [Sutemaru]. It is impossible to praise enough its magnificence."[81] In other words, Shōunji was constructed about 1591 or 1592, immediately after Sutemaru's death (and probably with urgency), its sponsor was Hideyoshi, it was built close by Hideyoshi's Great Buddha Hall, and it was judged an excellent creation. We know, too, that in 1596 Hideyoshi granted the temple an income of 300 koku.[82]

Political machinations and natural disasters have obscured the original state of this crucial Momoyama site. Soon after Tokugawa Ieyasu annihilated the Toyotomi family in 1615, he deconsecrated Shōunji and gave its precincts to the temple that still stands there, Chishakuin. In converting this Toyotomi temple to one historically allied with the Tokugawa, Ieyasu was seeking to erase all vestiges of Toyotomi greatness, all visible traces around which nostalgic fidelity to the Toyotomi house might coalesce.[83] In 1682 the original Shōunji buildings were destroyed by fire; over their ashes were raised new Chishakuin buildings, many of which then burned in 1947. Few Shōunji documents are known to have survived these several calamities, nor have any surfaced at Myōshinji, where the chief abbot of Shōunji moved when it was closed after 1615. Many of the concrete traces of Shōunji's considerable status during its brief period of activity, both as an institution and a physical presence, have consequently been lost.

Hideyoshi undoubtedly used all available means to make Shōunji a fitting memorial to his intended heir. First, it is reasonable to assume that Shōunji included both the large and small buildings typical of a Zen complex. Excavations in 1992 of the foundations of Shōunji's original Main Hall and its garden revealed how astonishingly large it had been: at thirty-six meters wide, it was twice the size of most contemporaneous buildings of its type.[84] Its size alone attests to the statement of grandiosity that Hideyoshi intended to make.[85]

A visitor to Chishakuin in 1679 described this building, then designated the Lecture Hall, as both impressively wide and tall, with colorful paintings on gold-leafed grounds adorning its interior.[86] These are likely to have been the well-known monumental paintings of floral subjects still preserved at Chishakuin, which an Edo-period inventory records as produced by the Hasegawa workshop and belonging originally to the Shōunji Main Hall *(Fig. 44)*.[87] In their ambitiousness and quality these paintings suggest the highest levels of patronage, thereby supporting the inventory's claims: their size would have required a spacious building, if not the excavated Main Hall, then some other large building at Shōunji; their boldly depicted floral forms, executed in gold-leaf and polychromy, recall the innovative style of the recently deceased Kano Eitoku, which in the post-Eitoku era was continued by the Hasegawa.

Such a decorative program for one of the major Shōunji buildings was entirely consistent with Toyotomi commemorative practice. The Main Hall at Tenzuiji, which Hideyoshi had built several years earlier for his mother, was the largest building of its type at Daitokuji, and it was filled with paintings. Although it was dismantled when Tenzuiji was closed in 1874, and its contents lost, information about its grand program of paintings is preserved in Edo-period documents and sketches.[88] In four of the eight rooms of the Main Hall the walls bore polychrome paintings on gold-leafed grounds, each of a different floral theme—pine, bamboo, plum (cherry according to another source), and chrysanthemum. The Edo-period documents attribute these to Kano Eitoku—one

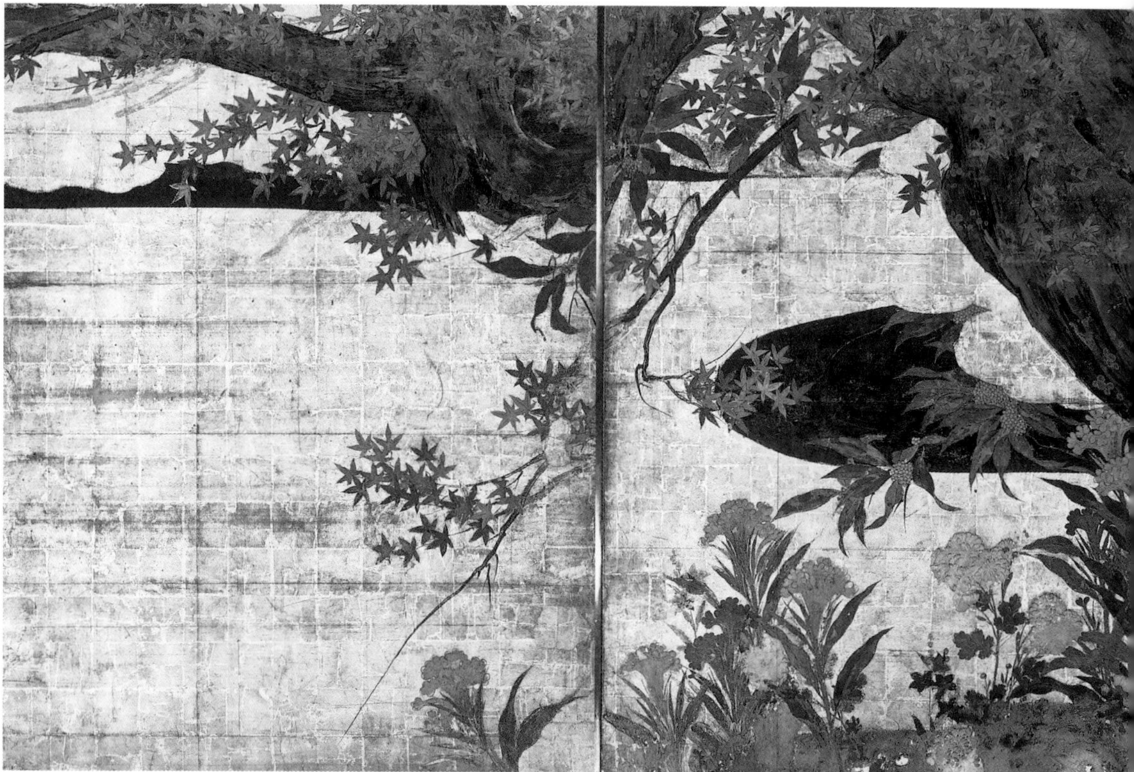

of the major commissions Eitoku filled toward the end of his life. Tenzuiji was Hideyoshi's first memorial building for a beloved relative; spectacular though it was, from the evidence of the Hasegawa paintings, Shōunji may well have surpassed it.

Hideyoshi assigned the most eminent of his associates to Shōunji. Its construction was overseen by Maeda Gen'i, Hideyoshi's Kyoto magistrate, who also had supervised the building of the Great Buddha Hall. Its founding abbot was Nanka Genkō (Sutemaru's eulogist), one of the highest-ranking and most accomplished clerics of his day. Although he later returned to Myōshinji, where he died in 1604, Nanka remained the abbot of Shōunji for life, and even when he resided elsewhere the temple was never left unattended.[89]

The new temple immediately became a major presence in Kyoto's cityscape, its own impressive precincts infused with the reflected grandeur of its neighbor, the Great Buddha Hall. Its importance is manifest in the prominence of Chishakuin, and thus of Shōunji which preceded it, in the previously discussed seventeenth-century *Sights in and around the Capital,* where the precinct is depicted prominently (though partly cloud-covered), just above the Great Buddha Hall *(Figs. 26, 45).*[90] Together, the two precincts acted as a salient assertion of Toyotomi eminence in the sacred realm.

That Shōunji was an independent temple also signifies its special status. By custom, the family of a deceased member of the warrior elite sponsored construction of a subtemple where memorial rites were conducted, within one of the established Kyoto Zen monasteries; the prevalence of this practice assisted such temples as Daitokuji and

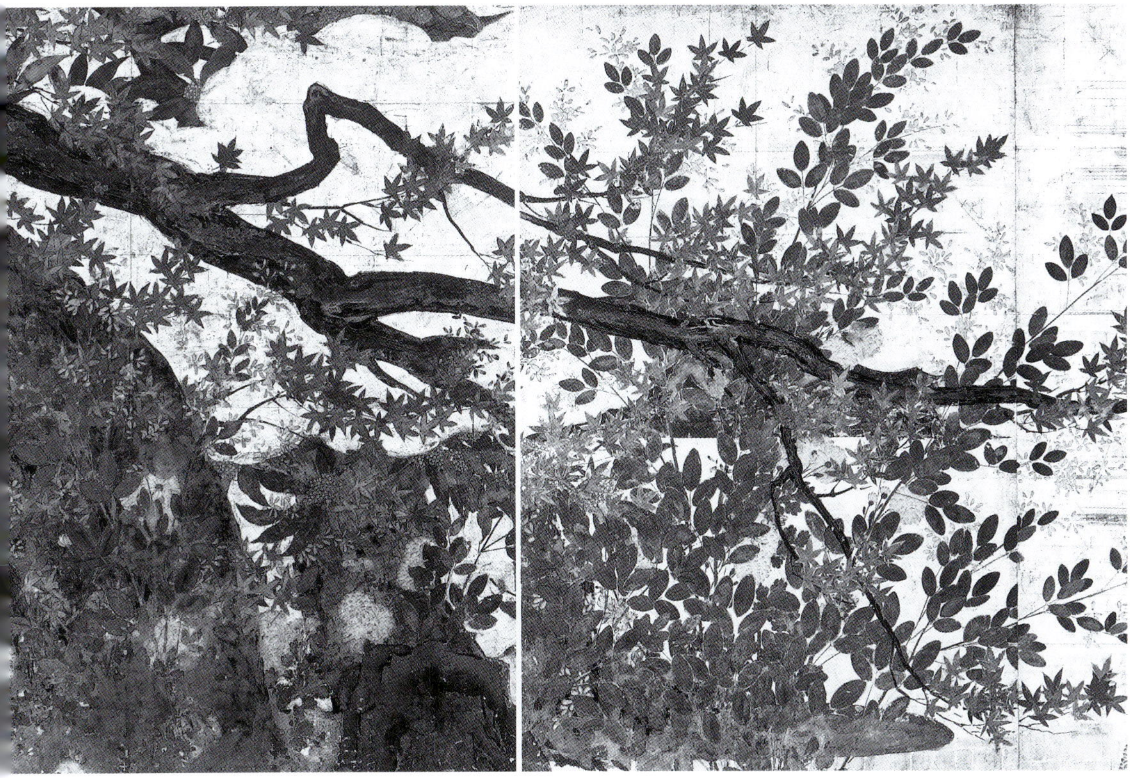

FIG. 44 Hasegawa workshop. *Maple Tree and Autumn Plants.* Late sixteenth century. Four sliding-screen panels; ink, color, and gold leaf on paper. Chishakuin, Kyoto. Photograph by Kyoto National Museum.

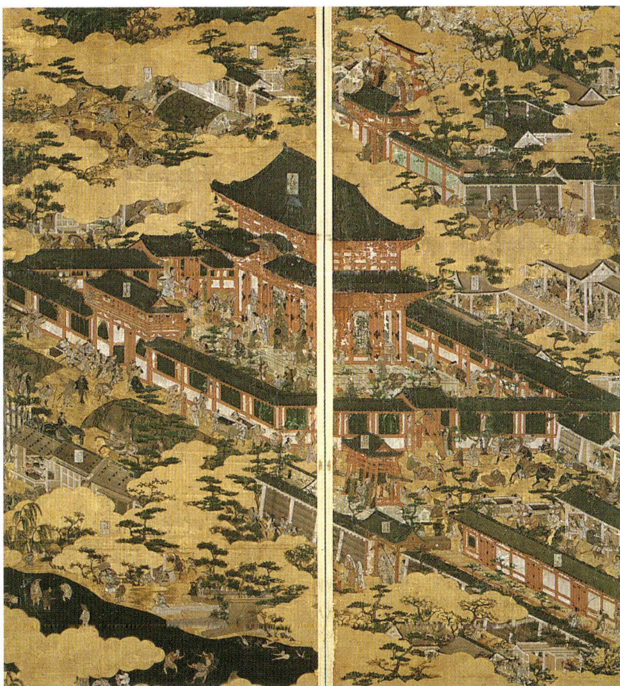

FIG. 45 Detail of Chishakuin, above Great Buddha Hall, from Fig. 26.

Myōshinji to rebuild after the enormous destruction suffered in a century of internecine warfare.[91] In fact, a small memorial hall *(tamaya)* for Sutemaru was built within such a subtemple of Myōshinji, the Gyokuhōin *(Fig. 46)*.[92] But Sutemaru's loss required more than what was customary and afforded the Toyotomi the opportunity to proclaim in architecture the dynastic ambitions that his death had frustrated. Though lost as a standard-bearer, he could still be an occasion of Toyotomi aggrandizement. Shōunji was the architectural simulacrum for the dead Sutemaru, and as such a cogent symbol of Toyotomi ambition.

THE 1596 EARTHQUAKE AND ITS AFTERMATH

Hideyoshi's new Kyoto bespoke a civil order such as had not obtained for centuries. Peace was the norm there, and the sacred realm was reconstituted: Hideyoshi allowed the old temples to rebuild (if not always on their previous sites) and added impressive new temples, especially Hōkōji. More quickly than it rose, however, Hideyoshi's rebuilt capital was devastated and its magnificent Great Buddha fell, victims of the greatest natural disaster ever to hit the Kyoto area.

Sometime in the night hours of the Rat or the Ox, between the twelfth and thirteenth days of the seventh intercalary month of 1596, a great earthquake shattered Kyoto. Reports of its ruin fill all the diaries. The Buddhist priest Bonshun (1553–1632) brushed an immediate stunned assessment: "Tens of thousands died, temples throughout Kyoto collapsed, Fushimi Castle and its town crumbled, and, at the Great Buddha, the earthen walls surrounding the compound and the main image ruptured"; the following day he notes that everyone in Kyoto, men and women alike, is now sleeping outdoors.[93] The courtier Yamashina Tokitsune begins his entry for the thirteenth by quoting an old man who said there had been no disaster like it in memory.[94] He then summarizes the damage, which was centered in the lower part of Kyoto, listing by name the toppled and bent buildings and noting the numberless dead at various locations; at Hōkōji, he writes, the Great Buddha Hall survived although its pillars were compromised, and the Great Buddha suffered damage from the chest down.

Gien echoes these horror-struck reports, noting that Kyoto's dwellings collapsed and countless people died.[95] Predictably, he writes in greater detail, especially about a select few of the most important monuments and how they weathered the quake. At the imperial compound the carriage approach and its corridor collapsed, and the emperor fled. For Tōji, Gien names eight structures that toppled, including the Great South Gate and Lecture Hall, and more than ten others that survived, some with partial damage; he also notes that most of the boundary wall collapsed. Fushimi Castle suffered extensive damage, with countless men and women perishing in its rubble (and, Gien reports several days later, he has heard that Hideyoshi has moved to temporary shelter). Gien devotes one long section to Hōkōji: the Great Buddha Hall survived, "miraculously," but the Great Buddha suffered serious damage: its left hand fell off, the chest collapsed,

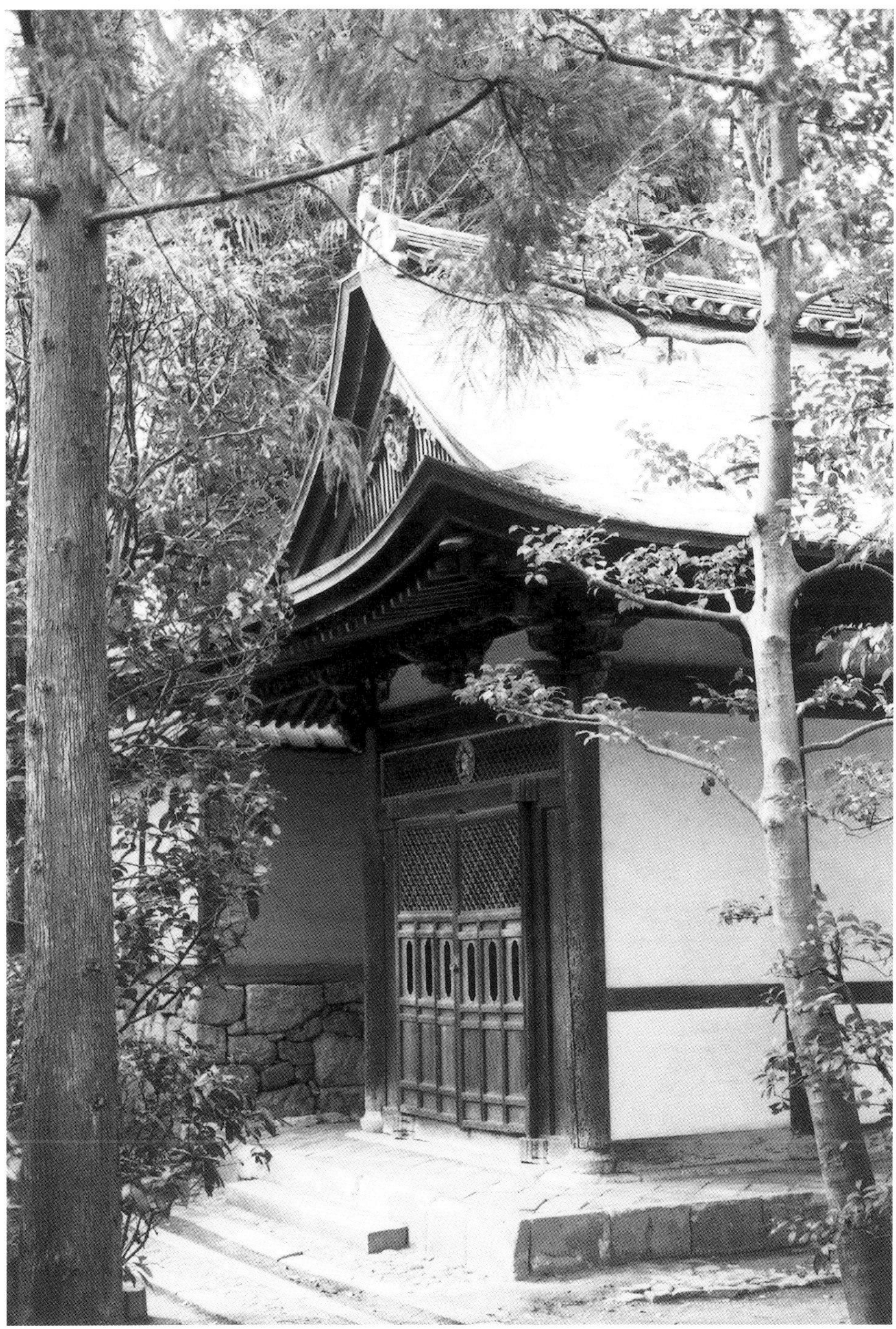

FIG. 46 Tamaya of Sutemaru, exterior. Late sixteenth century. Gyokuhōin, Myōshinji, Kyoto. Photograph by the author.

and cracks developed overall; the Great Middle Gate survived, though some of its pillars bent.

Weeks of aftershocks aggravated the damage to Kyoto and to the nerves of its inhabitants, already demoralized as the full extent of the initial damage was perceived. Two days after the quake Gien reports the rumor that representatives from Ming China, visiting the port of Sakai, died in the upheaval. He also describes a surreal, horrific aftereffect: hair, white, black, or red and of various lengths, apparently from the tails of horses, fell from the sky over Kyoto and over Gien's own temple of Daigoji.[96] Gien offers no explanation for this unnatural happening, which may have resulted from fires started by the earthquake that consumed the stabled animals and sent their remains into the atmosphere. Aftershocks, some of great intensity, continued to rattle Kyoto every day for most of the following month, and people lived in terror of another earthquake as strong as the first.[97] Amidst this, a typhoon hit Kyoto, causing flooding and additional death and destruction.[98] Repeated surveys of the important places brought discouraging reports: two weeks after the initial quake Gien hears a rumor of new, catastrophic damage to the Great Buddha: the statue had fully ruptured and scattered across the tatami mats of its enormous hall.[99] Hideyoshi's attempt to secure the protective powers of Buddhism had failed.[100]

RECONSTRUCTING KYOTO

To this tremendous devastation, the Toyotomi responded with another round of reconstruction, although apparently less systematically than before. In the second month of 1597, for example, the rumor circulated that Hideyoshi's wife, Kita no Mandokoro, would sponsor repairs of Tōji's vast precincts, though there is no indication that the work was begun in Hideyoshi's lifetime.[101] That same month Gien reports that at his own temple of Daigoji Hideyoshi will restore the tenth-century five-story pagoda, which "since the great earthquake last year . . . has been in disrepair" *(Fig. 47)*.[102] Gien's diary record of the progress of this lengthy restoration reveals Hideyoshi's increasing unpredictability and quixotic behavior at this, the end-stage of his life: his munificence now seems to be governed less by purpose than by whim. A carpenter was soon sent to Daigoji (described as the "Daibutsu *banshō*," or "Great Buddha carpenter") and the cost of the repairs estimated at 3,500 koku, an enormous sum, which Gien reported to the magistrate, Maeda Gen'i.

On the eighth day of the following month the project received a singular boost when Hideyoshi visited Daigoji to view its famous cherry trees, then in full blossom.[103] Hideyoshi and his party (which included Tokugawa Ieyasu) walked through the Daigo temple grounds, stopping here and there to admire the blossoms, and finally coming upon the broken-down pagoda; although he does not say so, we can imagine that Gien planned the route so that Hideyoshi would see the ravaged building set against the luxuriant flowers. Gien notes that Hideyoshi inspected the pagoda carefully and offered 1,500 koku toward its repair (Gien writes, with satisfaction, "how wonderful!") before continuing along the viewing route. After a stop for a rest and a meal—Gien reports that Hideyoshi was in a good mood, which made everyone "feel relieved"—Hideyoshi proceeded to Daigoji's upper precincts, in the mountains, to view the cherry trees there, while Gien stayed below. Gien rejoined the group to pay respects to the departing Hideyoshi, who in a stroke of generosity offered a vermilion-seal document prohibiting the removal of stones and trees from Daigoji; more than simply giving funds, Hideyoshi was lending his awesome authority to protect the temple's resources.

Actual repair of the pagoda did not begin until early 1598, after months of additional discussions between Gien and Toyotomi bureaucrats, but was completed in little more than a month, just in time for Hideyoshi's visit to the temple once again for cherry blossom viewing. On the sixth day of the third month Gien notes that the blossoms are just beginning to open and will be ready for viewing on the twelfth or thirteenth, and that the pagoda restoration is finally complete.[104] Preparations for Hideyoshi's visit, more

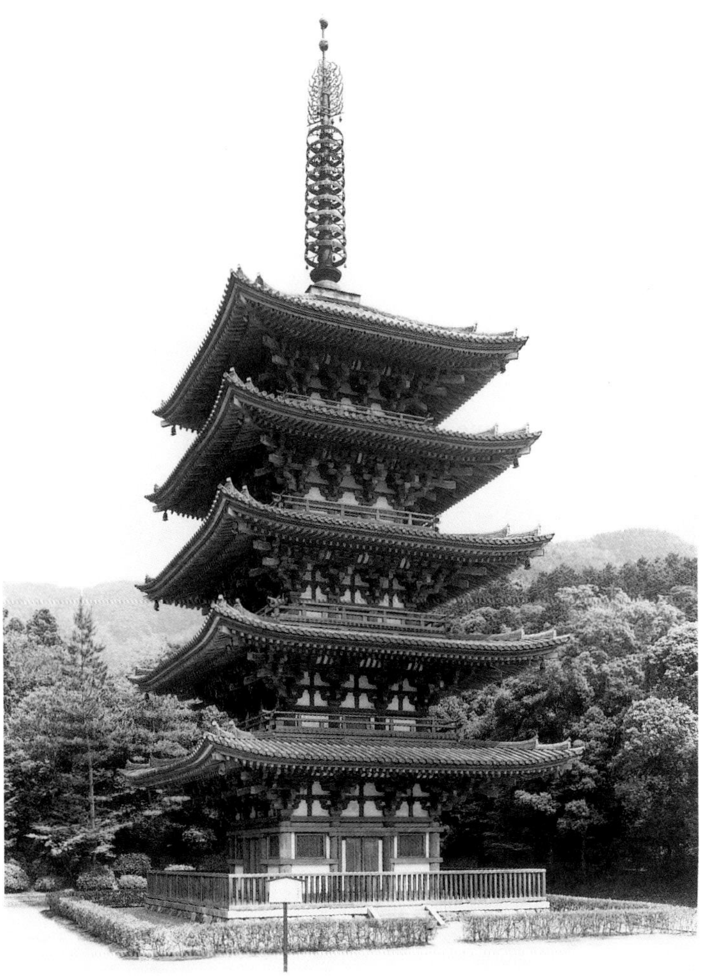

FIG. 47 Five-Story Pagoda, 951. Daigoji, Kyoto.

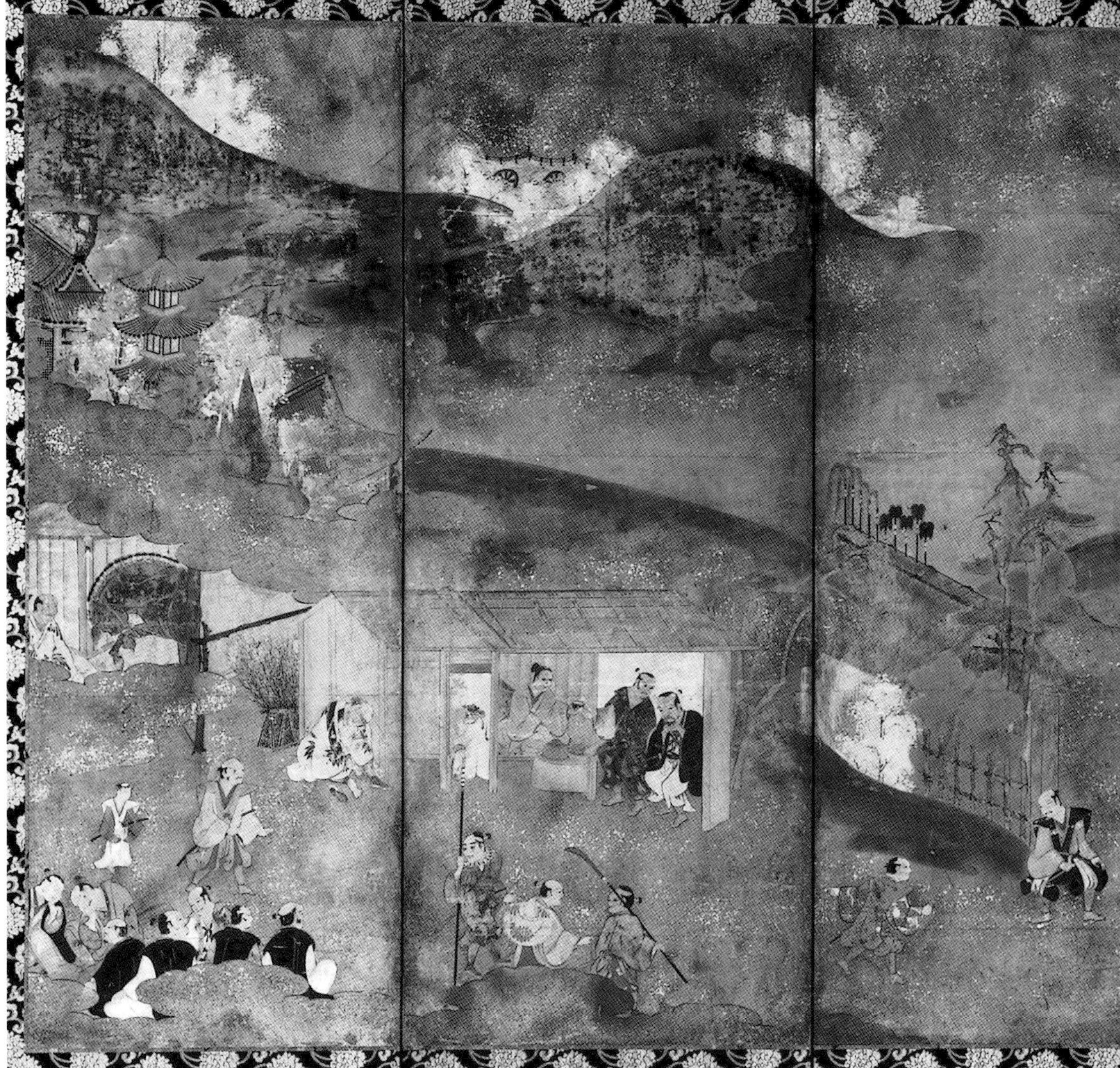

elaborate than the previous year, included construction of a stage in front of the newly restored pagoda, presumably for performances during the visit; not coincidentally, such would have drawn attention to Hideyoshi's pious act of reconstruction. The visit took place on the fifteenth—and it was quite a party, attended by several hundred people—an entire day devoted to amusements under the cherry trees, enjoying tea and other diversions *(Fig. 48)*; as Gien sums up, "The entire temple was filled with great pleasure, everyone was satisfied."

While restoring the pagoda, and during periodic visits in early 1598 leading up to the great cherry blossom party, Hideyoshi became increasingly engrossed in the affairs of Daigoji, as epitomized by three excursions there in the second month: on the ninth day, arriving with his wife Kita no Mandokoro and his young son Hideyori to enjoy plum blossoms, he ordered repairs for the Niō Gate and new buildings for the upper

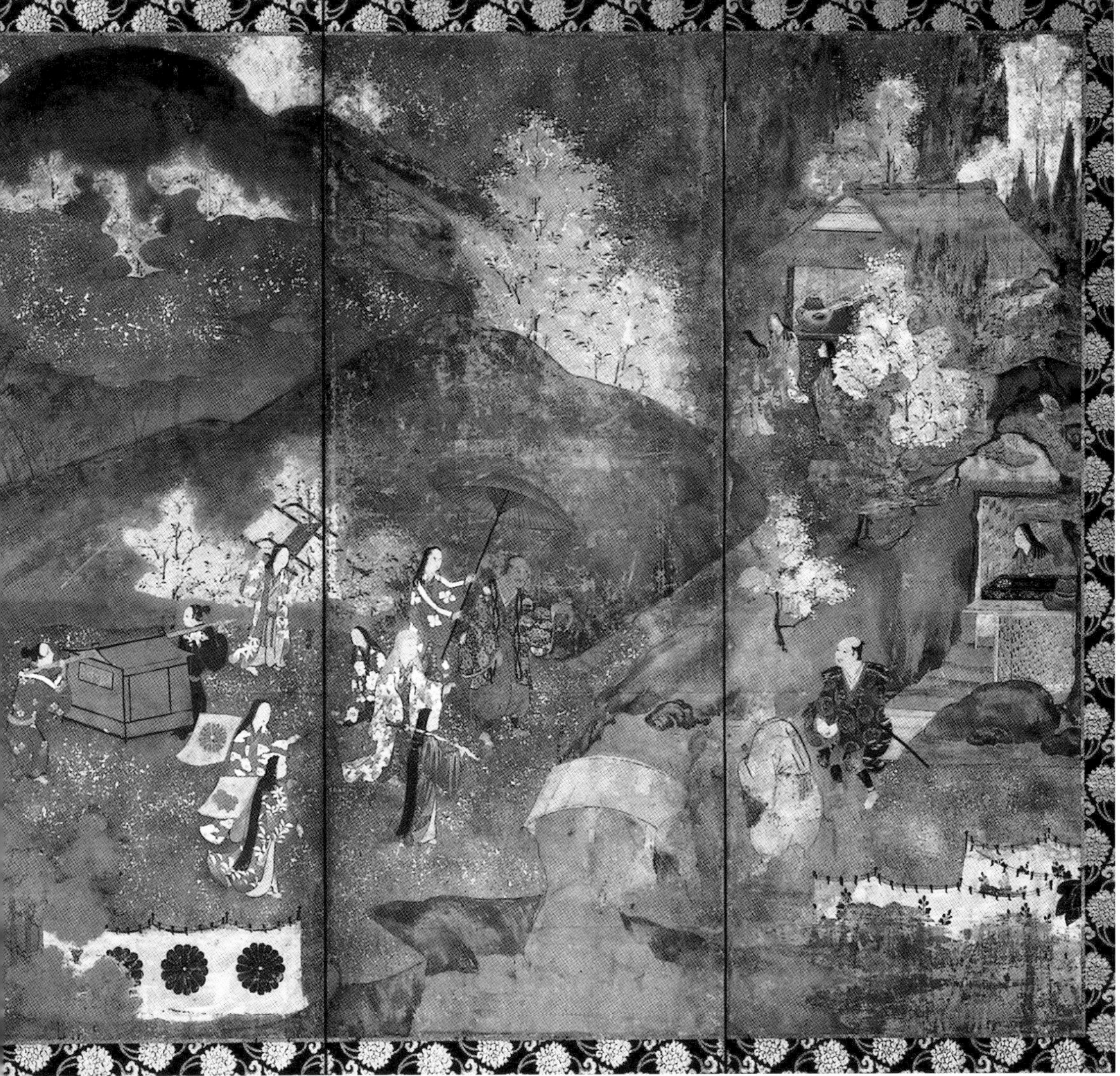

FIG. 48 *Viewing Blossoms at Daigo.* Late sixteenth century. Six-fold screen; ink and color on paper. National Museum of Japanese History, Chiba Prefecture. Photograph by Kyoto National Museum.

precincts before the cherries next blossomed (and, thus, before his visit to view them); on a return visit of the sixteenth Hideyoshi ordered construction of a *shinden*-style building at the Sanbōin and repairs to the old Golden Hall; on the twenty-third Hideyoshi surprised Gien with a list of eight projected structures; Daigoji would, Gien remarked, "surpass the form of even ancient times."[105] All this largesse was surely motivated in part by Hideyoshi's understanding of Daigoji's importance as a religious institution and his concomitant desire to act the role of its savior. An even keener spur to his generosity seems to have been the pleasure he obviously derived from his visits—part lordly progress, part lavish party—to its famed blossoming cherries. Whatever his motives, his interest was of supreme value to the beneficiary.

REPLACING THE GREAT BUDDHA

Post-earthquake, the Great Buddha was the restoration project in which Hideyoshi undoubtedly had the most visible stake and which inspired in him a most extraordinary response. In the fifth month of 1597, after personally inspecting the ruined statue at Hōkōji, Hideyoshi commanded its immediate refabrication.[106] The Great Buddha had been Hideyoshi's most conspicuous Buddhist contribution to Kyoto, and it likely surprised no one that he wished it rebuilt. This grand plan, however, was soon superseded by another, even more remarkable: Hideyoshi had an oracular dream in which the Shinano (present-day Nagano) temple Zenkōji's Amida triad, the most famous Buddha statue in Japan (though a secret image, never actually seen) and widely believed to be the Living Buddha, stated its wish to be moved to Hōkōji. Hideyoshi abandoned his initial scheme and gave orders to follow the marvelous request.[107]

The dream, in fact, was probably inspired by the precedent of the icon's recent peripatetic history. Battles in 1555 had left Zenkōji in ruins, and one of the combatants, Takeda Shingen (1521–1573), took the Amida triad (and other Zenkōji treasures) to Kōfu in Kai Province, where he built a temple, also called Zenkōji, to house them.[108] After Shingen's premature death from illness in 1573, however, the Takeda clan was eliminated by Oda Nobunaga's armies, and in 1582 Nobunaga's son Nobutada (1557–1582) transferred the Zenkōji statue to his base in Mino Province, where it was installed at a temple there. When Nobunaga and his son met their demise a few months later, another of Nobunaga's sons, Nobukatsu (1558–1630), moved the statue to a temple in Owari Province. Then, on Tokugawa Ieyasu's orders, it was sent back to the Kōfu Zenkōji, where it remained until Hideyoshi's dream. In 1597 the statue began its journey to Kyoto, carried along the Tōkaidō route in a great procession of five hundred warriors led by Hideyoshi's vassal Asano Nagayoshi (later Nagamasa, 1544–1611); local daimyo provided additional security along the way, and on the eighteenth day of the seventh month the statue arrived in Ōtsu, just north of Kyoto, where it was met with great fanfare by 150 Tendai and 150 Shingon monks and other important religious figures. There the great convoy prepared to enter Kyoto and, finally, the Great Buddha Hall.

Hideyoshi orchestrated the statue's arrival at the Great Buddha Hall to be a momentous event, and it inspired comment from all who kept diaries. With typical brevity the courtier Yamashina Tokitsune recalled the devastation of the Great Buddha in the earthquake and then described the Zenkōji triad's procession from Ōtsu to the Great Buddha Hall, noting the participation of musicians on horseback, aristocrat-abbots *(monzeki)*, and Asano Nagayoshi; suggesting the pageantry of the event, he ends by saying that he must describe it more fully sometime (though he never does).[109] Others comment more completely, in keeping with the magnitude of the occasion. Reflecting on the implications of the transfer, the abbot of the Rokuon'in subtemple at Shōkokuji describes Hideyoshi's displeasure with his Great Buddha, which was reduced to ruin so quickly. He hails the notion that the Zenkōji statue, despite its small size, had greater spiritual power than the ill-fated colossus, and sees the episode as a metaphor for Hideyoshi's supremacy, likening the failed Great Buddha to the vanquished Nobunaga (and the earthquake to his killer Akechi Mitsuhide [d. 1582]) and the Zenkōji statue to Hideyoshi.[110]

Gien drew no such malicious conclusions regarding the original Great Buddha, but celebrated with tremendously detailed description the magnificent pageant that brought the Zenkōji statue from the penultimate stop in Ōtsu to its new home in Kyoto.[111] In one of the longest entries of his prolix diary, he lists group after group of participants: palanquins carrying famous people, groups of aristocrat-abbots, thousands of guards, and hundreds of warriors in full armor. The Zenkōji icon itself, he writes, was concealed in a gold-brocaded palanquin, which was set atop another palanquin decorated with phoenixes. The gist of all writings on the topic was that the arrival of the famous icon was a magnificent response to disastrous circumstances. Thereafter, the Zenkōji Amida became a regular focus of ritual activities at Hōkōji,[112] although its ritual never displaced the Sensōe, which Gien continued to refer to in his diary as the "Daibutsu Sensōe."

Ultimately, however, this arrangement proved to be even less propitious than the original. Less than a year later, toward the end of the sixth month of 1598, Hideyoshi fell into what would prove to be his final illness, and the Toyotomi ordered temples around Japan to perform rituals for his recovery. Early in the seventh month, for instance, the Toyotomi administrators Maeda Gen'i, Mashita Nagamori, and Asano Nagamasa (who had overseen the conveyance of the Zenkōji triad to Hōkōji) sent a letter to Gien commanding rituals in the name of Hideyoshi's wife Kita no Mandokoro, who paid for them with five pieces *(mai)* of gold; the ceremonies were conducted the following day.[113] On the ninth the powerful daimyo and Toyotomi supporter Date Masamune (1567–1636) sent ten coins *(ryō)* of gold for similar rituals. On the tenth Gien noted that ceremonies were conducted, too, at the Imperial Court; he was also relieved to learn that Hideyoshi had improved.

Hideyoshi soon worsened, however, and death was understood to be imminent: on the twenty-fifth day of the month, Gien reports that an "unprecedented" quantity of bequests were distributed to the various Toyotomi constituencies: the aristocrat-abbots, courtiers, the emperor, and others in the imperial line received suitable amounts of silver or gold; Daigoji received three mai of gold; the daimyo received larger sums of gold (300 mai) as well as swords and other goods.[114] Early the next month, the rumor circulated that Hideyoshi's condition had worsened—Gien writes on two occasions that there is nothing left to do but conduct rituals[115]—and the senior vassals made their famous pact of allegiance to Hideyoshi's son, Hideyori. Gien was summoned to Fushimi Castle to conduct Buddhist rituals there on the sixteenth.

The following day, the seventeenth, Gien and others report that the Zenkōji Nyorai had been sent from the Great Buddha Hall back to its home province of Shinano.[116] These short but remarkable references are amplified by Bonshun in his diary: he writes that Hideyoshi had another oracular dream and as a result the Zenkōji Nyorai was abruptly returned, without fanfare, to Shinano.[117] The implication is that the presence of the icon had worked against Hideyoshi's well-being—the Takeda and Oda clans had, it was likely recalled, met misfortune soon after previous moves of the statue—and so it was banished from the Great Buddha Hall. This action apparently came too late, for on the very next day Bonshun reports the dreaded news: Hideyoshi had died.[118]

What remains of Hideyoshi's grand projects in the Kyoto region? Many were destroyed well before our time: by later rulers, who wished to erase his memory with finality and so deconsecrated his temples (Shōunji, as noted above) or burned his castles (Osaka in 1615); or by later fire (most of the Shōunji buildings, which were the property of its successor, Chishakuin); or, much later, by anti-Buddhist persecutions in the nineteenth century (Tenzuiji). Still, some important reminders endure: Daigoji remains a repository of Hideyoshi's munificence—the Sanbōin and the repaired early pagoda, for instance, and portions of the surrounding wall. The Hasegawa paintings at the Chishakuin likely once decorated the main hall of Shōunji. And one Kyoto building from Hideyoshi's period remains today on the island of Chikubushima, the core of the Tsukubusuma Main Hall; as we will next explore, it provides insights into the particulars of how, with architecture and ornament, Hideyoshi honored the sacred.

3

Encoding the Sacred

DISCOVERING THE KYOTO BUILDING WITHIN THE PRESENT TSUKUBUSUMA MAIN HALL

Hideyoshi marked his tenure as ruler by sponsoring the largest remaking of Kyoto's cityscape since it was first constructed in the eighth century as Japan's capital. Just beyond the city wall, Hōkōji and its Great Buddha Hall—the largest building in Kyoto (and indeed in all of Japan)—dominated the southeast section, along with Shōunji, the magnificent mortuary temple for his much-mourned young son; impressive temples were revived or built anew throughout the city; Hideyoshi raised his own splendid palace, Jurakutei, and commanded other elite warriors to surround it with their own mansions. Mostly unseen and marginalized today, however, is one building that was originally part of Kyoto's architectural efflorescence: the small structure that is the *moya* of the present Tsukubusuma Main Hall (the former Benzaiten Hall).

It was, as we have seen, manufactured in Kyoto near Hōkōji, sometime after the middle 1580s, and stood—somewhere in Kyoto—as an independent building until 1602. A more precise date of manufacture can be surmised from the loss and fading to the exterior lacquer now concealed by the *hisashi.* Such damage could have occurred only before the small Kyoto building was enveloped within the protective sheath and darkness of the Benzaiten Hall. In other words, the Kyoto building was exposed to the outside elements for some time before its move in 1602, and therefore was most likely made sometime in the years before Hideyoshi died in 1598. That the building stood in Hideyoshi's Kyoto we know, but nothing about its role or function there.

Since this structure was incorporated into another building after leaving Kyoto, can we even know what it looked like before it was moved, or was it so transformed in the process of incorporation into the Benzaiten Hall that its original appearance has been lost? The conservation project of 1936–1937, which involved the complete dismantling, "repair," and reassembly of the Main Hall, went a long way in recovering the moya's pre-move appearance (although it also produced, as we shall see, new problems). Evidence for this conclusion is contained in photographs taken before the 1936–1937 project, which reveal a configuration notably different from the Main Hall's present, post-conservation appearance *(Figs. 18–21).* Visualizing the preconservation configuration, admittedly difficult, is made easier by reading the text in close conjuction with the illustrations. The key characteristics of the Main Hall before the restoration project are

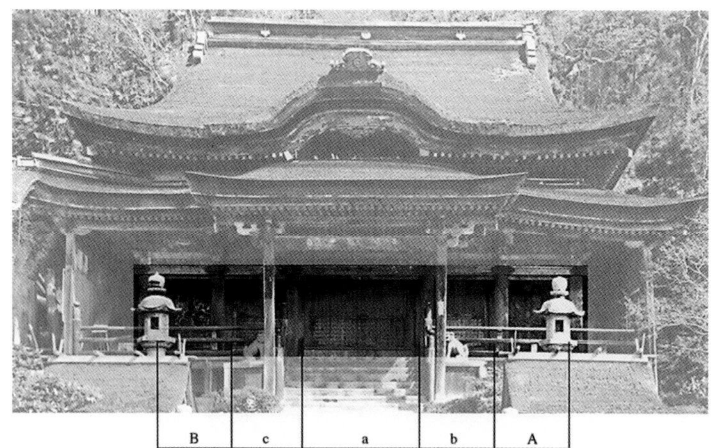

FIG. 49 Diagram of Tsukubusuma Main Hall before 1936–1937 repairs. Exterior, south side (front). Prepared with the aid of Dax Kajiwara, based on Fig. 18.

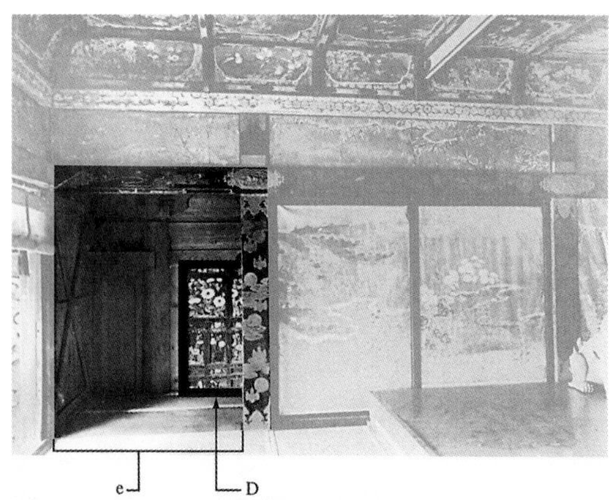

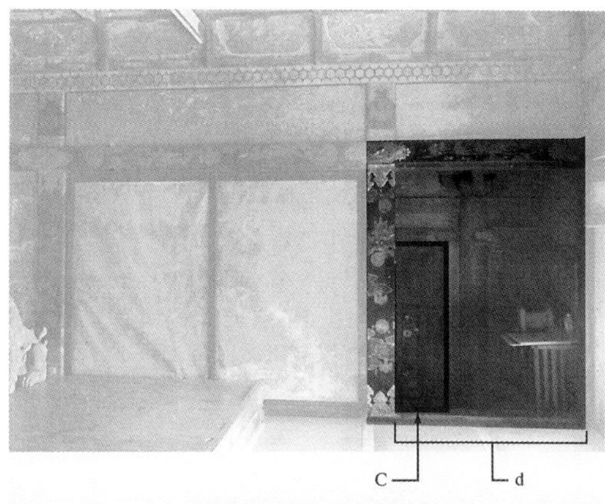

FIG. 50 (right) Diagram of Tsukubusuma Main Hall before 1936–1937 repairs. Moya interior, east side. Prepared with the aid of Dax Kajiwara, based on Fig. 21.

FIG. 51 (left) Diagram of Tsukubusuma Main Hall before 1936–1937 repairs. Moya interior, west side. Prepared with the aid of Dax Kajiwara, based on Fig. 20.

highlighted in Figures 49–51, diagrams based on the pre-restoration photographs (*Fig. 52* is a plan of the pre-restoration building keyed to the diagrams, with the hidden corridor indicated in gray).

> On the exterior, the three central bays at the front of the Main Hall building (i.e., the three front bays of the moya) held flap-down shutters (*Fig. 49*, bays a, b, c). These shutters are clearly seen in their closed position in Figure 19.
>
> Flanking the three moya bays at the front on either side is a one-bay wall that connects the moya with the hisashi; these two flanking bays are filled with monumental carvings, one with the plant known as *fuyō*[1] and the other with chrysanthemums (*Fig. 49*, bays A, B).
>
> On the interior, the most dramatic difference from the present state appears in photographs of the east and west sides of the moya *(Figs. 20, 21)*, which show no wall separating the bay closest to the front from the U-shaped corridor between the moya and the hisashi (*Fig. 50*, bay d, and *Fig. 51*, bay e).
>
> In addition, two pairs of swinging doors covered with relief chrysanthemum carvings were inserted into the east and west walls of the hisashi (*Fig. 50*, bay C, and *Fig. 51*, bay D).

It will never be possible to confirm that these early photographs show the Benzaiten Hall as it looked immediately after it was created in the seventeenth century by combining the moya with the hisashi, though in a later chapter I give reasons to suspect that they do.

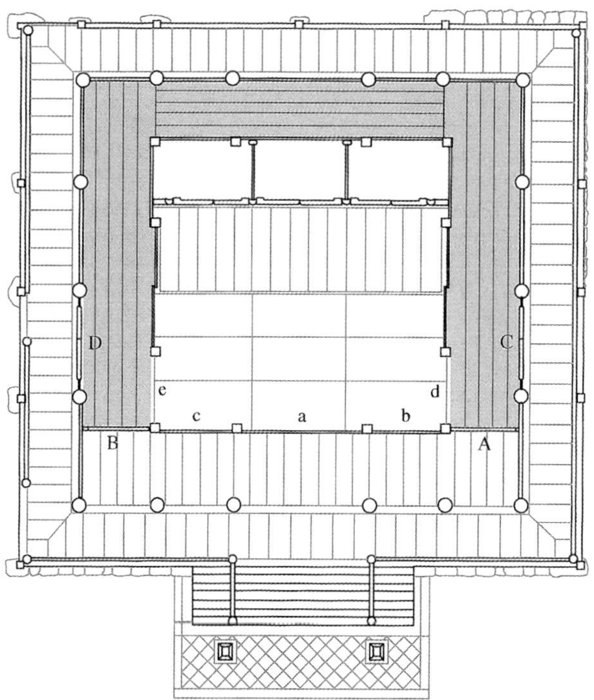

FIG. 52 Tsukubusuma Main Hall before 1936–1937 repairs. Plan. Prepared with the aid of Dax Kajiwara, adapted from *KTJHSKH*, pl. 48.

It is certain, however, that the changes the conservators made in their "repairs" reveal perplexity over how to understand a building that has had more than one "original" history. In their report, the series of changes they made to create the present arrangement is characterized as a "restoration," and they present evidence to support each change. The changes they made can be still seen in today's Main Hall and in the post-restoration photographs *(Figs. 2, 3, 8, 10)*, as diagrammed in Figures 53–55; Figure 56 is a plan of the post-restoration building keyed to these diagrams.

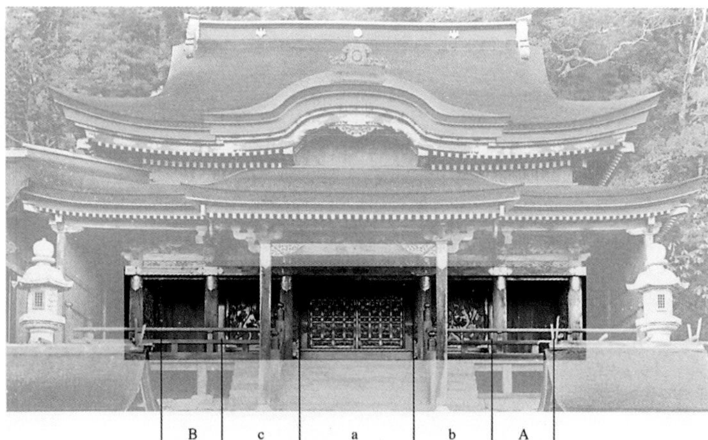

FIG. 53 Diagram of Tsukubusuma Main Hall after 1936–1937 repairs. Exterior, south side (front). Prepared with the aid of Dax Kajiwara, based on Fig. 2.

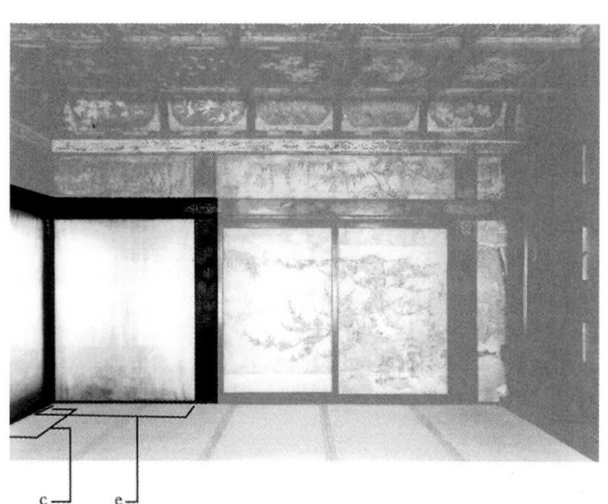

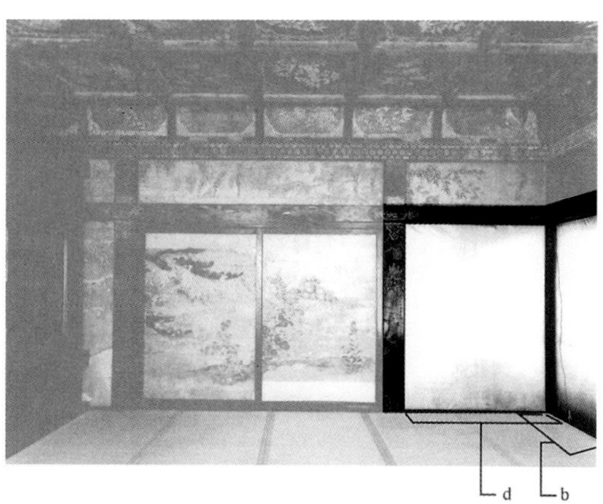

FIG. 54 (right) Diagram of Tsukubusuma Main Hall after 1936–1937 repairs. Moya interior, east side. Prepared with the aid of Dax Kajiwara, based on Fig. 8.

FIG. 55 (left) Diagram of Tsukubusuma Main Hall after 1936–1937 repairs. Moya interior, west side. Prepared with the aid of Dax Kajiwara, based on Fig. 10.

At the central bay of the front of the moya, for example—where the restorers found flap-down shutters—holes on the underside of the lintel-beam and the presence of door-jambs suggested that this bay at one time held swinging doors. It was no coincidence, they reasoned, that the two pairs of swinging doors covered with relief chrysanthemum carvings, awkwardly inserted into the east and west walls of the hisashi, had shafts that precisely fit the holes.[2] It was clear, moreover, that the doors had been trimmed width-wise to make them fit into the hisashi bay; when returned to their full proportions, one pair of these doors perfectly fit the moya's front central bay.[3] Accordingly, one pair was installed in this position (*Fig. 53*, bay a), and the other in the corresponding bay at the back of the moya, which presented a similar configuration (*Fig.6* and *Fig. 56*, bay h).

The two other moya bays that held flap-down shutters, on either side of the front central bay, also showed evidence of change: traces of wood-carving frames and grooves. These traces, considered in light of the aforementioned panels of fuyō and chrysanthemum carvings on the walls connecting the front of the moya with the hisashi—which match carvings in the bays of the moya hidden within the U-shaped corridor—suggested to the restorers that the carvings on the two connecting walls had originally belonged to walls in the two flanking bays of the front of the moya; therefore, walls were installed and the carvings were accordingly moved (*Fig. 53*, bays b, c). (The two connecting walls that had held these carvings, bays A and B, were then filled with plain plank walls.)

The interior faces of these two newly installed walls they covered with gilt paper, in the evident belief (though this is not stated in the report) that the original walls had held paintings, like the interior faces of the extant walls of the other outermost bays (*Fig. 54*, bay b, and *Fig. 55*, bay c; see also *Fig. 14*).

Similarly, they closed off the open southernmost bays of the east and west sides in the moya with walls covered on their interior faces with gilt paper (*Fig. 54*, bay d, and *Fig. 55*, bay e).

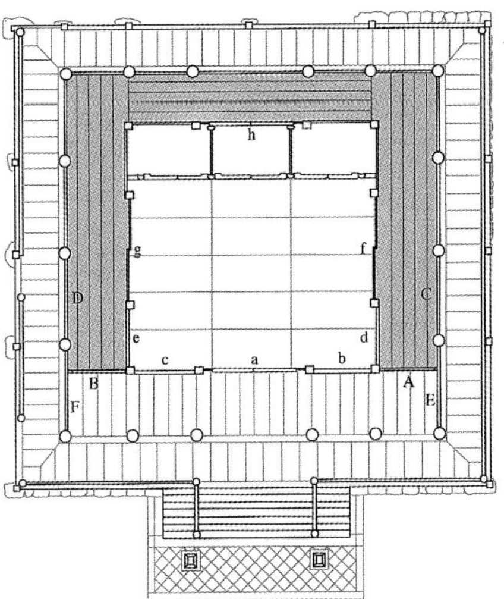

FIG. 56 Tsukubusuma Main Hall after 1936 1937 repairs. Plan. Prepared with the aid of Dax Kajiwara, adapted from *KTJHSKH*, pl. 37.

> These original walls presumably had carvings on their exterior (like the other exterior moya walls), but in the absence of spare carvings, the conservators left them blank (the blank wall on the west side is visible at the far right of *Fig.7*).

And so the present configuration of the building was created.

What the conservators apparently did not fully consider, reflected in the report's silence on the matter, is what exactly they thought they had restored. In a building composed of disparate parts, each with an earlier history, physical evidence of change will necessarily abound. What that evidence reveals, however, is often unclear. In the case of the Tsukubusuma Main Hall, all of the "restorations" described above most likely reinstated aspects of the moya as it stood in Kyoto as an independent building: the moya afforded physical evidence of having once contained components that in 1936–1937 were found elsewhere on the Main Hall but were clearly aberrant in their positions. The possible shortcomings of the conservators' choice to make these "restorations" is another matter, one to which we will return later. For now, we must acknowledge the conservators for uncovering valuable evidence of the original state of these aspects of the moya.[4]

One additional major change to the Kyoto building occurred at the time of the 1602 move, although it was not addressed in the 1936–1937 project: in the central bays of what are now the east and west walls of the moya, pairs of solid heavy wood *mairado* sliding doors replaced much thinner and fragile sliding closures, perhaps *fusuma* (sliding

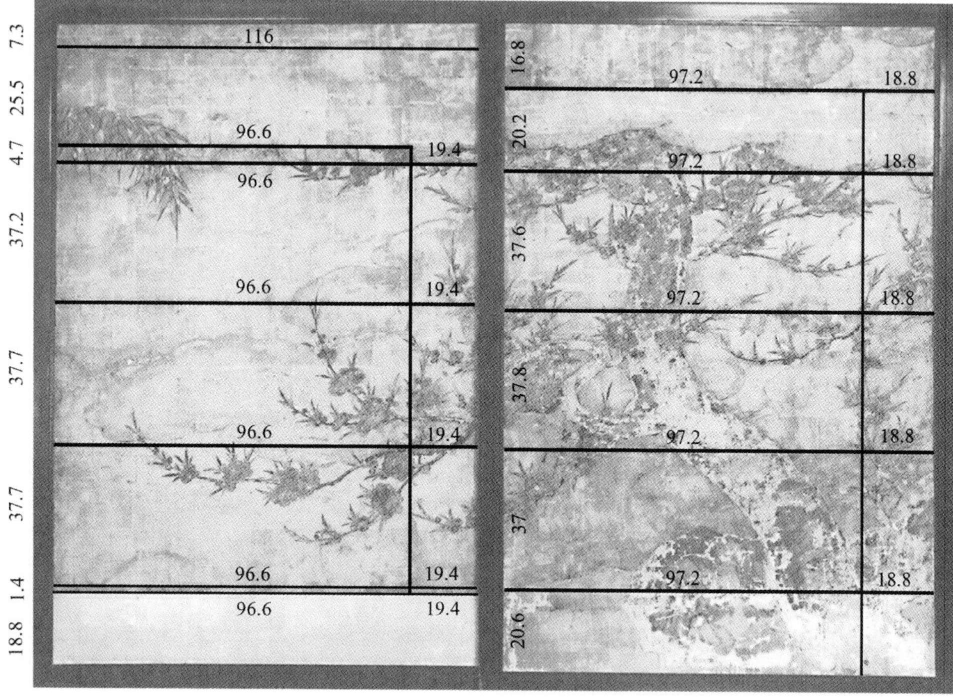

FIG. 57 Tsukubusuma Main Hall. Diagram of mairado paintings, west side. Prepared with the aid of John Boorsch and Dax Kajiwara, based on Fig. 11.

screens) *(Fig. 8–11)*.[5] Affixed to the mairado were the polychrome paintings they still hold, which were—from the clear evidence of anomalous sections at the sides, top, and bottom of each panel—cropped from a larger original state *(Figs. 57–58)*.[6] Their stylistic similarity to, as well as motival unity with, the other paintings in the moya argue that all of them originated in the same project. I surmise that the paintings now on the mairado were located originally on the interiors of the moya walls that were removed in 1602 at the time of the refabrication of the Benzaiten Hall, to allow passage between the moya and the corridors (on the east and west sides) or to be replaced by the flanking flap-down shutters (at the front). To preserve portions of them in the new building, they were attached to stable mairado, which then replaced the flimsier original sliding doors. These changes were part of the process of assembling the new building, of making a new whole from previously inviolate parts.

With this basic understanding of the moya's appearance as it once stood in Kyoto, it is possible to begin a consideration of the moya's conspicuously abundant ornament and its meanings. One caveat is in order. Until a more precise identification is reached below, I shall refer to the structure that is the focus of this discussion as the moya. It is important to keep in mind, however, that in its original context in Kyoto it was not a moya at all—that is, the *core* of a building—but rather an independent building. What, then, can we learn about the moya when it was an independent building in Kyoto?

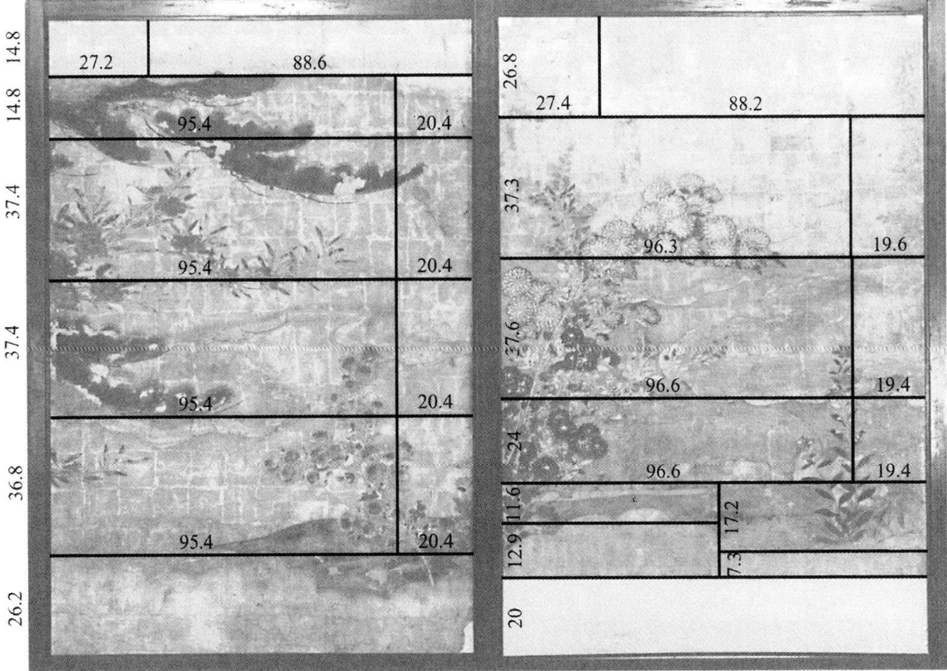

FIG. 58 Tsukubusuma Main Hall. Diagram of mairado paintings, east side. Prepared with the aid of John Boorsch and Dax Kajiwara, based on Fig. 9.

NUMINOUS MEANING IN MUNDANE MOTIFS

Even cursory examination reveals the moya to be worthy of close scrutiny. It is wholly covered with decoration in several mediums *(Figs. 3–17)*. Inside, polychrome paintings cover the ceiling and the gold-leafed walls (and, of course, the mairado, though those paintings too once graced the walls). The exterior faces of the moya walls hold large panels of high-relief wood carvings. Both inside and out, black and gold makie lacquer sheathes the pillars and lintel-beams. Finely embossed gilt metalwork marks the places where the pillars and lintel-beams meet *(Fig. 59, 60)*. Now-faded colors tint the wood carvings, and intricate multicolored geometric patterns envelop all other wood surfaces not coated with lacquer. The subject matter is manifestly unified and therefore easily discerned and engaging: with few exceptions, it is entirely floral—plants and trees—and the exceptions (such as *shishi* [lion-dogs] in the metalwork) only accentuate the characteristic oneness of the program. In short, no surface above the floor and below the roof remains unadorned: this structure demands notice.

And yet the effect is one not of excess but of restraint. The gold leaf of the interior walls does not glitter: in the dim light allowed in by the doorways, it gently glows. Makie lacquer is a reflective material but not radiant: its black ground absorbs light and reflects it back with soft luminosity. Though high-relief and massive, the large panels of wood carvings are subdued: they depict their subjects—either fuyō or chrysanthemum plants—as delicate, attenuated forms that comfortably fill their designated space. A sense of deliberateness stems from perceptible patterns in the distribution of the floral ornament: the paintings below the lintel are dominated by large but elegantly curving trees; just above the lintel, the interior is entirely encircled with a frieze of delicate pendent branches of wisteria and cherry trees; each exterior side of the structure holds one wood-carved bay of fuyō and another of chysanthemums. This tendency toward repeated and often symmetrical patterns persists throughout the moya, and so the decoration unfolds in an altogether deliberate manner. The total effect—of both materials and subject matter—is visually disciplined, unified, and complete. Intuitively, the viewer perceives the moya to be a carefully programmed ensemble of decoration.

Although this resplendent structure is the most fully realized monumental ensemble surviving from the Momoyama period, no comprehensive attempt has ever been made to retrieve precise information about its pre-Chikubushima history. It would seem a task unlikely to yield substantial results. The building that is now the moya has been removed from its original context. No known document records its original site or function or patron. Its past is further clouded by layers of persistently repeated traditional history, none supported by concrete evidence.[7] And what of its copious ornament? Was its purpose only aesthetic diversion, or are there deeper meanings to be found in the flowers and trees that dominate the decoration? The floral decoration contains no narrative element and little that immediately reveals itself as specifically meaningful. These are common flora, and long custom had made each of them into a rebus of auspicious meanings for the Japanese. No deeper significances

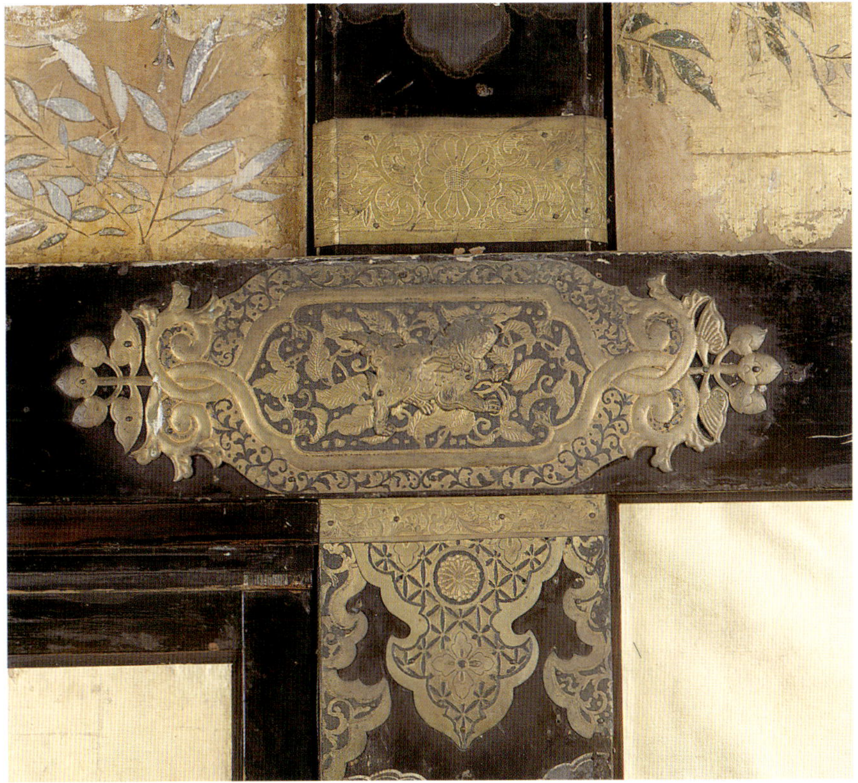

FIG. 59 Tsukubusuma Main Hall. Metalwork panel of shishi (lion-dog). Moya interior. Chikubushima, Shiga Prefecture.

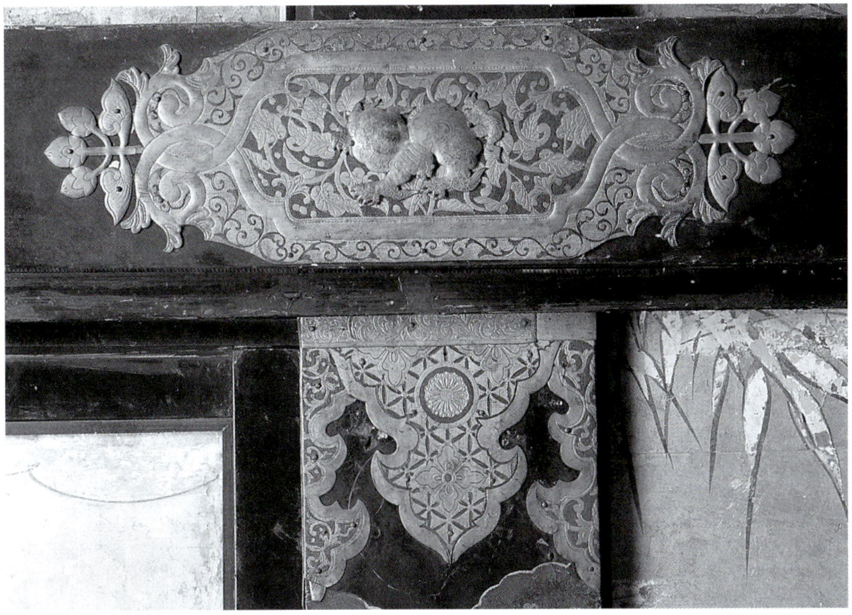

FIG. 60 Tsukubusuma Main Hall. Metalwork panel of shishi (lion-dog). Moya interior. Chikubushima, Shiga Prefecture.

are immediately apparent to the modern eye, nor have any efforts been made to discover if they might exist.

And yet, as we have seen in the case of *Maple Viewing at Mount Takao (Fig. 30)*, art historians recently have sought and found more complex meanings in art once viewed as only secular. Pivotal to this new approach is the awareness that the secular and sacred were intertwined inextricably in the Momoyama period, and that separating the two will diminish our understanding; for the Momoyama monuments were often the product of dual sacral-secular motivations. Not all of them, of course, possess this dual character, but to discover those that do, we must give sensitive attention to a wide range of possibly revelatory aspects, including multiple meanings of the depicted motifs and contextual evidence such as the location of a monument, its function, and its patron. When a work is examined in this manner, the capacity to read its significance—or to understand the limits of its significance—is greatly increased. And so it is with the moya ensemble. Indeed, it is only through such research that its floral subjects may be understood to be imbued with additional levels of supramundane, even soterial, significance. As we shall see, many of the floral motifs in the moya served—when this structure stood in Kyoto—as numinous references to the Buddhist realm of the Pure Land, while others referred to a deceased individual translated (it was hoped) to that realm.

PURE LAND REPRESENTED: THE DECORATIVE PROGRAM OF THE INTERIOR

The very lavishness of the moya decoration is informative. Only the powerful few commanded the resources to build a monument with such abundant and exquisitely crafted decoration.[8] The decoration tells us, at the very least, that the structure was important and that its sponsor was a person of great consequence.[9] Did this floral decoration, however, convey more specific meaning to its original audience and, if so, to what degree can this meaning now be recovered? Motifs had symbolic associations in the Momoyama period that are no longer current today. Typically, several symbolic associations coexisted in a single motif. Moreover, meaning often was keyed to the original location and function of a monument, and so the meaning of the decoration of the moya is unusually difficult to recover.

Among the decorative components, the most easily interpreted are the numerous paired chrysanthemum and paulownia crests. They are widely distributed throughout the structure, both inside and out, in lacquer, metalwork, and in the gold-leafed paper frames that surround the ceiling paintings *(Fig. 61)*. This pairing of crests had unmistakable significance and was strictly controlled during the period when the moya was originally built and decorated.[10] Awarded by the Imperial Court to the temporal ruler of the country, Toyotomi Hideyoshi, the paired crests became symbols of the Toyotomi regime and were often incorporated into the decoration of Toyotomi belongings. The Toyotomi closely guarded the use of the two crests, issuing prohibitive regulations that

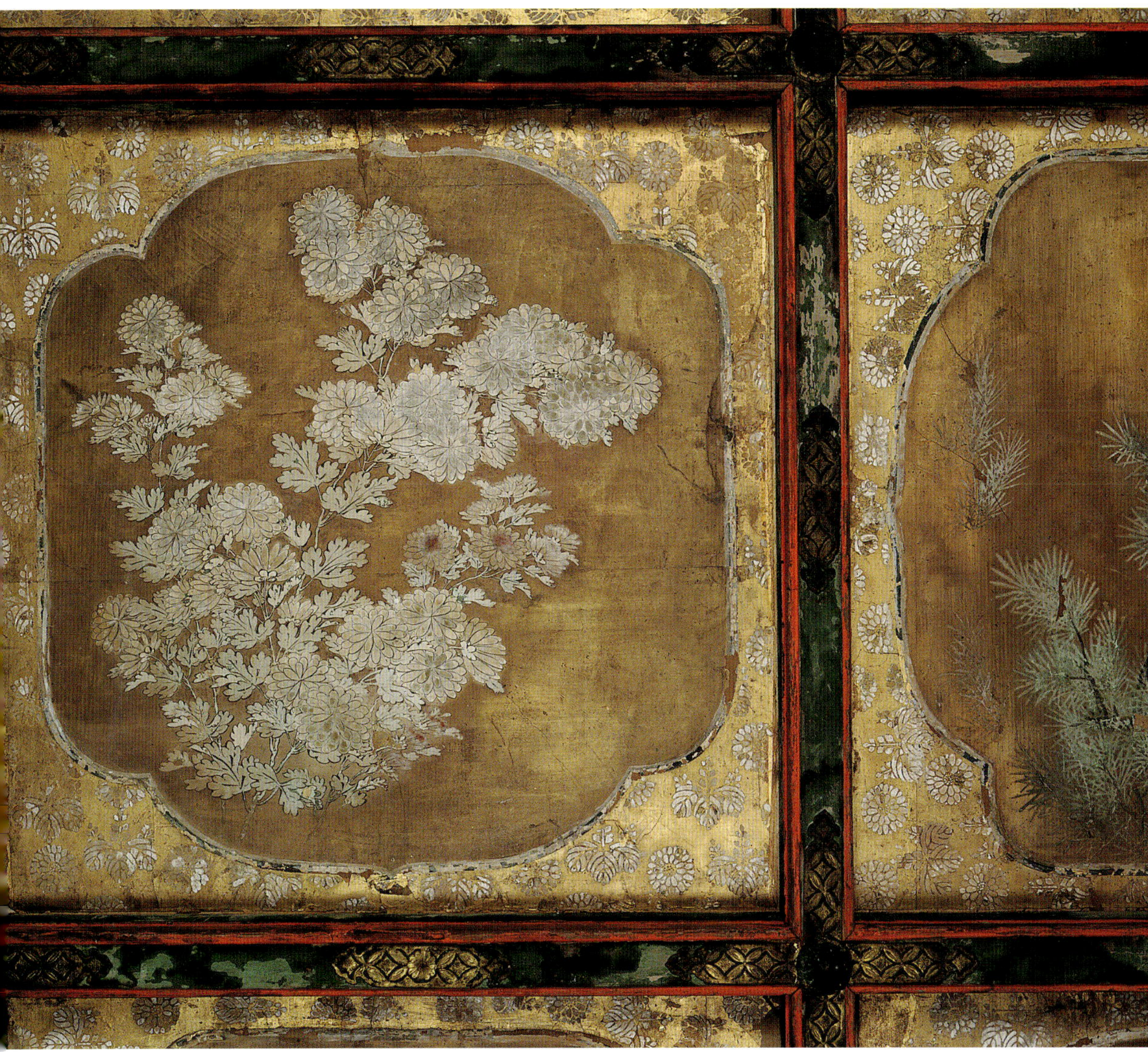

FIG. 61 Tsukubusuma Main Hall. Ceiling painting of chrysanthemums. Moya interior. Chikubushima, Shiga Prefecture.

were repeated in local law codes. The chrysanthemum and paulownia crests, clearly visible from virtually any viewing perspective, graphically state that the patron of the moya was the ruling Toyotomi clan.

The subject matter and mediums of the decorative program suggest the general function of the moya before its move. Abundant decoration of primarily floral subjects on both the interior and exterior of a building, as seen here, is a feature shared by many extant late sixteenth- and early seventeenth-century structures that were built to commemorate the deceased. The lavish use of gold, especially in the interior of the moya, is also characteristic of many death-memorial buildings. Hideyoshi, for example, was commemorated in death at Kōdaiji, where memorial rituals were conducted at a small

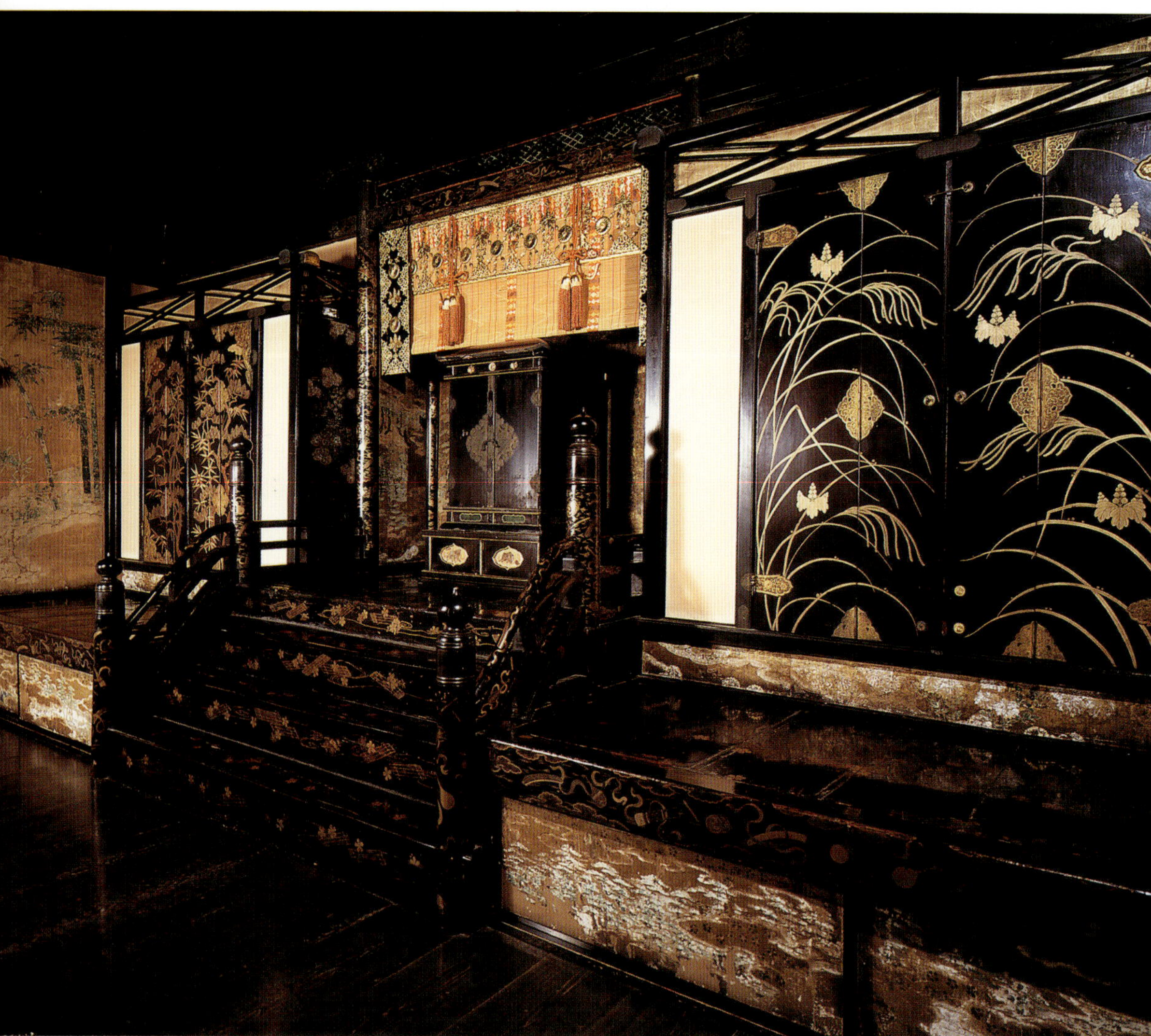

FIG. 62 Tamaya of Toyotomi Hideyoshi and Kita no Mandokoro, interior. Early seventeenth century. Kōdaiji, Kyoto. Photograph by Kyoto National Museum.

mortuary building, a *tamaya*.[11] The interior of the Kōdaiji tamaya is richly decorated with floral motifs in paintings on gold-leafed grounds, with gold makie lacquer, and with gilt metalwork *(Fig. 62)*. The exterior of the building was covered with black lacquer and architectural coloring.

The heavily decorated Momoyama memorial building was an important model for subsequent seventeenth-century structures of this type, especially those built for powerful military-class patrons.[12] The tamaya built for Nanbu Toshiyasu (d. 1631) of Mutsu (present-day Aomori Prefecture) is sheathed inside and out with gold, and its wood structural members are covered with black lacquer *(Figs. 63, 64)*. Its interior walls and ceiling are dominated by a program of Four Seasons floral paintings, including pine trees, chrysanthemums, peonies, and lotus plants, and a limited number of wood carvings adorn

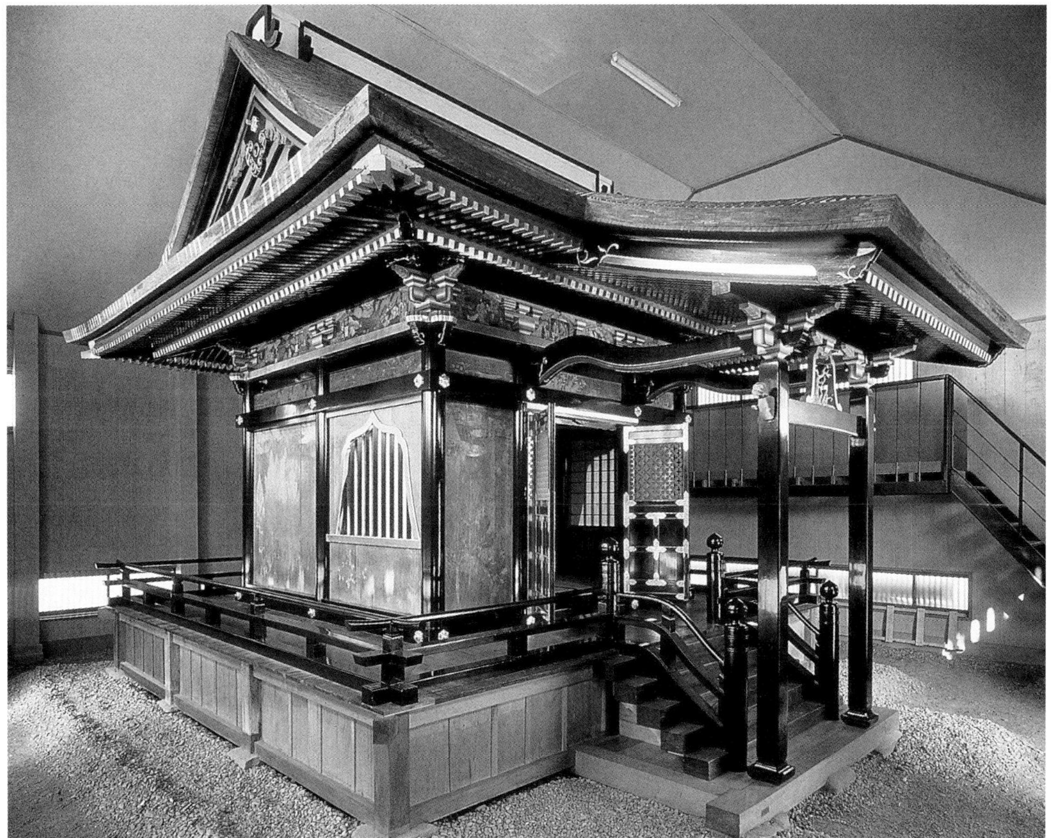

FIG. 63 Tamaya of Nanbu Toshiyasu, exterior. Mid-seventeenth century. Sankōji, Aomori Prefecture. Photograph by Shibundō.

the exterior. Also of relevance to our study of the moya is the tamaya built in memory of Sanada Nobuyuki (1566–1658), first daimyo of the Matsudaira domain in present-day Nagano Prefecture *(Figs. 65, 66)*.[13] The interior of this mortuary building is fully covered with decoration, including paintings of floral subjects, such as pine, peonies, and lotuses, against a gold-leafed background. Floral wood carvings and architectural coloring decorate the exterior. These examples indicate that copious floral and gold decoration was considered desirable for buildings constructed in memory of elite warriors, and support the possibility that the moya was once such a structure.[14]

Floral imagery so often predominates in the decoration of these mortuary buildings that we must consider its possible allusory significance. A crucial beginning was made by Bettina Klein in her discussion of a pair of fifteenth-century gold-leafed folding screens *(kinbyōbu)*, now owned by the Agency for Cultural Affairs in Tokyo, depicting Flowers, Birds, and Insects of the Four Seasons.[15] Klein reviews the evidence

FIG. 64 (overleaf) Tamaya of Nanbu Toshiyasu, interior. Mid-seventeenth century. Sankōji, Aomori Prefecture. Photograph by Shibundō.

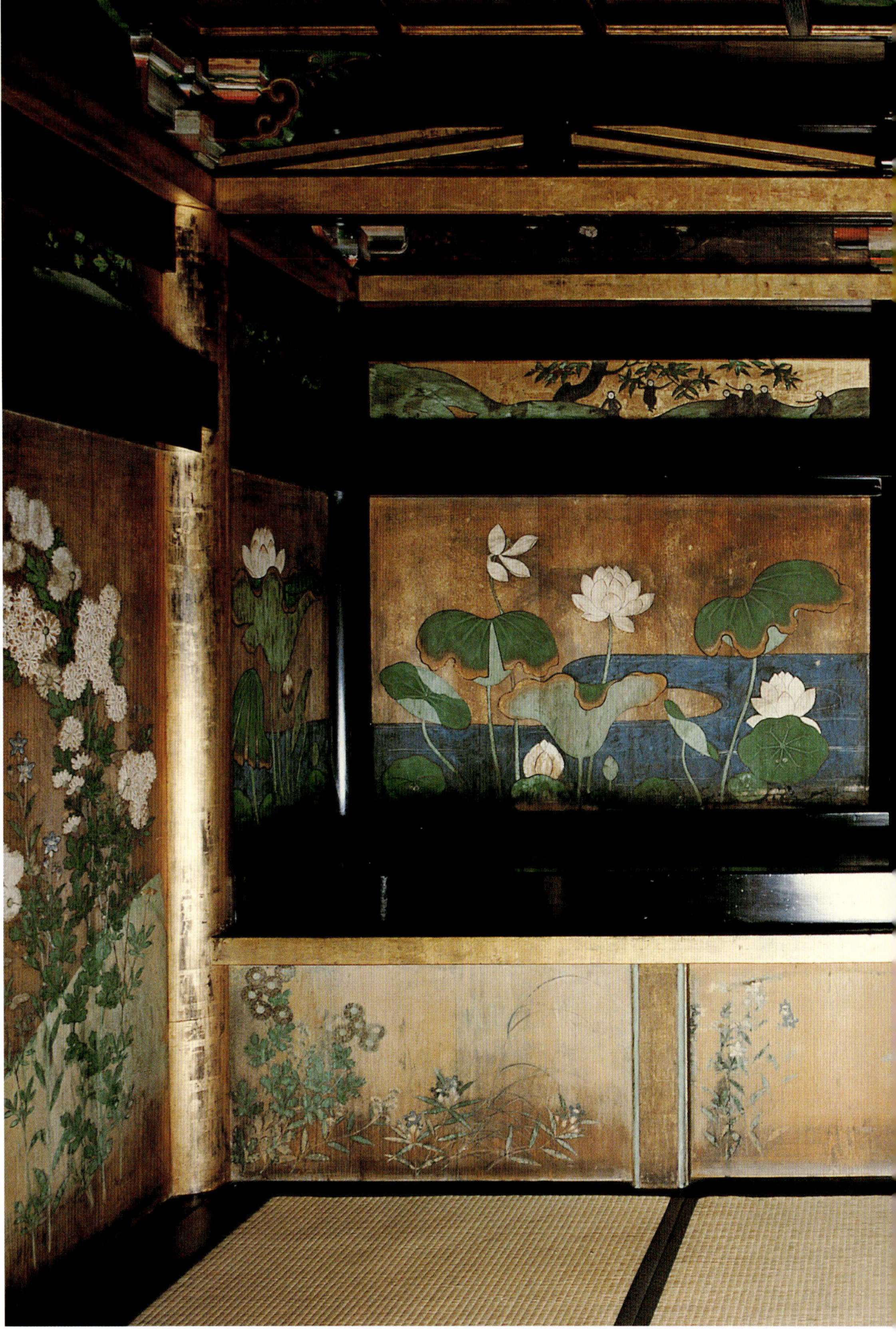

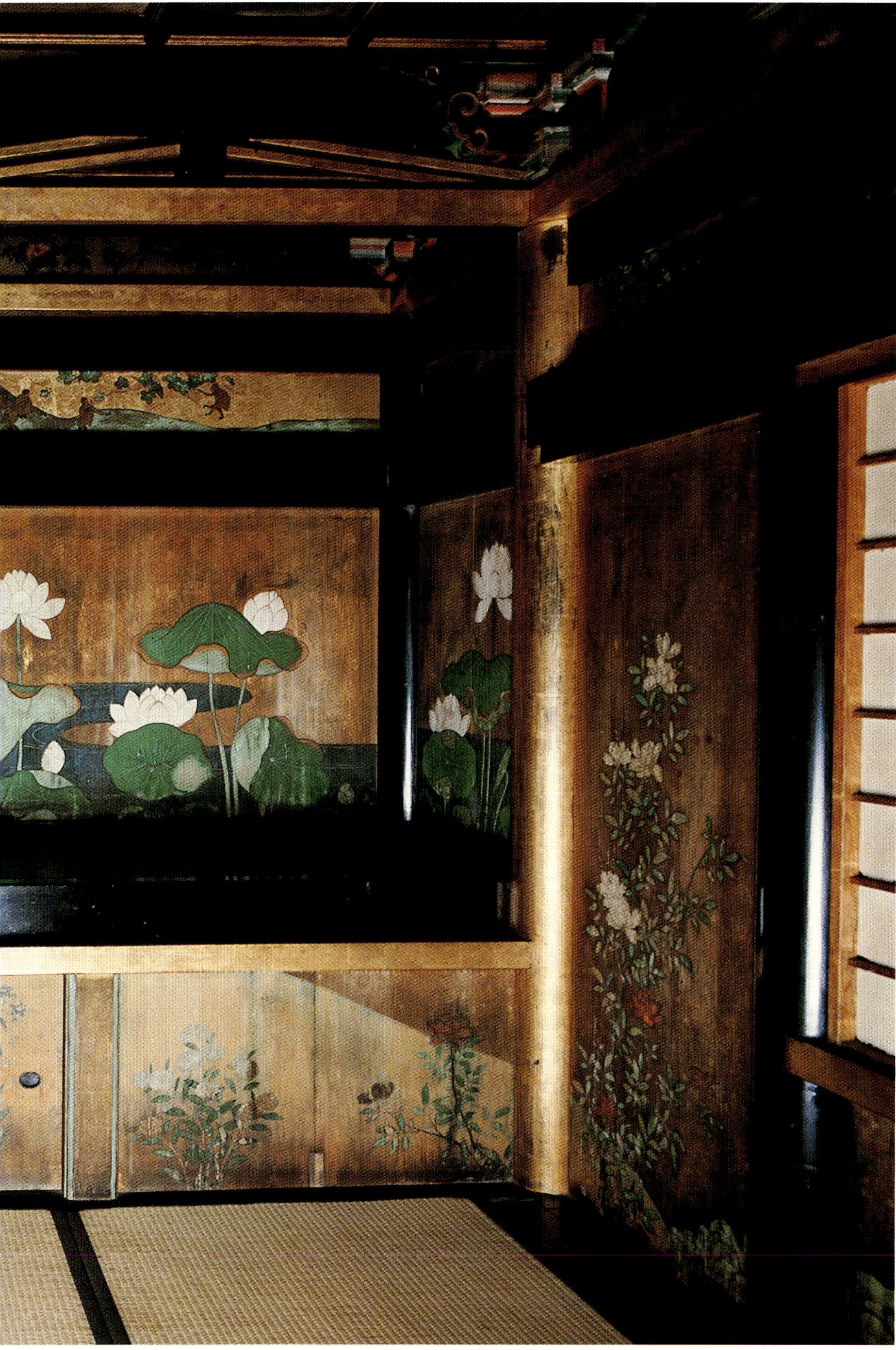

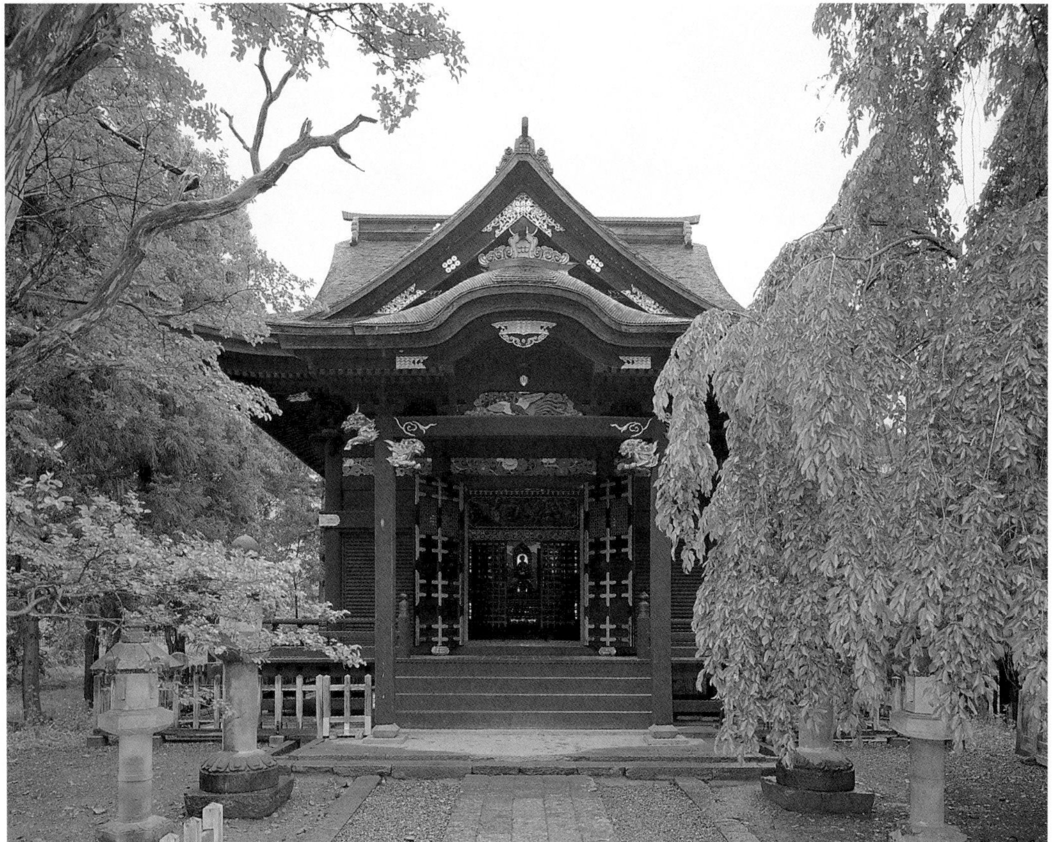

FIG. 65 Tamaya of Sanada Nobuyuki, exterior. Seventeenth century. Chōkokuji, Nagano Prefecture. Photograph by Shibundō.

that late fifteenth-century gold-leafed folding screens with floral subjects functioned in large part as funerary decoration. Citing descriptions of Amida's Western Pure Land in Jōdo-school texts, she argues that such screens were modelled on gardens created by Jōdo devotees to resemble that imagined Jōdo Pure Land. Klein concludes that the Agency for Cultural Affairs screens were likely used in Jōdo funerary rituals and that the theme of Flowers, Birds, and Insects of the Four Seasons was meant to evoke the Pure Land of the West. Sometimes, however, the gold-leafed folding screens used in funerals depicted only floral themes, suggesting that birds and insects were incidental: gold and flowers were the key emblems.[16]

Klein's general thesis is convincing: in certain contexts, representations of floral subjects combined with gold were used to evoke associations with the Western Pure Land. I submit that their use was not restricted to Jōdo adherents, for the Pure Land of the West was a destination that had wide appeal in Japan. Is it not possible, even likely, that this is the association evoked in the Kōdaiji, Nanbu, and Sanada tamaya, all located in Zen complexes? All three monuments share several significant characteristics: their decoration is primarily floral in theme and liberal in the use of gold, and they are all mortuary in func-

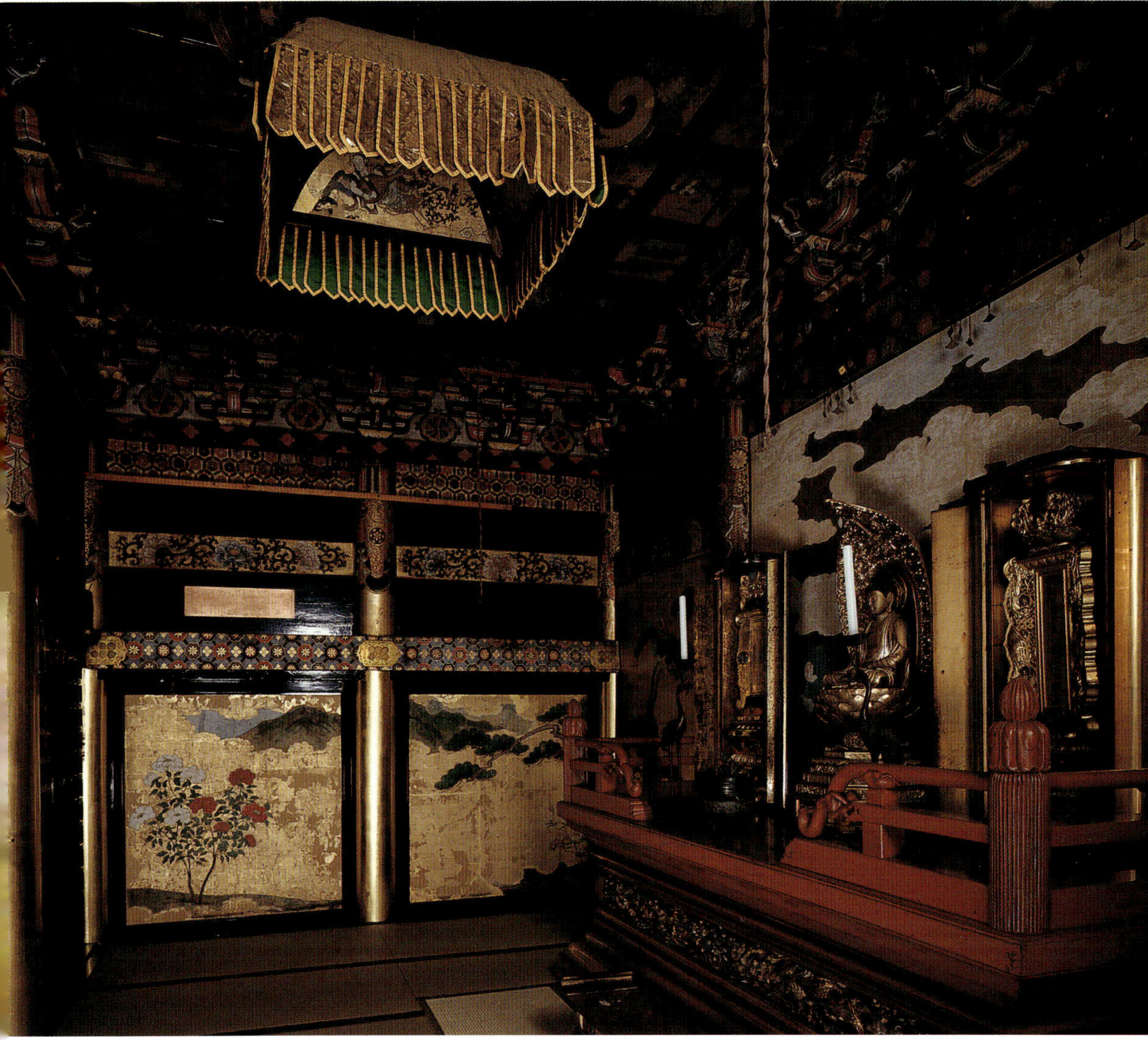

FIG. 66 Tamaya of Sanada Nobuyuki, interior. Seventeenth century. Chōkokuji, Nagano Prefecture. Photograph by Shibundō.

tion. That context suggests that their floral decoration held paradisal associations.[17]

Let us now turn back to the gold and floral decoration on the moya interior. The decorative program of the interior delineates the Four Seasons on a gold-leaf ground. The paintings on the mairado of the east side include flowers associated with autumn: chrysanthemums, bush clover, and oleander *(Figs. 8, 9)*. The paintings on the west-wall mairado depict a peach tree in full bloom, evoking spring *(Figs. 10, 11)*. Other wall paintings show the winter subject of snow-covered bamboo *(Fig. 67)*. Several sections of the wail paintings are now lost, but considering the content of the extant large-scale paintings, they may well have represented summer flora. Above the lintel-beams on all four walls, moreover, are paintings of blossoming cherry trees and wisteria *(Figs. 8, 10, 14, 68,*

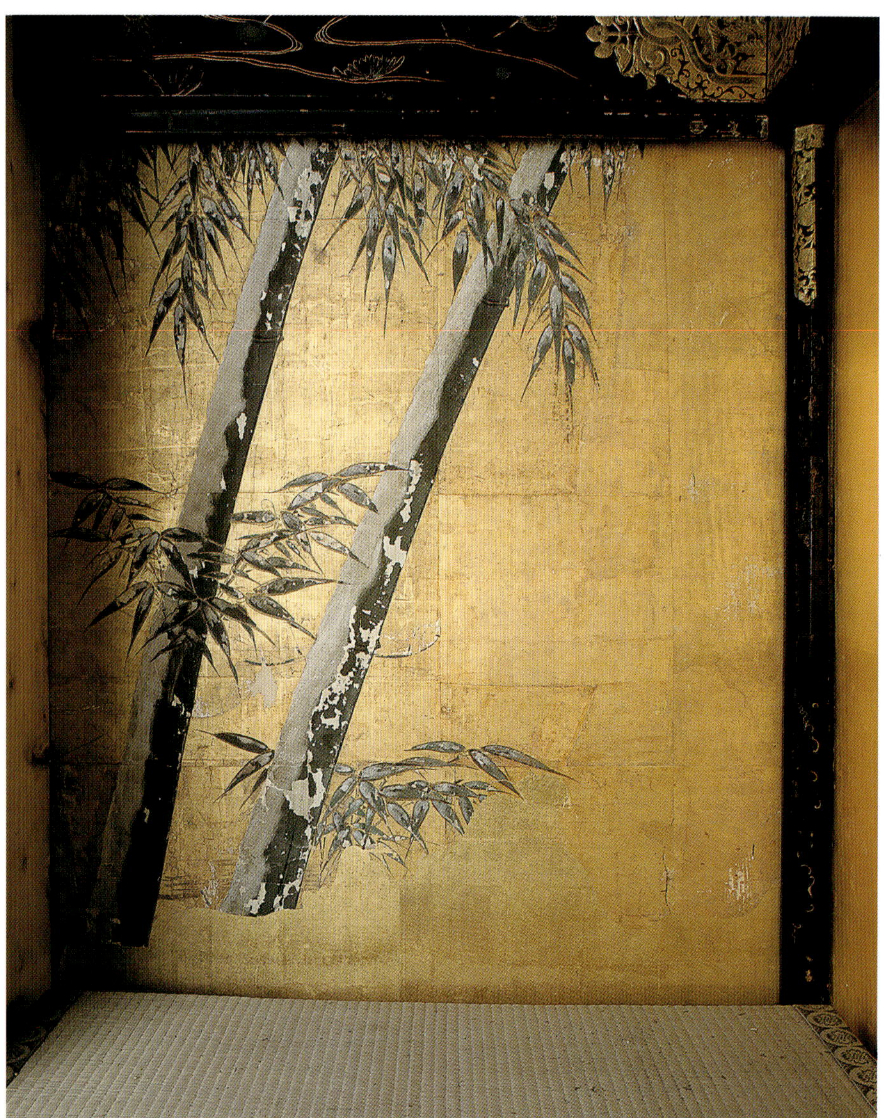

FIG. 67 Tsukubusuma Main Hall. Wall painting within zushi. Moya interior, west side. Chikubushima, Shiga Prefecture.

FIG. 68 (top) Tsukubusuma Main Hall. Painting above lintel-beam of blossoming cherry tree. Moya interior, south side. Chikubushima, Shiga Prefecture.

FIG. 69 (bottom) Tsukubusuma Main Hall. Painting above lintel-beam of wisteria. Moya interior, west side. Chikubushima, Shiga Prefecture.

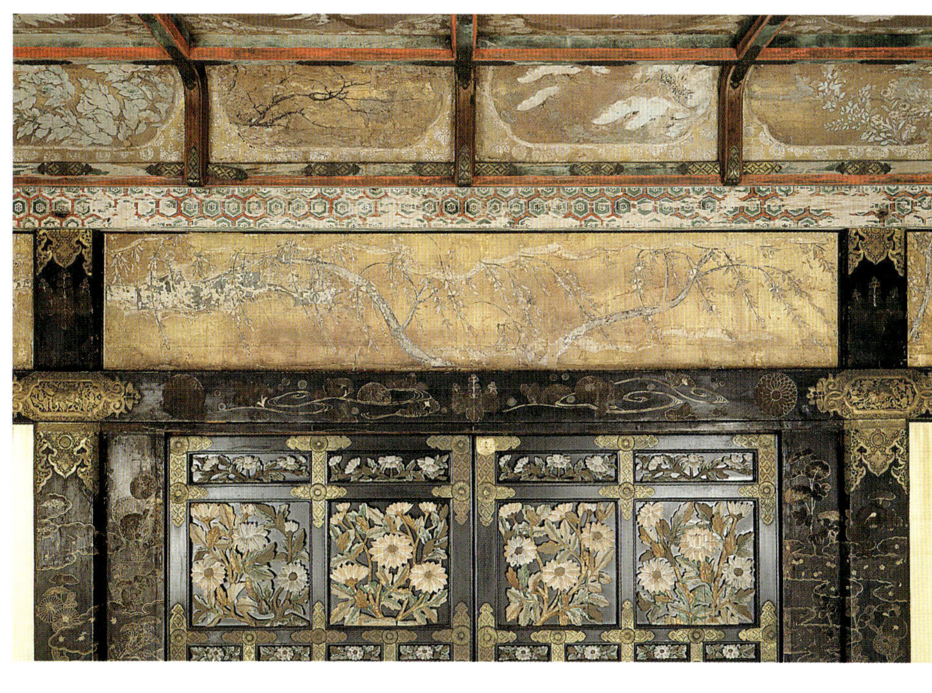

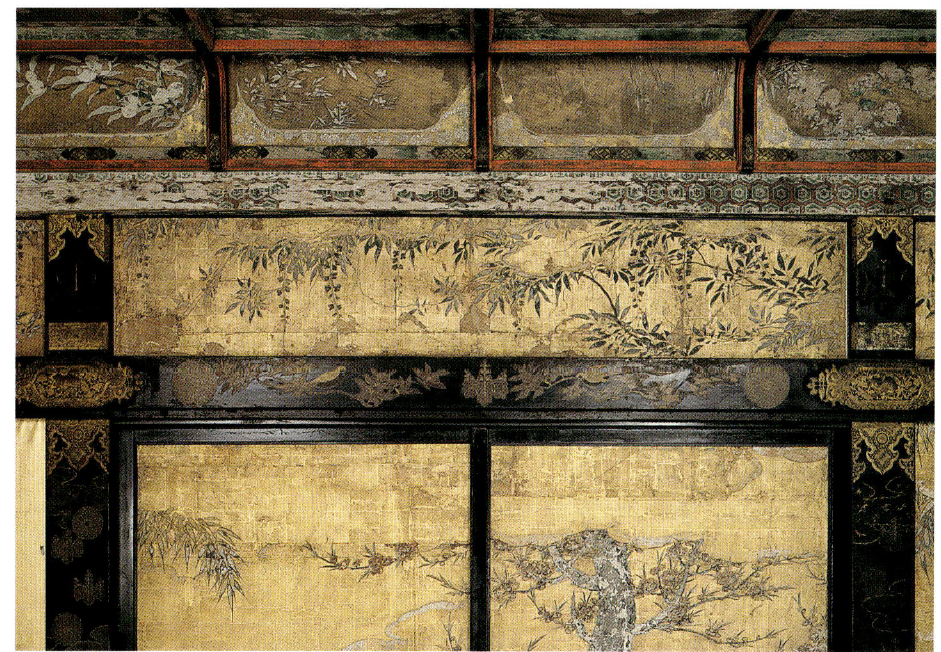

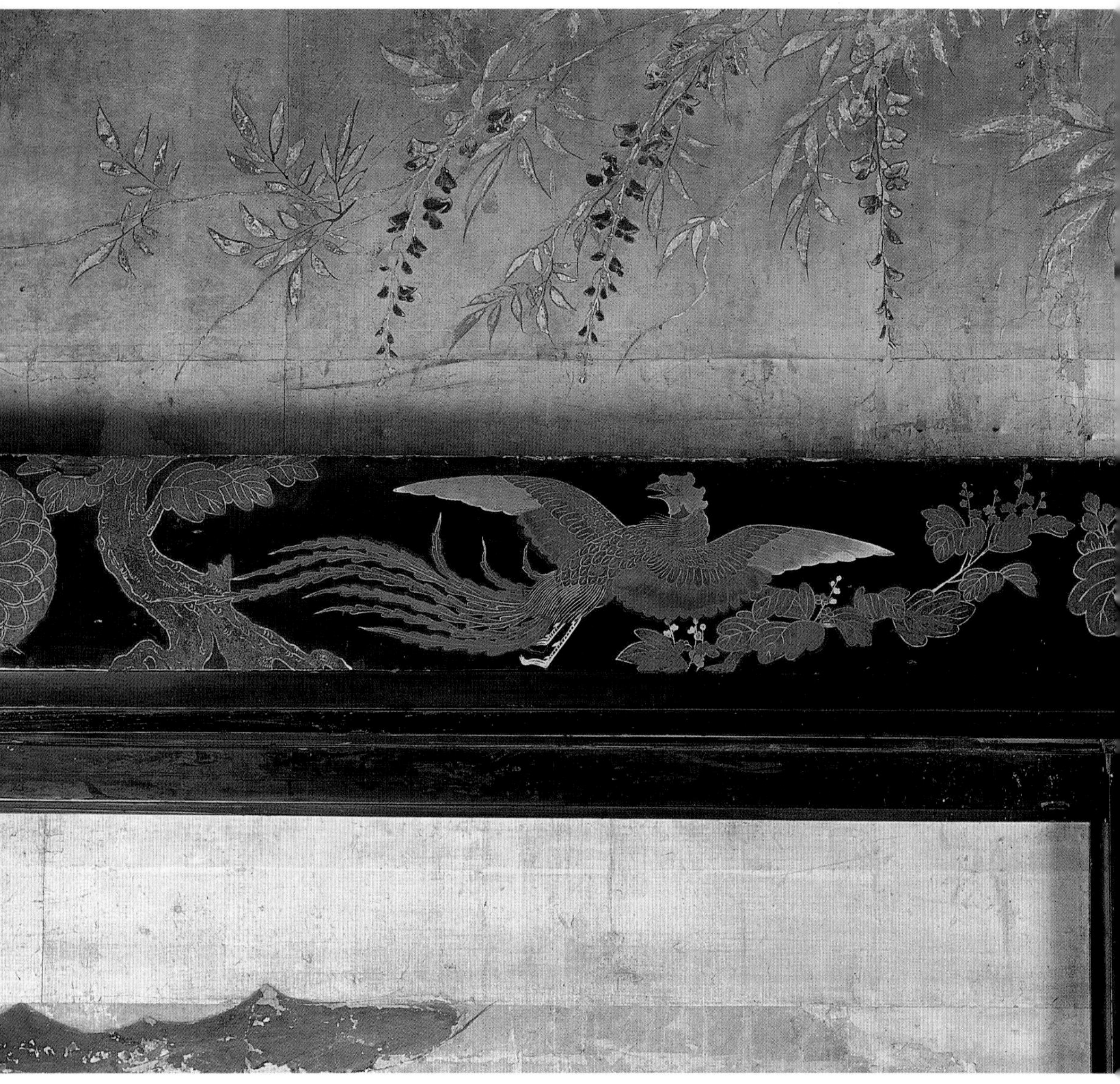

FIG. 70 Tsukubusuma Main Hall. Phoenix and paulownia. Makie lacquer. Moya interior, east side, lintel-beam of central bay. Chikubushima, Shiga Prefecture.

69). Floral subjects and clouds filled with all manner of floral detail cover the pillars and lintel-beams in makie lacquer; avian themes are introduced in makie lacquer on the east and west lintel-beams: phoenixes perched on paulownia, and long-tailed birds on camellia *(Figs. 8–12, 70).*[18]

The magnificent coffered ceiling comprises a total of sixty individual paintings of divers flowers and trees of the four seasons, amplifying this paradisal evocation *(Figs. 8, 10).* The splendor of this arching floral display recalls scriptural descriptions of the Pure Land. The *Muryōju kyō,* for example, describes the offerings made in the Pure Land to the Buddhas and to their assemblies of bodhisattvas and disciples, marvelous offerings that, when presented, "remain suspended in the sky and transform into canopies of flowers. Their radiance dazzles and their fragrance permeates everywhere. The flower [canopies] range in size from those of four hundred *ri* in circumference up to those large enough to cover the universe of three thousand million worlds."[19] I suggest that the coffered ceiling alludes to such textual descriptions of the paradisal floral canopies, thereby participating in a tradition of Pure Land allusions in such memorial buildings as the tamaya for Sanada Nobuyuki *(Fig. 66)*.[20] In toto, then, the interior decoration of the moya significantly resembles that of the three tamaya, suggesting that it too was originally a mortuary structure. And if it was, its gold and floral decoration was likely intended as an allusion to the Pure Land.

THE GRAPEVINE

That reading of the interior decoration is supported by the subject matter on the underside of the lintels over three of the four entrances: grapevine, executed in makie lacquer *(Fig. 71)*.[21] Grapes occur only once more in the decoration, in the floral canopy painted on the ceiling *(Fig. 72)*. The entrances, however, offer an especially prominent location, and there grapevines are the dominating motif. By the Momoyama period the grape had—in certain contexts—acquired sacred meaning, specifically an association with the Pure Land of the West, and this meaning may well have guided the decision to place the motif in such conspicuous locations.[22] The sacred association appears to have occurred even though the grape is not mentioned by name in the chief sutras that describe the Pure Land. Not all sacred meaning necessarily derives from direct sutra references; such meaning can also be created through a sacralization process that develops less explicit textual information. The mention of "purple-gold fruits" in the *Muryōju kyō*'s Pure Land, for example, may refer to the grape or may have been so interpreted later.[23] It is clear, in either case, that a well-developed association between the grape and the Pure Land of the West was reinforced and disseminated through the visual arts; paintings by the thirteenth-century Chinese monk-painter Riguan (d. 1295), admired in Japan from an early period and inspiration for Japanese painters such as Gukei Yūe (act. 1361–1375), are especially helpful in exploring this range of meanings.[24]

Native neither to Japan nor China, the grape entered East Asia from lands farther west.[25] In art it became a symbol of those lands, and inscriptions on grape paintings often allude to its geographic origins. A self-inscribed grape painting by Riguan added a spiritual dimension to an association with the West:

> The bow is relaxed and hung on the wall, the pellet has not fallen;
> the dragon rises in anger and bursts through the eye of the cloud;
> I know this species came from the western pass,
> carried on the reed twig, speaking of Zen.[26]

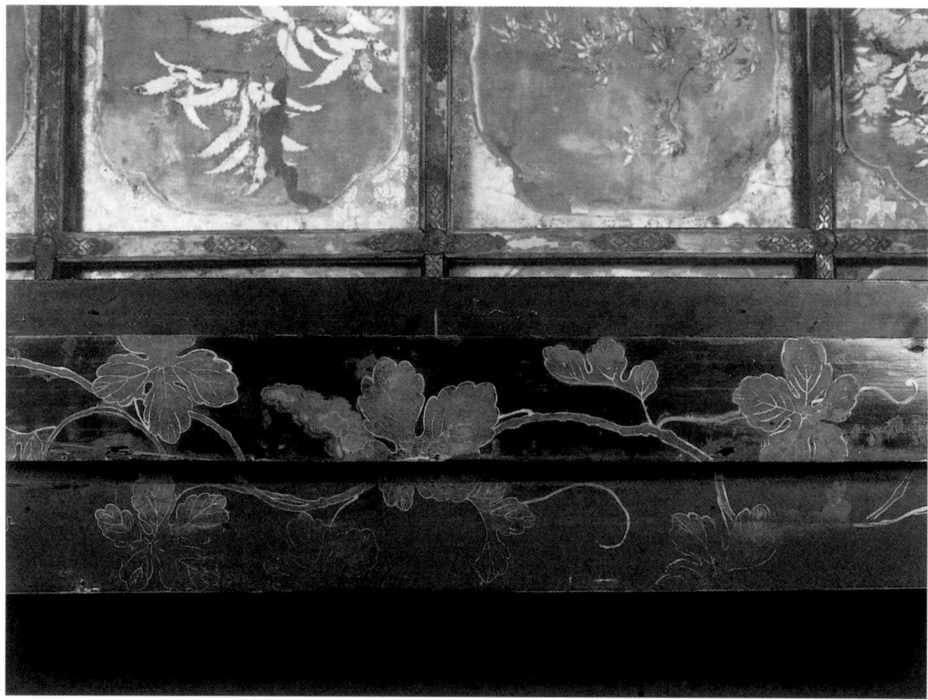

FIG. 71 Tsukubusuma Main Hall. Grapevines. Makie lacquer. Moya, underside of lintel-beam. Chikubushima, Shiga Prefecture.

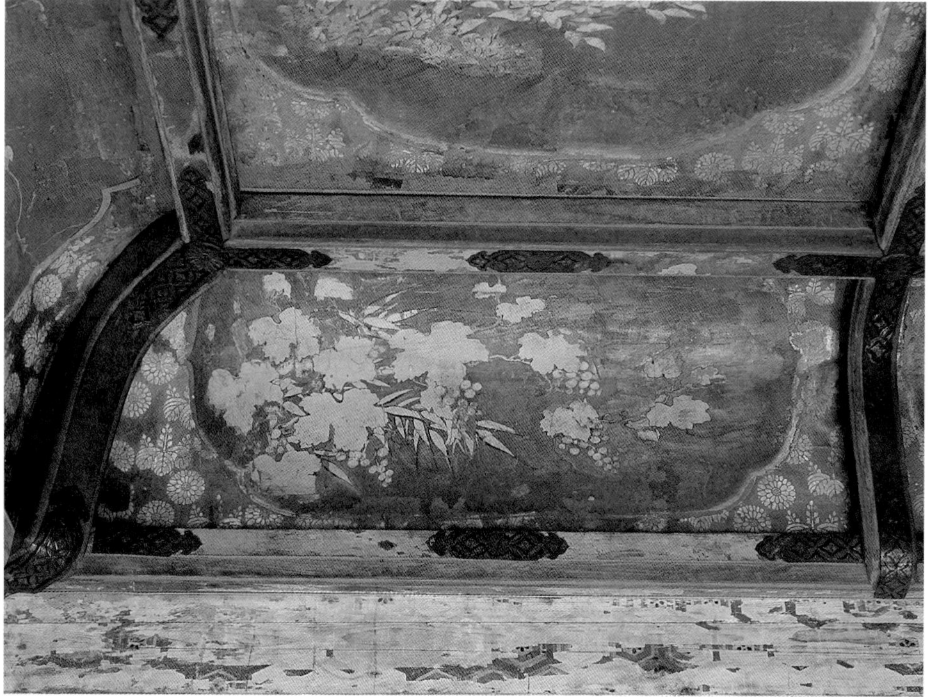

FIG. 72 Tsukubusuma Main Hall. Ceiling painting of grapevines. Moya interior. Chikubushima, Shiga Prefecture.

The poem gives the geographical source of the grape: this "species"—this fruit—was brought from the West. The grape is then concretely and compellingly linked with Zen, another "species" that came from the West. As Riguan presents it, the grape is simultaneously an exotic fruit, a symbol of western lands, and a metaphor for Zen Buddhism. This painting itself is no longer extant. It and its inscription are known today only as recorded in the *Bokuseki no utsushi,* a journal of calligraphies copied by the Zen monk and 156th Chief Abbot of Daitokuji, Kōgetsu Sōgan (1574–1643).[27] This voluminous compilation is valuable not only for its information on art now lost, but also as an inventory of the artists and themes that were highly regarded in Momoyama Japan. From it, we know that Riguan's grapevine paintings and calligraphies were then included in the canon of esteemed works, and that his connection between grapes and Zen was current at that time.[28]

Riguan invoked these links of the grape with the West and with Buddhism to amplify his paintings of grapevines with connotations of the Pure Land of the West. This association is most clearly evident in a painting *(Fig. 73),* formerly in the Inoue collection, on which his inscription reads:[29]

> Once a person skilled at chanting
> the sutra of Bianji[30]
> came to the place where I play with the brush;
> he delighted me and I created this painting
> and inscribed on it a poem that I had earlier composed;
> it is about longing for the Realm of Peace and Sustenance, my old home;
> the poem reads:
>
> The rain helps ripen the fragrant rice;
> my pious heart grows old and turns to ash;
> the sun sets and my return path nears;
> the dream of my hometown day by day lingers.

The author prefaces the poem by stating that he longs for the Realm of Peace and Sustenance *(annyō),* another name for the Pure Land of the West.[31] In the poem itself he alludes to his impending death: his path mirrors that of the sun which sets in the west, toward the Pure Land, and he regularly dreams of his home there. It is significant that Riguan inscribed this particular poem on a painting of grapevines and prefaced it with a prose explanation that reveals its paradisal significance. Here the grape is not merely an exotic fruit but, more importantly, a symbol of the Pure Land. An extant Kano copy of this painting (one of many Kano copies of grapevine paintings attributed to Riguan), attests that it was known in Japan during the Edo period (1615–1868) *(Fig. 74).*[32]

The Kano copies and Kōgetsu's *Bokuseki no utsushi* show that in Japan Riguan was a highly regarded early master of grape painting. Cultured Japanese of the Momoyama period knew that Riguan's grape paintings carried several layers of meaning, defined by

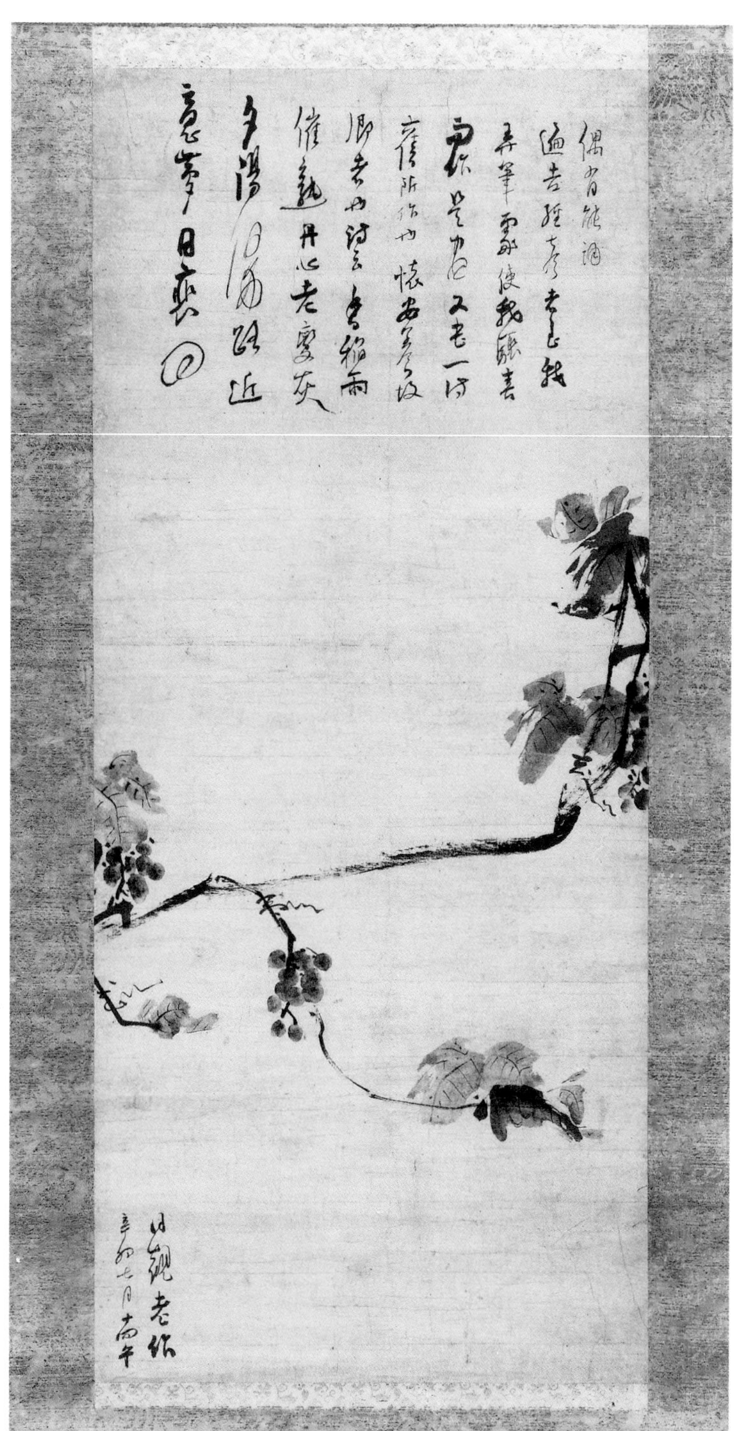

FIG. 73 (left) Riguan. *Grapevines.* Dated to 1291. Hanging scroll; ink on paper. Sunritz Hattori Museum of Arts, Nagano Prefecture.

FIG. 74 (right) Kano copy of painting by Riguan. *Grapevines.* Edo period. Ink on paper. Tokyo National Museum.

五五ノ二

the inscriptions on the paintings. The spiritual connotations of his works, best illustrated in the ex-Inoue collection scroll, are emphasized in another calligraphy copied by Kōgetsu, which states that Riguan is an artist who "uses ink play to create Buddhist things."[33] From as early as Riguan's lifetime and lasting certainly through the Momoyama period, the grape acquired and retained in the visual and literary arts the several meanings discussed above.

In the moya the placement of grapevines above each doorway—above each threshold leading from the mundane world outside to the sacred space within—suggests that the motif was intended as an allusion to the Pure Land, an allusion that would be taken up and amplified by the golden floral decoration of the interior. In this context grapevines are unlikely to have been purely decorative, or to have symbolized a direction or a season; they are very likely, in this context, to have connoted a sacred space.

ANNOUNCING SUTEMARU: THE DECORATIVE PROGRAM OF THE EXTERIOR

Above, we have seen that the moya shares significant characteristics with buildings that are known to have served as memorials. The comprehensive decoration, both interior and exterior, the seasonal groupings of plants and the use of gold in the interior paintings, and the depictions of grapes at the entrances all support the likelihood that the structure was built to commemorate a deceased individual. That hypothesis is supported by the decoration on the exterior of the moya, which is as allusive as that on the interior, though not to the Western Pure Land; rather, much of it specifically concerns the deceased.

The decoration on the exterior is very limited in subject matter. Two motifs carved in wood predominate, the chrysanthemum and the fuyō *(Figs. 3–7, 75)*. They are set in the flanking bays of each of the four walls; six sections of relief carvings from the original eight remain, four of the fuyō and two of the chrysanthemum. The very structure of the exterior concentrates our attention on these carvings: each compartment of carvings is the entire width of a bay and the carvings reach from the floor to the lintel-beam, framed by the compartment so as to emphasize the importance of the carved flower. Literary evidence from the period further suggests that both motifs were appropriate to a memorial building.

FIG. 75 Tsukubusuma Main Hall. View of moya exterior, east side, looking into moya interior, north side, through open central-bay mairado. Chikubushima, Shiga Prefecture.

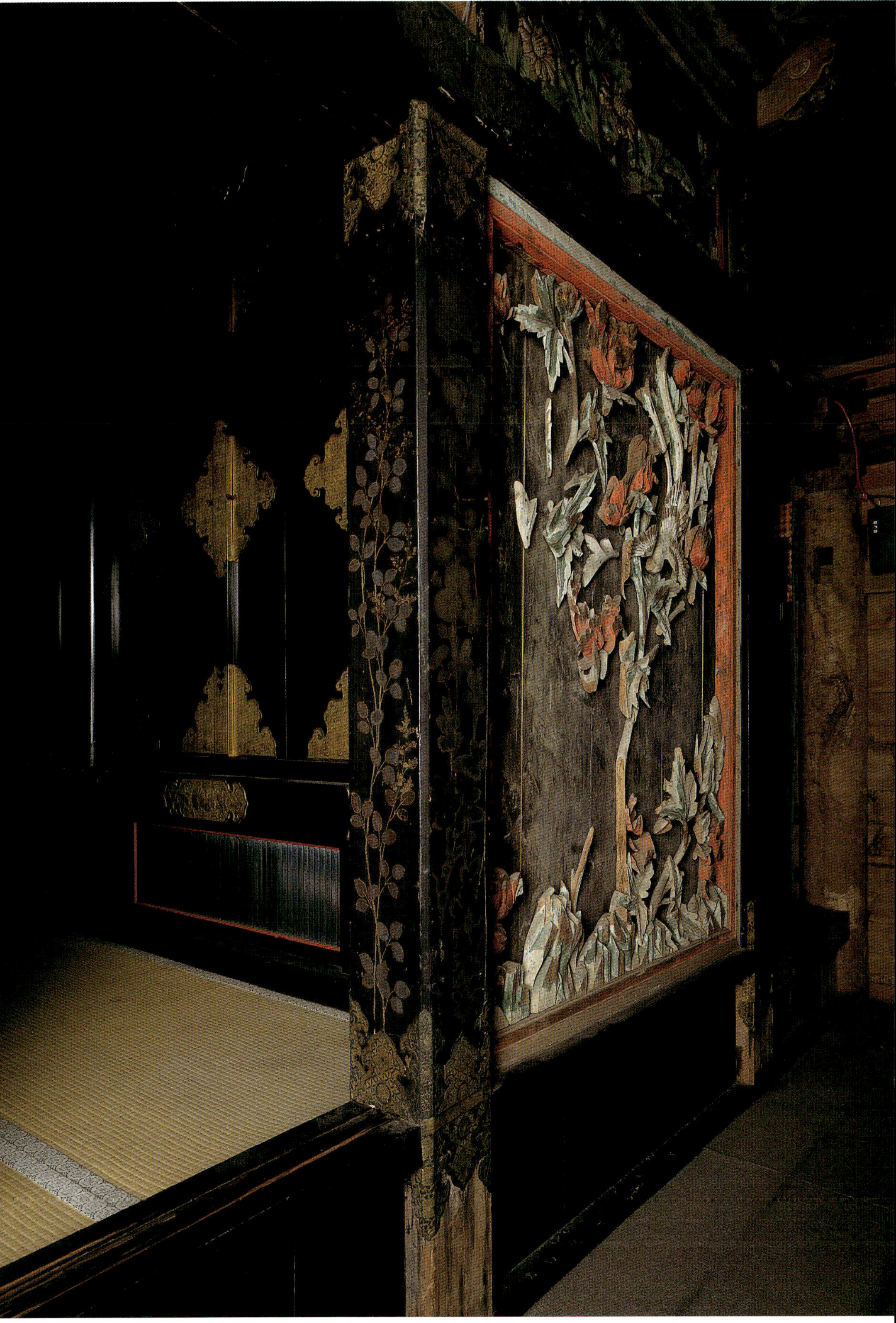

Chrysanthemum

One of the most commonly depicted motifs in all of Japanese art, the chrysanthemum had several associations when the moya was first created. These we know from literary evidence; as with the grapevines, however, context determines which association is operative in any given case. We have already encountered two common associations of the chrysanthemum. During the period when the moya was made, the chrysanthemum, depicted as a crest in combination with the paulownia crest, was exclusively an emblem of the Toyotomi family *(Fig. 13)*. In the interior paintings, which compose a Four Seasons floral program *(Fig. 9)*, the chrysanthemum, along with oleander and bush clover, is employed to indicate autumn. This use of the chrysanthemum, as a seasonal attribute, is its most common function in the arts of Japan.

The chrysanthemums carved on the exterior differ notably from those of the interior, whether rendered as makie crests or as painted emblems of autumn. Most fundamentally and conclusively, they are not reduced to virtually abstract linear pattern, as was typical Japanese practice in depicting a crest. Furthermore, unlike the painted chrysanthemums of the Four Seasons wall paintings, they are not accompanied by other motifs signifying autumn. Finally, they are far larger in proportion to their space than the painted chrysanthemums on the interior.

In the late sixteenth century the chrysanthemum had an additional association especially appropriate to the commemorative context. An alternate name for chrysanthemum in this period was *katamigusa* ("remembrance plant").[34] In usage, *katami* signified a thing—a piece of clothing, for example—that stood for something else, usually a person from whom one was separated by distance or by death. Hideyoshi used the term himself, in a poem he wrote shortly after his toddler son Sutemaru (1589–1591) died: "On the katami of the deceased, I leave my tears; I don't know where he's gone, only that he's disappeared."[35] As katamigusa, a plant was an object of remembrance, and figured as such in poetry: "I come and see / the katamigusa / of the deceased; each time I go / I wet my sleeves."[36] The speaker in the poem is brought to tears upon seeing katamigusa, remembering one who has passed away.

This sense of katamigusa is invoked also in the visual arts, notably in the mortuary context, where the "remembrance plant" is specifically a chrysanthemum. Several late sixteenth-century posthumous portrait paintings include the chrysanthemum as part of the composition, and in all of them, I believe, the chrysanthemum functions as katamigusa—as "flower of remembrance." One of the paintings, now in Keiunji in Hyōgo Prefecture, depicts an unknown young boy *(Fig. 76)*.[37] Save for the raised tatami mat on which he sits, the setting is unelaborated. The youngster wears samurai garb and holds in his left hand, silhouetted against his black belt, a spray of chrysanthemum.

At the top of the painting is an inscription written by the prominent Zen priest Nanka Genkō (1538–1604). As is common in Japanese painting, the inscription adds nuance to the painted image, making an analogy between the boy and the chrysanthemum,

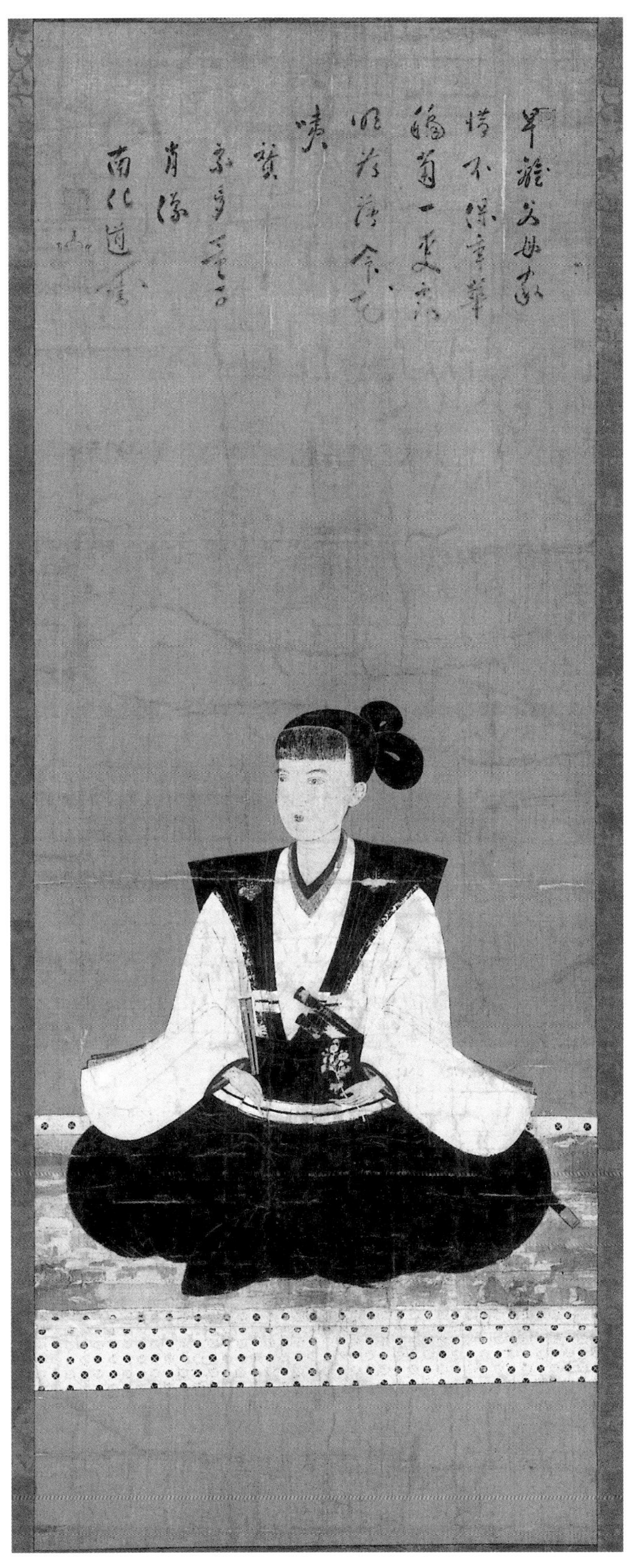

FIG. 76 *Portrait of Young Boy.* Late sixteenth–early seventeenth century. Hanging scroll; ink and color on silk. Inscription by Nanka Genkō. Keiunji, Hyōgo Prefecture. Photograph by Museum Yamato Bunkakan.

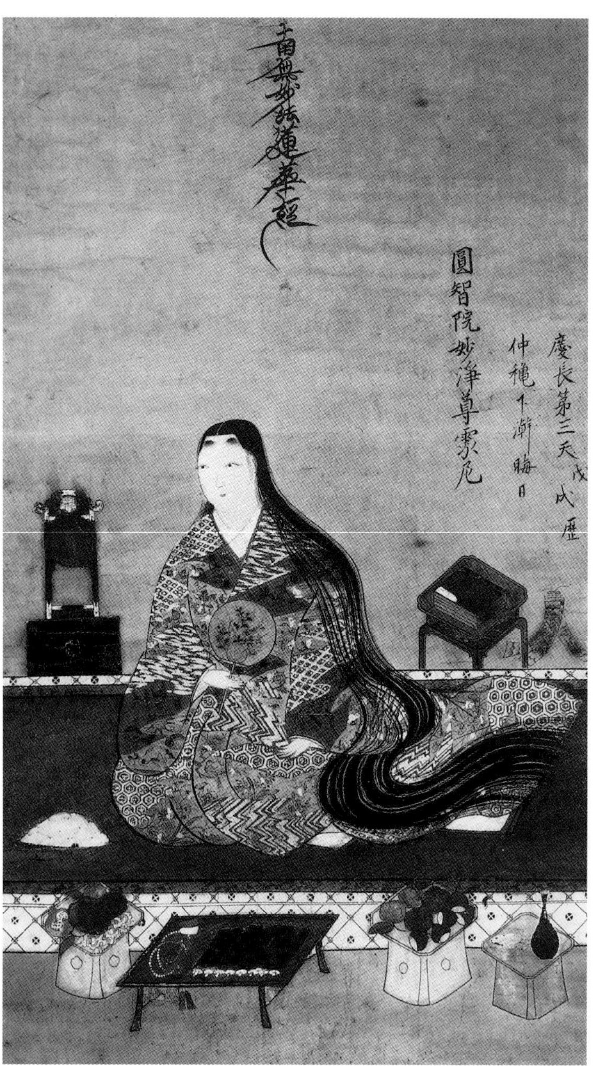

FIG. 77 *Portrait of Wife of Shinohara Kazutaka.* Dated to 1598. Hanging scroll; ink and color on paper. Myōhōji, Ishikawa Prefecture. Photograph by Ishikawa Prefectural Museum of Art.

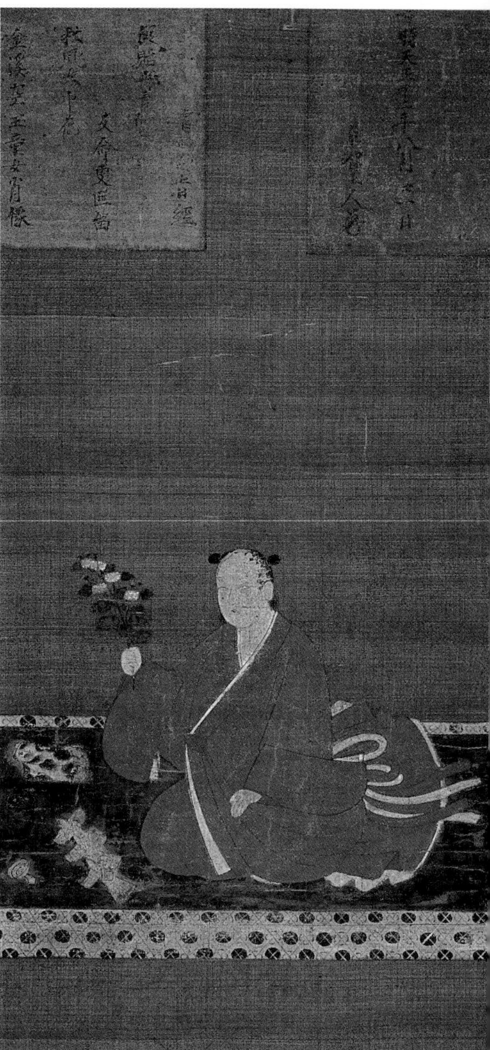

FIG. 78 *Portrait of Maeda Kikuhime.* Dated to 1584. Hanging scroll; ink and color on silk. Saikyōji, Shiga Prefecture. Photograph by Kyoto National Museum.

> Early he parted from the home of his father and mother;
> sadly, the blossoming years did not last;
> the dew on the single branch of autumn chrysanthemum;
> clearly, the life of the flower is brief.

The painting associates the boy and the chrysanthemum, and Nanka's eulogistic poem resonates with the depiction, equating the tragically short life of the boy with the bloom of the chrysanthemum, the flower of remembrance.[38]

This is likely the case also in a portrait of the wife of a warrior of the Kaga domain, Shinohara Kazutaka *(Fig. 77)*.[39] The painting shows the sitter with many of her possessions—including books and religious implements—and holding in her right hand, at the center of the portrait, a fan on which is depicted chrysanthemums. The brief inscription notes that she died in the autumn of 1598. The chrysanthemum is appropriate to the season of her death, but in this context probably functions also as the flower of remembrance.

A third portrait from this period, even more deeply layered with such associations, depicts Maeda Kikuhime (1578–1584), daughter of the powerful Kaga daimyo Maeda Toshiie (1538–1599), who was adopted soon after birth by Hideyoshi and died at the age of seven *(Fig. 78)*.[40] Seated amongst her toys, the child clutches in her right hand a branch of chrysanthemum. On one level, the chrysanthemums refer to the literal meaning of Kikuhime, "Chrysanthemum Princess."[41] Because Kikuhime died in the eighth month of 1584, the chrysanthemum is also appropriate seasonal imagery, and this connotation is reinforced by a phrase in the poetic inscription on the portrait, "the autumn wind blows the grass and flowers." Other flowers, though, symbolized autumn as unmistakably as did chrysanthemums. As in the Keiunji painting, the decision to depict the sitter holding a chrysanthemum rather than any other autumn flower was likely also guided by its specific import in the memorial context—as katamigusa, a flower-symbol of a loved one lost.

Thus, in the appropriate context, the chrysanthemum can be interpreted as katamigusa, a flower which stands in memory of one who has died. The above posthumous portraits show that the chrysanthemum was used as katamigusa in the visual arts and, significantly, that it bore this connotation in mortuary contexts of the late sixteenth century. It is my contention that the highly visible, even dominating presence of carved chrysanthemums on the exterior of the moya was intended to convey this memorial meaning.

Fuyō

The validity of this interpretation of the chrysanthemum carvings is substantiated by the other major carved motif on the exterior, the fuyō *(Figs. 5, 7, 75)*.[42] The four relief carvings of fuyō are exceptionally rare: in no other architectural context in Japan is fuyō as prominent as it is here, and nowhere else is it shown as the equal of the chrysanthemum.

FIG. 79 Fuyō. Dated to 1485. Hanging scroll; ink and color on paper. Masaki Museum of Art, Wakayama Prefecture.

These panels are, indeed, the earliest known large-scale depictions of this subject carved in wood in all of Japan. Their distinctive presence demands close examination.

The fuyō entered Japan from China, at least in painted representations, no later than the fourteenth century and was eventually incorporated into Japanese paintings.[43] The *Sancai tuhui,* a Chinese encyclopedia by Wang Qi (act. 1565–1614) first published in 1607 but based on earlier books, contains an illustration of the same broad-leafed, large-petalled fuyō plant that is represented in the carvings.[44] Over the illustration appears its name, a two-character compound read in Chinese as *furong* and in Japanese as fuyō. So named, the plant entered Japan. The link in Japan between this particular plant and the characters for fuyō is exemplified by a Japanese painting now in the Masaki Museum of Art, dated to 1485. The image clearly depicts the plant in question, and the inscription identifies it by the name fuyō *(Fig. 79).*[45]

Religious texts written in the 1590s suggest that the informed elite of the late sixteenth century would have recognized fuyō as a motif linked specifically to the youngest member of the Toyotomi family, Sutemaru. As related in the previous chapter, Sutemaru predeceased his father, Hideyoshi, succumbing to illness in 1591 at the age of two and a half.[46] During his short life, he was the only heir fathered by the aging Hideyoshi, his sole hope for dynastic continuity.

The Toyotomi solemnized Sutemaru's death with the proper Buddhist funeral rites and memorial rituals. They commissioned eulogies for these rituals from Nanka Genkō, inscriber of the Keiunji portrait painting examined above and founding abbot of Shōunji, the Kyoto temple Hideyoshi erected in memory of Sutemaru. Three of those eulogies have been preserved: those written for the seventh day after death *(shonanoka)* and for the third and seventh death anniversaries.[47] In each of these texts, the word fuyō occurs once, each time directly linked with Sutemaru. It is the only floral reference that appears in all three eulogies. The texts reveal yet another instance of the metaphorical linking that was common practice in the late sixteenth century—in this case, the linking of Sutemaru and fuyō.

In the first eulogy, Nanka makes an analogy between Sutemaru and fuyō:

> [Sutemaru's] splendor is like a spread-out brocade, his beauty is like a cherished jewel;
> his elegant bearing surpasses the opening of a fuyō in the morning;
> his delicate nature is like the closing of the rose mallow in the evening sun.[48]

Sutemaru is compared with several precious things, including the fuyō and the rose mallow—both beautiful, both poignantly short-lived. Each blossom opens with the morning sun but fades by the end of the day. Their beauty, fragility, and brevity made them appropriate metaphors for the dead child.

In the eulogy for the third anniversary of the boy's death, written in 1593, Nanka identifies Sutemaru with fuyō even more specifically:

> I have watched the moon illuminate the pine for three years since [Sutemaru's] death;
> the morning fuyō expresses him in life;
> extinguished, he has become the long-lasting rain that drenches the realm.[49]

Explicitly, fuyō reminds Nanka of Sutemaru as he was in life; implicitly, its brief bloom brings to mind the brief life of the child.

In the eulogy written in 1597 for the seventh anniversary, the shortest of the three texts, the reference to fuyō is keyed to the earlier eulogies.[50] It begins by stating that incense is offered on behalf of Sutemaru, and then offers a poetic trope, "The dew of the fuyō becomes the rain of the rose." Sutemaru is thereby linked with fuyō by juxtaposition. The transformation of the dew of the fuyō to the rain of the rose recalls the third-anniversary analogy, in which fuyō represented Sutemaru in life and the rain signified Sutemaru in death. Again, Sutemaru is equated with the fuyō plant by those in the world of the living.

In all three eulogies the word fuyō stands specifically for Sutemaru. This correspondence requires further clarification, however, because in the sixteenth century the word fuyō could signify two different plants. The first is the broad-leafed, large-petalled fuyō depicted in the 1485 Masaki painting noted above. Long before the word fuyō was used to refer to this plant, however, it denoted the lotus. Traditional glosses to Chinese sources from the Han and Tang periods define furong as lotus.[51] This definition was also known in Japan: the sixteenth-century Chinese encyclopedic text of the natural world, *Bencao gangmu* by Li Shizhen (1518–1593), notes that furong is another name for the lotus,[52] and Hayashi Razan (1583–1657) obtained this text in Nagasaki in 1607.[53] By the sixteenth century fuyō had come to denote the plant pictured in the Masaki painting, but had not entirely lost its earlier association with the lotus.

It is clear, however, that the primary association of the word fuyō in Momoyama Japan was not lotus. The 1603 *Vocabvlario da Lingoa de Iapam* defines "fuyō" as "*flor aßischanada,*" or "the flower that is called by this name."[54] In other words, fuyō denoted a plant which was then unknown in the West and therefore had no name in Portuguese. This ad hoc definition of fuyō did not refer to the lotus. The Portuguese Jesuits who compiled the *Vocabvlario* were familiar with the lotus and with its common Japanese name, *hasu,* which they translated into Portuguese as "*golfao,*" that is, lotus.[55] If the primary meaning of fuyō at this time had been lotus, surely the Jesuits would have translated it as "gol*f*ao." Fuyō could thus denote two different plants in Momoyama-period Japan. Its primary and current meaning—the one the Jesuits learned—was the large-petalled plant; its secondary, archaic meaning, still known but obscure, was lotus.

Understanding the etymology of fuyō is critical for evaluating Nanka Genkō's eulogies for Sutemaru. To which of the two possible meanings of fuyō did Nanka refer? In a Buddhist eulogy the lotus, so often an element in Buddhist iconography, may seem immediately more appropriate, but Nanka's own writings indicate that he meant the other plant. Nanka's collected writings include a total of twenty-seven eulogies composed for twenty-one individuals, including Sutemaru. In the eulogies for nine persons Nanka uses the character *hasu* to designate the lotus; he also uses it several times in referring to the *Lotus Sutra.* When Nanka wished to denote the lotus flower, he used the character *hasu.*[56]

Clearly, in his eulogies Nanka used the word fuyō to indicate the non-lotus flower. Mundane floral images, including pine, plum, peach, bamboo, and peony, are common in Nanka's eulogies, typically in contexts that do not point primarily, if at all, to a Buddhist connotation. Sometimes the flower refers to a season, for example, "the spring orchids and the autumn chrysanthemums."[57] Sometimes the flower is chosen for its association with the month in which the person died,[58] and this may be one sense of fuyō in the eulogies for Sutemaru: contemporary texts describe fuyō as a flower of the eighth and ninth months, and Sutemaru died in the eighth month.

In each of his three eulogies for Sutemaru, then, we can confidently infer that Nanka used the word fuyō to concretely link the boy with the large-leafed plant: fuyō connotes the month when Sutemaru died, and its fragile bloom was an apt image for a child who died so young. Nanka's eulogies record an association between Sutemaru and fuyō that was current within the Toyotomi milieu at least during the first seven years after the boy's death, spanning most of the 1590s. It is, moreover, especially significant that in all of the twenty-four eulogies that Nanka wrote for other individuals, only three references are made to fuyō and none of these references date between 1591 and 1597, the period of Sutemaru's eulogies.[59] In that period, in certain contexts, fuyō had acquired a particular association with Sutemaru.[60]

The question follows: does the presence of fuyō in the moya decoration have the same significance as Nanka's use of the word fuyō in the eulogies? The fuyō in the interior, in the ceiling, would appear to lack such significance *(Figs. 15, 16).* As one of many flowers in the paradisal floral canopy, it is too inconspicuous to be significant. In contrast, the fuyō carvings on the exterior are not only very conspicuous but also, as noted above, remarkably uncommon. The decision to use fuyō so prominently in that medium was not likely a casual one. I contend that the planner of the moya decoration featured fuyō on the exterior because it was, in that context, an especially meaningful motif.

The known facts concerning the moya and the eulogies argue that the fuyō carvings, like the word fuyō in Nanka's eulogies, functioned as a symbol of Sutemaru. The eulogies for Sutemaru were written within the period when the moya was built; in other words, the association between fuyō and Sutemaru was current among the Toyotomi at the time the carvings were made. Moreover, the Sutemaru eulogies were written at the request of the Toyotomi family, who were sponsors also of the moya. Imagery shared by two commemoratives sponsored at the same time by the same patron may well share a common meaning. This is especially likely here, since fuyō was otherwise uncommon in the wood carvings and eulogistic literature of this time. As exemplified by the portraits discussed above, mortuary art of the 1590s commonly related the deceased to a floral symbol in both text and image; in the Keiunji portrait, Sutemaru's eulogist Nanka himself echoed and commented on the pictorial association of youngster and chrysanthemum. I suggest that this type of association between a flower and a deceased person—specifically, in Nanka's eulogies, between fuyō and Sutemaru—was realized visually on the moya exterior, and that the association would have been understood by the learned audience of the 1590s.

Crane and Pine

One final motif on its exterior links the moya to Sutemaru: the combination of crane and pine. In the present configuration of the moya, the two are not found together; the present configuration, however, is problematic. Physical evidence reveals that the exterior portions of the lintel-beams on the east and west sides of the moya are not in their original positions. (Each lintel-beam consists of two long planks of wood—one facing the interior and one the exterior—each notched on its inner surface so that they could be sandwiched around the pillars with which they intersect.) The diagrams in Figure 80 represent the present juxtaposition of these exterior lintel-beam planks with the pillars of the central bays on the moya's east and west sides. Two rectangular holes, one above the other, pierce each of these central-bay pillars at the point where the pillar meets the lintel-beam (the holes are represented in black in the diagram). Likewise, a rectangular notch indents the upper edge of each lintel-beam plank where it meets the pillar (the notches are designated in the diagram with a stipple pattern). The holes and notches are thus paired, suggesting that they once functioned together to hold now-lost structural elements *(Fig. 81)*.[61] In their present pairings, however, the pillar holes and corresponding lintel-beam notches are not the same width, nor are they centered in relation to each other.

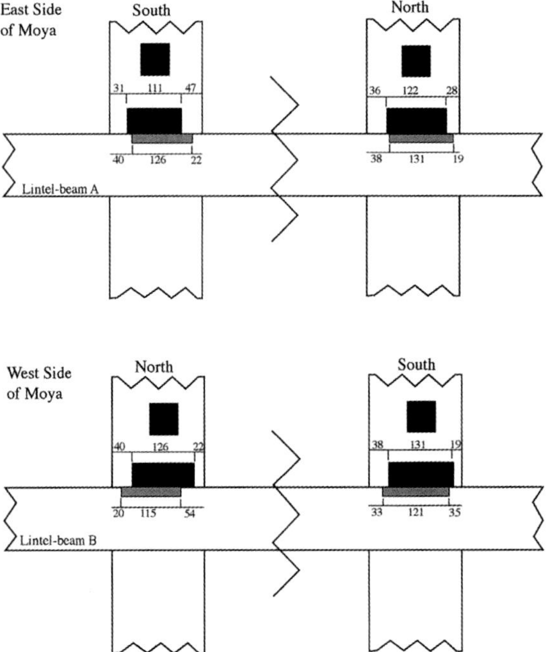

FIG. 80 Tsukubusuma Main Hall. Diagram of lintel-beam and pillar alignments of east and west sides, present state. Prepared with the aid of John Boorsch and Dax Kajiwara.

But if we were to interchange the two lintel-beams (as represented in *Fig. 82*, moving lintel-beam A from the east side of the moya to the west side, and lintel-beam B from the west side to the east side), the pillar holes would be markedly more congruent with their lintel-beam notches. In this configuration, the holes and notches of the west side are of the same width and are precisely centered in relation to each other. The match on the east side is only slightly less exact.[62] The key point is that the lintel-beam

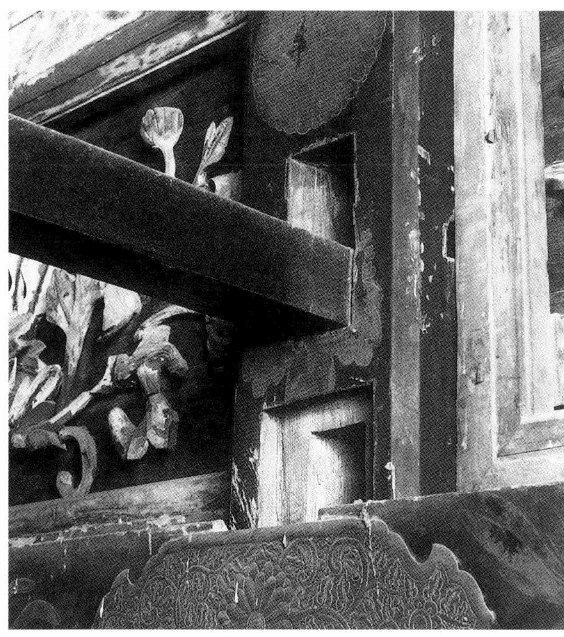

FIG. 81 Tsukubusuma Main Hall. Lintel-beam and pillar alignment, west side.

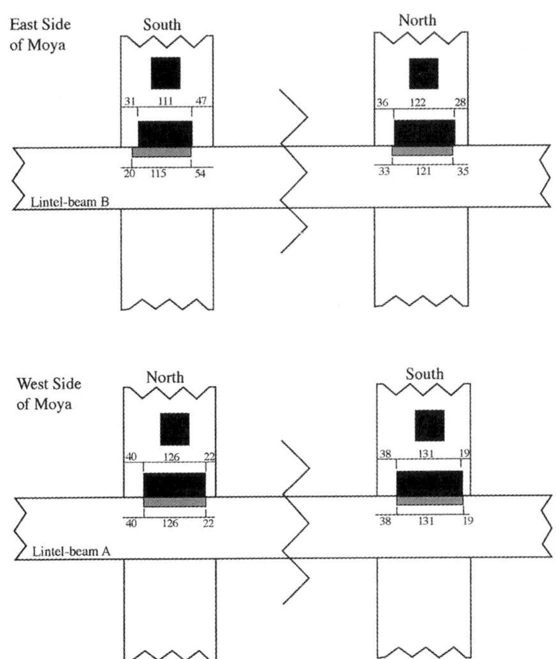

FIG. 82 Tsukubusuma Main Hall. Diagram of lintel-beam and pillar alignments of east and west sides, proposed reconstruction. Prepared with the aid of John Boorsch and Dax Kajiwara.

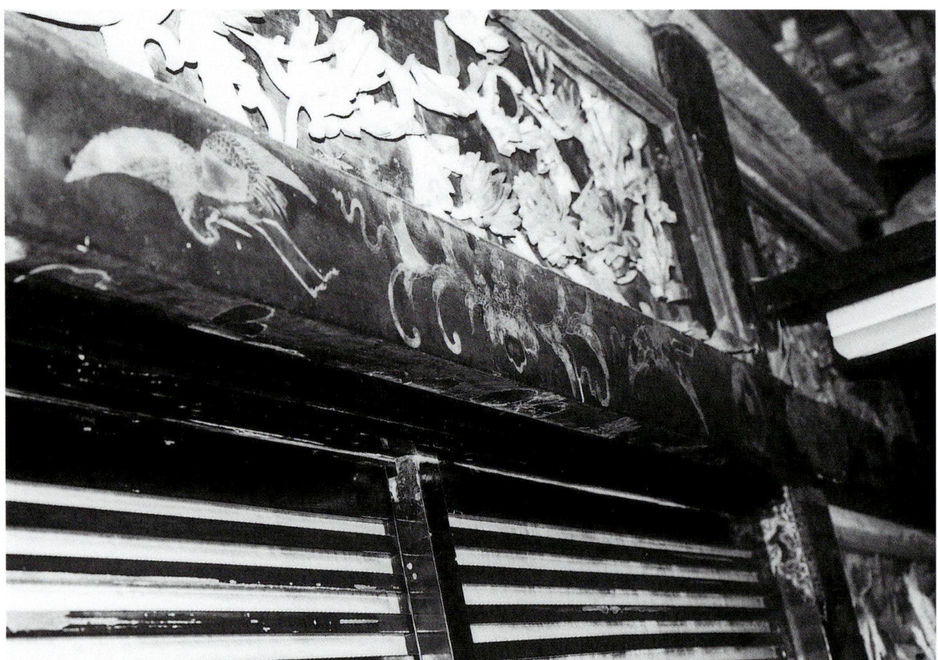

FIG. 83 Tsukubusuma Main Hall. Cranes. Makie lacquer. Moya exterior, east side, central bay, lintel-beam. Chikubushima, Shiga Prefecture. Photograph by the author.

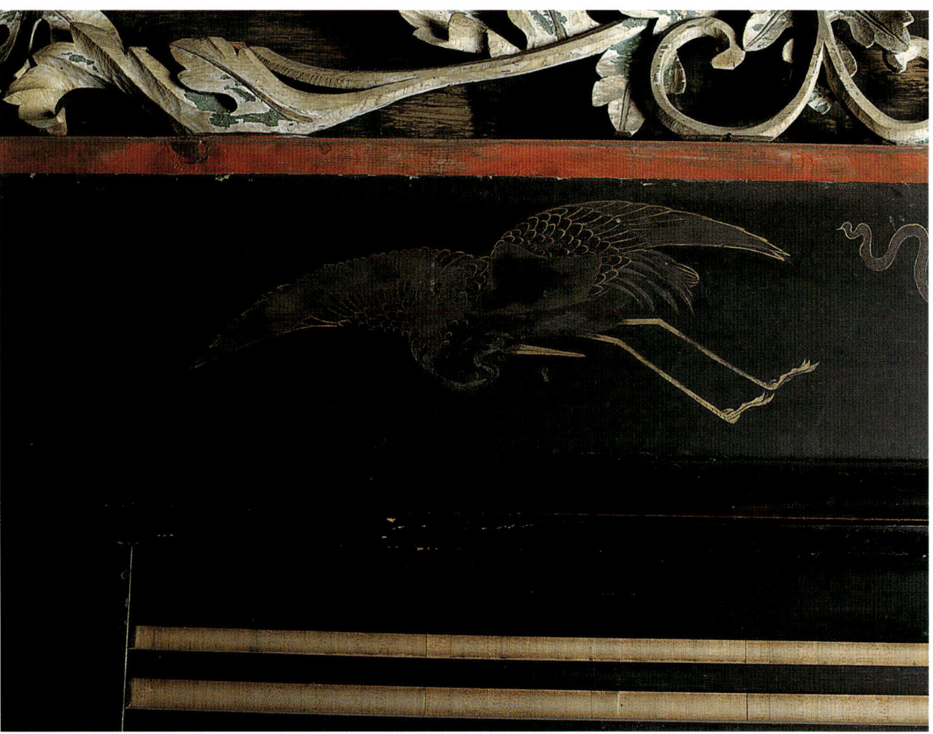

FIG. 84 Tsukubusuma Main Hall. Crane. Makie lacquer. Moya exterior, east side, central bay, lintel-beam. Chikubushima, Shiga Prefecture.

now on the east side of the moya aligns perfectly with the pillars on the west side; this lintel-beam must at one time have been paired with those pillars.[63]

This proposed realignment also yields a pattern of decoration that is far more logical than the present arrangement. Overall, the decoration on the exterior is characterized by a systematic repetition of motifs. The same subject appears at the same place on each of the four sides; the exterior faces of all four corner pillars, for example, have the same floral scroll with crests *(Fig. 6)*. There are only two exceptions to this pattern. All four lintel-beams are covered with a shell-and-seaweed motif; all, that is, except for the central-bay portion of the lintel-beam now on the east side (lintel-beam A), which is decorated with a pair of cranes *(Figs. 83, 84)*. Similarly, three of the four pairs of central-bay pillars are covered with the same motif, chrysanthemum plants *(Fig. 85)*. The fourth pair, on the west side, however, bears pine trees draped with wisteria *(Fig. 86)*. The proposed realignment, moving lintel-beam A to the west side of the moya, not only achieves a perfect match between the notches and holes on that side, but also brings together the only exceptions to the otherwise repeated motifs on the exterior: the cranes on lintel beam A join the pine trees on the west-side pillars. The conjunction of crane and pine greatly impacts our understanding of the moya decoration as a whole.

The crane-and-pine motif has long symbolized longevity or immortality in Japan,[64] but it gained additional significance in the late sixteenth century largely through its use by the Toyotomi family. The motif embellishes two sets of children's armor said to have

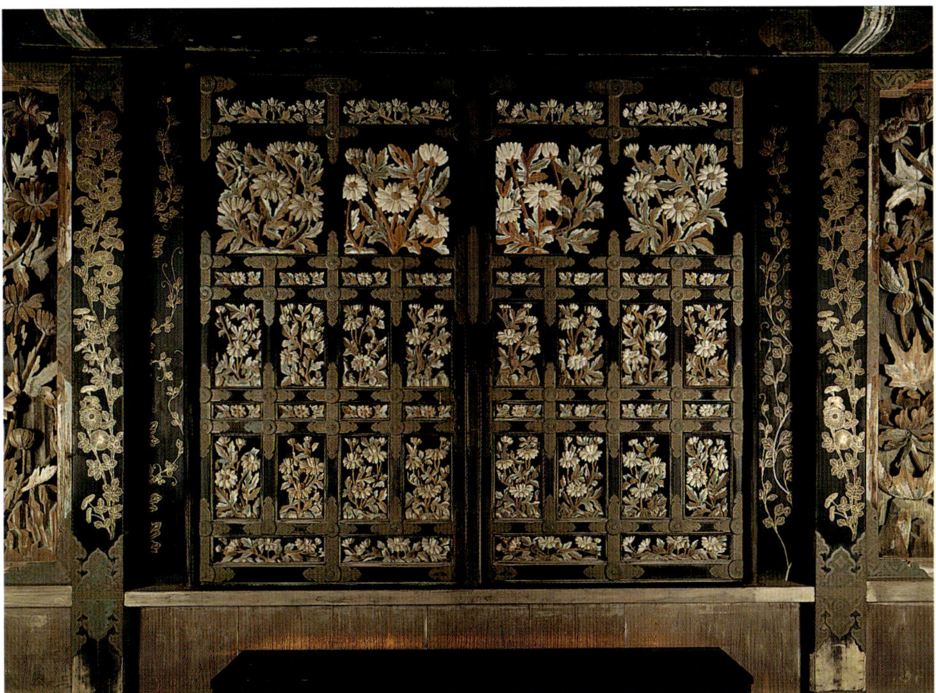

FIG. 85 Tsukubusuma Main Hall. Moya exterior, south side, central bay. Chikubushima, Shiga Prefecture.

been owned by Sutemaru and donated by Hideyoshi after the boy's death to Myōshinji, a temple in Kyoto lavishly sponsored by the Toyotomi and the site of Sutemaru's funeral *(Figs. 87, 88)*.[65] Both cuirasses are decorated with the crane-and-pine motif, one painted in colors on a gold-leafed background and the other embroidered on cloth. Certainly the motif was applied to the young heir's armor for its traditional auspicious meaning. But in addition, the Japanese words for crane and pine, *tsuru* and *matsu,* formed the boy Sutemaru's nickname; Hideyoshi himself, in a letter to his young son, addresses the boy as Tsurumatsu.[66] The nickname associated Sutemaru with the auspicious connotations of crane and pine; simultaneously it associated the crane and pine motif with Sutemaru.

Accordingly, on objects sponsored by the Toyotomi for Sutemaru during this period, the depiction of the crane-and-pine motif was probably intended to evoke the name Tsurumatsu. Armor owned by Sutemaru would have borne the crane-and-pine motif partly for its auspicious meaning and partly because it was a rebus of the child's nickname. Similarly, the crane-and-pine motif on the exterior of the Toyotomi-sponsored moya, unique and prominent on the moya, was placed there not only for its propitious associations, but also as an emblem of the deceased in whose memory the moya was originally created.

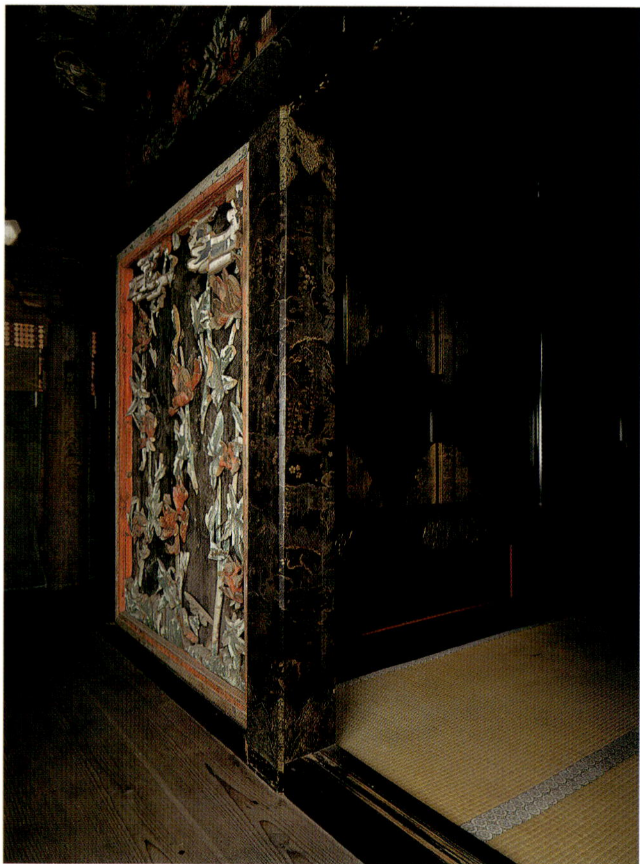

FIG. 86 Tsukubusuma Main Hall. View of moya exterior, west side, looking north through open central-bay mairado. Chikubushima, Shiga Prefecture.

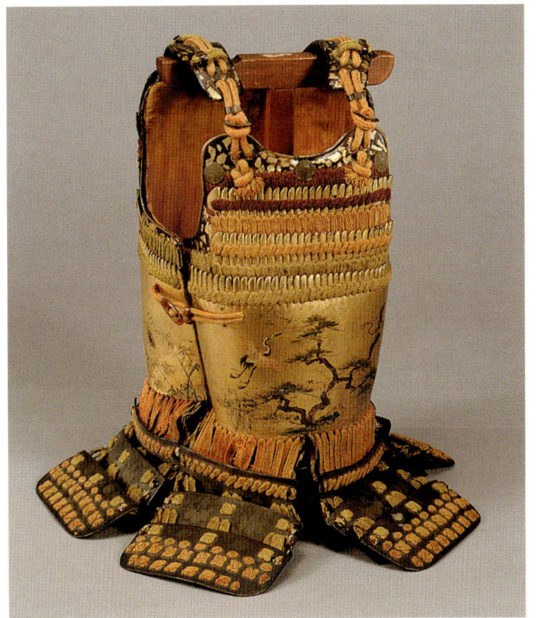

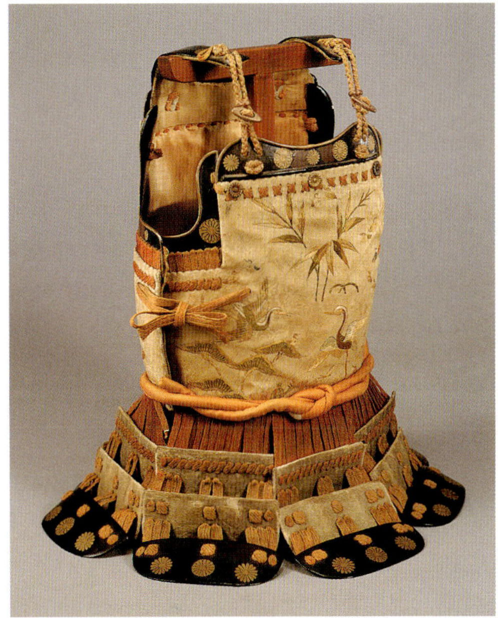

FIG. 87 (left) Armor cuirass. Late sixteenth century. Color and gold leaf on leather. Myōshinji, Kyoto. Photograph by Kyoto National Museum.

FIG. 88 (right) Armor cuirass. Late sixteenth century. Embroidery on cloth. Myōshinji, Kyoto. Photograph by Kyoto National Museum.

RECOVERING THE ORIGINAL KYOTO SITE OF SUTEMARU'S BUILDING

The moya was decorated so as to proclaim its Toyotomi sponsorship. Many of the motifs carry memorial symbolism, arguing for the building's mortuary function. The prominent fuyō carvings and the single makie crane-and-pine motif on the exterior may well have referred specifically to the young boy Sutemaru. He is the most likely candidate for such a building in this period, and this is reflected in much of the decoration.

Linking Sutemaru and the moya raises important questions. The first concerns the original location of this mortuary building. The most likely site would have been Shōunji, Sutemaru's mortuary temple, which neighbored the Great Buddha Hall, nearby which, the epigraphic evidence introduced above tells us, the moya was originally created. As we have seen, Sutemaru's eulogist Nanka Genkō wrote that Shōunji was sponsored by Hideyoshi, that it was built in the early 1590s, and that it was magnificent. The recent excavations at its former site confirm that Hideyoshi made Shōunji a temple of great size, as was appropriate to the memory of his intended heir, and the three-bay-square moya could easily have fit into such a complex.

If the temple Shōunji stood intact until at least 1615, however, why would this building have been removed in 1602? The answer to this question lies partly in certain distinctive aspects of the moya. Its small size and plan argue that when it was an independent structure, it was not one of the main halls of the temple, but a subsidiary building. The extensive makie lacquer on the exterior suggests that the moya was never intended as a permanent structure. No other extant building has such ample makie on its exterior, and the written descriptions of now-lost constructions suggest that such use of makie was rare.[67] Makie was not normally used on building exteriors, and for good reasons. Exposure to the elements ruins it, and unlike plain black lacquer, which was often used on exteriors, makie designs cannot easily be repaired once damaged.[68] These problems were no doubt understood, and explain why makie was generally avoided on the exteriors of buildings. The extravagant use of makie on the exterior here reflects the importance of the building for the Toyotomi.

I suggest that the moya was originally built as a subsidiary and temporary structure. Further research is needed to determine its precise purpose, but perhaps it was created for a specific occasion, such as one of Sutemaru's death anniversaries. Given the significance of Sutemaru's death to Hideyoshi and the prodigious resources Hideyoshi allocated for devotional worship on behalf of the dead boy, such lavish and costly decoration, even of a temporary structure, would not be unexpected. By 1602 the structure would have been deemed expendable at Shōunji because it had served its role and its exterior makie was irreversibly deteriorating. Why it was then moved to Chikubushima is a question for later chapters.

The moya has not received the art-historical attention it deserves, though its premove incarnation (as deduced above) makes it one of the most important extant monuments of the Momoyama period. It has been slighted for several reasons. Chikubushima is inconveniently located, a remote place not conducive to concentrated research. More significant an impediment, however, is the tendency of modern art historians to analyze the structure and each of its decorative mediums independently, which prevents seeing the whole monument as an integrated expression of a particular intention. As a result, separate studies of the structural anomalies of the architecture, the authorship of the paintings, and the cataloguing of the makie motifs have dominated the limited research.[69] Although these are important contributions, such disjointed analysis does not reveal the full accomplishment of the decoration or the possible concatenation of allusory meanings. It is, ultimately, the very interconnectedness of the motifs in the several mediums and the careful coordination of their placement that permit the decoration to communicate its multivalent significances. By considering the moya as a whole, we can begin to recover its full and complex identity—its original location and configuration, as well as the supramundane meanings embedded in its secular-seeming motifs.

Finally, the moya—which I shall hereafter refer to as Sutemaru's building—has been neglected, I believe, because modern art historians have accorded the mediums of its decoration far less esteem than they commanded at the time they were created. And so it is to a reconsideration of those materials, individually and in combination, that we will next turn.

4

The Material of the Sacred

AESTHETIC EXCELLENCE

Today, the importance of Sutemaru's building is most readily grasped through the symbolic information conveyed by its pictorial program: because the iconography indicates that the building memorialized the ruler Hideyoshi's dead son, we can deduce that it was, in its time, a structure of great consequence. The structure also lends itself to an equally persuasive, more sensual, more immediate mode of analysis. Even before decoding the building's symbolic meanings, many of its first viewers would have perceived it to be remarkable by virtue of its constituent materials. They were accustomed, by Momoyama convention, to admire certain materials per se, irrespective of what they were used to depict and of the symbolic content of these depictions; lucid meaning and value inhered in the materials themselves.

But are these meanings and values still knowable? Standards change over time, obscuring once prevalent perceptions. Especially since the Meiji period (1868–1912), when Western conceptions of art were first endorsed in Japan, objects that do not fit into the Western categories of fine art, such as those made of the Asian material lacquer, have been assigned much lower value in the Japanese art hierarchy than they originally enjoyed.[1] Even the value of things that may seem to fit comfortably within those categories, such as paintings, has not necessarily been static or commensurate with the value accorded them in the West. Recovery of pre-Meiji perceptions, understanding the earlier hierarchies, allows us to enter otherwise lost realms of appreciation. Japanese of the Momoyama period reveal distinctive Momoyama standards in the objects they commissioned and made, in their writings about these objects, and in the connotations of the vocabulary they used in these writings. The commentaries of foreigners then in Japan, often astute and educated observers (though, as we shall see, not always), shed additional light. All of this evidence allows us to discern that the materials composing Sutemaru's building were then the most highly esteemed in Japan, and that the orchestrated combination of them over an architectural framework—the ensemble—was especially prized. The Japanese and European predilections and insights help explain why Hideyoshi, in response to his son's death, mediated the sacred realm with this particular, and particularly splendid, building.

Unfamiliar kinds of excellence, however, can be hard to recognize. Witness the struggle of Alessandro Valignano (1539–1606), a Jesuit missionary who spent a decade in Japan over the course of the late sixteenth and early seventeenth century. Valignano was an attentive observer of Japanese culture and wrote for his brethren in Europe detailed, if often perplexed, accounts of what he observed. In this initial age of direct contact between Europe and Japan, he was particularly struck by how widely and profoundly this culture differed from his own, notably in its value judgments about art. "It is . . . astonishing," he wrote, "to see the importance that they attach to things which they regard as the treasures of Japan, although to us such things seem trivial and childish; they, in turn, look upon our jewels and gems as worthless."[2]

He illustrates his point with the example of *chanoyu,* which he briefly describes and rightly identifies as a fundamentally important practice in Momoyama Japan, one that bespoke and reinforced elite status (and was, we can imagine, thoroughly bewildering to his European readers). He discusses the many utensils required for chanoyu and how demand had created a market in these objects and driven their prices to extraordinary heights. He writes, "Among these vessels is a certain kind which is prized beyond all belief and only the Japanese can recognize it. Quite often one of these vessels, tripods, bowls or caddies will fetch three, four or six thousand ducats and even more, although to our eyes they appear completely worthless." In a most vivid example of divergent values, he tells of a powerful ruler in Japan who "once showed me a small earthenware caddy for which, in all truth, we would have no other use than to put it in a bird's cage as a drinking-trough; nevertheless, he had paid 9,000 silver *taels* (or about 14,000 ducats) although I myself would certainly not have given two farthings for it."

Despite his puzzled disparagement of the objects themselves, Valignano perceptively recognized that there existed in Japan a set of standards wholly different from the European standards by which the relative quality of an object was judged and by which hierarchies of art were created. He noted, with surprise, that countless numbers of seemingly similar objects were by no means similarly appraised. What he calls the "prized pieces" were made by "certain ancient masters," and the Japanese connoisseur could quickly recognize them. No European could learn to appreciate these objects, to practice such connoisseurship, because no European could "manage to understand in what consists their value and how they are different from the others." He applied this statement, as well, to Japanese objects other than those specifically associated with chanoyu, such as monochrome ink paintings and arms and armor. In his struggle to understand Japanese connoisseurship, Valignano ultimately admitted defeat. He did perceive, though, that

Japanese standards and hierarchies were as meaningful to the Japanese as European standards and hierarchies were to the European. A mind-set that he acknowledged without comprehending produced, among the Momoyama Japanese, general consent that certain objects were unquestionably better than others.

AESTHETIC EXCELLENCE AND THE ENSEMBLE

Valignano's insights (and his bafflement) epitomize the problem of perceiving excellence in the visual arts, of understanding accepted hierarchies, especially in a context as foreign and distant from our experience as Momoyama Japan. There existed at this time no single, universally applicable Japanese locution for artistic distinction, and this should encourage us to consider what terms the Japanese used to designate what they considered distinguished objects. Valignano grants that certain objects are much more highly valued than others (even if *he* can't recognize them). Was there, in Japan, special language with which to designate and describe such things? Were there other means by which such objects were recognized? Even more important, how might an understanding of these means affect the ability of an outsider—of that time or our own—to recognize that which was, according to Momoyama standards, most excellent?

Chanoyu, for example, which so puzzled Valignano, is rich in language that denotes exceptional quality. The *Yamanoue no Sōji ki,* the most important chanoyu treatise of the period, evaluates and ranks objects according to an accepted hierarchy.[3] It employs terms such as "tenka ichi"("first in the realm") or "meibutsu" ("famous object") to distinguish the best objects. The ability to discern the quality of these objects, however, was a gift that only enlightened tea people possessed, and they typically exercised their connoisseurship within private buildings constructed specially for chanoyu.[4] The treatise is full of language that expresses this exclusivity: "good" objects first beget and thereafter are comprehended through "mitsuden" ("secret teachings") and "kuden" ("oral traditions"), unavailable to all but the insider. More than a few Japanese would have been as perplexed as Valignano by standards that were a private knowledge-hoard of the chanoyu elite.

Momoyama-period aesthetic excellence, however, was not singular but rather exuberantly diverse. The standards associated with the ever-evolving chanoyu itself changed dramatically and swiftly, even over the relatively brief span of the Momoyama period. In many areas of creative production outside the lofty realm of chanoyu, the Japanese sought kinds of excellence that were—again, by Momoyama standards—more self-evident and often more publicly displayed. Many of the newly built structures in and around Kyoto, for example, unlike the enigmatic aesthetic constructs of chanoyu, were designed to elicit the attention and admiration of the multitude. (Even some of Valignano's compatriots perceived and praised their more discernible value.) Nobunaga and Hideyoshi used such architecture to proclaim their power: as we have seen, both built impressive castles and residences, and Hideyoshi, during his tenure, energetically rebuilt temples and commissioned religious buildings of grand size and public impact.

Contemporary writings reflect the conspicuousness of this architecture. Momoyama diarists chronicled the many buildings going up around them and typically recorded such factual information as the patron, site, and progress of construction.[5] They did not, generally, describe the aesthetic qualities of the buildings or their personal reactions to them. The buildings were significant as restorations or additions contributing to the revival of the capital; they were important less for their qualities than for their very presence.

THE PRE-MOMOYAMA ENSEMBLE

Certain buildings, though, were too remarkable for their appearance to pass without diaristic comment. The immensity of the Great Buddha Hall, for example, could not be ignored. Some diary accounts, as well as extant monuments, reveal also the prominence in the period of a distinctive type of structure, ornamented in several mediums expressly to capture the eye. This fusion of architecture and abundant decoration, in which all elements were synthesized to create a cohesive whole, is most succinctly expressed with the word "ensemble," usefully defined in the *OED* as "all the parts of anything taken together so that each part is considered only in relation to the whole."[6] Although no single Japanese word encompasses this broad meaning, a point to which we shall return later, it is clear from the documentary record and from extant monuments that the Momoyama period privileged the architectural ensemble of multiple mediums.

By no means, however, were large-scale ensembles a Momoyama invention. The earliest notable extant example is the 1053 Byōdōin Phoenix Hall in Uji *(Fig. 89)*.[7] Here, a massive gold-covered wood sculpture of Amida is seated within a heavily decorated architectural setting. The walls and doors hold polychrome paintings representing the nine levels of Amida's descent from his Pure Land to earth, to greet and escort the deceased believer back to the Western Pure Land. Relief wood carvings of bodhisattvas and of heavenly musicians and dancers, all borne on clouds, attach along the upper registers of the walls. Intricate patterns in metalwork and lacquer with inlaid shell once shimmered on the ceiling and on the sculpture's platform and canopy. Architectural coloring made brilliant much of the upper levels of the building. The whole palatial structure is sited on the west side of a pond in a garden. By this coordination of mediums, the monument successfully creates in our world a cohesive vision of Amida's realm, the Western Pure Land.

The twelfth-century Konjikidō at Chūsonji in Iwate Prefecture *(Fig. 90)* brilliantly combines architecture, lacquer, gold leaf, metalwork, and a group of Buddhist sculptures (as well as the mummified remains of its patron and two of his heirs).[8] All sur-

FIG. 89 Phoenix Hall. 1053. Byōdōin, Uji. Photograph by Benridō.

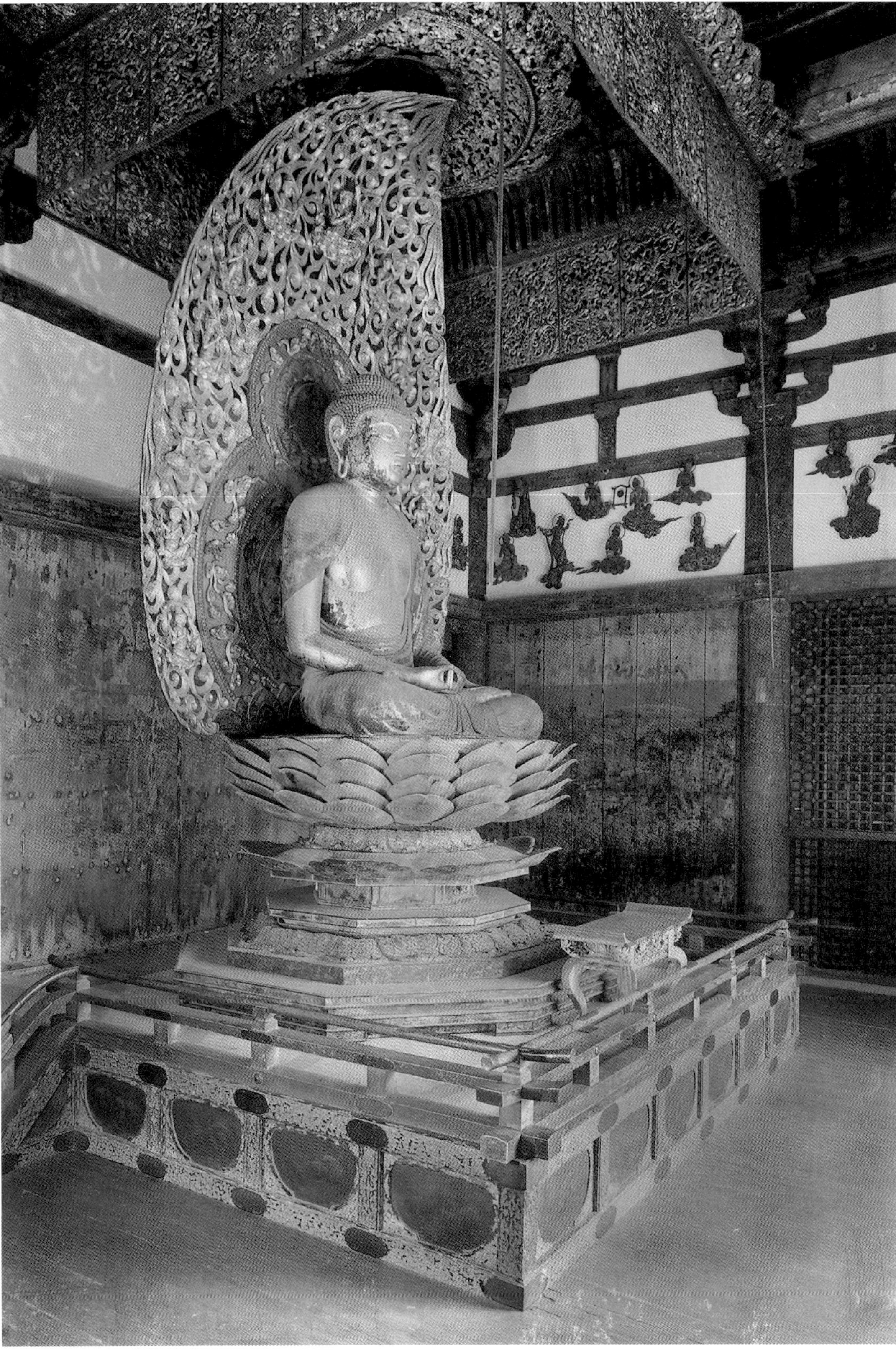

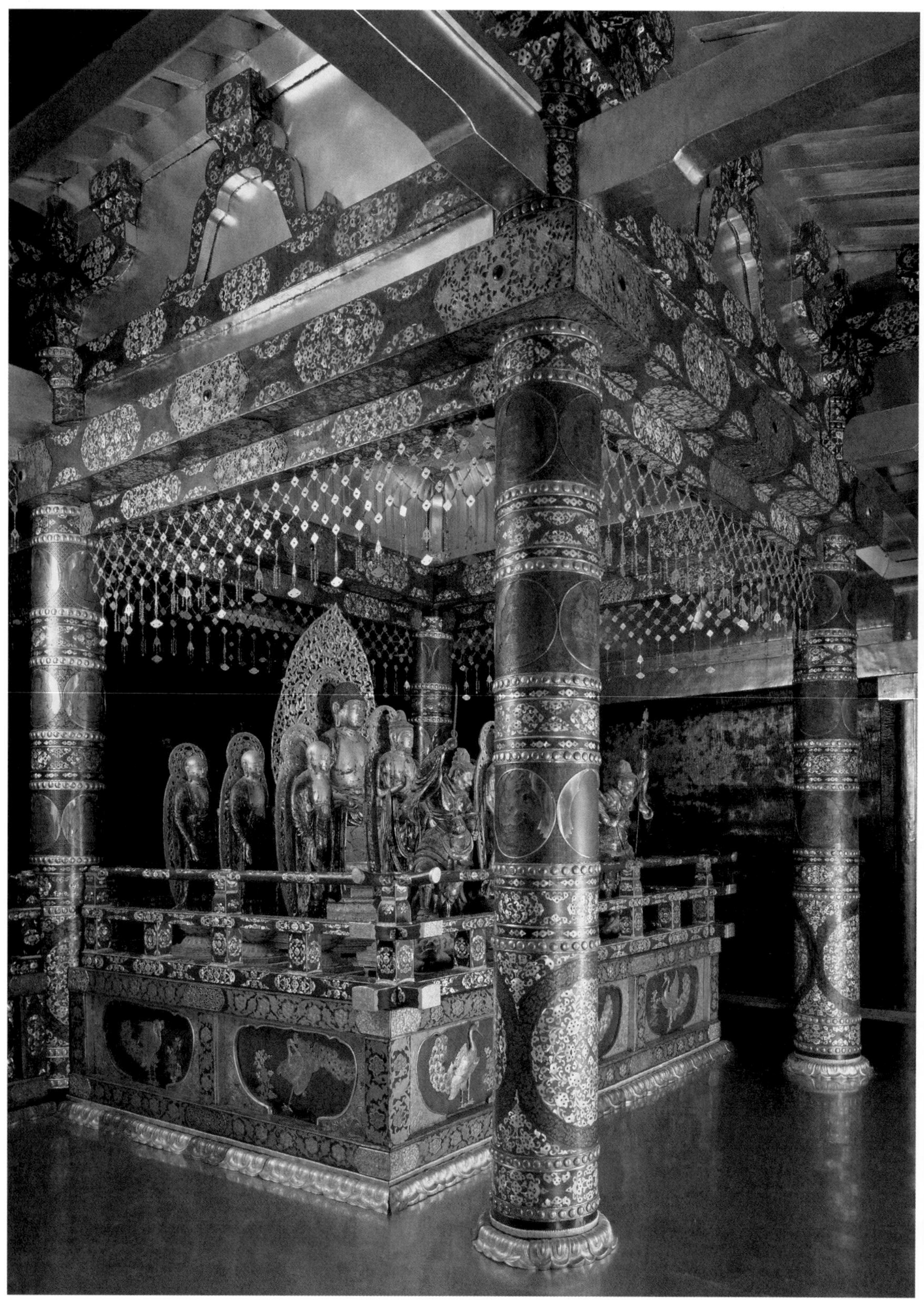

FIG. 90 Konjikidō. Twelfth century. Chūsonji, Iwate Prefecture. Photograph by Kōdansha.

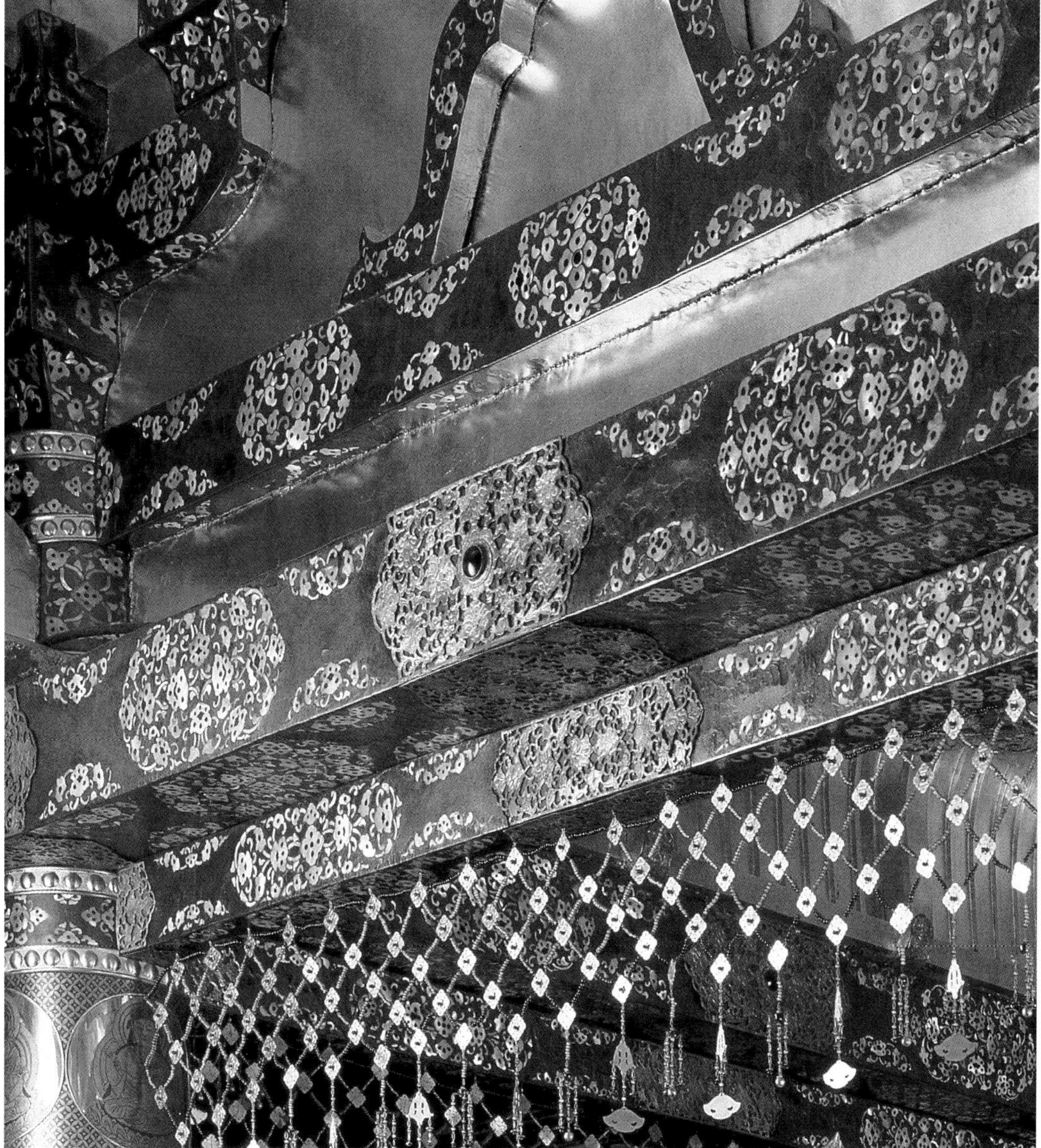

FIG. 91 Detail of Fig. 90.

faces of the vertical and horizontal architectural members of the structure are completely covered with metalwork or makie along with shell-inlaid lacquer. The careful coordination of this ensemble is revealed in passages of decoration almost identically depicted in different mediums: on the beam illustrated in Figure 91, for example, an oblong motif filled with interlacing floral scroll appears both in openwork metal plates and in shell-inlaid lacquer. Technical constraints limit the amount of detail achievable in shell, but the two mediums clearly share the same conception of the complicated design.[9]

THE MOMOYAMA ENSEMBLE

The practice of grand ensemble-making flowered especially in the Momoyama period, starting with Nobunaga's Azuchi Castle. Japanese descriptions emphasize that workers in different mediums collaborated on its renowned decorative program, which on the interior comprised paintings, lacquer, and metalwork; among those to whom payments were recorded are the most famous Kano workshop painters of the day (namely, Eitoku [1543–1590] and Mitsunobu [1565?–1608]) and the metalworker Gotō Heishirō.[10] Information about the appearance of such collaboration is helpfully provided by a curious European observer of Japanese building interiors, the French merchant François Caron (1600–1673), who wrote that "the walls of their chambers are also for the most part painted with [a] variety of figures, and laid with gilt paper so curiously, as if it were but one large sheet; the boards round about being beautified with lists of black Wax, very artificially wrought; most of their rooms are divided with shuts, prepared and painted as the walls are, which being taken out, enlarges the rooms at pleasure."[11] He thus describes the prevailing decorative scheme of walls and sliding doors covered with paintings on gold-leafed paper and pillars and beams coated with black lacquer, which he mistakes for wax.

Its massive size and magnificent decoration made Azuchi Castle a potent symbol of Nobunaga and his rule; perhaps for that reason, after his death in 1582, the combatants contesting power immediately destroyed it. Most of the other magnificent ensembles of the day were likewise destroyed, including Osaka Castle, which was demolished in 1615, and Jurakutei, which Hideyoshi dismantled himself. The evidence for the large Momoyama ensemble is now preserved in writings and in the few examples that remain: Sutemaru's building, incorporated into the Tsukubusuma Main Hall as its *moya,* is the most significant, more fully decorated with the full complement of accepted mediums than any other that survives.

ANALYZING THE ENSEMBLE

Common sense suggests that an ensemble, conceived as an integral whole, cannot be adequately analyzed piecemeal. Indeed, the aesthetic concept that without question governs Sutemaru's ensemble, *shōgon*—decoration used to glorify and express the sacred—is often predicated on a combination of materials to achieve a single glorious whole. And yet, to assess a Momoyama ensemble according to the standards its audience would have used, it is informative to first consider its constituent mediums separately, to recollect the place of privilege that each one held within premodern Japanese art-making. Three mediums dominate Sutemaru's ensemble: polychrome paintings, on the interior; relief wood carvings, on the exterior; and makie lacquer, both inside and out. They are augmented by two other, less pervasive, mediums, gilt metalwork and architectural coloring. Each of the three predominant mediums individually occupied an especially honored place within Momoyama visual culture, and so we will examine each in turn before considering them together.

PAINTING: THE PRINCIPAL ART

João Rodrigues (1561–1633) was generally correct when he wrote of the Japanese in *The History of the Church of Japan* that "among their other mechanical arts, the principal one is the art of painting."[12] Even a cursory glance at Japan's pre-Momoyama visual arts shows that painting had long been an admired medium, the most widely and diversely practiced of the representational arts. Great painters of the past were remembered by name, rulers characteristically employed painters on retainer or for specific projects, and religious institutions for about a millennium had been commissioning painters to produce devotional images. Painting enjoyed a favored position among the figurative arts, and was diverse in its functions, its impact, and its particular characteristics. It is in such characteristics—the scale, materials, and perceived novelty—that the contemporary audience detected excellence in some Momoyama painting.

From the mid-sixteenth century the status, and tangible presence, of painting in Japan increased with the surge of enormous architectural projects that included correspondingly large-scale paintings. As we have seen, leading warriors vaunted their position with buildings of exceptional size—Nobunaga's Azuchi Castle in the 1570s set the early precedent—and painting was the largest component of the interior decoration. Rodrigues succinctly describes these enormous images: "The inner surface of these walls is lined with paintings executed on many layers of paper like thick parchment," depicting a great variety of favored subjects, including scenes of nature, human activity, and ancient legends. "Thus the inner surface of the walls is excellently decorated with a variety of painting, and there is always someone admiring them and enjoying the sight of their great variety and beauty, for they are painted by famous artists for whom the Japanese have a very high regard."[13] Newly empowered warrior autocrats embraced painted representations, writ large on their walls by acknowledged masters, as a most effective device to impress rival or allied warriors, Buddhist clergy, and European visitors.

Paintings made for these public and semipublic contexts oftentimes were executed in vivid colors and gold leaf, creating a visual presence that dominated its setting. Rodrigues describes the preferred types of painting and their typical uses: monochromatic ink, for example, was a favorite medium of "celebrated ancient artists" and, in his experience, was used often in the inner private rooms of residences and in the context of chanoyu.[14] This he contrasts with the paintings used in more public spaces, whose function was to impress in less subtle ways: "The rooms and apartments where guests are received have rich gilding and paintings in color." This oversimplifies the dichotomy between ink and color—in fact, monochrome ink paintings also sometimes graced recep-

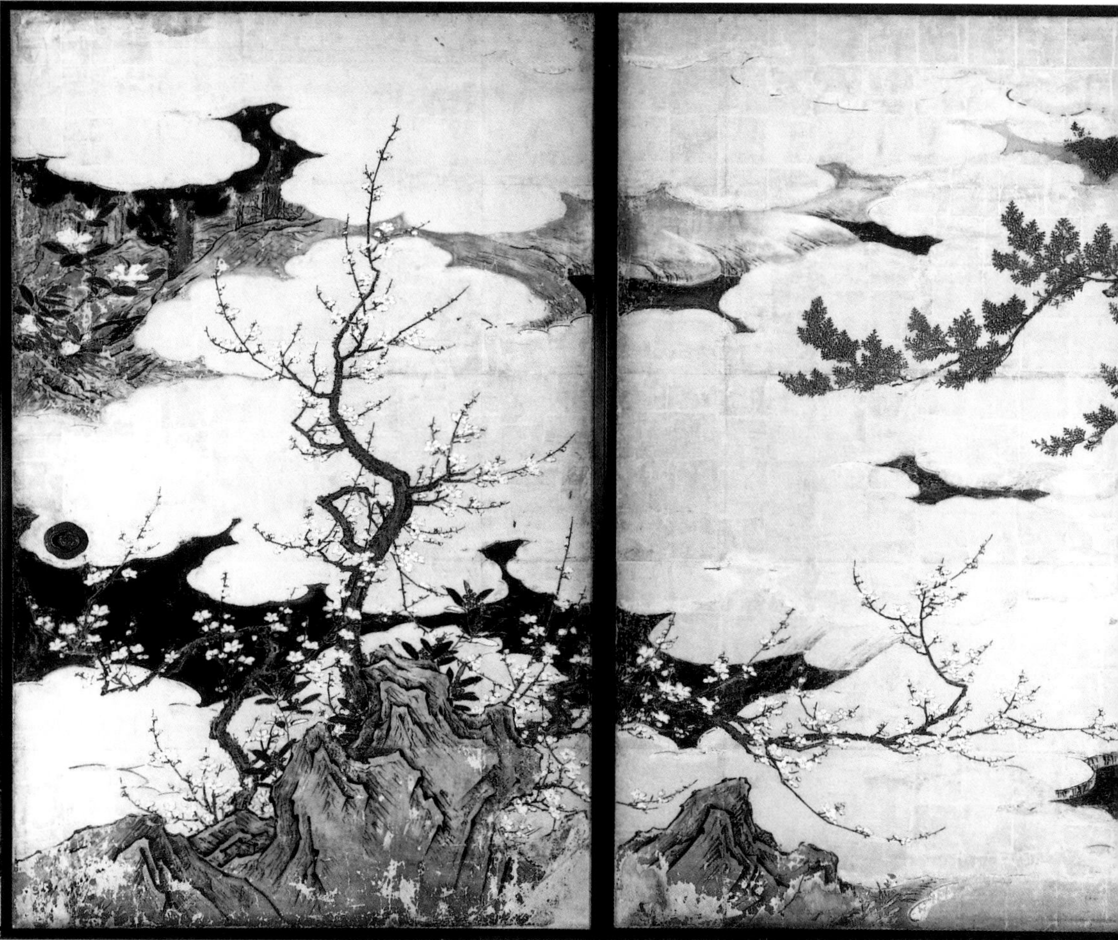

tion rooms. Nevertheless, on the whole, paintings in colors and gold were the favored, impressive medium of many Momoyama patrons.

Ōta Gyūichi (b. 1527), devoted annalist of Nobunaga's life, describes countless rooms throughout the seven-storied keep of Azuchi Castle, filled with a program of paintings famously directed by the leading painter of his day, Kano Eitoku.[15] Some of the paintings were executed in monochrome ink and touches of gold, but the prevailing, most innovative, and ultimately most celebrated painting mode at Azuchi combined polychrome and gold leaf. Luis Frois (1532–1597), having seen them, wrote that "the walls are decorated with designs richly painted in gold and different colours."[16] These resplendent paintings filled the public audience and entertainment rooms, on the third and fourth floors, and encompassed a vast range of subjects, including flowers and birds (individually and in assorted groupings); animals such as civets, horses, dragons, and tigers; and didactic exemplars and episodes taken from ancient Chinese lore. The more private sixth level was entirely Buddhist in theme, creating in colors and gold a realm filled with representations of the Buddha, his disciples, and attendant divinities. This program was nothing if not overtly celebratory of Nobunaga's kingly and ultimately godly

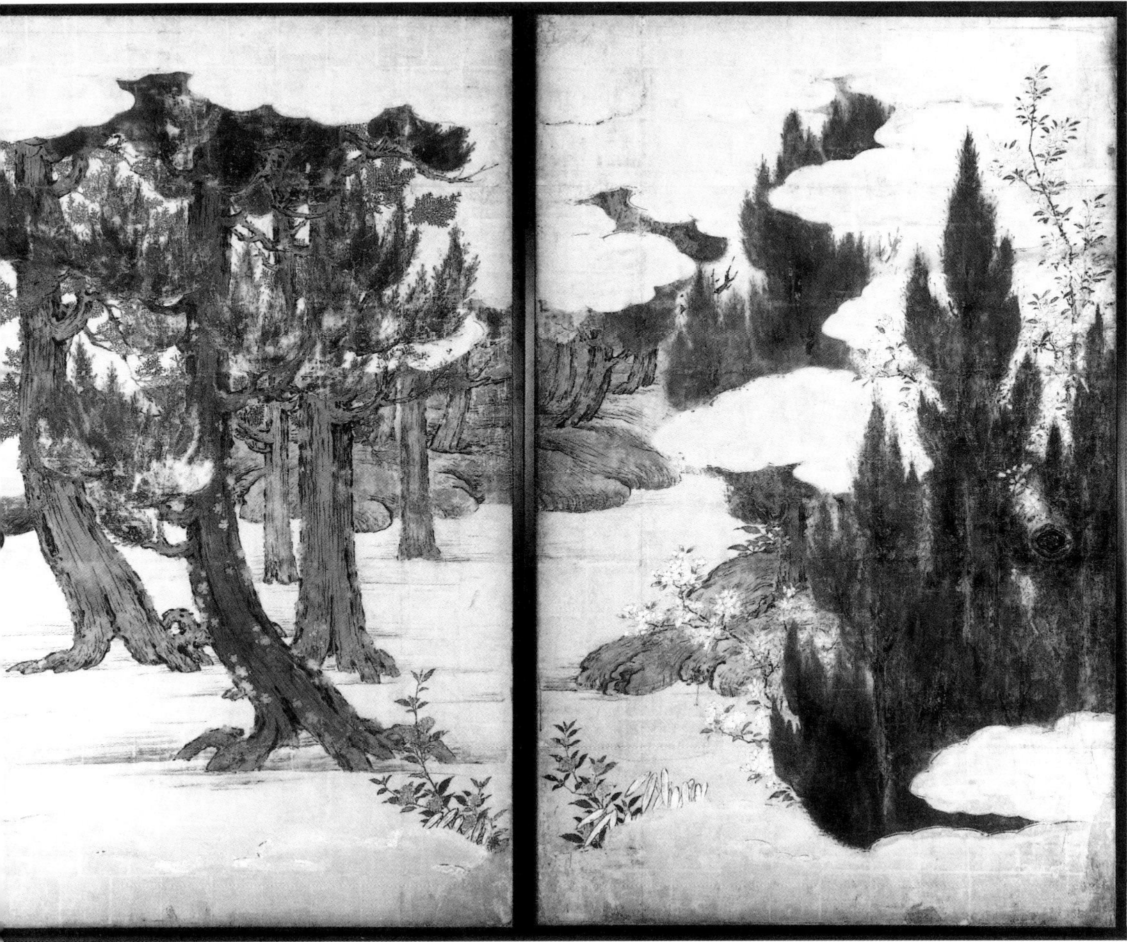

FIG. 92 Kano Mitsunobu. *Flowers and Birds of the Four Seasons.* 1600. Sliding-screen panels; ink, color, and gold leaf on paper. First Room, Kangakuin, Onjōji, Ōtsu.

ambitions, not only in its ranges of themes but also in its colorful, glowing, and visually commanding manner of describing them. While it stood, Azuchi captured the viewer's eye, and even after its destruction set the tone for subsequent projects.

Azuchi's prescription of grandly scaled gold-and-polychrome paintings was repeated, with numerous variations, in the most important buildings erected in the following decades. Gifu Castle, another of Nobunaga's now-lost grand edifices, is described by Luis Frois as a labyrinth: "Leading off from the first gallery there would be about 15 or 20 *zashiki* [rooms], all decorated with *byōbu,* or screens painted with gold, with the locks and fittings of pure gold." Frois also describes buildings within Hideyoshi's Osaka Castle compound that especially impressed him, for they "are adorned with a great variety of paintings depicting scenes from nature and events in the ancient histories of Japan and China."[17]

These precedents help explain why, beyond the iconographic demands of its program, the interior of Sutemaru's building is so thoroughly covered with its luxuriantly painted compendium of floral subjects. Most of the wall and sliding-door surfaces, from

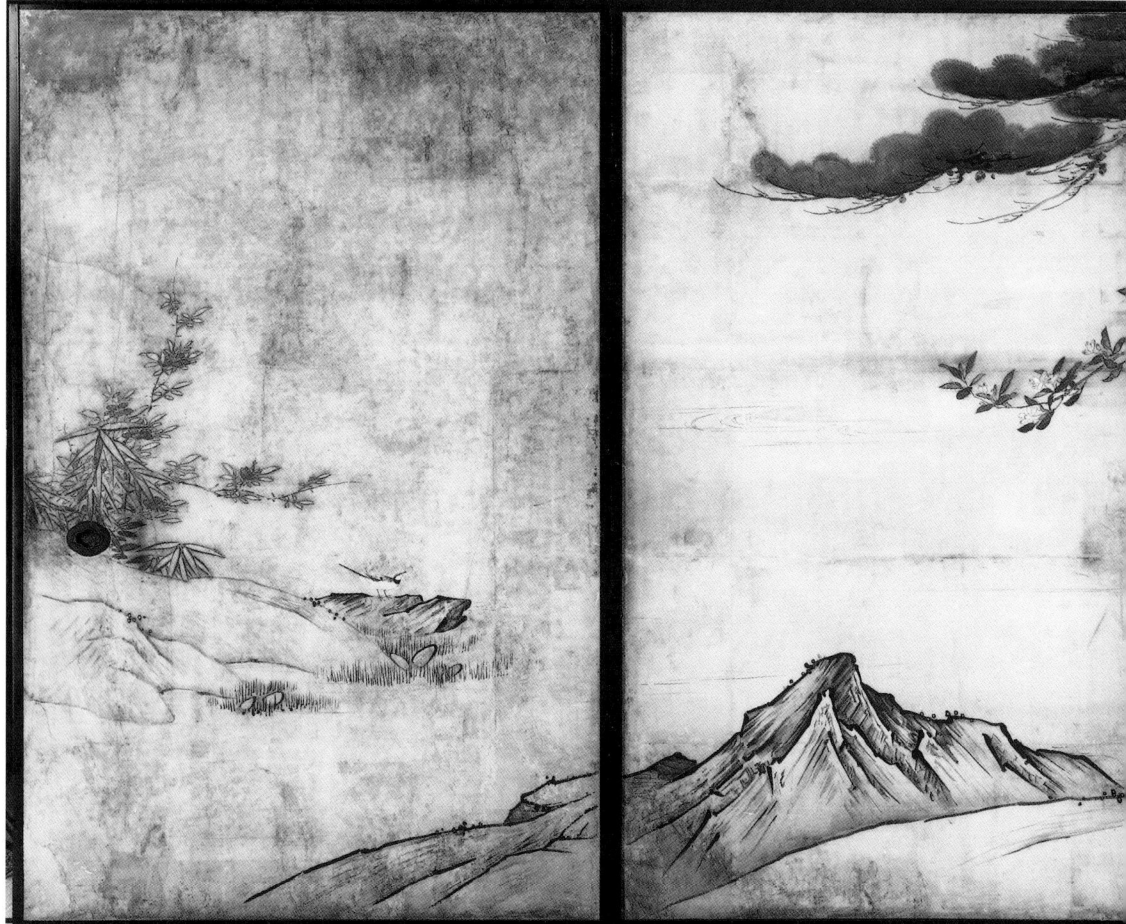

floor to ceiling, are covered with polychrome and gold-leaf paintings of flowers and trees;[18] even in the space between the lintels and the ceiling a painted frieze of wisteria and blossoming cherry trees encircles the room. The sixty coffers of the raised ceiling each contain an individual polychrome painting, surrounded by a gold-leafed paper frame, of a tree or flower subject. The natural luxuriance of the subject matter is matched by the artistic lushness of the color and gold leaf, which, of course, serves to enhance the elysian effect. It is difficult to imagine an essay in floral and paradisal imagery more suitably conveyed by its medium.

The importance of the project would imply a painter of major standing and, based on stylistic analysis, scholarly opinion has reasonably attributed the paintings to Kano Eitoku's son Mitsunobu and his workshop.[19] For this attribution the most important benchmark is the Guest Hall of the Kangakuin, a Toyotomi-sponsored subtemple of Onjōji in Ōtsu, and its Mitsunobu paintings dated to 1600 and divided between the First Room and Second Room.[20] In the polychrome-and-gold paintings of the First Room several varieties of flowers and trees, many in full bloom, are distributed across the broad horizontal expanse of the panels *(Fig. 92)*.[21] Though these are concentrated mainly within a

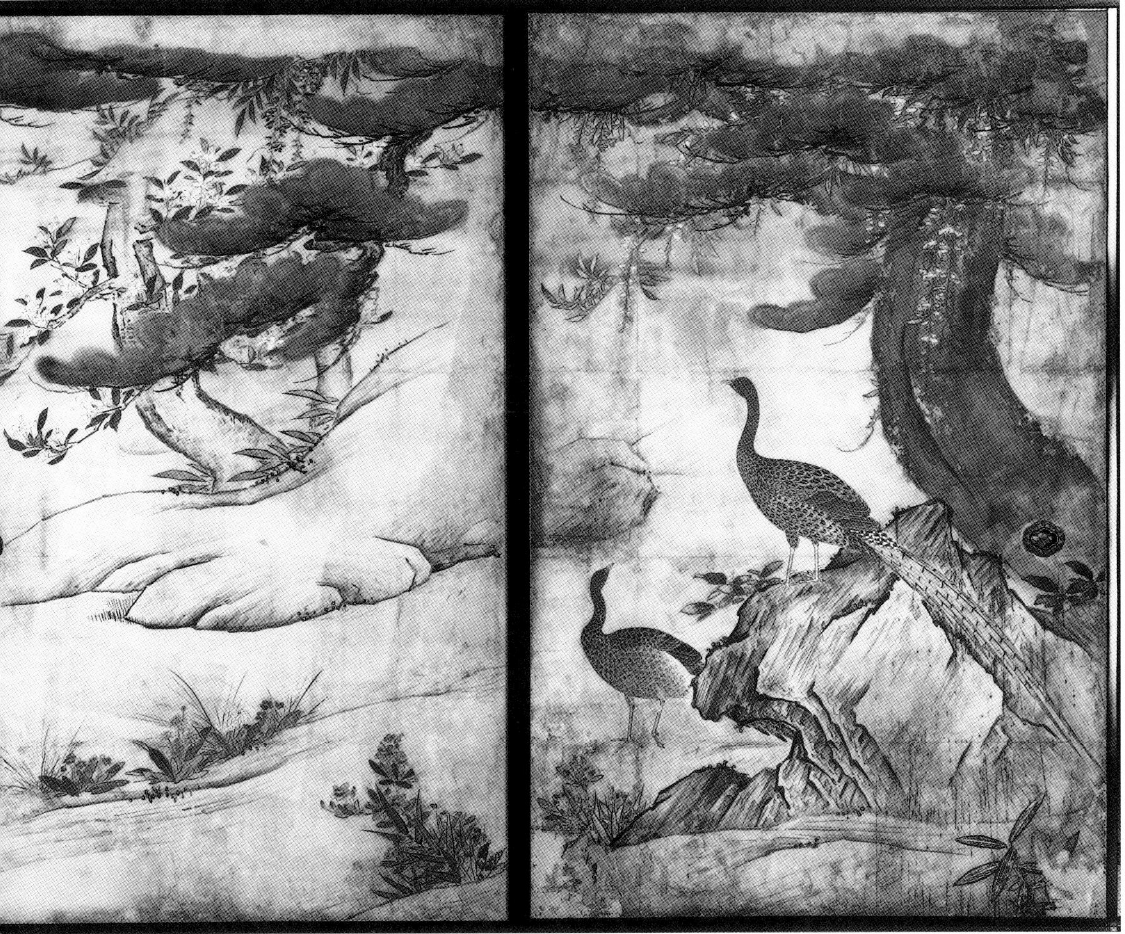

FIG. 93 Kano Mitsunobu. *Flowers and Birds of the Four Seasons.* 1600. Sliding-screen panels; ink and color on paper. Second Room, Kangakuin, Onjōji, Ōtsu.

deep foreground space, recession into an even deeper middle ground is indicated by trees, glimpses of landscape, and diagonal paths breaking here and there through the otherwise enveloping gold clouds. In the Second Room no gold leaf is employed, and most of the background landscape is executed in ink, but major motifs such as trees, flowers, and birds are represented in color *(Fig. 93)*.[22] Recession is described into a vague middle distance.

Although Sutemaru's paintings, in which dense gold clouds deny recession beyond the foreground, lack the conspicuous depth of the Kangakuin works, they share other telling features. Both buildings contain similar passages of description—of luxuriant fuyō plants *(Figs. 15, 94)*, for example—that strongly suggest the same workshop at both sites. In addition to individual correspondences, and of greater significance, however, is a nearly equivalent approach to the overall characterization of subject matter.

Mitsunobu's distinctive delicacy of form appears similarly achieved in both buildings. For example, a gentle attenuation of form marks the chrysanthemums in Sutemaru's building *(Fig. 9)* and the thin plum branch that glides across two panels in the

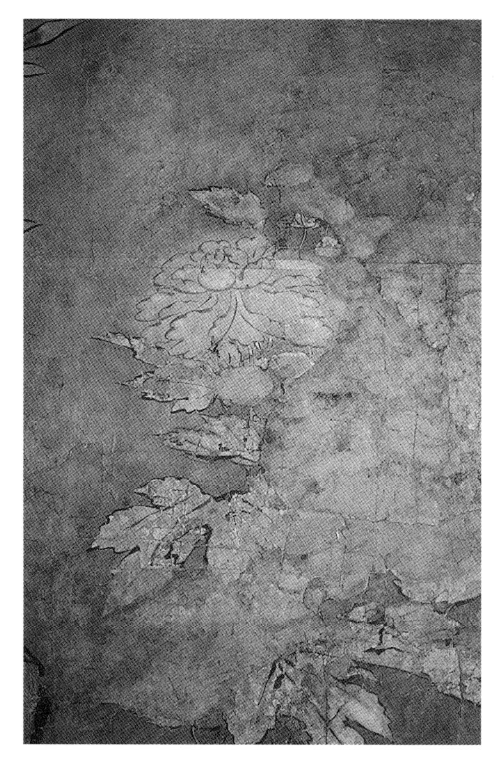

FIG. 94 (top) Kano Mitsunobu. Detail of fuyō from *Flowers and Birds of the Four Seasons.* 1600. Sliding-screen panels; ink and color on paper. Second Room, Kangakuin, Onjōji, Ōtsu. Photograph by the author.

FIG. 95 (bottom) Attributed to Kano Eitoku. *Cypress Tree.* Late sixteenth century. Six-fold screen; ink, color, and gold leaf on paper. Tokyo National Museum.

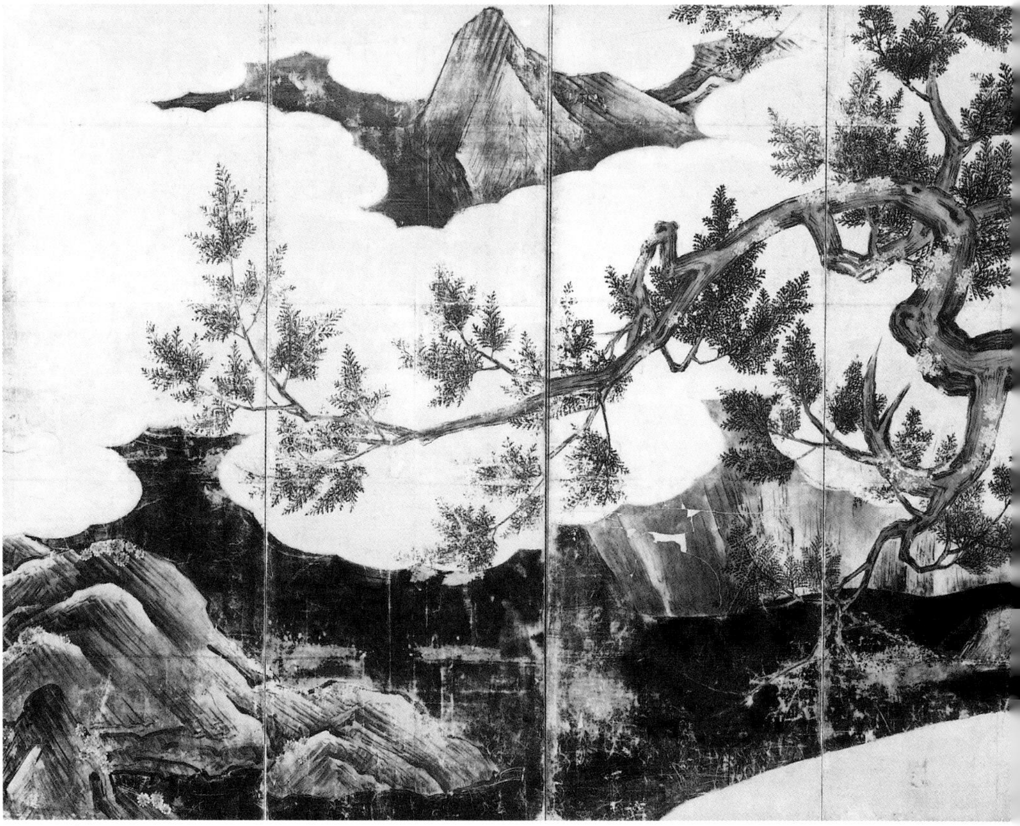

Kangakuin First Room *(Fig. 92)*. In both sites, even the largest trees have gently curving trunks *(Figs. 11, 93)*, in marked contrast to the more dynamic, muscular tree trunks favored by Mitsunobu's father, Eitoku *(Fig. 95)*. In this first decade after Eitoku's death, Mitsunobu led the Kano workshop away from the vigorous, energized painting style of his father, and it is Mitsunobu's style that clearly characterizes the paintings of Sutemaru's building. Though Sutemaru's paintings deny recession past the foreground, in contrast to the conspicuous deeper space in the Kangakuin paintings, the evidence of our eyes suggests that paintings in Sutemaru's building may be fairly credited to Mitsunobu's circle, if not given to Mitsunobu himself.

In light of the Toyotomi sponsorship of Sutemaru's building, it is not surprising to find Kano Mitsunobu playing a leading role in the project. Mitsunobu closely served the warrior rulers of the late sixteenth and early seventeenth centuries, from Oda Nobunaga through Tokugawa Ieyasu, and enjoyed an especially active artist-patron relationship with the Toyotomi. While still in his early twenties Mitsunobu probably assisted his father Eitoku on two important commissions for Hideyoshi: the decoration of Osaka Castle in 1585 and of Jurakutei in 1587.[23] A Kano workshop lineage informs us that in the ninth month of 1590, following Eitoku's death, Hideyoshi granted Mitsunobu land in Ōhara near Kyoto with an annual stipend of 100 *koku*.[24] In 1592 Mitsunobu executed paintings for Hideyoshi's Nagoya Castle in Kyushu (the base from which he launched the Korean

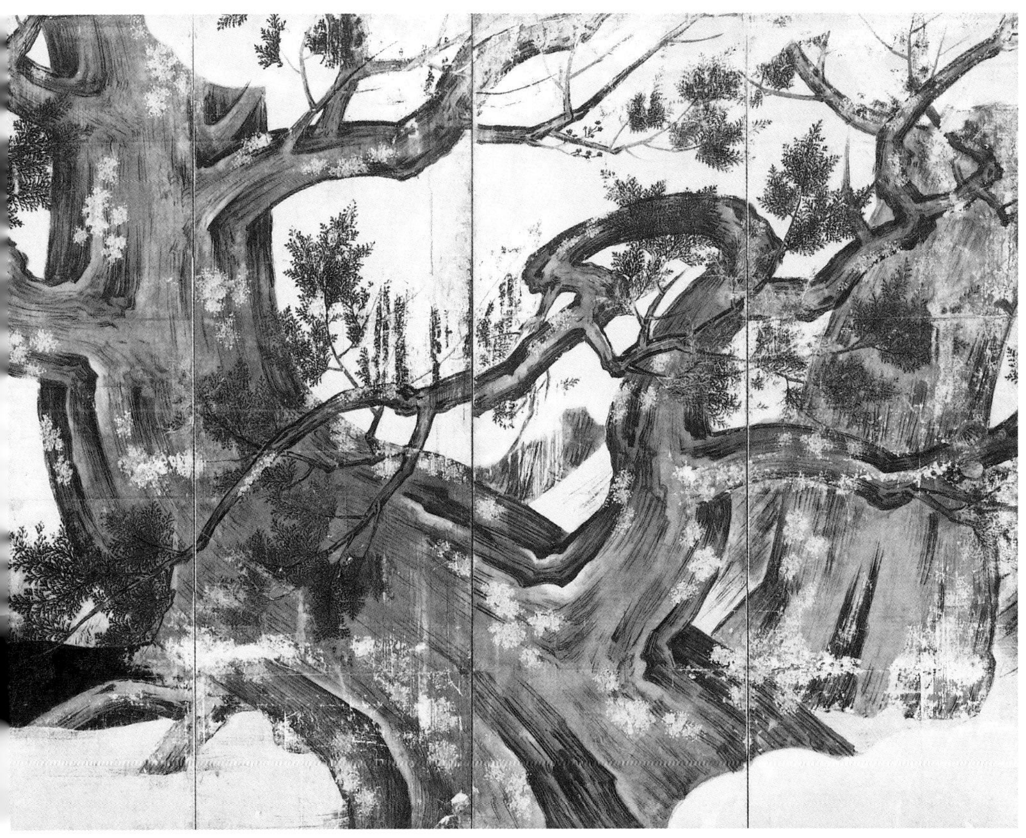

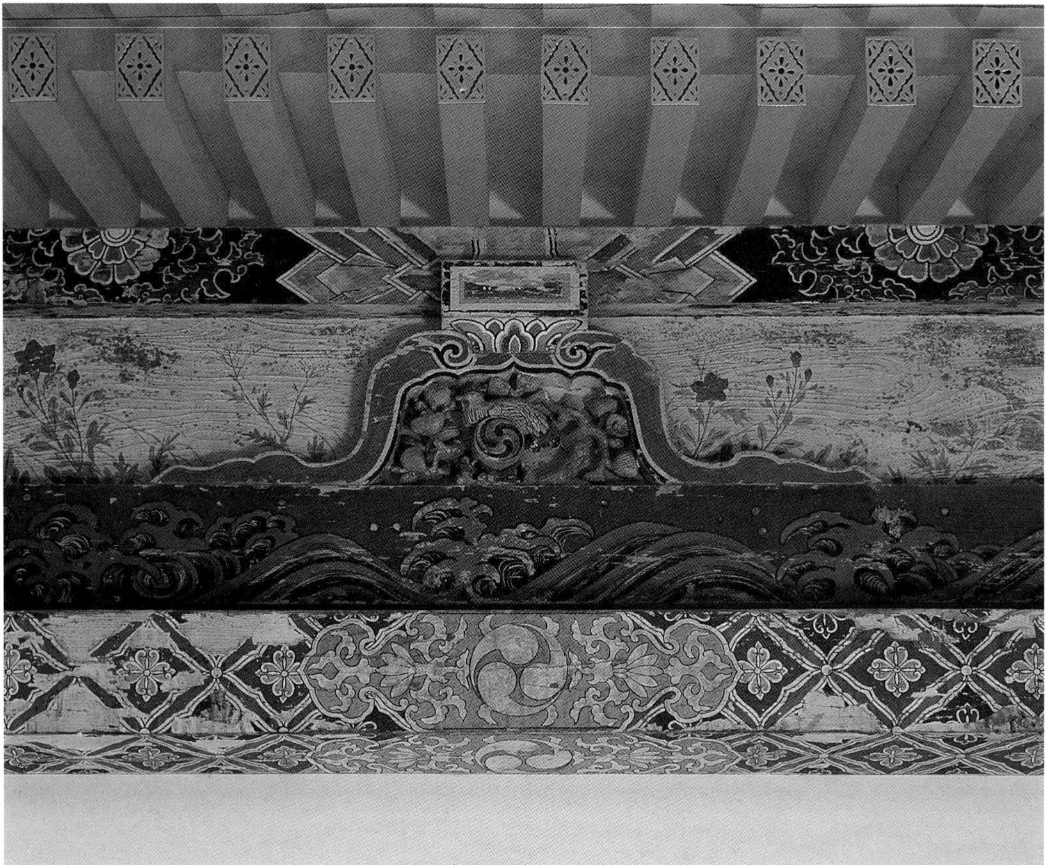

FIG. 96 Kaerumata wood carving. 1522. Sannōin, Kongōbuji, Wakayama Prefecture. Photograph by Aihara Isao, provided by INAX.

invasions), and scholars surmise that two years later, in 1594, he worked with Kano Sanraku on the decoration of Fushimi Castle.[25] In a letter of 1602 Mitsunobu mentions official commissions in both Fushimi and Osaka, so we know that Mitsunobu continued to work for the Toyotomi even following Hideyoshi's death in 1598.[26] This is confirmed by the extant Kangakuin paintings, as well as by the ceiling he painted for the Shōkokuji Dharma Hall, built with Hideyori's sponsorship in 1605.[27] A painter of Mitsunobu's high status was the logical choice for a monument as important as Sutemaru's building. How material was his role in its decoration is a question we shall consider below.

RELIEF WOOD CARVINGS

New to sixteenth-century Japan was a permutation of the old medium of architectural wood carving: relief sculptures of pictorial subjects applied to buildings, most often on the exterior. Earlier practice, as seen in the 1522 Sannōin at Kongōbuji, for instance, mostly limited these carvings to small architectural fields located high up on a building,

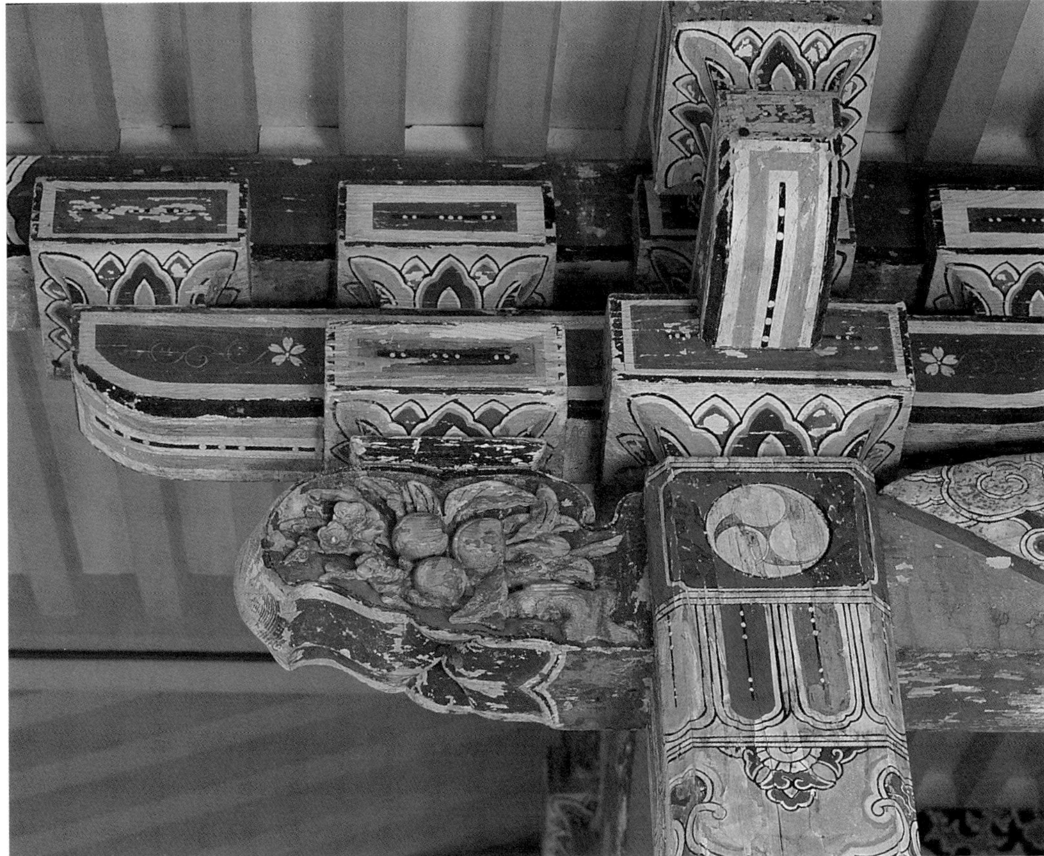

FIG. 97 Tabasami wood carving. 1522. Sannōin, Kongōbuji, Wakayama Prefecture. Photograph by Aihara Isao, provided by INAX.

such as *kaerumata* braces *(Fig. 96)*, beam ends *(tabasami) (Fig. 97)*, and the long horizontal friezes above the lintel; some Shinto shrines, such as the Ōsasahara Jinja Honden in Shiga Prefecture, had larger panels of relief carvings on exterior walls at the rear of the building *(wakishōji, Figs. 98, 99)*.[28] Never were these carvings the centerpiece of the architectural whole; rather they helped to frame the mostly unadorned facades of Buddhist temples and Shinto shrines.

The mid-sixteenth century saw a sudden vogue for enormous, usually wall-sized, architectural carvings embellishing the exteriors of important structures. The inspiration for this trend is unclear—similar architectural carvings, popular in Ming China, may have had an impact in Japan—but the trend itself is unmistakable and the carvings inspired comment. The English shipmaster Ralph Coppindall, for one, who visited Japan in the early seventeenth century, wrote home about the many "handsome" wooden bridges built in Osaka by the Toyotomi rulers, whose chief castle was located there, "all of them richly ornamented with carved work, while the main posts of the railing were mounted with thick copper. In the whole course of my life, I never saw anything equal to . . . these bridges."[29] Under the Toyotomi, even the public thoroughfares

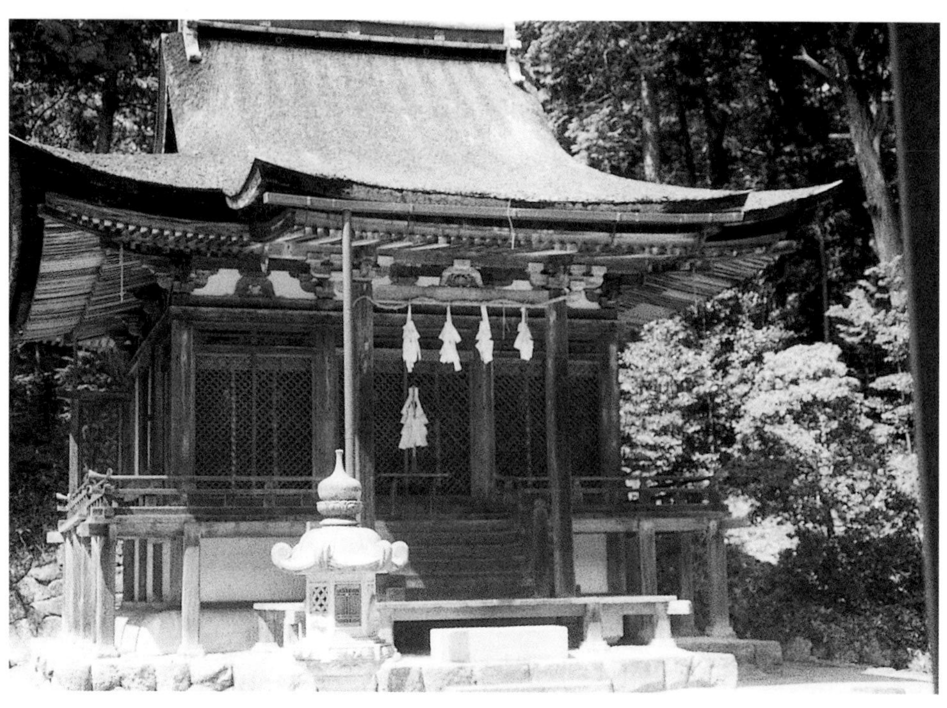

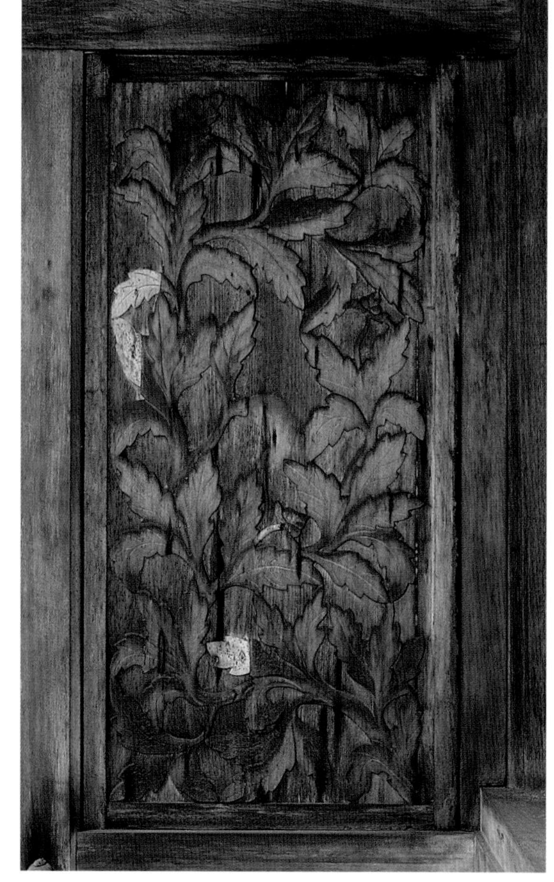

FIG. 98 (top) Ōsasahara Jinja Honden. 1414. Shiga Prefecture. Photograph by the author.

FIG. 99 (bottom) Wakishōji panel wood carvings. 1414. Ōsasahara Jinja Honden, Shiga Prefecture. Photograph by Aihara Isao, provided by INAX.

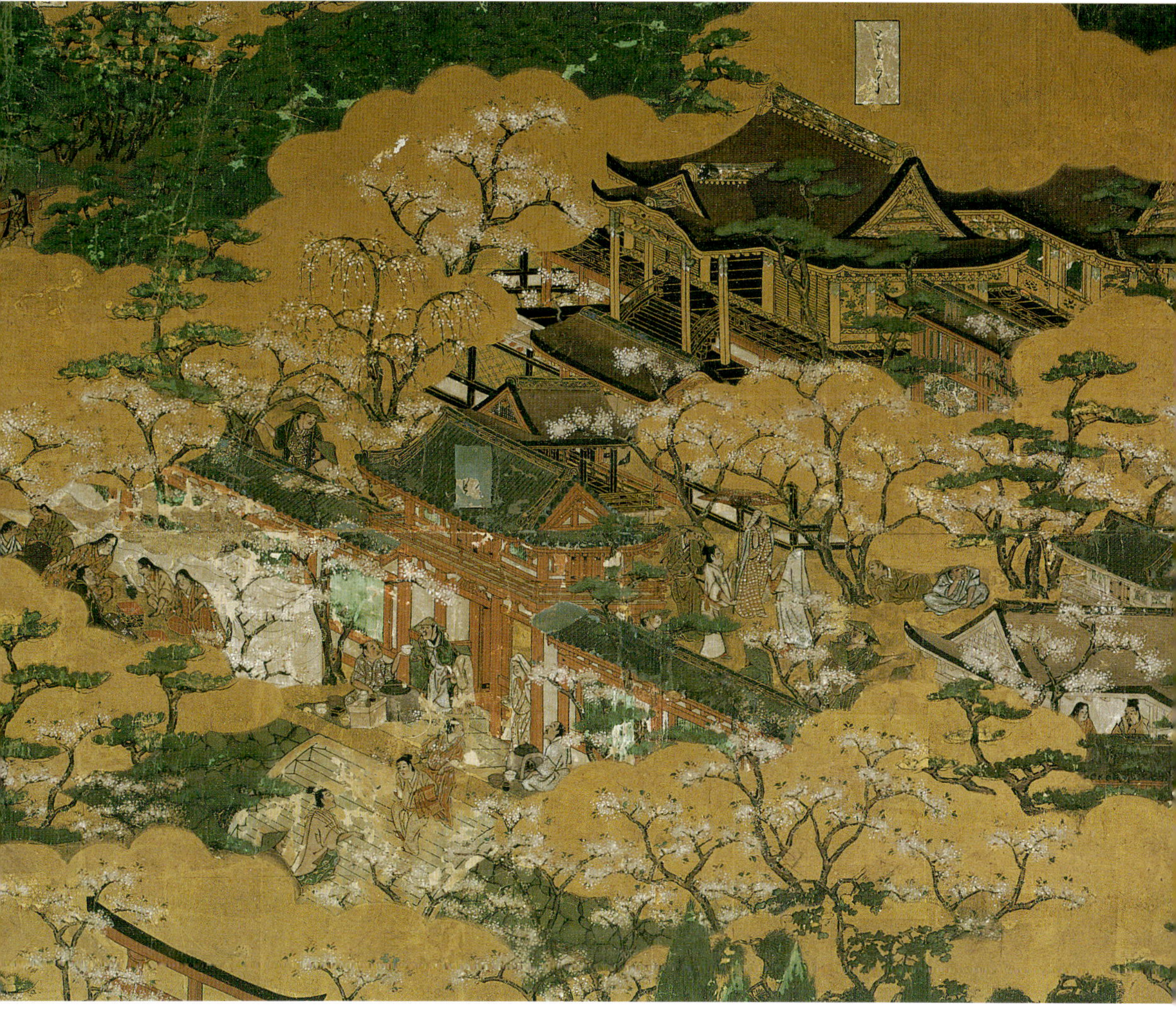

FIG. 100 Detail of building labelled as "Toyokuni," from Fig. 26.

of their chief castle town and bustling commercial port were thus made magnificent with this newly fashionable embellishment.

Osaka's carving-laden bridges are long gone, but pictorial representations of architectural structures and extant monuments attest the florescence of this new fashion. In the upper right corner of the ex-Funaki collection *Sights in and around the Capital,* for example, set in a grove of blossoming cherry trees, within a walled temple precinct just above the Great Buddha Hall, is a building with a hip-and-gable roof, a projecting porch, and—notably—floral carvings on its exterior *(Figs. 26,100).*[30] A cartouche identifies the building as part of "Toyokuni," Hideyoshi's vast memorial complex in Kyoto, the Toyokuni Shrine.[31] The carving-embellished edifice occupies one of the critical sacred spots in Kyoto, and proclaims its significance not by massive size, as did the Great Buddha Hall, but by its conspicuous exterior ornament of wood carvings.

Several of the most important surviving examples are gates, structures that stand

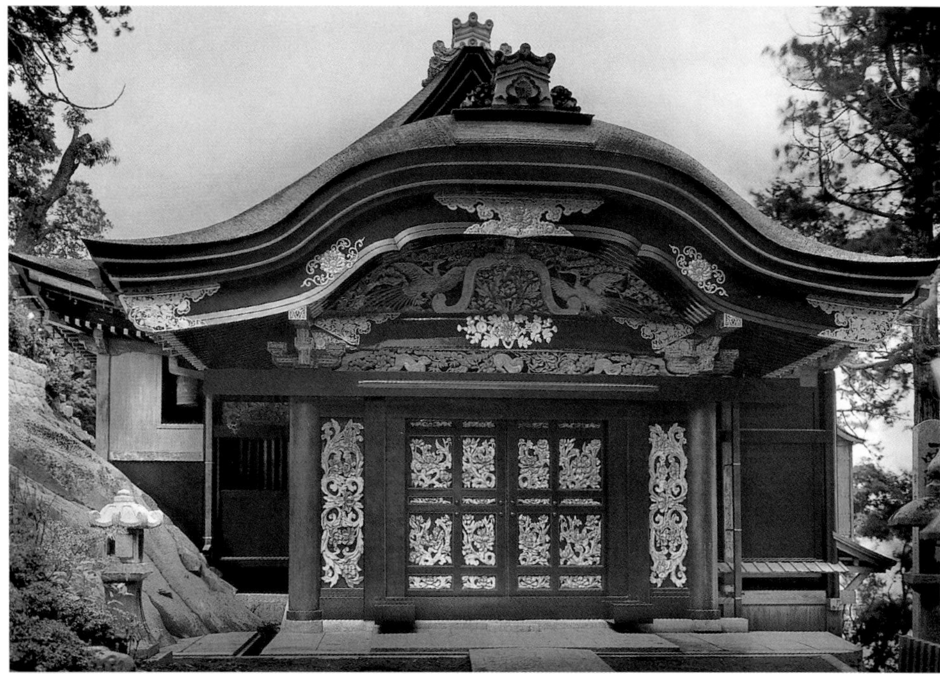

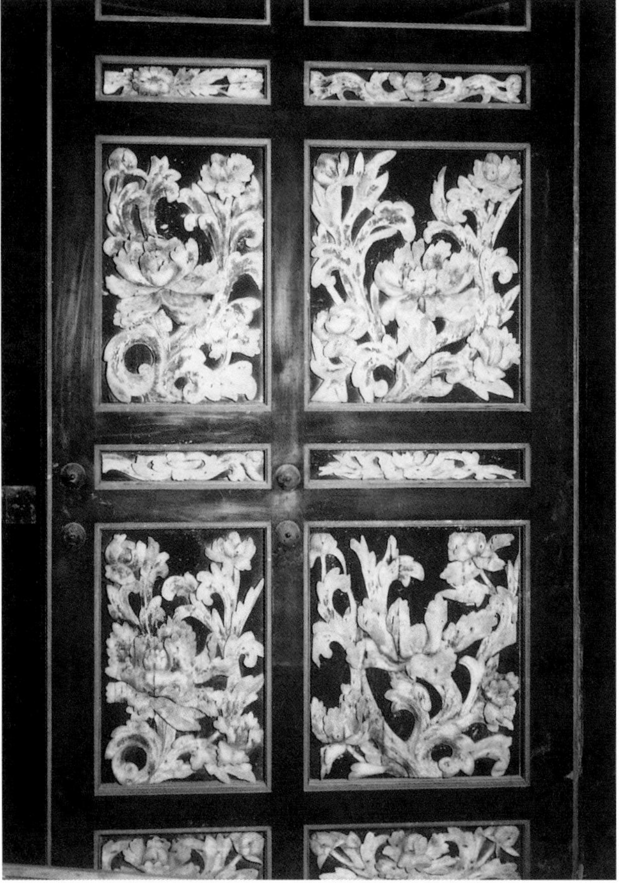

FIG. 101 (top) Karamon. Late sixteenth century. Hōgonji, Chikubushima, Shiga Prefecture. Photograph by Nara National Cultural Properties Research Institute.

FIG. 102 (bottom) Karamon. Wood carvings of peony scroll. Late sixteenth century. Hōgonji, Chikubushima, Shiga Prefecture. Photograph by Kōrinsha.

as the public face of, and entryway into, restricted inner precincts.[32] The Karamon of Hōgonji, once part of the Toyokuni Shrine, was removed to its present location on Chikubushima in 1602 *(Figs. 101, 102).*[33] Its lavish carvings comprise a busy tangle of floral peony scrolls, a meandering vine-like adaptation of the peony-plant motif that earlier was favored for carved friezes encircling the upper reaches of a building. Here, the peony scroll covers much of the gate, including the many rectangular compartments of the doors and their surrounds, ineluctably drawing attention to the gate and to the structure it introduces. The Karamon of Daigoji's Sanbōin, smaller but with equally conspicuous reliefs, was constructed in 1598 with Hideyoshi's sponsorship *(Fig. 103).* Here, two immense pairs of chrysanthemum and paulownia crests, symbols of the Toyotomi house, are carved front and center across the four doors of the gate, announcing the patron of the magnificent building and garden within. Architectural relief carvings were an effective means to make a public statement—doubtless one strong reason for their popularity.

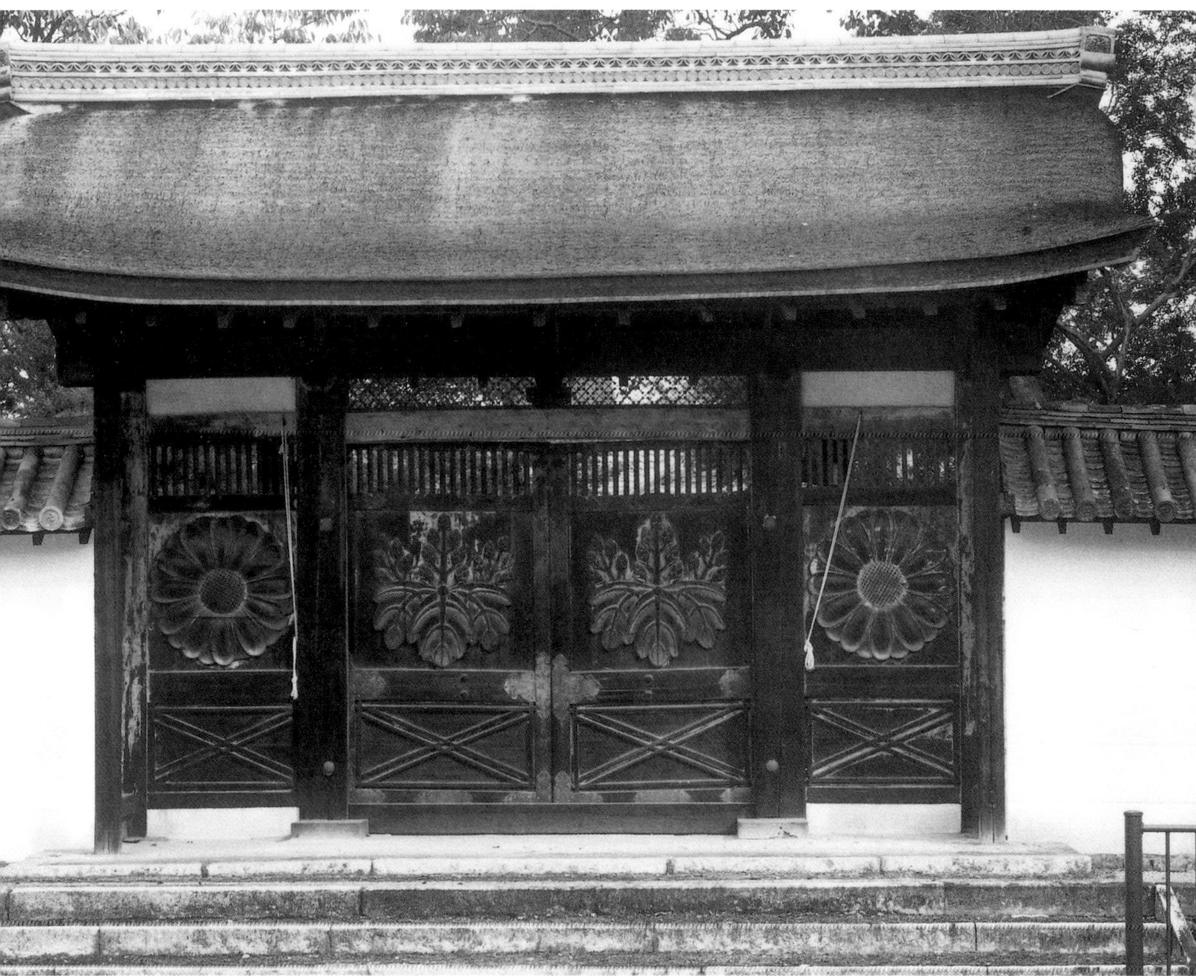

FIG. 103 Karamon. Late sixteenth century. Sanbōin, Daigoji, Kyoto. Photograph by Kyoto National Museum.

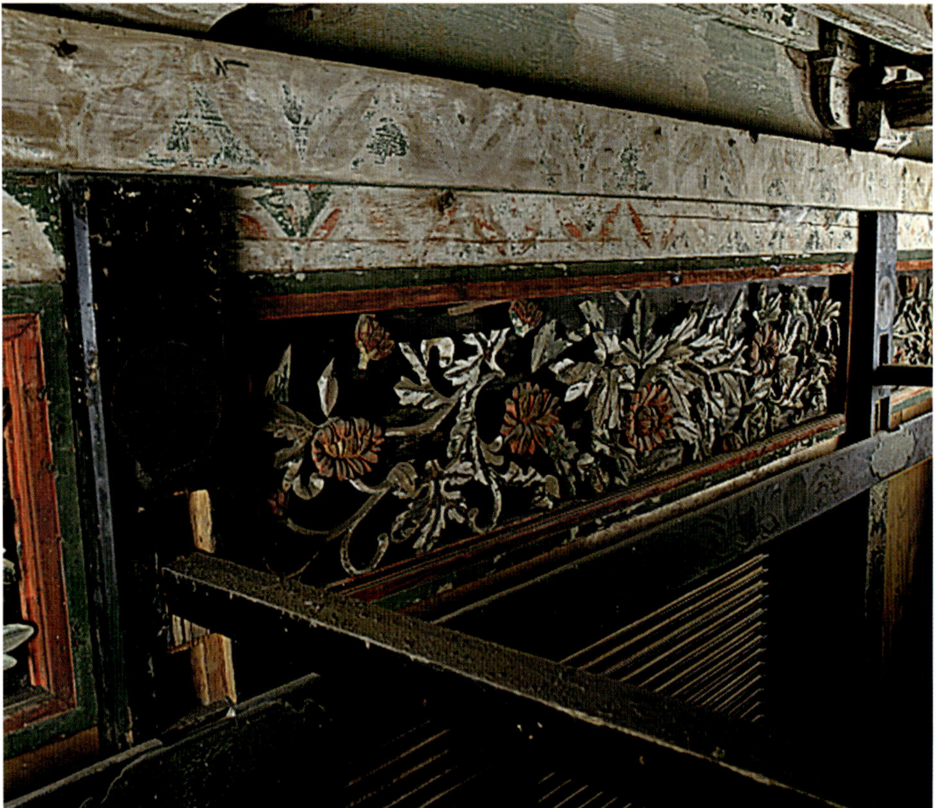

FIG. 104 Tsukubusuma Main Hall. Wood carvings of floral scroll above lintel-beam. Moya exterior. Chikubushima, Shiga Prefecture.

Sutemaru's monument, the earliest extant building with all-over architectural carvings, well demonstrates the potential of this freshly reconfigured medium. Some of the reliefs are of the older variety: repeated tendrils of a floral scroll, for example, fill the elevated frieze and embellish this framing element of the building in the time-honored manner *(Fig. 104)*. More conspicuous and especially novel, however, are the massive carvings that originally covered the walls of all eight flanking bays of the building's four sides; six walls of carvings remain today *(Figs. 3–7, 105)*.[34] Each bay features either chrysanthemum or fuyō plants, innovative subject matter in this medium that was dictated by the iconographic program. Perhaps reflecting the newness of these subjects in massive relief carvings and hence their not-yet-standardized depiction, several walls contain apparently unscripted elements along with the overwhelmingly dominant plant: one contains a passage of clouds; two more, a couple of long-tailed birds; yet another, a boldly protruding rock form. These details add visual diversity without distracting from the commanding presence of the iconographically required subject matter.

Unlike the highly stylized carvings found on the two gates and in the frieze of Sutemaru's building, the plants as represented in the bays convey some sense of their natural state: in place of a continuous vegetal scroll, individual plants are depicted growing

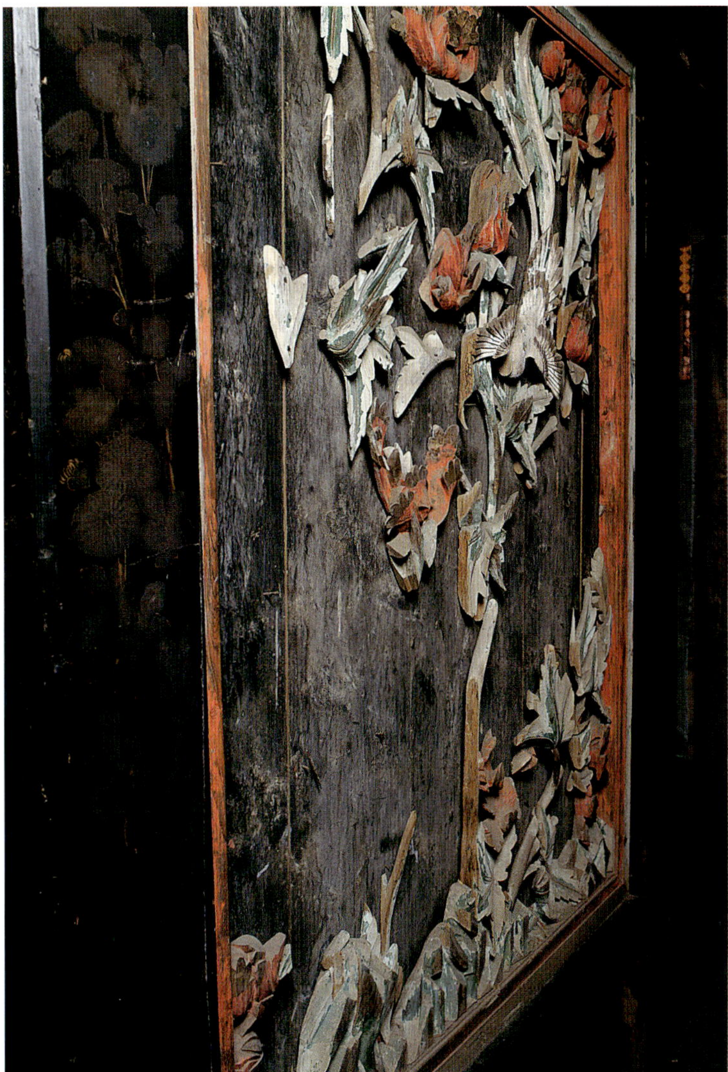

FIG. 105 Tsukubusuma Main Hall. Wood carving of fuyō. Moya exterior, east side, north bay. Chikubushima, Shiga Prefecture.

from a rocky landscape and in varied states of bloom. The intent, however, was not naturalism. Displaying a perfect regularity not found in our everyday world, the plants trace a controlled, sinuous ascent and spread across their space with an artificial evenness. They are impossibly large, magnificent specimens that dwarf their natural models. These adaptations make the plants easily legible and also identify them as the principal carriers of meaning on the exterior. To enhance the legibility, the carvings were colored with bright pigments, now partially abraded.

Carvings allowed pictorial representation out of doors, the exterior counterparts to the large-scale paintings on paper used within this and other important Momoyama buildings. They had the physical substance to withstand weather that would have quickly destroyed fragile paintings, and the three-dimensionality to exploit strong and shifting exterior daylight so as to create dramatically lit and shadowed pictures. Not only did they convey essential symbolic meanings, but equally important, they called attention to a structure even amid busy outdoor surroundings. Conspicuous, and in the Momoyama period novel, the carvings proclaimed that this building deserved to be noticed.

Large-scale architectural relief carvings that created highly figured, conspicuous facades continued even more popular in the early seventeenth century. As we shall see in the following chapter, many were commissioned by the Toyotomi in their home territory surrounding Osaka. In the early Edo period the Tokugawa adopted this mode of ornament as the family style for Tōshōgū, the many memorial shrines to Ieyasu, of which Nikkō's was only the most elaborate.

MAKIE LACQUER: "THE MOST UNIVERSAL ART OF THE KINGDOM"

For the Momoyama viewer, the medium that most clearly distinguished Sutemaru's ensemble as exceptional was the makie lacquer. This is also perhaps the material most difficult for the modern observer to fully appreciate. Even present-day Japanese, though more familiar with lacquer than their Western counterparts, often unconsciously accept a Western paradigm of the arts that disparages lacquer as a "minor art." For native English speakers, the difficulty is built into their very language, in which the word "lacquer" designates a wide range of materials; the dictionary defines lacquer as a spirit varnish, such as shellac, of either natural or synthetic origin, a sweeping definition that fails to specify the essential qualities of the material used in Japan.[35] Little of what the word *lacquer* denotes, in other words, applies in any meaningful way to this Japanese substance; and because the English term is at once so broad and so familiar, it has worked against a precise and accurate understanding of Japanese lacquer. It is important, therefore, to recover the specific implications that made lacquer so important in Momoyama Japan.

During the Momoyama period itself Europeans then in Japan were first attempting to explain to their compatriots back home what this unfamiliar material was and why it was so highly regarded.[36] Of those explanations, the most perceptive was written, not surprisingly, by João Rodrigues in *The History of the Church of Japan.*[37] Rodrigues combined an insider's understanding of the substance with an outsider's awareness of what his European audience would need explained, along with the ability to explain those things clearly.

He begins, "There is a universal art throughout the whole kingdom that has something in common with painting. This is the art of varnishing, which we call here *uruxar,* from the word *urushi.*" Rodrigues thus plainly and forcefully states the relative importance in Japan of this thing he is about to describe: it is practiced countrywide and is in some way comparable with painting, a tantalizing point he returns to later in his discussion. He calls it by a word familiar to his European audience, "varnishing," but in the same sentence also identifies it by its Japanese name, urushi, and states that "we," meaning the Europeans then in Japan, refer to the use of this material as "uruxar." That hybrid term, neither

Japanese nor Portuguese, was invented by the European cognoscenti in Japan, who combined the Japanese word *urushi* with the Portuguese verb ending *xar*.[38] In other words, the Europeans fabricated a hybrid neologism to denote this thing they encountered in Japan. They did so because something, or some things, about this newly encountered and unusual material made them realize that their own language had no adequate designation for it.[39]

Rodrigues then relates some of the basic facts about Japanese lacquer. It is, he writes,

> . . . made from the gum of a certain tree. They tap the trunk at a certain time of the year and draw off an excellent gum that is used as varnish; these trees are also found in China, Cauchi, Cambodia, and Siam. But of all these nations the Japanese stand supreme in this art, for they are so skilful that they can make a varnished object look as if it were made of smooth shiny ivory.

Japanese lacquer is made from the sap of a tree indigenous to Asia *(Rhus verniciflua)*, and the Japanese have mastered the making and using of it to a degree unmatched elsewhere. Rodrigues goes on to explain that this material is widely employed in Japan, from "all their tableware, such as bowls, tables, and other vessels and utensils, as well as the tables and trays from which they eat" to "the handles of lances, and the sheathes of their blades, and a multitude of other things," that is, on all sorts of portable household and personal objects. He notes its wonderful physical properties: strength, imperviousness to water and heat, and, as he noted previously, a sensuous surface, like "smooth shiny ivory." In essence, Rodrigues tells his audience that the material in question is a quintessentially Japanese product and needs to be thought of as fundamentally different from anything known in Europe. He ends this descriptive part of his account by calling it "the most universal art of the kingdom."

What Rodrigues found most intriguing and impressive was not merely the ubiquitousness of the material in Japan or its admirable durability. More than these things, he admired how the Japanese, in their use of this material, transcended utility and created beauty:

> This [Japanese lacquer] has a certain affinity to the art of painting in that some of these craftsmen gild in a special way the finest examples of this work in the discovered world. Using pure gold powder, they paint various objects in which they set flowers made of gold and silver leaf and mother-of-pearl.

Some lacquerwork resembles painting in that it incorporates pictorial imagery; it differs from painting in depicting the images with precious materials. Without relating in detail how these pictorial lacquers were made, Rodrigues was describing what the Japanese called makie lacquer, or "sprinkled-picture" lacquer. In this technique, metal particles, usually gold or silver, are sprinkled onto still-damp lacquer to create an image or pattern; the lacquer acts as an adhesive to the metal particles, and when it has hardened, the two mediums together create a lustrous, adamantine picture.

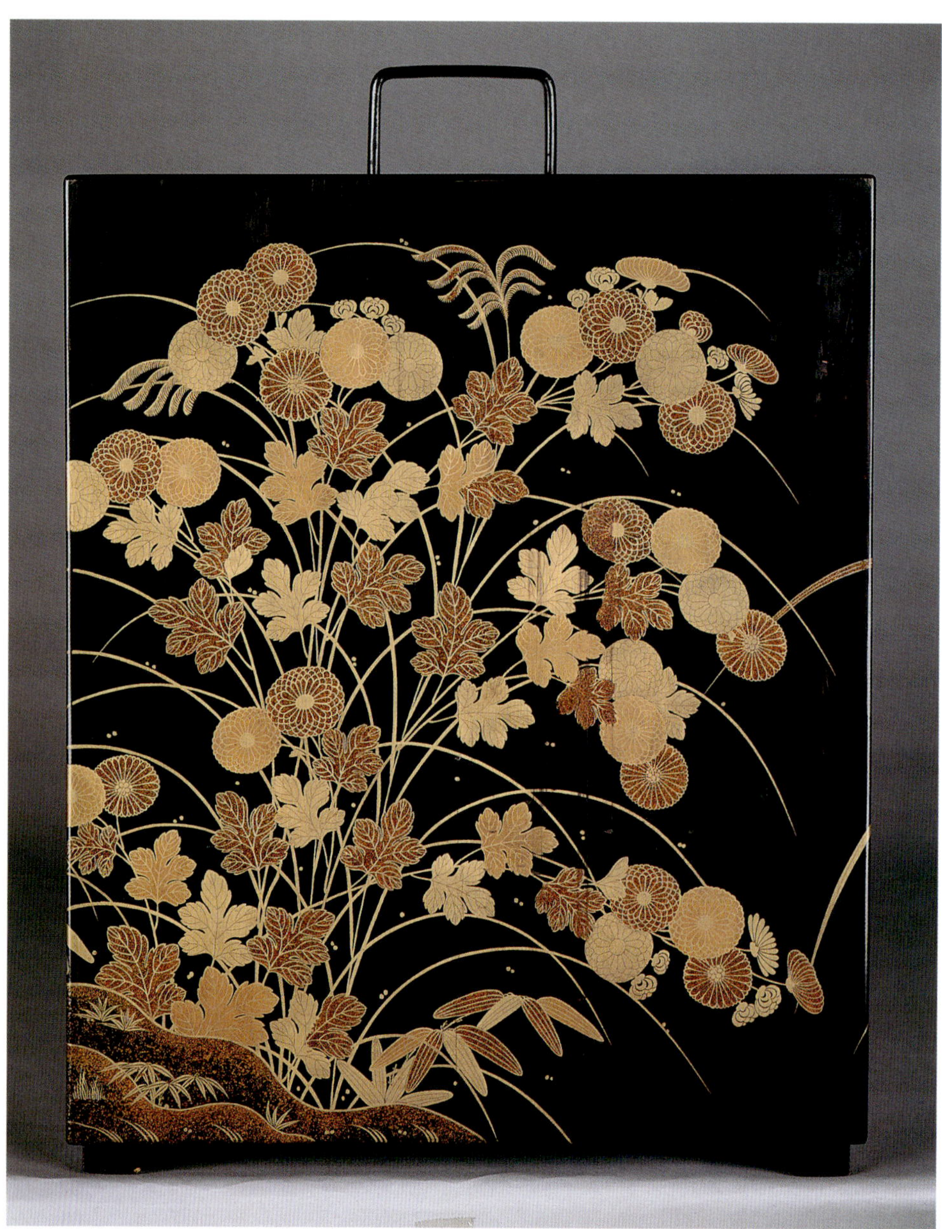

FIG. 106 Chest of drawers, back. Early seventeenth century. Makie lacquer on wood. Kōdaiji, Kyoto. Photograph by Kyoto National Museum.

FIG. 107 (opposite) Portable altar. Late sixteenth–early seventeenth century. Makie lacquer and inlaid mother-of-pearl on wood. Nagoya City Museum. Photograph by Kyoto National Museum.

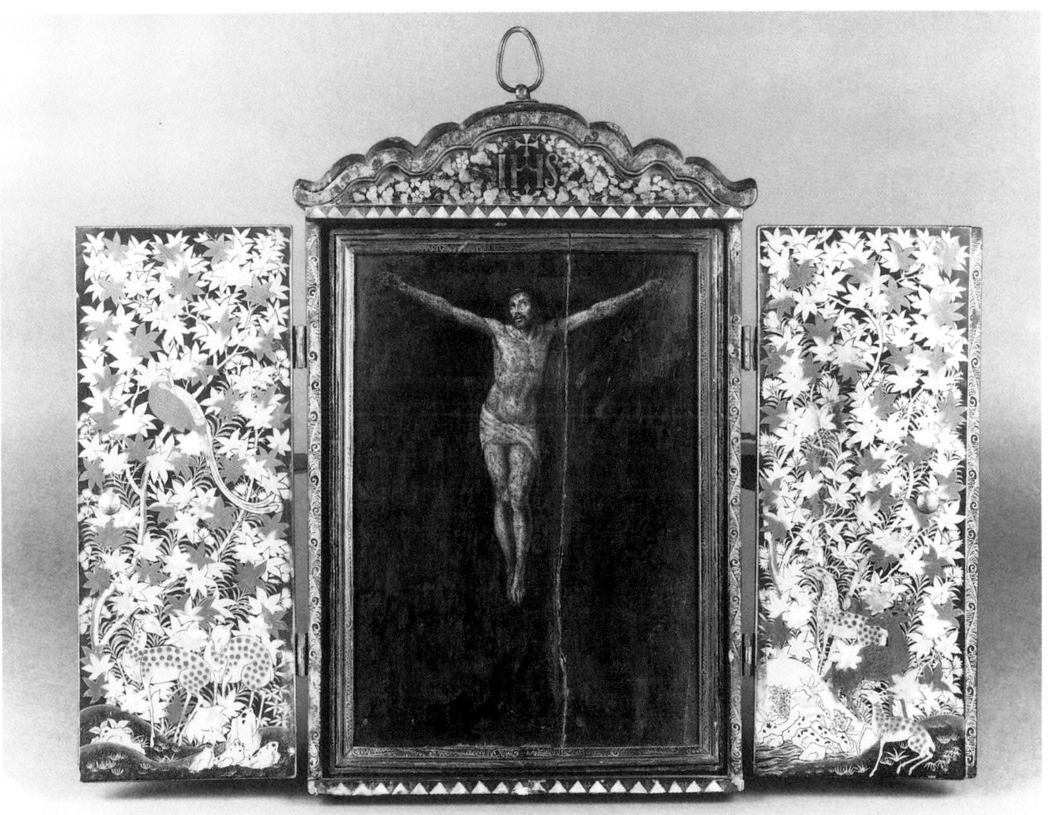

Excellent Momoyama examples of makie lacquer abound, well represented by a small chest from the Kyoto temple Kōdaiji (*Fig. 106* shows the back of the chest),[40] on which some parts of the design (e.g., many of the leaves) were executed with very fine gold powder, so densely sprinkled that it appears to be solid gold. To achieve the speckled look of some of the leaves and blossoms, on the other hand, larger particles of metal, which remain individually distinct, were sprinkled. Rodrigues also mentions "flowers made of gold and silver leaf and mother-of-pearl," a mode of decoration especially prevalent in lacquers made specifically for the European market—so-called Nanban lacquers *(Fig. 107).*

The costliness and opulence of these lacquers made the boxes appealing to the Momoyama audience. Rodrigues noted particularly that makie lacquer incorporates luxury materials, including gold and silver. Precious metals alone, however, would not have made makie lacquers so extraordinarily desirable—as we have seen, Japanese paintings, including those in Sutemaru's structure, frequently employ gold, but the lacquer itself displays these radiant materials to unique advantage. Lacquer transmits light, which is then reflected by the ground to which the lacquer is applied, making for a superbly lustrous surface. By embedding shell and particles of gold and silver in a multilayered coat of lacquer, the Japanese created pictures of a glowing richness unmatched in any other material.

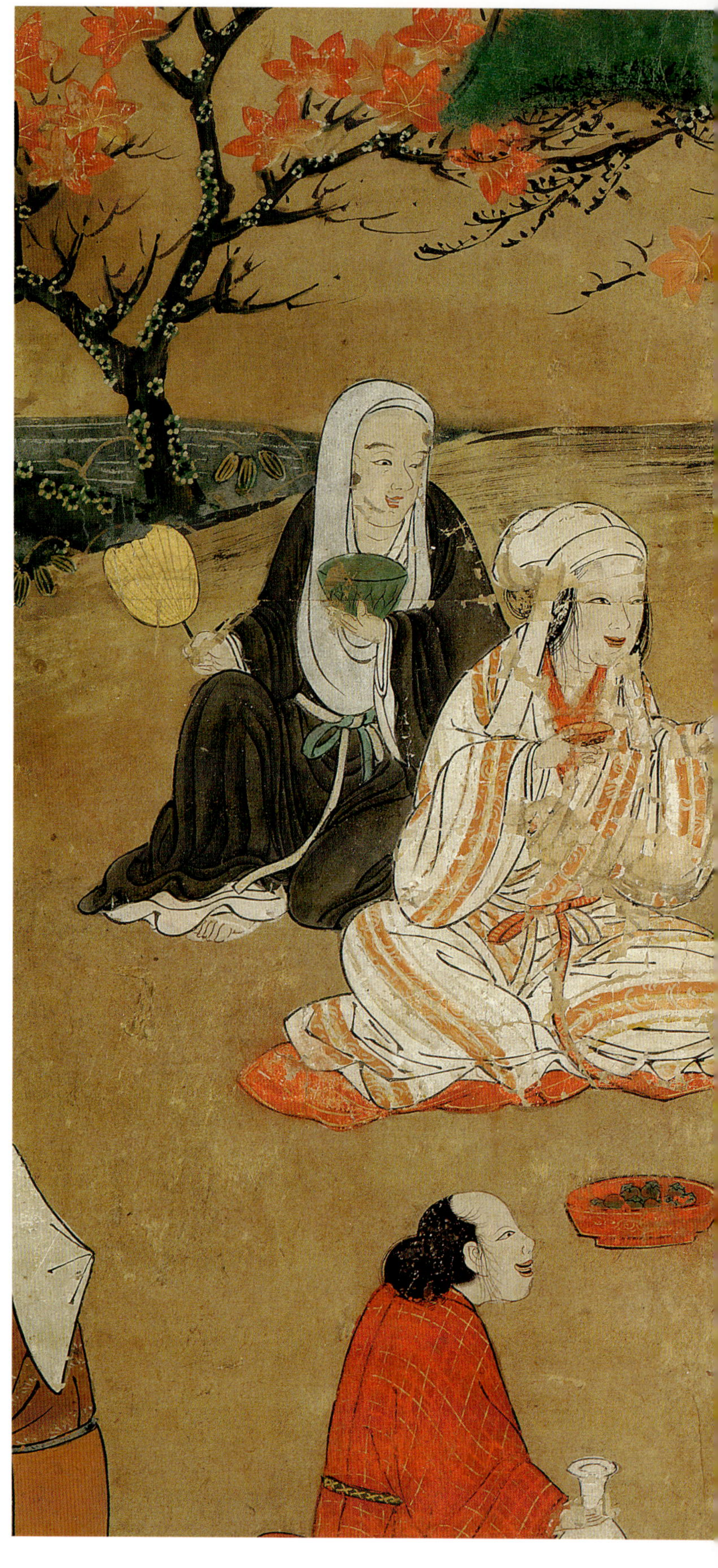

FIG. 108 Detail of Fig. 30.

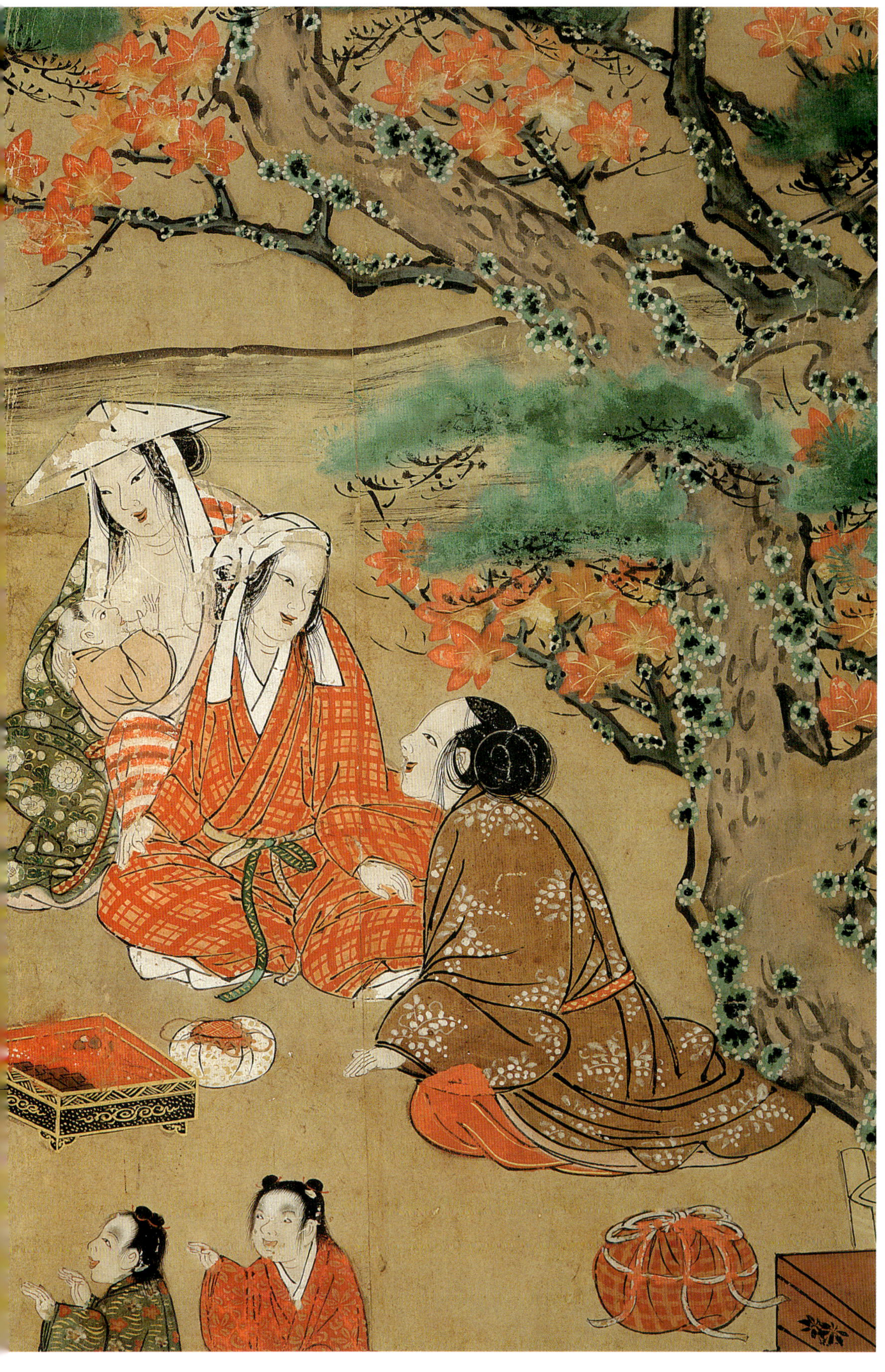

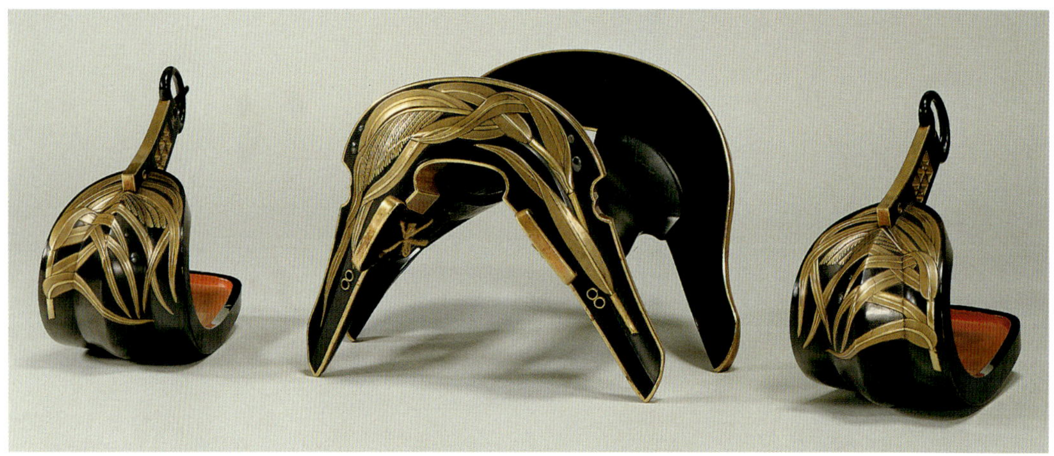

FIG. 109 Saddle and stirrups with design of reeds and dew. Late sixteenth century. Makie lacquer on wood. Tokyo National Museum.

Rodrigues also noted that, however ubiquitous lacquer might be in Japan, pictorial lacquers "are so splendidly made that they have no superior, but they are very costly and only lords and the wealthy can afford them." He concludes by remarking that although the Chinese, too, "have a large variety of gilded things and use a great deal of this varnish, they highly admire and value the gilt and varnished work of Japan, because for all their skill they cannot equal the Japanese in this art." Albeit the degree of Ming Chinese esteem for Japanese lacquer is debatable, these last remarks were clearly meant to establish the preeminence of Japanese pictorial lacquer throughout Asia and the world.

Rodrigues, in short, left no doubt as to the perceived excellence and desirability of Japanese lacquer. He emphasized the value placed on this material by the Japanese, and enumerated some of the qualities for which they esteemed it so greatly, commenting also on the costliness of the finest pictorial lacquers. He stressed lacquer's uniqueness to Asia, and thus its virtual unknowability in the West. These are the essential points to know about Japanese lacquer, and for this reason Rodrigues' remarks are invaluable. They are, however, only introductory.

To understand Momoyama lacquer more fully, to fill out the picture begun by Rodrigues, we must seek additional information from descriptions by the Japanese themselves and from the many extant Momoyama objects.[41] Virtually every Momoyama painting that represents elite personages, for instance, includes as a requisite motif objects made of makie lacquer. The well-dressed members of the merrymaking warrior elite pictured in *Maple Viewing at Takao* eat and drink out of makie lacquer vessels *(Figs. 30, 108)*. In their diaries prominent Japanese single out for mention plates, sake cups, writing boxes, and the like that were made from either black or makie lacquer; these were everyday objects, of which many were made in materials other than lacquer; of those, the diarists took no note.[42] Lacquer, and especially makie lacquer, was the element that transformed the utilitarian into the extraordinary. Because the value of lacquer was so generally understood in Japan, there was no more self-evident way to render a thing admirable than to cover it with makie lacquer.

And so makie lacquer was applied to a wide variety of objects in Japan. Many elite warriors lavished lacquer decoration on their saddles, accoutrements closely identified with their social status. Not only did Hideyoshi own a saddle with decoration of reeds done in makie lacquer *(Fig. 109)*; the drawing of it *(Fig. 110)*, which bears his cipher at bottom, suggests that he approved the design before it was made.[43] An object important enough to warrant makie decoration might well have required the patron's preliminary approval of the design.

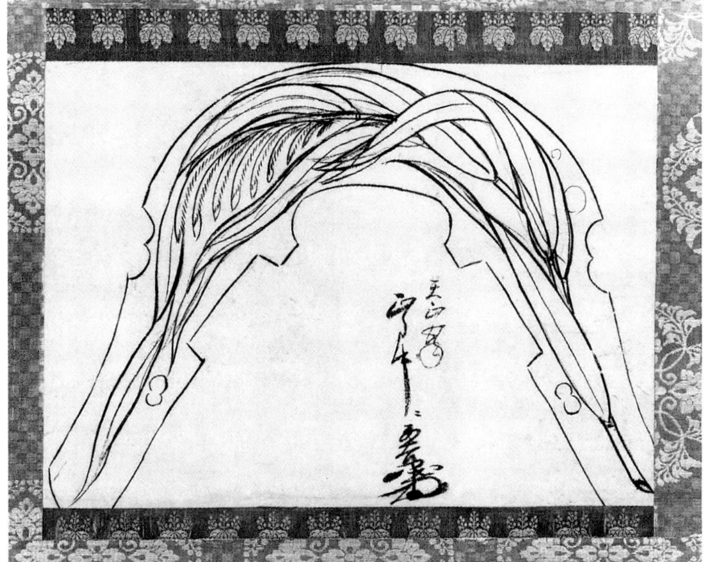

FIG. 110 Attributed to Kano Eitoku. Design for saddle. Late sixteenth century. Ink on paper. Tokyo National Museum.

LACQUER AND SACRED ADORNMENT

Lacquer was also regarded as an appropriate material with which to manifest the concept of shōgon and thereby honor the deities. Japanese elites donated extravagant makie lacquer versions of secular objects—boxes to hold cosmetic equipment, writing implements, and mirrors—to Shinto and Buddhist complexes; it is recorded, for example, that a group of cosmetics boxes were offered to the Shinto center Kumano Hayatama Taisha by the shogun Ashikaga Yoshimitsu (1358–1408) and others in 1390.[44] One of these, illustrated in Figure 111, together with its contents of exquisitely crafted personal effects such as combs, a bronze mirror, teeth-blackening utensils, and their small lacquer or bronze containers, required the most labor-intensive techniques of a generally labor-intensive medium to produce. These spectacular renderings of everyday articles survive because they were donated to temples or shrines, where they were carefully preserved as gifts to the gods.

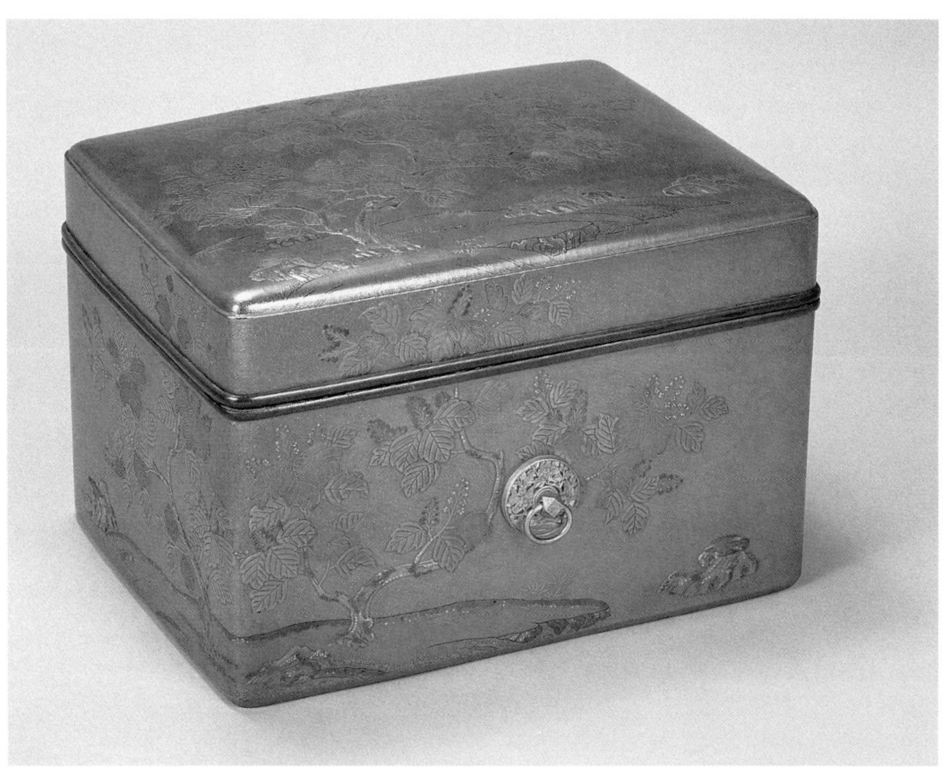

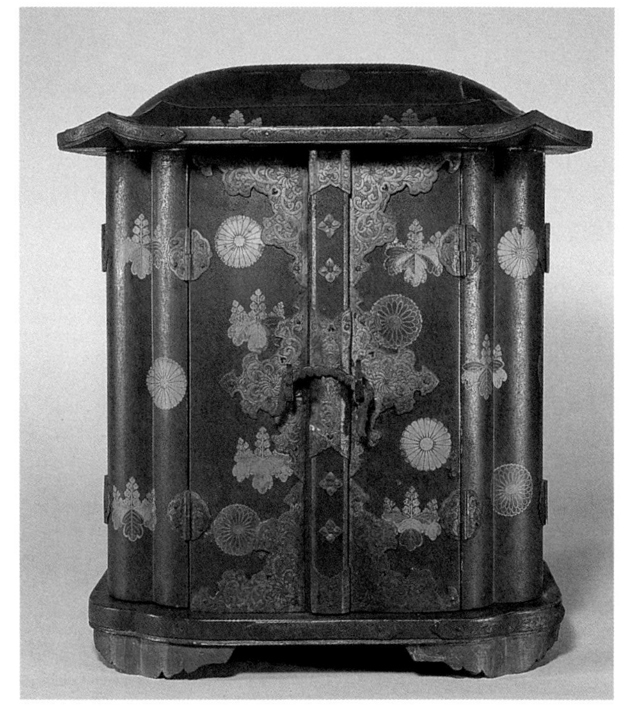

FIG. 111 (top)
Cosmetics box. 1390. Makie lacquer and gilt bronze on wood. Kumano Hayatama Taisha, Wakayama Prefecture. Photograph by Kōdansha.

FIG. 112 (bottom)
Zushi containing statue of Toyotomi Hideyoshi, exterior. Seventeenth century. Makie lacquer on wood. Hōjuin, Hyōgo Prefecture. Photograph by Osaka Castle.

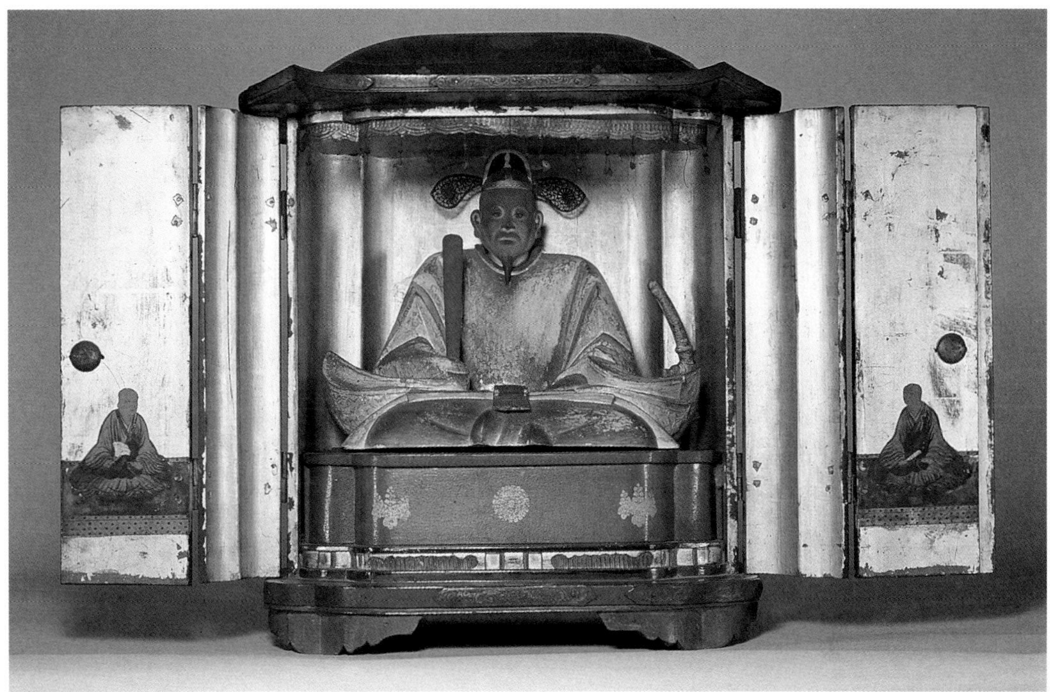

FIG. 113 Zushi containing statue of Toyotomi Hideyoshi, interior. Seventeenth century. Makie lacquer on wood. Hōjuin, Hyōgo Prefecture. Photograph by Osaka Castle.

Lacquer was also used on objects more inherently religious in function, such as sutra containers and *zushi;* the latter were, in effect, miniature buildings, which both protected and glorified through adornment the deity or deceased person represented within.[45] Both inside and out, the zushi illustrated in Figures 112 and 113, created to house a sculpture of Toyotomi Hideyoshi, is covered with the Toyotomi chrysanthemum and paulownia crests in makie lacquer.[46] This sculpture and zushi are preserved in the temple Hōjuin in Hyōgo Prefecture; another such unit is extant, and a third, now lost, is known to have been donated to a temple by Kuwayama Shigeharu (d. 1606), a daimyo who thrived under Hideyoshi's rule and showed his reverence through this sacred fabrication.

Such zushi, which ranged greatly in size—Hideyoshi's is about a foot and a half tall, but many are much larger—preceded even more spectacular uses of lacquer in Momoyama Japan: indeed, one of the periods distinctive visual expressions was the use of lacquer to embellish large freestanding structures. This practice was not entirely unknown earlier (recall the Konjikidō), but was still rare and remarkable in the Momoyama period. Lacquer lent magnificence: when Hideyori repaired a building at Kuramadera in 1607, according to the anonymous *Tōdaiki* diarist, the results were less than satisfactory, and so he re-engaged the project in the summer of 1608 and "the pillars of the hall were covered with lacquer, and it was truly wonderful."[47] Gien (1558–1626) describes a gate under construction within the precincts of his temple, Daigoji, in 1599: "From the pillars down, it is entirely [covered with] black lacquer, and the doors and other parts have metalwork with the chrysanthemum crest in gold—it is beautiful."[48]

In 1607 another priest, describing "an elegant meeting in a black-lacquered chamber," suggests the cultivated effect of this material.[49] If small lacquers were sumptuous, large ones were even more impressive: size amplified the impact.

None of the three above-mentioned structures survives, but not all lacquered monuments of the period are known only through description. Two major examples, both employing pictorial makie lacquer, remain from the Momoyama period: the *tamaya* at Kōdaiji and Sutemaru's building. Kōdaiji, today the better known of the two sites, was the Zen temple-residence of Hideyoshi's widow, Kita no Mandokoro (1549–1624); Buddhist memorial rites were offered there for Hideyoshi at the tamaya, a small mortuary building, and, after she died, for Kita no Mandokoro as well. The exterior of the Kōdaiji tamaya is austere, mostly bare wood with some painted coloring and limited amounts of black lacquer; within the building, however, the large altar space where rituals were conducted is densely covered with makie lacquer decoration *(Fig. 62)*.[50] Many of the motifs speak explicitly of the paradisal realm where the deceased reside. The musical instruments scattered throughout, for example, evoke the omnipresent music in the Pure Land that Buddhist texts so often describe. Other motifs, less specifically Buddhist in connotation, such as the floral rafts, can be understood from the context to contribute to the overall construction of a sacred space. Even before the specific iconographic content of the decoration is decoded, however, the soft glow and subdued opulence of the makie lacquer lends this ritual space its character, which the context tells the viewer is meant to be interpreted as ethereal.

SUTEMARU'S LACQUER

Sutemaru's building is an even more unusual and spectacular example of large-scale architectural makie lacquer. As a commemorative structure built by the era's most powerful patron for his deeply mourned firstborn son, this building was meant to be magnificent, an intent accomplished largely by its decoration. Particularly remarkable in this regard is that all of its pillars and beams, both interior and—even more extraordinarily—exterior, are covered with pictorial makie lacquer. It is the only extant building in Japan whose exterior boasts so much makie lacquer.

The makie in this building offers a catalogue of Momoyama motifs of the natural world, with seasonal flowers and trees and several species of birds filling every available bit of exposed pillar and beam. As we have seen, some are specifically emblematic of the commemorated little boy or of his family who sponsored the building: the pine and the crane, a rebus for Sutemaru's nickname; the paired chrysanthemum and paulownia crests, graphic symbols of the Toyotomi family and regime. Few of the lacquer motifs in this building are unique to the site, but nowhere else are they present in such great variety and volume. The floral and avian assemblage seems designed to overwhelm the viewer with visual density. As in the Kōdaiji tamaya, the makie on the interior casts an appropriate ethereal glow; unlike Kōdaiji, here the makie extends to the exterior, a ges-

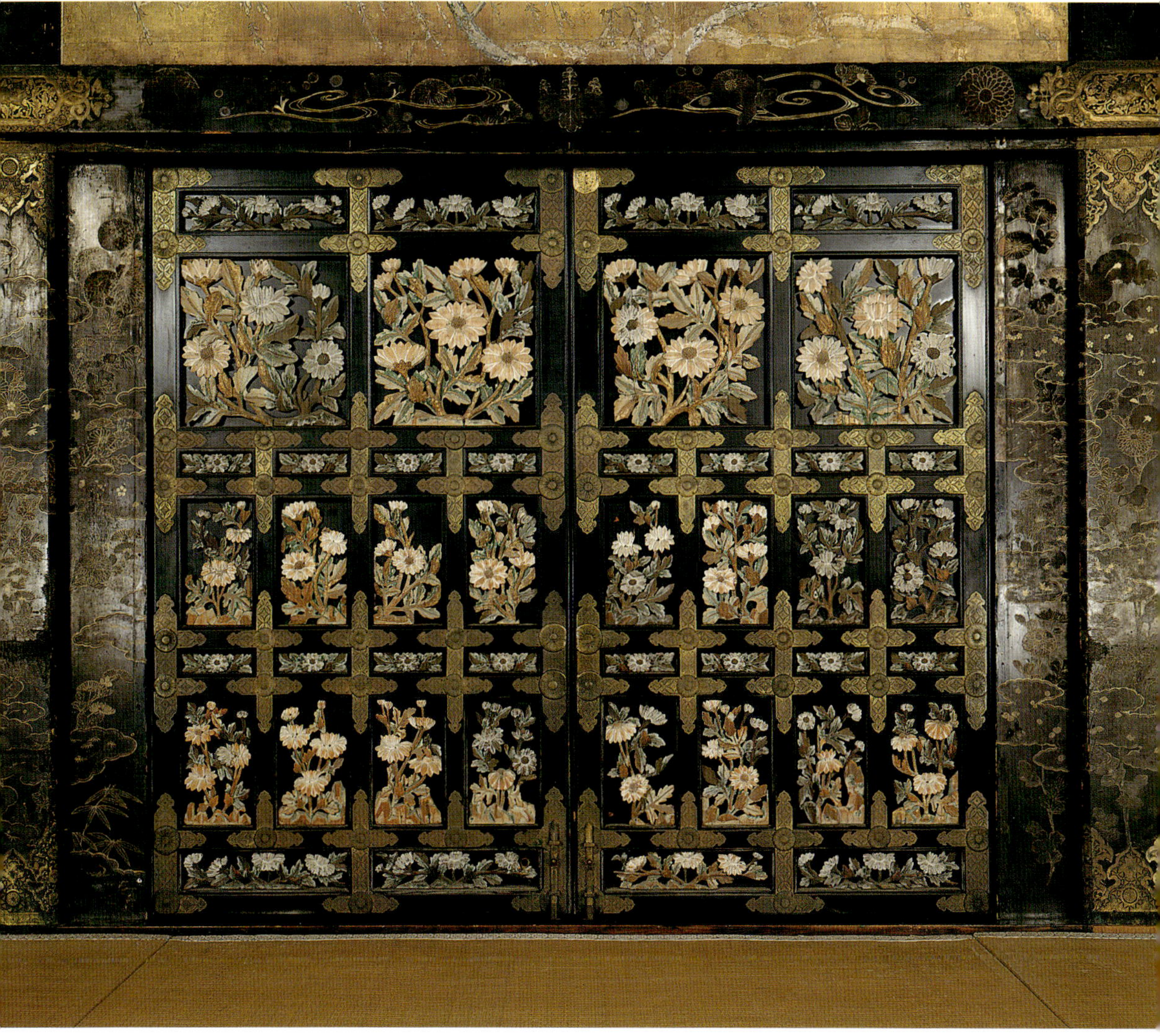

FIG. 114 Tsukubusuma Main Hall. Moya interior, south side, central bay. Chikubushima, Shiga Prefecture.

ture of opulence that surely signified to viewers the importance of the structure.

On the building's peripheral framing elements (rather than at focal points), most of the makie motifs are floral subjects ubiquitous in Momoyama lacquer; they were used here not only for their symbolic content but also simply for their ornamental appeal. On the interior pillars and on the door jambs flanking what is now the entrance, for instance, extending from the floor up to the lintel, is a luxuriant growth of chrysanthemums, a flower that in nature grows tall and so lends itself pictorially to vertical extension *(Figs. 114, 115)*. It was one of the most common of all Momoyama lacquer motifs, found on any number of smaller objects of credible provenance, including the small Kōdaiji chest *(Fig. 106)* and an inkstone case, whose lacquered lid the Hizen warrior Gotō Harumasa (1548–1612) received in award from Hideyoshi (to create this case,

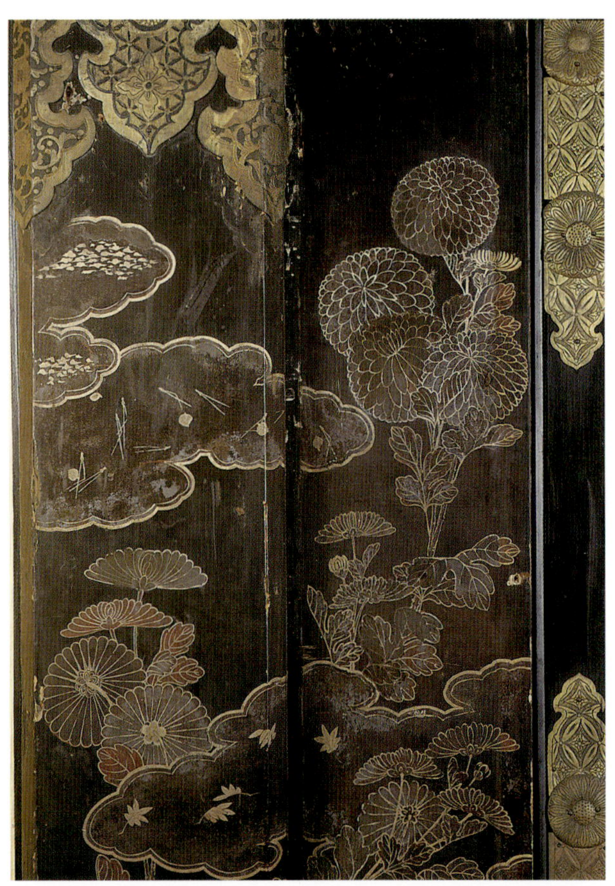

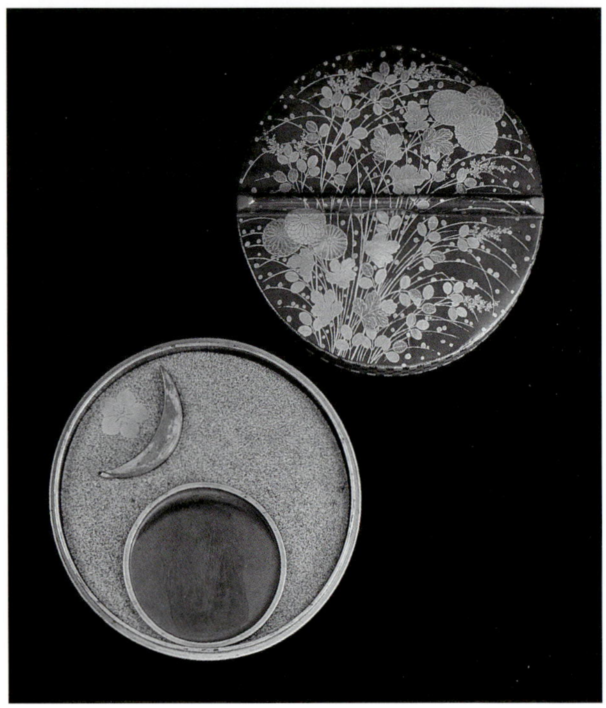

FIG. 115 (top) Tsukubusuma Main Hall. Chrysanthemum plants. Makie lacquer. Moya interior, south side, east pillar of central bay. Chikubushima, Shiga Prefecture.

FIG. 116 (bottom) Inkstone case. Late sixteenth century. Makie lacquer on wood. Osaka Castle.

Harumasa had a box fitted to the lid *[Fig. 116]*).[51] There were conventional ways to depict this plant in lacquer, and so it is no surprise that it is similarly characterized in all three instances: the thin stem tautly arcs, the broad leaf is shown either entire and flat against the picture plane or folded over on itself, and the flower is variously seen from above, from below, or from the side. The variations are most numerous in the building, whose greater size allowed the artist to explore countless permutations of the same basic form. Within the expanse of a lacquered building, even a motif primarily peripheral to the symbolic schema might be explored thoroughly for its potential to glorify through elaborate adornment.

MAKING SUTEMARU'S LACQUER

However expert the explorations of pictorial form on these objects, none of them were made using the most elaborate lacquer techniques, although these had been known for centuries. Indeed, on some of the most important Momoyama lacquers, the most time-consuming and intricate traditional techniques are conspicuously absent. In these three examples, the chrysanthemum plants are represented in the most basic of makie techniques: *hiramakie,* or "flat makie." In hiramakie, pictorial forms are depicted by sprinkling gold or silver powder onto a damp lacquer base in the form of the desired design, allowing the lacquer to harden slightly and then applying a thin coating of lacquer over the metal powder to strengthen the bond; the density of the powder can make the design appear as a smooth expanse of gold or silver. Sometimes large metal particles are applied to the damp lacquer ground in the form of the motif, and the whole surface of the object is then given a coating of lacquer; here, the individual particles of metal remain distinct. Diversity of pictorial effect is thus achieved by varying the kind of metal used and the density and size of the particles. With hiramakie, lines can be incised through the powdered metal—either while the lacquer is still damp or after it has hardened—to produce fine internal detailing, a simple technique known as *harigaki* (literally, "drawing with a needle").

The preference for these makie techniques over other traditional methods made for significant differences in both the production process and the appearance of the works. In earlier and later lacquerwork *takamakie,* or "raised makie" lacquer, was a much favored technique; it is expertly exemplified in the fourteenth-century box at Kumano *(Fig. 111).* Takamakie is created by molding the raised design forms out of a pasty mixture of lacquer and ground shell or other dry matter, allowing this mixture to harden, then applying the finish coats of lacquer and the sprinkled designs. This allows for volumetric and tactile variation in the lacquer, so that rocks, for example, can be represented as three-dimensional forms with surfaces variously rough or smooth. But this technique is also extremely labor-intensive, requiring an investment of time that, on the evidence of many extant Momoyama works, which employ only the non-relief techniques described above, was often deemed unnecessary or undesirable. This is not to say that takamakie was not used in the Momoyama period; it was (see, for example, the reeds on Hideyoshi's saddle *[Fig. 109]*), which makes its absence in certain objects even more obviously a matter of choice.

Even the non-relief makie techniques were further simplified to make the makie lacquer on Sutemaru's building. The wood beams and pillars were covered, as was common in most lacquerwork, with a coating of *jinoko,* a fine earth-based material that filled the grain of the wood and produced a smooth surface for the application of lacquer. Over this, it appears, only a single layer of black-colored lacquer was applied to produce the black background, in contrast to the more traditional practice of applying several layers of black lacquer and allowing each to harden before applying the next layer. On this hardened background, the design elements, greatly simplified, were roughly sketched out in red lacquer. Some of these red underdrawings are still visible: for a chrysanthemum flower, for example, the outliner simply drew a large red circle, indicating the outer contour, and small circle within to indicate the flower's center *(Fig. 117).*

The designs were completed in minor variations of non-relief makie lacquer, each of which created a slightly different golden hue. Many motifs—especially delicate ones, such as the attenuated bush clover—were done with dense applications of gold powder on top of the black ground creating the appearance of solid gold, and many of these passages preserve today much of their pristine glow *(Fig. 118).* The other designs were produced with larger particles, many not with gold but with silver; through the translucent

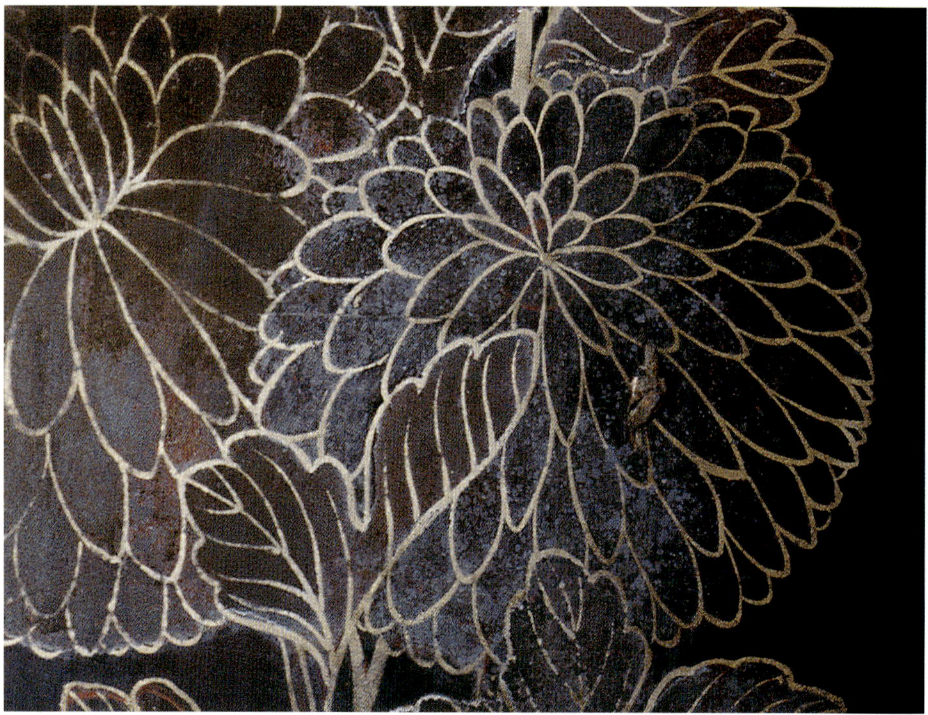

FIG. 117 Tsukubusuma Main Hall. Red underdrawing of chrysanthemum flower. Makie lacquer. Moya interior. Chikubushima, Shiga Prefecture. Photograph by the author.

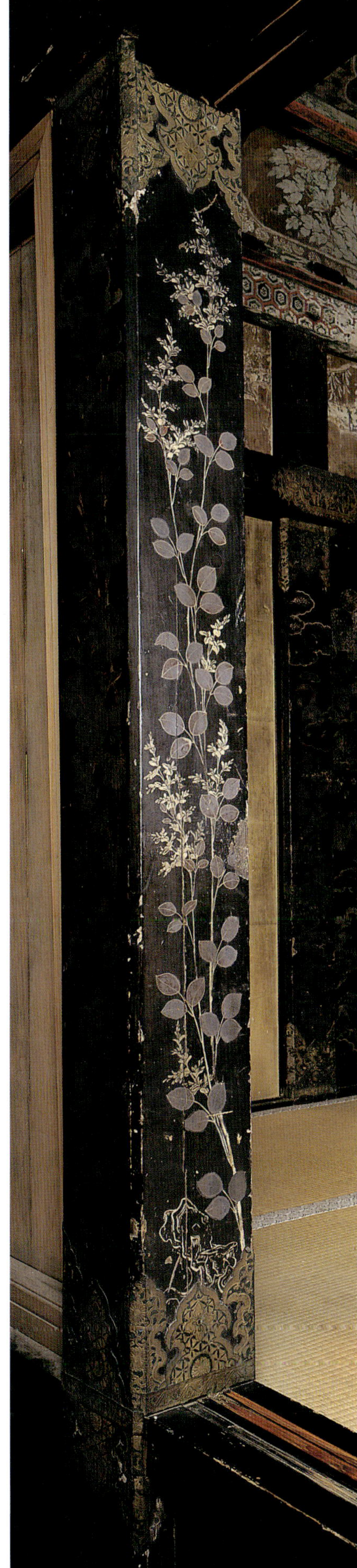

FIG. 118 Tsukubusuma Main Hall. Bush clover. Makie lacquer. Moya interior, east side, pillar of central bay. Chikubushima, Shiga Prefecture.

lacquer applied over these particles, the silver appears reddish-gold, different though allied in hue to hiramakie executed in gold. Silver has the unfortunate property of darkening and bleeding over time, however, so most of the designs rendered in silver are today muddy gray in color and blurred in definition (for example, *Fig. 6*). Yet another variation appears to employ a mixture of gold and silver particles, again covered with translucent lacquer, that created yet another slightly different golden hue. That mixture was used more sparingly, but at highly conspicuous points of the building—for example, for the two pairs of birds on the interior lintel-beams and the cranes on the exterior. The breasts of the long-tailed birds on an interior lintel were executed in this mixture, which, like the silver designs, has deteriorated over time, losing its original vibrant tonality *(Fig. 12)*. The birds' wings show a gossamer web of internal detailing, a linear pattern that effectively conveys the internal structure of the feathers, created by drawing lines in gold hiramakie *(Fig. 119)*. In short, pictorial interest was achieved in the lacquer of Sutemaru's building not through technical complexity, but through sheer abundance of motifs and the coloristic variation of the basic golden palette against a black ground.

The prevalence of non-relief golden-hued makie designs—primarily of floral subjects—on a black ground, seen in Sutemaru's building, in the Kōdaiji tamaya, and in the other smaller objects examined above, is characteristic of a style of lacquer decora-

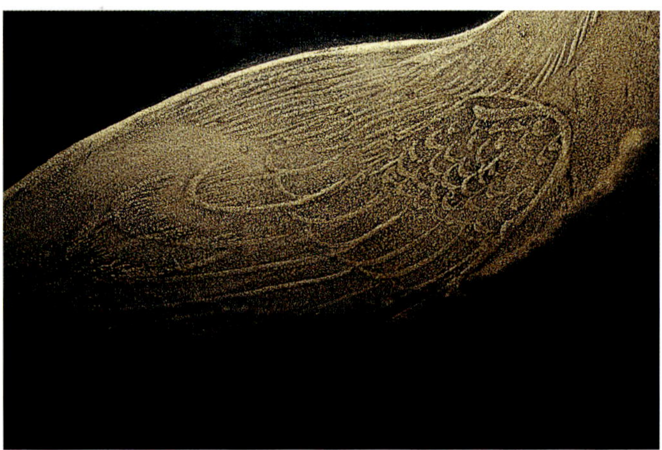

FIG. 119 (left) Tsukubusuma Main Hall. Detail of long-tailed bird. Makie lacquer. Moya interior, west side, lintel-beam of central bay. Chikubushima, Shiga Prefecture. Photograph by the author.

FIG. 120 (below) Sword sheath. Makie lacquer on wood. Sword dated to 1538. Tsurugaoka Hachimangū, Kanagawa Prefecture.

FIG. 121 (opposite) Drum body. Dated to 1566. Makie lacquer on wood. Tokyo National Museum.

tion that appears, on the basis of surviving objects, to have been extremely popular during the Momoyama period. The actual origins of this style are still not well understood and are obscured by the term used today to designate it—Kōdaiji makie—which misleadingly suggests that the temple Kōdaiji is its type site, and perhaps its place of invention.[52] In fact, the technical and stylistic characteristics of what many scholars now more cautiously call Kōdaiji-type makie may predate the Momoyama period by several decades.

Key evidence is a trio of sword sheaths in the Tsurugaoka Hachimangū in Kamakura, donated along with their swords to the shrine in 1538 by the swordsmiths, who wished (according to the inscriptions on the tangs) to give thanks to the deities who had realized their requests (*Fig. 120* illustrates one of them).[53] All three sheaths share the same basic design of paulownia crests interspersed with phoenixes, executed in gold hiramakie on a dark black ground (which has, over the centuries, changed to a dark amber color). The internal linear detailing in the motifs is executed primarily with harigaki. (Also evident is another, more painstaking, technique known as *kakiwari,* not typically used in Kōdaiji-type lacquer, in which a thin line of ground is carefully left exposed between two areas of makie, thereby creating a delicate black border separating the two zones of gold.) The sheaths are perhaps the earliest datable objects possessing several of the characteristics, both stylistic and technical, of what we have come to call Kōdaiji-type makie, and they suggest its early and perhaps—if the sheaths were made in the Kamakura area—geographically diffuse origins.

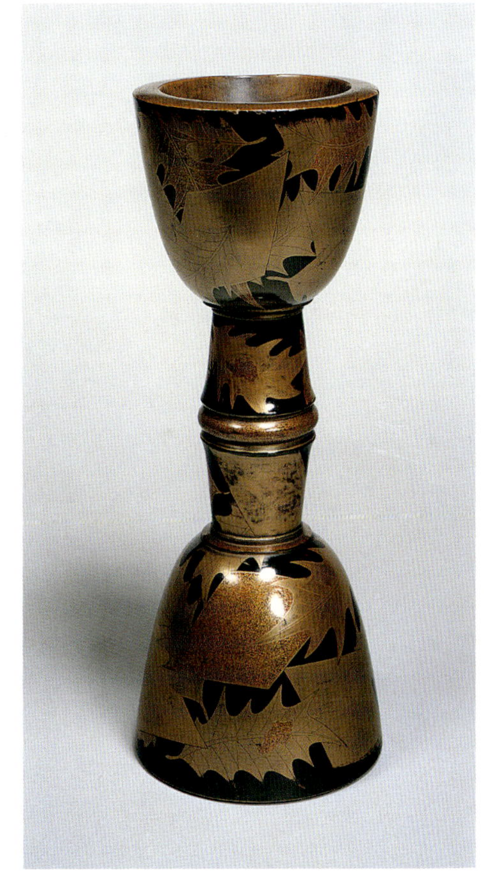

Also important to our understanding of these origins is a makie-covered drum body that bears an inscribed date of 1566, almost at the beginning of the Momoyama period *(Fig. 121).*[54] In certain aspects it anticipates the type of lacquer that soon thereafter reached an apex of popularity: its decoration is a bold floral pattern in gold—scattered holly leaves, along with diamond shapes—dramatically silhouetted against a dense black ground, and rendered entirely in non-relief makie techniques. In its fastidiousness of execution, however, it resembles the more complex lacquerwork favored in the pre-Momoyama era. Many pictorial elements on the drum are depicted so as to appear overlapping, and in each instance, the two overlapping motifs are depicted with two different sorts of gold hiramakie. Because the overlapping motifs are (by definition) contiguous, both procedures would have required that one motif be sprinkled, lacquer-coated, and allowed to harden before its overlapping motif was begun. Many of the single motifs on this drum were likewise depicted with two kinds of makie and would likewise have required two separate operations. Razor-thin lines of expertly executed kakiwari accentuate the common borders (attesting to the careful planning that went into the design). Most of the motifs are outlined with a thin line of gold hiramakie, applied only after the main area of the motif had hardened; this device much resembles the internal detailing of the long-tailed birds' wings on Sutemaru's building, but here the line of hiramakie is applied at the very perimeter of the motif, an unforgiving location that requires absolute precision. Moreover, this rigorous outlining was applied not to one motif but to many across the drum body. The enormous technical demands of this piece of lacquerwork differentiate it from some of the most important Momoyama lacquers. And yet, in its use of only non-relief techniques and in its penchant for floral patterns of gold-on-black, it can be seen to anticipate Momoyama predilections.

MAKING SUTEMARU'S LACQUER BUILDING

The extreme reduction in technical complexity characteristic of Momoyama lacquer should not be interpreted as a lessening of production standards; it represents, rather, a shift in priorities that permitted the manufacture of new types of lacquer objects. A lacquer commission of the magnitude of Sutemaru's building was extraordinarily rare in Japan—perhaps the only similarly ambitious structures are the Kōdaiji tamaya and twelfth-century Konjikidō, and on these the makie lacquer is limited to the interior of the building. Sutemaru's lacquer encouraged—or, more likely, required—a rethinking of the traditionally favored intricate makie lacquer techniques. The impatient patron and (if indeed the building was used for one of the death anniversaries) the need to have the building ready in a timely fashion probably necessitated relatively expeditious production.

Japanese construction practices made the physical task of creating a lacquered building less formidable than it might immediately seem, and we can speculate with reasonable certainty about how this building was produced. The load-bearing skeleton of a typical Japanese building comprises its posts (or vertical pillars) and lintels (or horizontal beams), and these pieces can be made individually in a workshop for eventual assembly on site. It is precisely these parts of Sutemaru's building that are covered with lacquer. Before assembly they were transported to a lacquer workshop, where all of the necessary materials were gathered and, quite probably, where the proper temperature and humidity controls necessary for the lacquer to cure could be maintained. As we

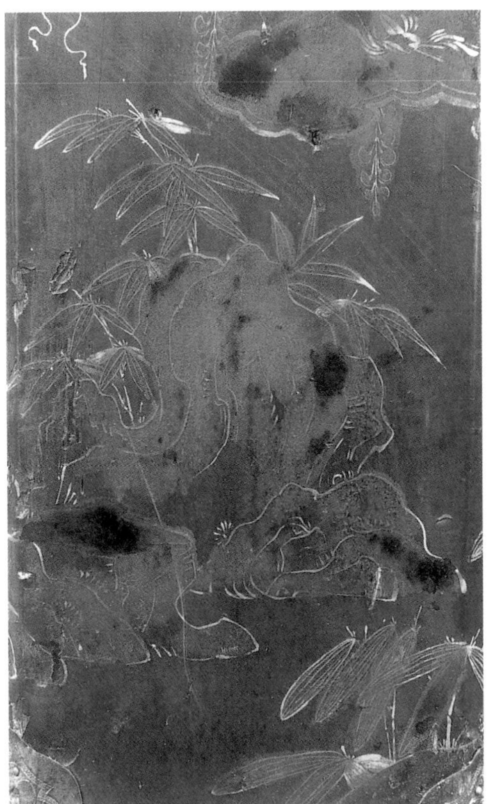

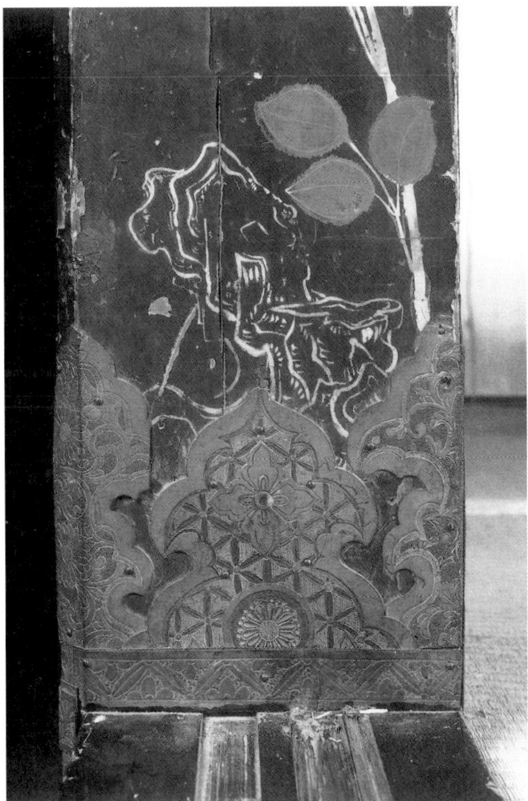

FIG. 122 (left) Tsukubusuma Main Hall. Rocky landscape. Makie lacquer. Moya interior, west side, north pillar of central bay. Chikubushima, Shiga Prefecture.

FIG. 123 (right) Tsukubusuma Main Hall. Rocky landscape. Makie lacquer. Moya interior, east side, south pillar of central bay. Chikubushima, Shiga Prefecture.

have seen, the workshop that did the lacquering for this building was located in southeastern Kyoto near Hideyoshi's Great Buddha Hall, and it was here that the pillars and beams, in their still-unassembled state, received their makie lacquer.

To have produced such a large amount of pictorial lacquer in a relatively short time implies a sizable work force and considerable division of labor. Each pillar and beam first received its jinoko coating, then its base of black lacquer, following which the designs were roughed-in in red; the more painstaking work of completing the designs in makie was the work of yet other craftsmen. A comparison of makie depictions of rocks at two locations within the structure clearly shows more than one hand at work in applying the makie *(Figs. 122, 123)*. Each rock cluster occupies a separate pillar base, and from each a plant grows to the full height of the pillar. The one cluster of rocks is expertly rendered, drawn with a subtly modulating line that well evokes the illusion of volume and faceting; from the crevices of the rocks grow tufts of bamboo and moss, affording a sense of setting as well as scale. This practiced excellence is entirely typical of most of the lacquer on the building. In stark contrast, the rocks at the base of the other pillar

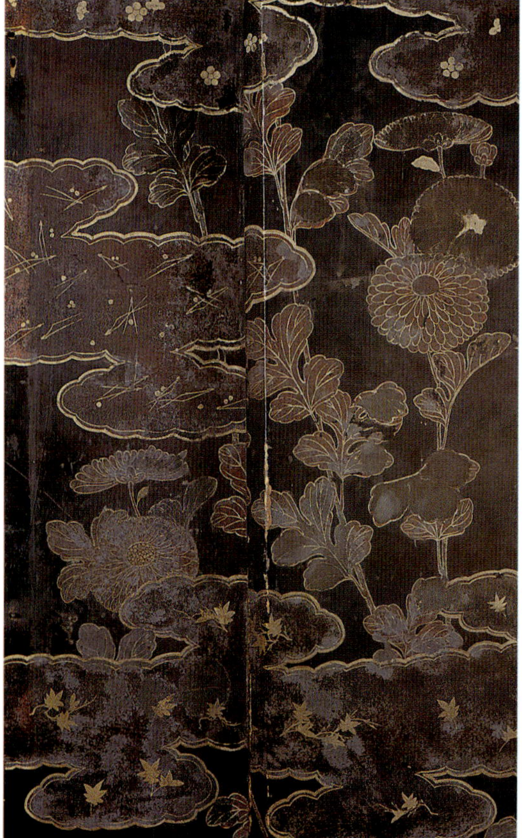

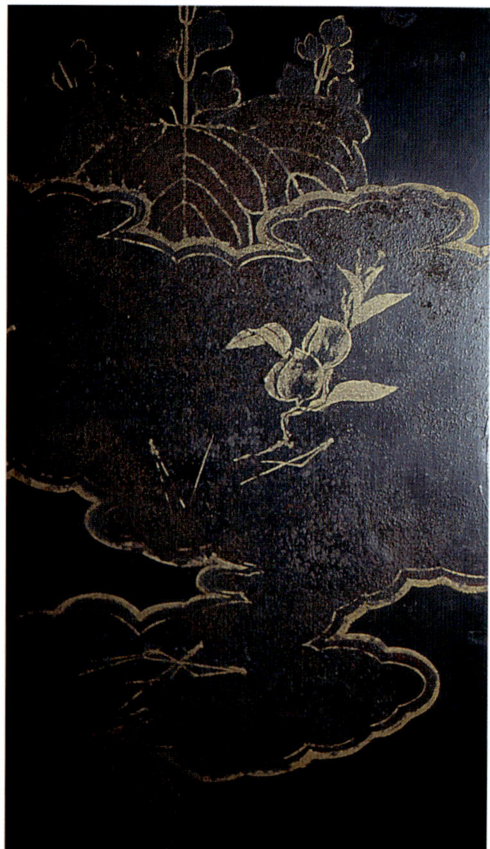

FIG. 124 (left) Tsukubusuma Main Hall. Clouds enclosing miniature pine needles, plum blossoms, and maple leaves. Makie lacquer. Moya interior. Chikubushima, Shiga Prefecture.

FIG. 125 (right) Tsukubusuma Main Hall. Clouds enclosing miniature peaches. Makie lacquer. Moya interior. Chikubushima, Shiga Prefecture.

are an obtrusively awkward protuberance, delineated by a thick, even clumsy, line. Apparently, the person who drew this one rock was allowed to do no more makie, for no other similar depiction appears elsewhere in the building. This is the sole lapse of dexterity in an otherwise fluent and consistently expert effort.

Although the most prominent motifs were determined by the iconographic requirements of the building, it appears as though the lacquer artist had freedom of choice in certain details. The lacquer designs, paintings, and carvings are visually linked by depictions of clouds that waft throughout the building, and the still-visible red underdrawings indicate that the makie clouds were a preplanned part of the composition. Filling the clouds, however, are miniature renderings of all manner of auspicious and floral subjects, such as pine needles, maple leaves, peaches, plum blossoms, bamboo, and paulownia crests, and there is no evidence (such as red underdrawings) that any of these were scripted *(Figs. 8–11, 124–27).* On the evidence of other Momoyama objects, we can conclude that these miniatures constitute a repertoire of motifs that were most popular in

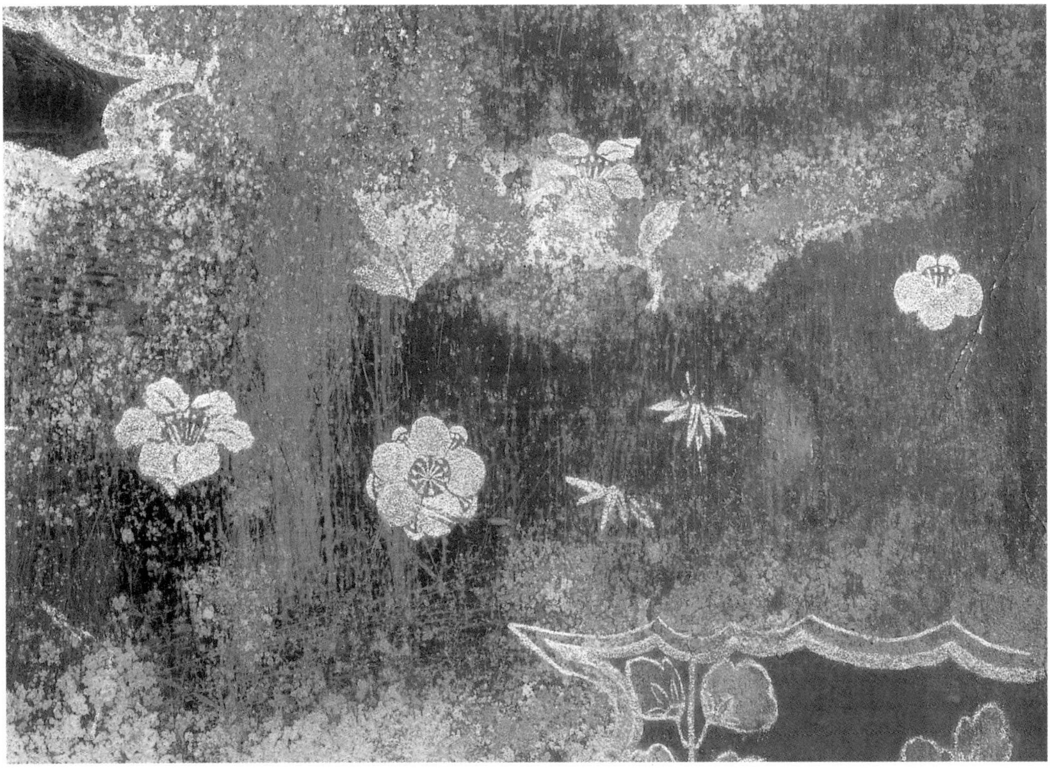

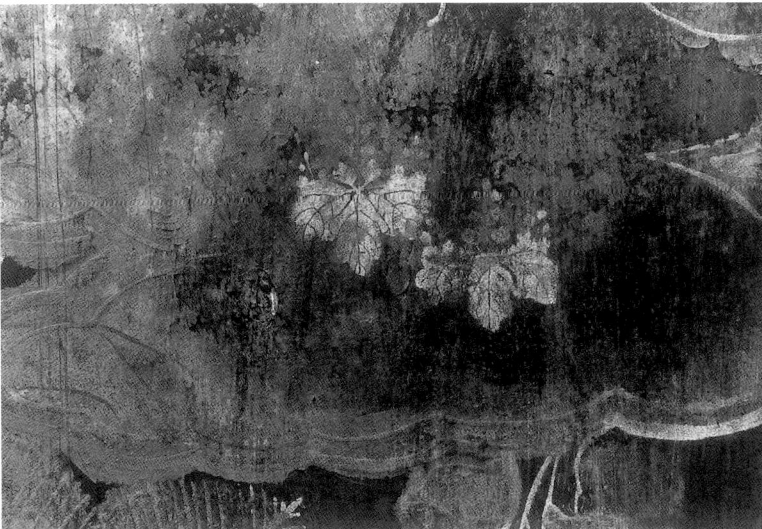

FIG. 126 (above) Tsukubusuma Main Hall. Clouds enclosing miniature plum blossoms and bamboo. Makie lacquer. Moya interior. Chikubushima, Shiga Prefecture.

FIG. 127 (below) Tsukubusuma Main Hall. Clouds enclosing miniature paulownia crests. Makie lacquer. Moya interior. Chikubushima, Shiga Prefecture.

Momoyama lacquerwork and hence most familiar to the practiced lacquerer. It would appear that the lacquerer was free to fill the obligatory clouds with whatever he wished, to animate the larger program with unprogrammed, but highly favored and appropriately propitious, lacquer motifs.

Sutemaru's building is unmatched in the volume, variety, and allover expanse of its lacquerwork. In sheer quantity the floral and avian lacquer assemblage, both large and miniature, seems designed to overwhelm the viewer with visual density and luxuriousness: the richness of the lacquer here outshines any other example from the period. Makie lacquer was only one element in Sutemaru's ensemble, but arguably the most impressive element to its period audience.

EVALUATING THE ENSEMBLE

Each of the mediums surveyed above ranked high within the Momoyama hierarchy of visual arts, and patrons commissioned grand synchronic ensembles of them to produce out-of-the-ordinary visual effects, unrealizable in less heterogeneous constructions. Consequently, people noticed them. One of the most articulate Momoyama commentators on the ensembles being built in the capital was the Daigoji monk Gien, an aesthete who travelled about Kyoto and recorded his views on new structures. He was particularly impressed by a gate he saw being assembled at the Toyokuni Shrine, near Hōkōji, in 1600. After remarking on its monumental size, two stories tall and about thirty-six meters wide, he records its physical appearance: "The central bay's second story is taller than the other ones, and from the pillars down, it is entirely [covered with] makie lacquer. The round pillars of the lower story are completely [covered with] black lacquer. The roof brackets are painted with colors."[55]

This is precise and illuminating description. Gien notes the coordination of ornament and architecture that was typical of the Momoyama ensemble, clearly distinguishes between the plain black lacquer (lacquer without designs) and the pictorial makie lacquer, and also remarks on the architectural coloring of the roof brackets, which played bright pigments against the lustrous blackness of the lacquered pillars. The importance of architectural coloring, either geometric or completely unpatterned, is suggested in diary references to it, including one by a Shōkokuji priest, which notes a visit to the temple by Katagiri Sadataka (1560–1627), a retainer of the Toyotomi family, specifically to discuss the architectural coloring of a pagoda then being constructed.[56] Today, no Momoyama gate survives with the prodigious dimensions or copious ornament described by Gien, and we can only imagine its visual impact. Gien ends his comments by declaring the gate to be "rather amazing to the eye and the ear *[kekkō kyōmokuji]*"—in other words, visually impressive and almost unheard of. In the context of normally reticent Momoyama diaristic prose, this is an effusive assertion, and one that marks its object as especially praiseworthy.

The language of positive description is also revealed in other Japanese sources. The courtier Funabashi Hidekata (1575–1614), for example, reports in his diary on a newly constructed building in Kyoto that he himself did not see; he was told that "everything is gold and it surprised the eye";[57] later he notes that the "pillars and so on" of a building being constructed at Shōkokuji "are beautiful and surprise the eye *[kirei kyōmoku]*."[58] A prominent Buddhist priest writes of a pair of ceremonial boats, unlike any he had seen before; one was covered with "black lacquer; its edges [are decorated with] makie lacquer and metalwork; the *yakata* [cabin-like structure] is immeasurably dazzling. The other boat is bright vermilion. The boats have the bodies of dragons and the heads of birds."[59] These comments tell us, again, that certain characteristics—the conspicuous presence of gold, for example, or the combination of metalwork with black and makie lacquer—yielded structures dazzling and beautiful to the eye of the Momoyama viewer. It is important to reiterate that, although many structures were commented on in passing in contemporary writings, expressions of praise were reserved for the few that boast such decoration. And those that combined various mediums inspired the most enthusiastic acclaim.

One of the most informative appreciations of the Momoyama ensemble again comes from the diarist-priest Gien, describing a building being constructed in 1606. The building, now lost, was located within an ancient temple-shrine complex just south of Kyoto, the Iwashimizu Hachimangū precinct at Otokoyama. In the fifth month of that year Gien wrote in his diary, "I went to see the construction of the shrine building at Otokoyama. It is a structure ordered by Hideyori Kō. From [the top of] the pillars down the building is entirely coated with black lacquer and pictures are painted. Even the flap-down shutters *[shitomido]* are [covered with] black lacquer."[60] On seeing the completed building several months later, Gien reiterated and elaborated, "Udaijin Toyotomi Ason Hideyori Kō constructed [the Otokoyama Hachimangū]. . . . The flap doors and so on of the new structure are [covered with] black lacquer. [The building] is painted with colors, and so on."[61]

Gien was recording what he thought important about this monument. In both entries, he scrupulously noted that the patron was Toyotomi Hideyori, which immediately lent the building status. He also meticulously observed that the decoration was of several different types—black lacquer, pictures, colors—and was distributed over the architectural framework. It is noteworthy that Gien felt no need to enumerate every medium employed. He specified black lacquer and color, but then lumped the rest together in a nonspecific "and so on." Having designated precisely some of the areas where the mediums were applied—the black lacquer covers the pillars and the flap doors—he was content to note vaguely that other parts were also so embellished. This coupling of precise and imprecise reporting suggests that the combination of mediums to create a significant monument was prevalent enough to obviate minutely detailed description.

Finally, Gien ended his account with an emphatically positive judgment of the whole, one that is based on the totality of its contextual and visual characteristics. The expression he uses, "jinzen jinbi," is fervent praise: the building was "perfectly good and perfectly beautiful." This is a phrase replete with classical significance, both Chinese and Japanese. It originates in a passage from Book Three of the *Analects of Confucius.*[62] "The Master said of the *shao* [the music of King Shun] that it was both perfectly beautiful and perfectly good, and of the *wu* [the music of King Wu] that it was perfectly beautiful but not perfectly good."[63] This passage was glossed by the influential twelfth-century Neo-Confucian scholar Zhu Xi (1130–1200), who explained, "'Beauty' refers to the pageantry of the music and the performance. 'Goodness' refers to the content of the beauty."[64] Zhu Xi went on to spell out that the music of the Shun was not only perfectly beautiful, aesthetically pleasing, it was also perfectly good (in the sense of virtuous) because Shun came to power through peaceful succession. The music of the other ruler, Wu, was perfectly beautiful, but it was not perfectly virtuous, because Wu came to power by conquest (even though his conquest was justified and ultimately, though imperfectly, virtuous). So glossed, this passage asserts that a piece of music can have both aesthetic and moral implications, and that its beauty can be linked with moral goodness. It is important to recognize, too, that Zhu Xi's use of the term "pageantry," or *shengrong* in Chinese, refers not only to the sound of music but also to the appearance of the performance[65]; the aesthetics of music; in other words, are not only aural but also visual.

There is little doubt that Gien, a learned monk well versed in the venerable Chinese Classics, knew both the original and its commentary and well understood their implications. Neo-Confucianism and especially the works of Zhu Xi were introduced into Japan by the thirteenth century; over the succeeding centuries they achieved a wide audience and were of great interest to learned Japanese throughout the Momoyama period.[66] Gien's use of "jinzen jinbi" is but one reflection of the current high regard for Confucian thought, a regard which was variously and conspicuously expressed: the top floor of Nobunaga's Azuchi Castle, for example, was entirely devoted to imaginary portraits of ancient Chinese culture heroes, including Confucius himself and his followers.[67]

Gien was likely aware, too, that the term had been used previously in Japan to extol excellent objects in religious contexts. In the Heian period the phrase "jinzen jinbi" surfaces in the vocabulary of praise applied to decorated sutras (sponsored as a way of gaining spiritual merit, much as one sought salvation through sutra chanting or by sponsoring religious buildings).[68] The powerful twelfth-century warrior aristocrat Taira no Kiyomori (1118–1181), for example, employed the term in his dedicatory inscription for the *Heike nōkyō,* acclaiming that magnificent illustrated sutra as "perfectly good and perfectly beautiful." These Heian uses apply the term not to music (as Confucius did), but to objects perceived visually. Gien uses the term in the same sense, applying it to an object he deemed remarkable-looking by accepted Momoyama standards. The Iwashimizu building was not only beautiful but bespoke the virtuous character of its patron. This was a monument that epitomized aesthetic and moral excellence in the Momoyama period.

CREATING SUTEMARU'S ENSEMBLE

Gien's Iwashimizu building and the other notable Momoyama ensembles celebrated in writing are all lost, and while the interpretive comments they inspired are informative and intriguing, they are inevitably incomplete. They lack the specificity that only the concrete object provides, the particulars that elucidate the indefinite "and so on" and the complexities of form that defy complete description. This kind of information is provided by the rare examples that survive, such as the Kōdaiji tamaya and Sutemaru's building. Sutemaru's is the most complete and elaborate, the model for analysis not only of symbolic content, but also of the characteristic interaction among mediums. It is this interaction that, to a large degree, governed the appearance of the ensemble and the primary responses to it. An arresting appearance, as the previous Momoyama accounts suggest, was the prime requisite for acclamation.

One's initial impression of this ensemble is established by its distinctive formal cohesiveness, accomplished through patterns of decoration repeated across the architectural framework (as described in the previous chapter), through motifs similarly described in different mediums, and through a remarkably consistent treatment of pictorial space. These features indicate a high degree of central coordination, a supervisor who orchestrated this visual content. We have no written record of this supervisor's existence, only the concrete results of his endeavors, which suggest that the painter Kano Mitsunobu most likely served in this capacity. Under his direction, a great variety of artists engaged in a dynamic exchange of visual information, filtered through the traditional practices of each artist's own particular medium. Though Mitsunobu's coordination left ample room for variations, there is sufficient conformity to crystallize the decoration into a consistent vision of pictorial harmony.

When necessary, Mitsunobu assisted in such matters as the description of form. For instance, the fuyō plant, represented in carvings *(Fig. 5)* and in paintings *(Fig. 15)*, is one of many motifs for which it is clear that paintings served as models for the carvers—though only for one part of the motif. The wood-carving tradition of that time afforded no models of fuyō plants per se.[69] But generic similarities between the large-blossomed, many-petalled *fuyō flower* and the large-blossomed, many-petalled *peony flower* provided the wood carvers with a model for the *flower* from within their own medium, for the peony was a longstanding and common subject of wood carving. Sutemaru's carved fuyō exhibit the same emphatically asymmetrical and irregular rendering of the flowers as we find in the numerous wood-carved peonies, such as those on the Hōgonji gate *(Fig. 102)*.[70] It is significant of the resemblance that modern observers have often misidentified the carved fuyō on Sutemaru's structure as peonies. Iconographically, however, it was necessary to make clear that these were not peony but fuyō. This could be achieved through accurate portrayal of the fuyō *leaves*, which are notably broader than peony leaves. No model being available in their own tradition, it appears that the wood carvers followed instructions provided by Mitsunobu, for the wood-carved fuyō leaves strikingly resemble those in Mitsunobu's paintings: large, windblown, foreshortened, and folding in on themselves (even though, again, the blossoms differ radically from Mitsunobu's neat, symmetrically ordered fuyō blossoms; see *Fig. 15*). This is just one of many instances in Sutemaru's ensemble in which the Kano workshop seems to have been the source for a specific form as represented in a medium other than painting.[71]

If these examples all point to Mitsunobu's role in resolving questions of form, then it is reasonable to conclude that he also played the principal role in determining other aspects of the appearance of this ensemble. In short, I suggest that Mitsunobu's orchestration of mediums was not confined to the local description of form but extended into the more broadly conceived realm of pictorial space. One consistent characterization of

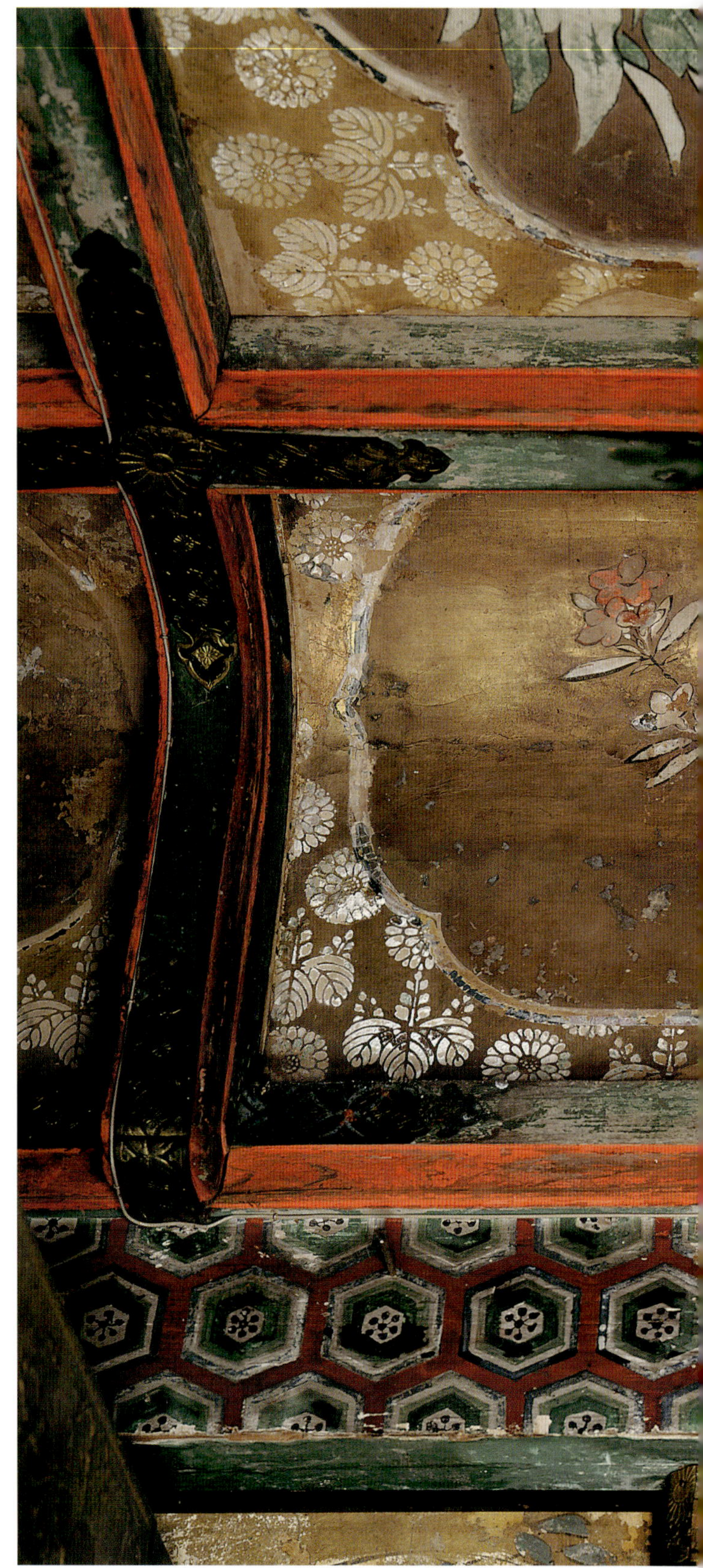

FIG. 128 Tsukubusuma Main Hall. Architectural coloring. Moya interior. Chikubushima, Shiga Prefecture.

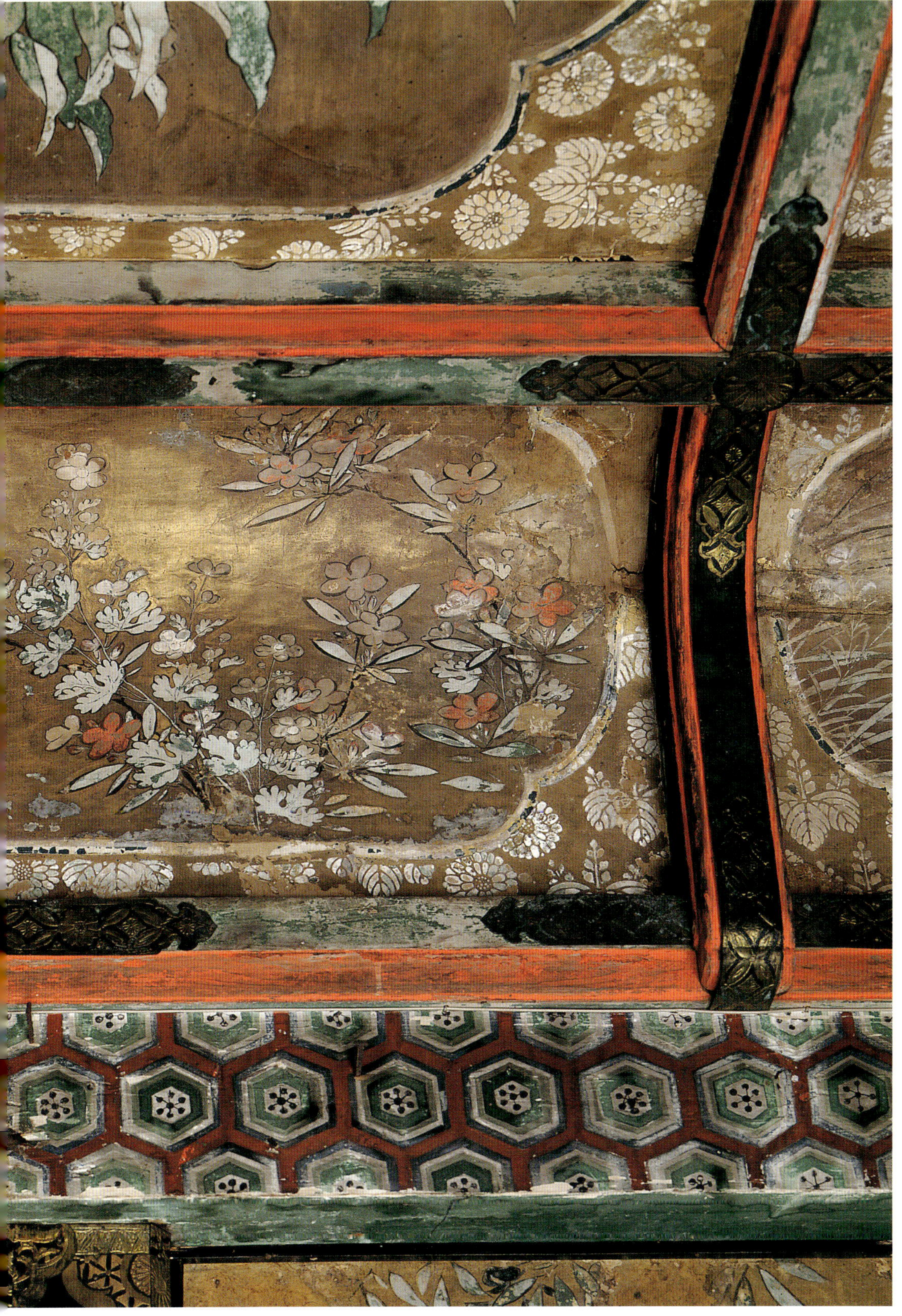

space dominates this ensemble: a shallow foreground with no indication of recession to a middle or far distance. Whether depicted in carvings, paintings, or lacquer, the flora and trees spread horizontally and vertically, they twist and turn in their immediate surrounding space, but they never penetrate beyond a foreground delimited by clusters of rocks and dense clouds. Such uniformity is the most important determinant of the optical unity of the ensemble. It could not be achieved by chance, but only by careful design.

In no medium was such a depiction of pictorial space the only, or even most typical, option. The tradition of relief wood carving in Japan held precedent for at least two characterizations of pictorial space: the shallow space dominant here *(Figs. 4, 5);* and an equally well established convention of absence of recession, i.e., an allover flat floral pattern, as seen, for example, in the floral scroll in the exterior frieze above the lintel *(Fig. 104).* Historically, makie lacquer depictions of plants encompassed an even great variety of spatial options, from the deepest recession to absolute graphic flatness. This latter option is also found in Sutemaru's building, in the depiction of the characteristically flat chrysanthemum and paulownia crests *(Fig. 13).* For the whole plants that occupy the largest part of the lacquer program, however, a shallow pictorial space was favored *(Figs. 114, 115, 118, 122).* This same convention was followed in the paintings *(Figs. 9, 11),* a decision especially telling because Mitsunobu's Kangakuin paintings, those most closely related in style to the paintings here, as well as countless other contemporary Kano works, show that Kano artists typically incorporated into their paintings at least some views into the far distance. Notwithstanding this tradition, the painter of Sutemaru's building chose to depict only limited recession, a choice which maintained the visual unity of the ensemble.

The predominance of shallow space is emphasized by contrast with the areas of depiction having no illusory space, found on those parts of the building that frame the major pictorial elements. No illusion of spatial recession is suggested, for example, in the lacquer on the four corner pillars: the exterior faces are filled with a floral scroll of paulownia and chrysanthemum crests, and either peony flowers or bellflower crests *(Figs. 6, 7),* while the thin interior portions are likewise covered with a floral scroll and bellflower crests. Nonrepresentational architectural coloring is applied to other framing elements: dense geometric patterns are painted directly on the wood just below the roof on the exterior *(Fig. 17);* they also cover the beams running just below the ceiling in the interior *(Figs. 8, 10, 14, 128);* the frames of the carving-filled exterior walls are colored with bright pigments (*Figs. 3–7*), as is the wood grid that contains the numerous ceiling paintings *(Figs. 8, 10, 14).* As we have already seen, the ceiling paintings themselves are framed by gold-leafed paper borders filled with a stencilled pattern of paulownia and chrysanthemum crests. These passages of flat decoration all act as boundaries to passages of spatial illusion; the flat ornament draws attention to, but does not distract from, the primary shallow-spaced pictorial program contained within its frames.

The consistency of these spatial descriptions in Sutemaru's building decoration reveals the high degree of coordination that Mitsunobu exercised in this ensemble of multiple mediums. His willingness to suppress his own workshop's tendency toward deeper pictorial space reveals the importance attached to the choice. This consistency helps blend the disparate mediums into a single unified vision. One is encouraged not to look into a fictive distance, but rather to concentrate on a fictive foreground that contains all of the pictured elements, the carriers of the all-important symbolic meaning. It has the effect, too, of keeping one's eye on the surface of this sensual ensemble, where the material and visual richness of the ensemble is most apparent. The elegant glow of the gold and black lacquer, the gleaming opacity of the gold-leafed and painted polychromy, the deeply carved facets of the wood carvings, the variegated brilliance of the architectural coloring, the luminescence of the gilt metalwork—these coalesce in our experience of the initial, powerful attraction of the object. Their commingling makes one notice and be drawn to Sutemaru's building.

The proof of Mitsunobu's directing role is entirely visual. No documentary evidence supports this thesis, and considering the structure's eventual dislocation and the destruction of Shōunji, no such evidence is likely ever to surface. In the Momoyama period, however, Kano artists frequently functioned as guiding directors of diverse armies of artists in lacquer, metalwork, wood carving, and painting: we have seen Mitsunobu's father, Eitoku, in this role during the creation of Nobunaga's Azuchi Castle. A couple of generations later Kano Tan'yū (1602–1674) may have served in the same capacity in the creation of Nijō Castle.[72] Documentary evidence of exchange between artists working in different mediums suggests that the painter typically provided drawings as models for artists in the other mediums. This occurred, for example, between the Kano painters and the Gotō metalworking workshop, as recorded in the *Gotō kafu,* which states that Kano Motonobu (1476–1559) and Gotō Kōjō lived near each other; that Kōjō offered critiques of Motonobu's completed works; that Kōjō requested drawings from Motonobu; and that Motonobu's sketches were preserved in the Gotō house.[73] A passage in the 1678 *Honchō gashi (The History of Painting in This Realm),* admittedly a biased Kano-authored text,[74] states that the excellence of Gotō Yūjō's metalworking technique derived from Kano Motonobu's paintings.[75]

Such written evidence documents the fact of interaction but does not convey its processes or results. They tell us only that an artist in one medium occasionally provided drawings or criticism to an artist in another medium, but not how the drawing or criticism was then used. The material evidence preserved at Sutemaru's ensemble reveals the dynamic of the exchange between artists. Even conspicuous instances of direct inter-medium borrowing, such as the fuyō, show that such borrowing was in no way constrictive. The artist who did the borrowing did not merely copy the model, he adapted it by exploiting his own tradition. Even within the fictive shallow space of the lacquer, the artists found leeway to include within the clouds the cornucopia of miniaturized auspicious motifs—these do not distract from the otherwise consistent illusion of space, but rather contribute to the overall sense of abundance in the paradisal program. Although exchange and overall coordination of the various mediums shaped the formal character of the ensemble, they in no way led to mechanical production. Working freely within prescribed boundaries, the artists created an ensemble in which the individual characteristics of each medium contribute to the brilliant effect of the whole.

How would Sutemaru's ensemble have been received by the Momoyama viewer? Certainly its target audience of elites would have easily appreciated it on the basis of iconography. And doubtless they would have appreciated it equally as a sensual visual experience. This dense compendium of floral and avian motifs, rendered in the period's most respected mediums of polychrome-and-gold painting, relief sculpture, makie lacquer, gilt metalwork, and architectural coloring, forms a seamless program of decoration that well performs the task of sacred commemoration.

This ensemble is the Momoyama archetype of shōgon: the celebration of a sacred manifestation—a religious building, a sculpture or a painting of a Buddha—by means of impressive adornment. Shōgon, as revealed in all of the examples noted above, is often achieved not by a single medium alone, but rather by the combination of mediums. This expression of aesthetic intent was used by the Japanese to describe fine religious buildings. In 1598, when Hideyoshi's restoration of Daigoji's deteriorated tenth-century pagoda was completed and the scaffolding was removed, Gien registered his praise with the exclamation "shōgon, very commendable," meaning that the structure had been returned to a physical glory appropriate to its sacred status.[76] In a sense, shōgon is the religious equivalent of the phrase "jinzen jinbi," which connotes an aesthetic goodness that bespeaks moral goodness; shōgon reveals the inner sacredness of something through glorious outward appearance. But whereas "jinzen jinbi" was an erudite, perhaps even arcane expression—Gien's diary, where it occurs, was written for himself alone—shōgon was in that period a term of wide currency and commonly understood implications. To memorialize his son with a fitting Buddhist monument, Hideyoshi required a magnificence of decoration that made the structure the very embodiment of shōgon.

5

After Hideyoshi: Hideyori's Enlistment of the Sacred

REMAINING RELEVANT AFTER HIDEYOSHI

Abruptly, in the first years of the seventeenth century, Sutemaru's building lost its original bearings. Until then, from the time it was built in the 1590s, this remarkably cohesive and praiseworthy ensemble stood in Kyoto as a monument answering the specific memorial needs of its Toyotomi patrons. And then, as suggested in the 1602 Benzaiten Hall ridgepole placard and by the epigraphic and physical evidence on the ensemble itself, the Toyotomi shipped it to Chikubushima and inserted it into a building constructed on the island some forty years earlier. It became a building core, a *moya,* surrounded by a *hisashi* adapted from the older building. From the two structures plus additional carvings of unclear origin, was created a single new building, a new Benzaiten Hall. But the question remains, why?

The re-creation of the Benzaiten Hall transpired amidst the political flux of the years after Hideyoshi's death in 1598. Whereas Sutemaru's building expressed a limited, essentially familial response to a discrete event, the Benzaiten Hall was remade in conjunction with gradually unfolding circumstances that were overtly more public in character. During those years Hideyoshi's heir, Hideyori, putatively sponsored many construction projects at temples and shrines, and so consideration of the re-created Benzaiten Hall requires, first, an overview of that broader effort. In that effort the Toyotomi are the central actors, but their activities are fully meaningful only in relation to the Tokugawa, the other family that dominated Japan in the early years of the seventeenth century. The Tokugawa soon came to rule Japan virtually unopposed for a full two and a half centuries, but until 1615 the Toyotomi remained a political force and were considered by many a viable, even preferable, alternative.

Though Hideyoshi on his deathbed attempted to secure with solemn oaths the transfer of power to his seven-year-old heir, Hideyori, once he was gone those oaths of allegiance rapidly unravelled, leading to the pivotal (though in truth inconclusive) Battle of Sekigahara in 1600. Even before Sekigahara the Toyotomi camp recognized the instability of its position and responded by promptly adopting a policy that continued and expanded Hideyoshi's campaign of building—concretely and conceptually—Japan's sacred realm. They created one major new religious site, the Toyokuni (also read Hōkoku) Shrine in Kyoto, which became the stage for Toyotomi-centered fanfare in the capital. Most fundamentally, however, the campaign comprised the repair or reconstruction of old religious sites both in Kyoto and outside it, in their home territory and far beyond it. To some of these Hideyoshi had pledged assistance before his death; others were newly selected. The Kyoto centerpiece of this restorative effort was, unsurprisingly, Hōkōji—the inauspicious Zenkōji triad had been exiled, and the Great Buddha was still in shambles—a project that consumed the Toyotomi until their demise. The Toyotomi thereby rebuilt and enlarged the sacred realm, attempting, by positioning themselves as mediators between it and our mundane world, to achieve their own political regeneration.

REAPPRAISING THE POST-HIDEYOSHI TOYOTOMI

Traditionally, the post-Hideyoshi period was characterized as one of quick Tokugawa ascent and corresponding Toyotomi decline, but scholarly re-examination has revealed the Toyotomi as a more considerable force until their ultimate demise in 1615.[1] Nonetheless, the often-repeated interpretation of Toyotomi patronage of religious construction, including the Chikubushima project, casts Hideyori and the entire Toyotomi clan as little more than puppets expertly played by Ieyasu.[2] In this scenario Hideyoshi had inadequately prepared for the preservation of Toyotomi ascendancy during his son's childhood, leaving the Toyotomi politically powerless and Ieyasu on the rise. As a strategy to drain the rich economic resources of the Toyotomi and thereby eliminate their potential for opposition, Ieyasu, under the pretense of respect for Hideyoshi's memory, encouraged the Toyotomi to finance costly building projects. Hideyori's primary administrator of the projects, Katagiri Katsumoto (1556–1615), was a perfidious vassal, opening the Toyotomi coffers at Ieyasu's behest.

This interpretation ignores or at least oversimplifies the significance of Toyotomi sponsorship of religious construction and ritual in the power politics of early seventeenth-century Japan. By claiming responsibility for monuments freighted with associations both venerable and vital, and by lavishing them with patronage intended to appear unprecedented, the Toyotomi were attempting to improve their political standing in the post-Hideyoshi era. The eventual Tokugawa triumph and subsequent two hundred and fifty years of uninterrupted hegemony should not mislead us into thinking that the Toyotomi vanished from the center stage of Japanese politics on Hideyoshi's death.

Tokugawa domination of the Japanese government was not the immediate result of a single event, but rather an incremental triumph achieved over more than fifteen years. Hideyoshi had empowered two administrative offices, the Five Regents (the Gotairō) and Five Administrators (the Gobugyō)—in essence, two coalitions of his most powerful vassals—to carry out the business of government after his death in the name of Hideyori, binding them with mighty oaths to serve Hideyori's interests and to relinquish their authority to the young man when he came of age.[3] After Hideyoshi died in 1598, the system functioned only briefly as planned. The inherent volatility of the coalitions, composed of warriors with conflicting interests, allegiances, and power bases, soon degenerated from friction to mobilization for war. In the ninth month of 1600 two huge armies, the Eastern and Western, fought the great day-long Battle of Sekigahara on the outskirts of the eponymous village near the northeastern shore of Lake Biwa. The Eastern forces, led by Ieyasu, soundly defeated Ishida Mitsunari's fractured Western army, and so Ieyasu emerged as the single most powerful military figure in the country.

Even with that victory, however, Ieyasu could not claim to have entirely displaced the Toyotomi regime. Indeed, both sides at Sekigahara fought on the pretext of defending Hideyori, and even after the battle, orders were issued with reference to Hideyoshi's directives.[4] Although Ieyasu gained widely recognized political powers soon after Hideyoshi's death, the coalition of warrior might backing his authority was not absolutely secure: it was newly formed and subject to unpredictable shifts in allegiance.[5] In fact, the Tokugawa as well as the Toyotomi sought for a time non-hostile coexistence, embodied in marriage alliances: the young Hideyori was married to Ieyasu's granddaughter Sen Hime (1597–1666) in the seventh month of 1603; Ieyasu wed Hideyoshi's younger sister; and Ieyasu's heir Hidetada (1579–1632) betrothed an adopted daughter of Hideyoshi.[6]

The Toyotomi, on the other hand, were well positioned to wait on the future. Hideyori, as Hideyoshi's designated heir, was an excellent vehicle by which Toyotomi aspirations for a larger role in Japan's power structure eventually could be realized. His youth—Hideyori was only seven when Hideyoshi died—encouraged the Toyotomi to work slowly toward achieving their potential.[7] Patience was feasible, in part, because the family retained a substantial stake in the post-Sekigahara settlement. From their apparently impregnable base at Osaka Castle, built by Hideyoshi and thus a monumental reminder of the family's once unmatched authority, the Toyotomi controlled a reduced but still massive domain of 657,000 *koku,* covering the three well-located provinces of Settsu, Kawachi, and Izumi (contained within the present-day prefectures of Osaka and Hyōgo).[8] The Imperial Court and many warrior elites regularly sent seasonal greetings and gifts to the Toyotomi throughout the period, showing a deference they would not have tendered to a family they regarded as no more than an equal among the many regional daimyo.[9] Even after Sekigahara there still remained important warrior leaders fiercely committed to the Toyotomi. All understood that the Toyotomi's strength was lessened but not eliminated: in 1601 the powerful Tokugawa vassal Date

Masamune (1567–1636) counselled, "In Osaka, if you treat it casually, there are those who wait for the right time to cause trouble in the realm, and will attempt to make Hideyori leader."[10]

Although the child heir Hideyori was, at the start, a figurehead for the Toyotomi cause, behind him stood his sharp and ambitious mother, Yododono (d. 1615). In her early years Yododono had already been tempered by the vacillations of warrior-class fortune.[11] Her father was Asai Nagamasa (1545–1573), the powerful ruler of northern Ōmi who, as we have seen, was defeated by Oda Nobunaga's forces in 1573 and his domain awarded to Hideyoshi. Yododono's widowed mother (Nobunaga's younger sister) then married Shibata Katsuie, but in 1583 Katsuie lost a battle to Hideyoshi, and he and Yododono's mother took their own lives. Orphaned and still in her teens, Yododono entered Hideyoshi's care and eventually became one of his consorts. From these precarious beginnings, Yododono emerged as one of the most powerful women of those dangerous times.

She rose to prominence within Hideyoshi's entourage by bearing him his only two children, both sons: the frail Sutemaru, born in 1589 (only to die in 1591), and then Hideyori, born in 1593. Hideyoshi favored Yododono with attention. He built her a castle residence in Yodo, south of Kyoto, and when they were separated, he wrote to her of his longing to have her at his side, summoning her to his battle camp in Odawara and to Nagoya Castle in Kyushu.[12] After Hideyoshi's death Yododono moved with Hideyori to Osaka Castle and was an active leader in the creation of Toyotomi policy. Although Hideyori is the central Toyotomi figure in the official documentary record from 1598 until the destruction of the clan in 1615, Yododono emerges occasionally in private writings—diaries and letters—as a figure who wielded substantial power.

Hideyori's high Imperial Court rank contributed greatly to the Toyotomi's continued significance after Sekigahara.[13] Though itself powerless, the Court arbitrated the legitimacy of others' claims to temporal authority. As Hideyoshi's recognized heir, Hideyori had a justifiable claim to official eminence, which the Court recognized by steadily elevating him through its ranks. In the fourth month of 1603, when he was eleven, Hideyori was appointed to the high rank of Naidaijin.[14] Ieyasu, too, notwithstanding his military advantage sealed by the victory at Sekigahara, sought to reinforce his and his family's authority by accepting court titles, including in the second month of 1603 that of Seiitaishōgun, the highest military rank within the Court. In the fourth month of 1605 he yielded this exalted title to his son Hidetada, completing in his lifetime the transfer of legitimated authority to his heir that neither Nobunaga or Hideyoshi had achieved. In this context Ieyasu could not forcibly eliminate Hideyori without appearing to disregard the authority of the Court, thereby endangering the Tokugawa claims to legitimacy that he so carefully fostered.

Ieyasu moved gradually to make Tokugawa ascendancy firm.[15] After retiring from the post of shogun in 1605, he moved from Kyoto to Sunpu, in the east. There he worked to form an effective governing apparatus, recognizing from recent precedent that without an administrative structure to complement military influence, Tokugawa hegemony would not last. By the beginning of the second decade of the seventeenth century, the Tokugawa position of authority in Japan was nearly unassailable, and from this time it becomes increasingly clear (certainly to us and no doubt to some contemporaries) that peaceful coexistence between the two clans was untenable. Ieyasu gained control over much of the Court's affairs, and in the third month of 1611 he received Hideyori at Nijō Castle in Kyoto, a symbolic display of Tokugawa dominance over the Toyotomi that he had failed to achieve six years earlier, in 1605. Ieyasu extracted pledges of fealty from daimyo throughout Japan, solidifying his position among the regional rulers as their supreme leader.

The Toyotomi, however, remained on Japan's stage. From 1612, having turned twenty and thus attained adulthood—when he could be expected to assert his bequeathed authority—Hideyori granted stipends to warriors in his service, including lands in Kawachi and Settsu, but also in areas beyond his supposed domain, in the provinces of Yamashiro, Ōmi, and Bitchū. In doing so, he was asserting authority over those lands as well as the right to reward those who served him.[16] In the sixth month of 1614 Hideyori enlarged the holdings of Katagiri Katsumoto, administrator of many Toyotomi construction projects, by adding 10,000 koku from lands even more widespread, in Yamato, Ise, Mino, Tanba, and, on the island of Shikoku, Sanuki and Iyo; that same month Hideyori also increased the domain of Katsumoto's younger brother Sadataka (1560–1627), by over 5,000 koku.[17] As late as the seventh month of 1614 Hideyori's retainers were awarded court rank without the petition of Ieyasu, the only warrior-class group so distinguished.[18] About this time the Court was considering bestowing on Hideyori the rank of *kanpaku*, the highest Court position held by his father. Hideyori was manifesting the aura and actions of traditional power.

Ieyasu needed to act decisively, and the Tokugawa position was now secure enough

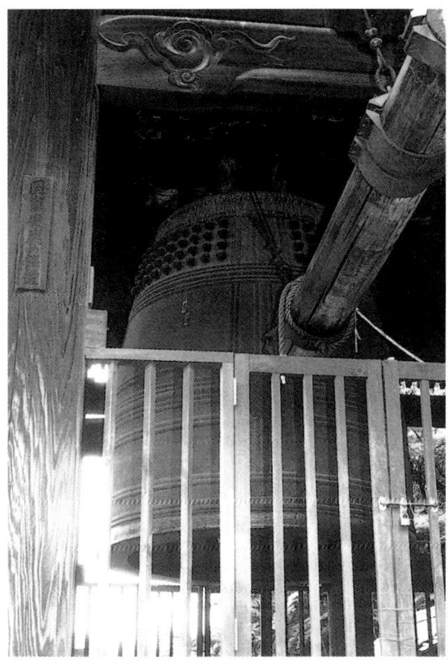

FIG. 129 Bell. 1614. Hōkōji, Kyoto. Photograph by the author.

to do so. A pretext for confrontation was found in the inscription on an enormous bell that Hideyori commissioned as part of the reconstruction of his father's Hōkōji *(Fig. 129)*. The inscription could be interpreted, the Tokugawa contended, to solicit support for the Toyotomi cause, and moreover included the two characters that form Ieyasu's name divided—maliciously, the Tokugawa averred—by a third character. Using the purported threat and insult as justification, Tokugawa forces attacked and eliminated the Toyotomi with bloody finality in the two Osaka Campaigns of 1614 and 1615, and so extinguished the possibility of a Toyotomi succession.[19] To those who remained loyal to the extinct Toyotomi, it could have been of some solace that even as Ieyasu took his last breath, he was unsure of this achievement: rumors that Hideyori had survived the Osaka attacks, and was waiting for his opportunity to rise again, persisted well into 1616; Ieyasu died in that year without the security of knowing that this potential rallying point against Tokugawa hegemony had, in fact, perished.[20]

THE TOYOTOMI AND RELIGION IN THE POST-HIDEYOSHI ERA

A full fifteen years passed between the Sekigahara and Osaka battles, an extended period in which the relationship between the Toyotomi and the Tokugawa was not uniform but changeable. The early seventeenth-century construction project on Chikubushima, including the restoration of the Benzaiten Hall, reflects in microcosm the early stage of the evolving relationship between the two families. Examination of the Chikubushima project in this light replaces the orthodox interpretation (the Toyotomi as hapless puppets of the Tokugawa) with a far more balanced reading of the roles of the participants; equally important, it reveals the importance of the sacred in the Toyotomi's efforts to retain hegemony. Our analysis thus begins with the larger context of activities of which the Chikubushima project forms one important part.

Although the Toyotomi surely desired to topple the Tokugawa from their increasingly commanding position of political authority, they refrained from explicit challenge or provocation. Instead, in the first decade of the seventeenth century they created a religious platform from which they might claim a position of legitimated dominance. When the Tokugawa were able to aver such an intent, in the Hōkōji bell inscription incident of 1614, they used it to justify elimination of the Toyotomi. Two sets of circumstances spurred the Tokugawa drive to eliminate Hideyori: first, the latter had reached his twenties and might have emerged a forceful leader of the Toyotomi cause, and second, the Tokugawa concluded correctly that they had not only the need but the military and political capacity to act decisively. Until that time the Toyotomi needed only to sustain the memory of the glorious—and very recent—Toyotomi past, manifested in Hideyoshi, whom the Toyotomi had deified, and to project an equally promising future, embodied in the young Hideyori. By engaging accepted religious practice, the Toyotomi tapped the authority that the sacred was widely believed to hold and made it the foundation for their political strategy.

SPONSORING THE SACRED

In the post-Hideyoshi era, with most of the actual administrative authority in the hands of the Tokugawa, there were few activities the Toyotomi could pursue that would convincingly advocate their continued relevance. Almost immediately after Hideyoshi's death, therefore, they embarked on massive sponsorship of the sacred, a campaign which might promise political as well as spiritual salvation. The most effective acts were those that were most conspicuous: the reconstruction of buildings not only in their home territory within and around Osaka, but also in Kyoto and throughout Japan, and the conduct of spectacular, often public rituals at these sites. These activities were open and striking, but the Toyotomi also engaged in religious ritual at Osaka Castle that was more private in nature, explicitly performed to benefit the Toyotomi family. It is evident, however, that even this was designed to have an impact that transcended family bounds, for the Toyotomi never lacked an audience: the constant presence at Osaka Castle of military, Court, and religious figures insured that many of the Osaka ceremonies had a public aspect, and the magnificence of the ceremonies—and the Toyotomi's energetic conduct of them—were apparent for all to see.

Illuminating accounts of Toyotomi "private" religious practice can be gleaned from contemporary diaries, especially Gien's, which indicate that the family ordered ceremonies to address internal problems as they arose. During the disquiet of 1600, shortly after Fushimi Castle burned and five weeks before the confrontation at Sekigahara, a messenger from Osaka informed Gien that on the tenth day of the eighth month he was to chant a sutra, the *Daihannya kyō,* for Hideyori, for "tranquillity in the realm and everlasting fortune in war."[21] Unusual natural phenomena near the castle brought orders from the Toyotomi for ritual performance, as in 1608 when a shining object was seen flying through the skies of Osaka, and in 1609 when it was noticed that "the calls of the crows were inauspicious and the foxes were wandering about."[22] These requests came directly from Osaka, and when Gien performed the requested ceremony at Daigoji, as opposed to traveling to Osaka, he would typically send scrolls recording the ritual *(kanju)* to Osaka on completion of the ceremony. Despite its recent ineffectiveness in Sutemaru's and Hideyoshi's final illnesses, Toyotomi faith in the curative power of ritual continued, as was entirely typical of Japan's elites. Gien provided Buddhist services when Hideyori or Yododono was unwell;[23] Bonshun, too, records in his diary that Osaka requested him to conduct seven days of ceremonies at the Yoshida Shrine for Yododono when she was ailing in 1613.[24] Ieyasu made similar petitions: Gien conducted rituals when Ieyasu fell ill in 1601, again when Ieyasu's mother was stricken the following year, and then in 1604 for the recovery of Ieyasu's son.[25] Temporal figures sponsored worship in response to private crises, fueling the rituals with substantial financial reward to the institutions where they were held.

The Toyotomi also adhered to a regular schedule of Buddhist ceremonies at Osaka Castle, not in response to acute problems but to facilitate the family's general welfare. The annual Toyotomi liturgical calendar began with a *Daihannya kyō* ceremony, which from 1601 through 1614 was held on the sixteenth day of the first month, and for which

Gien always travelled to Osaka Castle. This New Year's practice in fact was instituted in the second month of 1600, when the ceremony, termed "rites for the beginning of the year," was attended by many powerful daimyo; Gien describes the event as "jinzen jinbi" ("perfectly good and perfectly beautiful"), and his detailed account indicates that it was a magnificent spectacle.[26] Gien also offered Buddhist ceremonies for Hideyori on the third day of many months, Hideyori having been born on the *third day* of the eighth month of 1593.[27] Appeals to the sacred were, simply, the accepted manner of mediating all important aspects of life.

DEPLOYING THE DEIFIED HIDEYOSHI

The balance of public to private intent in the religious practice at Osaka was wholly reversed in the ceremonies and the buildings constructed for them that the Toyotomi sponsored in Kyoto, still the conceptual center of Japan. In Kyoto remained the Emperor and his Court, the traditional fount of authority that ambitious warriors still tapped for the imprimatur of legitimacy. Important warrior families maintained residences in Kyoto, foremost among them the Tokugawa, who constructed Nijō Castle there from 1602. Kyoto was a major commercial center and home to the producers of luxury goods—paintings, lacquer, textiles, metalwork, and ceramics—required by the elites. The sacred presence in the city was formidable, and now shorn of its earlier potential for discord: Enryakuji protected all from its towering mountain site; temples dotted the urban landscape, with a particular concentration in three districts; even Honganji was re-established there (see p. 72). And, fortunately for the Toyotomi, much of Kyoto's urban design still spoke plainly of Hideyoshi and his refabrication of the city. Within two decades Kyoto would lose its focal status and role, transferred eastward by the Tokugawa to their new capital at Edo, but for now it was the chief site for civic display, and the Toyotomi took full advantage.

In Kyoto the Toyotomi carried out the central sacred project of the post-Hideyoshi era: the deification of the recently deceased Hideyoshi and the concurrent creation of Toyokuni Shrine, the grand Shinto complex in which he was worshipped.[28] The process began to unfold concretely on the sixth day of the ninth month of 1598—less than a month after Hideyoshi's death—when, as Gien reports, the Toyotomi magistrate Maeda Gen'i (1539–1602) began to survey a site near Hōkōji for a "shrine building in the eight-ridge style *(yatsumune zukuri)*, like Kitano Shrine" (an ancient precinct in Kyoto shortly thereafter restored by Hideyori).[29] Several days later, he reports that the new shrine is to be the *chinju*—the protector—of the Great Buddha, that the pillars of the temporary structure were to be raised on the sixteenth, and that included in the plans was the construction of twelve subsidiary buildings, all to be realized with the support of various daimyo.[30] At the request of the Mount Kōya monk Ōgo (1536–1608), Gien performed a ground-breaking ceremony on the fifteenth.[31]

A mammoth project was fully underway, though Gien, like many others, may still have been unaware of its true purpose. Bonshun's is the only period diary to mention Hideyoshi's death when it actually occurred (see p. 100), and apparently it was not widely announced until several months later. Those who normally had access to Hideyoshi, however, and were privy to his long illness and ever-worsening appearance, might quickly have surmised his death. Toward the end of the year Gien first alludes to his suspicions: on the sixth day of the twelfth month he recalls that Hideyoshi made a promise, which he describes as perhaps a "dying wish" *(yuigon),* to donate twenty koku each to the upper and lower precincts of Daigoji;[32] on the eighteenth day he notes that Ieyasu and several daimyo went to the "Great Buddha chinju," and he speculates that perhaps it was Hideyoshi's *kinichi,* that is, his memorial day (the day of the month on which he died).[33] A month later, early in the new year, Gien notes that Hideyoshi's death had been kept a secret until recently.[34] The reasons for concealment are unexplained, and those closest to the center of political power surely knew of the event, but it is clear that behind the scenes and unknown to many was unfolding a remarkable Toyotomi enterprise to transform Hideyoshi from human to deified object of worship.[35] Toward the end of 1598 Maeda Gen'i met to discuss the shrine (and perhaps the uncommon process of apotheosis[36]) with Yoshida Kanemi (1535–1610), scion of a family which had long advised the Court on Shinto matters.[37]

Once Hideyoshi's death was public knowledge, apotheosis quickly followed and the nature of the new project became more precisely known. In early 1599 Gien reports that he had heard the deity of the new protector shrine of the Great Buddha was to be Hideyoshi.[38] In the third month the Toyotomi petitioned the Court regarding this Shinto deification, stating that it was Hideyoshi's "dying wish to be worshipped at a great shrine on Amidanotake," that is, the mountain overlooking the Great Buddha Hall where the new shrine was being built.[39]

A rapid succession of events in the following month defined the new sacred presence.[40] On the thirteenth Hideyoshi's body was moved from Fushimi Castle to the mountain. On the sixteenth the deity was ritually transferred to temporary quarters. The next day Emperor Goyōzei (1571–1617) decreed the deity's name to be Toyokuni Daimyōjin, "Most Bright God of Our Bountiful Country,"[41] a name whose component parts advanced the Toyotomi claims: the first character, *toyo* 豊, is the first character of Toyotomi, and the second character, *kuni* 国, means "country," thereby joining this family and Japan in symbiotic inseparability; the two characters also begin and end several compounds that were ancient names of Japan, some of which occur in the *Kojiki* and the *Nihon shoki,* eighth-century imperially sponsored histories of Japan. Hideyoshi's divine name condenses and subsumes Japan as it was designated in these earliest and much revered chronicles.[42] On the eighteenth Toyokuni Daimyōjin was formally installed into the permanent shrine hall, while enormous crowds of Kyotoites gathered and the various courtier houses and aristocrat-abbots *(monzeki)* donated large sums of money. On the nineteenth the Court conferred on him the highest rank within the Shinto hierarchy, and homage was paid by many elite warriors, including Tokugawa Ieyasu. Over the next two weeks a variety of rituals and performances were conducted, and Hideyori, his mother Yododono, Ieyasu, and many other elite persons donated enormous sums of silver and gold to the shrine.

And so in a month's time Hideyoshi was reinvented as a Shinto deity of the highest order and installed at a site neighboring Hōkōji. He was transformed from temporal intermediary of sacred protection of Japan (through his sponsorship of the Great Buddha) to the eternal, deified agency of protection itself. His family hoped to be elevated by relationship with this suddenly manifested god to a correspondingly privileged standing; Hideyori was the most closely related to Toyokuni Daimyōjin, an association the Toyotomi sought to perpetuate and publicize. To this end, the young Hideyori brushed numerous calligraphies of the deity's name, typically one vertical line of boldly brushed (if not yet expert) characters on a long piece of paper, and, at the lower left, his own name and age. Many examples are extant, and it appears that the Toyotomi sent them as precious talismanic objects to temples and shrines throughout Japan. Gien mentions receiving one such calligraphy, which he sent to have mounted for preservation and display and which remains today in Daigoji *(Fig. 130)*.[43] The Toyokuni compound was carefully maintained until 1615,[44] and its financial security was assured in the seventh month of 1601, when Hideyori awarded it the enormous income of 10,000 koku a year.[45] Hideyoshi's deification at the Toyokuni Shrine was the opening bid by the Toyotomi to assume sacred preeminence and thereby remain broadly relevant even after Hideyoshi's death.

Although the original shrine is long lost, its glorious appearance is confirmed in contemporary writings. Richard Cocks (1566–1624), director of the short-lived English factory in Hirado, described the buildings in his diary in 1616, when they were still in good condition. The Toyokuni Shrine is, he wrote,

> a thinge to be wondred at, and rather to be admired then to be discribed. It is a hudge big howse, of an admerable workmanshipp both within and without, far excelling either of the other temples, and within it many pillars covered with bras enameled and gilded over with gould; and the flowre of plankes very black, shynyng lyke ebony. But we could not be sufferd to enter, but only to look in a wyndor or grates. And to the place where the corps (or ashes) are set, yow must assend up 8 or 9 steps or degrees, very lardge, made parte of gilded bras and parte of black wood or ebony. And by the corps borneth a contynewall lampe, watched by a *boz* or pagon prist. And for the workemanshipp about that place, it exceedeth my memory to discribe it; only, all I can say, it may well befitt the entering of so famouse an Emperour.[46]

Unsurprisingly, the monumentally large main shrine and the building holding Hideyoshi's remains were spectacular; the shrine's pillars were covered with gilt metalwork and gold lacquer and the floor glowed with black lacquer. The best pictorial evidence for the shrine's appearance is found in paintings that record the shrine's function as a center of Toyotomi worship, as we will examine below. The Toyokuni Shrine was the platform from which the Toyotomi proclaimed their continued presence as a contender

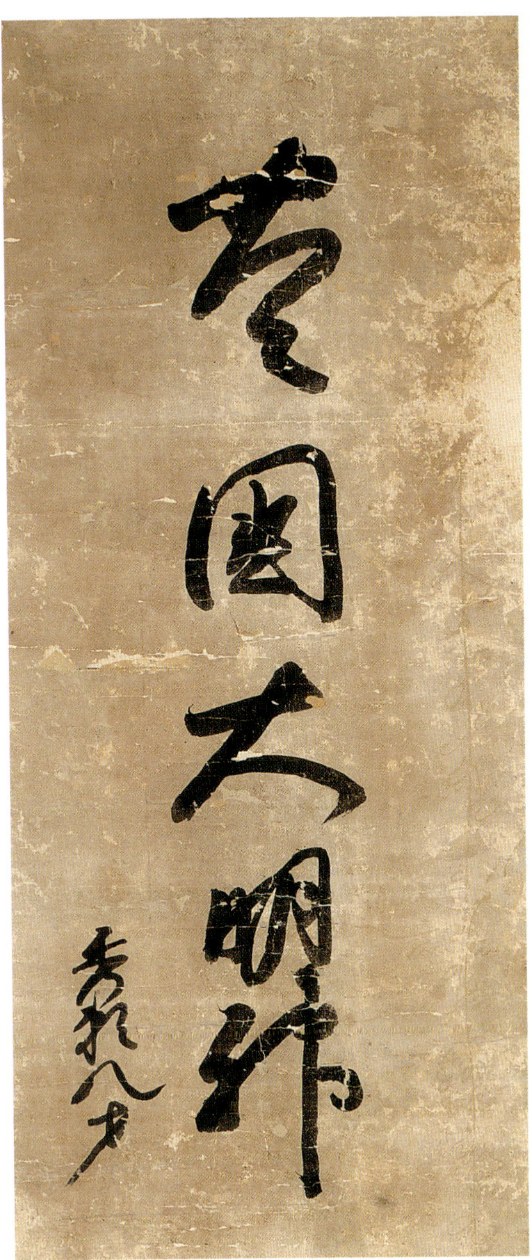

FIG. 130 Toyotomi Hideyori. Calligraphy reading "Toyokuni Daimyōjin." Early seventeenth century. Hanging scroll; ink on paper. Daigoji, Kyoto.

for countrywide power, and this they did through monumentally conceived, gloriously executed religious ceremonies.

Daimyo built branches of Kyoto's Toyokuni Shrine in other parts of Japan, thereby spreading the Hideyoshi cult and providing additional focal points for support of the Toyotomi.[17] Kato Kiyomasa (1562–1611), for example, who had long served under Hideyoshi (but fought on the Tokugawa side at the Battle of Sekigahara), established a branch shrine in his domain in Kyushu in the eleventh month of 1599, only a half-year after the founding of the main shrine in Kyoto. In Nagahama, the seat of what had been Hideyoshi's first domain, another branch was established in 1600, for which Emperor Goyōzei calligraphed the name plaque. Hideyori established one in Osaka Castle in 1606, facilitating worship at the central Toyotomi stronghold. Gien, the head priest at Daigoji and especially favored recipient of Hideyoshi's largesse, established a branch shrine within the precincts of his temple and thereafter, each month on the eighteenth day (the day Hideyoshi died), sponsored ritual dance *(kagura)* followed by Buddhist ceremonies.[48]

THE TOYOKUNI FESTIVALS

In short order, in 1599, semiannual observances began at Kyoto's Toyokuni Shrine. Many diaries of the period note these activities, though none are as complete as the diary kept by Bonshun, head priest of the temple associated with the Toyokuni Shrine. On the eighteenth day of the eighth month of 1599, the first anniversary of Hideyoshi's death, Bonshun records ceremonies at the shrine, including ritual dance performances, attended by representatives from the Court and from Osaka and by Ieyasu as well.[49] Ceremonies had begun the previous day, and a program of Nō was performed on the nineteenth. Gien notes in his diary that daimyo from all the provinces, without exception, attended the shrine on the eighteenth; he himself did not attend, but merely reported what he had heard. He had heard a great deal, however: the observances at the Toyokuni Shrine were much discussed in Kyoto, and that is precisely as the Toyotomi wished.[50]

The 1599 ceremonies set the precedent for the Toyokuni Festival, large-scale semiannual worship at the Toyokuni Shrine.[51] Every year thereafter, until the commencement of the Osaka battles in 1614, the Festival took place over a three-day period centered on the eighteenth day of the fourth and eighth months, respectively the anniversaries of the ritual installation of the deity and of Hideyoshi's death. The proceedings followed a fixed schedule. On the seventeenth day of both months the ceremonies were attended by Court and military figures bearing offerings for Toyokuni Daimyōjin, usually money but also objects such as robes, swords, and fans; typically on this day Hideyoshi's widow, Kita no Mandokoro, would make an appearance. Ceremonies and often performance of some kind, such as kagura, were held. The eighteenth featured donations by representatives of the Court and of Hideyori. The third day, the nineteenth, comprised a program of Nō dramas, well attended by military and Court figures; at least twice over the lifetime of the Festival the Nō drama *Chikubushima* was performed, a point we will return to below.

The semiannual Toyokuni Festivals were, however, only the most important commemorative event in a crowded calendar of worship. In each of the remaining ten months the eighteenth day was distinguished by what Bonshun refers to as "the matter of the *kami*," a small-scale version of the semiannual event. And a continual stream of donations arrived from a wide range of constituents, from Hideyori and Yododono, on whose behalf ritual was then conducted, as well as from other members of the Osaka entourage, from daimyo, and from representatives of the Court.

The Toyokuni Festival of 1604

Among all activities at the Toyokuni Shrine, one event stands out. On the occasion of Hideyoshi's seventh death anniversary, in 1604, the eighth-month ceremony was expanded into week-long festivities that sparked high excitement in Kyoto, the Toyokuni Special Festival (Toyokuni Rinjisai or Toyokuni Rinjisairei). The Toyotomi's largest public display in the post-Hideyoshi period, it glorified the deified Hideyoshi and, by association, his survivors, and by design involved the active participation of all sectors of Kyoto's population, from the highest to the lowest classes.

Although a Special Festival was also held in 1610, the thirteenth death anniversary, the one in 1604 was the most ambitious and conspicuous declaration of the Toyotomi's ambition to remain a strong presence in Japan.[52] As described in Bonshun's unadorned daily chronicle of the proceedings, the festival began on the twelfth day of the eighth month with a purification ritual, the *yudate no shinji,* and was then followed on the fourteenth by a huge procession (postponed from the day before because of rain) led by two people wearing ceremonial garb, the one on the left carrying a *nusa,* or Shinto offering of white folded paper, and the one on the right a seven-foot-tall gold-foiled *sakaki,* the sacred Shinto tree.[53] They were followed by a retinue of one hundred attendants in white Shinto robes. After these came two hundred people on horseback, mostly Shinto priests from Kyoto shrines and also fifteen musicians. Following the procession, *dengaku* (a form of liturgical dance and music) was performed by thirty people, and after that came presentations of Nō by the four established troupes, the Konparu, Kanze, Hōshō, and Kongō; to each of the four, Osaka gave payment in a ceremony that took place at the gate of the Toyokuni Shrine.

The next day, the fifteenth, brought together five hundred townspeople from all over Kyoto who convened in front of the Great Buddha Hall to perform dance in five groups, each with one hundred dancers. On this day, too, twenty koku of rice (enough to feed over seven thousand people) were distributed at the Great Buddha Hall as alms to the outcastes, thereby expanding the event to incorporate Hideyoshi's greatest Buddhist building and expressing the ecumenical nature of the Toyotomi's occupation of the sacred realm. On the sixteenth the Court sponsored kagura at the Toyokuni Shrine. The next two days followed the busy ceremonial schedule typical of the seventeenth and eighteenth days of the eighth-month event. On the nineteenth *bugaku* ritual dance was performed, but the scheduled performances of Nō were cancelled. On the twentieth Bonshun travelled to Osaka to inform Hideyori that the events had gone well, and to present him, Yododono, and several others with gifts. Bonshun's disciplined, detached diary entries thus record the factual sequence of events.

He left it to others to commemorate the colorful pageantry, the orderly tumult, the splendid excitement of this happening that transfixed and transformed Kyoto. Virtually all extant diaries of the period contain accounts of the 1604 Special Festival, some prosaic, others lively and enthusiastic at what the author had observed and, equally important, what he had heard from others. The anticipation with which Kyoto awaited the

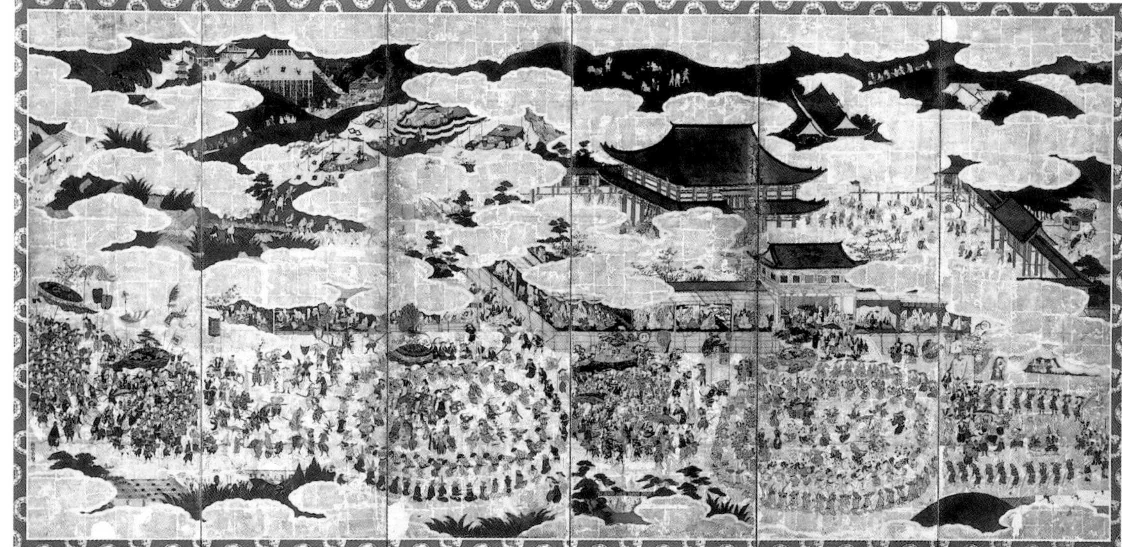

FIG. 131 (this page and opposite page) Kano Naizen. *Toyokuni Special Festival.* Early seventeenth century. Pair of six-fold screens; ink, color, and gold leaf. Toyokuni Jinja, Kyoto. Photograph by Kyoto National Museum.

long-planned festival is captured by the courtier Yamashina Tokitsune (1543–1611), who wrote on the twelfth, "Tomorrow, the fashionable from throughout Kyoto will go to the Toyokuni Shrine, so I will go with Kujō Dono to watch"; two days later he confirms that, although the events of the thirteenth were postponed, he was there for the dengaku, the grand mounted procession, Nō performances, and other activities during the fine weather of the fourteenth.[54] "The horses," Gien tells us, "were supplied by the various daimyo," and their equipage dazzles him: "the red tassels, red ropes, and gold and silver saddles—the beauty surprised the eye."[55] Ōta Gyūichi (b. 1527), warrior-biographer of Nobunaga and Hideyoshi, also left a detailed day-by-day record of the proceedings, which lists in great detail the various activities, even to naming many of the participants in the parades; he included, too, the lyrics sung by the dancers, including some they chanted on their way through Kyoto to the festival site: "The power of the Toyokuni god is boundless. It will be celebrated for eternity. We raise our voices in song."[56] The entire city, it seems, was caught up in the festive atmosphere.

Representing the 1604 Festival

The Toyotomi too commemorated the Special Festival of 1604, commissioning a pair of folding-screen paintings depicting the festival and donating them to the Toyokuni Shrine on the second anniversary of the event, the thirteenth day of the eighth month of 1606; the screens were set up in the lower chamber of the main worship hall in time for Hideyoshi's death anniversary on the eighteenth, Bonshun tells us, and many people viewed them.[57] The audience for such a painting likely comprised the unending stream

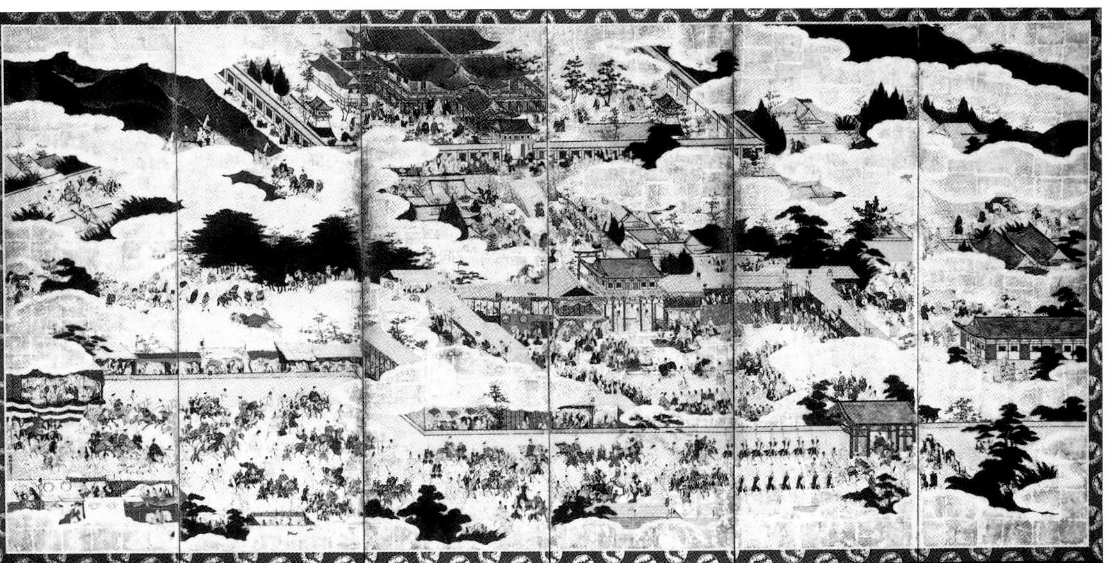

of shrine visitors—perhaps it was set up for viewing during the semiannual celebrations—and so it regularly disseminated the Toyotomi's reading of the event.

The immediate fate of these paintings during the shrine's dissolution after 1615 is unknown, though several pairs of Toyokuni Special Festival screens are extant. One of these, which bears the signature of Kano Naizen (1570–1616) and pictures the first two days of the 1604 festival, is generally accepted as the Toyotomi-commissioned paintings donated in 1606 *(Fig. 131)*.[58] Its recent history supports this possibility: it was donated to the Toyokuni Shrine in 1883 (shortly after the shrine was reopened) by Yoshida Nagayoshi, descended from the Shintoist Yoshida Kanemi, who had advised the Toyotomi during their planning of the Toyokuni Shrine. Tradition holds that the paintings had been in the Yoshida family since they were removed from the shrine sometime after the fall of the Toyotomi in 1615, a likely possibility given the Yoshida links with the shrine.[59]

In content, the ex-Yoshida screens seem the kind of paintings that the Toyotomi would have wanted as a commemorative, for they represent the festival in a manner distinctly favorable to the Toyotomi. Each densely populated screen is devoted to one day's principal event, one to the great procession and the performances of the fourteenth, the other to the frenetic dancing of the fifteenth, and each has as its compositional framework the architectural complexes where the events were staged, respectively the Toyokuni Shine and the Great Buddha Hall. Holding the festivities at both temple and shrine displayed the Toyotomi's syncretic conception of the sacred, a conception rehearsed, with emphasis, by pairing the two complexes on the screens. Typical of monumental polychrome screen paintings by the Kano workshop, scrims of gold clouds waft across the broad expanse of the horizontal format, concealing and revealing scenes and linking all in their weave. The screens portray a population joined in diversely expressed and magnificently realized mass veneration at a series of magnificent buildings that together form a religious epicenter.

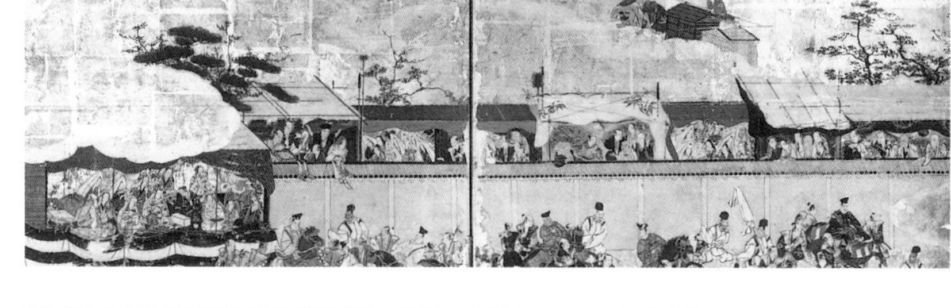

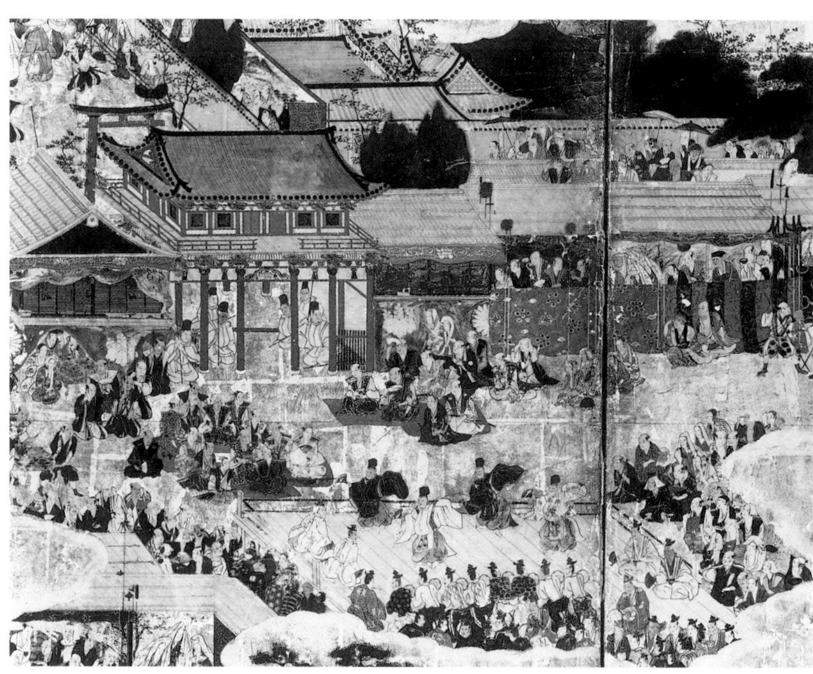

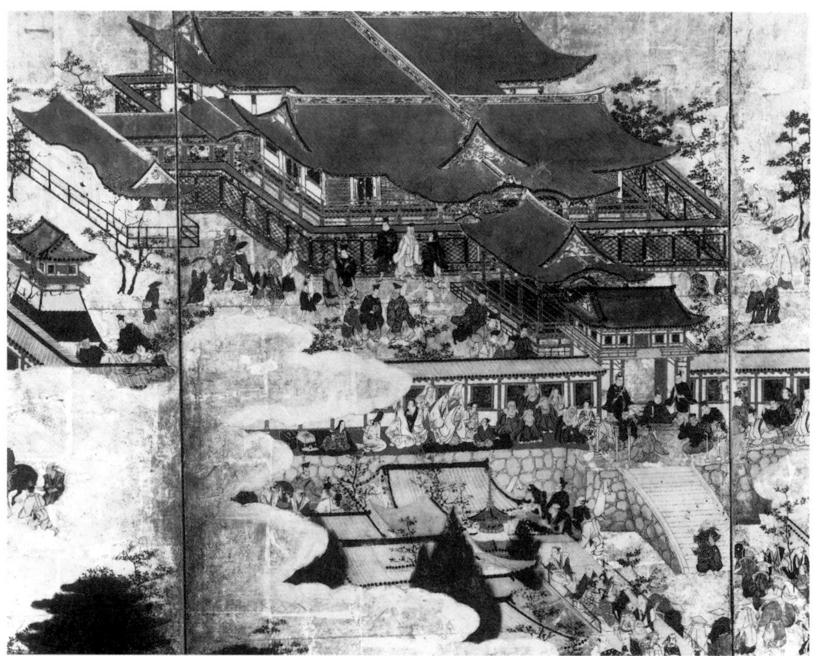

The right-hand screen captures the fourteenth at its peak: a crowd fills the precinct, its numbers ever swelled by the lengthy train still entering at the outermost shrine gate. White-garbed figures (the Shinto priests of Bonshun's account) mill outside the precinct's outer walls, scattered along the horizontal length of the bottom of the screen. More numerous still are foot soldiers who form the retinues of the many finely dressed elite warriors arriving on horseback to view the proceedings. The screen painter has depicted each rider in rich detail, just as he delineated the elaborate temporary viewing booths set against the walls; most of the latter are fitted with gold-and-polychrome wall paintings, and each accommodates well-dressed men, women, and children *(Fig. 132)*. Most of the occupants appear to be of the warrior class, though some may be courtiers, wealthy merchants, and clergy; we see them drinking and eating from fine makie and ceramic wares to sustain them through the long festivities. By its choice of subjects, the painting stresses the Toyotomi's wish to incorporate Japan's secular elites into their sacred event and thereby to demonstrate their continuing hold over them. Gien writes, in fact, that the whole spectrum of Kyotoites witnessed the revelry of the fourteenth, though lesser people and even many of the upper classes were confined to the streets: "between the area of the bridges at Fifth Street and Third Street, and up to the [Toyokuni Shrine]," quite a distance, "there was no empty space; there was nothing but crowds of people, high and low."[60]

The painting's composition is tipped forward and seen from above, permitting a privileged view of the vast shrine grounds (though they were so extensive, the artist chose not to contain them even within the oversized screen's six panels) and the throngs of people that filled them that day. Sturdy roofed walls, each penetrated by a single imposing gate, divide the shrine precinct into outer, middle, and inner zones, imposing an architectonic order on the unwieldy crowds. Within the outer zone, lowest on the screen, a Nō performance is observed by a crowd of mainly warrior-class men and women, on the ground and in the raised booths (several festooned with cloths bearing the Toyotomi's paulownia and chrysanthemum crests) *(Fig. 133)*. The middle zone holds a number of subsidiary buildings and, again, numerous elite spectators—here plainly more diverse, with Buddhist monks, Shinto priests, and courtiers joining the warriors—watching an impressive exhibition of juggling visible at the bottom right of Figure 134 (the pantaloon-garbed man has eight batons in the air!).

The innermost zone, at the top center of the painting and reached by a broad stone staircase leading to a gate, contains the majestic principal building of the Toyokuni Shrine, pictured on an angle that allows its full grandeur to be appreciated *(Fig. 134)*. Closed off from its surroundings by a latticed fence, the building consists of two linked structures on axis, a worship hall in front of a main hall, creating a doubled and therefore amplified presence.[61] The two sets of majestic, sweeping roofs are embellished with architectural coloring, prominent end tiles, and elaborate metalwork. Before the fence stand warriors, women, Buddhist monks and nuns, courtiers, and, closest to the building, a

FIG. 132–134 (opposite) Details of Fig. 131.

single Shinto priest dressed in white robes. In stark contrast to the commotion elsewhere in the precincts, this area is tranquil and solemn: many figures face the shrine in silent contemplation, awed by the magnificence of the grand structure (as was Richard Cocks) and by Toyokuni Daimyōjin, the august sacred presence within.

The variegated festivities of the fourteenth were followed, the next day, by the more focused activities at the Great Buddha Hall, pictured on the left-hand screen. Again, the architectural setting determines the composition: the massive hall—largest building in all Japan—spreads across four of the six panels and towers above the human actors before it. Its obliquely viewed rectangular shape is precisely echoed by walls that define the outer perimeter of its broad precinct. Adding to its monumentality is the dark, double-tiered, deeply curved roof, which pierces the clouds that enfold much of the rest of the screen. In front of its perimeter walls, viewed by privileged spectators in elaborately embellished booths, the townspeople's dance is underway; the courtier Funabashi Hidekata (1575–1614) records three hundred participants from Upper Kyoto and two hundred from Lower Kyoto, all holding artificial flowers and effecting an extraordinary beauty.[62]

Two groups perform simultaneously, while three others watch and wait their turn: each gathers around its unwieldy float, centered on an oversized parasol of rich brocades topped with an enormous floral arrangement (one also incorporates a peacock) *(Fig. 135)*. The similar appearance of the two active groups confirms the established nature of the choreography. Each group is circumscribed by two concentric rings of dancers wearing the same brightly patterned robes: the outer ring comprises seated figures defining a fixed perimeter, while the inner one consists of dancers bending at the waist and gesticulating dramatically in unison with tree branches and, as Gien describes it, "gold and silver fans"; Gien was equally impressed that "even their sashes and sandals were of gold and silver." In the center of each circle, within these orderly boundaries, ecstatic disorder reigns: diversely garbed figures gyrate in unregimented abandon; according to Gien, "they [were dressed as] the Shitennō, or as a Chinese, or as Daikoku, Ebisu, or the Kōya saint Oi. They took all possible forms, [dancing] to the musical accompaniment of *tsuzumi* and *ōtsuzumi* drums and flutes. It is difficult to describe in words." The painting confirms his account, capturing the musicians and the astonishingly varied and extravagant dress of the great throngs of central dancers—including some not mentioned in Gien's catalogue, such as figures in Western dress, another dressed as a long-nosed *tengu*—all orbiting the huge parasol-float that gives each dynamic, fluid group its focus.

This performance was extraordinary and memorable—the brilliant costumes, astounding floats, the rapture of the dancers surely inspired the writer and painter—but in addition, this kind of dance, known as *fūryū odori,* literally, "wind-flowing dance," had a prior history that influenced its meaning at Hōkōji in 1604.[63] During the chaotic wartime years of sixteenth-century Kyoto, before Nobunaga's ascendance, townspeople performed fūryū dance at night throughout the city, in defiance of official prohibitions. Dance was dangerous: it was political spectacle, demonstrating the commoners' potential for organized action and their willingness and ability to brave the authorities. By

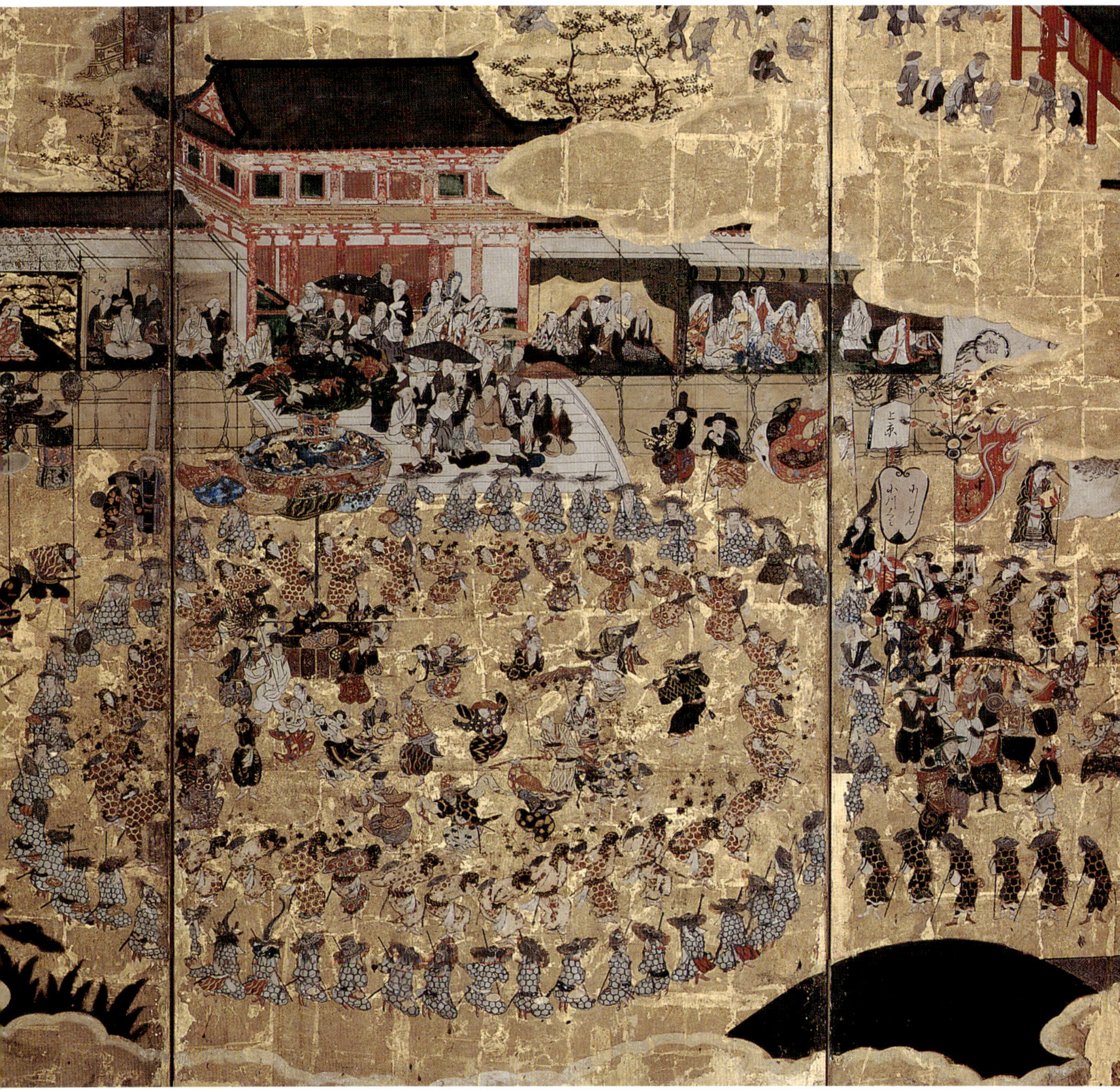

FIG. 135 Detail of Fig. 131.

the last quarter of the sixteenth century, however, potent rulers had regained control over Kyoto and its inhabitants, and fūryū dance was stripped of its illicit overtones; in the context of the Toyokuni Special Festival, indeed, its meaning was reversed: the fūryū dancers were willing participants in the Toyotomi's design to gather all Kyoto in celebration of the deified Hideyoshi, and by extension, of his progeny; here it was a dance of unity. In the painting, the vigorous performers confine themselves within boundaries imposed by the Toyotomi's great Buddhist precincts, a dutifulness witnessed by the elites of Kyoto and, of course, by the viewers of the painting. Pictured too are the beggars noted by Bonshun, rough-shod and wasted, gathered at the door of the Great Buddha

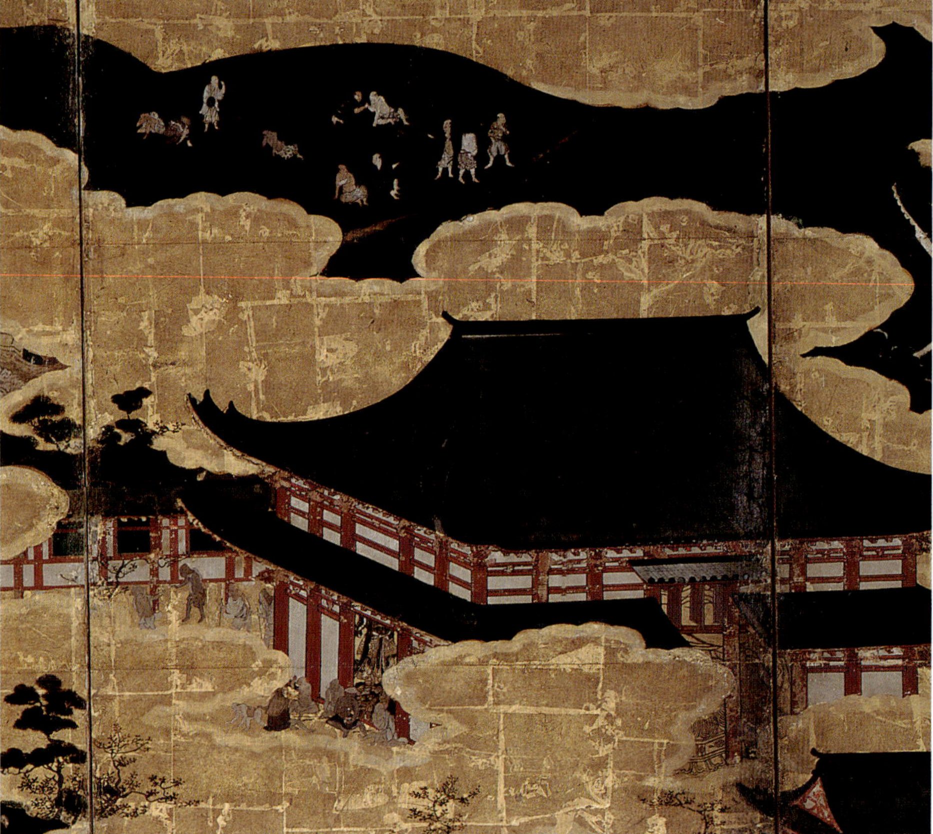

FIG. 136 Detail of Fig. 131.

Hall—framed by clouds and thereby highlighted—to receive alms, thus completing the roster of Kyoto inhabitants incorporated into this idealized vision of the Toyotomi's sympathetic munificence *(Fig. 136).* The festival continued on for several more days, but the two days immortalized on this pair of screens were its high point.

REBUILDING AND REPRESENTING THE GREAT BUDDHA HALL

The centrality of the Great Buddha Hall in the 1604 commemoration, as depicted in these screens, conflicts with other records regarding a project that occupied the Toyotomi immediately after Hideyoshi's death: the repair of Hōkōji and refabrication of the Great Buddha and its hall. The Toyotomi would not allow the Great Buddha, destroyed in the 1596 earthquake and its aftershocks, to remain a ruin, nor neglect its damaged precincts, so along with construction of the Toyokuni Shrine in southeastern Kyoto they undertook the equally ambitious project of renewing Hōkōji. Unlike its wood predecessor, the new Great Buddha was to be cast of bronze, which various daimyo were commanded to provide.[64] Gien reports having heard that casting of the new statue was in progress in late 1599, and that by the third month of 1600 surveying had begun for a seven-story pagoda, a lecture hall, and a boundary corridor.[65]

Gien also travelled to view the reconstruction in the fifth month of that year and provided the most concrete firsthand description of the colossal project in progress.[66] The huge lotus pedestal of the Great Buddha was being cast, and he was amazed at the enormous size of the figure, whose torso was being prepared for casting; the arms were made of wood, and sculptors were busy refining parts here and there. He then visited the nearby Sanjūsangendō and its thousand sculptures of Kannon, where he learned that Hideyori had promised twenty thousand koku of funds, an enormous amount, for repairs to the sculptures' arms and the objects they held, a project that would keep all of Kyoto's Buddhist sculptors busy (by calculating the total number of arms and objects of the one thousand many-armed sculptures, one easily sees the truth in this statement); he heard also of plans to expand the Great Buddha precincts to incorporate the Sanjūsangendō. Finally, completing this tour of the Toyotomi's expanding sacred territory, he described the great gate, some of whose pillars were decorated with makie lacquer, that was being built to the west of the Toyokuni Shine torii.[67]

In 1602, however, on the morning of the fourth day of the twelfth month, misfortune struck yet again. During the casting process, Gien heard, fire leapt from the statue, spread to the mandorla behind and then to Great Buddha Hall, and by the afternoon, all had turned to ashes: "in a matter of three hours, the mountain trees gathered from the sixty-odd provinces of Japan were destroyed, the several years of meritorious deeds *[rōkō]* by Taikō [Hideyoshi] so quickly perished"; the fire then spread and burned the eastern portion of the corridor around the perimeter (a quick response saved the other three sides), though the Toyokuni Shrine and its precincts were spared; six days later the fire still smoldered.[68] Other diarists recorded virtually the same account, with minor additions, suggesting the buzz of information that circulated around Kyoto: Yamashina Tokitsune noted that the Second Gate and a storage building were spared,[69] and Bonshun wrote that the Kōyashū buildings were all burned.[70] The Rokuon'in diarist heard that a bellows had started the blaze; a day later, he returned to examine the ruined precincts and, reflecting on the loss, wrote, "The Gion Shōja of old, too, with the passage of time could not escape turning into scorched earth."[71] He refers, of course, to the famous message of impermanence in the opening lines of the *Tale of the Heike:* "The sound of the Gion Shōja bells echoes the impermanence of all things; the color of the *śāla* flowers reveals the truth that the prosperous must decline. The proud do not endure, they are like a dream on a spring night; the mighty fall at last, they are as dust before the wind."[72] "And now," the diarist continued, "the Great Buddha's time has come; it is beyond words." Although a few subsidiary structures remained, the Great Buddha Hall and its statue were altogether lost. Kyoto was in shock.

The confirmed documentary record is silent again until 1608, when the author of the *Tōdaiki* mentions hearing of plans to rebuild the Great Buddha the following year: "Hideyori will supply the funds, Ieyasu will receive them and also supply provisions; in addition, Hideyori will provide gold, silver, and lumber"; the following year he again reports the news that Hideyori of Osaka would rebuild the Great Buddha that spring.[73] In 1610 reconstruction formally commenced with a *chōnahajime,* the ceremonial first stroke of the adze, on the twelfth day of the sixth month, duly noted in period diaries.[74] Another entry in the *Tōdaiki* speaks of 180 enormous pillars gathered for the reconstruction, comments on their great cost, and notes a rumor that the project will drain the Toyotomi treasury. Gien stopped by the construction site in the eighth month and heard that the first three pillars were to be raised the next day; their immensity, he wrote, beggared description. In the fourth month of 1611 Gien notes that all of the pillars had been raised; recalling that the chōnahajime had taken place less than a year earlier, he marvels at the rate of progress. Just after the turn of 1612 Gien heard a rumor that the Great Buddha Hall would be completed within four or five months; late that year he visited the site, which he found still unfinished but impressive: the gold leaf had been applied to the Great Buddha, the lotus pedestal was almost complete, and most of the stone floor had been laid.

Richard Cocks viewed the completed ensemble in 1616, while it was still new, just after the Toyotomi's demise.

> I went to se the monumentes of the towne, viz. the temple of Dibottes, with the hudge collosso or bras imadg (or rather idoll) in it, it being of a wonderful bignes, the head of it reaching to the top of the temple, allthough he sat crose-legged, it being all gilded over with gould, and a great wall or plate behind the back of it the lyke, whereon was carved the pickture of the son. The temple of it selfe is the hugest peece of building that eaver I saw, it not haveing any other thing in it but the idoll, which standeth in a cercle or chappell just in the midell thereof, with 4 rowes of pillars of wood, 2 on eather side, from the on end of the temple to the other, each one reaching to the top of it; the compose of each pillar being 3 fathom, and all dyed over with red occar, as all the temple within is the lyke. And a littell from the north end of the temple is a tower with a bell hanging in it, the bigest that ever I saw. And from the easter dore of the temple stand two rowes of ston pillars, of som dozen in a rowe, a pretty distance on from the other. . . . The truth is, all of it is to be admired.[75]

Finally, the entire precincts were complete: the Great Buddha Hall, of inconceivable size and with an interior resplendent with red lacquer; the enormous gold-covered statue of the Buddha, seated against an equally large mandorla; the bell with its inscription allegedly offensive to the Tokugawa hung outside (perhaps the only component of the temple still extant, *Fig. 129*); the gate flanked by two enormous statues of Guardian Kings. Finally, the temple recaptured the magnificence it had possessed, briefly, during Hideyoshi's lifetime.

But this chronology based on contemporary diaries seems to contradict the ex-Yoshida Festival screens. According to the diaries, reconstruction following the 1602 conflagration began only *after* the 1604 festival (and had barely begun by the time of the smaller one in the eighth month of 1610). Was the Great Buddha Hall, pictured so prominently in the screens and noted as the site of major events even in the diary accounts, still a ruin during the 1604 Toyokuni festival? Did enough of it remain to evoke its previous grandeur? Were there additional, now forgotten, stages in the reconstruction campaign? Present information cannot conclusively answer these questions. What is known, however, raises the distinct possibility that the Great Buddha Hall was more a conceptual than physical presence in early seventeenth-century Kyoto, and as such remained, even in its much-damaged and incomplete state, a monument evocative of the perseverance and power of the Toyotomi. Its wholeness in the painting most likely portrays an imagined ideal; its employment as a festival site and the contemporary writings describing it as such indicate that, ruined or not, the Great Buddha Hall still functioned as a major monument in Momoyama Kyoto. By 1614 the Toyotomi finally completed their renewal of Hōkōji, though its planned dedication never transpired: the Tokugawa would soon begin their campaign of extermination against the Toyotomi.

INTERPRETING THE 1604 FESTIVAL

How are we to interpret the 1604 festival and its remembrances? The correspondence among the written accounts indicates, presumably, a reality observed; the screens, commissioned by the Toyotomi, a reality desired. The former confirms an overwhelmingly positive reception: the comments are attentive, respectful, and awestruck. The latter mines the potential of painting to selectively distill, modify, and picture any situation according to the desire of its patron: in it, the participants and observers are unified in fervent celebration of Toyokuni Daimyōjin, a celebration occurring among the monuments of Toyotomi architecture. Despite these different perspectives, however, there is remarkable agreement between the writers' perceptions and the patrons' requirements as portrayed in the screens: in the overwhelming judgment of those involved, participant or patron, this religious festival was well executed and wildly popular. And so the Toyotomi's objectives were met: to surpass any other public demonstration of its time; to elevate the still-living Toyotomi by virtue of their place in the lineage of a god; and, ultimately, to create a positive impression of Toyotomi suitability to rule.

That such screens were painted at all indicates the distinction of the 1604 Toyokuni Special Festival. No earlier festival painting in the monumental folding-screen format is known. Previously, religious celebrations had been incorporated into large-scale paintings as one of many activities—as, for instance, the Gion Festival was included in *Rakuchū rakugai* screens (and that was still a relatively recent invention) *(Fig. 26);* or, if the festival was the sole subject, it would be depicted in the more intimate hanging-scroll format, as in the case of the Chikubushima Festival painting *(Fig. 33)* This 1604 celebration was so impressive in size and conception that only a correspondingly grand format could serve for its depiction. The Toyokuni Special Festival screens also exemplified another new type of painting that emerged in the early seventeenth century: the representation of recent history with the intent of glorifying a patron. In the 1610s the Tokugawa commissioned paintings of the Battle of Sekigahara to commemorate what was, in retrospect, one of the defining moments of their ascent.[76] The 1604 Festival was, for the Toyotomi, an event of similar magnitude, and had they survived and flourished as the Tokugawa did, it would have held a similar place of glory in the construction of their history. In 1606, when the screens were unveiled, hope for such a future was still possible.

And where in all of this were the Tokugawa? In his entry for the fifteenth day of the eighth month, 1604, Bonshun notes that Ieyasu had been informed periodically of the proposed events throughout the planning stages. This statement is confirmed in his diary entries beginning in the fifth month of that year, when Bonshun first informed Ieyasu that a Toyokuni Special Festival would be held.[77] On the sixteenth day of the eighth month Bonshun and Katagiri Katsumoto travelled to Fushimi Castle to report to Ieyasu that the first two days of the festival had gone well, and he was, by Bonshun's account, pleased to hear this. A European report from this period, sent to Rome by João Rodrigues (1561–1633), even suggests that Ieyasu was a willing sponsor of the Special Festival (though this cannot be confirmed): "This year the festival made for him by Cubo [Ieyasu] was to confirm [Hideyoshi's] dignity and false divinity as a kami, and was the most impressive festival, not only among the festivals made up to now for Taikō [Hideyoshi] but also among all of such events ever made in all of Japan."[78] Ieyasu's acceptance of the Special Festival is additional evidence that the Tokugawa were not yet securely dominant over the Toyotomi. An attempt to prevent or disrupt observance of this important death anniversary would have constituted a challenge to the Toyotomi that Ieyasu was, apparently, not yet willing to make. Conversely, by lavish observance of the anniversary, the Toyotomi were proclaiming that they remained a major force in Japan.

TOYOTOMI CONSTRUCTION AT RELIGIOUS SITES OUTSIDE KYOTO

Although Kyoto was Momoyama's political and social center—the logical location for the Toyotomi to construct their new shrine and sponsor communal acts of persuasion—it was not its sole place of importance; long-revered wellheads of divine power, places at which previous sovereigns had demonstrated their wisdom by constructing outstanding buildings, punctuated the whole of the archipelago. Comparison with these revealed the shortcoming of the marvelous Toyokuni Shrine. Its newness was in part a virtue—the Toyotomi were able to institute practices there that were advantageous to the family—but it was at the same time a weakness. The shrine could claim no place in deep historical memory, no tradition of past sacred achievement, no precedent of benefaction by the rulers of antiquity, and these were all attributes crucial in the legitimating structures of Japanese power.

The Toyotomi thus looked elsewhere in the sacred realm, beyond and in addition to their new shrine, to consummate their incompletely substantiated claims of legitimacy. And so, from 1599 through 1614, they sponsored new construction and repairs at no fewer than ninety separate temple and shrine complexes, many of these efforts involving multiple structures.[79] To realize this massive undertaking, they engaged hordes of workmen, in some places employing locals long associated with the temple or shrine under construction, in others (especially those near their domain) sending men to the site from Osaka; a Toyotomi administrator was responsible for each project, most often Katagiri Katsumoto, though other names appear in the documentary record, reflecting the need to delegate authority with so many projects underway simultaneously.[80] Their campaign far exceeded anyone else's, then or in recent memory; the Toyotomi, in short, became the chief patron of sacred Japan. For most projects, the individual credited as patron was Hideyori, still a child in the early seventeenth century but the embodiment of Toyotomi authority. His was an authority that, like his court rank, was primarily symbolic, and at that time did not impact actual governance, but this symbolism lent it a weight and authenticity that mere power could not confer. The Toyotomi tied their fortunes to it, hoping that symbolic could be transformed to actual over time and through sacred acts that accrued power.

Within the Home Domain

Like other local rulers, the Toyotomi were active in their own domain; daimyo throughout Japan in this period sponsored the construction of temples and shrines, invoking the sacred realm for the protection of their local interests.[81] What differentiated the Toyotomi from other daimyo is the remarkably large number of projects they sponsored: even the expected they did exceptionally. In the first decade of the seventeenth century the Toyotomi completed projects at more than forty religious sites within their territory of Settsu, Kawachi, and Izumi provinces, including the ancient Shitennōji, Sōjiji, Honzanji, Konda Hachimangū, and Kanshinji. Hideyori is named as the patron behind construction at a group of shrines in Izumi, among which the Katano Jinja, Anashi Jinja, Tsugawa Jinja, and Hijiri Jinja are still well preserved; the boldly carved and polychromed wood carvings on these buildings are the stylistic descendants of those on Sutemaru's building, maintaining an ornamental tradition that spoke of earlier Toyotomi power.

Outside the Home Domain: Following Hideyoshi's Lead

Less expected of a ruler with only local ambition were projects executed outside his own domain, and in this regard no one in the post-Hideyoshi period was more active than the Toyotomi, especially before 1606. They sponsored projects at temples and shrines in Kyoto, in the eighth-century capital of Nara, in the provinces surrounding those cities, and along far-flung pilgrimage routes encompassing the ancient shrines of Ise, Kumano, and Izumo. Their criteria for choosing a site varied, though several distinct patterns can be ascertained.

Some were places that Hideyoshi had included in his program of restoring religious sites consumed in sixteenth-century warfare or in the 1596 earthquake, or that were linked to a renowned event in Hideyoshi's life. At Yoshino, for example, deep in the mountains outside Nara, Hideyori rebuilt the Mikumari Jinja and the Great Bridge. Hideyoshi had sponsored construction at Yoshino's most eminent Buddhist temple, Kinpusenji, and he particularly favored the area because of its famous cherry trees. On his grand flower-viewing expedition there in 1594, Hideyoshi went accompanied by a host of retainers and—to properly commemorate the occasion—poets, including the famous Satomura Jōha (1525–1602); a Nō drama was even composed about the event, *Yoshino mōde (Pilgrimage to Yoshino),* and in performance Hideyoshi played the role of Zaō Gongen, chief deity at Kinpusenji—an appropriate role, it seems, for a man who himself would later be transformed into a Shinto deity.[82] For the Toyotomi, Yoshino was an area replete with the aura of Hideyoshi, who had endorsed its natural beauty and patronized its important religious sites, and so they chose it as a site for major restoration.[83]

We have seen that the Toyotomi repeatedly rebuilt Hideyoshi's most important creation, Hōkōji, and they also reconstructed the Kitano Shrine, where Hideyoshi had held his famed colossal tea gathering in 1587.[84] At Tōji, Hideyori is the patron who ultimately realized work that Hideyoshi's wife had earlier promised to sponsor after the 1596 earthquake.[85] The Toyotomi sponsored work at many other significant Kyoto temples with Hideyoshi associations, including Shōkokuji, Nanzenji, Seiryōji, Enryakuji on Mount Hiei, and one we earlier observed in some detail, Daigoji. Hideyoshi had restored Daigoji's venerable five-story pagoda, and after his cherry-blossom outing there in 1598 promised reconstruction of its Golden Hall and, a week later, of a long roster of other structures. He died before this pledge could be carried out, leaving it to his descendants to fulfill in 1600.

Gien, head priest of Daigoji and therefore intensely interested in these proceedings, recorded in his diary the text of the Golden Hall's commemorative ridgepole placard, which he brushed on a Japanese cypress board.[86]

> Regarding this hall, in 1598 Daishōkoku Denka [Hideyoshi] repeatedly gave strict orders for its reconstruction, but in the past two years [work on the building] has stagnated. Then this year, again, Kōmon Denka [Hideyori] ordered Tokuzen'in Gon no Sōjō Gen'i [Maeda Gen'i] and provided funds [for reconstruction]. Accordingly Kōzan Shōnin Ōgo [the Mount Kōya monk Ōgo] served as administrative coordinator, and . . . the construction was quickly completed. Accordingly, the warrior house will last eternally *[bumon chōkyū].*

At first glance, these words may seem no more than predictable gratitude for beneficence, but mere sycophancy would not have required the detailed information that Gien incorporates. Reconstruction was initially commanded by an imperially titled—that is, legitimated—ruler, but lay dormant until the next similarly legitimated magnate appeared, released funds, and empowered those at his behest (Hideyoshi's trusted Kyoto magistrate and the Mount Kōya monk who was his project manager) to realize the holy work with due efficiency. For such beneficence to the sacred realm, this well-run house will triumph over time and the manifest uncertainty of warrior life.

Circumstances at the time appeared to justify Gien's good augury. The recent historical context seemed hopeful for the Toyotomi: in the first years of the seventeenth century the cult of Hideyoshi—carefully constructed even while he was alive[87] and enhanced by his posthumous deification—was a potent dynamic; as his son and designated heir, Hideyori was seen by many as the rightful and still conceivable successor to his authority. The sacred, moreover, was fully rehabilitated after the sixteenth-century upheaval: Nobunaga's incorporation of numinous aspects into his grand scheme and Hideyoshi's concentrated attentions made it a visible and forceful presence, one that was deemed, as it had long been, essential in protecting Japan.

The Daigoji Golden Hall project conflated the dynastic claims of the Toyotomi with the countrywide relevance of the sacred, and though on its own it would carry little influence, it was not a singular occurrence. In 1606, several years after completing the Golden Hall, Hideyori sponsored the reconstruction of several other structures at Daigoji, including the Mieidō, Godaidō, and Nyoirindō in the upper precincts, which had burned the previous year.[88] These buildings, erected under the most difficult of construction conditions at the top of a steep mountain, received long, often historically contextualized ridgepole placard texts, similar to the Golden Hall's, glorifying Hideyori's efforts.[89] For certain projects of special significance to the Toyotomi and to Japan as a whole, long texts were composed, intended by their length and number to compound significance and make a grand statement.

Hideyori also performed good works at the ancient and important Shinto center of Ise, again following in his father's footsteps. Tradition called for rebuilding Ise every twenty years, though this long-observed practice of renewal had lapsed for over a century before Hideyoshi provided the funds to revive it in 1585.[90] Ise's extensive precincts unfold within a verdant preserve separated from our mundane world by the Isuzu River and reached by a long wooden span, the Uji Bridge. In 1601, however, fire destroyed the bridge, a disaster the Toyotomi promised to rectify. By 1604 the bridge had still not been rebuilt, apparently precipitating an anxious query, to which Hideyori's mother, Yodo-dono, responded by the following letter to the nun Keikōin Shuyō (d. 1611):

> As I told you on the first, regarding the Uji Bridge to be laid by Hideyori, I have carefully instructed Ichinokami [Katagiri Katsumoto] to complete this before the transfer of the deity. Accordingly, Ichinokami will appoint an administrator and make certain that the bridge is laid; you should rest assured. For this reason [Ichinokami] even sent a person and strictly gave the order that an administrator be appointed, so rest assured. I will have the Third Rank person inform you of the details.[91]

Yododono—here revealed as the orchestrator behind Hideyori's concerted efforts—has instructed Katagiri Katsumoto to activate the administrative machinery to insure that the project is carried out in a timely fashion, before the planned completion of the reconstructed shrine buildings in 1609.[92]

Outside the Home Domain: Expanding Hideyoshi's Legacy

The Toyotomi campaign transcended even the parameters of domainal responsibility and family precedent, extending to projects in places well beyond Osaka and not associated with Hideyoshi. It ranged widely, seeking sites of consequence within Japan's deep sacred past and then committing funds to revitalize them. These places existed in a sphere that transcended local political controls, unlike secular sites and their buildings (such as castles), and by sponsoring them the Toyotomi could assert their claim to relevance beyond their territory. At distant and ancient Izumo Shrine, for instance, a place commensurate with Ise as a prime locus of Shinto veneration, Hideyori in 1609 sponsored a major rebuilding of the neglected and decayed site.[93]

In Nara Hideyori sponsored extensive repairs from 1600 through 1606 on many of the buildings at ancient Hōryūji.[94] Some of the major themes espoused by the Toyotomi in much of their far-reaching campaign were here carefully articulated in the placard texts, which were signed—and thereby sanctioned—by two representatives of the Toyotomi administrator Katagiri Katsumoto. The underlying theme of the 1606 text for the Denpōdō (a hall in Hōryūji's Eastern Precinct), for example, is Toyotomi concern for the spiritual, and hence overall, welfare of Japan.

> Hōryū Gakumonji, in Heiguri County of Yamato Province, is the first temple of the Buddhist law and a holy site for the protection of the nation. Now, more than one thousand years since it was founded by Shōtoku Taishi, Toyotomi Ason Udaijin Hideyori Kō ordered Katagiri Higashi Ichinokami to rebuild and repair all of the buildings within the four sides of the temple precincts with a succession of chief priests. This is because [this project] well matches the year of future repairs recorded [i.e., predicted] by Daishō [Shōtoku Taishi], and recalls the poetic description of [Shōtoku Taishi's] follower. Without doubt, [Hideyori] should be respected, he should be revered.[95]

The entire Hōryūji complex is presented as a place of unsurpassed historical importance, not only a fountainhead of Japanese Buddhism (as the Ise and Izumo shrines were of Shinto, a fact the Toyotomi were careful to announce), linked to Prince Shōtoku (574–622), the first major imperial patron of Buddhism in Japan, but also a fortification in Japan's defense. As the placard claimed, a full millennium had elapsed since Hōryūji's predecessor, Wakakusadera, was founded, and Hideyori is credited with understanding and responding to the vital need to repair the temple's physical decay; even more wondrous, however, the wise Shōtoku had foreseen the distant future need for these repairs, a need met by the sagacity of Hideyori. There is in this claim an assertion of Hideyori's singular suitability, even inevitability, to take his proper place not only in his father's line, but in the lineage of Japan's most illustrious leaders: his link to revered Prince Shōtoku further justifies Hideyori's claim to power.

COMMEMORATING SACRED CONSTRUCTION

The Toyotomi hoped the Momoyama audience would accept their claims for the import of all their projects. Each project was commemorated in a ridgepole placard, some long and detailed like the examples above, others much shorter but never omitting the vital information that the patron of the shrine or temple structure was none other than Toyotomi Hideyori. To whom, however, were these placards directed? The term *munafuda,* "ridgepole placard," literally suggests a board attached to the highest point of a building, which would render it unreadable, and so, apparently, not intended to be read.

This was not the case. First, we cannot dismiss an audience the Toyotomi wished to reach, one perceived to be all-powerful: the deities themselves, for whom the buildings were created, to whom the Toyotomi appealed for their very survival, and in whom all the Toyotomi's other sacred activities evince a strong belief. A mundane but important audience comprised the people who created the placards: those (often clerics) who composed and then calligraphed the text onto the wooden placard and the Toyotomi administrators with whom they consulted and who approved the final text. The Shōkokuji diarist of the *Rokuon nichiroku* wrote that he met with the chief Toyotomi administrator, Katagiri Katsumoto, to discuss a placard (for an unspecified building).[96] Gien wrote several placards, including the long Hōryūji text. In his diary, he notes conferring with the monk and Toyotomi associate Ōgo about the text for the Daigoji Golden Hall placard three days before actually brushing it onto the board;[97] similarly, after remarking that the ridge-raising ceremony for Hideyori's Tōji Golden Hall project would be held in a few days, he mentions discussing the placard text, which he proceeded to write the following day.[98] And we should not dismiss the power of hearsay to spread news in this period. Those engaged in producing placards would have interacted with their peers—other elites whom the Toyotomi wished to impress—and would doubtless have mentioned the ideas expressed in the placards. Finally, it appears that not all placards were relegated to the unreadable upper reaches of the building they commemorated; some were hung within easy view from ground level.[99]

Friction over the wording of the placard for Hideyori's reconstructed Hōkōji suggests, too, the general importance accorded this object: in the months preceding the final confrontation between the Toyotomi and the Tokugawa, it was not only the bell inscription which Ieyasu found offensive but also the placard, delivered to Sunpu by Katagiri Katsumoto and reviewed by Ieyasu in the eighth month of 1614.[100]

From the placards themselves, from conversations about them, and from reports of them, the Toyotomi gloss on these sacred activities reached its intended audience. In

1599, on his journey to Osaka to read the *Daihannya kyō* for the first time, Gien wrote in his diary that he stopped at the recently devastated temple of Tennōji (more commonly referred to today as Shitennōji) in Osaka.

> I made a pilgrimage to Tennōji, [the first time] since perhaps last year. Hideyori Kyō has restored it all, and it was a marvel to my eyes. It is the revival of one of the first holy temples of the Buddhist law, and is highly esteemed. In past years the Ikkō sect and Nobunaga Kyō fought repeated battles and, because of the Ikkō sect, not a single building remained, all were burned. This construction [by Hideyori] is the result of the authority of [Shōtoku] Taishi; it is a miracle.[101]

In this private diaristic reading of the place Gien interweaves the Toyotomi's self-promoted self-image and the realities of contemporary history. Gien knew, of course, of Shitennōji's calamitous destruction during Nobunaga's assault on Honganji and the Ikkō sectarians. He blamed the havoc not on Nobunaga but on the sectarians, perhaps implying that their downfall was owing to their spiritual decline. More to the point, he appreciated the significance of the temple as an early and respected site of Buddhist worship in Japan, and he once again made the all-important connection between the first sponsor of the temple, Prince Shōtoku, and the present patron, Hideyori. Gien, of course, had an insider's awareness of churchly matters, and was a Toyotomi partisan, but his words provide us with a fair sense of how a well-informed person of the time would have construed Toyotomi religious construction.[102]

Another seventeenth-century writer, the anonymous author of the *Tōdaiki,* saw the Toyotomi sponsorship of religious construction projects as one part of the family's broad range of sacred work, motivated not only by family interests, but often by the wish to benefit Japan as a whole. In a 1604 entry he mused, "For the past two or three years, Hideyori Kō has constructed temple buildings in the various provinces; could it be that it is because in his heart he is offering vows *[ryūgan]*?"[103]—thus proposing a spiritual motive for the extensive Toyotomi religious construction throughout Japan. In 1607 the same observer expanded upon this hypothesis:

> From this time, Hideyori Kō of Osaka is rebuilding Kitano Shrine; not only Kitano, but all temple and shrine buildings in recent years are constructed [by him]. Hideyori Kō is but a child, and it is said that perhaps [such reconstruction] is the vow *[hatsugan]* of his mother [Yododono], which is wonderful. The rumor throughout Kyoto is that this is because [Yododono] has repeatedly had auspicious dreams.[104]

The passage echoes the contents of the 1604 letter to Keikōin Shuyō: the boy Hideyori was nominally the sponsor of Toyotomi religious construction, but Yododono was the true principal. Her motive was to realize, with the help of sacred powers, a wish of unspecified content, manifested in repeated auspicious dreams. This account is not the opinion of a lone onlooker, moreover; throughout Kyoto there circulated the perception that the Toyotomi projects were inspired by the hope of enlisting the sacred in the restoration of Toyotomi political dominance. At this time, still, the possibility of Toyotomi revival seemed realistic.

EBBING FORTUNES

As the century progressed, however, doubts about the Toyotomi's future began to emerge. The author of the *Tōdaiki* recorded a rumor, alluded to above, regarding the impact of the 1610 rebuilding of the Great Buddha Hall on the Toyotomi treasury: "It is said that the gold and silver in Taikō's [Hideyoshi's] hoard will be depleted at this time." Here, a decade into the seventeenth century, is the first hint that the Toyotomi's extensive construction projects might bring the family to financial, and thence comprehensive, collapse. By this time the Toyotomi's position with respect to the Tokugawa was deteriorating markedly, and although in the end military defeat overtook economic ruin, the statement seems prescient of apparent florescence masking an ineluctably ebbing fortune.

Another account pertaining to the same project—Gien's official record of the 1610 groundbreaking ceremony—emphasizes that the Toyotomi were the Great Buddha Hall's chief sponsors (i.e., the moving spirits and principal paymasters of its restoration), and that the splendor of the groundbreaking ceremony and of the restoration itself redounded primarily to their credit and bespoke the undiminished eminence of their position.[105] Gien begins by stating the roles of the two principals in the project: Ieyasu ordered (that is, permitted) restoration of the hall the previous year; Hideyori will provide the funds. This uncluttered statement of fact contains no hint of the friction between the two camps and no interpretation of either's motives. Ieyasu is respectfully mentioned as a recognized authority whose consent for this mammoth mission was received. Gien explained Hideyori's source of funding. When Toyokuni Daimyōjin (Hideyoshi) was alive, he prudently supplied his young son with gold cast into blocks of one thousand *mai* each, of which Hideyori allocated twenty for the present project, an amount sufficient for the restoration. The ceremony itself was splendid: the carpenter (a man who usually worked for Ieyasu, Gien notes) used an adze decorated with makie lacquer, and everything, including the robes, was—using for this Buddhist undertaking the locution of high acclamation—"perfectly good and perfectly beautiful." Gien adds that reconstruction of the temple was "the necessary path for the protection of the nation *[chingo kokka]*." Gien's account emphasizes the unmatched wealth of the Toyotomi and their use of it for the protection of Japan; Ieyasu is credited for his support but allotted a strictly supporting role.[106]

What of the rumor reported in the *Tōdaiki*? It is easy to imagine such an idea originating in hopes held by Toyotomi foes, especially the Tokugawa. It appears, too, to support the conventional interpretation noted earlier—that the Tokugawa forced the

Toyotomi to undertake these projects in order to drain their financial resources and, in turn, their potential to resurrect their fortunes. Neither the *Tōdaiki* hearsay, however, nor any extant Momoyama record explicitly asserts Tokugawa intent or ability to coerce the Toyotomi into ruinous expenditures.[107] Such an interpretation exaggerates the ability of the Tokugawa to manipulate the Toyotomi in the first decade of the seventeenth century and, moreover, underestimates Toyotomi strength. The Toyotomi demonstrated their capacity to withstand Tokugawa attempts to weaken Toyotomi status. Yododono, as noted above, resisted Tokugawa requests in 1605 that she and Hideyori travel to Kyoto to visit Ieyasu, a visit that would have signified Toyotomi obeisance to the Tokugawa, as a daimyo to the hegemon.[108] The massive 1604 Toyokuni Special Festival would not have occurred had the Tokugawa been able to constrain the Toyotomi. The Tokugawa may have hoped that the Toyotomi would ruin themselves through too-assiduous reconstruction of religious sites, and there may have been people who viewed the events in this way. That possibility notwithstanding, we have ample evidence that the Toyotomi acted according to their own needs as they perceived them. Nor, in the end, did their construction projects bleed them dry; they continued to sponsor such construction until 1614, the year of the Tokugawa's first attack. The Toyotomi were overwhelmed not by self-inflicted financial adversity, but by Tokugawa political and military preponderance, progressively won and promptly exploited.

Momoyama people assumed cultivation of the sacred to be an efficacious and indispensable means to achieve desired ends. Believing in the possibility of direct spiritual furtherance to mundane purposes, they sponsored religious ceremonies, both private and, as in the Toyokuni Special Festival of 1604, spectacularly public. Like ritual in times of illness or natural disasters or anomalies, the deification and veneration of the deceased Hideyoshi was performed with the conviction that it was a spiritually meaningful act, its spirituality in no way diminished by its political ramifications. With public religious activities, such as the apotheosis of Hideyoshi, the Toyotomi articulated temporal goals: Hideyoshi's deification implied especially intimate clan connections with the spiritual realm and so proclaimed the importance of the Toyotomi in this world. The continuous worship at the Toyokuni Shrine, regularly intensifying in semiannual ceremonies and climaxing in the more elaborate festivals on major death anniversaries (where even dieties, as Gien described, danced in celebration of Hideyoshi), institutionalized communal tribute to the deified Hideyoshi and, by virtue of patrimony, to Hideyoshi's descendants. The prominence given Hideyori's offerings on the pivotal day of the three-day festivals asserted, ritually, that the young but impressively titled heir was paramount among the living within this lineage. Attendance at these ceremonies by leading warriors, clergy, and courtiers attested and simultaneously disseminated the continuing moral authority of the Toyotomi. The buildings at these sites and the abundant construction at religious sites elsewhere served as material symbols of Hideyori's links to spiritual power, established either by his father Hideyoshi or by the ancient, prescient forerunners who were his adopted ancestors. The Toyotomi remained a major presence in Japan during this period through their substantial claim to be conduits of the spiritual power crucial to the preservation of Japan.

To a large degree, Ieyasu ceded the sacred realm to the Toyotomi, asserting his authority through secular means. Primarily this entailed building a bureaucracy that effectively administered the temporal needs of Japan.[109] But like most Japanese rulers before him, Ieyasu also sought to demonstrate his greatness through impressive buildings, and so became a notable patron of secular architecture. In the first years of the seventeenth century he constructed a castle at Edo—the undeveloped headquarters of the domain to which Hideyoshi had transferred him in 1590—and, after ceding the post of shogun to his son in 1605, rebuilt another at his post-abdication seat of power at nearby Sunpu. Ieyasu also sought a major architectural presence in the capital district, most importantly realized at the palatial Nijō Castle in Kyoto and, just to the south, at Fushimi Castle, which he had received after Hideyoshi's death and proceeded to rebuild in the early seventeenth century.[110] As we will see, it was his progeny who recognized the value of the sacred realm and sought to reclaim it soon after Ieyasu's, and the Toyotomi's, demise.[111]

Even under Ieyasu's leadership the Tokugawa did not entirely neglect religious construction. Although in the years before 1615 they did not match the Toyotomi's level of activity, they sponsored structures at Chion'in (to house memorial rites for Ieyasu's mother), Kōdaiji, Shōkokuji, Kiyomizudera, Nanzenji, the Yasaka Jinja, and several other Kyoto temples and shrines, and at Ise.[112] Significantly, they also contemplated the monumental task of reconstructing Nara's Great Buddha and its hall.[113] The Toyotomi never tended to this site, primarily because they were devoted to its replacement in Kyoto at Hōkōji, and yet within the sacred realm of Japan, it remained a place of great historical significance, one that could confer great benefits on its supporters. A great typhoon in 1610 inflicted severe damage on the incompletely restored statue and its temporary shelter, and spurred the Tōdaiji monks to seek funds for more permanent and complete restoration. From 1613 they travelled repeatedly to Sunpu, petitioning the Tokugawa for assistance in the project. They showed Ieyasu an autograph letter by Minamoto no Yoritomo (1147–1199) regarding the Kamakura-period reconstruction, appealing to Ieyasu's sense of himself as the inheritor of Yoritomo's legacy. Ieyasu responded to this opportunity. He authorized the temple to collect funds and promised to make up whatever was lacking. Plans were drawn up for the repairs and budgets estimated. But the project was not immediately realized because matters more important to Ieyasu's larger designs intervened: the battles of Osaka.

Nor was the significance of the Toyotomi religious activity as a symbol of Toyotomi power lost on the Tokugawa. One gauge of their awareness is the rapidity with which the Tokugawa dismantled the Toyokuni Shrine after the fall of Osaka in 1615. Over the course of several months in mid-1616 the Tokugawa transferred the deity Toyokuni Daimyōjin from the shrine to the Great Buddha Hall, revoked the shrine's income, gave the shrine's bell (and thirty of its tatami mats) to Chishakuin and some of its ritual paraphernalia to the Yoshida Shrine, dismantled some of its buildings, nailed shut the doors to the inner sanctum, and thereby brought about the shrine's demise; by the 1650s the grounds where the shrine had stood were renowned for their cherry tree.[114] Equally significantly, the Tokugawa then followed the Toyotomi example, elevating Ieyasu to the status of a Shinto deity (named Tōshō Daigongen) in the year after his death, and constructing the Tōshōgū shrine complexes at Kunōzan, Nikkō, and elsewhere, where the deity was venerated.[115] It well suited a ruling clan—the Toyotomi had shown and the Tokugawa accepted—to worship its progenitor-turned-god.

6

Hideyori and Chikubushima's New Ensemble

LAYING CLAIM TO CHIKUBUSHIMA

Within a decade of its creation in the 1590s, the Toyotomi uprooted the jewel-like ensemble that functioned as a Kyoto setting of remembrance for Hideyoshi's son Sutemaru. They did so because exposure to the elements was beginning to mar the makie lacquer on its exterior; remaining outside at Shōunji would have turned this spectacular monument to a lost son into a ruinous profanation. Their options were to demolish the structure or to find it a less exposed setting. They chose the latter, placing it within the protective cocoon of Chikubushima's main building, a hall built about forty years earlier and dedicated to the worship of Benzaiten.

This was no simple task. The Kyoto building had to be disassembled and shipped overland to Lake Biwa and thence by boat to the island. To accommodate it, the pre-existing Benzaiten Hall was extensively and precisely modified: its core was removed and its east and west sides altered to the exact dimensions necessary to encompass the new component. Sutemaru's structure was inserted as the new core, with its southern wall left exposed to form the entrance. Linking elements *(ebikōryō)* were appended, and monumental relief wood carvings were added to the exterior of the sparsely decorated older structure. The result was a building formed of pre-existing unrelated parts, today called the Tsukubusuma Main Hall. Even by Momoyama's famously latitudinarian architectural criteria—which encompassed Hideyoshi's portable tea house surfaced entirely in gold, and Taian, the small stationary tea house made of mud, straw, bamboo, and raw wood, along with divers other extraordinary buildings whose likenesses have been preserved on monumental folding-screen paintings—this was an unusual fabrication. In Momoyama eyes it was also useful, appropriate to its site, and, moreover, beautiful. And in uniting an embodiment of *shōgon* with a site of great spiritual significance, it perfectly served the larger Toyotomi strategy of laying claim to the sacred realm.

CHIKUBUSHIMA AND BENZAITEN IN THE POST-HIDEYOSHI ERA

In the early seventeenth century, recent Momoyama history—the age of Nobunaga—was already the stuff of official legend: according to his biographer Ōta Gyūichi (b. 1527), Nobunaga in the spring of 1581 made a remarkable pilgrimage to the island just visible from his castle mount in Azuchi:

> Nobunaga summoned five or six attendants and made a pilgrimage to Chikubushima. They travelled on horseback to Hashiba Chikuzen's [Hideyoshi's] place in Nagahama, and from there traversed the five *ri* over water by boat. Together the water and land portions of the trip amounted to some fifteen ri each way, and the thirty ri of the round trip were covered in a single day; truly, this was an amazing feat.[1]

Amazing, indeed—and, since one ri equals almost four kilometers, highly improbable. (So speedy was Nobunaga, the narrative continues, that many at Azuchi—counting on Nobunaga's longer absence—left their posts for various amusements, triggering Nobunaga's wrath on his return that same evening to an understaffed castle.) Although the account is factually questionable (and there is, as we have seen, more reliable evidence for Nobunaga's true involvement with the island), the inclusion of Chikubushima in this early effort at establishing a canonical account of Nobunaga's life is intriguing. Ōta Gyūichi had begun his work on Nobunaga's biography no later than 1598 (when Gien mentions it in his diary), and it is thought that he continued to revise it until completing it about 1615.[2] At the time he was writing, Gyūichi deemed the island important enough to merit, if only on paper, his protagonist's arduous holy journey there.

In part because of Nobunaga's actual and apocryphal attentions—and more especially due to the island's deep and enduring links with Hideyoshi—the centuries-long reverence for Chikubushima as a sacred site intensified and expanded in the Momoyama period, as did regard for its resident deity, Benzaiten. Benzaiten had secured a toehold in the Japanese pantheon no later than the eighth century, when imperially sponsored worship employed the *Sutra of Golden Light,* a sutra in which Benzaiten figures as one of many deities who protect Buddhism.[3] Foremost among her many powers, according to the sutra, are the abilities to grant eloquence and wisdom, and significantly, she was associated as well with military prowess: she is "superior like a lion among beasts," and she is eight-armed, with a different weapon in each of many hands.[4] She was, in other words, an impressively capable sacred force, but not yet independently worshipped. A second major form of Benzaiten emerged in Japan which emphasized Benzaiten's aspect as a goddess of music, and in this aspect she came to be depicted with only two arms and holding a lute *(biwa)*.[5]

Benzaiten emerged as a focus of independent veneration in Japan about the thirteenth century. About this time there appeared three texts devoted to her, the *Benten sanbukyō (Three Sutras of Benten)*, which were fabricated in Japan.[6] In these, Benzaiten is eight-armed and she still holds various weapons, but her attributes also include the wish-fulfilling jewel *(hōju)* and a key, thus emphasizing Benzaiten's aspect as a goddess of fortune. She is associated with the indigenous harvest god Ugajin, who is himself connected with the snake god and dragon god. Finally, Benzaiten's potency is enhanced by her Fifteen Attendants, each with his own attributes.

Surviving from the late fourteenth century onward are numerous paintings and sculptures depicting the so-called Uga Benzaiten, often with the Fifteen Attendants.[7] Many such images are found at Chikubushima, including sculptures commissioned and donated for the annual Lotus Festival. One from 1614 exemplifies the type *(Fig. 137)*. Benzaiten is eight-armed; she holds several weapons, in the central left hand the wish-fulfilling jewel, and in the corresponding right hand a sword; on her head is a Shinto torii gate and Ugajin, depicted with the body of a snake and the head of an old bearded man. The *Benten sanbukyō*'s additional layers of textual exegesis, here impressively realized in visual form, have transformed Benzaiten into a more powerful presence, one especially well acclimated to Japan.

The puissant Benzaiten was widely venerated in the Momoyama period, not only at Chikubushima but in the surrounding Ōmi area, in the capital, and far beyond. A Benzaiten Hall built in 1550 at Chōjuin, for example, not far from Chikubushima, suggests the diffusion of Benzaiten belief from Chikubushima into the immediate Ōmi area.[8] Closer to Kyoto, Gien writes in his diary that "the first cherry blossoms and leaves at the Benzaiten have opened," indicating that within the Daigoji complex was a hall that housed Benzaiten.[9] Within the Misu Jinja complex near Fushimi is a Benzaiten Hall that, according to its ridgepole placard, was rebuilt in 1606, after being "a place that for 120 years was neglected."[10] In 1596 the courtier Yamashina Tokitsune (1543–1611) mentioned in his diary possessing a painting of Benzaiten and the Fifteen Attendants.[11] Funabashi Hidekata (1575–1614), a scholar who served the Court, made a pilgrimage in 1603 to "the Take no Benzaiten," referring probably to the major cult center in Tennokawa.[12]

Benzaiten also attracted major warrior sponsors, perpetuating into the Momoyama period an association she historically enjoyed (as demonstrated when Minamoto no Yoritomo [1147–1199], the first shogun of Japan, sought divine assistance from the Benzaiten enshrined on Enoshima before a battle with the Hiraizumi Fujiwara in 1182).[13] Nobunaga, as we have seen, prominently displayed at Sōkenji, his temple complex within Azuchi Castle's precincts, an image of Benzaiten which he had brought from Chikubushima (see p. 60). Hideyoshi paid her homage throughout his adult life. The daimyo Kobayakawa Takakage (1533–1597), to whom Hideyoshi awarded a large northern Kyushu domain in 1587, was patron of a Benzaiten Hall in his castle town at Najima (in

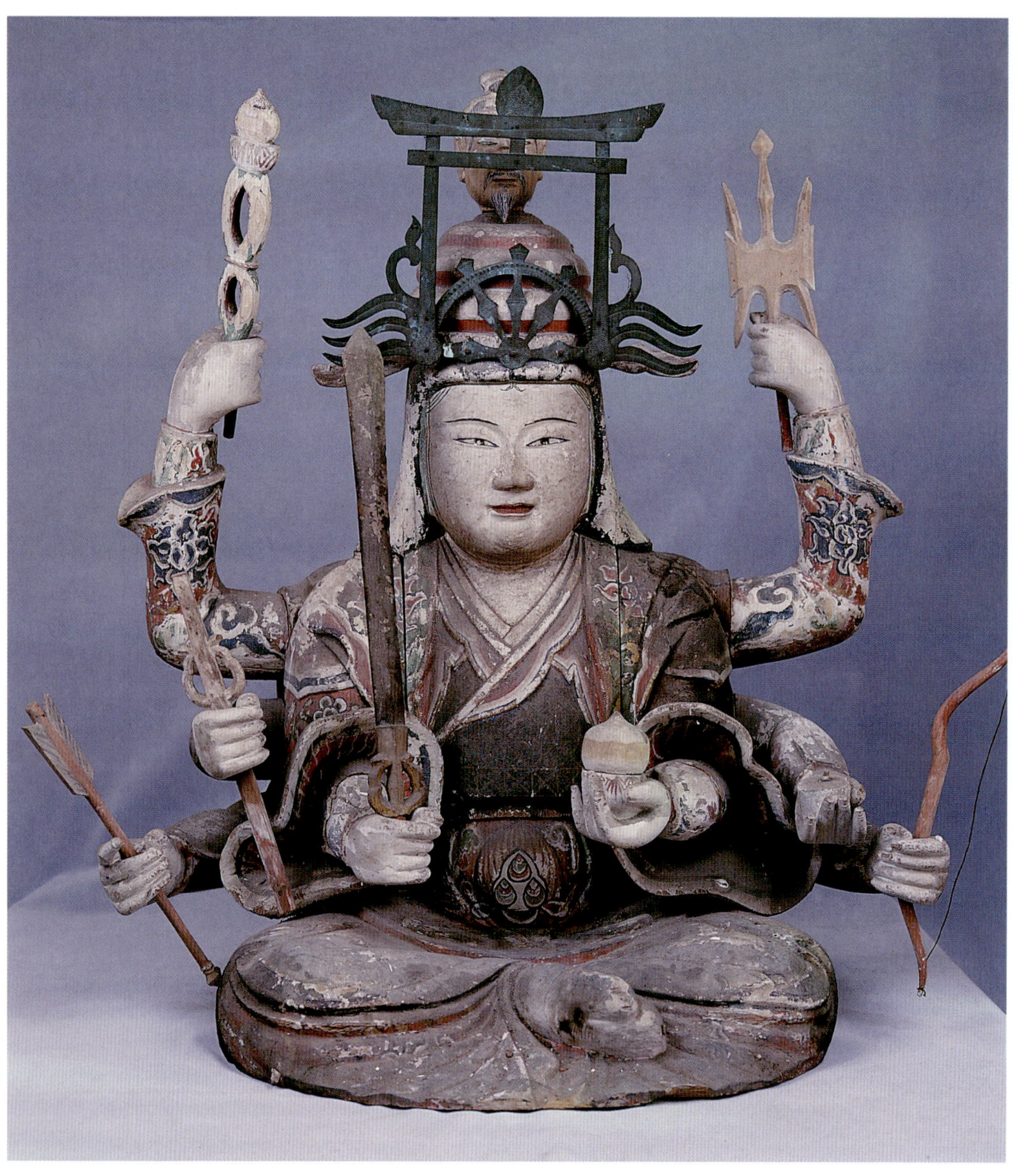

FIG. 137 *Benzaiten.* Dated to 1614. Polychromed wood. Hōgonji, Chikubushima, Shiga Prefecture. Photograph by Shiga Kenritsu Biwako Bunkakan.

present-day Fukuoka Prefecture); it may have been located within the castle precincts, suggesting that Benzaiten served as guardian deity of the clan.[14] Kuwayama Shigeharu (d. 1606), another of Hideyoshi's daimyo vassals, rebuilt the Hyōgo Prefecture temple Hōjuin, whose central deity was Benzaiten (an icon reputedly admired by Hideyoshi).[15] Benzaiten's martial character, a character that was particularly emphasized in Japan, apparently made her appealing to warriors as a tutelary deity.[16]

THE LOTUS FESTIVAL IN THE POST-HIDEYOSHI ERA

In this period Chikubushima was a paramount Benzaiten cult center. Despite its difficulty of access—numerous pilgrims drowned making the trip[17]—leading figures of the Momoyama religious establishment went there. Gien made the journey once, if not twice, as he related in a 1597 entry in his diary: "Two years ago at the time of my pilgrimage [I stayed] at the temple lodgings of Myōkakuin on Chikubushima in Ōmi; next time I will lodge at the same place."[18] Bonshun recorded in his diary a journey to Chikubushima in 1603: "Within Shiga County, I stopped at a place called Komatsu, and then, from my lodgings at Imazu, made a pilgrimage by boat to Chikubushima."[19] Both Gien and Bonshun use the term *sankei,* or pilgrimage, to denote the nature of their visits to the island; Bonshun so differentiates the sacred character of Chikubushima from Komatsu, the previous stop on his journey.

Regular participation in Chikubushima ceremonial affairs by highly placed temporal figures, often warriors, was institutionalized in the annual Lotus Festival, which from as early as the late tenth century was Chikubushima's festival dedicated to Benzaiten.[20] On the fourteenth day of the sixth month it reached its culmination with a performance of *bugaku* dance in front of the Benzaiten Hall, continuing the next day with a procession to the island of participants in colorfully decorated boats, followed by the eye-opening ceremony of a new sculpture of Benzaiten.[21] Preparations for the Lotus Festival began shortly before the turn of the new year, with the selection of sponsors (*tōnin,* literally, "Head People") from among laymen who lived or had familial roots in northern Ōmi. The sponsors followed a series of ceremonial procedures over the six-month period after their selection, and undertook the costly duty of commissioning a new Benzaiten sculpture. Many of these sculptures are still preserved, ranging in size from less than twenty centimeters to monumental seated figures almost one and a half meters in height (the one dated to 1614, *Fig. 137,* is 65 centimeters tall), and all depict the deity in her eight-armed Uga Benzaiten manifestation.[22]

Although the Momoyama record is incomplete, available information confirms that it was local warrior and political figures of high standing, as well as well-to-do villagers, who were awarded the prestigious sponsor's role.[23] As we have seen, the Asai served in this capacity several times in the 1560s, when they were the ruling daimyo family of the area encompassing Chikubushima.[24] In the post-Hideyoshi period, the most detailed insight into temporal participation in the Lotus Festival is conveyed in a letter sent to the island on the twelfth day of the fifth month of 1604 by Tanaka Yoshimasa, a Tokugawa vassal with roots in Ōmi:

> In accordance with the vows I fervently offered several years ago [in 1600] when I made a pilgrimage [to Chikubushima], I should like the customary *shinji* of Chikubushima, in the sixth month of 1605, to be conducted as prayer rituals for us, husband and wife. For this purpose, we will send 100 *koku* of rice. Tonda Kyūzaemon will speak to you.[25]

Yoshimasa had already made one pilgrimage to Chikubushima in the year of Sekigahara, perhaps in connection with a letter of protection for the island that he issued immediately after the battle.[26] His letter of 1604 expresses his long-standing desire to participate in the Lotus Festival, which he refers to as the *shinji,* literally, "god-event," and offers a sizable donation of 100 koku of rice. He received the recommendation of another warrior, Tonda Kyūzaemon who, in another letter to the island of the same date, reiterates Yoshimasa's request and discusses in detail the implementation of the proffered donation, indicating that it will be sent in the form of cash.[27] It is unclear whether Yoshimasa was petitioning Chikubushima for the privilege of serving as sponsor for the 1605 Lotus Festival or accepting their invitation to serve, though he unquestionably met the qualifications. His family had strong ties with northern Ōmi, he had already made a pilgrimage to the island, and he had ample financial resources: his fief after Sekigahara was more than quintupled, from 57,000 koku to 300,000 koku.[28] The incomplete documentary record does not reveal whether Yoshimasa ever fulfilled his wish, but it makes clear that this eminent warrior considered service as sponsor an honor to be sought.

THE NŌ PLAY *CHIKUBUSHIMA* IN THE POST-HIDEYOSHI ERA

Chikubushima's renown, chronicled and thus augmented in prominent ancient texts such as the *Tale of the Heike* and the *Keiran shūyōshū,* continued to grow. No vehicle was then more important than Nō, the meta-religious performance art that was the preferred theatrical diversion of all Momoyama elites—Hideyoshi was not only a patron of Nō but an eager performer as well.[29] Chikubushima was a prominent Nō presence, in a self-titled drama that was widely performed at divers places and for divers occasions and audiences. In 1601 *Chikubushima* was the first play in an all-day program at the Imperial Palace;[30] in 1605 it was the first of five plays performed in a temple setting;[31] in 1606 and then again in the following year it was included in the repertoire performed during the semi-annual three-day ceremonies at the Toyokuni Shrine.[32] The *Nō no tomechō,* a record of Nō performances in the Momoyama period, lists nine performances of *Chikubushima* between the years 1608 and 1615 in a variety of settings, including Honganji, Edo Castle, and Nijō Castle.[33] Performances of *Chikubushima,* always for elite audiences, powerfully sustained the distant island's vital presence in Kyoto and other urban centers of Japan.

The theme of the Nō play *Chikubushima* is its characterization of the island as a sacred place where Benzaiten dwells and manifests her wondrous benefits.[34] Its structure is a common Nō type: characters that first appear as mortals reveal themselves as deities in the course of the drama. It is set in ancient times—a golden age of munificent rule by the emperor Daigo (885–930)—and begins with a court official announcing his intention to make a pilgrimage to Chikubushima in Ōmi Province, to offer his vows to the deity there. There follows a description of his journey, progressing from Kyoto to the western shore of Lake Biwa. Seeing a fishing boat in the lake, the official calls out to ask for a ride to the island for himself and his companions. The occupants of the boat are an old man and a woman. In response to the old man's protestation that the vessel is only a fishing boat, the official describes it as a "boat of the vow," appropriate to his journey. They board the boat and head for Chikubushima.

Finally reaching the distant island, they disembark. The old man leads the visitors to the hall dedicated to Benzaiten and beckons them to offer their supplications. The court official remarks on the wonder of the place, even more marvelous than he had heard, and asks how it is that a woman (the fisherman's attendant) is allowed on the island's holy ground. The old man chastises him for his ignorance, telling him that Benzaiten is an "incarnation of eternal enlightenment," and that women in particular make the pilgrimage to Chikubushima. The chorus adds that Benzaiten makes her appearance in the form of a woman; she is the Tennyo, the "Celestial Woman," of wondrous divine virtue; she "made the vow of compassion and many years have passed since she reached enlightenment. From long ago . . . her benefits have not decreased." Now the old man and woman reveal their true natures. The woman states, "I am not human," opens the door of the Benzaiten Hall, and enters. The old man announces, "I am the ruler of the lake," and disappears beneath the waters. The woman, a humble fisherman's attendant whose presence on the island the court official had questioned, is the deity Benzaiten.

After a short interlude, a return to the main drama is announced by the chorus, "The hall shakes violently, and the sun and the moon, their light shining, rise over the mountains, and Benzaiten appears."[35] She emerges from the hall in splendid dress, announcing, "Indeed, I am Benzaiten. I live on this island and protect all sentient beings." Music emanates from the heavens, flowers rain down, and Benzaiten begins a dance to the stately chanting of the chorus. Next the Dragon God, a water deity, emerges from the waves, and performs a dance to fast, high-pitched flute music and the chanting of the chorus. The chorus announces that salvation appears in various forms, including Tennyo (that is, Benzaiten), who answers the entreaties of believers, or the Dragon God (who is probably one of Benzaiten's manifestations). The drama ends with the chorus describing the return of Benzaiten to her hall, and of the Dragon God to the lake. The frequency with which *Chikubushima* was performed, and the variety of important venues, insured that this awe-inspiring image of the island and its resident deity was well established in the minds of the Japanese elite: within a hall at this sacred place, far removed physically and spiritually from the mundane world, resides the female deity Benzaiten who offers salvation to her many believers.

STUDYING CHIKUBUSHIMA

Chikubushima also appeared in a forum less public than Nō, though with an audience of equally great significance. In 1600 Gien transcribed into his diary portions of a manuscript concerning such eminent Buddhist centers as Tōji, Mount Kōya, and Kiyomizudera.[36] He does not name the manuscript, but it would appear that he found it worthy of consultation and that it included intriguing bits of information about each place. He cites it, for example, as stating that the Bishamonten statue at Kuramadera, "is in truth Kannon; it is a Kannon made of lotus tree." Regarding the Main Hall at Mount Kōya, he quotes, "Kūkai built it from the ninth day of the second month of 819, but on the sixth day of the seventh month of 994 it was struck by lightning and burned. Over the course of thirteen years, from 1100, it was rebuilt, and then in 1149 it was struck by lightning and burned." This miscellany of Japan's sacred places piqued Gien's curiosity, and so he copied it into his journal.

Gien also records a reference in the text to Chikubushima:

> The same record, on the matter of the Chiku[bu]shima Benzaiten, states that "the *Kegon Sutra,* in the *Bosatsubon,* states, 'East of here, there is one small country, and in the country is a large lake, and in the lake there is a lone island, and there Benzai Tennyo has gained her living body and endured; she lives at this place.'"[37]

The unnamed record connects Chikubushima with an island purportedly described in the *Kegon Sutra,* and there identified as a spot where Benzaiten resides. The passage is very close, of course, to the one cited in the fourteenth-century *Keiran shūyōshū,* and even closer in its specific wording to the one in the fifteenth-century Chikubushima temple solicitation register *(kanjinchō),* differing from the latter only in that it omits a part of the book chapter title (see pp. 55–57). Because Gien never names his source, possible links between this quotation and the others cannot be discovered. In all these documents the attribution of the passage regarding Chikubushima to the *Kegon Sutra* appears to be spurious; nevertheless, it enjoyed great currency.

Gien's interest in this remarkable passage is easy to understand. As a scholar of the sacred in Japan, Gien possibly already knew the claim from the *Keiran shūyōshū* itself or, since he had been to Chikubushima just a couple of years earlier, from the kanjinchō or from monks on the island who continued to repeat it. If so, he would have been impressed not by the newness of the information, but rather by its reaffirmation in yet another apparently credible text. Knowing Gien's habits as we do from his diary (and one of his habits was to spend considerable time doing services for his Osaka patrons), we can imagine he might have shared this piece of scholarship with the Toyotomi, who would have been duly pleased to hear confirmation of the special status of this site that had once been so closely associated with Hideyoshi.

THE TOKUGAWA AT CHIKUBUSHIMA IN THE POST-HIDEYOSHI ERA

Chikubushima was common ground for the Tokugawa and Toyotomi early on in their ultimately unsuccessful period of coexistence. Ieyasu's most visible mark on the island today is the magnificent entrance gate of Hōgonji, the temple neighboring the Tsukubusuma Main Hall *(Fig. 101)*. This gate was initially part of the Toyokuni Shrine and, as recorded by Bonshun, Ieyasu removed it from there in 1602 and donated it to the island.[38] Bonshun does not suggest an ulterior motive for this donation, which is often cited as an example of Ieyasu's attempt to rid Kyoto of reminders of Hideyoshi, one more stroke in his campaign to eliminate the Toyotomi. If that was Ieyasu's intent, which is unlikely, it was unusually unsuccessful, for, as Bonshun notes, at the very same time that Ieyasu was having this gate moved, Hideyori was building a new one at the Toyokuni Shrine.

Ieyasu's fine gift of the Toyokuni gate is one indication of his high regard for the island, but was less significant for Chikubushima than the alert bureaucratic consideration his new administration offered, best demonstrated in its resolution of a serious land-related problem that had long plagued the island. Control of land rights was, arguably, the greatest power Ieyasu gained in the post-Sekigahara settlement, and he wielded it deftly, asserting Tokugawa authority throughout Japan with confiscations, reductions, and increases of warrior domains, and strategic transfers of military allies and foes to new locations.[39] To determine the yield of the land he dispersed, Ieyasu conducted cadastral surveys, including one in Ōmi that began in the spring of 1602 and lasted until the eleventh month.[40] Although Chikubushima's annual income had been determined by Hideyoshi to be 300 koku, Ieyasu's survey found that a portion of the island's holdings was not producing the expected yield; the shortage is described in a set of internal Chikubushima regulations issued in 1603 as "the deficiency of 47 koku, 5 *to*, 4 *shō* from within the 300 koku, revealed during the cadastral survey ordered by Naifu [Ieyasu]."[41] The deficient fields are likely those referred to in Bokushinsai Nobusada's letter, dating to Hideyoshi's rule, as "temple-donation land frequently affected by water damage";[42] by decreasing yield, such damage created a potentially serious economic problem that, despite Nobusada's assurances, was not resolved during Hideyoshi's lifetime.

The Tokugawa not only identified the problem, they resolved it quickly and to the exact amount. In the third month of 1603 a Tokugawa official by the name of Ogawa Ichizaemon sent a memo to Chikubushima pledging that the deficiency would be made up; he lists first an amount of slightly over 252 koku, described as "the portion as from before," and then the amount of "47 koku, 5 to, 4 shō" that will be given Chikubushima "from within the village of Hayasaki," all together making the entire 300 koku.[43] Other Tokugawa correspondence refers in even more minute detail to the compensation of the forty-seven koku deficit, itemizing the transfer of "16 koku, 6 shō" as "the supplementary part of the Hayasaki Village Chikubushima holdings of 300 koku."[44] For their part, Chikubushima sent the Tokugawa appropriate gifts, sake in one instance, and, no doubt, letters voicing their concerns.[45] Subsequently the Tokugawa also issued vermilion-seal letters endorsing the island's annual income: in 1613 Ieyasu followed precedent and confirmed Chikubushima's claim to the 300 koku within Hayasaki[46]; Ieyasu's two Tokugawa successors—Hidetada (1579–1632) and Iemitsu (1604–1651)—also sanctioned the 300-koku income, stating in their letters that they were following earlier Tokugawa precedent.[47] The transfer of jurisdiction over land rights from the Toyotomi to the Tokugawa was complete, and Chikubushima reaped the bureaucratic benefits.

THE TOYOTOMI AT CHIKUBUSHIMA IN THE POST-HIDEYOSHI ERA

By deftly alleviating Chikubushima's worldly distress over its terrestrial holdings, the Tokugawa made themselves an indispensable ally; they were no match, however, for the Toyotomi in their solicitude for Chikubushima's halls of worship. In 1602 and 1603 the Toyotomi sponsored a substantial construction campaign on the island, which rebuilt its religious infrastructure. Its scope is suggested by three extant ridgepole placards: the first, dated to the sixth day of the ninth month of 1602, celebrates completion of the Benzaiten Hall and lists Katagiri Katsumoto as the chief administrator and four local Ōmi assistants, Amenomori Chōsuke, Ōnoki Gorōzaemon, Ōne Ichizaemon (Takanori), and Nishimura Kiyoemon;[48] the second placard, from two weeks later, the nineteenth, commemorates another, unnamed building in the campaign, credits Hideyori as its patron, Katsumoto as the administrator, and then names the same four men;[49] the third, dated to the sixth month of 1603, marks completion of the entire island-wide undertaking.[50] At some point in the proceedings Chikubushima expressed its gratitude by sending Hideyori appropriate ceremonial gifts as well as records of rituals performed for him; in response Amenomori Chōsuke, one of the four local administrators working under Katagiri Katsumoto, returned a letter to the island conveying Hideyori's pleasure with the gifts as well as his promise to next construct a Sutra Hall on the island, a project that would be carried out in consultation with Katsumoto.[51] It is not known whether this building was completed, but Hideyori's promise suggests the all-encompassing attention the Toyotomi directed to the sacred island.

The 1603 placard, a large and well-preserved panel of Japanese cypress, wholly covered with precisely calligraphed columns of writing, provides the most substantial documentary evidence for the Toyotomi campaign's intended significance *(Fig. 138)*. The lengthy text of over six hundred characters links sacred and temporal history, articulated in three distinct sections: the first and third describe normally unnoticed divine events

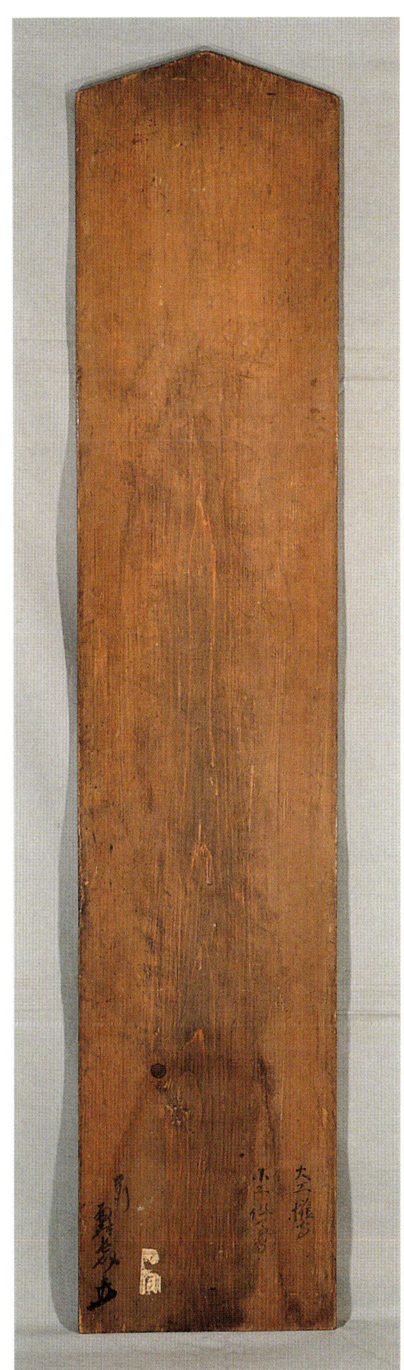

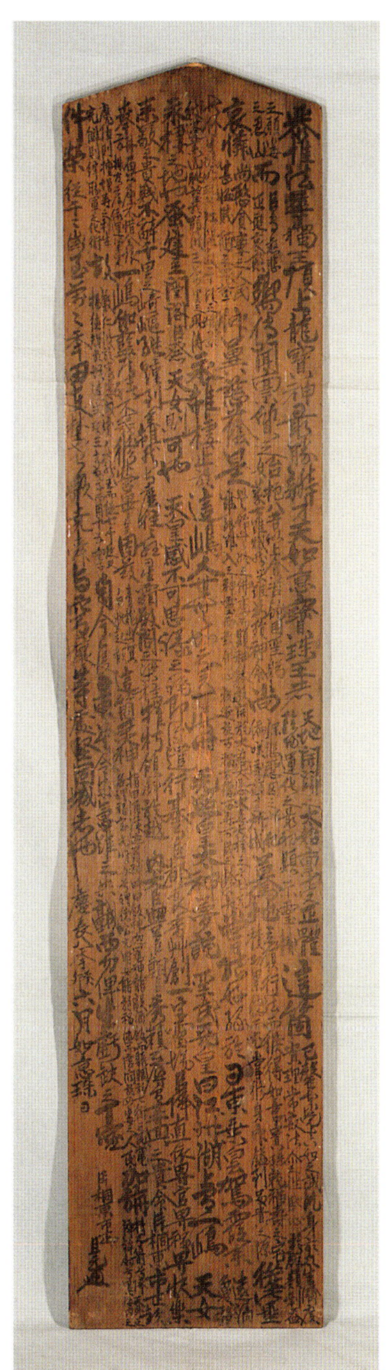

FIG. 138 Ridgepole placard; front (right), back (left). Dated to 1603. Chikubu-shima, Shiga Prefecture. Photograph by Nagahama Castle Historical Museum.

involving Benzaiten; the middle section is historical, concerned primarily with secular personalities and centered on the Momoyama patron Hideyori. The text conveys Benzaiten's magnificence with literary care: many of the passages that concern her comprise sentences paired by parallel grammar and content and by graphic similarity, being written in twinned columns of small characters. Other parts, including the historical section describing Hideyori's actions, are written entirely in bold, larger-sized characters in a single column. The text, in other words, was composed and executed with the attention befitting an undertaking of great consequence.

The first section provides a detailed hagiography of Benzaiten. It begins with a lengthy rendering of her name: Lotus-Law Solitary-Ruler Dragon-Treasure-Deity-on-Head Most-Excellent-Eloquence-Talent-Deity Wish-Granting-Jewel Ruler. She reached enlightenment long ago, and is praised for her single-minded devotion to the salvation of all beings. The text backtracks to describe the difficult path she travelled to achieve enlightenment. Then she is again extolled for her devotion to the salvation of people, particularly the impoverished and lowborn.

The second section, a historical account of Benzaiten's association with Japan, opens with her arrival, poetically described:

> Long ago [Benzaiten] knotted her fortuitous karma with Japan, and [she] came riding on the clouds and borne by the mist;
>
> [Benzaiten] settled on this distant Chikubushima and sang of the misty scenes of the several thousand *kei* of the lake of Ōmi;
>
> [Benzaiten] moved to this far-off Mount Hōrai and gazed over the gentle waves of the thirty thousand ri of wind-swept water.

Although the people did not know of her presence, the text continues, the emperor Shōmu (701–756) had a vision in which the deity Amaterasu Ōmikami appeared and informed him that Benzaiten had long lived on Chikubushima and thus buildings should be constructed and the deity worshipped. Accordingly, Emperor Shōmu sent the priest Gyōki (668–749) and the poet Miyako no Yoshika (834–879) to Chikubushima and they constructed a religious building there.[52] People rich and poor made the arduous journey to Chikubushima in great numbers. The text then jumps to the early seventeenth century, when the buildings on the island fell into desperate need of repair: "Dust gradually accumulated and over time the beams and pillars of the buildings decayed and passed the point of just bending." At this critical juncture appeared Toyotomi Hideyori, referred to by his court rank of Naidaijin, and he issued the order for restoration. The project was administered by Hideyori's magistrate Katagiri Katsumoto, and with no expense spared—"the government storehouses were opened" and "gold and silver were used without restraint"—the construction was quickly completed.

The final section reprises the initial theme of Benzaiten's boundless divine qualities, now revealed because of Hideyori's actions. The Blue Dragon and White Snake, both manifestations of Benzaiten, appeared in celebration of Hideyori's project, and people throughout the world rejoiced. Responding to the requests of people throughout Japan, Benzaiten bestowed on everyone sake, rice, fortune, and goodness. The attributes of Benzaiten are described in greater detail than before. She is a fierce protector, using sword as well as bow-and-arrow to defeat her enemies; she is "devoted to the arts of military victory." In her several manifestations and with her Fifteen Attendants, Benzaiten brings only good to the world. Under her mindful care Japan will encounter no disaster. Of this prosperity, and thus of the benevolence of Benzaiten, the old men of the countryside sing in praise. The placard is dated to "the day of the *nyoishu,*" referring to the wish-fulfilling gem that is one of Benzaiten's main attributes, in the sixth month of 1603, and is signed by Katagiri Katsumoto.

This text conveys a well-defined image of both site and patron, deftly combining previously stated conceptions with new ones to create a singularly attractive narrative. It repeats themes that correspond to the Uga Benzaiten manifestation described in the *Benten sanbukyō:* Benzaiten's Fifteen Attendants; her capacity to grant good fortune; her attainment of the hōju (wish-fulfilling jewel) and the key. None of the finely crafted, elaborate descriptions of Benzaiten are direct quotes from any known version of the *Benten sanbukyō* or other sutra, though it is possible they were taken from a now-lost text then used in Japan.

The characterizations of Chikubushima, too, are not exact quotations of recognized texts, but they evoke familiar themes. The comparison of Chikubushima to Mount Hōrai is a claim made in the *Tale of the Heike,* and the prominent role of the renowned monk Gyōki echoes information revealed in Chikubushima's *engi.* This is the first recorded association of Emperor Shōmu with Chikubushima, though it is a reasonable extrapolation if we accept Gyōki's connection with the island: Shōmu employed Gyōki for his most remarkable projects, including Tōdaiji's Great Buddha Hall, and to include him here makes a claim of merit for the island that the Toyotomi desired. It restates Hideyoshi's own preoccupation with Shōmu, as manifested in his construction of Hōkōji, and it recalls the parallel that the Toyotomi sought to draw between Hideyori and another revered ancient ruler, Prince Shōtoku.

At the same time, information clearly specific to this project is also emphasized, such as the description of the state of the buildings and the role of Hideyori in repairing them. Hideyori, first, is included in a prestigious lineage. As sponsor of Chikubushima and Benzaiten, Hideyori carries on a tradition originating in an act of Emperor Shōmu, who was himself motivated by a vision of Amaterasu Ōmikami. Both men were inspired by religious devotion, which was based in their concern for all the people of Japan. Benzaiten is emphasized throughout the text as savior of the poor as well as the prosperous. Accordingly, the activities of both Shōmu and Hideyori are described as bringing benefits for everyone. Following Emperor Shōmu's sponsorship, good fortune was bestowed and "rich and poor . . . made the pilgrimage." Hideyori's activities directly benefitted "the people of the Seven Paths," and "the people of the Four Seas" (people, that is, throughout Japan) were provided with both food and good fortune.

Other considerations, though unstated in the placard, motivated the Toyotomi in

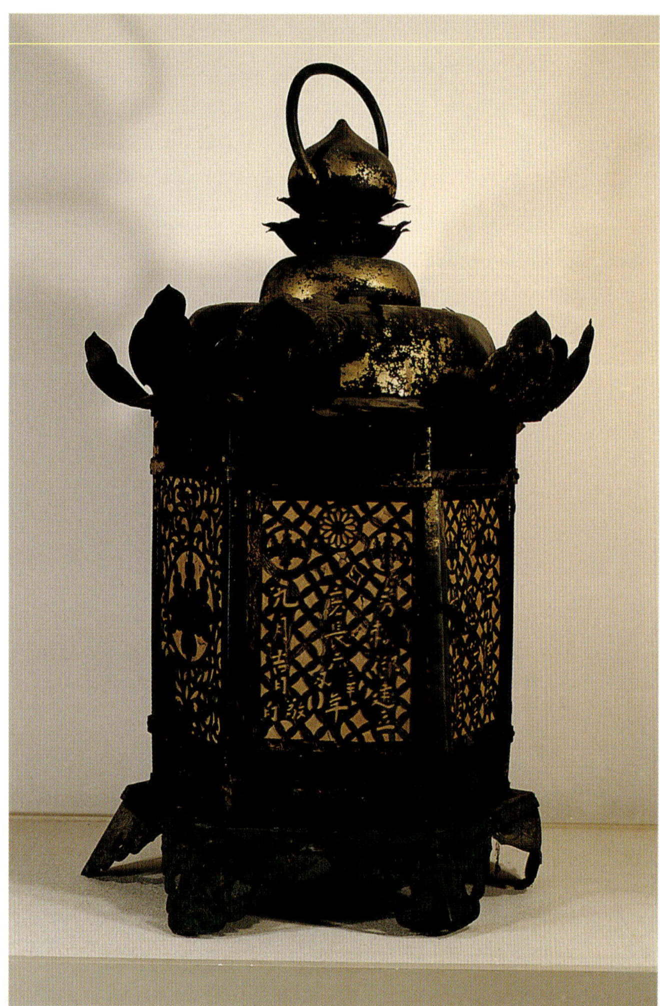

FIG. 139 Lantern. Dated to 1601. Bronze. Jōshinji, Kinomoto, Shiga Prefecture. Photograph by Nagahama Castle Historical Museum.

their work at Chikubushima. The most important, of course, was Hideyoshi's prior involvement with the island—forged in the earliest stages of his career, when he was still a retainer of Oda Nobunaga, and maintained throughout his tenure as ruler of Japan—and this made the place as attractive and sensible a site of Toyotomi patronage as any in Japan. That patronage was stimulated as well by the connections of other clan members to the surrounding area. Yododono was born and raised there, daughter of Asai Nagamasa, daimyo of the area before Hideyoshi and an active sponsor of the Lotus Festival and generous donor to Chikubushima. Yododono's interest in Chikubushima may also have been amplified by the island's unusual benevolence toward women worshippers, as the Nō play suggests. Katagiri Katsumoto, too, came from the area and entered Toyotomi service while Hideyoshi was based in Nagahama.

With this in mind, it is not surprising that Chikubushima was not the only religious site in northern Ōmi where the Toyotomi constructed holy works in the first years of the seventeenth century.[53] In the ninth month of 1601 Hideyori sponsored the building of the Jizō Hall at Jōshinji, a temple in nearby Kinomoto, a deed commemorated in two bronze lanterns (one is pictured in *Fig. 139*), four baluster caps, and a bronze gong—intricately wrought metalwork objects that exalt through ornament and commemorative inscriptions. The baluster caps and gong also list the project administrators as Katagiri Katsumoto and Amenomori Chōsuke, both participants in the construction at Chikubushima.[54] The Toyotomi sponsorship at Jōshinji conformed to a common pattern: in 1585 Hideyoshi had granted the temple permission to solicit funds to build a Jizō Hall, but the project apparently languished until Hideyori filially assumed its patronage and supplied the funds to bring it to completion. Another bronze gong preserved at Jōshinji bears an inscription dated to the sixth month of 1602 that proclaims Hideyori patron of the Gosha Jinja of Kinomoto, and Amenomori Chōsuke its administrator.[55] In 1601 Hideyori, Katsumoto, and Amenomori Chōsuke were responsible for a reconstruction project at nearby Ifufura Jinja, and in 1603 for another at Shirahige Jinja, farther south in Ōmi.[56] The region was busy with Toyotomi projects, all administered by local men who coveted the assignments. Amenomori Chōsuke petitioned Katagiri Katsumoto to be selected for one of the Kinomoto projects and was appointed to work with Katsumoto's brother-in-law, Ōne Takanori; Katsumoto sent Takanori a letter to this effect, also instructing him to go to Chikubushima during lulls at Kinomoto: in these years the major Toyotomi endeavor in this area, which required constant attention, took place on Benzaiten's island.[57]

APPROPRIATION AND ASSEMBLAGE

The depth of these synchronic familial, sacred, literary, and historical resonances made Chikubushima a logical site for the Toyotomi's architectural campaign. Their choice of seemingly complicated means to carry it out—instead of simply building anew, moving one entire building and radically altering another—fits into larger patterns of period architectural practice. Although not a Momoyama invention, the appropriation of preexisting architecture—moving structures large and small, in whole or in part—was conducted then with unusual energy and innovation. Ieyasu's transfer of the Toyokuni Shrine gate to Hōgonji is an unusually well documented extant example, but many other destabilized structures, now lost and mostly forgotten, are recorded in period writings.[58]

To a degree, appropriation was stimulated by historical events. Momoyama battles brought the victors architectural spoils: Hideyoshi's subjugation of Negoroji in 1585 prompted a plan to move the Main Hall of one of its subtemples to Tenshōji, then under construction, and the building was dismantled in preparation for the transfer (p. 76); ultimately, the supervising monk-administrator, Kokei Sōchin (1532–1597), sent the building not to Kyoto but rather to Sakai, to revive a temple there.[59] Available buildings deemed worthy—for their perceived architectural excellence or their patrons' fame—or simply expedient would be dismantled and moved from their original context to a new one. Indeed, the black and makie lacquer gate whose construction at the

Toyokuni Shrine Gien described so carefully in 1600, was built, at least in part, from portions of Osaka Castle's Gokuraku Bridge, which Hideyori apparently had dismantled and moved to Kyoto.[60]

The dismantling of a building was, in and of itself, not anomalous in the context of Japanese building practice, for it was simply the reverse of a common method of construction, prefabrication. Sutemaru's building was made in this way: its pillars and beams were cut and shaped, then makie-lacquered in a workshop near the Great Buddha Hall, and only then moved to their "original" location for final assembly (pp. 184–85). Gien writes in his diary that all of the several large structures that Hideyori sponsored for Daigoji's upper precincts in 1606 were prepared in Osaka and assembled on site.[61] Considering that location, a narrow clearing near the top of a steep and high mountain, prefabrication was the logical method. And if a building was so prepared and then moved to its original site, there was no reason why it should not be moved again to a second site.

Today, many buildings said to have been moved during Momoyama are claimed, often without credible substantiation, to have originated in one or another of Hideyoshi's monumental architectural projects. A survey of Kyoto's presumed Momoyama buildings yields numerous structures for which distinguished provenances, rarely supported by evidence, have been alleged—at Nishi Honganji, for example, the Hiunkaku purportedly comes from Jurakutei and the Karamon from Fushimi Castle.[62] Extant examples whose Toyotomi provenance actually can be corroborated, such as the Hōgonji gate, are the rare exceptions, but dubious assertions of such a provenance are not simply a function of the post-Edo desire to be linked to Hideyoshi's glory. They also reflect the reliable lore that buildings were often moved during Momoyama, so that such a claim is not ipso facto preposterous.

In truth, Hideyoshi may have stimulated the trend himself when he dismantled and dispersed his celebrated Kyoto palace, Jurakutei, which he had completed in 1587 and lived in for several years. In 1592 Hideyoshi shifted his headquarters to Fushimi Castle, his final residential fortress near Kyoto, and into Jurakutei moved his adopted nephew and appointed successor, Hidetsugu. Soon thereafter, however, the birth of Hideyoshi's son and new heir, Hideyori, exacerbated tensions that led to Hidetsugu's downfall, and in 1595 he was forced to commit suicide. The entire complex, tainted by his occupancy, was effaced: "Today, returning to [Daigoji], I took a look at Juraku—it is all a wild field," Gien wrote in 1596, "I wept; it is like a dream."[63] In this drastic transformation from splendor to void, however, the buildings were not destroyed. Hideyoshi had some of them transferred to Fushimi Castle, where the change in context purified these marvelous structures of Hidetsugu's defilement and afforded them new status as pieces of Hideyoshi's final residence.[64] (Most, presumably, were soon lost in the 1596 earthquake.) Jurakutei's garden stones were carried off, too, including one named Fujito, formerly owned by Nobunaga, which was transferred to Hideyoshi's remodelled garden at the Sanbōin subtemple of Daigoji; there it serves as an important visual focus of a garden that contains more than six hundred stones *(Figs. 140, 141)*.[65]

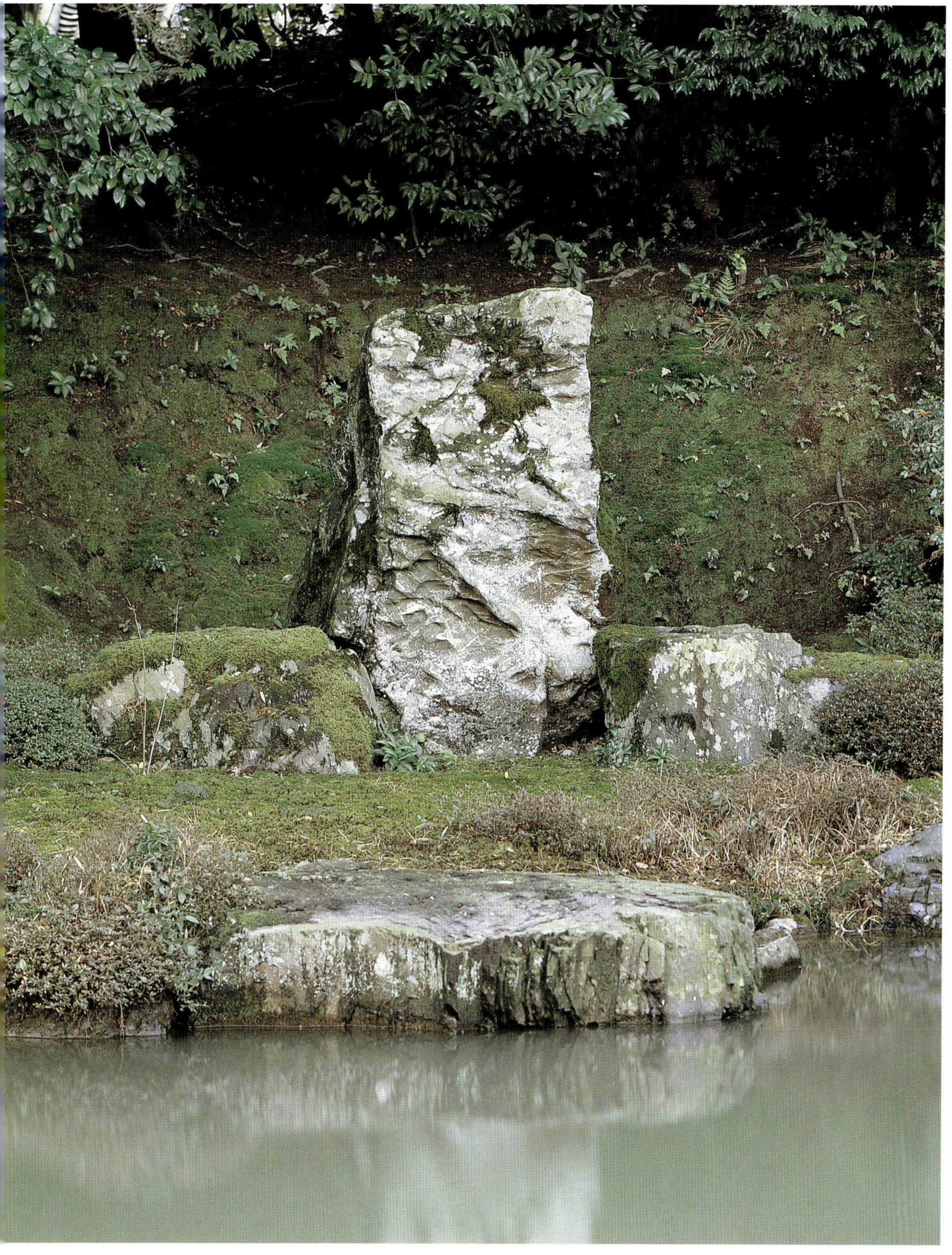

FIG. 140 Garden stone, named Fujito. Sanbōin, Daigoji, Kyoto.

FIG. 141 (overleaf) Garden. Sanbōin, Daigoji, Kyoto.

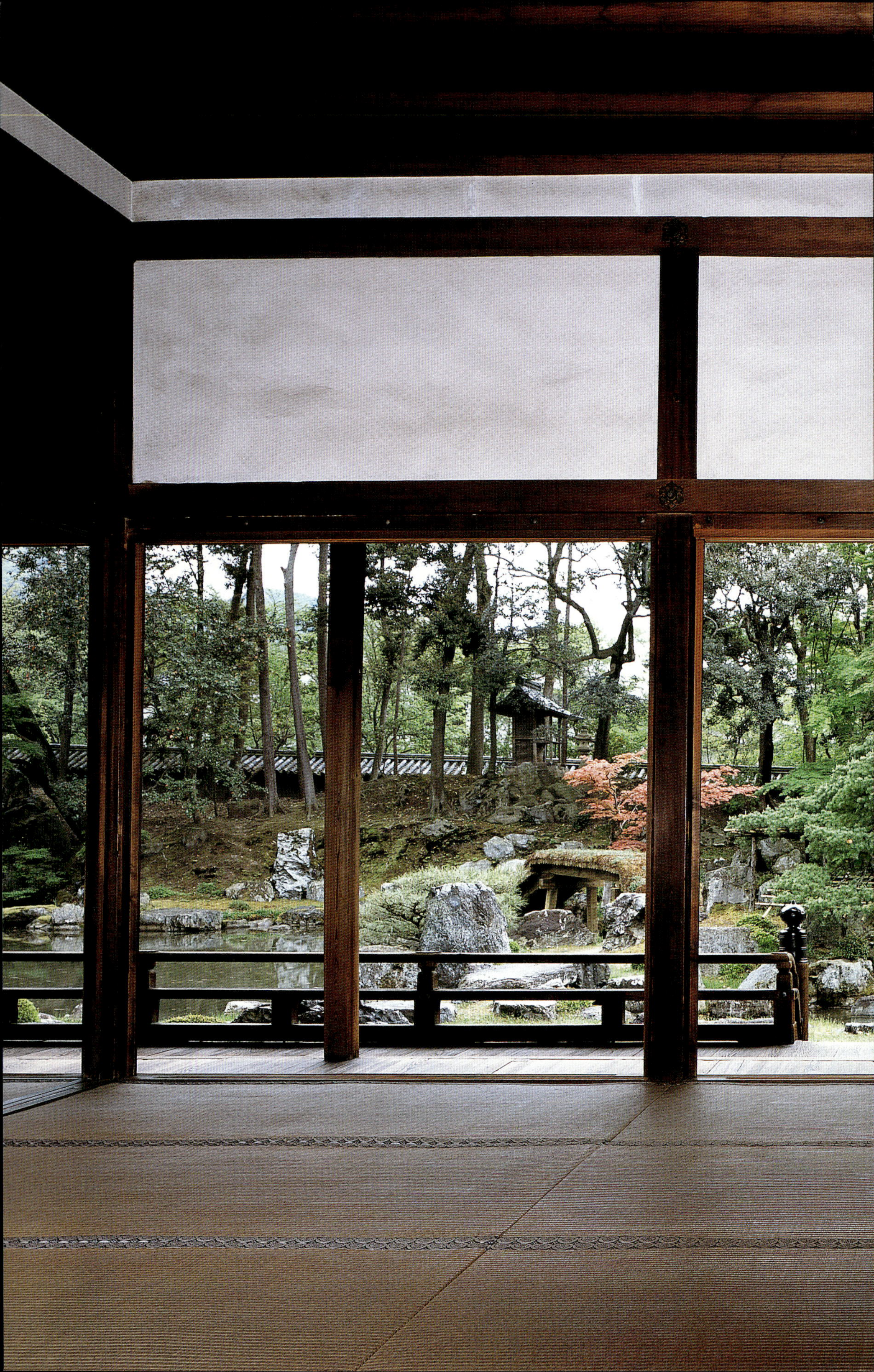

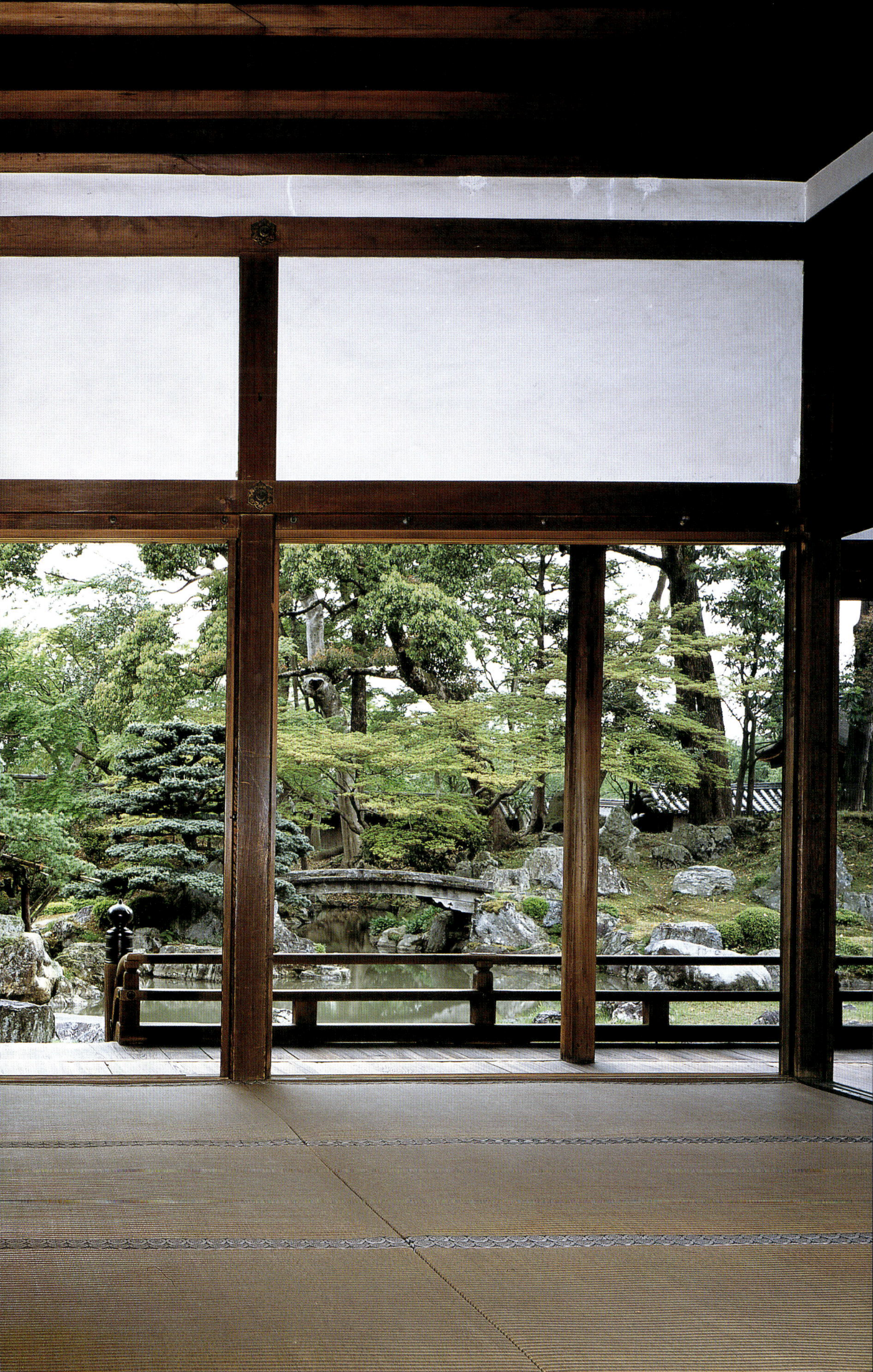

Gien and the Practice of Appropriation

Gien recounts several transfers of buildings in which he was involved, each different. The first took place within Gien's Daigoji, and demonstrates how a structure might be adapted to serve a different purpose:

> The Yamagami Morishita tea house was dismantled. It will be built as the guardhouse of the *monzeki.* This tea house was built at the time of Taikō's blossom-viewing last year. It is two and a half *ken* wide and five ken deep, with a panel roof.[66]

The tea house, first built on the mountainside of Daigoji for Hideyoshi's famed 1598 cherry-blossom celebration, was an impermanent structure by design. When that occasion was past, it was disassembled, moved to Daigoji's lower precincts, and rebuilt at the Sanbōin subtemple (the monzeki), where it served as a guardhouse. Why the building was reused, Gien does not say, though practicality was probably one reason. Doubtless the building's association with Hideyoshi conferred prestige, and perhaps it bore emblems of its original patron (such as the Toyotomi's paulownia and chrysanthemum crests) that would have befitted the new location at the Sanbōin, site of Hideyoshi's rock-filled garden.

Very often, however, moves entailed much more than simply reusing what one already owned. Gien describes the transfer of a number of buildings from Fushimi Castle. Extensive damage, sustained during the turmoil that preceded the Battle of Sekigahara in 1600, inspired a reconstruction campaign during which dilapidated or unwanted buildings were dispersed.[67] During this reconstruction phase, buildings from a temple precinct within the castle complex were given to other religious establishments. They were highly coveted, for their Toyotomi associations and for the quality of construction that such sponsorship implies. Gien, the longtime Toyotomi associate, wrote from Daigoji in the third month of 1601 about his efforts to obtain a gate from the temple:

> At Fushimi Castle there is a Niō Gate that was built by Taikō [Hideyoshi]. I wished to have it moved to this temple. It is said that Shōkōin appealed to Naifu [Ieyasu] and the gate is to be built as the Miidera gate. Today I received a message and sent money to Fushimi. The matter had already been decided, however, and I heard that everything was dismantled and taken to the Ishida boat landing. I am greatly angered.[68]

Despite Gien's overtures, then, which included a gift of money, the structure had already been prepared for shipment to Miidera, that is, Onjōji in Ōtsu, where it continued (as it does today) to function as a Niō Gate *(Fig. 142).* This was not, in fact, the gate's first move. Inscriptions on the two Niō sculptures and a placard indicate that the gate dates from the mid-fifteenth century and that Hideyoshi had brought it to Fushimi from

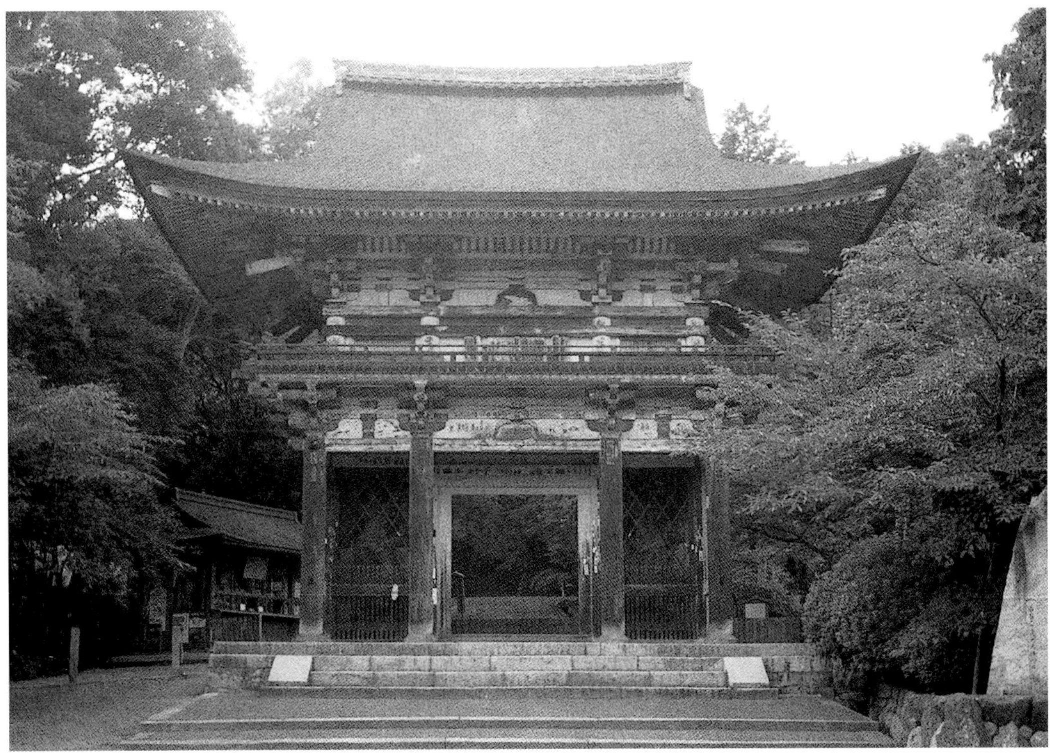

FIG. 142 Niō Gate. Onjōji, Ōtsu, Shiga Prefecture. Photograph by the author.

another temple, Jōrakuji, northeast of Onjōji in Shiga Prefecture.[69]

Gien's ire at losing the gate did not impede him from immediately lobbying for another Fushimi building,

> Yesterday I spoke to the priest Enshun and told him that there may be religious buildings left at Fushimi Castle and that he should go see them. It is said that there are two pagodas, a bell tower, and a three-bay-square hall. In my heart I desire to have the three-bay-square hall as the Mieidō for this temple. I think I will make an appeal for it.[70]

Enshun, probably a monk under Gien at Daigoji, was to inspect the remaining religious structures at the castle. Gien specifically wanted the three-bay-square building for use as a Mieidō, or Founder's Hall, at Daigoji. It would have replaced a Mieidō in Daigoji's lower precinct, which had been rebuilt as a three-bay-square hall after a fire in 1470 but over the years had deteriorated, as Gien described it, into "a half-built old structure."[71] Although the original function of the Fushimi building is unclear, its size made it apt for Gien's purpose. Alas for Gien, this petition too was denied, and Daigoji's old Mieidō stood as it was until 1605, when it was dismantled and then reconstructed within the Golden Hall, where it continued to be used thereafter for rituals for the founder.

These various moves all were predicated on the assumption that buildings are, in the context of Japan's tradition of wood architecture, fundamentally impermanent. This perception was understandably deep-rooted in a country frequently wracked by natural disaster, especially earthquakes and their ensuing fires, and—in the Momoyama period and the century that preceded it—by human depredation. No building was immune, not even the exalted ones, such as Hideyoshi's Great Buddha Hall (or Emperor Shōmu's, for that matter), Nobunaga's Azuchi Castle, or any of the many temple halls that were casualties of the 1596 earthquake. This is not to say that devastation was accepted as irreversible. Hideyori's restorations proceeded from the certitude that reclaiming worthy religious buildings was meritorious labor, welcomed by the deities who were venerated in them and who protected Japan. And in this regard it is important to emphasize that Hideyori most often engaged in the *restoration* of religious buildings—rather than in the construction of new ones—repairing and therefore preserving older buildings whose places in the sacro-historical record rendered them important to the preservation of Japan. It was on the currency of this belief that the Toyotomi staked their very survival, and in this belief that they embarked on their especially ambitious project at Chikubushima.

Chanoyu: A Model of Appropriation and Assemblage

The Toyotomi restoration of Chikubushima's Benzaiten Hall—which, as it turned out, constituted a re-creation—was a more complex architectural event than any described by Gien, and turned on another Momoyama activity that complemented the practice of appropriation: the assemblage of discrete, once-unrelated objects into a single unified ensemble. Together, appropriation and assemblage act to transform objects into something entirely new. Appropriation alone changes an object's meaning greatly if the new context differs dramatically from the old, as in Hideyoshi's tea house turned guardhouse, but very little if the contexts are similar, as in the case of Fushimi's Niō gate. Assemblage, however, almost always alters the appropriated object's meaning profoundly, by shifting it into a new context and submerging its independent identity in a new unity, which selectively highlights some of the object's elements, both physical and conceptual, and correspondingly de-emphasizes others. In an assemblage, the appropriated object cannot but be something different from what it was, an effect that Momoyama people brought about in their buildings and, indeed, in all sorts of things.

Especially from the mid-sixteenth century, manifold ways of appropriating and assembling objects were widely essayed in that quintessential Momoyama activity, *chanoyu*. Although chanoyu's explicit goals were the proper preparation and drinking of a bowl of tea, achieving these goals depended upon the host's calculated selection of the objects needed to create, in combination, a suitable chanoyu ensemble: bowls from which to drink, containers to hold water and leaf or powdered tea, kettles and braziers to boil water, and paintings, calligraphies, and vases to decorate the tea room. Tea masters accumulated these objects and then combined them in as many permutations as they deter-

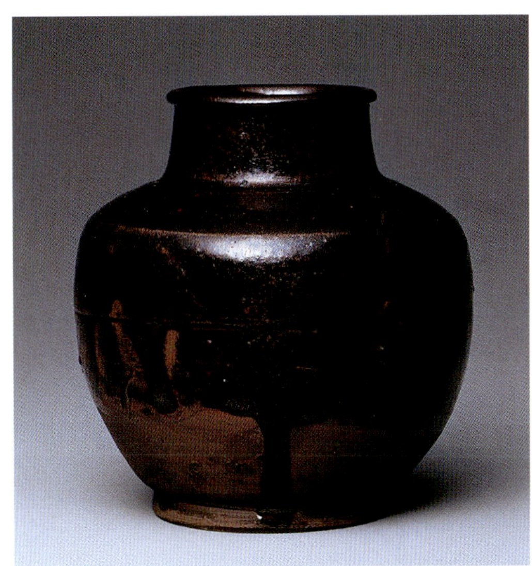

FIG. 143 Tea caddy, named Enza. Southern Song dynasty, thirteenth century. Glazed ceramic. Gotoh Museum, Tokyo.

mined, according to the evolving chanoyu precepts, would make good chanoyu sense.

Many chanoyu objects were not made expressly for chanoyu; one of a tea master's important skills was the ability to find interesting objects outside the chanoyu realm that could serve one of the necessary functions in the tea room. At first, the most desirable of these adoptees were antique and long-prized Chinese objects—many jars used in Japan for holding powdered tea, for instance, had been made in China for the purpose of storing medicine *(Fig. 143)*. Over time, with chanoyu's rising popularity and the concomitant escalating demand for appropriate paraphernalia, tea masters searched widely for newer and less scarce objects that could serve effectively in the chanoyu environment. This often involved appropriating objects of little status in their original settings for use in the elevated context of chanoyu. In short, chanoyu exploited the potential of an object to accumulate new value and meaning through a change in context.

The unglazed vessel in Figure 144, for example, was originally made in Southeast Asia for everyday, utilitarian use; it was not technically complex to make, it was not rare, and it was not expensive.[72] After it was brought to Japan, the eminent tea master Takeno Jōō (1502–1555) employed it in chanoyu as a fresh-water container *(mizusashi)*, and its new elevated function transformed it into an object of high value. Of course, provenance had much to do with this elevation: the humble pot rose in status when Jōō acquired it, and even more when it passed into Hideyoshi's possession; soon the pot-turned-mizusashi was judged to be, according to the Momoyama chanoyu treatise *Yamanoue no Sōji ki*, "tenka ichi," or "first in the realm."[73] It was also awarded a name, Jōō Imogashira, acknowledging its initial noted owner and describing its rotund shape, like that of an *imo*, or potato; being named both signified and enhanced its distinction. Eventually it was acquired by Tokugawa Ieyasu, whose descendants still own it today.[74] The genesis of its lofty status, however, lay in Jōō's act of appropriation, in the eminent tea master's choice to remove it from its lowly context and declare it to be something else.

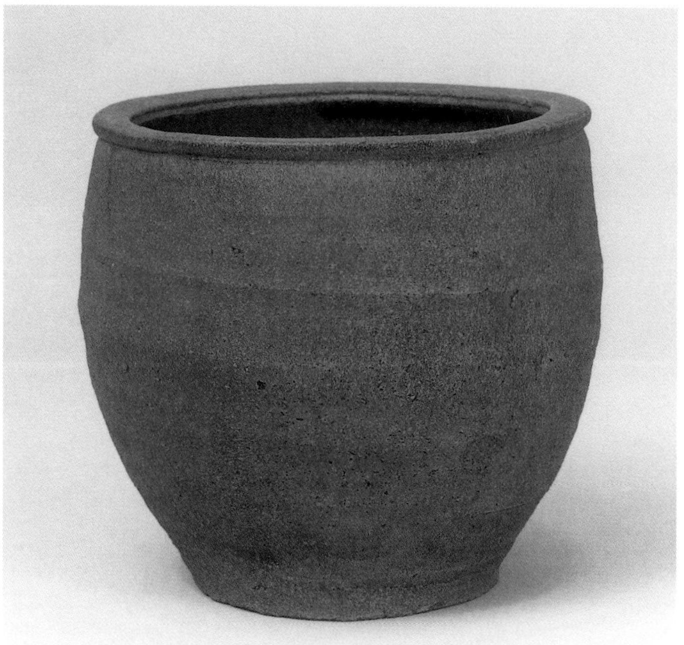

FIG. 144 Fresh-water jar, named Jōō Imogashira. Southeast Asia, sixteenth century. Unglazed stoneware. Tokugawa Art Museum, Nagoya.

Assemblage was always a core chanoyu activity: it was axiomatic that each gathering was unique, hence it was incumbent upon the host to create for each a new combination of objects from among those he owned that alluded to aesthetic principles, the guests' interests, and other variables. For each gathering, the host experimented with new relationships among disparate objects, and thereby created an interesting, if temporary, totality with them. Assemblage allowed Imogashira not only to transcend its original low function, but to speak in more subtle ways. It was used, for example, in a gathering Hideyoshi hosted in the first month of 1582, where it was combined with an iron kettle with a hailstone pattern of decoration, a bronze flower container also once owned by Jōō, and a Chinese tea bowl of a type particularly favored by Hideyoshi.[75] The reasons for this combination are unstated, though some can be surmised: by conjoining the pot with another object once owned by Jōō, its rarity and privileged provenance were highlighted; by juxtaposing the pot's rustic surface against the polish of the metal Chinese flower container, the stippled dark surface of the iron kettle, and the gloss of the glazed Chinese tea bowl, Hideyoshi's aesthetic subtlety was demonstrated.

Hideyoshi employed Imogashira again one year later, for guests among whom were the elite of the chanoyu world (who were also leading merchants, including dealers in firearms): Imai Sōkyū (1520–1593), who had been Nobunaga's chief tea master, and Sen no Rikyū (1522–1591), the merchant who soon replaced Sōkyū as tea master to the ruler.[76] For this group Hideyoshi combined Imogashira with objects that raised some altered associations: the kettle was Otogoze, a famed one noted in the *Yamanoue no Sōji ki;*[77]

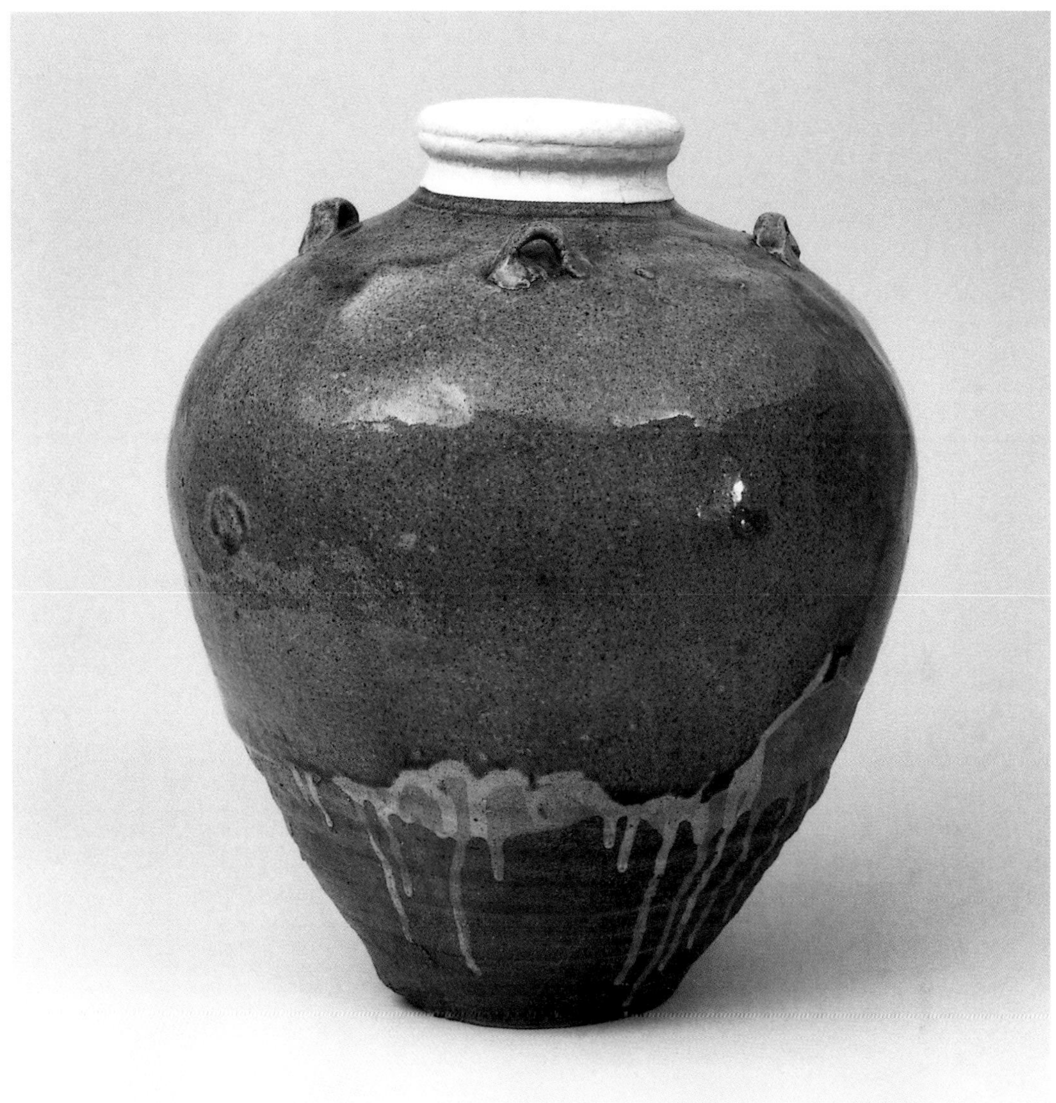

FIG. 145 Large tea jar, named Shōka. Southern Song–Yuan dynasty, thirteenth–fourteenth century. Glazed ceramic. Tokugawa Art Museum, Nagoya.

displayed in the alcove were a renowned calligraphy by the distinguished thirteenth-century Chan master Xutang Zhiyu (1185–1269)[78] and the large tea jar Shōka (still extant, *Fig. 145*), then one of the most famous in all Japan and previously owned by Nobunaga;[79] also used were an Ido teabowl, that is, a glazed Korean bowl appropriated from its original utilitarian context to be used in chanoyu, and a waste-water container made of metal. These juxtapositions reflect aesthetic criteria similar to those of the 1582 gathering: the rough earthen surface of Imogashira contrasted with the smooth glazes of Shōka and the Ido teabowl and the sheen of metal surfaces (the specific effects, of course, were subtly different, since the only constant in the two assemblages was Imogashira). In its meanings, however, this combination of objects was quite distinct from the earlier assemblage.

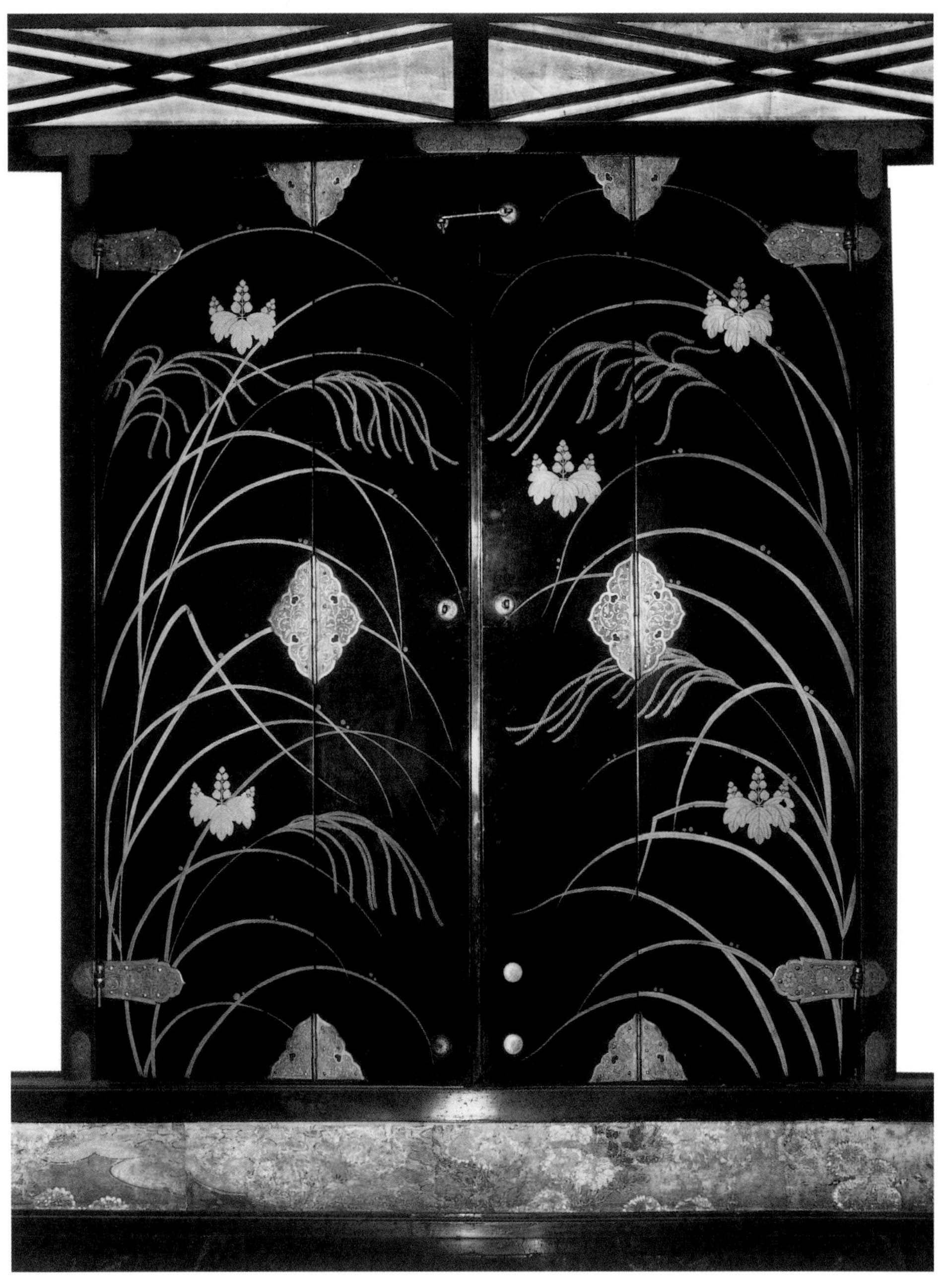

FIG. 146 Doors of Hideyoshi's zushi. Late sixteenth–early seventeenth century. Makie lacquer on wood. Kōdaiji, Kyoto. Photograph by Kyoto National Museum.

This gathering, held soon after Hideyoshi's elevation to ruler of Japan following Nobunaga's death, conjoined Imogashira—one of Hideyoshi's first tea objects with a famous provenance—with several other of the most celebrated objects in the land, including one of Nobunaga's prized possessions that Hideyoshi had only recently come to acquire. In creating this assemblage, Hideyoshi was proclaiming his newly won authority to an audience over whom he urgently wished to assert this authority.

Such were the aesthetic and symbolic constellations that could be created in an assemblage, and in the Momoyama period they were highly valued. It is no surprise that the Momoyama term closest to the English word "assemblage" is found in the context of chanoyu: *toriawase,* literally, "to take and combine," which is defined in the 1603 Portuguese dictionary of Japanese, *Vocabvlario da Lingoa de Iapam,* as "to combine things that are different and see if they go well together."[80] Widely popular, this notion of toriawase encouraged the creation of hybrid ensembles in many spheres. The urge to create new meaning through transformative appropriation and assemblage energized Momoyama object making. Such experiments created treasures out of clay, the phenomenon that so mystified the Jesuit missionary Alessandro Valignano (1539–1606) in his critique of chanoyu (see pp. 144–45).

But toriawase did not function exclusively to elevate the humble. The practice also allowed objects already valued to be reused in different and newly meaningful contexts. The doors of Hideyoshi's *zushi* in the Kōdaiji *tamaya (Fig. 146),* for instance, a pair of monumental two-fold panels decorated front and back with floral designs in gold makie lacquer, are inscribed with the date 1596, two years before Hideyoshi died and ten before Kōdaiji was established about 1606. What purpose the doors served before being moved to Kōdaiji is not known (though it certainly differed from the one they came to serve after Hideyoshi's death), but they appear to have been cut down and installed back to front, in other words, refashioned to make them suitable for the commemorative ensemble at Kōdaiji.[81] So, too, the new Benzaiten Hall was a work of appropriation and assembly: Chikubushima's old Benzaiten Hall, Sutemaru's marvelous but vulnerable structure, and other wood carvings of unknown origin were merged and thereby transformed into a new building well suited to house the venerated deity.

RECONFIGURING THE BENZAITEN HALL

How, then, was Hideyori's new Benzaiten Hall configured? The answer to this question, sadly, is obscured by today's Tsukubusuma Main Hall, which no longer preserves the reconstituted building's original form: the questionable "restorations" of 1936–1937, which recovered pre-move aspects of Sutemaru's structure, had an understandably pernicious impact on the post-move assemblage. (What they resulted in, in effect, was the creation of yet another new building.) Precious evidence of the building's appearance before 1936—and, as we will argue below, of its appearance in the early seventeenth century—is preserved in the several preconservation photographs introduced in Chapter 3.

To restate and further explicate this evidence, the pre-conservation front facade and interiors, pictured in Figures 18–21 and diagrammed in Figures 147–49, reveal a rearrangement of the formerly unrelated structures that differs greatly from the present, post-conservation state; Figure 150 is a plan of the prerestoration building keyed to the diagram, with the hidden corridor indicated in gray. The exterior presents the following form:

> In the three central bays—those of the moya (*Fig. 147,* bays a, b, c)—three sets of flap-down shutters replace the swinging doors and the fuyō and chrysanthemum carvings that originally ornamented Sutemaru's building (and which were returned to those positions in 1937).

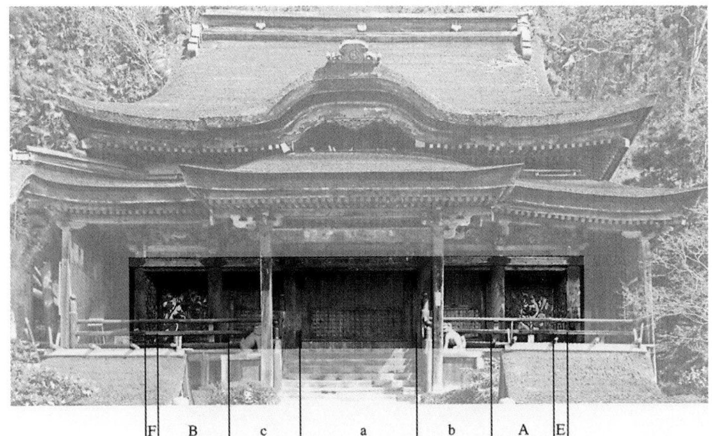

FIG. 147 Diagram of Tsukubusuma Main Hall before 1936–1937 repairs. Exterior, south side (front). Prepared with the aid of Dax Kajiwara, based on Fig. 18.

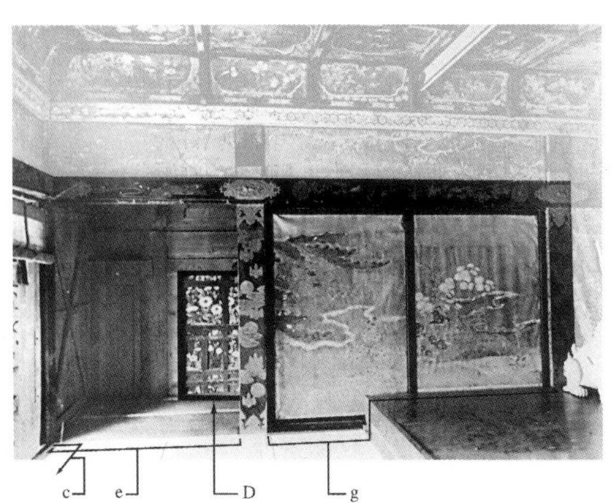

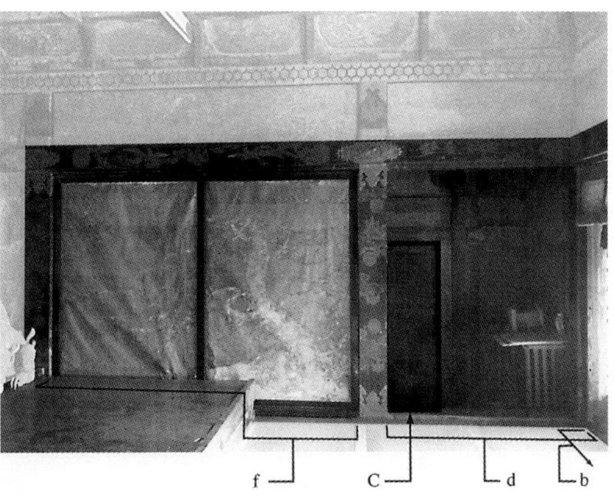

FIG. 148 (right) Diagram of Tsukubusuma Main Hall before 1936–1937 repairs. Moya interior, east side. Prepared with the aid of Dax Kajiwara, based on Fig. 21.

FIG. 149 (left) Diagram of Tsukubusuma Main Hall before 1936–1937 repairs. Moya interior, west side. Prepared with the aid of Dax Kajiwara, based on Fig. 20.

In turn, those carvings flank the flap-down shutters (*Fig. 147,* bays A, B), on walls that were built to bridge the pillars of the two coupled structures (replaced in 1937 with unadorned walls).

On the east and west hisashi walls, where they extend one bay past the facade (*Fig. 147,* E, F), are boldly stylized peony-scroll carvings that were taken from an unknown source (repaired and left there in 1937; *Fig. 3* shows this bay on the east).

The preconservation interior shows similarly dramatic differences from the present state:

The moya bays closest to the front on the east and west sides are open (*Fig. 148,* bay d, and *Fig. 149,* bay e), the walls of Sutemaru's building having been removed, thus providing easy access to the corridor. (These openings were filled in 1937 with gold-papered walls.).

Within the corridors, the hisashi walls east and west just opposite these openings (*Fig. 148,* bay C, and *Fig. 149,* bay D) each contain one bay of carving-laden panels. (These panels originally formed the swinging doors of Sutemaru's structure; in 1937, when they were restored to the moya, they were replaced with plank walls.)

A wide rectangular altar platform extends from the rear wall to well beyond the midpoint of the moya, providing a spacious elevated ritual area (replaced in 1937 by a tall zushi along the back wall, *Fig. 151*).

The photographs preserve an attempt, in short, to redistribute the decorated portions of Sutemaru's building throughout the refurbished Benzaiten Hall.

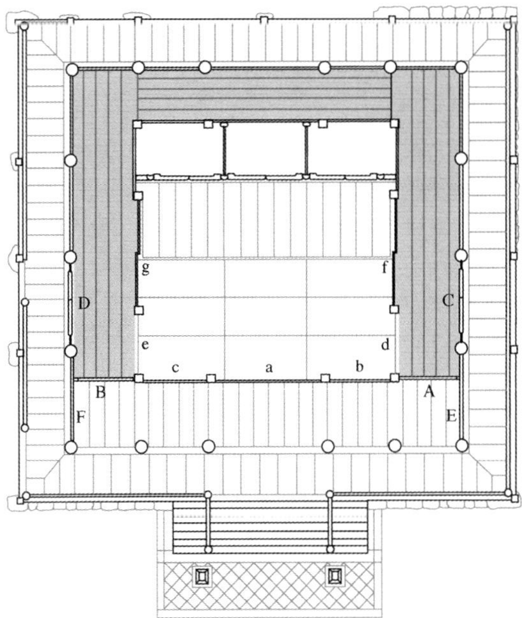

FIG. 150 Tsukubusuma Main Hall before 1936–1937 repairs. Plan. Prepared with the aid of Dax Kajiwara, adapted from *KTJHSKH,* pl. 48.

But when were these various distributions made? One illuminating piece of evidence (created, ironically, by the conservators themselves) strongly supports an early seventeenth-century origin for most, if not all, of these reconfigurations. When the conservators (re-)installed the swinging doors in the central bay of the moya's facade, they apparently found that the ebikōryō prevented the doors from opening fully; to solve this problem, they evidently (there is no *written* reference to this matter in their report) cut deep notches into the ebikōryō to permit the doors free passage *(Fig. 152).* Before the repairs, as a photograph confirms *(Fig. 19),* the ebikōryō were intact.[82]

From this one fact, we can deduce, with some confidence, the simultaneity of all of the changes described above. To begin, we must presume that Hideyori's workers attempted to create a building in which the appropriated parts were assembled to create a suitably unified appearance and to function well as a hall for the veneration of Benzaiten. If we accept that the ebikōryō were added during this effort—to link the different parts of the new building in the traditional manner—then it follows that the flap-down shutters in the central bay were added concomitantly, in part to avoid the problem that disconcerted the conservators. The flap-down shutters in the moya's front flanking bays are identical to those in the central bay, which suggests that they too were added at this time.

Most of the other changes then unfold as a function of the desire to reuse the displaced, and therefore available, parts of Sutemaru's building.

> The flap-down shutters in the central bay displaced carving-filled swinging doors (*Fig. 147,* bay a), which were then fit into the hisashi wall within the corridor (*Fig. 148,* bay C, and *Fig. 149,* bay D).
>
> To allow access to the corridor and these carvings, the foremost bay of the east and west walls of the moya was removed (*Fig. 148,* bay d, and *Fig. 149,* bay e).
>
> The other flap-down shutters displaced the moya's front flanking walls (*Fig. 147,* bays b, c), and the fuyō and chrysanthemum carvings on the walls' exteriors were moved one bay over, to the walls newly constructed to link the moya and hisashi (*Fig. 147,* bays A, B).
>
> The paintings on the inner faces of all four removed moya walls (fig. 148, bays b, d, and *fig. 149,* bays c, e)—polychrome and gold leaf on a paper support—were detached and applied to the newly created mairado, which were inserted into the moya's east and west central bays (*Fig. 148,* bay f, and *Fig. 149,* bay g); because the paintings were larger than the mairado could accomodate, their edges were cropped.[83]

Although it will never be possible absolutely to confirm this scenario, what we know of the circumstances makes it the most reasonable hypothesis.

From Sutemaru's ensemble and the other parts was created, in other words, a composite ensemble well suited to its high patron and its venerated goddess. When compared with Sutemaru's ensemble, the newly formed building on Chikubushima presents

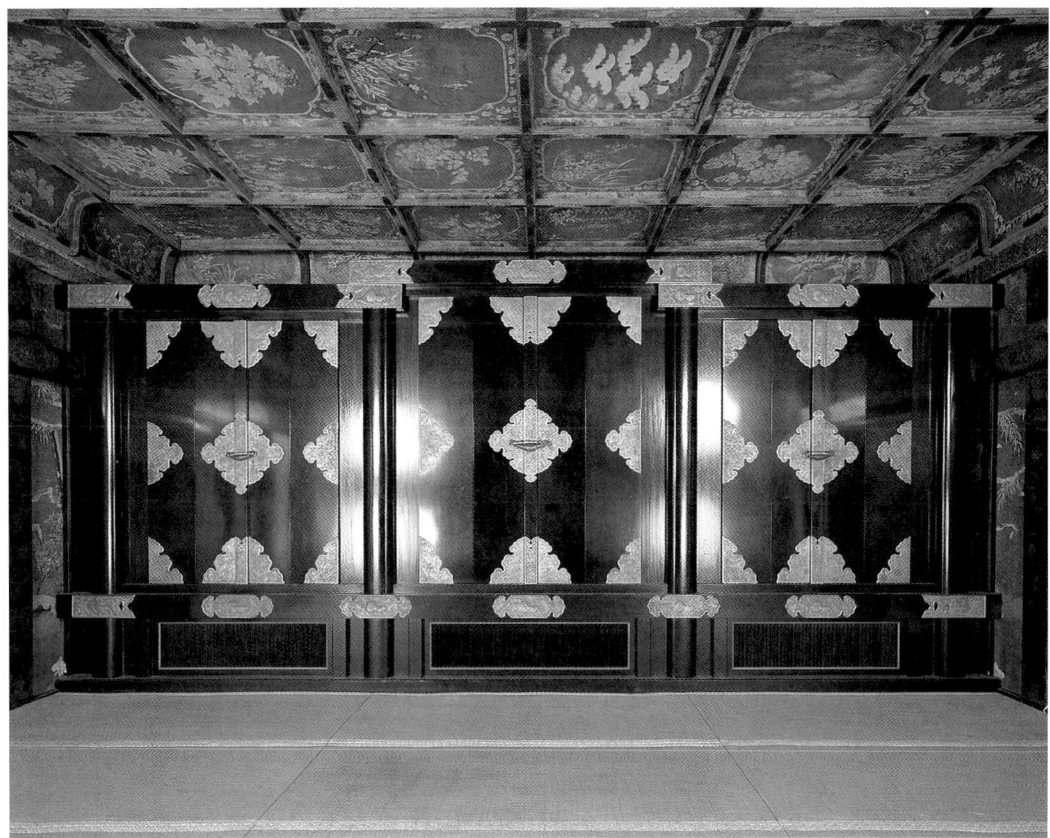

FIG. 151 Tsukubusuma Main Hall. Interior, north side, showing zushi. Chikubushima, Shiga Prefecture.

a measure of what we might perceive as formal dissonance. It joined a part with fully lacquered pillars and lintel beams (the moya) with a part made of unlacquered wood (the hisashi). Because a portion of the moya's original decoration was dislocated, especially at the new building's front, and that which remained intact on the rest of the exterior was obscured by the hisashi, patterns in the distribution of motifs—as well as exceptions to the patterns—were no longer discernible, and the moya's striking thematic logic was disturbed. Other ornament on the new building's exterior speaks of mixed origins: the relief carvings added to the hisashi depict an abstracted peony scroll entirely lacking any illusion of space, and they seem overscaled for their compartments; Sutemaru's carvings, on the other hand, represent more naturalistic fuyō and chrysanthemum plants within a shallow pictorial space, and are appropriately scaled to their surrounds.

But these dissonances stand out only through comparison with the original form of Sutemaru's ensemble, a comparison the casual viewer is unlikely to undertake. And the new patterns in the distribution of ornament created new symmetries which were pleasing in their own way. The facade presented three central bays of flap-down shutters, flanked on either side by a bay of naturalistic carvings and, extending forward at

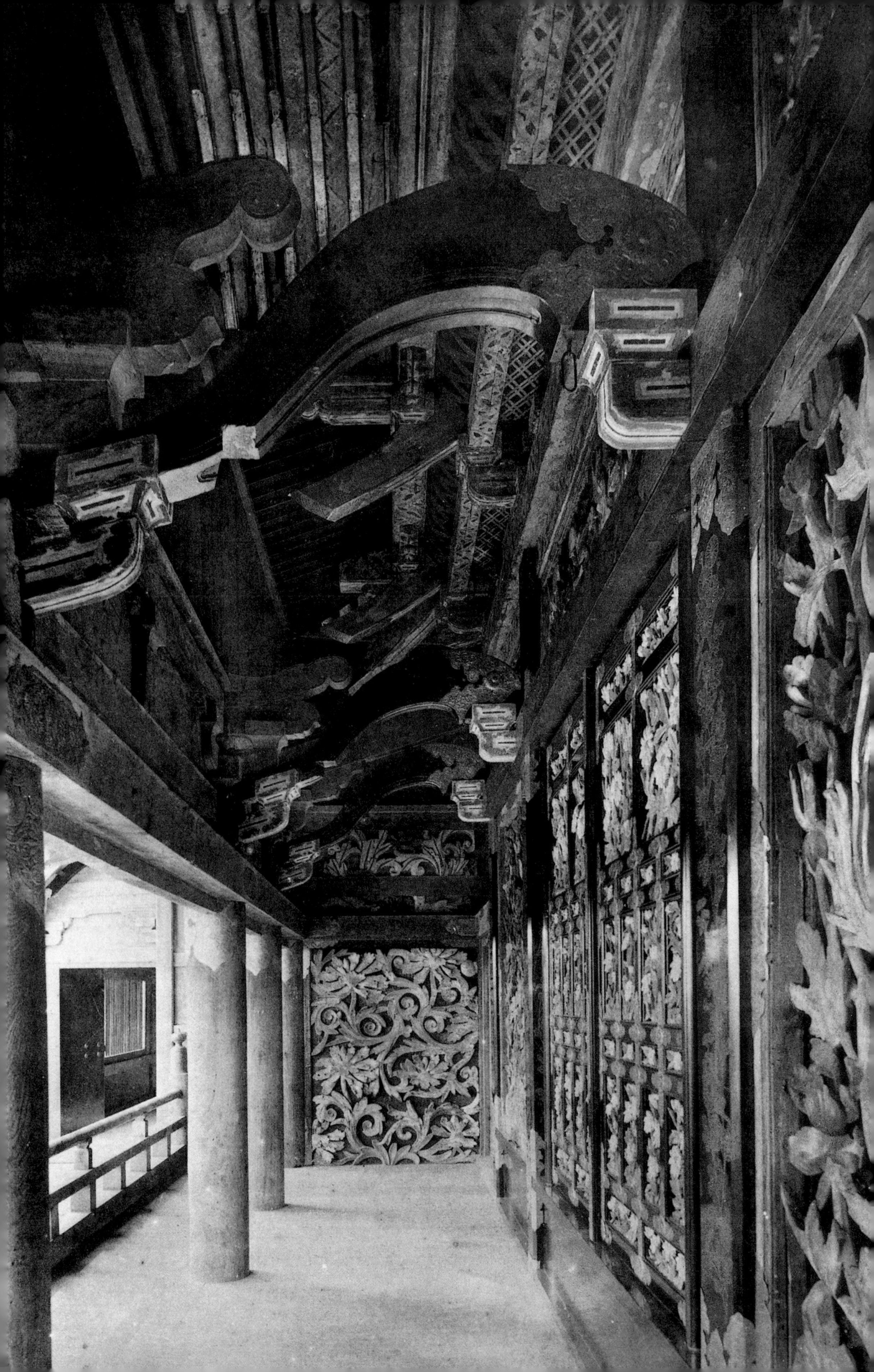

right angles to the facade, a bay of peony scroll. The central part of the new facade was coated with makie lacquer and retained, above the lintel, the moya's decorative floral-scroll wood carvings. All of this was enveloped by the now heavily ornamented hisashi. Sheltering the whole was the massive roof, which was, as we've seen, deceptively well incorporated into the building.

Inside, the lacquered lintels and beams remained in place and thereby preserved their sense of unity. The cropping of the mairado paintings might seem odd, but in the normally low light, the combined effect of all of the paintings (on the walls, above the lintel, and in the ceiling) was splendid. The dimmer light of the corridor precluded close examination of the decoration there, but what was visible—especially the carving-laden doors inserted into the hisashi walls just opposite the openings (and closest to the source of light)—would still have carried ornamental power. In this new ensemble, in short, the appropriated and assembled parts were sufficiently well integrated to persuade the viewer that this configuration was right and complete; the visitor unfamiliar with the hall's complex history, not alert to and thereby not perceiving discordances, would have accepted the object as a given.[84]

GENERATING NEW MEANINGS FOR OLD PARTS

The Benzaiten Hall's success as an assemblage must also be measured by the new meaning it generated for its old parts. To a large degree, Sutemaru's once lucid ensemble was expunged. Some of its most articulate parts were no longer even visible: the pine and crane makie lacquer, originally a central focus of attention on the exterior and perhaps even at the front of the building, was now concealed within the dark inner corridor and rendered entirely mute. Separated from Shōunji—and in fact, moved one bay away from the moya—the one highly visible panel of fuyō carvings became unintelligible as a rebus for Sutemaru; nor is there an instructive context to tell the viewer that the visible panel of large chrysanthemum carvings might be interpreted as katamigusa. The Four Seasons imagery of the interior, disconnected from its memorial context, was no longer obviously paradisal in character. The iconographic links to Sutemaru were effectively broken.

Although these changes thus silenced some of Sutemaru's principal symbolic elements, they correspondingly amplified others, and in combination with new ornament, created new meanings. The visible moya carvings remained impressive as floral decoration and in their new setting served to call attention to this house of Benzaiten. The peony-scroll reliefs attached to the hisashi added to the external embellishment, thereby heightening the efficacy of Sutemaru's carvings as exaltation through adornment, or

FIG. 152 Tsukubusuma Main Hall. View of Main Hall exterior, south side, looking west from east corner. Chikubushima, Shiga Prefecture. Photograph after *KTJHSKH*, pl. 5.

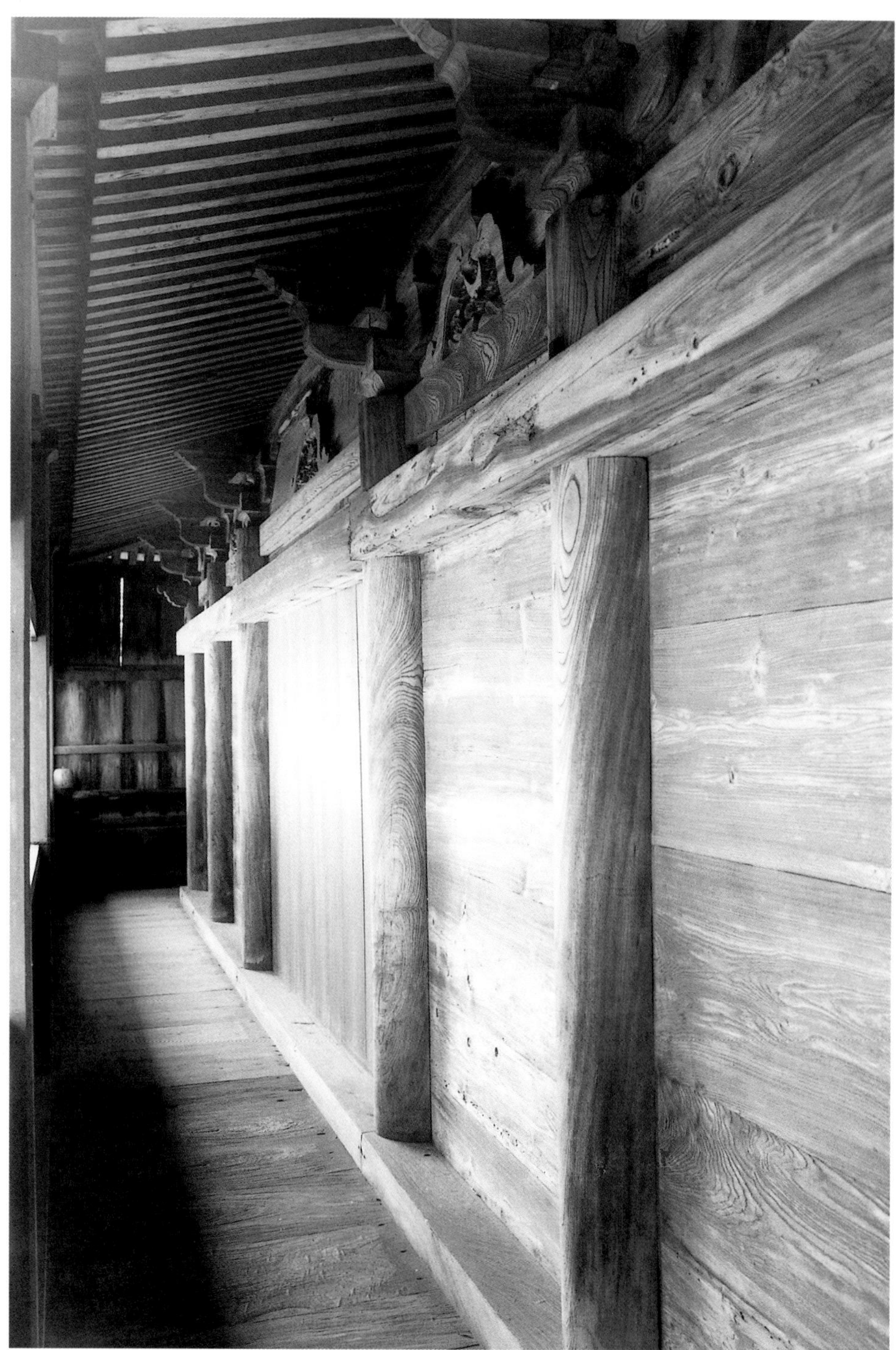

FIG. 153 Tsukubusuma Main Hall. Hisashi, north side, outer face, looking east from north-west corner. Chikubu-shima, Shiga Prefecture.

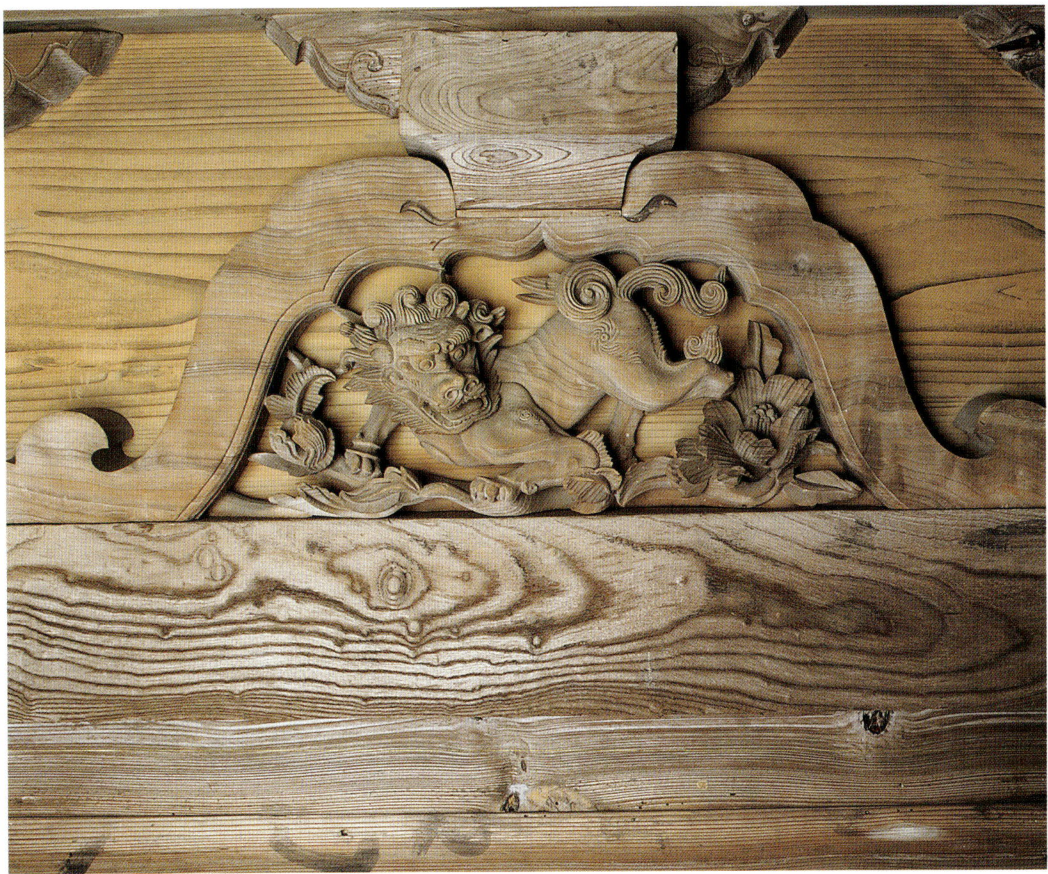

FIG. 154 Tsukubusuma Main Hall. Kaerumata with wood carving of shishi (lion-dog). Hisashi exterior. Chikubushima, Shiga Prefecture.

shōgon *(Figs. 37–39)*. That these reliefs are not fuyō but the visually similar and more common peony abetted the reading of the adjacent fuyō as nonspecific ornament. (The rear of the old hisashi, on the other hand, was not enhanced with peony-scroll carvings *[Fig. 153]*: apparently it was deemed unnecessary to update this normally unseen part of the building; the only carvings here are the small ones that originally graced it, above the lintel within the *kaerumata* braces *[Fig. 154]*.)

The interior, still glorious with paintings, lacquer, metalwork, and architectural coloring, metamorphosed conceptually into a resplendent setting for Benzaiten worship, outfitted with the Buddhist paraphernalia appropriate to Benzaiten rituals. No seventeenth-century itemization of this paraphernalia exists, but some notion might be gleaned from an inventory of objects in the hall in 1871, when the building was being transformed from Buddhist to Shinto.[85] The inventory begins by describing the contents of the building as "the shōgon [sacred adornment] of a Buddhist sculpture," and lists the following: a zushi placed along the rear wall; one standing sculpture of Benzaiten; a divine mirror on a lotus pedestal with a relief of a seated Buddha on the reverse; flanking sculptures of Daikokuten and Bishamonten (Benzaiten's traditional accompanying figures) as well as sculptures of Benzaiten's Fifteen Attendants; a five-piece altar set (comprising a censer, a pair of vases, and a pair of candlesticks); a gong in front of the building; and, also at the front of the building, a plaque that read "Benzaiten." The building was, in other words, fully equipped for the worship of Benzaiten.

Overall, the Benzaiten Hall—assembled from visually impressive appropriated parts and ritual objects—would have been read as a manifestation of sacred adornment, that is, as shōgon, and it is here that the meaning and importance of shōgon can best be understood. The concept of shōgon—the revelation and celebration of the sacred through extraordinary ornament—is one meaning of the moya's whole program of decoration that survived the move from Kyoto to Chikubushima, and perhaps even was enhanced by the moya's inclusion in the larger building at this geomantically important location. On the island, Sutemaru's building was absorbed into a larger ensemble, creating a magnificent example of shōgon composed in celebration of the all-powerful Benzaiten.

Finally, and perhaps most significant in the early seventeenth century, the assemblage of the new Benzaiten Hall directed attention to its patrons. Many of the omnipresent chrysanthemum and paulownia crests in Sutemaru's building were left as visible in the transformation as they had been in the original manifestation, though applied to a new purpose. They remained the most resonant of the motifs in Sutemaru's ensemble, clearly proclaiming the patron of this building to be the Toyotomi family. Once the building was ensconced on Chikubushima, however, not Hideyoshi but his surviving son, Hideyori, was the munificent patron, a meaning that was emphasized by the 1603 placard, by the other buildings constructed on the island by the Toyotomi at this time, and by the other religious projects that they sponsored throughout the country.[86]

Benzaiten's new home was an assemblage of the very distinguished Toyotomi trophy and the pre-existing Benzaiten Hall, originally rather plain but now modernized with exterior relief carvings. With it, the Toyotomi called attention to their historical association with the sacred island, to their concern for the spiritually derived well-being of Japan, and, implicitly, to their political legitimacy in the post-Hideyoshi era. That the Toyotomi ultimately failed to regain hegemony in Japan should not blind us to the skill with which they wielded—and welded—ethereal and material culture in the post-Hideyoshi era. Until their demise in 1615 the Toyotomi were a conspicuous and spiritually privileged presence in the highest forums of the Japanese elite; their restoration of Chikubushima's Benzaiten Hall is an especially elaborate example of the means by which they achieved this status. It is this ensemble that remained intact for more than 250 years, until the prefectural directives of 1871 evicted Benzaiten from her home, which the restorations of 1936–1937 unwittingly disassembled. Still today, notwithstanding two major reconfigurations and countless accidents of survival and retrieval, the Tsukubusuma Main Hall—formerly the Benzaiten Hall—remains, as it was in 1603, an epitome of Momoyama shōgon.

EPILOGUE

Chikubushima in Post-Toyotomi Japan

Even after the destruction of its Toyotomi patrons in 1615, Chikubushima remained a site of mysterious divine favor. Its special status was noted in a history of Japan by the Dutch physician Engelbert Kaempfer (1651–1716), one of the few Western visitors to a mostly sequestered Japan in the late seventeenth century. He relates that certain places were seemingly immune from the natural disasters, especially earthquakes, suffered elsewhere in the country:

> [S]ome particular places in Japan are observ'd to be free from all manner of succussions. The Japanese reason variously upon this Phænomenon. Some attribute it to the holiness and sanctity of the place, and to the powerful protection of its Genius, or tutelar God. Others are of opinion, that these places are not shook, because they immediately repose upon the unmov'd Center of the Earth. The fact itself is not call'd in question, and there are noted for having this singular Privilege, the Islands of Gotho, the small Island Sikubusima, on which stands a most stately Temple of Bonzes, being one of the first that was built in the Country, the large mountain Kojasan near Miaco, famous for the number of its Convents, Monasteries and Monks, besides some few others.[1]

Kaempfer's account reflects then-current knowledge in Japan, what he had heard and what we can assume most people would have known: Chikubushima—one of a very select group of unusually sacred places—was a bastion of uncommon solidity in a physically unstable and precarious country, and a site notable for its ancient holiness and

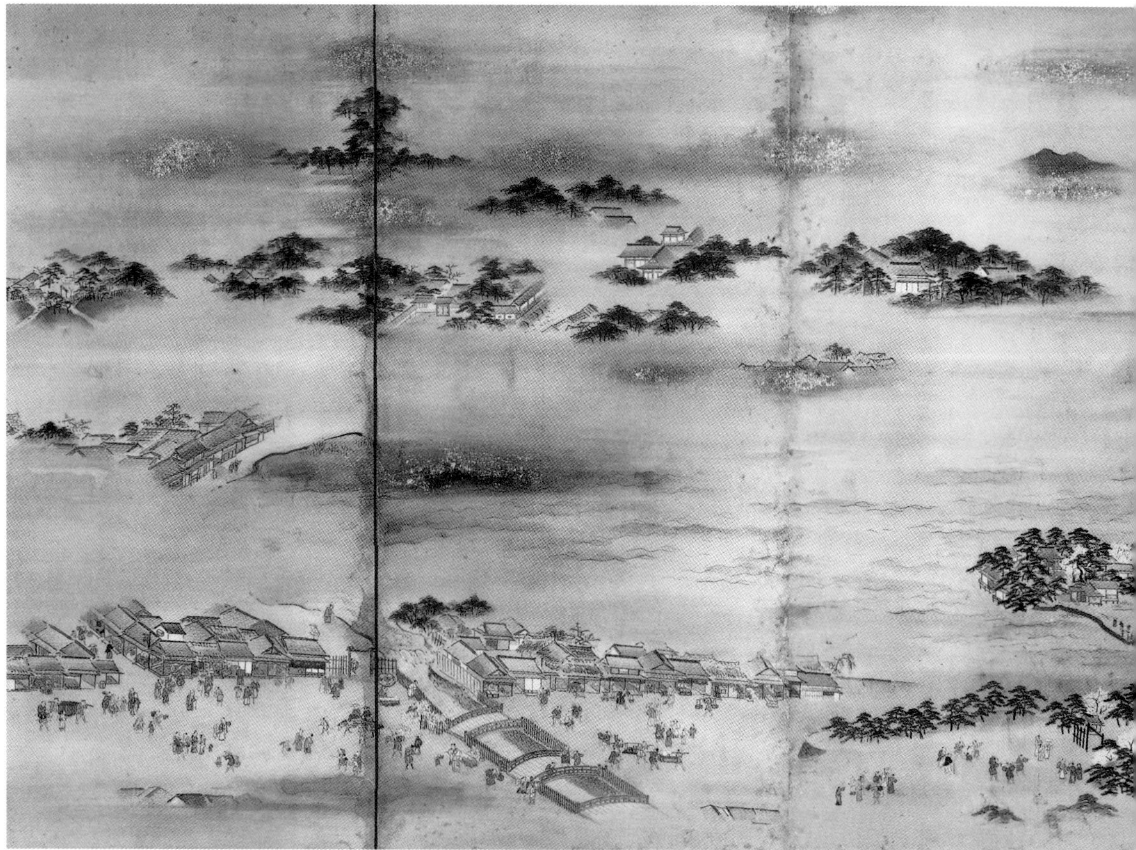

FIG. 155 Kano Sokuyo. *Pilgrimage to Kan'eiji.* Six-fold screen; ink, color, and gold leaf on paper. Itabashi Art Museum, Tokyo.

admirable religious architecture. And so people continued to journey there. A fervor for pilgrimage brought many visitors to Chikubushima, long counted among the thirty-three stations of the Kannon pilgrimage route in western Japan. To an even greater degree the sacred island remained significant for its local constituency, who continued to support the costly Lotus Festival in the Edo period.

Even so, Chikubushima was no longer as eminent a countrywide presence as it had been for the Momoyama elites, primarily because Japan now had a new political center of gravity: the shogunal capital had been moved far to the east to Edo, Ieyasu's seat of power since the 1590s. Because Kyoto had long been the locus of actual and symbolic political power in Japan, the Tokugawa rulers may have felt compelled to quit it so as to distance themselves from its constricting traditions. Because it had been the capital for centuries, however, Kyoto also possessed the full complement of cultural and commercial resources necessary for the conduct of official business and of elite private life. Kyoto and its environs also encompassed the ancient, hallowed religious sanctuaries that allowed Japanese leaders based there to conduct the weighty business of sacred ritual.

At the time of the Tokugawa arrival Edo was underdeveloped and sorely lacked many of the basic necessities of a domainal, let alone shogunal capital.[2] This problem

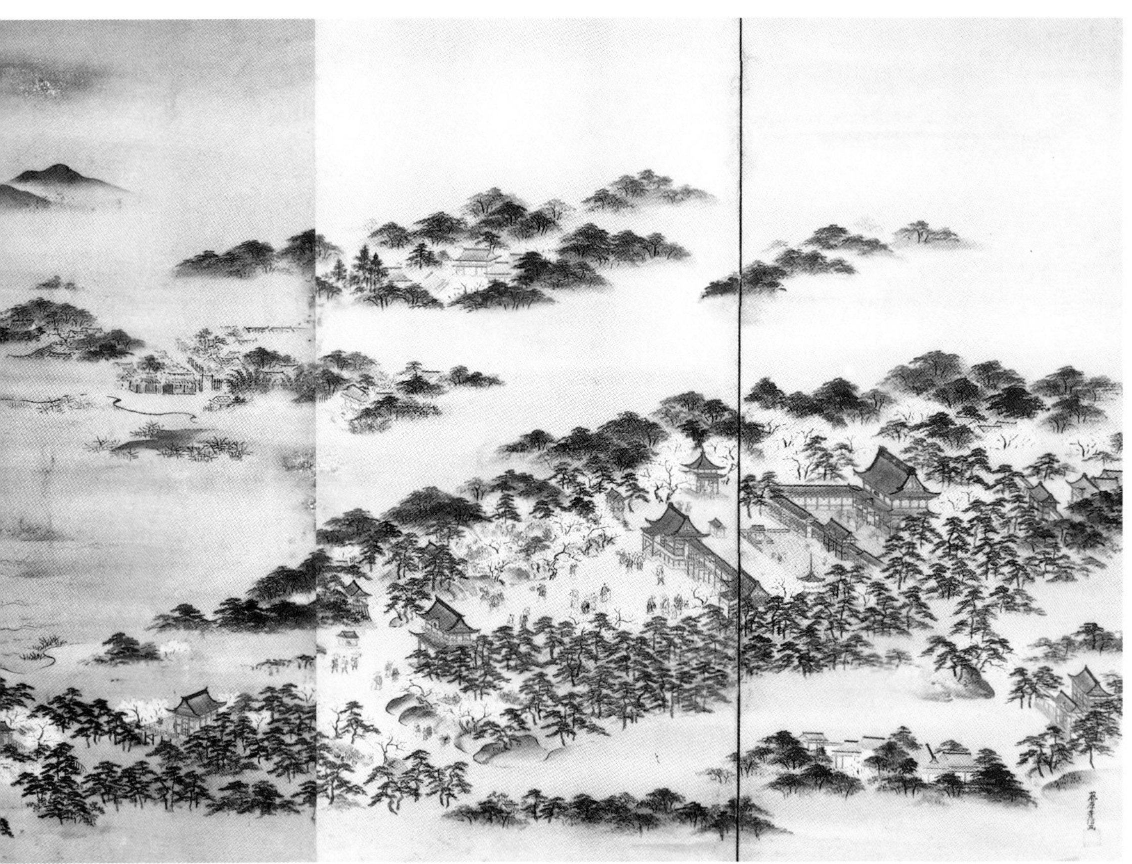

the new rulers quickly addressed. The Tokugawa soon rebuilt Edo Castle on the grandly imposing scale befitting their seat of government, and the castle became Edo's focal point. Its role as the center of command, symbolically as well as operationally, is reflected in the castle's location and size in the many pairs of screens representing the new city—screens which were the Edo equivalents of the *Sights in and around the Capital* screens of Kyoto.[3]

The dearth of significant religious sanctuaries in Edo spurred the Tokugawa and their religious advisers to an enormous enterprise of temple construction, thereby creating a new geography of sacred power with the new capital as its center. To this end, they identified key temples in and around Kyoto and reproduced the most important ones in Edo. In the 1620s the shogunate confiscated hilly land near Edo Castle and designated it the simulacrum of Kyoto's great sacred mountain, Mount Hiei, and on it they erected religious buildings to represent Enryakuji, the Tendai center on Hieizan. They linked the two sites by name, combining the character for "east" 東 (describing the new location in relation to the original site) with the second character of Hiei, *ei* 叡, and the word "mountain" 山: Tōeizan, the "Eastern Ei Mountain."

Chikubushima was similarly replicated. Near the new copy of Mount Hiei, a 1626 entry in the diary *Kanmei nikki* notes, "was a pond—Shinobazu Pond is its name—that

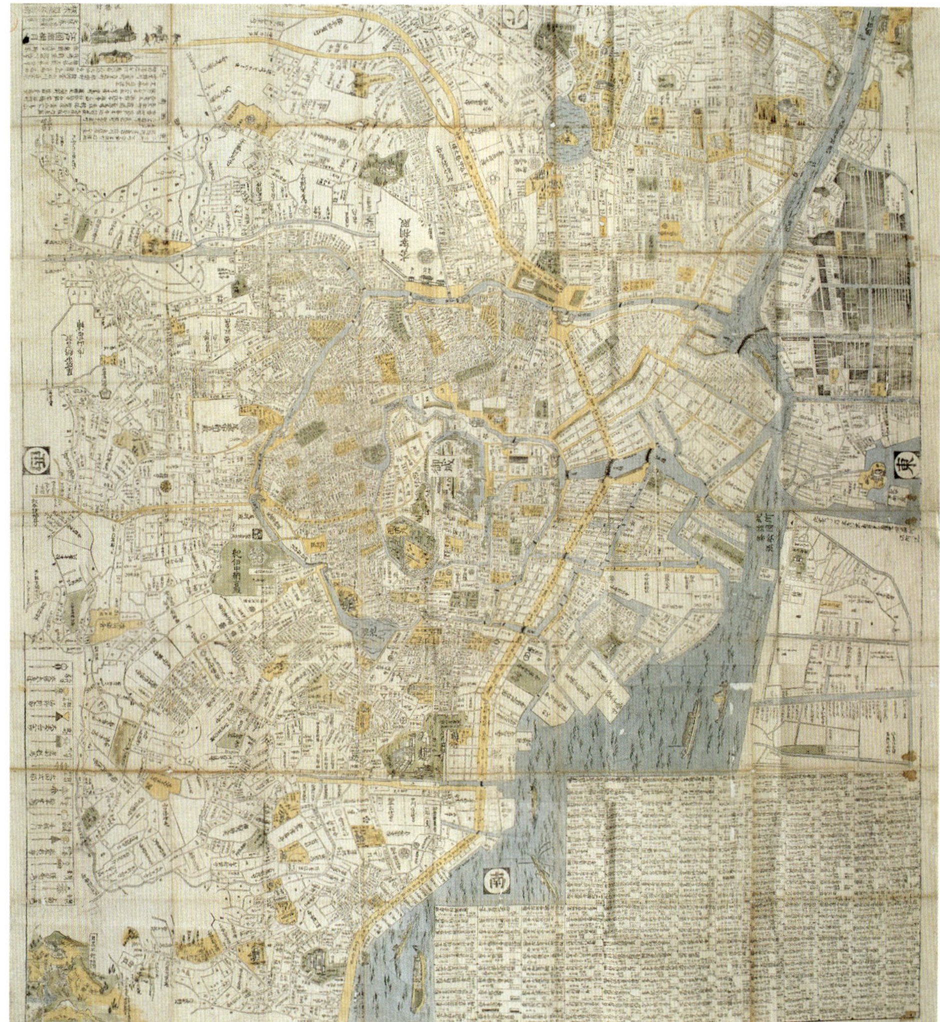

FIG. 156 Ishikawa Ryūsen. *Edo zukan kōmoku, kon.* 1689. Print; ink and color on paper. Tokyo Metropolitan Central Library.

imitates Lake [Biwa]; [in the pond was] fabricated an island, and on the island was built a Benzaiten Hall; this imitates Chikubushima."[4] Shinobazu Pond was, in other words, a naturally occurring body of water in Edo that the government designated to be the equivalent of Lake Biwa, and within this pond, earth was piled to create an island. Tenkai (d. 1643), the Buddhist monk who served as a key advisor to the Tokugawa, indicates that the island took ten days to build.[5] On that equivalent of Chikubushima (which, like the original, even included a small islet just off its shore) the deity Benzaiten could live, and buildings in which to worship her were constructed. One six-fold screen of Edo by Kano Sokuyo (act. 1722), in the Itabashi Museum of Art, focuses on this area of the city, with its rolling hills and the many Buddhist temples and Shinto shrines tucked among them *(Fig. 155)*.[6] Shinobazu Pond extends horizontally through the middle of

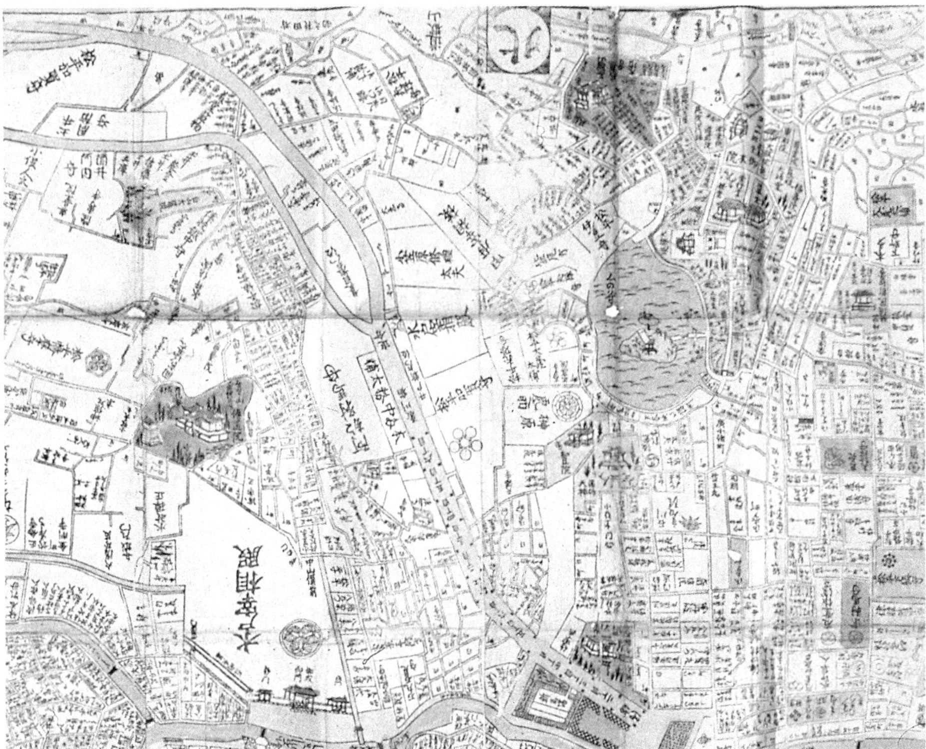

FIG. 157 Detail of Fig. 156.

the screen, and at the center is depicted its replicated Chikubushima, represented as a popular destination, with several figures crossing the bridge and spit of land that spanned the pond to the island.[7]

Maps of Edo, which proliferated from the seventeenth century onward, suggest why, among the many sacred places near Kyoto, Chikubushima was chosen to be replicated. The 1689 *Edo zukan kōmoku, kon* (Outline Map of Edo, Part I) *(Fig. 156),* for example,[8] shows the castle at the center, typical practice for representing the actual and conceptual heart of the city; surrounding it, in concentric rings of power, are the mansions of the various daimyo families, who each built a residence in the new capital, and enclosing this center of secular power is a great moat. Interspersed among the grand mansions and especially just within and beyond the moat are areas marked in yellow, indicating main roads as well as the precincts of temples and shrines. Within this matrix, Shinobazu Pond (identified in writing) and the island home of Benzaiten are depicted clearly, including the religious halls and the separate islet *(Fig. 157).*

Indicated on the map are the four cardinal directions, allowing analysis of the geomantic relationships among the different parts of the city. The pond and replicated island are north and east of the castle, thus duplicating the position of Lake Biwa and Chikubushima in relation to Kyoto (as depicted in the overall map of Japan now in Jōtokuji; *Fig. 28*).[9] Northeast—the cosmological direction from which the most malevolent dangers emanated—was where Benzaiten was stationed with respect to Edo Castle, just as

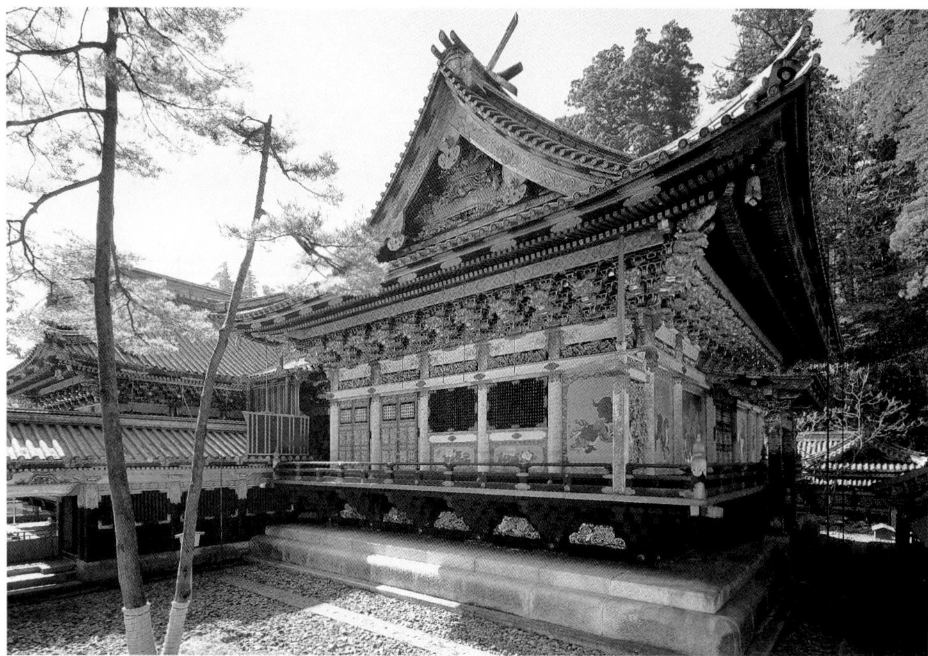

FIG. 158 Tōshōgū Main Hall, exterior. 1636. Nikkō, Tochigi Prefecture. Photograph by Kōdansha.

she had been stationed with respect to the old capital, to better protect the new center of authority and, by extension, the realm.

Replicating Chikubushima in Edo was an astute move on the part of the new Tokugawa rulers. By 1626, when Tenkai recorded the replication of Chikubushima in Shinobazu Pond, the original island of Chikubushima resonated in Japanese consciousness more than ever before. Not only was it the home of Benzaiten, it was also strongly linked with the prestige of the most important recent secular rulers—Oda Nobunaga and especially Toyotomi Hideyoshi and Tokugawa Ieyasu—so that it combined exceptionally meaningful secular and sacred auras. These associations made Chikubushima a place in the pre-Edo-period sacred geography of Japan that the Tokugawa rulers could ill afford to leave behind when they moved east. They replicated the island at Edo to gain for the new capital the ancient spiritual authority and recent political associations of the place that was Chikubushima.

Although Shinobazu Pond was a natural feature, the new island in it was a man-made construction, a representation that reproduced the physical existence of the original island as well as its sacredness. And this island, in turn, spawned the production of other representations, such as paintings and maps, that recorded the celestialized component of the new city, and so helped to legitimate Tokugawa rule.

The Tokugawa also adopted and adapted the Momoyama visual language of sacred adornment, most obviously and meaningfully for buildings that enshrined their progenitor, Tokugawa Ieyasu.[10] The Tōshōgū, as these shrines were known (incorporating the deified Ieyasu's appellation, Tōshō Daigongen—Great Avatar Illuminating the East),

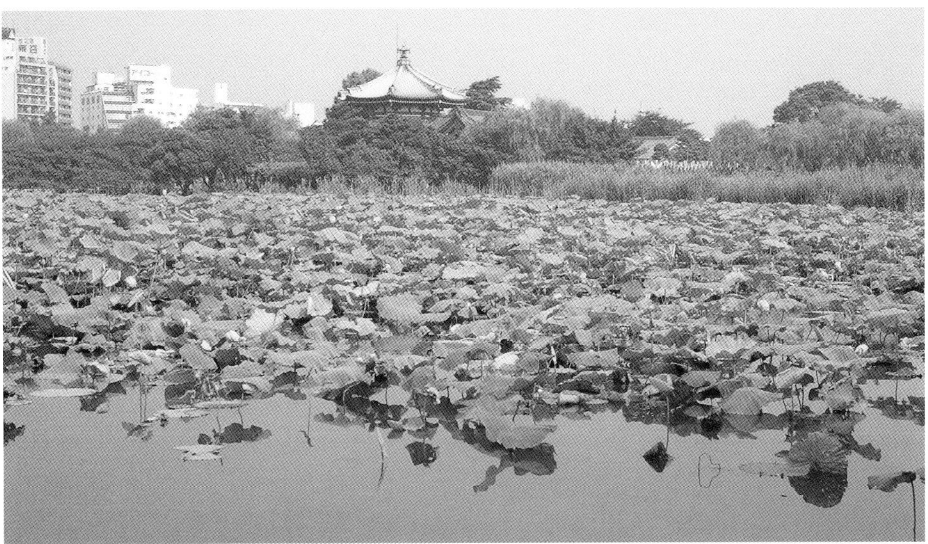

FIG. 159 View of Shinobazu Pond. Tokyo. Photograph by the author.

were constructed throughout the country by the provincial daimyo rulers, thereby creating throughout Japan a network of religious monuments to Tokugawa hegemony. Chief among these was the one at Nikkō, north of Edo, for which in 1636 the third Tokugawa shogun, Iemitsu (1604–1651), opened the shogunal coffers to replace the initial structures of 1617 with the grand ones that stand today. Its vast precincts cover much of Mount Nikkō, and teem with buildings and paths; torii gates and, at the boundary between inner and outer sacred space, the elaborate Yōmeimon gate[11] demarcate the stages of the ascent, which increase in divinity as they approach the main hall *(Fig. 158)*, where ceremonies for Tōshō Daigongen were conducted. In its materials this building's ornament—paintings, wood carvings, lacquer, metalwork, architectural coloring—recalls the ensembles favored in the Momoyama period. At Nikkō, however, the materials have been orchestrated to create an abundance of embellishment that is more dense, more rigid in execution, more colorful, and ultimately a more ornate interpretation of *shōgon,* the art of sacred adornment. Thus, quite early in the Tokugawa era, the Momoyama legacy was transformed, reshaping the received ensemble of multiple mediums into one whose visual language became firmly associated with the new regime.

Ōmi's replicated sacred geography—the pond and the island (and a recently reconstructed Benzaiten hall)—still stand in Tokyo, just a stone's throw from the Tokyo National Museum and the Ueno Zoo. Chikubushima remains, of course, in its place. But both sites have current associations more vivid than their historical links to Benzaiten and to the Toyotomi and Tokugawa: Chikubushima is a popular boating destination and is better known for the worship of the popular Buddhist deity Kannon than it is for the protector manifestation of Benzaiten; Shinobazu Pond and its island are noted for abundant lotus flowers *(Fig. 159)*.

For the Benzaiten worshipper, however, both islands remain places of potent spiritual power. In a recent conversation, the Head Priest of the Tsukubusuma Jinja explained it as follows, "The believers in Benzaiten are devoted; they know where she resides, and that is why they come here." For those who understand, in other words, both islands retain their sacred character: Benzaiten resides on these islands and protects Japan, as the 1603 ridgepole placard proclaims, from those "demons and evils that emanate from outside the heavens." Divine safeguard is the meaning conveyed by all these various manifestations of the island—the original Chikubushima, its replication in Edo/Tokyo, and its representations in the paintings and maps—and by the glorious buildings that house the deities there: these places, depictions of places, and ensembles speak powerfully of the place of the sacred in Japan.

Notes

Introduction

1. Most of the extant text of this work, *História da Igreja do Japão* in the original Portuguese, is translated in Michael Cooper, ed., *João Rodrigues's Account of Sixteenth-Century Japan,* ser. 3, vol. 7 (London: Hakluyt Society, 2001); for this passage, which is one part of a longer description of Japanese faith, p. 126. Rodrigues' fascinating career is explored in Michael Cooper, S. J., *Rodrigues the Interpreter: An Early Jesuit in Japan and China* (New York and Tokyo: Weatherhill, 1974).

2. The extensive modern literature on the sacred also has guided my thinking. For a general treatment, see Mircea Eliade, ed., *The Encyclopedia of Religion* (New York: Macmillan Publishing Company, 1987), s.v. "The Sacred and the Profane," by Carsten Colpe. To stress the impossibility of formulating a universal definition of the sacred, Colpe writes (and I agree), "It is necessary to suppress one's own conclusions about how and in what dimensions the sacred might exist, and what it 'is,' . . . conclusions may only be drawn case by case, in the light of the data and the theoretical arguments presented, and may well come out differently in every instance. Only with such reservations in mind can we consider the nature of the sacred and the profane."

Also, and with regard as well to the concept of sacred space, see Allan G. Grapard, "Flying Mountains and Walkers of Emptiness: Toward a Definition of Sacred Space in Japanese Religions," *History of Religions* 21, no. 3 (February 1982), pp. 195–221; Jonathan Z. Smith, "The Bare Facts of Ritual," in *Imagining Religion: From Babylon to Jonestown* (Chicago and London: University of Chicago Press, 1982), pp. 53–65; and Jonathan Z. Smith, "The Wobbling Pivot," in *To Take Place: Toward Theory in Ritual* (Chicago and London: University of Chicago Press, 1987), pp. 88–103.

3. The reprint of the Bodleian Library copy of the original 1603 edition is published as Doi Tadao, ed., *Vocabvlario da Lingoa de Iapam, Nippo jisho,* (Tokyo: Iwanami Shoten, 1960). The dictionary has been translated into modern Japanese in Doi Tadao, Morita Takeshi, and Chōnan Minoru, eds., *Hōyaku Nippo jisho* (Tokyo: Iwanami Shoten, 1980). For a discussion of the Jesuits' treatment of Buddhist terms in the *Vocabvlario,* see Michael Cooper, "The Early Jesuits in Japan and Buddhism," in *Portuguese Voyages to Asia and Japan in the Renaissance Period,* ed. Peter Milward (Tokyo: Renaissance Institute, Sophia University, 1994), pp. 43–57.

4. For the "work of sacralization," see David Chidester and Edward T. Linenthal, "Introduction," in *American Sacred Space,* ed. David Chidester and Edward T. Linenthal (Bloomington and Indianapolis: Indiana University Press, 1995), p. 6.

5. The Shinto-Buddhist amalgam, known in Japanese as *shinbutsu shūgō,* is discussed in Toshio Kuroda, "Shinto in the History of Japanese Religion," *Journal of Japanese Studies* 7, no. 1 (1981), pp. 1–21; and Neil McMullin, "Historical and Historiographical Issues in the Study of Pre-Modern Japanese Religions," *Japanese Journal of Religious Studies* 16, no. 1 (March 1989), pp. 4–12. For a helpful recent compilation of essays on Shinto, see John Breen and Mark Teeuwen, eds., *Shinto in History: Ways of the Kami* (Honolulu: University of Hawai'i Press, 2000).

6. Religion and politics had long been intertwined in Japan, as is well delineated in McMullin, "Historical and Historiographical Issues in the Study of Pre-Modern Japanese Religions," esp. pp. 12–25, 30–33. For the same author's discussion of a tenth-century instance of this commingling, in which "to do religion was to do politics, and vice versa," see Neil McMullin, "The *Lotus Sutra* and Politics in the Mid-Heian Period," in *The Lotus Sutra in Japanese Culture,* ed. George J. Tanabe, Jr. and Willa Jane Tanabe (Honolulu: University of Hawaii Press, 1989), pp. 119–41.

7. For a succinct, excellent discussion about the nature of Japan's isolation in the Edo period (and other persistent clichés), see Henry D. Smith, II, "Five Myths about Early Modern Japan," in *Asia in Western and World History: A Guide for Teaching,* ed. Ainslie T. Embree and Carol Gluck (Armonk, N.Y. and London: M. E. Sharpe, 1997), pp. 514–22.

8. An excellent study of this period, known as the Era of Warring States, with a focus on the impact on Kyoto, is Mary Elizabeth Berry, *The Culture of Civil War in Kyoto* (Berkeley, Los Angeles, London: University of California Press, 1994).

9. Many scholars bemoan the inadequacy of the term Momoyama for this period—although most admit that convention and convenience will ensure its longevity. See, for example, Saiki Kazuma, "Momoyama jidai to iu koshō," *Nihon rekishi,* no. 209 (October 1965), pp. 84–85; Wakita Osamu, *Ōsaka jidai to Hideyoshi,* Shōgakukan Raiburari, no. 127 (Tokyo: Shōgakukan, 1999). Some historians use the term Shokuhō for the period, a combination of the first characters of Oda and Toyotomi, though the aptness of this term is lost in romanization.

10. See, for example, George Elison, "The Cross and the Sword: Patterns of Momoyama History," in *Warlords, Artists, and Commoners: Japan in the Sixteenth Century,* ed. George Elison and Bardwell L. Smith (Honolulu: University of Hawaii Press, 1981), pp. 61–62.

11. The most recent and complete scholarship on *Rakuchū rakugai* is Matthew Philip McKelway, "Capitalscapes: Painting and Politics in 16th–17th Century Japan" (Ph.D. diss., Columbia University, 1999); see also, by the same author, "In or Out of the Capital? Reading Point of View in *Rakuchū Rakugai Zu:* The Case of the Sanjō Version," *Transactions of the International Conference of Eastern Studies,* no. 40 (1995), pp. 100–118; and "The Partisan View: Rakuchū Rakugai Screens in the Mary and Jackson Burke Collection," *Orientations* 28, no. 40 (February 1997), pp. 48–57.

12. The precise dating of these widely published screens is unsettled, although scholars agree that, on the basis of style, the buildings depicted, and the funds-solicitation scene, they were painted after the early seventeenth century; whether they pre- or postdate the destruction of the Toyotomi in 1615 is still under debate. Though having that information would afford a more exact and nuanced interpretation of the painting's meaning, for our purposes it is sufficient to see the screens as representing a moment before the destruction of the Toyotomi in 1615, no matter whether they were painted as contemporary record or as later recollection. See, for example, Tsuji Nobuo, "Funaki ke kyūzōbon rakuchū rakugai zu byōbu no kento," in *Fūzokuga: Rakuchū rakugai,* ed. Takeda Tsuneo, pp. 122–29, vol. 11 of *Nihon byōbue shūsei* (Tokyo: Kōdansha, 1978); Sandy Kita, *The Last Tosa: Iwasa Katsumochi Matabei, Bridge to Ukiyo-e* (Honolulu: University of Hawai'i Press, 1999), pp. 170–80; Okudaira Shunroku, *Rakuchū rakugai zu, Funakibon: Machi no nigiwai ga kikoeru* (Tokyo: Shōgakukan, 2001).

13. Likewise new to the period were portraits of individual famous Momoyama buildings. From an episode of the early 1580s we see that these buildings were conceived as surrogates for their patrons: the first Momoyama ruler, Oda Nobunaga, presented a pair of screens depicting his great castle at Azuchi to the Jesuit missionary Alessandro Valignano (1539–1606), who then conveyed them to Pope Gregory XIII (1502–1585). This painting—its whereabouts now unknown though, intriguingly, perhaps still in the Vatican—is discussed in McKelway, "Capitalscapes: Painting and Politics in 16th–17th Century Japan," pp. 153–60.

14. On the screen a partially abraded cartouche apparently identifies Shōunji as Chishakuin, the temple that received Shōunji's site and buildings after 1615. Some scholars take this to attest a post-1615 date for the entire screen, but the cartouche may have been a later addition to a pre-1615 screen.

15. The well-known Jōtokuji screens are widely published; see, for example, Yoshiaki Shimizu, ed., *Japan: The Shaping of Daimyo Culture, 1185–1868* (Washington, D.C.: National Gallery of Art, 1988), cat. no. 110. The other screen in this pair shows a map of the world; both maps were based on European models. The date of the screens is disputed, ranging anywhere from the late sixteenth century through the 1640s, though the Japanese places distinguished as important by means of graphic highlighting, as discussed below, undoubtedly reflect Momoyama perceptions.

16. A collection of essays on Osaka's history, with a focus on the post-Momoyama period but with enlightening attention paid to earlier matters as well, is James L. McClain and Wakita Osamu, eds., *Osaka, the Merchant's Capital of Early Modern Japan* (Ithaca, N.Y.: Cornell University Press, 1999).

17. In 1953 the Japanese government conferred its highest cultural distinction on the Tsukubusuma Jinja Honden by designating it a National Treasure; this designation, however, did little to clarify the complicated history of the building. As part of the designation process, a draft text explaining the building's suitability for such official recognition was submitted to the government committee that made the final decision on registration. After a brief (and incorrect) comment on the building's religious history, the text describes its architectural past (the unpublished record is preserved in the Architecture and Other Structures Division of the Agency for Cultural Affairs):

> Since it was first built, the Honden has been destroyed by fire several times, and after a fire in 1558, the present Honden was rebuilt in 1567, and then in 1602 Toyotomi Hideyori *donated a building from Fushimi Castle* and with Katagiri Katsumoto as the administrator, remade the old Honden, and combined it with the moved building, and this is the present Honden. The Honden's three-bay-square

moya *was a surviving structure from Fushimi Castle,* and the surrounding hisashi and kōhai are the 1567 rebuilt parts. Furthermore, the carvings in the hisashi bays and transom were brought *from Fushimi Castle,* cut down and inserted. The moya is decorated with lacquer, gold makie, carvings, architectural coloring, and gilt metalwork, and is extremely lavish, and technically excellent, and therefore is an exemplary building of the Momoyama period.

The committee, however, did not accept this draft without objection: it crossed out the sentences asserting the notably high provenance (in italics in the translation)—that part of the building came from Hideyoshi's final residence, Fushimi Castle—and replaced them in the final text with more restrained claims:

> . . . the present Honden was rebuilt in 1567, and then in 1602 Toyotomi Hideyori, with Katagiri Katsumoto as the administrator, remade the old Honden, and combined it with the moved building, and this is the present Honden. The Honden's three-bay-square moya, *which is said to be a surviving structure from Fushimi Castle,* is the building that was moved, and the surrounding hisashi and kōhai are the 1567 rebuilt parts. Furthermore, the carvings in the hisashi bays and transom *were brought along with the moya from somewhere else,* cut down and inserted.

With these emendations (and without an alternative theory regarding provenance), the hall was designated a National Treasure: its securely known history (as a building remade by Toyotomi Hideyori), its unusual structure (a combination of buildings), and its outstanding decoration were sufficient reason. Although even this final version is not entirely accurate, all evidence supports the committee's concluding assertion that "it is an exemplary building of the Momoyama period" and encourages fuller inquiry into the matters only briefly touched on in the official précis.

For a brief but excellent discussion of the Japanese government's systems of registering objects, see Christine Guth's essay in Money L. Hickman et al., *Japan's Golden Age: Momoyama* (New Haven and London: Yale University Press, 1996), p. 15; for a more detailed explication, see Knut Einar Larsen, *Architectural Preservation in Japan* (Trondheim, Norway: Tapir Publishers, 1994).

The building was also registered under an earlier system, for reasons no longer known; the remaining records from this designation, which occurred in 1899, only note the form of the building, and are published in Zaidanhōjin Bunkazai Kenzōbutsu Hozon Gijutsu Gyōkai, ed., *Shiryō kyūkokuhō kenzōbutsu shitei setsumei* (Tokyo: Zaidanhōjin Bunkazai Kenzōbutsu Hozon Gijutsu Gyōkai, 1982), p. 15.

18. The pioneering study of this painting is Suzuki Hiroyuki, *Kano Hideyori hitsu, Takao kanpūzu byōbu: Kioku no katachi,* E wa kataru, vol. 8 (Tokyo: Heibonsha, 1994). For a similarly complex and important analysis of Muromachi-period screens, which suggests the immediate precedent for Momoyama-period attitudes, see Melinda Takeuchi, "The Golden Link: Place, Poetry, and Paradise in a Medieval Japanese Design," in Taizō Kuroda, Melinda Takeuchi, and Yūzō Yamane, *Worlds Seen and Imagined: Japanese Screens from The Idemitsu Museum of Art* (New York: Asia Society Galleries, 1995), pp. 30–53.

19. Christine Guth succinctly discusses the importance of the functional aspects of portraiture in her essay in Hickman et al., *Japan's Golden Age: Momoyama,* pp. 59–64. For a penetrating treatment of sixteenth-century portraiture and the larger architectural and devotional context in which it was used, see Gregory P. A. Levine, "Jukōin: Art, Architecture, and Mortuary Culture at a Japanese Zen Buddhist Temple" (Ph.D. diss., Princeton University, 1997).

20. See, for example, Nobuo Tsuji, "Ornament (Kazari)—An Approach to Japanese Culture," *Archives of Asian Art* 47 (1994), pp. 35–45.

21. A brief but informative discussion of shōgon is found in Elizabeth ten Grotenhuis, *Japanese Mandalas: Representations of Sacred Geography* (Honolulu: University of Hawai'i Press, 1999), p. 9. See also Ueyama Shunpei, ed., *Kenkyū happyō to zadankai: Bukkyō bijutsu ni okeru "shōgon,"* Bukkyō Bijutsu Kenkyū Ueno Kinen Zaidan Josei Kenkyūkai, report no. 15 (Kyoto: Bukkyō Bijutsu Kenkyū Ueno Kinen Zaidan Josei Kenkyūkai, 1987); Kawada Sadamu, *Busshari to kyō no shōgon, Nihon no bijutsu,* no. 280 (Tokyo: Shibundō, 1989); Sekine Shun'ichi, *Hotoke, bosatsu to dōnai no shōgon, Nihon no bijutsu,* no. 281 (Tokyo: Shibundō, 1989).

22. Doi Tadao, ed. *Vocabvlario da Lingoa de Iapam, Nippo jisho,* p. 620; Doi, Morita, and Chōnan, eds., *Hōyaku Nippo jisho,* p. 791.

23. For a study and reconstruction of this lost building, see MOA Museum of Art, ed., *Ōgon no chashitsu, chadōgu* (Shizuoka: MOA Museum of Art, 1988).

1 Chikubushima, from Its Origins to the Ascendancy of Hideyoshi

1. For a translation and analysis of Kūkai's text on the sacredness of Mount Futara, see Allan Gra-

pard, "On Kūkai's Stone Inscription for Shōdō," in *The Mountain Spirit,* ed. Michael Charles Tobias and Harold Drasdo (Woodstock, N.Y.: Overlook Press, 1979), pp. 51–59. Dōgen's more broadly conceived discussion of the sacredness of mountains is examined in Carl Bielefeldt, "Dōgen's Shōbōgenzō Sansuikyō," in *The Mountain Spirit,* pp. 37–49. For China, see Munakata Kiyohiko, *Sacred Mountains in Chinese Art* (Champaign, Ill.: Krannert Art Museum, University of Illinois at Urbana-Champaign; Urbana: University of Illinois Press, 1991).

2. Mount Murō's caves and resident dragon are well explored in Sherry Fowler, "In Search of the Dragon: Mount Murō's Sacred Topography," *Japanese Journal of Religious Studies* 24, nos. 1–2 (Spring 1997), pp. 145–61.

3. For a discussion of waterfalls and their associated deities, see Mark H. Sandler, "Water Dragons: Sacred Cataracts in Japanese Art," *Asian Art and Culture* 8 (Spring/Summer 1995), pp. 74–91; Nezu Institute of Fine Arts, ed., *Nachi no taki: Kumano no shizen to shinkō no zōkei* (Tokyo: Nezu Institute of Fine Arts, 1991).

4. The abundant green of Chikubushima has been severely diminished in recent years by the noxious droppings of myriad cormorants who have taken residence in the island's trees, presumably displaced from mainland roosts by ever-expanding development; various measures have been taken to discourage their presence, some seemingly inappropriate for a sacred haven, but none have had the desired effect.

5. According to the cadastral surveys of 1598, Ōmi was second only to Mutsu Province in rice yield. Fujita Tsuneharu, "Keichō nananen Ōmi no kuni kenchi o megutte," *Hisutoria,* no. 129 (December 1990), p. 165.

6. The centrality of Benzaiten within the Chikubushima religious complex is discussed in Itō Futoshi, "Chūsei kōki ni okeru Ōmi Chikubushima no jiji to shakai" (M.A. thesis, Kokugakuin Daigaku, 1990), p. 15.

7. Kageyama Haruki, "Chikubushima saireizu," *Yamato bunka,* no. 27 (September 1958), pp. 39–47; Museum of Modern Art, Shiga, and Kyōto Shinbunsha, eds., *Tokubetsuten: Ōmi hakkei: Kokoku fūkeiga no seiritsu to tenkai* (Ōtsu: Museum of Modern Art, Shiga, and Kyōto Shinbunsha, 1988), cat. no. 12; Michael R. Cunningham, *The Triumph of Japanese Style: Sixteenth Century Art in Japan* (Cleveland: Cleveland Museum of Art, 1991), cat. no. 34.

8. The fire is the subject of a letter, written that year, which is discussed below.

9. Sasaki Takamasa, "Chikubushima ni okeru shinbutsu bunri ni tsuite," *Ōtani gakuhō* 55, no. 2 (September 1975), pp. 1–13. Similar separations of Buddhism and Shinto at religious complexes in Japan were common in the early Meiji period, a time when promotion of "indigenous" Shinto at the expense of the alien Buddhism was seen as a necessary corollary to the restoration of imperial rule. For the Meiji-period separation of Shinto and Buddhism, see Allan G. Grapard, "Japan's Ignored Cultural Revolution: The Separation of Shinto and Buddhist Divinities in Meiji *(shimbutsu bunri)* and a Case Study: Tonomine," *History of Religions* 23, no. 3 (February 1984), pp. 240–65; Martin Collcutt, "Buddhism: The Threat of Eradication," in *Japan in Transition: From Tokugawa to Meiji,* ed. Marius B. Jansen and Gilbert Rozman (Princeton: Princeton University Press, 1988), pp. 143–67; James Ketelaar, *Of Heretics and Martyrs in Meiji Japan: Buddhism and Its Persecution* (Princeton: Princeton University Press, 1990).

10. Conversely, other buildings on the island were designated as Buddhist.

11. The list of shrines is included in the *Engi shiki,* a tenth-century collection of government codes. *Engi shiki,* in vol. 26 of *Shintei zōho kokushi taikei,* ed. Kuroita Katsumi (Tokyo: Kokushi Taikei Kankōkai, 1937), p. 246. An English translation of the first ten parts of the text is published as Felicia Gressitt Bock, trans., *Engi-shiki: Procedures of the Engi Era,* 2 vols. (Tokyo: Sophia University, 1970–1972); the reference to the Tsukubusuma Jinja is on p. 142 of vol. 2.

12. Several records illustrate this point. For example, a *kanjinchō* (contribution book) dated to 1326 begins with a reference to the "*hōden* of Benzaiten"; a document from 1466 refers to the "Tennyo *onbyō*"; a ridgepole placard dated to 1602 commemorating the completion of a building refers to "construction of Benzaiten." These three examples are published in *Higashi Asai Gun shi,* 4 vols. (1927; reprint, Nagaokakyō: Nihon Shiryō Kankōkai, 1975), vol. 4, pp. 568–71, 206, and 615, respectively; hereafter, *HAGS.* The name Tsukubusuma Jinja does not appear in any of the many pre-1871 documents preserved on Chikubushima and now held in the Nagahama Castle Historical Museum in Shiga Prefecture.

13. In recent years, the Tsukubusuma Jinja has purchased or commissioned images of Benzaiten and installed them on the altar, thus reintroducing Benzaiten as a focus of worship.

14. The cusped gable, or *karahafu,* which was used on important buildings, is well discussed in William Howard Coaldrake, "Gateways of Power: Edo Architecture and Tokugawa Authority 1603–1651" (Ph.D. diss., Harvard University, 1983), pp. 121–48.

15. This project was initiated to repair damage following a typhoon in 1934. Dramatic newspaper accounts described the extent of destruction to the area around Chikubushima. A headline in the *Ōsaka Asahi shinbun* proclaimed, "Great Typhoon Sweeps Through the Kinki Area—An Unprecedented Disaster" (*Ōsaka Asahi shinbun,* 22 September 1934, p. 1). Several days after the typhoon, the *Ōsaka Mainichi shinbun* published an article on the destruction in Shiga Prefecture, "Chikubushima, which floats its dream-like island silhouette and temples on Lake [Biwa], sustained such heavy damage as to transform its shape" (*Ōsaka Mainichi shinbun,* 26 September 1934, p. 17). The report of this project is published as Kokuhō Tsukubusuma Jinja Keidai Shuppansho, ed., *Kokuhō Tsukubusuma Jinja Honden shūri kōji hōkokusho* (Shiga Prefecture: Kokuhō Tsukubusuma Jinja Keidai Shuppansho, 1937); hereafter, *KTJHSKH.*

16. The sections are reproduced in *KTJHSKH,* plates 41, 42; see also Sakurai Toshio, "Tsukubusuma Jinja Honden," in *Shaden 3,* vol. 3 of *Nihon kenchiku shi kiso shiryō shūsei,* ed. Ōta Hirotarō (Tokyo: Chūō Kōron Bijutsu Shuppan, 1981), figs. 4–5.

17. *KTJHSKH,* p. 15.

18. *KTJHSKH,* p. 16. Today the wood is the same throughout, which probably indicates that the restorers replaced wood as part of the project.

19. A pair of documents record *chōnahajime* ceremonies (marking the ritual start of construction), one on 1558.11.17, and the second ten days later. The documents are published in *HAGS,* vol. 4, pp. 14–15, nos. 38 and 39, respectively; in *KTJHSKH,* p. 29; and in Sakurai Toshio, "Tsukubusuma Jinja Honden," p. 46, n. 7. The latter two sources suggest, without explanation, that the documents refer to the reconstruction of the Tsukubusuma Main Hall, though in fact neither document specifies what building is being commemorated.

20. The 1937 restorers raised several pieces of evidence, none conclusive, that suggest that the building was in the process of being constructed in 1567. For a review of this evidence, see Andrew M. Watsky, "The Art of the Ensemble: The Tsukubusuma Sanctuary, 1570–1615" (Ph.D. diss., Princeton University, 1994), pp. 37–40.

21. *KTJHSKH,* p. 20. The same inscription also lists Yoshizō. Other inscriptions on the moya apparently name lacquer craftsmen of the Seiami workshop. The inscriptions read, "Seiami Yōzaemon"; "lacquerer Fusai Uchishōzaemon, lacquerer Fusai." The term *nushi* is preceded by an honorific, which one would not write in reference to oneself, suggesting that someone other than the lacquerers themselves wrote these inscriptions.

22. Yokota Fuyuhiko, "Kinsei toshi to shokunin shūdan," in vol. 3 of *Nihon toshi shi nyūmon,* ed. Takahashi Yasuo and Yoshida Nobuyuki (Tokyo: Tōkyō Daigaku Shuppankai, 1990), p. 39.

23. This and two other Chikubushima placards related to this project are discussed in Chapter 6, pp. 240–43.

24. Directional characters recorded on various parts of the moya suggest that it was differently oriented in its original location than it is now. *KTJHSKH,* p. 15. The 1937 report does not provide photographs of the characters, nor does it specify the number of characters found.

25. Both versions of the engi are published in *KTJHSKH,* pp. 23–26. For a discussion of the *Chikubushima engi,* see Mori Masato, "Chikubushima," *Kokubungaku kaishaku to kanshō* 47, no. 3 (March 1982), pp. 120–21.

26. Mori Masato also speculates that this later engi was written partly to aid in soliciting funds; Mori, "Chikubushima," p. 120.

27. The character 生, which among many other things often means "to grow," can also be translated as "grove."

28. Some of the dates given in the two texts differ slightly; I follow the dates of the 1415 version.

29. The pre-Momoyama period saw other construction projects undertaken on the island after the ones noted in the engi, though they were not celebrated in such public texts. For a review of the evidence for these projects, see Sasaki, "Chikubushima ni okeru shinbutsu bunri ni tsuite," p. 3.

30. This pilgrimage route is studied in James H. Foard, "The Boundaries of Compassion: Buddhism and National Tradition in Japanese Pilgrimage," *Journal of Asian Studies* 41, no. 2 (February 1982), pp. 231–51, and, along with the larger context of Kannon worship, in Mark Wheeler MacWilliams, "Kannon *Engi:* Strategies of Indigenization in Kannon Temple Myths of the *Saikoku sanjūsansho Kannon reijōki* and the *Sanjūsansho bandō Kannon reijōki*" (Ph.D. diss., University of Chicago, 1990).

31. The diary in question, *Rokuon nichiroku,* was kept from 1487 through 1651 by a succession of priests at the Rokuon' in subtemple of Shōkokuji. It is published as *Rokuon nichiroku,* ed. Tsuji Zennosuke, 6 vols. (1934–1937; reprint, Tokyo: Zoku Gunsho Ruijū Kanseikai, 1961–1962); separate index vol. ed. Tsuji Zennosuke and Nomura Tsuneshige (Tokyo: Zoku Gunsho Ruijū Kanseikai, 1962); hereafter *RN.* For the passage cited here, *RN,* vol. 1, p. 233 (1536 [Tenbun 5].6.15).

32. My translation of the passage is based on *The Tale of the Heike,* trans. Helen Craig McCullough (Stanford: Stanford University Press, 1988),

p. 226, and *Heike monogatari,* ann. Kajihara Masaaki and Yamashita Hiroaki (Tokyo: Iwanami Shoten, 1993), vol. 2, pp. 8–9.

33. In this passage, I differ substantially from McCullough's translation, which renders Tennyo as "heavenly maidens"; given the religious focus of Chikubushima and references in various historical documents (discussed below), the term is clearly meant to refer specifically—and meaningfully—to Benzaiten.

34. The Ichinotani battle and the parade of heads taken there are described in *The Tale of the Heike,* translated by McCullough, pp. 310–27.

35. Since it was first composed, *Heike* has provided narrative material for other mediums, such as Nō, Kabuki, and various song forms, which further disseminated the text; see the essays in Yamashita Hiroaki, ed., *Heike monogatari: Hihyō to bunkashi* (Tokyo: Kyūko Shoin, 1997).

36. Kōshū, *Keiran shūyōshū,* in *Taishō shinshū Daizōkyō,* ed. Takakusu Junjirō, Watanabe Kaigyoku, et al. 85 vols. (Tokyo: Taishō Issaikyō Kankōkai, 1924–1934), 2410.76.503–888; for this passage, p. 519c. Hereafter, the *Taishō shinshū Daizōkyō* is referred to as *T.* The term "eloquence" refers to Benzaiten, being a translation of the first character of her name. A similar observation is also made later in the *Keiran shūyōshū,* p. 625a.

37. Kōshū, *Keiran shūyōshū,* p. 626a–b.

38. For an overview of the *Keiran shūyōshū,* explicating the text's essence as both cultic and political document, see Allan G. Grapard, "*Keiran-shūyōshū:* A Different Perspective on Mt. Hiei in the Medieval Period," in *Re-Visioning "Kamakura" Buddhism,* ed. Richard K. Payne, Kuroda Institute: Studies in East Asian Buddhism 11 (Honolulu: University of Hawai'i Press, 1998), pp. 55–69.

39. Kōshū, *Keiran shūyōshū,* pp. 625b–626a. I thank James Robson for sharing his translation of this portion of the text with me. Another version of this claim is made in the earlier portion of the *Keiran shūyōshū,* p. 519b.

40. For the earliest complete translation of the *Kegon Sutra* (full title in Japanese *Dai hōkōbutsu Kegon kyō*), directed by the Indian monk Buddhabhadra (359–429), see *Kegon kyō, T.* 278.9.395–788. For the second translation of the *Kegon Sutra,* directed by the Khotanese monk Shikshananda (652–710), see *Kegon kyō, T.* 279.10.1–444; this version has also been translated into English: Thomas Cleary, trans., *The Flower Ornament Scripture: A Translation of the Avatamsaka Sutra* (Boulder and London: Shambhala, 1993); Cleary gives a lucid introduction to the sutra, pp. 1–53, including the above information regarding translations (p. 2).

41. This document is published in *HAGS,* vol. 4, pp. 572–73, no. 8.

42. Neil McMullin, *Buddhism and the State in Sixteenth-Century Japan* (Princeton: Princeton University Press, 1984), p. 43.

43. Berry, *The Culture of Civil War in Kyoto,* pp. 164–67. Doctrinal rivalries were partly to blame for this bloody clash, though Berry persuasively locates the roots of the conflict in the aversion of a traditional elite (Enryakuji) toward a commoner group (Hokke adherents) which had recently begun to assume certain functions of government. See also McMullin, *Buddhism and the State in Sixteenth-Century Japan,* p. 55.

44. The best discussion of this period, focused on events in Kyoto but equally articulate about national implications, is Berry, *The Culture of Civil War in Kyoto.*

45. The confrontation between Nobunaga and Honganji is examined in McMullin, *Buddhism and the State in Sixteenth-Century Japan,* pp. 100–145; Mary Elizabeth Berry, *Hideyoshi,* Harvard East Asian Series, no. 97 (Cambridge, Mass.: Harvard University Press, 1982), pp. 63–64; Herman Ooms, *Tokugawa Ideology: Early Constructs, 1570–1680* (Princeton: Princeton University Press, 1985), pp. 31–34; Elison, "The Cross and the Sword," pp. 70–73.

46. For Nobunaga's treatment of Enryakuji, see McMullin, *Buddhism and the State in Sixteenth-Century Japan,* pp. 145–51; Berry *Hideyoshi,* pp. 45–51,

47. Part of a longer description translated in Ryusaku Tsunoda et al., eds., *Sources of Japanese Tradition,* 2 vols., paperback ed. (New York: Columbia University Press, 1964), vol. 1, pp. 305–8.

48. *Tokitsugu Kyō ki,* cited in McMullin, *Buddhism and the State in Sixteenth-Century Japan,* p. 147.

49. Michael Cooper, S. J., comp. and ann., *They Came to Japan: An Anthology of European Reports on Japan, 1543–1640* (Berkeley and Los Angeles: University of California Press, 1965), pp. 98–99.

50. McMullin, *Buddhism and the State in Sixteenth-Century Japan,* p. 142.

51. Okuno Takahiro, *Zōtei Oda Nobunaga monjo no kenkyū,* 3 vols. (Tokyo: Yoshikawa Kōbunkan, 1988); the letters of protection and those specifying or attesting preferential treament for certain temples are found throughout this collection, which organizes all known Nobunaga documents chronologically, from 1549 through his death in 1582.

52. Cited in Cooper, comp. and ann., *They Came to Japan,* p. 134.

53. The preeminent Japanese studies of Azuchi Castle are, first, Naitō Akira, "Azuchijō no kenkyū," *Kokka,* no. 987 (February 1976), pp. 7–117; no. 988 (March 1976), pp. 7–63, which presents what Naitō argues is a copy of plans for the castle and other related materials, from which he proposes a reconstruction (this research has recently been republished in Naitō Akira, *Fukugen Azuchijō: Nobunaga no risō to ōgon no tenshu* [Tokyo: Kodansha, 1994]); and second, Miyakami Shigetaka, "Azuchijō tenshu no fukugen to sono shiryō ni tsuite: Naitō Akira shi 'Azuchijō no kenkyū' ni taisuru gimon," *Kokka,* no. 998 (March 1977), pp. 7–26; no. 999 (April 1977), pp. 5–27, which disputes some of Naitō's sources and conclusions. In English, see Shun'ichi Takayanagi, "The Glory That Was Azuchi," *Monumenta Nipponica* 32, no. 4 (Winter 1977), pp. 515–24; Elison, "The Cross and the Sword," pp. 63–66; for an excellent study of the paintings, Carolyn Wheelwright, "A Visualization of Eitoku's Lost Paintings at Azuchi Castle," in *Warlords, Artists, and Commoners: Japan in the Sixteenth Century,* ed. George Elison and Bardwell L. Smith (Honolulu: University of Hawaii Press, 1981), pp. 87–111.

54. The *Shōchū Gōka okibumi,* dated to 1608.1.5, describes the principal image of Sōkenji's five-bay-square Hondō as Kannon, but also notes the presence of Benzaiten. The 1745 *Enkeizan Sōkenji Zenji kōkatsuchō* indicates that the Benzaiten was moved at some point from Sōkenji's Hondō to its Pagoda and that Nobunaga acquired it from Chikubushima. Both are quoted and discussed in Akita Hiroki, *Oda Nobunaga to Azuchijō* (Osaka: Sōgensha, 1990), pp. 195–97.

55. An excellent discussion of Nobunaga's use of the sacred as a basis of his own authority (and other matters related to his rise to power) is contained in Ooms, *Tokugawa Ideology,* pp. 18–39; my citation is on p. 38.

56. For Frois' text, see Cooper, comp. and ann., *They Came to Japan,* pp. 101–2.

57. Asao Naohiro proposed the argument for Nobunaga's self-deification, based on Frois' writings: see Asao Naohiro, "'Shōgun kenryoku' no sōshutsu," parts 1–3, *Rekishi hyōron,* no. 241 (August 1970), pp. 70–78; no. 266 (August 1972), pp. 46–59; no. 293 (September 1974), pp. 20–36; "Bakuhansei to tennō," in *Kinsei,* vol. 3 of Taikei Nihon kokka shi, ed. Hara Hidesaburō, Minegishi Sumio, Sasaki Junnosuke, and Nakamura Masanori (Tokyo: Tōkyō Daigaku Shuppankai, 1975), pp. 187–222. Others have disputed Asao: see Elison, "The Cross and the Sword," pp. 71–75; W. J. Boot, "The Death of a Shogun: Deification in Early Modern Japan," in *Shinto in History: Ways of the Kami,* ed. John Breen and Mark Teeuwen (Honolulu: University of Hawai'i Press, 2000), pp. 144–66. For a rebuttal to Elison's counter-argument, see Herman Ooms, "Neo-Confucianism and the Formation of Early Tokugawa Ideology: Contours of a Problem," in *Confucianism and Tokugawa Culture,* ed. Peter Nosco (Princeton: Princeton University Press, 1984), p. 41, n. 41.

58. The letter is published in *HAGS,* vol. 4, p. 235, *CM* no. 157. For a translation, see Appendix, document 1.

59. *HAGS,* vol. 3, pp. 558–60.

60. For the Asai and their relationship with Chikubushima, see Miyajima Keiichi, "Asai shi kenryoku no keisei: Chikubushima shihai o chūshin ni shite," in *Daimyō ryōgoku o aruku,* ed. Nagahara Keiji (Tokyo: Yoshikawa Kōbunkan, 1993), pp. 175–99; see also *HAGS,* vol. 3, pp. 1–568.

61. The first edict is dated Eiroku 3 (1560).12.13 (*HAGS,* vol. 4, p. 225, doc. 124); the second is only inscribed 12.27 (*HAGS,* vol. 4, p. 232, doc. 150), though from context it is thought to date from about 1566. For a brief discussion of these two documents, see *HAGS,* vol. 3, pp. 176–78.

62. Miyajima, "Asai shi kenryoku no keisei," pp. 191–92. See also Nagahama Castle Historical Museum, ed., *Tokubetsuten: Chikubushima Hōgonji* (Nagahama: Nagahama Castle Historical Museum, 1992), p. 71; hereafter, *TCH.*

63. A letter addressed to Chikubushima, for example, dated the twenty-fifth day of the fourth month of Eiroku 4 (1561), records Nagamasa's gift of three thousand *hiki. HAGS,* vol. 4, p. 226, doc. 127.

64. Miyajima, "Asai shi kenryoku no keisei," p. 191.

65. This letter, dated 10.12, is transcribed in *HAGS,* vol. 4, p. 225, *CM* no. 123. See Appendix, document 2. The 1558 fire is also referred to in later Edo-period documents. Describing three swords in the Chikubushima collection, an inventory record dated to 1719 notes, "At the time of the conflagration of the buildings on the island in 1558, it is said that they were caught in the flames." Transcribed in *TCH* p. 100. Satō Sōjun cites an unspecified document that describes the great destruction of the 1558 fire; see *Meishō shiseki: Chikubushima hozon kanri keikaku* (Ōtsu: Shiga Ken Kyōiku Iinkai, 1979), p. 9. In conversation, Professor Satō informed me that he believed the document to date from the Edo period.

66. *HAGS,* vol. 4, p. 235, *CM* no. 158.

67. *HAGS,* vol. 4, p. 235, *CM* no. 159. For a full translation, see Appendix, document 3.

68. The detailed annals of Nobunaga's activi-

ties are provided in Okuno, *Zōtei Oda Nobunaga monjo no kenkyū;* a useful chronology is also available in Yamamoto Hikari, ed., *Oda Nobunaga: Tenka fubu e no michi,* Bessatsu rekishi dokuhon, vol. 14, no. 6 (Tokyo: Shin Jinbutsu Ōraisha, 1989), pp. 50–79.

69. The document, dated to 1573 [Genki 3].7.1, is published in *HAGS,* vol. 4, p. 236, *CM* no. 163. See also Okuno, *Zōtei Oda Nobunaga monjo no kenkyū,* vol. 1, pp. 638–39 (doc. 374). For a full translation, see Appendix, document 4.

70. The document, dated to 1573 [Tenshō 1].12.21, is published in *HAGS,* vol. 4, p. 237, *CM* no. 166. See also Okuno, *Zōtei Oda Nobunaga monjo no kenkyū,* vol. 1, pp. 639–40 (reference document). For a translation, see Appendix, document 5.

71. The letter is dated the sixth day of the ninth month. No year is given, but scholars date it to this period. *HAGS,* vol. 4, pp. 236–37, *CM* no. 165. See also Okuno, *Zōtei Oda Nobunaga monjo no kenkyū,* vol. 1, pp. 675–76 (doc. 398). For a full translation, see Appendix, document 6.

72. For a discussion of Nobunaga and tea, see Andrew M. Watsky, "Commerce, Politics, and Tea: The Career of Imai Sōkyū," *Monumenta Nipponica* 50, no. 1 (Spring 1995), pp. 47–65.

73. This letter is also dated the sixth day of the ninth month. *HAGS,* vol. 4, pp. 236–37, *CM* no. 164. See also Okuno, *Zōtei Oda Nobunaga monjo no kenkyū,* vol. 1, pp. 674–75 (doc. 397). For a full translation, see Appendix, document 7.

74. The diarist of the *Rokuon nichiroku* visited Chikubushima in 1626, during a *kaichō* exhibition of the island's treasures; he notes seeing the "Shizuka small drum" and many other objects, but makes no mention of the two flutes, further supporting the possibility that Nobunaga kept them. *RN,* vol. 5, pp. 247–48 (1626 [Kan'ei 3].5.1).

75. The history of this drum body is given in Haino Akio, "Raiun makie kodō," *Gakusō,* no. 5 (March 1983), pp. 121–28. See also *TCH,* pp. 95–96.

76. The document, dated only 9.3, is published in *HAGS,* vol. 4, pp. 241–42, *CM* no. 182. For a full translation, see Appendix, document 8.

77. An enlightening examination of Japan's forests and their use is Conrad Totman, *The Green Archipelago: Forestry in Preindustrial Japan* (Berkeley, Los Angeles, London: University of California Press, 1989).

78. The letter is dated 1.23 in the text,, and is published in *HAGS,* vol. 4, p. 237, *CM* no. 167. For a translation, see Appendix, document 9.

79. This letter is dated 3.22 and is published in *HAGS,* vol. 4, pp. 237–38, *CM* no. 168. For a translation, see Appendix, document 10.

80. Nagahama Castle Historical Museum, ed., *Kaikan go shūnen kinen tokubetsuten: Hashiba Hideyoshi to kohoku, Nagahama* (Nagahama: Nagahama Castle Historical Museum, 1988), p. 40.

81. The document, dated to 1574 [Tenshō 2].9.11, is published in *HAGS,* vol. 4, p. 238, *CM* no. 169. It is also discussed in *TCH,* pp. 122–23, cat. no. 71. For a translation, see Appendix, document 11.

82. The document dates from 1744 and is introduced in *TCH,* p. 123.

83. The document, dated only 12.8, is published in *HAGS,* vol. 4, p. 239, *CM* no. 174. For a full translation, see Appendix, document 12. That it dates to Hideyoshi's Nagahama period is indicated by the reference to Hideyoshi as Chikushū, a title which he used only at this time.

84. The document is published in *HAGS,* vol. 4, pp. 579–83. Photographs of the entire document, as well as a transcription and brief discussion, are found in Morioka Eiichi and Ōta Hiroshi, "Shiryō shōkai: *Chikubushima hōgachō,*" *Shiritsu Nagahamajō Rekishi Hakubutsukan nenpō,* no. 1 (March 1987), pp. 79–88. Not every entry in the document is dated, but the dates mentioned range from 1576 to 1588. The bulk of entries date from 1578 or earlier.

85. Literally described as "a table before the Tennyo," the entry is transcribed in Morioka and Ōta, "Shiryō shōkai: *Chikubushima hōgachō,*" p. 81, no. 33.

86. The late sixteenth-century *Yamanoue no Sōji ki* (also read by some scholars as *Yamanoue Sōji ki*), which describes famed tea objects and lists their previous and present owners, notes numerous objects owned by Nobunaga and lost in the attack on Honnōji. For a transcription of the text, see Tanaka Hiromi, ed., "Honkoku *Yamanoue no Sōji ki* Takeda ke otsubon," in *Yamanoue no Sōji ki kenkyū,* ed. Chanoyu Konwakai (Tokyo: Santokuan, 1994), vol. 2, pp. 83–128.

87. Indeed, the Court showed remarkable perceptiveness in reading Hideyoshi's potential, for they granted his first rank as early as 1582 [Tenshō 10].10.3, about a week before Hideyoshi sponsored Nobunaga's funeral; for a discussion of Hideyoshi's rise within the Court, see George Elison, "Hideyoshi, the Bountiful Minister," in *Warlords, Artists, and Commoners: Japan in the Sixteenth Century,* ed. George Elison and Bardwell L. Smith (Honolulu: University of Hawaii Press, 1981), pp. 230–33.

2 Hideyoshi and the Sacred: Manipulating Convention

1. These accolades by, respectively, John Saris, João Rodrigues, and Rodrigo de Vivero y Velasco, are quoted from longer, informative descriptions

contained in Cooper, comp. and ann., *They Came to Japan,* pp. 275–82. For a fuller description of Hideyoshi's remaking of the Kyoto cityscape, see Moriya Katsuhisa, "Toyotomi Hideyoshi no toshi kaizō," in *Hideyoshi to Kyōto—Hōkoku Jinja shahō ten: Hōtaikō botsugo yonhyaku nen kinen,* ed. Kataoka Hajime (Kyoto: Hōkoku Jinja, 1998), pp. 5–9; Hickman et al., *Momoyama, Japan's Golden Age,* pp. 35–40; Berry, *Hideyoshi,* pp. 193–203.

2. For excellent accounts of the construction, see Matsuoka Toshirō, *Ōsakajō no rekishi to kōzō* (Tokyo: Meicho Shuppan, 1988); Uchida Kusuo, "Toyotomi Hideyoshi no Ōsakajō kensetsu," in *Yomigaeru chūsei 2: Honganji kara tenka ichi e Ōsaka,* ed. Sakuma Takashi (Tokyo: Heibonsha, 1989), pp. 34–55.

3. See Kyōto Shi, *Kyōto no rekishi,* 10 vols. (Tokyo: Gakugei Shorin, 1968–1976), vol. 4, pp. 267–72; Hickman et al., *Momoyama, Japan's Golden Age,* pp. 35–38.

4. Cited in Cooper, ed., *João Rodrigues's Account of Sixteenth-Century Japan,* p. 165.

5. For discussions of temple and shrine patronage by Hideyoshi, see Kuwata Tadachika, *Toyotomi Hideyoshi kenkyū* (Tokyo: Kadokawa Shoten, 1975), pp. 343–46; Berry, *Hideyoshi,* pp. 202–3.

6. Ooms, *Tokugawa Ideology,* p. 48.

7. See Hickman et al., *Momoyama, Japan's Golden Age,* p. 39.

8. Cooper, comp. and ann., *They Came to Japan,* p. 111. For similar accounts of Hideyoshi's miraculous birth, see Berry, *Hideyoshi,* p. 9; Elison, "Hideyoshi, the Bountiful Minister," pp. 223–26.

9. Cited in Ooms, *Tokugawa Ideology,* p. 46.

10. Berry, *Hideyoshi,* pp. 85–86.

11. Kuwata, *Toyotomi Hideyoshi kenkyū,* pp. 343–44; Ōkuwa Hitoshi, "Tenshōji no sōken, chūzetsu kara Daibutsu zōei e: Tenshōki Toyotomi seiken to Bukkyō," *Ōtani gakuhō* 63, no. 2 (September 1983), pp. 33–34.

12. Berry, *Hideyoshi,* p. 86.

13. The document, dated to intercalary 4.15, is published in *HAGS,* vol. 4, p. 241, *CM* no. 181. The year 1585 is ascertained from the month, intercalary 4, which during this period occurred only that year. For a translation, see Appendix, document 13.

14. The three documents, dated 1.15, 1.16, and 1.23, are published in *HAGS,* vol. 4: respectively, p. 244, *CM* no. 192; p. 243, *CM* no. 188; and p. 244, *CM* no. 193. Although the years of these documents are unknown, they clearly postdate Hideyoshi's departure from Nagahama, when he first began to use the vermilion seal. For translations, see Appendix, documents 14, 15, and 16, respectively.

Kinoshita Yoshitaka, a Hideyoshi retainer, sent to Chikubushima an accompanying letter for document 15, dated to the same day. He assures Chikubushima that Hideyoshi received the gift and that he will send Hideyoshi's vermilion-seal letter, in other words, document 19. Yoshitaka's letter is published in *HAGS,* vol. 4, p. 243, *CM* no. 189. For a translation, see Appendix, document 17.

15. The document is published in *HAGS,* vol. 4, p. 241, *CM* no. 180. For a translation, see Appendix, document 18.

16. The text of this document, dated to 1591 [Tenshō 19].4.23, is not published. The document is recorded in a recent comprehensive survey of documentary materials related to Chikubushima that predate 1603: Shiga Ken Kyōiku Iinkai Jimukyoku Bunkabu Bunkazai Hogoka, ed., *Chikubushima Hōgonji monjo mokuroku* (Shiga Ken Kyōiku Iinkai Jimukyoku Bunkabu Bunkazai Hogoka, 1992), p. 21, no. 196. For a transcription of the document and a translation, see Appendix, document 19.

A second, slightly earlier letter of 1591 [Tenshō 19].3.29 from a Hideyoshi retainer informs Chikubushima that Hideyoshi will soon make the 300 koku donation, and discusses details regarding the source of a small portion of the total. The letter is published in *HAGS,* vol. 4, pp. 243–44, *CM* no. 190. For a translation, see Appendix, document 20.

17. The document is published in *HAGS,* vol. 4, p. 242, *CM* no. 185. The text contains only the date of 11.4; the year 1584 [Tenshō 12] is written on the paper wrapping of the document. For a translation, see Appendix, document 21.

18. The year is not specified in either letter, but the references to Hideyoshi and his schedule confirm that they postdate his departure from Nagahama. Bokushinsai Nobusada's letter is published in *HAGS,* vol. 4, p. 243, *CM* no. 187. For a translation, see Appendix, document 22. Itō Hidemori's letter is not published. It is recorded in Shiga Ken Kyōiku Iinkai Jimukyoku Bunkabu Bunkazai Hogoka, ed., *Chikubushima Hōgonji monjo mokuroku,* 26, no. 244. For a translation, see Appendix, document 23.

An earlier letter to Chikubushima from each of these two men also shows their connection with the affairs of the island during Hideyoshi's Nagahama period. The letters are published in *HAGS,* vol. 4, p. 240, *CM* nos. 176 (Itō Hidemori) and 177 (Bokushinsai Nobusada). For translations, see Appendix, documents 24 and 25. The exact years of the earlier letters are unknown, but their contents confirm that they were written while Hideyoshi was still based in Nagahama. Itō Hidemori's letter discusses the Hayasaki farmers' nonpayment of income they owed to Chikubushima, a matter that would have been handled at the local level, while Hidemori was still in Nagahama. Bokushinsai Nobusada's letter refers to Bessho Magoemon, that is, Bessho Shigemune (d. 1591). Bessho Shigemune was first a vassal of Nobunaga, and beginning in 1578, of Hideyoshi; after becoming Hideyoshi's vassal, he is unlikely to have been referred to with the deference implied in Nobusada's description of him as a "respected guest from another province."

19. The documentary evidence for the project described below—and an excellent analysis of it—is given in Ōkuwa, 'Tenshōji no sōken."

20. For a discussion of this project and of much of the documentary evidence for it, see Miki Seiichirō, "Hōkōji Daibutsuden no zōei ni kansuru ikkōsatsu," in *Chūsei, kinsei no kokka to shakai,* ed. Nagahara Keiji, Inagaki Yasuhiko, and Yamaguchi Keiji (Tokyo: Tōkyō Daigaku Shuppankai, 1986), pp. 185–213. The Yoshida Kanemi passage is cited on p. 188. See also Kyōto Shi, *Kyōto no rekishi,* vol. 4, pp. 274–77; Kyōto Shi, *Shiryō Kyōto no rekishi,* 16 vols. (Tokyo: Heibonsha, 1979–1991), vol. 10, pp. 412–14; and Tsuji Zennosuke, *Kinseihen no ichi,* vol. 7 of *Nihon Bukkyō shi* (Tokyo: Iwanami Shoten, 1952), pp. 373–408.

21. Cited in Miki, "Hōkōji Daibutsuden no zōei ni kansuru ikkōsatsu," pp. 188–89.

22. This report, dated by the Japanese calendar Tenshō 14 [1586].8.20, is translated in Murakami Naojirō, trans., *Iezusukai Nihon nenpō* (Tokyo: Yūshōdō Shoten, 1969), vol. 2, pp. 146–47; referenced in Miki, "Hōkōji Daibutsuden no zōei ni kansuru ikkōsatsu," p. 188.

23. Cooper, comp. and ann., *They Came to Japan,* p. 336.

24. Noted by Gaspar Vilela (1525–1572), a Portuguese Jesuit missionary who lived in Japan from 1554 until 1570. Cited in Cooper, comp. and ann., *They Came to Japan,* p. 282.

25. Tsunoda et al., eds., *Sources of Japanese Tradition,* vol. 1, pp. 98–99.

26. Tsunoda et al., eds., *Sources of Japanese Tradition,* vol. 1, pp. 104–5.

27. An exhaustive compilation of the documentary evidence related to the Great Buddha is contained in Maeda Taiji, Nishi Daiyū, Matsuyama Tetsuo, Totsu Keinosuke, and Hirakawa Shingo, *Tōdaiji Daibutsu no kenkyū: Rekishi to chūzō gijutsu,* 2 vols. (Tokyo: Iwanami Shoten, 1997). In English, see Naomi Noble Richard, ed., *The Great Eastern Temple: Treasures of Japanese Buddhist Art from Tōdai-ji* (Chicago: Art Institute of Chicago, 1986). For the Tōdaiji project, as well as the broader context of Nara-period Buddhist art, see Mimi Hall Yiengpruksawan, "The Legacy of Buddhist Art at Nara," in *Buddhist Treasures from Nara,* ed. Michael R. Cunningham (Cleveland: Cleveland Museum of Art, 1998), pp. 1–34.

28. Yoshiaki Shimizu, "The *Shigisan-engi* Scrolls, c. 1175," in *Pictorial Narrative in Antiquity and the Middle Ages,* ed. Herbert L. Kessler and Marianna Shreve Simpson, Studies in the History of Art, vol. 16 (Washington: National Gallery of Art, 1985), pp. 115–29; Karen Brock, "The Making and Remaking of *Miraculous Origins of Mt. Shigi,*" *Archives of Asian Art* 45 (1992), pp. 42–71.

29. *The Tale of the Heike,* trans. McCullough, pp. 195–96.

30. Yamashina Tokitsune's diary is published as *Tokitsune Kyō ki,* ed. Tōkyō Daigaku Shiryō Hensanjo, *Dai Nihon kokiroku,* 14 vols. (Tokyo: Iwanami Shoten, 1959–1991). In his diary he refers often to *Heike:* on 1596 [Keichō 1].9.11 he notes that he explained a passage of the text (*Tokitsune Kyō ki,* vol. 7, p. 216); on 1598 [Keichō 3].4.15 he records that he has discussed portions of the third *kan* of *Heike* (*Tokitsune Kyō ki,* vol. 8, p. 229); group discussions of *Heike* are held on 1599 [Keichō 4].4.5 (*Tokitsune Kyō ki,* vol. 9, p. 206), 1599 [Keichō 4].5.5 (*Tokitsune Kyō ki,* vol. 9, p. 222), and 1599 [Keichō 4].7.3 (*Tokitsune Kyō ki,* vol. 10, p. 2). The courtier Funabashi Hidekata (1575–1614) discusses *Heike* paintings in at least two entries of his diary, *Keichō nikken roku,* ed. Yamamoto Takeo, *Shiryō sanshū kokiroku hen* (Tokyo: Zoku Gunsho Ruijū Kanseikai, 1981–); hereafter, *Keichō nikken roku:* on 1604 [Keichō 9].12.30 Kano Naizen inquires about how to illustrate an episode of the *Heike* in painting (*Keichō nikken roku,* vol. 1, p. 151), and on 1605 [Keichō 10].1.6 a certain Kano Yōichi visits and similarly discusses a *Heike* scroll (*Keichō nikken roku,* vol. 1, p. 158).

31. The reception of *Heike* from the fifteenth through nineteenth centuries is reviewed in Shimizu Masumi, "*Heike monogatari* no juyō, kinsei (chūshaku shi o fukumu)," in *Heike monogatari: Hihyō to bunkashi,* ed. Yamashita Hiroaki (Tokyo: Kyūko Shoin, 1997), pp. 135–57.

32. Shimizu Masumi, "*Heike monogatari* no juyō, kinsei (chūshaku shi o fukumu)," p. 145.

33. For a discussion of the rebuilding project, see Richard, ed., *The Great Eastern Temple: Treasures of Japanese Buddhist Art from Tōdai-ji,* pp. 42–44; Yoshiaki Shimizu, ed., *Japan: The Shaping of Daimyo Culture,* pp. 47–48; and Maeda, Nishi, et al., *Tōdaiji Daibutsu no kenkyū,* vol. 1, pp. 53–71.

34. Cited in Berry, *Hideyoshi,* p. 80.

35. Maeda, Nishi, et al., *Tōdaiji Daibutsu no kenkyū,* vol. 1, pp. 72–73.

36. Maeda, Nishi, et al., *Tōdaiji Daibutsu no kenkyū,* vol. 1, pp. 73–75.

37. Tokyo National Museum et al., eds., *Tōdai-jiten* (Asahi Shinbunsha, 1980), p. 235. Parts of the body were recast in bronze, while the head, evidence suggests, was fabricated in bronze-clad wood. For a detailed discussion of the remaking of the Great Buddha, see Maeda, Nishi, et al., *Tōdaiji Daibutsu no kenkyū,* vol. 1, pp. 75–89.

38. Tokyo National Museum et al., eds., *Tōdai-jiten,* p. 235.

39. The portions of Gien's diary covering the years 1596 through 1604 have been published: *Gien Jugō nikki,* ed. Iyanaga Teizō et al., 3 vols., *Shiryō sanshū, kokiroku hen* (Tokyo: Zoku Gunsho Ruijū Kanseikai, 1976–); hereafter *GJN*. For this citation, see *GJN,* vol. 2, p. 259 (1601 [Keichō 6].2.11).

40. Miki, "Hōkōji Daibutsuden no zōei ni kansuru ikkōsatsu," p. 205. Kawauchi Masayoshi points out that there appear to be no period references to the name "Hōkōji"; instead, the temple was referred to by its central image or building: "Daibutsu" or "Daibutsuden" ("Kyōto Higashiyama Daibutsu Sensōe ni tsuite: Chūkinsei ikōki ni okeru kenryoku to shūkyō," *Nihonshi kenkyū,* no. 425 (January 1998), pp. 1–25; for a discussion of the name, see p. 3). It is unlikely that this absence indicates—as Kawauchi seems to suggest—that the name was invented only later, but rather that the temple was more familiarly known by its most noticeable building.

41. Tamon'in Eishun's diary is contained in *Tamon'in nikki,* ed. Tsuji Zennosuke, 5 vols. (Tokyo: Sankyō Shoin, 1935–1939); hereafter *TN;* for this entry, see *TN,* vol. 4, p. 121 (1591 [Tenshō 16].5.12).

42. *RN,* vol. 3, p. 24 (1591 [Tenshō 19].7.10).

43. Cited in *Shiryō Kyōto no rekishi,* vol. 10, p. 414.

44. *GJN,* vol. 1, pp. 9–21 (1596 [Bunroku 5].1.21; 1596 [Bunroku 5].1.28; 1596 [Bunroku 5].2.25).

45. Oze Hoan, *Taikōki,* ann. Hinotani Teruhiko and Emoto Hiroshi, Shin Nihon koten bungaku taikei, no. 60 (Tokyo: Iwanami Shoten, 1996), pp. 174–78.

46. John M. Rosenfield, in Hickman et al., ed. *Momoyama: Japan's Golden Age,* p. 88.

47. For a translation of the edict, see Berry, *Hideyoshi,* p. 198.

48. *GJN,* vol. 1, pp. 13–14 (1596 [Bunroku 5].1.29). The most recent and in-depth study of the Sensōe is Kawauchi, "Kyōto Higashiyama Daibutsu Sensōe ni tsuite." See also Tamamuro Fumio, *Nihon bukkyō shi: Kinsei* (Tokyo: Yoshikawa Kōbunkan, 1987), pp. 28–35.

49. *GJN,* vol. 1, p. 14 (1596 [Bunroku 5].1.29). This building was part of the temple Myōhōin, which was apparently subsumed within the larger Hōkōji precincts. For the several period references to the the Sutra Hall and the Myōhōin that link them specifically to the Daibutsu, see Kawauchi, "Kyōto Higashiyama Daibutsu Sensōe ni tsuite," pp. 2–3.

50. The letter is dated to 1596 [Keichō 1].intercalary 7.8, and is published in *HAGS,* vol. 4, pp. 244–45, *CM* no. 194.

51. For an excellent examination of the objects used in Buddhist ritual settings, see Anne Nishimura Morse and Samuel Crowell Morse, *Object as Insight: Japanese Buddhist Art and Ritual* (Katonah, N.Y.: Katonah Museum of Art, 1996).

52. *GJN,* vol. 1, pp. 13–14 (1596 [Bunroku 5].1.29).

53. Kawauchi, "Kyōto Higashiyama Daibutsu Sensōe ni tsuite," pp. 4–12; Tamamuro, *Nihon bukkyō shi: Kinsei,* pp. 32–35.

54. Kawauchi, "Kyōto Higashiyama Daibutsu Sensōe ni tsuite," p. 7.

55. The Nichiren debate is examined in Tamamuro, *Nihon bukkyō shi: Kinsei,* pp. 26–37; Kawauchi, "Kyōto Higashiyama Daibutsu Sensōe ni tsuite," pp. 16–22.

56. Tamamuro, *Nihon bukkyō shi: Kinsei,* p. 30. Maeda Gen'i sent similar letters to the other Buddhist sects as well, cited and discussed in Kawauchi, "Kyōto Higashiyama Daibutsu Sensōe ni tsuite," p. 4.

57. Miki, "Hōkōji Daibutsuden no zōei ni kansuru ikkōsatsu," p. 202; Kawauchi, "Kyōto Higashiyama Daibutsu Sensōe ni tsuite," p. 6.

58. The records of eleventh- and twelfth-century performances of the ceremony are compiled in Marinus Willem de Visser, *Ancient Buddhism in Japan, Sutras and Ceremonies in Use in the Seventh and Eighth Centuries A.D. and their History in Later Times* (Leiden: E.J. Brill, 1935), pp. 698–99.

59. Kawauchi, "Kyōto Higashiyama Daibutsu Sensōe ni tsuite," pp. 6–7, 16–22.

60. The biography and documentary evidence for Ōmandokoro is compiled in Watanabe Yosuke, *Hōtaikō no shiteki seikatsu,* Nihon bunka meicho sen (Osaka: Sōgensha, 1939), pp. 143–73.

61. For the founding of Tenzuiji, see Kawakami Mitsugu, *Zen'in no kenchiku: Zensō no sumai to saikyo* (Kyoto: Kawahara Shoten, 1968), pp. 239–42; and Watanabe, *Hōtaikō no shiteki seikatsu,* pp. 155–56, 167–69.

62. Sutemaru's biography is discussed in Watanabe, *Hōtaikō no shiteki seikatsu,* pp. 104–15; Kuwata Tadachika, *Yodogimi,* Jinbutsu sōsho, no. 7 (Tokyo: Yoshikawa Kōbunkan, 1958), pp. 48–65. Uncon-

firmed legend has it that while in Nagahama Hideyoshi had a son and a daughter, both of whom died in childhood; see Kuwata Tadachika, *Toyotomi Hideyoshi,* Kuwata Tadachika chōsakushū, no. 5 (Tokyo: Akita Shoten, 1979), pp. 109–13.

63. The birth and celebrations are reported in *RN,* vol. 2, p. 314 (1589 [Tenshō 17].5.28); *RN,* vol. 2, p. 315 (1589 [Tenshō 17].6.6); *RN,* vol. 2, p. 318 (1589 [Tenshō 17].6.29). The birth is also reported by Tamon'in Eishun; see *TN,* vol. 4, p. 182 (1589 [Tenshō 17].5.30). For the construction of Yodo Castle, see *Kyōto no rekishi,* vol. 4, pp. 272–74.

64. Translations and analysis of Hideyoshi's letters from this period are found in Adriana Boscaro, ed. and trans., *101 Letters of Hideyoshi, Monumenta Nipponica* monograph 54 (Tokyo: Sophia University, 1975), pp. 34–43.

65. The entries recording these activities are in *TN,* vol. 4, p. 248 (1590 [Tenshō 18].7.29), p. 281 (1591 [Tenshō 19].intercalary 1.3), and p. 282 (1591 [Tenshō 19].intercalary 1.11). Eishun notes another request for rituals for Sutemaru in the fifth month of 1590, reported in the entry for 1591 [Tenshō 19].7.28 (*TN,* vol. 4, p. 305); this does not specify illness as the reason. Many sources other than the *Tamon'in nikki* note other incidents when the performance of rituals was requested of a religious institution in response to Sutemaru being ill. See *Shiryō sōran,* ed. Tōkyō Daigaku Shiryō Hensanjo, 17 vols. (Tokyo: Tōkyō Daigaku Shuppankai, 1923–1963), vol. 12, pp. 316, 322.

66. This amount is confirmed in the entry dated to 1591 [Tenshō 19].intercalary 1.11 (*TN,* vol. 4, p. 282).

67. *Kanemi Kyō ki;* transcribed in unpublished volume of *Dai Nihon shiryō,* Tōkyō Daigaku Shiryō Hensanjo.

68. Tōkyō Teikoku Daigaku, ed., *Dai Nihon komonjo, iewake* (Tokyo: Tōkyō Teikoku Daigaku, 1905), vol. 1, pt. 3, pp. 53–54.

69. The unpublished letter, included in the *CM,* is preserved at the Nagahama Castle Historical Museum. See Appendix, document 26.

70. Watanabe, *Hōtaikō no shiteki seikatsu,* pp. 109–11.

71. *TN,* vol. 4, p. 307 (1591 [Tenshō 19].8.4).

72. For an accounting of Kōfukuji's economic straits in this period, see Izumiya Yasuo, *Kōfukuji* (Tokyo: Yoshikawa Kōbunkan, 1997), pp. 180–85.

73. *TN,* vol. 4, p. 307 (1591 [Tenshō 19].8.6).

74. *TN,* vol. 4, p. 308 (1591 [Tenshō 19].8.8). Hideyoshi's response to the death of Sutemaru is similarly described in many other sources, compiled in *Shiryō sōran,* vol. 12, p. 334.

75. *Kanemi Kyō ki;* transcribed in unpublished volume of *Dai Nihon shiryō,* Tōkyō Daigaku Shiryō Hensanjo.

76. Kajūji Haretoyo (1544–1602), *Haretoyo ki,* ed. Takeuchi Rizō, in vol. 9 of *Zoku shiryō taisei* (Kyoto: Rinsen Shoten, 1967), pp. 349–50 (1591 [Tenshō 19].8.5).

77. The invasion of Korea is discussed in Berry, *Hideyoshi,* pp. 207–17.

78. Tōkyō Teikoku Daigaku, ed., *Dai Nihon komonjo, iewake,* vol. 5, pt. 2, pp. 117–18. For Ishida Masazumi, see Nagahama Castle Historical Museum, ed., *Tokubetsu tenrankai: Ishida Mitsunari, dai ni shō—Sengoku o shissō shita Hideyoshi bugyō* (Nagahama: Nagahama Castle Historical Museum, 2000), p. 55.

79. *TN,* vol. 4, p. 307 (1591 [Tenshō 19].8.8); *Kanemi Kyō ki* (1591 [Tenshō 19].8.8), transcribed in unpublished volume of *Dai Nihon shiryō,* Tōkyō Daigaku Shiryō Hensanjo.

80. Kawakami Kozan and Ogisu Jundō, *Zōho Myōshinji shi* (Kyoto: Shibunkaku, 1975), pp. 298–303. The eulogies will be discussed below, Chapter 3, pp. 133–36.

81. This text is recorded in Nanka Genkō's collected writings, the *Jōe Enmyō Kokushi kyohakuroku,* published in 1753 in a woodblock-printed edition (preserved, among other places, at Kyoto University); hereafter referred to as *JEKK. JEKK,* vol. 2, p. 10, obverse.

82. Kawakami and Ogisu, *Zōho Myōshinji shi,* p. 303.

83. Chishakuin began as part of the Negoroji complex in present-day Wakayama Prefecture. A difficult period for Chishakuin ensued following Hideyoshi's subjugation of Negoroji in 1585. This period ended, however, in the early seventeenth century when Ieyasu became a patron of the temple; on 1615.7.19 Ieyasu gave the Shōunji site to Chishakuin. See Hayashida Kōzen, *Chishakuin shi* (Kyoto: Sōhonzan Chishakuin, 1915), pp. 4–12; Murayama Shōei, *Chishakuin shi* (Kyoto: Kōbō Daishi Onki Jimukyoku, 1934), pp. 60–65.

84. Kyōto Shi Maizō Bunkazai Chōsa Sentaa, ed., *Sōhonzan Chishakuin keidai: Shōunji Kyakuden ato no hakkutsu chōsa: Chishakuin Kōdō shinchiku keikaku yoteichi no maizō bunkazai hakkutsu chōsa hōkoku* (Kyoto: Sōhonzan Chishakuin, 1995). This study presents the findings of these excavations, and also condenses many of the important primary and secondary sources of information on Shōunji and Chishakuin.

85. Kyōto Shi Maizō Bunkazai Chōsa Sentaa, ed., *Sōhonzan Chishakuin keidai,* p. 79.

86. Cited in Kyōto Shi Maizō Bunkazai Chōsa Sentaa, ed., *Sōhonzan Chishakuin keidai,* p. 63.

87. The inventory records ninety-three large and small paintings from the former Main Hall by Hasegawa Kyūzō (1568–1593), the son of Hasegawa Tōhaku (1539–1610); it also states that in 1727 the paintings were reused in buildings throughout Chishakuin. Over the years a number of the paintings were lost through fires and unrecorded deaccessions; in 1952 the remaining paintings were designated National Treasures and placed in their present ferro-concrete building. For an extensive discussion of the much-debated history of these paintings, see Kyōto Shi Maizō Bunkazai Chōsa Sentaa, ed., *Sōhonzan Chishakuin keidai,* pp. 62–72.

88. For a discussion of the paintings, see Takeda Tsuneo, "Tenzuiji Kyakuden gakō: Eitoku taiga o megutte," in *Bijutsushi no danmen* (Osaka: Seibundō, 1995), pp. 317–33.

89. Nanka's Buddhist education began in Mino Province, where he was born. Moving to Kyoto in 1570, he entered Myōshinji, whence he advanced into the highest echelons of the Buddhist elite. In 1586 he became the founding abbot of the Myōshinji subtemple Daitsūin; in 1590 he revived Myōkōji in Owari Province. Hideyoshi selected him as founding abbot of Shōunji in 1591. Thereafter, he continued as abbot of Shōunji but returned to Myōshinji, where he founded the subtemples Chishōin in 1597 and Rinkain, his retirement temple, in 1599. After Nanka died in 1604, there was much discussion, mediated by the Toyotomi, to determine who would take over as head priest of Shōunji, and eventually, it seems, the temple was left unattended; see Kawakami and Ogisu, *Zōho Myōshinji shi,* pp. 304–5. Selections from the JEKK and other materials pertaining to Nanka Genkō are included in Kawakami and Ogisu, *Zōho Myōshinji shi,* pp. 279–332; *Dai Nihon shiryō,* ed. Tōkyō Daigaku (Tokyo: Tōkyō Daigaku, 1901–): vol. 12, pt. 2, pp. 252–68; *Dai Nihon shiryō* is hereafter referred to as DNS.

90. For the identification of Chishakuin in the Funaki screens, see Takeda Tsuneo, ed., *Fūzokuga: Rakuchū rakugai,* vol. 11 of *Nihon byōbue shūsei* (Tokyo: Kōdansha, 1978), pp. 164–65. The representation in the Funaki sceens, too, supports the idea that despite Nanka Genkō's phrase "the construction of a temple building," noted above, the precincts included many buildings.

91. The historical development of the subtemples at Daitokuji is examined in Kawakami, *Zen'in no kenchiku,* pp. 127–265; Levine,"Jukōin: Art, Architecture, and Mortuary Culture at a Japanese Zen Buddhist Temple," pp. 27–75; for Myōshinji, see Kawakami Mitsugu, "Myōshinji no jiiki keikan to kenchiku," in *Myōshinji,* vol. 24 of *Nihon koji bijutsu zenshū,* ed. Miya Tsugio (Tokyo: Shūeisha, 1982), pp. 93–94.

92. Little is securely known about the history of this building, though it is believed to date from the Momoyama period. Kyōto Fu Kyōiku Chō Bunkazai Hogoka Jūyō Bunkazai Myōshinji Daihōjō Shūri Jimusho, ed., *Jūyō bunkazai Myōshinji Daihōjō shūri kōji hōkokusho* (1959), pp. 30–35. Legend has it (and I know of no supporting evidence) that this small building was moved from Shōunji; see Murakami Jin'ichi, *Reibyō kenchiku, Nihon no bijutsu,* no. 295 (Tokyo: Shibundō, 1990), pp. 60–61.

93. Bonshun's diary is published as *Shunkyū ki,* ed. Kamata Jun'ichi, 5 vols., *Shiryō sanshū, kokiroku hen* (Tokyo: Zoku Gunsho Ruijū Kanseikai, 1970–1983); hereafter SK. For this reference, SK, vol. 1, pp. 51–52 (1596 [Bunroku 5]. intercalary 7.12, 13). For the biography of Bonshun, who becomes an increasingly important figure in the post-Hideyoshi period as the head priest of the temple associated with the Toyokuni Shrine, see Tsuda Saburō, *Hideyoshi, hideo densetsu no kiseki: Shirarezaru uramenshi* (Tokyo: Rokkō Shuppan, 1991), pp. 26–47. At the time of the earthquake, he was a priest at the temple Shinryūin in Kyoto.

94. *Tokitsune Kyō ki,* vol. 7, pp. 175–77 (1596 [Bunroku 5]. intercalary 7.13).

95. GJN, vol. 1, pp. 60–62 (1596 [Bunroku 5]. intercalary 7.13).

96. GJN, vol. 1, p. 62 (1596 [Bunroku 5]. intercalary 7.14).

97. *Tokitsune Kyō ki,* vol. 7, p. 178 (1596 [Bunroku 5]. intercalary 7.16).

98. GJN, vol. 1, p. 68 (1596 [Bunroku 5]. 8.6); SK , p. 54 (1596 [Bunroku 5].8.7).

99. GJN, vol. 1, p. 68 (1596 [Bunroku 5]. 8.2).

100. Luis Frois reported the breadth and tremendous devastation of the earthquake beyond Kyoto in a letter, quoted at length by Engelbert Kaempfer (1651–1716) in his book *The History of Japan, Together with a Description of the Kingdom of Siam, 1690–92,* 3 vols., trans. J. G. Scheuchzer (Glasgow: James MacLehose and Sons, 1906), vol. 1, pp. 162–63.

101. GJN, vol. 1, p. 110 (1597 [Keichō 2].2.18).

102. This early stage of the pagoda repairs is charted in GJN, vol. 1, pp. 109–13 (1597 [Keichō 2].2.17 and for several days after).

103. GJN, vol. 1, p. 114 (1597 [Keicho 2].3.8)

104. The references to this phase of the repairs appear frequently throughout the diary, from just after Hideyoshi's initial visit for cherry blossom viewing until the removal of the scaffolding on 1598 [Keichō 3].3.6 (GJN, vol. 1, p. 216).

105. GJN, vol. 1, pp. 208–213 (1598 [Keichō 3].2.9–23).

106. *GJN*, vol. 1, p. 137 (1597 [Keichō 2].5.23).

107. For accounts of this episode, see Donald F. McCallum, *Zenkōji and Its Icon: A Study in Medieval Japanese Religious Art* (Princeton: Princeton University Press, 1994), pp. 163–67; and Kitagawa Hiroshi, "Hōkōji Daibutsuden ni matsurareta Zenkōji Nyorai," *Kankō no Ōsaka*, no. 458 (July 1989), pp. 8–9; no. 459 (August 1989), pp. 8–9. For a discussion of the sculpture as a secret image, see McCallum, *Zenkōji and Its Icon*, pp. 54–55.

108. A full recounting of the movements of the Zenkōji Amida triad at this time is provided in McCallum, *Zenkōji and Its Icon*, pp. 160–63.

109. *Tokitsune Kyō ki*, vol. 8, p. 22 (1597 [Keichō 2].7.18). For a discussion of monzeki, Imperial Court aristocrats who held positions as temple abbots (also the temples in which they lived), see Mikael S. Adolphson, *The Gates of Power: Monks, Courtiers, and Warriors in Premodern Japan* (Honolulu: University of Hawai'i Press, 2000), pp. 71–74.

110. *RN*, vol. 2, p. 358 (1597 [Keichō 2].7.18).

111. *GJN*, vol. 1, pp. 148–50 (1597 [Keichō 2].7.17, 18).

112. In the seventh month of 1598 Gien notes he had heard that the "Zenkōji ritual" would take place the following month, as it had beginning the previous year, implying that this was a regular ceremony. See *GJN*, vol, 1, p. 273 (1598 [Keichō 3].7.26). (It was occasionally cancelled, as well, as noted in *GJN*, vol. 1, p. 164 (1597 [Keichō 2].9.23).

113. This round of ceremonies is reported in *GJN*, vol. 1, pp. 258–66 (1598 [Keichō 3].7.7–11).

114. *GJN*, vol. 1, pp. 272–73 (1598 [Keichō 3].7.25). A mai is 165 grams; Berry, *Hideyoshi*, p. 132.

115. *GJN*, vol. 1, p. 277 (1598 [Keichō 3].8.7) and *GJN*, vol. 1, p. 279 (1598 [Keichō 3].8.12).

116. *GJN*, vol. 1, p. 281 (1598 [Keichō 3].8.17); see also *Tokitsune Kyō ki*, vol. 9, p. 36; *Oyudono no Ue no nikki*, ed. Wada Masao and Saiki Kazuma, 11 vols., Zoku Gunsho Ruijū, hoi (Tokyo: Zoku Gunsho Ruijū Kanseikai, 1964–1966), vol. 9, p. 54.

117. *SK*, vol. 1, p. 146 (1598 [Keichō 3].8.17).

118. *SK*, vol. 1, p. 146 (1598 [Keichō 3].8.18). See Chapter 5 for further discussion of Hideyoshi's death, which was apparently kept secret from most until the end of 1598.

3 Encoding the Sacred

1. *Fuyō*, often referred to in English by the common but inexact name hibiscus, is identified more precisely by its botanical name, *Hibiscus mutabilis.*

2. These hisashi bays, furthermore, had grooves on the pillars and upper and lower frames, indicating that instead of such doors they once held wood panels, which accordingly were restored.

3. The 1937 report states that the doors had in the past been trimmed to make them fit into the hisashi bays (*KTJHSKH*, p. 18), and that the restored width of each pair fits the central bay of the south side of the moya (*KTJHSKH*, p. 19). This deduction is explicable once we know that horizontal and vertical slats divide both front and back surfaces of the doors into a grid of regularly-sized compartments, each of which is filled with wood carvings. A photograph of two of the doors before the restoration shows narrower compartments along the edges where the doors meet (*KTJHSKH*, p. 19, fig. 4; note that the illustration is reproduced upside-down). By increasing the width of the doors so that the edge compartments were once again exactly congruent with the other compartments, the conservators obtained doors of a size that exactly fit the central bay of the south side of the moya.

4. The common goal in Japanese conservation of restoring a building to its "original state" is well discussed in Siegfried RCT Enders and Niels Gutschow, eds., *Hozon: Architectural and Urban Conservation in Japan* (Stuttgart and London: Edition Axel Menges, 1998).

5. The evidence for this configuration is the absence of uneven fading in the lacquer on the pillars, fading which would be expected if the mairado had been in place while the building was outdoors, and also in the remains of tracks for thin sliding closures on the moya interior. See Watsky, "The Art of the Ensemble," pp. 61–65.

6. For a more complete discussion of the physical anomalies of these paintings, see Watsky, "The Art of the Ensemble," pp. 65–69. It is also worth noting that at some point (probably during the 1936–1937 restorations), for a now-unknown reason, the mairado paintings on the east wall were switched with those on the west; compare Figs. 8 and 10 with Figs. 20 and 21.

7. Unsubstantiated tradition states that the moya, like many Momoyama buildings without obvious provenance, was originally part of Hideyoshi's Fushimi Castle. Another often-repeated suggestion is that the moya came from the Toyokuni Shrine, Hideyoshi's memorial complex in Kyoto, because of reliable evidence that the Karamon gate of Hōgonji, also on Chikubushima, came from there; see, for example, Inagaki Eizō, *Jinja to reibyō*, vol. 16 of *Genshoku Nihon no bijutsu* (Tokyo: Shōgakukan, 1968), p. 161. The documentary evidence cited to support this provenance of the gate, an entry in Bonshun's diary that we will discuss below, states that the Toyokuni Shrine gate is being moved to Chi-

kubushima, but makes no mention of the moya, which argues against its hypothetical origin as part of the Toyokuni Shrine.

8. This is attested, for example, in the reports written by European visitors to Japan in the sixteenth century, as well as by the Japanese themselves. For a discussion of this evidence, see Watsky, "The Art of the Ensemble," pp. 11–15.

9. For an excellent discussion of the meanings of decoration, see Robert W. Bagley, "Meaning and Explanation," *Archives of Asian Art* 46 (1993), p. 18.

10. The history of the chrysanthemum and paulownia crests is extensively discussed in Numata Raisuke, *Nihon monshō gaku* (rev. ed., Tokyo: Shin Jinbutsu Ōraisha, 1972), pp. 156–57, 167–69, 209–15, 311–92.

11. Rituals were also offered there for Hideyoshi's widow, Kita no Mandokoro, after her death. See Kyōto Fu Kyōiku Iinkai Jimukyoku Shidōbu Bunkazai Hogoka Jūyō Bunkazai Kōdaiji Kaisandō Shūri Jimusho, ed., *Jūyō bunkazai Kōdaiji Kaisandō shūri kōji hōkokusho* (1951); Kyoto National Museum, *Kōdaiji makie* (Kyoto: Kyoto National Museum, 1971); San'yō Shinbunsha, ed., *Nene to Kinoshita ke monjo* (Okayama: San'yō Shinbunsha, 1982).

12. A review of daimyo mortuary architecture, especially that in the provinces, is given in Murakami, *Reibyō kenchiku,* pp. 60–80.

13. The significance of this tamaya, especially in relation to the interior decoration of the moya, cannot be overemphasized, and demands further study; Murakami, *Reibyō kenchiku,* figs. 19–20.

14. Extensive decoration was not, on the other hand, absolutely essential in mortuary buildings. Note, for example, the late sixteenth-century tamaya built to the memory of Sutemaru in the Gyokuhōin subtemple of Myōshinji (*Fig. 46;* Murakami, *Reibyō kenchiku,* fig. 107). It is subdued in its decoration, with only limited architectural coloring, mostly faded, a single wood carving on the exterior, and paintings of three heavenly musicians on the ceiling. Whereas Nanbu Toshiyasu's tamaya is elaborately decorated inside and out, that built for his father Toshinao, who died in 1632, is austere in appearance (Murakami, *Reibyō kenchiku,* fig. 115).

15. Bettina Klein; adapted and expanded by Carolyn Wheelwright, "Japanese *Kinbyōbu:* The Gold-leafed Folding Screens of the Muromachi Period (1333–1573)," *Artibus Asiae,* pts. 1–2, vol. 45, no. 1 (1984), pp. 5–34; vol. 45, nos. 2–3 (1984), pp. 101–74.

16. It is important to acknowledge that gold-leafed folding screens of floral subjects were also used in purely secular contexts. Additional external evidence is needed, therefore, to confirm that the Agency for Cultural Affairs screens in particular were used in a mortuary context, and as allusions to the Western Pure Land.

17. For a related study of pictorial decoration within a Zen mortuary context that explores the possible associations of natural imagery with rebirth and posthumous enlightenment, see Levine, "Jukōin: Art, Architecture, and Mortuary Culture within a Japanese Zen Buddhist Temple," pp. 480–526.

18. The phoenix-and-paulownia motif is often used in Japanese art for its auspicious association with good government, based on the Chinese legend that the phoenix, which feeds and roosts only on paulownia, appears only in times of just rule. In this Toyotomi monument, then, it functions to endorse Toyotomi rule. For a discussion of this motif and its dissemination in Japan, see Numata, *Nihon monshō gaku,* pp. 359, 764–67.

19. *Muryōju kyō, T.* 360.12.273c. My translation is based on those in Inagaki Hisao in collaboration with Harold Stewart, *The Three Pure Land Sutras: The Larger Sutra on Amitāyus* (*The Sutra on the Buddha of Infinite Life*) (*Taishō, Volume 12, Number 360*), *The Sutra on Contemplation of Amitāyus* (*The Sutra on Visualization of the Buddha of Infinite Life*) (*Taishō, Volume 12, Number 365*), *The Smaller Sutra on Amitāyus* (*The Sutra on Amitāyus Buddha*) (*Taishō, Volume 12, Number 366*), BDK English Tripitaka 12–II, III, IV (Berkeley: Numata Center for Buddhist Translation and Research, 1995), p. 61; and Luis O. Gómez, *The Land Of Bliss: The Paradise of the Buddha of Measureless Light, Sanskrit and Chinese Versions of the Sukhāvatīvyūha Sutras,* Studies in the Buddhist Traditions (Honolulu: University of Hawai'i Press; Kyoto: Higashi Honganji Shinshū Ōtani-ha, 1996), p. 194.

20. Other floral ceilings are found in contexts that are not mortuary. Fifty-three ceiling panels of floral themes stylistically similar to those in the moya cover a portion of the Ōsaki Hachiman Jinja in Sendai, built 1604–1607. Ōsaki, the family shrine of the Date daimyo, is not a mortuary structure. The floral ceilings at Nijō Castle and Nishi Honganji, of uncertain date and origin, need also to be further studied in this context.

21. An entrance is centered in each wall. At present, the grapes are preserved on three of the four moya entrance lintels. The lintel on the north side of the building, a replacement probably installed during the 1936–1937 repairs, holds no decoration; I surmise that the original beam held the grape motif as well.

22. I am indebted to Yoshiaki Shimizu for first

suggesting that I examine the grape for its Pure Land associations.

23. *Muryōjū kyō,* T. 360.12.270c; Inagaki in collaboration with Stewart, *The Three Pure Land Sutras,* p. 46; Gómez, *The Land of Bliss,* p. 179.

24. The most comprehensive study of Riguan and his grape paintings is Shimada Shūjirō, "Jikkan to boku budō," in *Chūgoku kaigashi kenkyū,* vol. 2 of *Shimada Shūjirō chosakushū* (Tokyo: Chūō Kōron Bijutsu Shuppan, 1993), pp. 136–51; first published in *Bijutsu kenkyū,* no. 337 (February 1987), pp. 102–12. For a general discussion of grape painting in the Chan/Zen context, see Helmut Brinker and Hiroshi Kanazawa, *Zen Masters of Meditation in Images and Writings,* trans. Andreas Leisinger (Zürich: Artibus Asiae, 1996), pp. 184–86.

25. The Chinese term for grape, *putao,* was a loan-word from lands west of China, in Central Asia; see Janusz Chmielewski, "The Problem of Early Loan-words in Chinese as Illustrated by the Word *p'u-t'ao,*" *Rocznik orientalistyczny* 22, no. 2 (1958), pp. 7–45; Janusz Chmielewski, "Two Early Loan-words in Chinese," *Rocznik orientalistyczny* 24, no. 2 (1961), pp. 65–86.

26. Takeuchi Naoji, *Kōgetsu Sōgan: Bokuseki no utsushi—Zenrin bokuseki kantei nichiroku—no kenkyū* (Tokyo: Kokusho Kankōkai, 1976–), vol. 1, p. 98.

27. Kōgetsu included as well information related to the works, such as descriptions of the paintings that held some of the calligraphies.

28. Grapes were also a well-recognized allusion to autumn, as demonstrated in another now-lost painting of grapes by Riguan recorded in the *Bokuseki no utsushi;* in the self-inscribed poem, the jewel-like grape represents the very essence of autumn:

> The fragile vine extends its slender tendrils;
> its pendent clusters glisten like crystal;
> I think back on the moon and a river journey;
> [the fruit] ripening on the autumn trestle in the wind and dew.

Takeuchi Naoji, *Kōgetsu Sōgan: Bokuseki no utsushi,* vol. 1, p. 799.

29. The painting, now in the Sunritz Hattori Museum of Arts, Suwa City, Nagano Prefecture, is published in Tokyo National Museum, ed., *Sōgen no kaiga* (Kyoto: Benridō, 1962), pl. 90.

30. Bianji is a Chinese name for the bodhisattva Samantabhadra (J: Fugen Bosatsu).

31. The currency of this particular meaning of *annyō* in the Momoyama period is reflected in the *Vocabvlario da Lingoa de Iapam,* which defines *annyōkai* as "Amida's paradise." For the original Portuguese, see Doi Tadao, ed., *Vocabvlario da Lingoa de Iapam, Nippo jisho,* p. 19; for a translation into modern Japanese, see Doi, Morita, and Chōnan, eds., *Hōyaku Nippo jisho,* p. 27.

32. The Kano copy of this painting is in the Tokyo National Museum, Kano copy no. 5502. An inscription on the painting includes the name of the copier, a certain Nakanobu; two Kano artists with this name are known, one of whom also used the name Ryūsetsu (1729–1774), and the other Tōsen (1811–1871). More significantly, the inscription contains the information that the original had been copied also by Kano Tan'yū (1602–1674), indicating that the painting was known in Japan at least as early as the seventeenth century. I have yet to examine the unpublished second half of *Bokuseki no utsushi* to see if this painting was also recorded by Kōgetsu Sōgan.

33. Takeuchi Naoji, *Kōgetsu Sōgan: Bokuseki no utsushi,* vol. 1, p. 881. The original of this calligraphy was written by the Chinese Chan monk Pingshi Ruzhi (1268–1357), and is still preserved at the Tokiwayama Bunko in Japan. It is published in Kanagawa Prefectural Museum, ed., *Tokiwayama Bunko meihin ten* (Yokohama: Kanagawa Prefectural Museum, 1983), cat. no. 88. For Pingshi Ruzhi, see Yoshiaki Shimizu, "Problems of Moku'an Rei'en (?- 1323–1345)" (Ph.D. diss., Princeton University, 1974), pp. 25, 93–98.

34. The *Zōgyoku wakashū,* a Muromachi-period text that interprets motifs employed in poetry, lists katamigusa as an alternate name for kiku (chrysanthemum), calling it "katamigusa that one does not take one's eye off, that one always wants to see; by custom it brings to mind memories of autumn." *Zōgyoku wakashū,* in *Gunsho ruijū,* vol. 16 (Tokyo: Zoku Gunsho Ruijū Kanseikai Yōsha, 1934), p. 278.

It is particularly relevant to the present discussion that the 1603 *Vocabvlario da Lingoa de Iapam* defines katami as "an object of remembrance." For the original Portuguese, see Doi Tadao, ed., *Vocabvlario da Lingoa de Iapam, Nippo jisho,* p. 84; for a translation into modern Japanese, see Doi, Morita, and Chōnan, eds., *Hōyaku Nippo jisho,* p. 107.

35. Kuwata, *Yodogimi,* p. 64.

36. This poem, from the Heian poetic compilation *Bakudenshō,* is cited in Shimonaka Yasaburō, ed., *Daijiten,* 26 vols. (Tokyo: Heibonsha, 1934–1936), vol. 6, p. 250.

37. Published in Museum Yamato Bunkakan, ed., *Tokubetsuten Nihon no shōzōga* (Nara: Museum Yamato Bunkakan, 1991), cat. no. 49.

38. The month of the sitter's death is unknown. Even if he died in autumn and the choice of flower was governed by its seasonal association, it would remain significant that, from among the several con-

ventional emblems of autumn, the flower chosen was chrysanthemum. The likely reason for that choice would have been the chysanthemum's association with katamigusa.

39. The painting, now in the Myōhōji in Ishikawa Prefecture, is published in Museum Yamato Bunkakan, ed., *Tokubetsuten Nihon no shōzōga,* cat. no. 44.

40. See Irita Seizō, "Maeda Kikuhime no gazō," *Bijutsu kenkyū,* no. 38 (February 1935), pp. 12–13.

41. For the earliest contemporary references to this girl under the name Kikuhime, see DNS, pt. 12, vol. 8, pp. 295–300.

42. See above, p. 288, note 1.

43. For a discussion of early depictions of fuyō in Japan, see Shimada Shūjirō and Iriya Yoshitaka, eds., *Zenrin gasan: Chūsei suibokuga o yomu* (Tokyo: Mainichi Shinbunsha, 1987), p. 433. The earliest example of fuyō cited, however—plants depicted in the background of the Kamakura-period portrait of Emperor Goshirakawa in the Myōhōin—are more likely peonies.

44. Wang Qi [Wang Ch'i], *Sancai tuhui* [*San-ts'ai t'u-hui*] (Taibei: Chengwen Chubanshe [Taipei: Ch'eng-wen Ch'u-pan-she], 1970), p. 2575.

45. The painting is published in Shimada and Iriya, *Zenrin gasan,* pp. 432–33.

46. Toyotomi sponsorship of the moya, announced in the conspicuous chrysanthemum and paulownia crests, strongly suggests that the moya originally commemorated a Toyotomi family member. Only three prominent Toyotomi figures died between the years 1586 and 1602, the period in which the moya must have been created: the ruler Hideyoshi, who died in 1598; Hideyoshi's mother, Ōmandokoro, who died in 1593; and Hideyoshi's son Sutemaru, who died in 1591 during his third year of life. The analysis below of the thematic content of the exterior decoration supports Sutemaru as the most likely subject of the moya.

47. The three Sutemaru eulogies are contained in JEKK, vol. 2, p. 4, obverse–p. 12, reverse. Selections from the JEKK and other materials pertaining to Nanka Genkō are included in Kawakami and Ogisu, *Zōho Myōshinjishi,* pp. 279–332; and DNS, pt. 12, vol. 2, pp. 252–68.

48. JEKK, vol. 2, p. 7, reverse–p. 8, obverse.

49. JEKK, vol. 2, p. 11, obverse.

50. JEKK, vol. 2, p. 11, obverse–p. 11, reverse.

51. Several sources are cited in Morohashi Tetsuji, ed., *Dai kanwa jiten,* 13 vols. (Tokyo: Taishūkan Shoten, 1955–1960), vol. 9, p. 526.

52. Li Shizhen, *Bencao gangmu,* 2 vols. (Beijing: Renmin Weisheng Chubanshe, 1982), vol. 2, pp. 2130–31.

53. Yoshiaki Shimizu, "Multiple Commemorations: *The Vegetable Nehan* of Itō Jakuchū," in *Flowing Traces: Buddhism in the Literary and Visual Arts of Japan,* ed. James H. Sanford, William R. LaFleur, and Masatoshi Nagatomi (Princeton: Princeton University Press, 1992), p. 226. This understanding of fuyō persisted through the Edo period. The *Honzō kōmoku keimō,* an early nineteenth-century botanical text, similarly states that "originally, fuyō was the name of the lotus flower"; see Ono Ranzan, *Honzō kōmoku keimō,* ed. Sugimoto Tsutomu (Tokyo: Waseda Daigaku Shuppanbu, 1974), p. 502.

54. For the original Portuguese, see Doi Tadao, ed., *Vocabvlario da Lingoa de Iapam, Nippo jisho,* p. 225; for a translation into modern Japanese, see Doi, Morita, and Chōnan, eds., *Hōyaku Nippo jisho,* p. 289.

55. For the original Portuguese, see Doi Tadao, ed., *Vocabvlario da Lingoa de Iapam, Nippo jisho,* p. 163; for a translation into modern Japanese, see Doi, Morita, and Chōnan, eds., *Hōyaku Nippo jisho,* p. 211.

56. The absence of any reference to hasu in Nanka's eulogies for Sutemaru is not anomalous. Eleven of Nanka's eulogies contain no reference to either fuyō or hasu, therefore the lotus could not have been an essential motif in his eulogies. Moreover, one of the eulogies mentions both hasu and fuyō, making it unlikely that both refer to the same flower. It is rather more likely that the former refers to the lotus and the latter to the *Hibiscus mutabilis.* JEKK, vol. 2, p. 21, reverse–p. 24, obverse.

57. JEKK, vol. 2, p. 35, obverse.

58. Plum blossoms are noted in the eulogy of a woman who died in early spring. JEKK, vol. 2, p. 33, obverse.

59. Twice fuyō appears in the eulogies for a woman who died in the eighth month of 1567, that is, almost twenty-five years before Sutemaru died. In these, too, fuyō means *Hibiscus mutabilis,* and was likely chosen as an allusion to the month in which she died. Fuyō does not always, however, reflect such an association. It appears also in Nanka's eulogy for a man who died in the second month of 1599. Nor was fuyō a necessary floral image in eulogies for people who died in the eighth month. At least one eulogy for a man who died in the eighth month contains no reference to fuyō.

60. As noted above, two other important Toyotomi family members died in the period during which the moya could have been first built, that is, between 1586 and 1602: Hideyoshi's mother, Ōmandokoro, who died in 1592, and Hideyoshi himself, who died in 1598. There is no evidence that either was associated with fuyō.

61. It is also clear that the holes do not predate the move of the moya to Chikubushima. The workmanship of the cuts is considerably less polished than that found on other parts of the building (*Fig. 81*). Moreover, the upper pillar holes deface paulownia crests, which would hardly have been acceptable while the moya was located in Kyoto, when these areas were clearly visible from the exterior. The ill-fitting beam visible in the upper hole in Fig. 81 is clearly a later addition.

62. The differences are relatively slight and may not be meaningful. Possibly, too, the exterior of the lintel-beam on the south side of the building may also have been moved. The areas where such holes in the pillars and cutouts in the lintel-beam would be located are now obscured by ebikōryō, which were added during the installation of the moya into the Tsukubusuma Main Hall. The lintel-beams now on the west and south sides of the moya may at some point have been switched. There is no evidence that there were ever holes in the pillars or cut-outs in the lintel-beam of the present north side of the moya.

63. Such a switch could easily have been made, since the dimensions of the lintel-beams are identical. It could have happened during the rebuilding of the moya after it was moved to Chikubushima. I suspect, however, that the switch may have occurred during the 1936–1937 repairs; although no mention is made in the 1937 report, a photograph taken during the repairs clearly shows that the lintel-beams were taken down (*KTJHSKH*, pl. 35).

64. For a discussion of the crane motif, primarily as a crest but also for its auspicious associations, see Numata, *Nihon monshō gaku*, pp. 730–43.

65. Absolute confirmation of Sutemaru's ownership of the armor or Hideyoshi's donation of the armor to Myōshinji is not possible. No known sixteenth-century documents record the donation, nor are the objects inscribed. I examined the armor on 92.7.13 with the armor conservator Nishioka Fumio, who is convinced of a late sixteenth-century date for both sets on the basis of workmanship. The painting on the one set has been discussed as a work in the style of Kano Mitsunobu; see Wakisaka Atsushi's comments in Miya, ed., *Myōshinji*, pl. 29.

66. The letter is published in Watanabe, *Hōtaikō no shiteki seikatsu*, p. 108. I wish to thank Kitagawa Hiroshi of Osaka Castle for his assistance in locating this reference.

67. Instances of small amounts of exterior makie lacquer are not entirely unknown. The frames of the cusped windows of the tamaya of Date Masamune in Sendai hold chrysanthemums executed in makie lacquer. For additional documentary evidence, see Watsky, "The Art of the Ensemble," pp. 13–14.

68. I thank Murose Kazumi, lacquer conservator and director of the Urushi Institute for Research and Restoration in Tokyo, and Katō Hiroshi, of the Department of Restoration Techniques, National Research Institute for Cultural Properties, Tokyo, for their explanations of lacquer restoration in general and their assistance in examining and interpreting the specific problems of the makie lacquer on the Tsukubusuma moya.

69. For the lacquer, see Haino Akio, "Tsukubusuma Jinja Honden no makie sōshoku," *Gakusō*, no. 3 (March 1981), pp. 53–86. Published comments on the paintings are universally brief. Shrine legend attributes these paintings to Kano Eitoku (1543–1590), a claim unsupported by documentary or visual evidence; see Doi Tsugiyoshi, "Tsukubusuma Jinja no tenjōga," *Kyōto* 20 (June 1952), p. 28. Tanaka Kisaku proposes Kano Sanraku in an early modern evaluation of the paintings, suggesting unspecified similarities with works at Daikakuji; see Bijutsu Kenkyūjo, ed., *Momoyama jidai kinpeki shōhekiga* (Tokyo: Otsuka Kōgeisha, 1937), p. 33. Doi Tsugiyoshi is convinced that the works are by Mitsunobu, as he states in "Tsukubusuma Jinja no tenjōga," pp. 27–29; in *Momoyama no shōhekiga*, vol. 14 of *Nihon no bijutsu* (Tokyo: Heibonsha, 1964), pp. 143–44; and in *Kano Eitoku, Mitsunobu*, vol. 9 of *Nihon bijutsu kaiga zenshō* (Tokyo: Shūeisha, 1978), p. 136. Other recent writers generally agree with Doi's attribution of the paintings to Mitsunobu. See, for example, Takeda Tsuneo, *Shōheiga*, vol. 13 of *Genshoku Nihon no bijutsu* (Tokyo: Shōgakukan, 1967), pp. 178–79; Takeda Tsuneo, ed., *Kano Eitoku, Nihon no bijutsu*, no. 94 (Tokyo: Shibundō, 1974), pp. 84–92; Kawai Masatomo and Wakisaka Atsushi, eds., *Momoyama no shōheiga: Eitoku, Tōhaku, Yūshō*, vol. 17 of *Nihon bijutsu zenshū* (Tokyo: Gakushū Kenkyūsha, 1978), pp. 156–57, 204; Ishimaru Shōun and Iso Hiroshi, *Ōmi no shōhekiga* (Kyoto: Kyōto Shoin, 1981), pp. 253–54; Takeda Tsuneo, ed., *Momoyama kaiga, Nihon no bijutsu*, no. 208 (Tokyo: Shibundō, 1983), p. 47; and Tsuji Nobuo, Kōno Motoaki, and Yabe Yoshiaki, eds., *Eitoku to shōheiga: Momoyama no kaiga, kōgei 2*, vol. 15 of *Nihon bijutsu zenshū* (Tokyo: Kōdansha, 1991), p. 127.

4 The Material of the Sacred

1. Before the late nineteenth century there was no Japanese term to designate what we now refer

to as "fine art." The modern word *bijutsu* was an invention of the Meiji period, when interest in things Western brought about the adoption of foreign concepts necessitating Japanese equivalents of terms such as "fine art." For the implications of the creation of the term *bijutsu* in the Meiji period, see Hiroyuki Suzuki, "The Reconstruction of the Body and the Inauguration of 'Bijutsu (Fine Arts)' in the Meiji Period," 1997 TMs [photocopy] prepared for College Art Association Conference. Suzuki notes that *bijutsu* did not appear until 1873, when it was used as a translation of the German term for "applied art," and did not until the late 1880s acquire the meaning of "fine arts." For a more complete discussion, see Satō Dōshin, *<Nihon bijutsu> tanjō: Kindai Nihon no "kotoba" to senryaku,* Kodansha sensho métier 92 (Tokyo: Kōdansha, 1996).

2. Valignano's discussion is cited in Cooper, comp. and ann., *They Came to Japan,* pp. 260–62.

3. Especially in the last several years scholarly literature on the *Yamanoue no Sōji ki* has become extensive. See, for example, the catalogue of a major museum exhibition, Gotō Bijutsukan Gakugeibu, ed., *Yamanoue no Sōji ki: Tenshō jūyon nen no me* (Tokyo: Gotoh Museum, 1995), and three volumes of papers that examine various aspects of the text, Chanoyu Konwakai, ed., *Yamanoue no Sōji ki kenkyū,* 3 vols. (Tokyo: Santokuan, 1993–1997). For the text, of which I am currently preparing an annotated translation, see Tanaka Hiromi, ed., "Honkoku *Yamanoue no Sōji ki* Takeda ke otsubon."

4. Exceptions to the exclusive nature of elite chanoyu are few in the Momoyama period; the most famous public gathering was the event sponsored by Hideyoshi at Kitano in 1587, which purported to engage all levels of Japanese society. See Louise Allison Cort, "The Great Kitano Tea Gathering," *Chanoyu Quarterly,* no. 31 (1982), pp. 15–20.

5. Recall, for example, Hideyoshi's repair of the pagoda at Daigoji (and eventually other buildings there as well), Chapter 2, pp. 94–97.

6. *The Oxford English Dictionary,* 1933 ed., reprint, 1961, s.v. "Ensemble."

7. Excellent illustrations of the Byōdōin Phoenix Hall are found in Akiyama Terukazu, Ōta Hirotarō, Nishikawa Shinji, and Fukuyama Toshio, eds., *Byōdōin taikan,* 3 vols. (Tokyo: Iwanami Shoten, 1987–1992).

8. For a recent study of the Konjikidō lacquer, including photographic documentation of the pre- and post-repair state of the decoration, see Nakasato Toshikatsu, *Chūsonji no shitsugei, Nihon no bijutsu,* no. 318 (Tokyo: Shibundō, 1992).

9. The Konjikidō is also an excellent example of an ensemble whose meaning can be elicited only by considering the whole; see recent studies by Mimi Yiengpruksawan: "The House of Gold: Fujiwara Kiyohira's Konjikidō," *Monumenta Nipponica* 48, no. 1 (Spring 1993), pp. 33–52, and *Hiraizumi: Buddhist Art and Regional Politics in Twelfth-Century Japan,* Harvard East Asian Monographs, no. 171 (Cambridge, Mass.: Harvard University Asia Center, 1998). Yiengpruksawan shows that the Konjikidō combines elements typical of the Heian Buddhism of the capital region with elements more characteristic of the northern Honshu–Siberian ancestry of its patron, Kiyohira of the Ōshū Fujiwara. In some respects the building is typical of a Kyoto Buddhist hall used for the worship of Amida. In others, however, it is absolutely anathema to such a tradition. No Amida Hall is known in which the mummified remains of the patron (and his heirs) are interred, as they are here, within the altar. The Konjikidō is thus unique in being a hall of worship for Amida and also a tomb for a mummy, and the allover use of gold may have been key to both aspects. In the relevant Buddhist texts, gold evokes the Western Pure Land of Amida. It may also have served to neutralize the defilement associated with death, so that the interred corpses did not profane the sacred precinct. Taken as a whole, the several components of the Konjikidō offer a complex assemblage of implications. In other words, only when considered as an ensemble of forms does the Konjikidō disclose its ensemble of meanings.

10. Yoshiaki Shimizu, "Workshop Management of the Early Kano Painters, ca. A.D. 1530–1600," *Archives of Asian Art* 34 (1981), p. 38. The identification of the artists involved in the decoration of the interior is discussed in Naitō, *Fukugen Azuchijō,* pp. 67–73.

11. François Caron, *True Description,* cited in Cooper, comp. and ann., *They Came to Japan,* pp. 218–19. Cooper notes that "artificially" at that time meant "skilfully" (p. 225).

12. From a long discussion by Rodrigues on painting in his *History of the Church of Japan,* cited in full in Cooper, ed., *João Rodrigues's Account of Sixteenth-Century Japan,* pp. 315–21. Gaspar Vilela (1525–1572) a Portuguese Jesuit, equated the function of Japanese screen paintings with the familiar decorative use in his native Europe of Gobelin tapestries to cover the walls. Gaspar Vilela, *Cartas,* cited in Cooper, comp. and ann., *They Came to Japan,* pp. 254–55.

13. Cooper, ed., *João Rodrigues's Account of Sixteenth-Century Japan,* p. 151.

14. Cooper, ed., *João Rodrigues's Account of Sixteenth-Century Japan,* p. 321.

15. For analysis of Azuchi's painting program, see Wheelwright, "A Visualization of Eitoku's Lost Paintings at Azuchi Castle."

16. Cooper, comp. and ann., *They Came to Japan,* p. 134.

17. Cooper, comp. and ann., *They Came to Japan,* pp. 132, 136.

18. Below the lintel in the southern bays of the eastern and western walls and on the southern wall (excluding the entrance door) the paintings have been lost, and their former locations covered with gold-leafed paper.

19. See Chapter 3, note 69 for a summary of the published comments on these paintings. For a recent review of the scholarship on Kano Mitsunobu, see Tsuji, Kōno, and Yabe, *Eitoku to shōheiga: Momoyama no kaiga, kōgei 2,* pp. 152–53, 208–10; and Doi Tsugiyoshi, *Kano Eitoku, Mitsunobu.* A useful chronology of the Kano workshop through the early seventeenth century can be found in Carolyn K. Wheelwright, "Kano Shōei" (Ph.D. diss., Princeton University, 1981), pp. 447–57.

20. A 1799 inscription discovered during a restoration of the Guest Hall (Kyakuden) in 1925 not only dates the building to 1600 and attributes the paintings to Mitsunobu, but, of particular interest in the context of this study, identifies the patron of the project as Hideyori. It may be translated as follows:

> This subtemple was constructed by Toyotomi Naidaijin Hideyori Kō; the *bugyō* was Mōri Terumoto of Geishū [Aki Province]; the pillar raising was on the tenth day of the fourth month of Keichō 5 [1600]; the paintings of both rooms are [from the] brush of Kano Ko Ukyō Mitsunobu; from that time for two hundred years the gold fusuma and *toko* [paintings] of the Kyakuden had not been rehung; now, due to damage, [they have undergone] restoration.

The 1600 date mentioned in the inscription is confirmed by other, earlier ink writings uncovered during the 1925 restoration, lending credence also, some scholars believe, to the other information, including the attribution of the paintings to Mitsunobu. For a summary of the scholarship on these paintings, see Doi Tsugiyoshi, *Kano Eitoku, Mitsunobu,* pp. 113–14; Tsuji, Kōno, and Yabe, *Eitoku to shōheiga: Momoyama no kaiga, kōgei 2,* pp. 208–9.

21. Thirteen sections of fusuma and wall paintings from the First Room are reproduced in black-and-white in Bijutsu Kenkyūjo, *Momoyama jidai kinpeki shōhekiga,* pp. 69–70, pls. II-1 through II-5; for their recent placement within the room, see the diagram and notations in the Accompanying Booklet 1, pp. 13–14, and, for installation photographs, p. 9 of the illustrations.

22. All twenty-four sections of fusuma paintings from the Second Room, referred to as the Higashi no Ma, are reproduced in black-and-white in Bijutsu Kenkyūjo, *Momoyama jidai kinpeki shōhekiga,* pp. 67–68, 71, pls. I-1 through I-10; for their recent placement within the room, see the diagram and notations in the Accompanying Booklet 1, pp. 13–14, and, for installation photographs, p. 8 of the illustrations.

23. Doi Tsugiyoshi, *Kano Eitoku, Mitsunobu,* p. 112.

24. Asaoka Okisada, *Koga bikō,* revised and enlarged by Ōta Kin as *Zōtei koga bikō,* 3 vols. plus separate index vol. (1904–1905; reprint, Kyoto: Shibunkaku, 1970), vol. 3, p. 1585.

25. Narazaki Muneshige, "Hizen Nagoyajō zu to Kano Mitsunobu," *Kokka,* no. 915 (June 1968), pp. 51–52.

26. The letter is dated the sixteenth day of the fourth month; the year is understood from context. Preserved only in transcription, it is published in Asaoka and Ōta, *Zōtei koga bikō,* vol. 3, p. 1608.

27. Published in Doi Tsugiyoshi, *Kano Eitoku, Mitsunobu,* pl. 53. This is the sole painting assigned by the *Honchō gashi* to Mitsunobu. See Kasai Masaaki, Sasaki Susumu, and Takei Akio, ann., *Yakuchū Honchō gashi* (Kyoto: Dōhōsha Shuppan, 1985), p. 347.

Considering the evidence of Mitsunobu's work for the Toyotomi, three portraits of Hideyoshi should also be noted, one preserved in Kōdaiji, a second in the Date Bunka Hozonkai, and a third, a preliminary sketch now in the Itsuō Art Museum. The Kōdaiji painting, dated by its inscription to 1598, is published in Shizuoka Prefectural Museum of Art, ed., *Kaikan sanshūnen kinen ten: Kanoha no kyoshōtachi* (Shizuoka: Kanoha no Kyoshōtachi Ten Jikkō Iinkai, 1989), cat. no. 21. The Date painting, dated by inscription to 1599, is published in Doi Tsugiyoshi, *Kano Eitoku, Mitsunobu,* pl. 35, and the Itsuō sketch in Doi Tsugiyoshi, *Kano Eitoku, Mitsunobu,* pl. 34. All three are attributed to Mitsunobu by some scholars, including Doi (Doi Tsugiyoshi, *Kano Eitoku, Mitsunobu,* pp. 117–18). This is a question that deserves further consideration.

28. For an excellent source of information about such architectural carvings, see Itō Nobuo, ed., *Daiku chōkoku,* Inax Booklet, vol. 6, no. 3 (Tokyo: Inax, 1988).

29. Cited in Cooper, comp. and ann., *They Came to Japan,* pp. 288–89.

30. For the Funaki screens, see Introduction, pp. 30–32.

31. The identification of the building is discussed in Tsuji Nobuo, "Funaki ke kyūzōbon rakuchū rakugai zu byōbu no kentō," p. 122.

32. For a discussion of the gate in Japanese architecture, see William H. Coaldrake, "Shogunal and Daimyo Gateways: The Intersecting Spheres of Arbitrary Will and Technical Necessity," in *Architecture and Authority in Japan* (London and New York: Routledge, 1996).

33. See below, Chapter 5. The Toyokuni Shrine itself was established only after Hideyoshi's death in 1598, and so the carvings can be reasonably dated within the brief span 1598–1602. The carvings are well reproduced in Chin Shunshin and Mine Kakukai, *Chikubushima Hōgonji,* vol. 3 of *Koji junrei: Ōmi* (Kyoto: Tankōsha, 1980), pl. 16.

34. The fate of the carvings on the other two walls is unclear. Possibly they were incorporated into other parts of the Tsukubusuma Main Hall and deteriorated over time or disappeared during the conservation work of 1936–1937 (see below, Chapter 6).

35. *Webster's Third New International Dictionary of the English Language Unabridged,* 1971 ed., s.v. "Lacquer."

36. For a recent study that examines the visiting Europeans' understanding of lacquer, with special attention given to the large number of technical terms included in the *Vocabvlario da Lingoa de Iapam,* see Leonor Leiria, "The Art of Lacquering According to the Namban-Jin Written Sources," *Bulletin of Portuguese/Japanese Studies* 3 (December 2001), pp. 9–26.

37. Rodrigues' discussion of lacquer, which I quote extensively on the following pages, is found in Cooper, ed., *João Rodrigues's Account of Sixteenth-Century Japan,* pp. 326–27.

38. I thank Michael Cooper for his assistance in understanding the etymology of the word *uruxar;* letter dated 98.7.8.

39. The 1603 Portuguese dictionary of the Japanese language, *Vocabvlario da Lingoa de Iapam,* has a similarly oblique way of referring to this novel substance, defining it (*vruxi*) as "the varnish of Japan." For the original Portuguese, see Doi Tadao, ed., *Vocabvlario da Lingoa de Iapam, Nippo jisho,* p. 577; for a translation into modern Japanese, see Doi, Morita, and Chōnan, eds., *Hōyaku Nippo jisho,* p. 733.

40. For this widely published chest, see Tsuji Nobuo, Hirai Kiyoshi, and Yabe Yoshiaki, eds., *Shiro to chashitsu: Momoyama no kenchiku, kōgei 1,* vol. 14 of *Nihon bijutsu zenshū* (Tokyo: Kōdansha, 1992), cpl. 79; and Kyoto National Museum, ed., *Hideyoshi to Nene no tera: Kōdaiji no meihō* (Kyoto: Kyoto National Museum, 1995), cat. no. 83.

41. Lacquer was so closely linked to Japan in the European imagination that varnishing was known as "japanning"; for an early European treatise on the art of lacquering, adapted to European specifications, see John Stalker and George Parker, *A Treatise of Japanning and Varnishing 1688* (Chicago: Quadrangle Books, 1960).

42. Such references are too numerous to comprehensively list; the following entries represent the types of reference most frequently made: *Tokitsune Kyō ki,* vol. 9, p. 141 (1599 [Keichō 4].1.18), notes a makie sake cup; *GJN,* vol. 2, p. 123 (1600 [Keichō 5].1.18), notes that Sūden of Nanzenji has brought a makie letterbox, presumably as a gift; *RN,* vol. 4, p. 247 (1605 [Keichō 10].5.18), mentions lacquered plates.

43. This saddle is widely published; see, for example, Hickman et al., *Japan's Golden Age: Momoyama,* p. 241.

44. Toda Teisuke, Kawakami Mitsugu, Nagai Norio, and Yabe Yoshiaki, eds., *Zenshū jiin to teien: Nanbokuchō, Muromachi no kenchiku, chōkoku, kōgei,* vol. 11 of *Nihon bijutsu zenshū* (Tokyo: Kōdansha, 1993), p. 234. For a good selection of other such donated objects, see Kyoto National Museum, ed., *Tokubetsu tenrankai: Makie—shikkoku to ōgon no Nihonbi* (Kyoto: Kyoto National Museum, 1995), pp. 41–79.

45. See Kyoto National Museum, ed., *Tokubetsu tenrankai: Makie—shikkoku to ōgon no Nihonbi,* pp. 29–40.

46. The zushi is well discussed in Osaka Castle, ed., *Seitan yonhyaku nen kinen tokubetsuten: Toyotomi Hideyori ten* (Osaka: Ōsakajō Tenshukaku Tokubetsu Jigyō Iinkai, 1993), cat. no. 35.

47. *Tōdaiki,* in vol. 2 of *Shiseki zassan,* ed. Hayakawa Junsaburō (Tokyo: Kokusho Kankōkai, 1911), p. 118 (1608 [Keichō 13].10.3).

48. *GJN,* vol. 2, p. 71 (1599 [Keichō 4].7.30).

49. *RN,* vol. 4, p. 386 (1607 [Keichō 12].11.20).

50. For Kōdaiji and its lacquer, as well as the biography of Kita no Mandokoro (Kōdaiin), see William H. Samonides, "Patronizing Images: Kōdai-in and Toyotomi Hideyoshi at Kōdaiji," *Nichibunken Japan Review* 7 (1996), pp. 99–125; Kyoto National Museum, ed., *Hideyoshi to Nene no tera: Kōdaiji no meihō;* Kyōto Fu Kyōiku Iinkai Jimukyoku Shidōbu Bunkazai Hogoka Jūyō Bunkazai Kōdaiji Kaisandō Shūri Jimusho, ed., *Jūyō bunkazai Kōdaiji Kaisandō shūri kōji hōkokusho;* San'yō Shinbunsha, ed., *Nene to Kinoshita ke monjo;* Kyoto National Museum, *Kōdaiji makie,* pp. 2–12. Precise

dating of the Kōdaiji lacquer is difficult, since it appears that the lacquered portions of the altar came from elsewhere.

51. The storage box of this inkstone is inscribed "Taikō [Hideyoshi]'s [sake] warmer lid, awarded to Gotō Harumasa." Published in Osaka Castle, ed., *Hideyoshi to Momoyama bunka: Ōsakajō Tenshukaku meihin ten* (Osaka: Mainichi Shinbun, 1996), cat. no. 144.

52. The term *Kōdaiji makie* dates only to the nineteenth century; Samonides, "Patronizing Images: Kōdai-in and Toyotomi Hideyoshi at Kōdaiji," p. 101.

53. Published in *Minamoto no Yoritomo Kō happyaku nensai kinen: Minamoto no Yoritomo ten* (Kamakura: Tsurugaoka Hachimangū, 1999), cat. nos. 14–16. I thank Katō Hiroshi for bringing these sheaths to my attention.

54. This drum body is published in Katō Hiroshi, "Kodō no kōzō to sōshoku," *Museum*, no. 449 (August 1988), pp. 4–17.

55. *GJN*, vol. 2, p. 170 (1600 [Keichō 5].5.12).

56. *RN*, vol. 4, p. 361 (1607 [Keichō 12].intercalary 4.18).

57. *Keichō nikken roku*, p. 142 (1604 [Keichō 9].11.20).

58. *Keichō nikken roku*, p. 189 (1605 [Keichō 10].5.19).

59. *RN*, vol. 3, pp. 10–11 (1591 [Tenshō 19].4.28).

60. *GJN*, cited in *DNS*, pt. 12, vol. 4, p. 484 (1606 [Keichō 11].5.17). For documents associated with this construction project, see Iwashimizu Hachimangū, ed., *Iwashimizu Hachimangū shi* (Tokyo: Zoku Gunsho Ruijū Kanseikai, 1932), vol. 1, pp. 501–9.

61. *GJN*, cited in *DNS*, pt. 12, vol. 4, p. 484 (1606 [Keichō 11].12.12).

62. Morohashi, ed., *Dai kanwa jiten*, vol. 8, p. 127.

63. Confucius, *The Analects* (*Lun yü*), trans. D. C. Lau, Penguin Classics (London and New York: Penguin Books, 1979), III.25.

64. Zhu Xi, *Sishu jizhu*, commentary on *Analects* 3:25 (*Sibu beiyao* ed.). I thank my colleague Bryan W. Van Norden for allowing me to use his translation of Zhu Xi's commentary. In full, it reads,

> "Shao" is the music of [Sage King] Shun. "Wu" is the music of King Wu. "Beauty" refers to the pageantry of the music and the performance. "Goodness" refers to the content of the beauty.
>
> Shun succeeded Yao to preserve orderliness. King Wu attacked [Tyrant] Zhou to save the people. Their achievements were one. Hence, the music of each was perfectly beautiful. Nonetheless, Shun's virtue was such that he "had it by nature." And he got the kingdom through deference. King Wu's virtue was such that he "returned to it." And he got the kingdom through a punitive attack. Hence, the content [of their achievements] had differences.
>
> Master Cheng said, "King Tang banished [Tyrant] Jie but felt remorse for so doing. So it was with [the action of] King Wu. Hence, they were 'not perfectly good.' [But] the standards of Yao, Shun, Tang and Wu were one. To launch a punitive attack was not what they wanted to do. It was a matter of the times they encountered being so."

65. Morohashi, ed., *Dai kanwa jiten*, vol. 12, p. 222.

66. See John Whitney Hall, ed., *Early Modern Japan*, vol. 4 of *The Cambridge History of Japan*, ed. John Whitney Hall, Marius B. Jansen, Madoka Kanai, and Denis Twitchett (Cambridge: Cambridge University Press, 1991), pp. 398–404.

67. Elison, "The Cross and the Sword," p. 65; Wheelwright, "A Visualization of Eitoku's Lost Paintings at Azuchi Castle," pp. 109–11.

68. Komatsu Shigemi, "Tokubetsuten: '*Nihon no sho*' e no tebiki," in *Tokubetsuten: Nihon no sho* (Tokyo: Tokyo National Museum, 1978), pp. 19–21. I thank John Carpenter for alerting me to these Heian-period precedents for *jinzen jinbi*.

69. Closest in date to the ones on Sutemaru's building are those found on the 1604 Mikumari Jinja in Yoshino, and they are a minor detail in the decorative program.

70. Also see the carvings on the large zushi at the 1604 Godaidō in Matsushima; Kokuhō Zuiganji Dainiki Shūri Iinkai, ed., *Kokuhō, jūyō bunkazai Zuiganji shūri kōji hōkokusho* (Miyagi Prefecture: Kokuhō Zuiganji Dainiki Shūri Iinkai, 1958), pls. 90–91. This publication also gathers documentary evidence related to the site, including a transcription and photograph of the 1604 ridgepole placard.

71. For other examples, see Watsky, "The Art of the Ensemble," pp. 80–117.

72. More research is needed to fully understand Tan'yū's role at Nijō.

73. The documentary evidence is compiled and discussed in Tsuji Nobuo, "Kano Motonobu," *Bijutsu kenkyū*, no. 249 (November 1966), pp. 138–39, 147–59.

74. For a critical discussion of this text, see Quitman E. Phillips, "*Honchō gashi* and the Kano Myth," *Archives of Asian Art* 47 (1994), pp. 46–57.

75. Kasai, Sasaki, and Takei, ann., *Yakuchū Honchō gashi*, p. 319.

76. *GJN*, vol. 1, p. 216 (1598 [Keichō 3].3.6). See Chapter 2, pp. 94–96 for this project.

5 After Hideyoshi

1. The transition from the Toyotomi to Tokugawa regimes is surveyed in Hall, ed., *Early Modern Japan*, pp. 141–47. Fujino Tamotsu describes three stages in the Tokugawa achievement of hegemony, marked by the Battle of Sekigahara, the Osaka Campaigns, and finally the creation of the countrywide *bakuhan* administrative establishment that characterized the Tokugawa regime; see Fujino Tamotsu, *Shintei bakuhan taisei shi no kenkyū* (Tokyo: Yoshikawa Kōbunkan, 1975), pp. 201–8. For an analysis of the transition that focuses on the role of the Court, see Asao, "Bakuhansei to tennō."

2. See, for example, *Kyoto no rekishi*, vol. 4, pp. 604–5, 609; Haino, "Tsukubusuma Jinja Honden no makie sōshoku," p. 59; and Tsuji Zennosuke *Kinseihen no ni*, vol. 8 of *Nihon Bukkyō shi*, pp. 1–5. More recently, some scholars have begun to see the limitations of such an interpretation; see, for example, Coaldrake, "Gateways of Power: Edo Architecture and Tokugawa Authority 1603–1651," pp. 169–71.

3. For a discussion of the oaths of fealty to Hideyori that Hideyoshi required of his vassals, see Berry, *Hideyoshi*, pp. 234–36.

4. In a letter Ieyasu writes that Ishida Mitsunari and Ōtani Yoshitsugu of the Western Army had committed "treason." Another document, written during a campaign after Sekigahara and sent to Fukushima Masanori and Kuroda Nagamasa, speaks of following Hideyoshi's directive. Both documents are cited in Asao, "Bakuhansei to tennō," p. 210.

5. Ieyasu's uncertain post-Sekigahara position, even with regard to his supposed allies, is discussed in Harold Bolitho, *Treasures among Men: The Fudai Daimyo in Tokugawa Japan* (New Haven and London: Yale University Press, 1974), pp. 1–7.

6. Ooms, *Tokugawa Ideology*, p. 53. The retrospective *Histoire de l'Eglise du Japon*, by R. P. Crasset, proposes that the betrothal of Hideyori and Sen Hime was initiated by Hideyoshi. This and other relevant materials are quoted in *DNS*, pt. 12, vol. 1, pp. 387–94.

7. Throughout this discussion Hideyori's age is computed in traditional Japanese fashion: the total number of calendar years during which one has lived.

8. The accuracy of this often-repeated dramatic reduction of Toyotomi holdings has been challenged recently by Kitagawa Hiroshi, who points out—as we will see below—that the Toyotomi were granting lands to others outside this domain. He also questions the veracity of the 657,000 koku figure, since the first document recording it is the early nineteenth century *Haizetsuroku*, but the slightly earlier *Dankafu*, of 1809, makes no mention of the Toyotomi at all; does the *Haizetsuroku* represent a late Tokugawa attempt at revisionism? Kitagawa Hiroshi, "Ōsaka no jin saikō," unpublished notes and handout for his lecture, Osaka, 1999.

9. Period diaries are filled with references to these events; Kitagawa Hiroshi alludes to a few representative examples in "Ōsaka no jin saikō"

10. Cited in Asao, "Bakuhansei to tennō," p. 211.

11. For the biography of Yododono, see Kuwata, *Yodogimi*; Nakamura Kōya, *Yododono to Hideyori* (Tokyo: Kokumin Bunka Kenkyūkai, 1966).

12. The documentary materials are introduced in Kuwata, *Yodogimi*, pp. 48–65.

13. See Asao, "Bakuhansei to tennō," and Asao Naohiro and Marius B. Jansen, "Shogun and Tennō," in *Japan before Tokugawa: Political Consolidation and Economic Growth, 1500–1650*, ed. John Whitney Hall, Nagahara Keiji, and Kozo Yamamura (Princeton: Princeton University Press, 1981), pp. 248–70.

14. The Court doubtless supported Hideyori, at least in part, as a counterweight to Ieyasu's ambitions for ultimate power.

15. Ieyasu's activities in this period are surveyed in Ooms, *Tokugawa Ideology*, pp. 50–54.

16. Shimomura Nobuhiro, "Aru Toyotomi Hideyori no monjo," *Nagoyashi Hakubutsukan dayori*, no. 110 (June 1996), p. 878. Presently six such grant letters are known, though Shimomura reasonably suggests that many others were lost in the aftermath of the Osaka Castle campaigns of 1614–1615.

17. Shimomura admits that more research is necessary to fully understand the implications of Hideyori's geographically wide-ranging awards to the Katagiri, questioning whether Hideyori had the authority to act independently of Ieyasu in these cases; the precise nature of Katagiri Katsumoto's close ties with the Toyotomi as well as with the Tokugawa—he received awards from them as well—makes this a more difficult case to assess.

18. Asao, "Bakuhansei to tennō," p. 216.

19. *Kyōto no rekishi*, vol. 4, pp. 606–9.

20. The rumors are reported throughout *Diary of Richard Cocks: Cape-merchant in the English Fac-*

tory in Japan, 1615–1622, with Correspondence, ed. Edward Maunde Thompson, 2 vols. (Hakluyt Society, First Series, no. 66, 1883; reprint, New York: Burt Franklin, n.d.).

21. *GJN,* vol. 2, p. 207 (1600 [Keichō 5].8.7). Also note in *GJN,* p. 165 (1600.5.1), Gien offers on Hideyori's behalf ritual performance for "everlasting military success."

22. *GJN,* cited in *DNS,* pt. 12, vol. 5, p. 580 (1608 [Keichō 13].6.5), and *DNS,* pt. 12, vol. 6, p. 380 (1609 [Keichō 14].6.4).

23. For Yododono, see *GJN,* vol. 2, p. 143 (1600 [Keichō 5].3.4), on which occasion Gien sends kanju; for Hideyori, see *GJN,* cited in *DNS,* pt. 12, vol. 5, pp. 423–24 (1608 [Keichō 13].2.24), and *DNS,* pt. 12, vol. 9, p. 467 (1612 [Keichō 17].2.29).

24. 1613 [Keichō 18].9.19–27, cited in *DNS,* pt. 12, vol. 13, pp. 9–10.

25. *GJN,* vol. 2, p. 303 (1601 [Keichō 6].7.3); *GJN* , vol. 3, p. 58 (1602 [Keichō 7].7.26); *GJN,* vol. 3, p. 220 (1604 [Keichō 9].5.10).

26. *GJN,* vol. 2, pp. 135–38 (1600 [Keichō 5].2.12–16). This entry provides Gien's most detailed description of the actual order and content of the *Daihannya kyō* ceremony proceedings. The *Daihannya kyō* ceremony was held not only at New Year's. In diary entries from the eleventh month of 1599 Gien describes his first *Daihannya kyō* ceremony at Osaka Castle, where Hideyori had taken up residence earlier that year. On the thirteenth Gien is preoccupied with preparations for the trip, leaves Kyoto the next day, stops at Tennōji the day following, and then on the sixteenth arrives at the castle for the ceremony. He names the fifteen monks in attendance, carefully lists the contents of the room within the castle where the ceremony took place, and notes how much the Toyotomi disbursed to the participating monks. The entries for 1599 [Keichō 4].11.13 through 1599.11.16 are found in *GJN,* vol. 2, pp. 96–98. He remarks that Hideyori is said to be slightly ill, so this service may well have been intended for Hideyori's recovery. In subsequent years Gien often performed the ceremony on the sixteenth day at Daigoji and then sent kanju to Osaka.

27. The sutra read on these occasions was either the *Daihannya kyō* or the *Ninnōgyō* (*The Sutra of Benevolent Kings*).

28. Much of the documentary evidence surrounding Hideyoshi's apotheosis and the creation of his shrine is presented in Miyachi Naokazu, "Hōtaikō to Toyokuni Daimyōjin," in *Jingi to kokushi* (Tokyo: Kokin Shoin, 1926), pp. 310–82, and two recent Japanese articles re-engage it: Miki Seiichirō, "Hōkokusha no zōei ni kansuru ichikōsatsu;" *Nagoya Daigaku Bungakubu kenkyū ronshū* 98, *Shigaku* 33 (1987), pp. 195–209, and Nishiyama Masaru, "Toyotomi 'shiso' shinwa no fūkei," *Shisō,* no. 829 (1993), pp. 83–100. See also Kawauchi Masayoshi, "Hōkokusha no seiritsu katei ni tsuite: Hideyoshi shinkakuka o megutte," *Hisutoria,* no. 164 (April 1999), pp. 56–70; Tsuda Saburō, *Hideyoshi, hideo densetsu no nazo: Hiyoshimaru kara Hōtaikō e,* Chūkō bunko, no. 800 (Tokyo: Chūō Kōronsha, 1997), pp. 13–32; for a useful chronology of events relating to the Toyokuni Shrine, Tsuda, *Hideyoshi, hideo densetsu no kiseki: Shirarezaru uramenshi,* pp. 200–234. For discussions of human deification in this period, including Hideyoshi's case, see Ooms, *Tokugawa Ideology,* pp. 36–62; Hall, *Early Modern Japan,* pp. 393–95; most recently and in great detail, Boot, "The Death of a Shogun: Deification in Early Modern Japan."

29. *GJN,* vol. 1, p. 299 (1598 [Keichō 3].9.7). This description refers to a specific sacred building comprising a worship hall and main hall in parallel and linked by an enclosed chamber. For a discussion of this building form as it was manifested in the Edo period, and the term by which it came to be called, *gongen zukuri,* see Coaldrake, *Architecture and Authority in Japan,* pp. 163–92. The "eight-ridge style," a popular term for the building, refers to the characteristically complex roof system (eight simply meaning "a great many"); Coaldrake, "Gateways of Power: Edo Architecture and Tokugawa Authority 1603–1651," pp. 166–68.

30. *GJN,* vol. 1, p. 301 (1598 [Keichō 3].9.11).

31. *GJN,* vol. 1, pp. 303–4 (1598 [Keichō 3].9.15).

32. *GJN,* vol. 1, p. 322 (1598 [Keichō 3].12.6).

33. *GJN,* vol. 1, p. 324 (1598 [Keichō 3].12.18). Gien was correct: Hideyoshi had died on the eighteenth day of the eighth month.

34. *GJN,* vol. 2, p. 8 (1599 [Keichō 4].1.5). He also reports news he heard surrounding Hideyoshi's death, including the unusual occurrence that top vassals had undone their topknots the previous year—much like Hideyoshi's response to the death of Sutemaru.

35. The secrecy surrounding the new site and its intended function is reflected in the several different names by which it was called during its construction, a circumstance well discussed in Kawauchi, "Hōkokusha no seiritsu katei ni tsuite: Hideyoshi shinkakuka o megutte," pp. 58–64.

36. Boot, "The Death of a Shogun: Deification in Early Modern Japan," p. 156.

37. *SK,* vol. 1, p. 161 (1598 [Keichō 3].3.12).

38. *GJN,* vol. 2, p. 8 (1599 [Keichō 4].1.5).

39. *Oyudono no Ue no nikki,* vol. 9, p. 90 (1599 [Keichō 4].3.5). The published version of this text, which I have translated, writes the place name as

"Amidanotake," though it is also known as "Amidagatake."

40. All of these events are reported in *GJN*, vol. 2, pp. 42–47 (1599 [Keichō 4].4.13–30].

41. The translation of the name is from Berry, *Hideyoshi*, p. 1.

42. For discussion of the name, see Ooms, *Tokugawa Ideology*, p. 50.

43. *GJN*, vol. 3, p. 262 (1604 [Keichō 9].10.17). The calligraphy is published in Sōhonzan Daigoji and Nihon Keizai Shinbun, eds., *Inori to bi no denshō: Daigojiten: Hideyoshi, Daigo no hanami yonhyaku nen* (Nihon Keizai Shinbun, 1998), cat. no. 104.

44. Bonshun's diary notes roof tile repairs, *SK*, vol. 2, p. 32 (1602 [Keichō 7].7.26), changing of tatami mats, *SK*, vol. 2, p. 34 (1602 [Keichō 7].8.11) and *SK*, vol. 2, p. 188 (1605 [Keichō 10].8.7), payments to various craftsmen, including the tiler, tatami maker, carpenter, and blacksmith, *SK*, vol. 2, p. 39 (1602 [Keichō 7].9.2). From late 1605 through 1606 Bonshun also notes the building of a new boundary corridor.

45. *SK*, vol. 2, p. 31 (1602 [Keichō 7].7.24).

46. *Diary of Richard Cocks*, vol. 1, pp. 201–2; also cited in Cooper, comp. and ann., *They Came to Japan*, p. 339. Another important written source of information about the shrine is the *Shōmei*, an early seventeenth-century architectural treatise compiled by architects who worked for the Tokugawa, well discussed in Coaldrake, "Gateways of Power: Edo Architecture and Tokugawa Authority 1603–1651," pp. 172–73.

47. Kondō Yoshihiro, "Toyokuni daimyōjin no bunshi ni tsuite," in *Ueki Hakase kanreki kinen kokushigaku ronshū* (Ueki Hakase Kanreki Kinen Shuku Gakkai, 1938), pp. 357–77; Ooms, *Tokugawa Ideology*, p. 58.

48. Tsuda, *Hideyoshi, hideo densetsu no kiseki*, pp. 176–88.

49. *SK*, vol. 1, pp. 188–89 (1599 [Keichō 4].8.17–19).

50. *GJN*, vol. 2, p. 78 (1599 [Keichō 4].8.18].

51. Contemporary records refer to the ceremony by several different names. Bonshun often does not call it by any name, simply describing the events as they take place. He uses the term "Toyokuni *shinji*," (*SK*, vol. 2, p. 17; 1602 [Keichō 7].4.17) or simply "shinji" (*SK*, vol. 3, p. 20; 1607 [Keichō 12].4.18). He refers to the week-long event in the eighth month of 1604 that attended the seventh anniversary of Hideyoshi's death as the "Toyokuni Rinji *no matsuri*," (*SK*, vol. 2, p. 124; 1604 [Keichō 9].5.19).

52. Much of the documentary evidence for the 1604 Special Festival, including the sources I cite individually below, is collected in *DNS*, pt. 12, vol. 2, pp. 496–511. For the 1610 Special Festival, see *DNS*, pt. 12, vol. 7, pp. 469–78. The festival planned for 1614, the seventeenth anniversary, was cancelled.

53. *SK*, vol. 2, pp. 135–37 (1604 [Keichō 9].8.13–21).

54. *Tokitsune Kyō ki*, vol. 13, p. 20 (1604 [Keichō 9].8.12–14).

55. *GJN*, vol. 3, p. 239 (1604 [Keichō 9].8.14).

56. Ōta Gyūichi, *Toyokuni Daimyōjin sairei ki*, in Zoku gunsho ruijū, ed. Hanawa Hokiichi, series 3, vol. 63, pp. 223–31 (Tokyo: Zoku Gunsho Ruijū Kanseikai, 1924). The songs are transcribed on p. 230.

57. *SK*, vol. 2, p. 248 (1606 [Keichō 11].8.18. Bonshun indicates that Katagiri Katsumoto, Hideyori's chief administrator, made the donation. In 1612 Bonshun notes a new pair of screen paintings in the lower chamber of the shrine, although he does not indicate what they depict; cited in *DNS*, pt. 12, vol. 9, p. 679 (1612 [Keichō 17].4.16).

58. This painting is widely published: see, for example, Suzuki Hiroyuki, "Byōbue ni okeru shajitsu: Naizenbon Hōkoku saireizu to chūkū no shikaku," in *Tōyō bijutsu ni okeru shajitsu: Kokusai kōryū bijutsushi kenkyūkai dai 12 kai shinpojiamu* (Osaka: Kokusai Kōryū Bijutsushi Kenkyūkai, 1994), pp. 71–79; Tsuji, Kōno, and Yabe, eds., *Eitoku to shōheiga: Momoyama no kaiga, kōgei 2*, p. 222; Tsuji Nobuo, "Toyokuni matsurie byōbu," *Kokka*, no. 924 (July 1970), pp. 23–31; Tanomura Tadao, "Hōkokusai zu byōbu," *Kokka*, no. 805 (April 1959), pp. 119–25; Tanaka Toyozō, "Hōkokusai no byōbu ni tsuite," *Kokka*, no. 352 (September 1919), pp. 90–102.

59. Kataoka Hajime, ed., *Hideyoshi to Kyōto—Hōkoku Jinja shahō ten: Hōtaikō botsugo yonhyaku nen kinen* (Kyoto: Hōkoku Jinja, 1998): cat. no. 47; Tanaka Toyozō, "Hōkokusai no byōbu ni tsuite."

60. *GJN*, vol. 3, p. 240 (1604 [Keichō 9].8.14).

61. This is the form of the actual building, as described in Gien's diary; see above, p. 204.

62. *Keichō nikken roku*, vol. 1, p. 115 (1604 [Keichō 9].8.15).

63. Pre-Momoyama fūryū dance is examined in Berry, *The Culture of Civil War*, pp. 244–59.

64. For a review of the rebuilding process, see Kyōto Shi, *Kyōto no rekishi*, vol. 4, pp. 602–9. An Edo-period source, the *Miyako meisho zue*, states that reconstruction began as early as the eighth month of 1598—the month of Hideyoshi's death—though no contemporary information corroborates this claim (Kyōto Shi, *Kyōto no rekishi*, vol. 4, p. 276).

65. *GJN,* vol. 2, p. 92 (1599 [Keichō 4].10.19), and vol. 2, p. 148 (1600 [Keichō 5].3.18).

66. *GJN,* vol. 2, p. 170 (1600 [Keichō 5].5.12).

67. For the gate, see Chapter 4, p. 188.

68. *GJN,* vol. 3, pp. 90–91 (1602 [Keichō 7].12.4 and 12.9).

69. *Tokitsune Kyō ki,* p. 345 (1602 [Keichō 7].12.4).

70. *SK,* vol. 2, p. 50 (1602 [Keichō 7].12.4). "Kōyashū buildings" have not been positively identified, though they were probably buildings at Hōkōji used by monks from Mount Kōya.

71. *RN,* vol. 4, pp. 72–73 (1602 [Keichō 7].12.4–5).

72. *The Tale of the Heike,* p. 23.

73. *Tōdaiki,* p. 118 (1608 [Keichō 13].10.3); p. 146 (1609 [Keichō 14].1.28).

74. For the diary entries discussed below, see *DNS,* pt. 12, vol. 7, pp. 294–313. *Kyōto no rekishi* (vol. 4, p. 604) notes that reconstruction began again early in 1609, but its sources are not cited and their reliability cannot be confirmed.

75. *Diary of Richard Cocks,* vol. 1, p. 200; also cited in Cooper, comp. and ann., *They Came to Japan,* pp. 337–38.

76. Yoshiaki Shimizu, ed., *Japan: The Shaping of Daimyo Culture, 1185–1868,* cat. no. 104.

77. The pertinent entries are conveniently collected in *DNS,* pt. 12, vol. 2, pp. 496–99.

78. Matsuda Kiichi, trans., *Jūroku, shichi seiki Iezusu Kai Nihon hōkoku shū* (Kyoto: Dohōsha, 1988), pt. 1, vol. 4, pp. 177–78.

79. The Toyotomi's post-Hideyoshi sponsorship of religious construction has attracted notable scholarly interest. The most recent—and most comprehensive—effort to quantify and analyze this campaign, incorporating informative chronological and geographical charts, is Kimura Nobuko, "Toyotomi Hideyori no jisha zōei ni tsuite," *Nihon kenchiku gakkai keikakukei ronbunshū,* no. 499 (September 1997), pp. 171–77. Among the earlier essays are: Kawakatsu Masatarō, "Hideyori no shaji kenchiku saikō," *Shiseki to bijutsu,* no. 71 (October 1936), pp. 589–600; Moku Masao, "Katagiri Katsumoto to Keichō no shūri," *Gekkan bunkazai,* no. 151 (April 1976), pp. 4–15; Fujii Naomasa, "Toyotomi Hideyori no shaji zōei to sono ikō," *Ōtemae Joshi Daigaku ronshū,* no. 17 (1983), pp. 48–72.

80. The most comprehensive study of the Toyotomi's organization of construction in the post-Hideyoshi era is Kimura Nobuko, "Toyotomi Hideyori no sakuji taisei ni tsuite," *Nihon kenchiku gakkai keikakukei ronbunshū,* no. 511 (September 1998), pp. 185–92.

81. The prevalence of such construction is affirmed by the numerous placards that remain from this period throughout Japan; see, for example, the many examples included in National Museum of Japanese History, ed., *"Hibunken shiryō no kisoteki kenkyū (munafuda)" hōkokusho: Shaji no kokuhō, jūbun kenzōbutsu nado: Munafuda meibun shūsei,* 6 vols. (Sakura: National Museum of Japanese History, 1993–1997).

82. For Hideyoshi's trip to Yoshino, see Hickman et al., *Momoyama: Japan's Golden Age,* p. 41. Two paintings of the event are known: a pair of six-fold screens in the Hosomi collection (*Kokka,* no. 795) and a single six-fold screen in the Powers collection (John M. Rosenfield in collaboration with Fumiko E. Cranston, *Extraordinary Persons: Works by Eccentric, Nonconformist Japanese Artists of the Early Modern Era (1580–1868) in the Collection of Kimiko and John Powers,* ed. Naomi Noble Richard, 3 vols. [Cambridge, Mass.: Harvard University Art Museums, 1999], 1, pp. 48–53).

83. See Yoshino Chō Shi Henshū Iinkai, ed., *Yoshino Chō shi,* 2 vols. (Nara: Yoshino Machiyakuba, 1972). For Mikumari Jinja, see Sakurai Toshio, "Yoshino Mikumari Jinja Honden," in *Shaden* 3, vol. 3 of *Nihon kenchiku shi kiso shiryō shūsei,* ed. Ōta Hirotarō (Tokyo: Chūō Kōron Bijutsu Shuppan, 1981), pp. 48–55.

84. For the period textual evidence of Hideyori's patronage, which includes a placard and inscribed baluster cap and mirror, see Kawakatsu Masatarō and Sasaki Rizō, *Kyōto komei shuki* (Kyoto: Suzukake Shuppanbu, 1941), pp. 334–37; for only the placard, see National Museum of Japanese History, ed., *"Hibunken shiryō no kisoteki kenkyū (munafuda)" hōkokusho, Kinki hen 1,* p. 140. For Hideyoshi's gathering, see Cort, "The Grand Kitano Tea Gathering."

85. See the placard Gien wrote for the reconstruction of Tōji's Golden Hall, as transcribed in his diary, *GJN,* vol. 3, pp. 62–64 (1602 [Keichō 7].8.29, 9.1). For the placard, as well as inscriptions found on the building itself, see Kawakatsu and Sasaki, *Kyōto komei shuki,* pp. 307–9, 311–12; for only the placard, see National Museum of Japanese History, ed., *"Hibunken shiryō no kisoteki kenkyū (munafuda)" hōkokusho, Kinki hen 1,* p. 165.

86. See *GJN,* vol. 2, pp. 159–61 (1600 [Keichō 5].4.18). The placard is transcribed in National Museum of Japanese History, ed., *"Hibunken shiryō no kisoteki kenkyū (munafuda)" hōkokusho, Kinki hen 1,* p. 187; and Kawakatsu and Sasaki, *Kyōto komei shuki,* p. 303.

87. For a recent discussion of this theme, see Yamamuro Kyōko, *Ōgon Taikō,* Chūkō shinsho, no. 1105 (Tokyo: Chūō Kōronsha, 1993).

88. For the documentary evidence surrounding this aspect of Hideyori's Daigoji project, especially Gien's careful diary notations, see *DNS,* pt. 12, vol. 4, pp. 216–29.

89. The ridgepole placard texts for the Nyoirindō and the Mieidō mention all three buildings. These texts were probably authored by Gien himself; in the text for the Mieidō his term of high praise, "jinzen jinbi," is applied to all three buildings. For the 1608 placard for the Nyoirindō, see National Museum of Japanese History, ed., *"Hibunken shiryō no kisoteki kenkyū (munafuda)" hōkokusho, Kinki hen 1,* pp. 187–88. For the 1606 placard text for the Mieidō, see *DNS,* pt. 12, vol. 4, pp. 224–25.

90. Ooms, *Tokugawa Ideology,* p. 49.

91. The letter is dated 7.26; the year can be ascertained from the reference in the letter to the birth of Ieyasu's son Iemitsu, which occurred on 1604.7.17. The letter is transcribed and discussed in Osaka Castle, ed., *Seitan yonhyaku nen kinen tokubetsuten: Toyotomi Hideyori ten,* cat. no. 123.

92. For some projects Yododono was the declared patron, as in the 1601 rebuilding of the Hondō at Hokkeji in Yamato; see Fujii Naomasa, "Toyotomi Hideyori no shaji zōei to sono ikō," p. 56.

93. For the extensive documentation surrounding this project, see *DNS,* pt. 12, vol. 6, pp. 205–14.

94. For a review of the dates of the various stages of the Hōryūji project and of the types of evidence that have been uncovered, see Moku, "Katagiri Katsumoto to Keichō no shūri," pp. 10–13.

95. The text of the placard is transcribed in Sawamura Masashi, "Hōryūji Tōin Denpōdō," in *Butsudō 1,* vol. 4 of *Nihon kenchiku shi kiso shiryō shūsei,* ed. Ōta Hirotarō (Tokyo: Chūō Kōron Bijutsu Shuppan, 1981), p. 50; and "Ko kenchiku meibun shū," pt. 6, *Kōkan bijutsu shiryō,* no. 93, 1957, TMs [photocopy], pp. 102–3. This same basic text is repeated as well in the placards written for other structures at Hōryūji repaired at this time, including the Nandaimon (Great South Gate) and Sankyōin; see "Ko kenchiku meibun shū," pt. 6, pp. 99–101.

96. *RN,* vol. 4, p. 348 (1607 [Keichō 12].2.29).

97. *GJN,* vol. 2, p. 158 (1600 [Keichō 5].4.15).

98. *GJN,* vol. 3, pp. 62–64 (1602 [Keichō 7].8.29–9.1).

99. Research on ridgepole placards does not yet allow firm conclusions about their placement. Evidence suggests, however, that placards were not always attached to the ridgepole. For example, the placard at Ima Hachimangū in Yamaguchi Prefecture, dating to 1668, was produced in duplicate; one was raised to the rafter and the other kept below, where it may have been viewable (see National Museum of Japanese History, ed., *"Hibunken shiryō no kisoteki kenkyū (munafuda)" hōkokusho, Chūgoku, Shikoku, Kyūshū hen,* p. 156). Modern architectural restorers note finding many placards within viewing range (in Shinto shrines, within the zushi) or in the precinct treasure house, although the location in which they were found is not necessarily the one in which they were originally placed. I am indebted to Hamashima Masaji, who helped direct the recent pioneering compilation of placard texts (National Museum of Japanese History, ed., *"Hibunken shiryō no kisoteki kenkyū (munafuda)" hōkokusho*), for sharing his findings on placards with me on 2000.5.17. For a basic study of placards, which focuses on Edo-period examples from Kyushu, see Satō Masahiko, *Tenjōura no bunkashi: Munafuda wa kataru* (Tokyo: Kōdansha, 1995).

100. *DNS,* pt. 12, vol. 14, pp. 451–71, 537–42; in fact, Katagiri Katsumoto began discussions with Ieyasu about the Great Buddha Hall ridgepole placard ceremony as early as 1612 (*DNS,* pt. 12, vol. 10, pp. 143–45).

101. *GJN,* vol. 2, p. 96 (1599 [Keichō 4].11.15).

102. It does not appear, however, that he was involved with the placard written for Tennōji. The only surviving reference to that placard appears in the diary of the aristocrat and famous calligrapher Konoe Nobutada (1565–1614), suggesting that it was discussed within courtier circles; see Konoe Nobutada, *Sanmyakuin ki,* ed. Konoe Michitaka, Nawa Osamu, and Hashimoto Masanobu, *Shiryō sanshū kokiroku hen* (Tokyo: Zoku Gunsho Ruijū Kanseikai, 1975), p. 56 (1598 [Keichō 3].1.10).

103. *Tōdaiki,* p. 83 (1604 [Keichō 9].5.3).

104. *Tōdaiki,* p. 109 (1607 [Keichō 12].9.10). This passage is cited in Fujii Naomasa, "Toyotomi Hideyori no shaji zōei to sono ikō," p. 56.

105. The document, part of the *Sanbōin monjo,* is transcribed in *DNS,* pt. 12, vol. 7, pp. 297–302.

106. Bonshun, too, highlights the Toyotomi role, noting in his diary his need to consult with the "Osaka mother," Yododono, about the Great Buddha construction; 1610 [Keichō 15].intercalary 2.18; cited in *DNS,* pt. 12, vol. 7, p. 303. Much like the rumors that circulated about the Toyotomi's motivations for their construction works, it is the perception of reality—how people understood the events unfolding around them—that provides illuminating commentary on the official record.

107. The sources cited as evidence in *DNS,* pt. 12, vol. 6, pp. 64–68, for example, appear to date from the Edo period.

108. For the documentary record, see *DNS,* pt. 12, vol. 3, pp. 193–97. Earlier precedent for this type of

event can be seen in Hideyoshi's reception of Emperor Goyōzei, which in turn followed precedents set by the Ashikaga shoguns Yoshimitsu and Yoshinori. See Chapter 2, p. 71.

109. Ieyasu did seek to control temples through legislation, as a means of incorporating them into his bureaucratic structure; see Peter Nosco, "Keeping the Faith: *Bakuhan* Policy towards Religions in Seventeenth-century Japan," in *Religion in Japan: Arrows to Heaven and Earth,* ed. P. F. Kornicki and I. J. McMullen (Cambridge: Cambridge University Press, 1991), pp. 135–55.

110. Tokugawa secular architecture is discussed in Coaldrake, *Architecture and Authority in Japan,* pp. 129–37.

111. *Shiryō Kyōto no rekishi,* vol. 10, p. 47.

112. *Kyōto no rekishi,* vol. 4, p. 613; *Shiryō Kyōto no rekishi,* vol. 10, p. 46. For Tokugawa policies towards temples and shrines in this period, see Itō Shinshō, "Keichōki ni okeru Tokugawa Ieyasu to Kinai jisha: 'Seishō Oshō bun'an' no bunseki o tōshite," *Machikaneyama ronsō,* no. 28 (1994), pp. 57–82.

113. Maeda, Nishi, et al., *Tōdaiji Daibutsu no kenkyū,* vol. 1, pp. 89–96.

114. Bonshun's diary reports of the 1616 events and the passage from the 1658 *Rakuyō meisho shū* are collected in *Shiryō Kyōto no rekishi,* vol. 10, pp. 453–56. For fuller discussion of Ieyasu's dismantling of the shrine, see Tsuda, *Hideyoshi, hideo densetsu no nazo,* pp. 89–134. The Meiji revival of the shrine is examined in Kitagawa Hiroshi, "Kami ni matsurareta Hideyoshi to Ieyasu: Hōkokusha, Tōshōgū," in *Yomigaeru chūsei 2: Honganji kara tenka ichi e Ōsaka,* ed. Sakuma Takashi (Tokyo: Heibonsha, 1989), pp. 220–25; and Tsuda, *Hideyoshi, hideo densetsu no nazo,* pp. 260–78.

115. See above, p. 298, note 28.

6 Hideyori and Chikubushima's New Ensemble

1. Ōta Gyūichi, *Shinchō Kō ki,* ann. Okuno Takahiro and Iwasawa Yoshihiko (Tokyo: Kadokawa Shoten, 1969), pp. 351–52.

2. See Tanaka Hisao, "Ōta Gyūichi *Shinchō Kō ki* seiritsu kō," *Teikoku Gakushiin kiji* 5, nos. 2–3 (November 1947), pp. 137–57.

3. The pioneering study of Benzaiten in Japan is Ōmura Seigai, "Benzaiten," pts. 1–2, *Mikkyō* 1, no. 1 (February 1911), pp. 84–105; no. 2 (May 1911), pp. 1–22. A survey of Benzaiten worship and its manifestation in the visual arts is found in Nedachi Kensuke, *Kichijō, Benzaiten zō, Nihon no bijutsu,* no. 317 (Tokyo: Shibundō, 1992). For the most in-depth and recent study of Benzaiten, see Catherine Ludvik, "From Sarasvatī to Benzaiten (India, China, Japan)" (Ph.D. diss., University of Toronto, 2001); this impressive study contains a long discussion of Benzaiten's presence in the *Sutra of Golden Light,* pp. 188–244.

4. Translation cited from Ludvik, "From Sarasvatī to Benzaiten (India, China, Japan)," p. 243. The only extant representation of Benzaiten from this period is a heavily damaged eight-armed sculpture in the Tōdaiji Hokkedō, illustrated in Nedachi, *Kichijō, Benzaiten zō,* fig. 135. Documentary references note now-lost sculptures and paintings at major Nara temples, including Kōfukuji, Saidaiji, and Gangōji, as well as another work at Tōdaiji, a painting executed at the scriptorium; see Nishigori Ryōsuke, *Tenbu no Butsuzō jiten* (Tokyo: Tōkyō Bijutsu, 1983), p. 124.

5. Ludvik, "From Sarasvatī to Benzaiten (India, China, Japan)," pp. 279–86. See, for example, the *Taizōkai mandala* wall painting in the five-story pagoda of 951 at Daigoji, and iconographic drawings such as that in the late Heian text *Besson zakki.* Sculptures of Benzaiten thought to date from this period have been extensively reworked, and reflect less the Heian imaging of Benzaiten than later developments. Nedachi, *Kichijō, Benzaiten zō,* pp. 64–65.

6. For the *Benten sanbukyō* and their implications for the representation of Benzaiten, see Ludvik, "From Sarasvatī to Benzaiten (India, China, Japan)," pp. 287–91.

7. Even earlier examples are known, including two eight-armed Uga Benzaiten preserved at Kakurinji in Hyōgo Prefecture and Seiryōji in Kyoto, both thought to predate the Nanbokuchō period. Nedachi, *Kichijō, Benzaiten zō,* pp. 67–71. What is thought to be the oldest extant sculpture with a contemporaneous figure of Ugajin on Benzaiten's head dates to the late thirteenth century; it is now in a private collection and held at the Tokyo National Museum and is illustrated in color in Nedachi, *Kichijō, Benzaiten zō,* cpl. 21. Muromachi-period paintings include two now preserved at Tōji in Kyoto, with the eight-armed Benzaiten seated on a rocky outcropping at the center, Ugajin on her head, and the Fifteen Attendants, each with an identifying attribute, in the lower half of the painting. Atypically, however, neither of these paintings shows a torii gate on Benzaiten's head. For reproductions, see Tōji (Kyōō Gokokuji) Hōmotsukan, ed., *Tōji no Tenbuzō* (Kyoto: Tōji (Kyōō Gokokuji) Hōmotsukan, 1993), pls. 28, 29. For a discussion of other representative paintings of the Uga Benzaiten, see Nedachi, *Kichijō, Benzaiten zō,* pp. 68–71.

Many later Edo-period paintings and prints closely follow the basic composition delineated in these paintings.

8. Jūyō Bunkazai Hensan Iinkai, ed., *Shin shitei jūyō bunkazai: Kaisetsuban* (Tokyo: Mainichi Shinbunsha, 1981), vol. 11, p. 137.

9. GJN, vol. 2, p. 134 (1600 [Keichō 5].2.10). Gien makes a similar report on 1602 [Keichō 7].2.18; GJN, vol. 3, p. 21.

10. Yamamoto Shinji and Mizuno Katsuhiko, *Kyō, Fushimi rekishi no tabi* (Tokyo: Yamakawa Shuppansha, 1991), pp. 30–32.

11. *Tokitsune Kyō ki*, vol. 7, p. 247 (1596 [Bunroku 5].11.9).

12. This is reported in *Keichō nikken roku*, vol. 1, p. 30 (1603 [Keichō 8].3.9).

13. Yiengpruksawan, *Hiraizumi: Buddhist Art and Regional Politics in Twelfth-Century Japan*, pp. 163, 165.

14. 'Kadokawa Nihon Chimei Daijiten' Hensan Iinkai, ed., *Kadokawa Nihon chimei daijiten*, 49 vols. (Tokyo: Kadokawa Shoten, 1978–1990), vol. 40, p. 999. The location of the hall is indicated on an undated map of the castle precincts. This same site served as the setting for the politicized pastime of chanoyu: Kamiya Sōtan (1553–1635), a merchant–tea master employed by Takakage and also favored by Hideyoshi, wrote in his diary in 1591 that Takakage ordered him to "make a tea house within the Najima Benzaiten shrine" precincts, which he did with the help of thirteen people; the warrior was reportedly pleased with the fine results and a tea gathering was held there. Sōtan's diary is transcribed and critically discussed in Kamiya Sōtan, *Sōtan nikki*, ed. Haga Kōshirō, in vol. 6 of *Chadō koten zenshū*, pp. 131–403 (Kyoto: Tankō Shinsha, 1958); the above entry is on p. 265 (1591 [Tenshō 19].4.10).

15. Osaka Castle, *Seitan yonhyaku nen kinen tokubetsuten: Toyotomi Hideyori ten*, cat. no. 35. This is the same man who donated a zushi and sculpture of Hideyoshi to Hōjuin; see Chapter 4, p. 175.

16. Recent research has shown that the eight-armed, martial Benzaiten was derived in large part from the Indian battle goddess Durgā; see Catherine Ludvik, "La Benzaiten à huit bras: Durgā déesse guerrière sous l'apparence de Sarasvatī," *Cahiers d'Extrême-Asie*, no. 11 (1999–2000), pp. 292–338; Ludvik, "From Sarasvatī to Benzaiten (India, China, Japan)," pp. 248–78.

17. Edo-period records of pilgrimages note such disasters, which surely happened earlier as well, and often describe the treacherous winds on Lake Biwa, which made the journey to Chikubushima hazardous. Tanaka Tomohiko, "Ishiyama yori gyakuuchi to tōgoku no junreisha: Saigoku junreiro no fukugen," *Kōbe Daigaku Bungakubu kiyō*, no. 15 (March 1988), pp. 1–23.

18. GJN, vol. 1, p. 127 (1597 [Keichō 2].4.1).

19. SK, vol. 2, p. 92 (1603 [Keichō 8].9.4).

20. For discussions of the Chikubushima Lotus Festival, covering both historical and contemporary versions, see Nakajima Seiichi, "Chikubushima rengee," in *Bukkyō gyōji saiji ki: Hachigatsu mandō*, ed. Setouchi Jakuchō, Fujii Masao, and Miyata Noboru (Tokyo: Nihon Aato Sentaa, 1989), pp. 175–84; and TCH, pp. 71–86. The latter also includes a survey of Lotus Festivals at other sites. The earliest documentary reference to the Lotus Festival is thought to be the 977 *Jie Daishi Sōjō shūiden*, which describes but does not name a festival following the procedures of what we now know to be the Lotus Festival. The first appearance of the term "Rengee" in the written record dates to 1299. By the Momoyama period the Lotus Festival was a well-established event (TCH, p. 71). A 1421 document relates, among other information, that the purpose of the Lotus Festival was to offer rites for rain. HAGS, vol. 4, p. 202, CM no. 33.

21. The Lotus Festival is depicted in two known paintings, each of which includes both the bugaku performances and the boat procession. For the earlier painting, preserved in the Tokyo National Museum, see Chapter 1, pp. 41–42 and *Fig. 33*. The second painting, from the Edo period and now in the Museum Yamato Bunkakan, is published in Kageyama, "Chikubushima saireizu." Both paintings are also reproduced in Museum of Modern Art, Shiga and Kyōto Shinbunsha, eds., *Tokubetsuten: Ōmi hakkei: Kokoku fūkeiga no seiritsu to tenkai*, cat. nos. 12, 13.

22. For a discussion of the Lotus Festival Benzaiten sculptures, including reproductions of several examples, see TCH, pp. 68–71 and cat. nos. 28, 80–84. Ink inscriptions on the donated Benzaiten sculptures, often giving the date and the names of both patron and sculptor, confirm that at least seven of the extant sculptures predate 1615 (*Fig. 137*). Six of these date to 1565, 1566, 1605, 1609, 1613, 1614, and one is dated to the Keichō era (1596–1615).

23. The *Rengee tōyaku kadofumi roku* lists the sponsors from as early as 1561 through 1853, but many of the years prior to 1645 are unrecorded, indicating that it was only in the mid-seventeenth century that regular record-keeping began. In the *Rengee tōyaku kadofumi roku* sponsors are recorded in the year they were selected, that is, the year before their actual service. For a discussion of this document, see TCH, cat. no. 89. The pre-1645 information was likely compiled from surviving documents reporting the selection of the sponsors for the com-

ing Lotus Festival and from the inscriptions on Benzaiten sculptures. Four pre-seventeenth-century documents recording the selection of sponsors for the Chikubushima Lotus Festival are known, dating to 1484, 1501, 1508, and 1552. For a discussion of these documents, as well as others from the Edo period, and transcriptions of the 1484 and 1508 examples, see *TCH*, pp. 134–35, cat. nos. 92–97. The 1508 example is also published in *HAGS*, vol. 4, pp. 213–14, *CM* no. 84.

24. *TCH*, p. 71.

25. This letter is transcribed and discussed in *TCH*, cat. no. 88. It is also published in *HAGS*, vol. 4, p. 248, *CM* no. 205. For a full translation, see Appendix, document 27.

26. Chikubushima was within the immediate area affected by the violence spinning out from the Battle of Sekigahara. Ieyasu or his vassals issued numerous proclamations protecting villages and religious complexes near the areas of hostilities, many dated to 9.16, the day after the battle, and addressed to places in northern Ōmi, including Chikubushima. These proclamations warned troops not to pillage or assault the local populations. Typical of most of the extant examples, the Chikubushima version comprises three articles; it prohibits military violence, arson, and general irresponsible behavior. The document, known in an Edo-period copy, is published in *HAGS*, vol. 4, p. 245, *CM* no. 197. For a translation, see Appendix, document 28.

For other examples of the post-Sekigahara proclamations, see Nakamura Kōya, *Tokugawa Ieyasu monjo no kenkyū*, 4 vols. (Tokyo: Nihon Gakujutsu Shinkōkai, 1958–1971), vol. 2, pp. 700–710; and Tokugawa Yoshinobu, *Shinshū Tokugawa Ieyasu monjo no kenkyū* (Tokyo: Tokugawa Reimeikai, 1983), pp. 287–90. Most of the non-Chikubushima documents prohibit the appropriation of agricultural products from fields. The absence of such a statement in the Chikubushima proclamation—where it is replaced with the prohibition of "irresponsible" behavior—reflects the entirely nonagricultural nature of the activities on the island.

27. Tonda Kyūzaemon's letter, which he sent from Fushimi Castle, is published in *HAGS*, vol. 4, p. 248, *CM* no. 206. For a translation, see Appendix, document 29.

28. For a brief biography of Tanaka Yoshimasa, see *TCH*, pp. 130–31.

29. See Elison, "Hideyoshi, the Bountiful Minister," pp. 241–44.

30. *Tokitsune Kyō ki*, vol. 11, pp. 136–37 (1601 [Keichō 6].8.21). This was the second day of a two-day presentation of Nō dramas.

31. *RN*, vol. 4, p. 263 (1605 [Keichō 10].8.26).

32. *SK*, vol. 2, p. 248 (1606 [Keichō 11].8.19); *SK*, vol. 3, p. 22 (1607 [Keichō 12].4.19).

33. The *Nō no tomechō* covers a period from 1588 through 1615. I examined the unpublished manuscript preserved in Kyoto University.

34. The drama is widely published in Japanese, including Koyama Hiroshi, Satō Kikuo, and Satō Ken'ichirō, eds., *Yōkyokushū* 1, vol. 33 of *Nihon koten bungaku zenshū* (Tokyo: Shōgakukan, 1973), pp. 87–96. A recent translation of *Chikubushima* into English is found in Royall Tyler, ed. and trans., *Japanese Nō Dramas* (New York: Penguin Books, 1992), pp. 58–67. My translations are based on both of the above texts. Royall Tyler includes a discussion of the play in his essay, "'The Path of My Mountain': Buddhism in Nō," in *Flowing Traces: Buddhism in the Literary and Visual Arts of Japan*, ed. James H. Sanford, William R. LaFleur, and Masatoshi Nagatomi (Princeton: Princeton University Press, 1992), pp. 149–79.

35. The interlude is known as the *aikyōgen*, a brief, often comical scene dividing the main drama into two acts.

36. *GJN*, vol. 2, pp. 183–87 (1600 [Keichō 5].6.26)

37. *GJN*, vol. 2, p. 186 (1600 [Keichō 5].6.26).

38. For this widely-quoted passage, see *SK*, vol. 2, p. 25 (1602 [Keichō 7].6.11). "Today the dismantling of the Toyokuni Gokuraku Gate was begun, as it is to be donated to Chikubushima by [Ieyasu]. A new shrine gate was ordered by [Hideyori]." Discussed also in Coaldrake, "Gateways of Power: Edo Architecture and Tokugawa Authority 1603–1651," pp. 174–76.

39. For a review in English of Ieyasu's post-Sekigahara land policies, see Hall, *Early Modern Japan*, pp. 144–45.

40. For a recent discussion of Ieyasu's 1602 survey in Ōmi, see Fujita, "Keichō nana nen Ōmi no kuni kenchi o megutte," pp. 157–84.

41. The document, dated to 1603 [Keichō 8].7.19, is published in *HAGS*, vol. 4, pp. 247–48, *CM* no. 203. For a translation, see Appendix, document 30.

42. See above, p. 75.

43. The document, dated to 1603 [Keichō 8].3.10, is published in *HAGS*, vol. 4, p. 246, *CM* no. 200. For a complete translation, see Appendix, document 31.

44. Two letters refer to the sixteen koku, six shō matter, dated to 1603 [Keichō 8].5.15 and 1603 [Keichō 8].10.16. They are published in *HAGS*, vol. 4, pp. 247–48, *CM* nos. 202, 204. For translations, see Appendix, documents 32, 33. The above passage is quoted from the earlier letter.

45. A letter noting a gift of sake and referring specifically to this matter, dated 5.15, is published in *HAGS*, vol. 4, p. 246, *CM* no. 201. For a translation, see Appendix, document 34.

46. The document is dated to 1613 [Keichō 18].4.10 and published in *HAGS*, vol. 4, p. 249, *CM* no. 209. For a translation, see Appendix, document 35.

47. The documents are dated to 1617 [Genna 3].7.21 and 1636 [Kan'ei 13].11.9, respectively, and published in *HAGS*, vol. 4, pp. 249–50, *CM* nos. 210, 211. For translations, see Appendix, documents 36, 37.

48. This placard is now preserved in the Treasure House of Hōgonji, also on Chikubushima. When it was taken out of the Tsukubusuma Main Hall, where it would normally be preserved, is not recorded; I suspect this occurred during the early Meiji period, when all traces of evidence linking the building to Benzaiten were removed. It is reproduced and transcribed in *TCH*, cat. no. 52; reproduced in *KTJHSKH*, pl. 36 (the small placard at the left); and transcribed in Sakurai Toshio, "Tsukubusuma Jinja Honden," p. 47, n. 12, no. 1.

49. This placard is preserved in the Treasure House on Chikubushima. It is reproduced and transcribed in *TCH*, cat. no. 53, and transcribed in *HAGS*, vol. 4, p. 615. The *HAGS* transcription refers to this placard as "supplementary" to the one which specifies Benzaiten, suggesting that the two formed a pair and that both refer to the Tsukubusuma Main Hall. The different dates and lack of specificity in the contents, however, argue against such a conclusion; it was more likely written for another building included in this project. It is unknown when the placard was removed from its building and under what circumstances.

50. This placard, preserved in the Treasure House on Chikubushima, is widely published. It is reproduced and transcribed in *TCH*, cat. no. 54; and in *KTJHSKH*, pl. 36 (the right-hand large placard shows the front and the left-hand large placard the reverse); it is transcribed in *HAGS*, vol. 4, pp. 616–17, and Sakurai Toshio, "Tsukubusuma Jinja Honden," p. 47, n. 12, no. 2. For a translation, see Appendix, document 39.

51. The document, dated only to the twentieth day, is published in *HAGS*, vol. 4, pp. 245–46, *CM* no. 198. For a translation, see Appendix, document 38.

52. The apocryphal nature of the story is evident from the dates of the supposed participants: Gyōki and Shōmu preceded Yoshika by about a century. Much the same story is related after an early-seventeenth century visit to Chikubushima, described in an entry in the *RN*, vol. 5, pp. 247–48 (1626 [Kan'ei 3].5.1). Also remarked upon in that entry are several treasures of Chikubushima, including a drum that Nobunaga had earlier inquired about (pp. 64–65), and the great beauty of the island setting.

53. The most complete compilation of the documentary materials related to these projects is Morioka Eiichi, "Katagiri Katsumoto no Kita Ōmi ni okeru jisha fukkō," *Shiritsu Nagahamajō Rekishi Hakubutsukan nenpō*, no. 7 (April 1998), pp. 69–75.

54. I thank Kimoto Kakusen, the Head Priest of Jōshinji, for allowing me to study the objects and documents preserved at the temple.

55. It is presently unclear whether the shrine, now lost, was part of the Jōshinji complex or occupied another site in Kinomoto.

56. The placards that detail Hideyori's involvement with the Shirahige project are transcribed in National Museum of Japanese History, ed., "*Hibunken shiryō no kisoteki kenkyū* (*munafuda*)" *hōkokusho, Kinki hen 1*, pp. 120–22; "Ko kenchiku meibun shū," pt. 5, pp. 91–94.

57. The letter, dated to the eighth day of the sixth month, is published in *HAGS*, vol. 4, p. 269, *Katagiri monjo* no. 1.

58. Gien records the moves of many structures, including—in addition to the ones we will discuss below—a guest hall from Yariyama; *GJN*, vol. 1, pp. 316–19 (1598 [Keichō 3].11.4–11.23). For important discussions of the movement of buildings, see Nishi Kazuo, *Kenchikushi kenkyū no shinshiten 1: Kenchiku to shōhekiga* (Tokyo: Chūō Kōron Bijutsu Shuppan, 1999).

59. Ōkuwa, "Tenshōji no sōken, chūzetsu kara Daibutsu zōei e," pp. 35–38.

60. For a discussion of this bridge's history at Osaka Castle, see Kitagawa Hiroshi, "Ōsaka fuyu no jin zu byōbu, natsu no jin zu byōbu ni egakareta Ōsakajō: Gokurakubashi no kentō," in *Sengoku gassen zu byōbu no sekai*, ed. Wakayama Prefectural Museum (Wakayama: Wakayama Prefectural Museum, 1997), pp. 13–17.

61. *GJN*, 1606 [Keichō 11].10.1; cited in Kimura, "Toyotomi Hideyori no sakuji taisei ni tsuite," p. 189.

62. The source of these pedigrees is unclear, though post-Edo-period Kyoto guidebooks sometimes tout buildings as having been located originally at either Jurakutei or Fushimi Castle. The 1915 guidebook *Kyōtobō mokushi, Shimogyō, ken*, for example, states that the Hiunkaku was moved from Jurakutei; *Kyōtobō mokushi, Shimogyō, ken*, vol. 17 of *Shinshū Kyōto sōsho* (Kyoto: Kōsaisha, 1969), pp. 208–9. Kitagawa Hiroshi has reasonably surmised, in conversation, that the construction of these pedi-

grees in the Meiji and Taishō periods probably resulted from the resurrection of interest in the Toyotomi legacy at that time, after 250 years of suppression by the Tokugawa during the Edo period.

63. *GJN,* vol. 1, p. 73 (1596 [Bunroku 5].9.19).

64. *Kyōto no rekishi,* vol. 4, p. 332.

65. Loraine Kuck, *The World of the Japanese Garden, from Chinese Origins to Modern Landscape Art* (reprint, with corrections, New York, Tokyo: Weatherhill, 1980), p. 182.

66. *GJN,* vol. 2, p. 58 (1598 [Keichō 3].11.18).

67. Hideyoshi began Fushimi Castle in 1592. Destroyed during the 1596 earthquake, it was rebuilt by the following year. For the history of Fushimi Castle in the Momoyama period, see Kii Gun Yakusho and Fushimi Chō Yakuba, eds., *Kyōto Fu Kii Gun shi, Fushimi Chō shi* (1915, 1929; reprint, Kyoto: Rinsen Shoten, 1972), pp. 94–113; and Sakurai Narihiro, *Toyotomi Hideyoshi no kyojō* (Tokyo: Nihon Jōkaku Shiryōkan Shuppankai, 1970).

68. *GJN,* vol. 2, pp. 271–72 (1601 [Keichō 6].3.21).

69. See Tendaishū Jimonha Goonki Jimukyoku, ed., *Onjōji no kenkyū* (Ōtsu: Tendaishū Jimonha Goonki Jimukyoku, 1931; reprint, Kyoto: Shibunkaku Shuppan, 1978), pp. 589–92.

70. *GJN,* vol. 2, p. 272 (1601 [Keichō 6].3.23).

71. The *Daigoji shin yōroku,* a record of Daigoji history compiled by Gien, contains detailed information on the buildings there, including two Mieidō, one in the upper precinct of the temple and another in the lower precinct; see Gien, *Daigoji shin yōroku,* ed. Daigoji Bunkazai Kenkyūjo, 2 vols. (Tokyo: Hōzōkan, 1991). The Mieidō in the upper precinct, rebuilt after a fire in 1361, apparently remained in place until it burned again in 1605 (Gien, *Daigoji shin yōroku,* vol. 1, pp. 215–18). For the discussion of the Mieidō in the lower precinct, see Gien, *Daigoji shin yōroku,* vol. 1, pp. 389–95.

72. For a discussion of this widely published vessel, see Gotō Bijutsukan Gakugeibu, ed., *Yamanoue no Sōji ki: Tenshō jūyon nen no me,* p. 55.

73. Tanaka Hiromi, ed., "Honkoku *Yamanoue no Sōji ki* Takeda ke otsubon," p. 95.

74. This mizusashi is listed in the Owari Ke Bon *Sunpu onbunbutsu ondōguchō,* an inventory written in 1616–1618, soon after Ieyasu's death, recording those of Ieyasu's possessions that passed into the hands of Tokugawa Yoshinao (1600–1650), Ieyasu's ninth son and the first-generation head of the Tokugawa branch family in Owari; it remained in the family into recent times, when it was deposited in the Tokugawa Art Museum. See Tokugawa Art Museum, ed., *Tokugawa Ieyasu tanjō yonhyaku gojū nen kinen: Ieyasu no isan—Sunpu onbunbutsu* (Nagoya: Tokugawa Art Museum; Mito: Tokugawa Museum, 1992), p. 237.

75. This gathering, hosted by Hideyoshi on 1582 [Tenshō 10].1.18, is recorded in the tea diary of Tsuda Sōgyū (d. 1591), who was a guest along with Yamanoue no Sōji; see *Tennōjiya kaiki,* ed. Nagashima Fukutarō, in *Chado koten zenshū,* ed. Sen Sōshitsu (Kyoto: Tankōsha, 1959), vol. 7, p. 357.

76. For this gathering, recorded in Imai Sōkyū's tea diary and held on 1582 [Tenshō 11].1.5, see Imai Sōkyū, *Imai Sōkyū chanoyu nikki nukigaki,* ed. Nagashima Fukutarō, in *Chadō koten zenshū,* ed. Sen Sōshitsu (Kyoto: Tankō Shinsha, 1961), vol. 10, p. 35. For a discussion of Nobunaga, Imai Sōkyū, and the other Sakai merchants, see Watsky, "Commerce, Politics, and Tea: The Career of Imai Sōkyū."

77. Tanaka Hiromi, ed., "Honkoku *Yamanoue no Sōji ki* Takeda ke otsubon," p. 94.

78. The *Yamanoue no Sōji ki* records two Xutang calligraphies owned by Hideyoshi, both famous, though one of them is called "tenka ichi no meibutsu," or a meibutsu that is number one in the realm; it is unclear which of the two Hideyoshi displayed on this occasion. Tanaka Hiromi, ed., "Honkoku *Yamanoue no Sōji ki* Takeda ke otsubon," p. 100.

79. Tanaka Hiromi, ed., "Honkoku *Yamanoue no Sōji ki* Takeda ke otsubon," p. 88. This jar eventually entered Ieyasu's collection and then, like Imogashira, passed to the Owari Tokugawa family and the Tokugawa Art Museum; see Tokugawa Art Museum, ed., *Tokugawa Ieyasu tanjō yonhyaku gojū nen kinen: Ieyasu no isan—Sunpu onbunbutsu,* p. 234.

80. For the entry in the reprint of the dictionary, see Doi Tadao, ed., *Vocabvlario da Lingoa de Iapam, Nippo jisho,* p. 524; for the modern Japanese translation, see Doi, Morita, and Chōnan, eds., *Hōyaku Nippo jisho,* p. 665.

81. Kyoto National Museum, *Kōdaiji makie,* pp. 6–8; William Harry Samonides, "The Kōami Family of Maki-e Lacquerers" (Ph.D. diss., Harvard University, 1991), pp. 160–68; Samonides, "Patronizing Images: Kōdai-in and Toyotomi Hideyoshi at Kōdaiji," pp. 110–12.

82. Hirai Toshiyuki, an architecture specialist with the Cultural Preservation Office of Kyoto, dated the notches on the ebikōryō to the 1936–1937 project. I am grateful to him for pointing this out to me.

83. Not all of the moya's decoration is accounted for: present evidence does not reveal what happened to some portions of the fuyō and chrysanthemum carvings; even today, some of the carvings are ill-attached to their supports and fragments occasionally fall off, suggesting that some of the carvings were

lost through natural attrition over time, or perhaps during the move from Kyoto to Chikubushima.

84. One of the most interesting and well documented examples of the reuse of building parts, although much more recent than Chikubushima's hall (dating to the nineteenth century), is Matsuura Takeshirō's One-Mat Room of 1886, composed of numerous pieces of wood gathered from ancient sacred and secular buildings from across Japan; see Henry D. Smith, II, *Taizansō and the One-Mat Room (Taizansō: Matsuura Takeshirō no ichijōjiki no sekai)* (Tokyo: Hachiro Yuasa Memorial Museum, International Christian University, 1993).

85. Sasaki, "Chikubushima ni okeru shinbutsu bunri ni tsuite," p. 6. As part of its effort to make the building a Shinto shrine, the government responded to this inventory—which clearly showed the building to be Buddhist—with a directive for the disposal of the various objects: the Benzaiten sculpture was to be relegated to the side rear, the mirror replaced, the five-piece altar set removed, the gong replaced with bells, and the plaque replaced with one that read "Tsukubusuma Shrine." Thus was the Buddhist hall transformed into a Shinto shrine.

86. For examination of a Buddhist statue in which the assemblage of originally unrelated parts generated new meaning, see Gregory P. Levine, "Switching Sites and Identities: The Founder's Statue at the Buddhist Temple Kōrin'in," *The Art Bulletin* 83, no. 1 (March 2001), pp. 72–104.

Epilogue

1. Kaempfer, *The History of Japan, Together with a Description of the Kingdom of Siam, 1690–92,* vol. 1 pp. 163–64. I thank Christine Guth for alerting me to Kaempfer's reference to Chikubushima.

2. For a discussion of the expansion of Edo in the first half of the seventeenth century, see Coaldrake, "Gateways of Power: Edo Architecture and Tokugawa Authority 1603–1651," pp. 26–46.

3. For a good collection of such screens, see Suwa Haruo and Naitō Akira, eds., *Edozu byōbu* (Tokyo: Mainichi Shinbunsha, 1972).

4. The *Kanmei nikki* is a record of matters concerning the Tokugawa shogunate from 1624 to 1657. Cited in Tōkyō To Daitō Kuyakusho, *Daitō Ku shi: Enkakuhen* (Tokyo: Tōkyō To Daitō Kuyakusho, 1966), p. 529.

5. See Kan'eiji, ed., *Jigen Daishi zenshū,* 2 vols., 1916 (reprint, Tokyo: Kokusho Kankōkai, 1976), vol. 2, 1 pp. 13–14. Jigen Daishi was Tenkai's posthumous honorific.

6. Published in National Museum of Japanese History, ed., *Egakareta Edo* (Sakura: National Museum of Japanese History, 1991), cat. no. 11.

7. A representation of Chikubushima was also found in Edo Castle. The castle was filled with Kano workshop paintings of a great variety of subjects; the walls of one space were filled with representations of the famous places of Ōmi, among them Chikubushima. The paintings are now preserved only in nineteenth-century copies; see Tokugawa Art Museum, ed., *Shōgun no goten: Edojō shōhekiga no shitae* (Nagoya: Tokugawa Art Museum, 1988), cat. no. 48–1.

8. This map was published by Ishikawa Ryūsen. For an excellent discussion of Ishikawa Ryūsen's maps and the broader issues of Tokugawa cartography, see Marcia Yonemoto, "The 'Spatial Vernacular' in Tokugawa Maps," *The Journal of Asian Studies* 59, no. 3 (August 2000), pp. 647–66.

9. That the relationship between these two cities was seen to be analogous is well reflected in a pair of six-fold screens that depicts the cities of Kyoto and Edo in the mid-seventeenth century, one city on each screen. The paintings show each city primarily as a grid of streets and waterways centered around the bastions of Tokugawa rule: Nijō Castle in Kyoto and Edo Castle in Edo. Only a limited number of sites are pictorially represented; on the Edo screen, these include Edo Castle, Mount Fuji, and, at the far right of the screen, Shinobazu Pond and its replicated island. The prominence of the pond and island in this screen is further evidence of the importance of the replication project. The screens are reproduced in Tokyo Metropolitan Edo-Tokyo Museum, ed., *Edo Tōkyō Hakubutsukan: Sōgō annai* (Tokyo: Edo Tōkyō Rekishi Zaidan, 1993), pls. 1, 2; they are briefly discussed on p. 21.

10. For Tokugawa memorial architecture, see Coaldrake, *Architecture and Authority in Japan,* pp. 163–92; for the deification of Ieyasu, see Boot, "The Death of a Shogun: Deification in Early Modern Japan."

11. For a thorough analysis of the Yōmeimon, and more broadly of the Tōshōgū precincts, see Karen M. Gerhart, *The Eyes of Power: Art and Early Tokugawa Authority* (Honolulu: University of Hawai'i Press, 1999), pp. 73–105.

Appendix

Note to reader: Documents 1–38 are translations of *Chikubushima monjo* documents referred to in the text. Most are published in volume 4 of *Higashi Asai Gun shi,* as indicated. Japanese characters are inserted into the translations for some terms and for most names; the characters are from the *Higashi Asai Gun shi* transcriptions, with a few amendments made after examination of the original documents. Documents 19,23, and 26 are unpublished and transcribed in full. Document 39 is a translation of the 1603.6 Chikubushima ridgepole placard discussed in Chapter 6.

DOCUMENT 1 Genki 1 [1570].7.25
Higashi Asai Gun shi, Chikubushima monjo no. 157

With regard to the 'Buddha fields' [*butsuden* 仏田], various donations, dormitory lands, dormitory-related domains, and purchased land [*baitokubun* 買得分] of this temple, the matter of unfair special taxes should be laid out as it has been up to now. Regarding the question of Hayasaki 早崎 Village, as for [the market activities] in front of the gate[1] the various matters should be carried out in accordance with the regulations of this temple. In addition, regarding such matters as the Tennyo 天女 rituals [*goku* 御供][2] and transportation boats [*tsūsen* 通船], they should be followed as before without deviation. It is so commanded.

[To] Chikubushima Sōchū 竹生嶋惣中 [From] Kinoshita Tōkichirō 木下藤吉郎
Hideyoshi 秀吉 (cipher)

DOCUMENT 2 10.12
Higashi Asai Gun shi, Chikubushima monjo no. 123

Your temple went up in flames, and I am beyond words. I fear you suffered much. On that occasion, you made it your first priority to save my belongings. You were truly compassionate and, in such a case, it is difficult to express my gratitude. Of the seven [objects that were] in the *goten* 御殿, four have arrived. Without fail, I will duly express [my indebtedness in a proper manner]. For now, I offer my thanks. Respectfully conveyed.

[To] Senhōbō 千宝坊 [From] Asai Sahyōe no Jō 淺井左兵衛尉
Gobōchū 御坊中 Hisamasa 久政 (cipher)

DOCUMENT 3 8.25
Higashi Asai Gun shi, Chikubushima monjo no. 159

Members of our naval forces took two transportation boats [*kayoibune* 通舟] from Hayasaki Village. Accordingly, I have ordered that [the boats] be returned. You took the trouble of sending cask[s of sake] and 20 *hiki* 疋 [of money]. I am humbly [grateful] for your frequent kindnesses. The details [of these matters] will be discussed with Minbukyō Dono 民部卿殿. Respectfully conveyed.

1. Hayasaki, though on the mainland, is the market area "in front of the gate" for the Chikubushima religious establishment.

2. *Goku* here probably indicates daily rituals, referred to in other documents as *hinogoku;* note in particular that the rituals referred to are those specifically for Tennyo, or Benzaiten. See Ito Futoshi, "Chusei koki ni okeru Ōmi Chikubushima no jiji to shakai," pp. 11–12 for discussion of fifteenth- and sixteenth-century references to *hinogoku.*

[To] Chikubushima 竹生嶋
Sōgobō Onchū 惣御坊御中

[From] Higuchi Saburōhyōe no Jō 樋口三郎兵衛尉
Naofusa 直房 (cipher)

DOCUMENT 4
Higashi Asai Gun shi, Chikubushima monjo no. 163 Genki 4[1573].7.1

The buildings and temple holdings of this temple should [be treated] according to precedent. There should not be even the slightest transgression. Without deviation, [precedent] should be followed energetically and with diligence. Isono Tanba no Kami 磯野丹波守 will report this. It is so commanded.

[To] Chikubushima 竹生嶋
Nengyōji 年行事

[From] Nobunaga 信長
(*Tenka fubu* 天下布武 seal)

DOCUMENT 5
Higashi Asai Gun shi, Chikubushima monjo no. 166 Tenshō 1 [1573].12.21

From this temple Tonosama has received [some] of the courtesy money. There should be no negligence [regarding payment of] the remaining portion. Respectfully conveyed.

[To] Chikubushima 竹生嶋
Nengyōji mairu 年行事まいる

[From] Isotan 磯丹
Kazumasa 員昌 (cipher)

DOCUMENT 6
Higashi Asai Gun shi, Chikubushima monjo no. 165 9.6

The flute named Aoba 青葉 has arrived. It is indeed a *meibutsu* 名物, truly fine. I will keep it for a short while, and after inspecting it, have it returned. I wonder about the circumstances of the donation of this flute to the mountain [i.e., Chikubushima] and who previously owned it. The small flute accompanies it. Please write down what is reliably known of their lineages and send it to me. Also, regarding the small drum [said to have been] owned by Shizuka 静, the makie lacquer design on the body is of thunder. Please take a look at it. Isono 磯野 will discuss this with you. Respectfully submitted.

[To] Chikubushima 竹生嶋
Sōyamachū 惣山中

[From] Nobunaga 信長 (vermilion seal)

DOCUMENT 7
Higashi Asai Gun shi, Chikubushima monjo no. 164 9.6

The flute named Aoba has been delivered to me. It is a *meibutsu.* [I wonder] who owned it in earlier times and according to what circumstances it was donated to Chikubushima. The small flute accompanies it. This [small flute], too, must have a lineage. Inquire carefully and make a written note of the things known [about the flutes], and have [the note] sent to me. Respectfully conveyed.

[To] Isono Tanba no Kami Dono 磯野丹波守殿

[From] Nobunaga 信長 (cipher)

DOCUMENT 8
Higashi Asai Gun shi, Chikubushima monjo no. 182 9.3[3]

The other day Tonosama 殿様 [i.e., Nobunaga] made a visit to the Tennyo 天女 and when he left, he sent a messenger to report to the effect that he saw there were people who sold the subtemple dormitories of your temple. This is not good. Previously, Chikushū 筑州 [i.e. Hideyoshi] was of the same opinion. Hereafter, for such sales, punishment will be administered. In addition, bamboo and trees in the island's forests are being felled too freely. This too is not good. Furthermore, with regard to the subtemple income donated from Hayasaki, people not in residence at the temple should not get a stipend. If there are people who

3. The unstated year is sometime before Nobunaga's death in 1582.6.2.

say they should get [the stipend], stop the matter and report to me. In regard to all [of the above matters Nobunaga] feels most strongly, which I report by way of this letter. Respectfully conveyed.

[To] Chikubushima 竹生嶋
Sōchū 惣中
Godōshukuchū 御同宿中

[From] Bokushinsai 卜眞齋
Nobusada 信貞 (cipher)

DOCUMENT 9
Higashi Asai Gun shi, Chikubushima monjo no. 167 1.23

Regarding the matter of lumber deposited on this island by Bizen 備前 [i.e., Asai Nagamasa], [the lumber] should be passed over without fail. If there are problems, serious repercussions will result. Respectfully conveyed.

[To] Chikubushima 竹生嶋
Jikechū 寺家中

[From] Hashiba Tōkichirō 羽柴藤吉郎
Hideyoshi 秀吉 (cipher)

Tenshō 2 [1574]

By these letters [i.e., documents 9 and 10], all of the lumber was passed over. [The matter] is resolved.
Representative Naihō Tōsuke 内保藤介

DOCUMENT 10
Higashi Asai Gun shi, Chikubushima monjo no. 168 3.22

Regarding the matter of lumber left [on Chikubushima] by Asai Bizen 淺井備前 [Nagamasa], Hatō 羽藤 [i.e., Hideyoshi] has issued a letter [i.e., document 9]. Provide a detailed statement [*chūmon* 注文] and send it. I will report the statement [to Hideyoshi]. The representative who kept [the lumber] from the beginning has been sent. Regarding the matter of the lumber, we will receive it directly.[4] Respectfully conveyed.

Also, I received [the letter] this past first month of the year, but as I was distracted by this and that, there has been this delay and it is only now that I pass on to you [Hideyoshi's letter].

[To] Chikubushima 竹生嶋
Gonengyōji 御年行事
Gobōchū 御坊中

[From] Ishikawa Mokuhyōe no Jō 石川杢兵衛尉
Mitsumasa 光政 (cipher)

Tenshō 2 [1574]

By these letters [i.e., documents 9 and 10], all of the lumber was passed over. [The matter] is resolved.
Representative Naihō Tōsuke 内保藤介

DOCUMENT 11
Higashi Asai Gun shi, Chikubushima monjo no. 169 Tenshō 2 [1574].9.11

I donate 300 *koku* 石 from within Hayasaki District of this county. It should absolutely be a temple contribution. Concerning the above, as before, there should be no negligence as regards the religious services. It is so commanded.

[To] Chikubushima 竹生嶋
Sōchū 衆中

[From] Hashiba Tōkichirō 羽柴藤吉郎
Hideyoshi 秀吉 (cipher)

DOCUMENT 12
Higashi Asai Gun shi, Chikubushima monjo no. 174 12.8

Regarding the matter of the *sairei* 祭礼, we have learned of the details by way of your monk representative and letter. Chikushū 筑州 [i.e., Hideyoshi] is in Gifu. On his return to the castle [in Naga-

4. The meaning of these two sentences is unclear.

hama], we will report this to him. Regarding the matters of Buddhist and Shinto *sairei* and other religious affairs, [Hideyoshi] generally accedes to precedent. Accordingly, we hear how things have been done until now, and follow that. Respectfully conveyed.

[To] Chikubushima 竹生嶋
Nengyōji 年行事
Gobōgochū 御坊御中

[From]: [Kuwayama 桑山] Shigekatsu 重勝(cipher)
[Bokushinsai 卜眞齋] Nobusada 信貞 (cipher)

DOCUMENT 13
Higashi Asai Gun shi, Chikubushima monjo no. 181 Intercalary 8.15

The gift of *shii* [*take* mushrooms] and *konbu* seaweed arrived. I am pleased. I will tell Ishida Yasō 石田彌三.

[To] Chikubushima Sōchū 竹生嶋惣中 [From] (Hideyoshi vermilion seal)

DOCUMENT 14
Higashi Asai Gun shi, Chikubushima monjo no. 192 1.15

The [gifts] for New Year's greetings have arrived. I am pleased. Ishida Yasō 石田彌三 will speak [to you directly of my thanks].

[To] Chikubushima 竹生嶋
Sōchū 惣中

[From] (Hideyoshi vermilion seal)

DOCUMENT 15
Higashi Asai Gun shi, Chikubushima monjo no. 188 1.16

The New Year's gift of prayer *kanju* 巻数 and 200 *hiki* arrived. I am pleased. Kinoshita Hansuke 木下半介 will report [to you directly of my thanks].

[To] Chikubushima Sōchū 竹生嶋惣中 [From] (Hideyoshi vermilion seal)

DOCUMENT 16
Higashi Asai Gun shi, Chikubushima monjo no. 193 1.23

The *kanju, konbu* seaweed, and stick of skewered persimmons for the New Year's greetings have arrived. I am pleased. Also, Kinoshita Hansuke 木下半介 will speak [to you directly of my thanks].

[To] Hōgonji 寶厳寺 [From] (Hideyoshi vermilion seal)

DOCUMENT 17
Higashi Asai Gun shi, Chikubushima monjo no. 189 1.16

The New Year's gift of prayer *kanju* and 200 *hiki* were shown [to Hideyoshi] just as they were sent. I have received the vermilion seal [i.e., document 19] and forward it to you. Next, we thank you for the 30 *hiki.* Respectfully conveyed. The end.

[To] Chikubushima Sōchū 竹生嶋惣中
Gobōchū 御坊中

[From] Kihansuke 木半介
[Kinoshita Yoshitaka 木下吉隆] (cipher)

DOCUMENT 18
Higashi Asai Gun shi, Chikubushima monjo no. 180 Tenshō 11 [1583].3

Prohibited: [in] Ōmi Province, Asai County, Hayasaki
<1> Disruption or violence by anyone with my military forces, high or low.
<2> Tearing down buildings, arson, and cutting down [requisitioning] *mugi*, etc.
<3> Bothering *jigenin* 地下人 without cause.

The above actions are strictly prohibited. Offenders will be promptly punished. By this command, it is so conveyed.

[From] Chikuzen no Kami 筑前守 (cipher)

DOCUMENT 19

Unpublished; original document preserved at the Nagahama Castle Historical Museum — Tenshō 19 [1591].4.23

於江州淺井郡早崎浦内合三百石事令寄附候訖
天正十九四月廿三日

[To] 竹生嶋 — [From] (Hideyoshi 秀吉 vermilion seal)

From within Hayasaki of Asai County in Ōmi Province, I donate a total of 300 *koku.*

[To] Chikubushima — [From] (Hideyoshi vermilion seal)

DOCUMENT 20

Higashi Asai Gun shi, Chikubushima monjo no. 190 — Tenshō 19 [1591].3.29

I hear that [Hideyoshi] will make a donation to this temple of 300 *koku* from within Hayasaki. Regarding this, it includes three *tan dai*[5] 反大 from Masuda ますた district, and so I enter it into our record book. The above three *tan* will be presented as part of the Hayasaki [total]. Please rest assured. Respectfully conveyed.

[To] Chikubushima 竹生嶋
Gojichū 御寺中
Gobōchū 御坊中

[From] Miyagi Chōjirō 宮木長次郎
Moritoyo 盛豐 (cipher)

DOCUMENT 21

Higashi Asai Gun shi, Chikubushima monjo no. 185 — 11.4

Regarding the matter of Benzaiten *mitarashi* reeds, following precedent, Hideyoshi will without doubt make a donation for prayer. Respectfully conveyed.

[To] Chikubushima 竹生嶋
Sōyama mairu 惣山参
Gobōchū 御坊中

[From]: Hayasaki Heisō 早崎平三
Iehisa 家久 (cipher)
Kannonji 観音寺
Kenchin 賢珍 (cipher)

DOCUMENT 22

Higashi Asai Gun shi, Chikubushima monjo no. 187 — 7.20

Shōkokusama 相國様 [i.e., Hideyoshi] has returned [to Osaka], and your monk messengers and the three hundred *hiki* have arrived. Considering the distance, time, and various other things, I expect it was quite troublesome. I have consulted with Itasa 伊太左 [i.e., Itō Tarōzaemon Hidemori 伊藤太郎左衛門秀盛] and [your letter and money] have been presented to [Hideyoshi]. The results will be conveyed to you by Kisshōbō 吉祥坊. I believe you will be satisfied, which is only right. I have also looked through the series of official documents, and was indeed surprised. I want [Hideyoshi] to be made aware of this, but on the twenty-third he will be going to Kyoto. Because he was long at the battle camp, [Hideyoshi] will go immediately to Kyoto and so I will be thoroughly engaged with both public and private matters. Soon thereafter [Hideyoshi] will go [to Osaka], and at that time I will pursue [this matter]. I am aware of the matter regarding the Rengee 蓮花会 and the letter to Asai County. It is a simple matter [to send the letter]. As I have said before, I have aged. I cannot perform my duties

5. *Dai* means "two thirds of one *tan*"; the total discussed here, then, is three and two-thirds *tan.*

as I have in the past and am refraining from engaging myself in things. I will, however, exert myself [on your behalf]. We should not be in the least negligent. The matter of the temple-donation land frequently affected by water damage is disturbing. I will address this concretely with Umemotobō 梅本坊, and so will not write much here. Respectfully conveyed.

In closing, we would like to thank you for taking the trouble to send us twenty *hiki.* We are very grateful indeed. In the future, though, this type of consideration is not necessary. We will report the details to your two messengers as I cannot, at this busy time, write everything in a letter.

[To] Chikubushima 竹生嶋
Gosōchū 御惣中
Gohō 御報

[From] Bokushinsai 卜眞齋
Nobusada 信貞 (cipher)

DOCUMENT 23

Unpublished; original document preserved at the Nagahama Castle Historical Museum

7.21

御状并鳥目三十疋被懸御意候御懇切之段過至極候殊

相國様へ御音信則卜真申合披露申候所御気嫌能納申候於拙者令満足候然者御寺之儀代々芳書拝見申候
一段殊勝ニ存候然間卜真候申合　御めにかけ可申候と存候◇さま御宝物なとも御座候て一両種被相副
被懸御目ニ候て可燃存候　相國様廿三日ニ被成御上洛候やかて可被成御下向候間其砌御使僧今一人も
被相加於大坂少御手間入申候共以御気嫌申上候此刻被入御精　御書御頂戴候て可燃存候不可有御由断
候萬事書中ニハ難聞候条於様子ハ吉祥坊へ申含候恐惶謹言
尚以蓮花会之儀者右之段相調候者其上を以折帋相認可進之候此段ハ両一日之御事候并本堂御建立之儀
モ懇ニ吉祥坊へ申渡候先々当座相調申様ニ可燃候ハんと存計候以上

七月廿一日
[To] 竹生嶋
御寺家中
御報

[From] 伊太左
秀盛 (cipher)

You took the consideration to send us a letter as well as thirty[6] *hiki* of *chōmoku.* We are very thankful for your kindness. Regarding your letter to Shōkokusama [i.e., Hideyoshi], after consulting with Bokushin[sai], I submitted it to him and he accepted it in a good mood. I was very pleased. Accordingly, regarding the matter of the temple, we looked at the successive letters; they are very impressive. I spoke with Bokushin[sai] Kō, and we think it is best to submit [the letters to Hideyoshi].—I think that the treasures, etc., also should be to shown [to Hideyoshi], along with the accompanying *ryōshu.* Shōkokusama will go to Kyoto on the twenty-third. Soon he will return [to Osaka]; at that time, send one more monk-messenger, and at Osaka, even if it takes some negotiations, approach him when he is in good spirits and make every effort to get the *onsho.*[7] There should be no negligence. It is difficult to convey everything in a letter, so about the details, I have spoken to Kisshōbo. Respectfully conveyed.

Regarding the matter of the Rengee, when the above matter is completed, at that time I will inform you by letter in a few days. Furthermore, regarding the construction of the Hondō, this also I have discussed in detail with Kisshōbo.

[To] Chikubushima
Gojikechū
Gohō

[From] Itasa
Hidemori (cipher)

6. This may be a mistake for three hundred.
7. The *onsho* may refer to a vermilion-seal document.

DOCUMENT 24
Higashi Asai Gun shi, Chikubushima monjo no. 176 4.16

I am grateful for your courteous letter. Regarding the matter of the Hayasaki portion [of income] not yet paid, that the farmers have been negligent, you must be troubled. I was not aware earlier and did not say anything, causing you much trouble. Hereafter, if there is such negligence you should inform me. I will take care of it quickly. I will discuss the details with your envoy. Respectfully conveyed.

In closing, I am thankful for your taking the trouble to generously send the cask [of *sake*] and fish. . . . I express my gratitude for this.

[To] Shima Nengyōji 嶋年行寺
Mairu gohenpō 参御返報

[From] [Itō] Hidemori [伊藤] 秀盛
(cipher)

DOCUMENT 25
Higashi Asai Gun shi, Chikubushima monjo no. 177 1.6

I reported the details this past winter and received your letter. Even after repeated inquiries, Hideyoshi's thoughts remain as we reported them last winter, so it would have been difficult to ask again. However, as Kuwayama 桑山 reports the communications [between you and Hideyoshi], in regards to your concerns, you should ask by way of Kuwashū 桑修. We too will give it some thought. Hideyoshi recently took healing baths. In addition, the visit of Bessho Magoemon 別所孫右衛門 of Banshū 播州, the respected guest from another province, distracts us greatly, so in any case we will not discuss the above matter anytime soon. Regarding the matter of the Ōtani 大谷 area, we haven't seen that person. Last winter you made a request, and you spoke to us.[8] Respectfully conveyed. As I write in haste, I cannot go into detail. The end.

[To] Chikubushima 竹生嶋
Nengyōji 年行事
Gohō 御報

[From] Bokushin[sai] 卜眞 [齋] (cipher)

DOCUMENT 26
Unpublished; original document preserved at the Nagahama Castle Historical Museum 8.3

今度若公様於御本復者最前之御立願米可令社納候其上重而可有五十石御奉加之由被仰出候条於神前可被抽懇祈事専用候無油断可有祈念候恐々謹言
為当座初花三百疋被遣候以上
八月三

[To] 竹生嶋惣中

[From]: 増田右衛門尉
長盛 (cipher)
小出播磨守
秀政 (cipher)
伊藤加賀守
秀盛 (cipher)
寺沢越中守
弘政 (cipher)
石川伊賀守
光重 (cipher)
民部卿法印
玄以 (cipher)

8. The meaning of these two sentences is unclear.

If Wakagimi recovers, a donation of *goryūganmai* [rice for rituals] will be made. In addition, furthermore, [Hideyoshi] proclaimed that there will be a donation of fifty *koku.* Saving-prayers should be conducted before the deity. Without negligence there should be prayer. Respectfully conveyed.

For the time being, three hundred *hiki* will be sent.

[To] Chikubushima Sōchū

[From]: Mashita Yuemon no Jō
Nagamori (cipher)
Koide Harima no Kami
Hidemasa (cipher)
Itō Kaga no Kami
Hidemori (cipher)
Terasawa Etchū no Kami
Hiromasa (cipher)
Ishikawa Iga no Kami
Mitsushige (cipher)
Minbukyō Hōin
Gen'i (cipher)

DOCUMENT 27

Higashi Asai Gun shi, Chikubushima monjo no. 205 Keichō 9 [1604].5.12

In accordance with the vows I fervently offered several years ago in [1600] when I made a pilgrimage [to Chikubushima], I should like the customary *shinji* 神事 of Chikubushima, in the sixth month of 1605, to be conducted as prayer rituals for us, husband and wife. For this purpose, we will send 100 *koku* of rice. Tonda Kyūzaemon 富田久左衛門 will speak to you.

[To] Chikubushima 竹生嶋
Jōgyōin 常教[行]院
Konzōbō 金藏坊
Dōji Sōchū 同寺惣中

[From] Tanaka Chikugo no Kami 田中筑後守
Yoshimasa 吉政 (cipher)

DOCUMENT 28

Higashi Asai Gun shi, Chikubushima monjo no. 197 Keichō 5 [1600].9.16

Prohibited: [in] Chikubushima
<1> Anyone with the military, high or low, causing disruption or violence.
<2> Arson.
<3> Irresponsible actions.
Anyone who disobeys the above prohibitions should be immediately reported. It is so commanded.

[From] Tanaka Hyōbu Shōyū 田中兵部少輔

DOCUMENT 29

Higashi Asai Gun shi, Chikubushima monjo no. 206 たつノ [1604].5.12

I take this opportunity to send you a note. I should pay a visit [to Chikubushima] to receive your opinion, but as I am still in Fushimi, I shall take the liberty to communicate with you by letter. Tanaka Chikugo Dono 田中筑後殿 has sent a *sashigami* さしかみ expressing his desire to [participate] in next year's Rengee and that [he] is directing 100 *koku* of rice be given to the *goryōnin* 御両人 in Osaka. The Osaka *bugyō* is also in Fushimi. Upon inquiry, [I was told that] the rice has not yet arrived from Western Japan, but when it arrives it will be passed over without fail. However, my plan, about which I consulted the *goryōnin* and discussed with the [Osaka] warehouse *bugyō,* is to sell [the rice] at the Osaka market and to give instead cash. We will receive the cash and deliver it. Respectfully conveyed.

Also, regarding the above cash, I will take special care with it, so on this point please rest assured. I will discuss details with the *goryōnin.* The end.

[To] Chikubushimasō Gobōchū 竹生嶋惣御坊中
Mairu Hitobito Onchū 参人々御中

[From] Ton[da] Kyūzaemon no Jō 富[田]久左衛門尉
Miyoshi [?] 身吉 (cipher)

DOCUMENT 30
Higashi Asai Gun shi, Chikubushima monjo no. 203 Keichō 8 [1603].7.19

The matter of the *jiryō okime* 寺領置目
<1> With regard to the deficiency of 47 *koku* 石, 5 *to* 斗, 4 *shō* 升 from within the 300 *koku,* revealed during the survey ordered by Naifu [i.e., Ieyasu], the *gobugyō* Katō Kizaemon 加藤喜左衛門 has made up the 47 *koku,* 5 *to,* 4 *shō* from the total of 300 *koku.* Thus we have the *tashi* たし of the 300 *koku,* but times being as they are, it will be divided among the active temples. However, if hereafter a *daikan* 代官 encroaches on the 47 *koku,* 5 *to,* 4 *shō* of unproductive fields [*eikō* 永荒], the *manzan* 満山 [i.e., Chikubushima] will protest, but if the argument is insufficient, following the above record of the 300 *koku,* without protest we will return [the disputed land].
<2> The division for the *hinogoku* 日御供 temples is also the same as before.
<3> The twenty-three active temples are as one, but if there is any negligence, the above apportionment will be taken back by the Sōchū 惣中.

[From] Ryō Nengyōji 兩年行事
Gyōkei 行慶 (cipher)
Gyōyū 行雄 (cipher)

Regarding the number of active temples:

Ruribō 瑠璃坊; Hōsōbō 實相坊; Getteiin 月定院; Kōjōin 高淨院; Jōgyōin 常行院; Kinchikubō 金竹坊; Keōbō 花王坊; Hōrin'in 法輪院; Hōsen'in 寶泉院; Fudōin 不動院; Bodaibō 菩提坊; Umemotobō 梅本坊; Ichijōin 一乘院; Myōōbō 明王坊; Seijubō 成就坊; Kinzōbō 金藏坊; Renzōbō 蓮藏坊; Onjōbō 圓城坊; Kichijōin 吉祥院; Myōkakuin 妙覺院; Seirinbō 西林坊; Sōjibō 惣持坊; Seihōin 西方院. The above, twenty-three.

The group that signs for the above:

Oshō 和尚 (cipher); Getteiin 月定院 (cipher); Onjōbō 圓城坊 (cipher); Hōjōbō 寶城坊 (cipher); Hōsen'in 寶泉院 (cipher); Hōrin'in 法輪院 (cipher); Kichijōin 吉祥院 (cipher); Bodaibō 菩提坊 (cipher); Seijubō 成就坊 (cipher); Hōsōin 實相院 (cipher); Kinzōbō 金藏坊 (cipher); Ichijōin 一乘院 (cipher); Tōzenbō 東善坊 (cipher); Kōjōin 高淨院 (cipher); Kinchikubō 金竹坊 (cipher); Fudōbō 不動坊 (cipher); Jōgyōin 常行院 (cipher); Umemotobō 梅本坊 (cipher); Jibukō 治部公 (cipher); Dainagon 大納言 (cipher); Jijōkō 侍從公 (cipher); Kunaikyō 宮内卿 (cipher); Jijūkō 侍從公 (cipher); Minbukō 民部公 (cipher); Shikibukō 式部公 (cipher); Ukyōkō 右京公 (cipher). The end.

It is so commanded.

DOCUMENT 31
Higashi Asai Gun shi, Chikubushima monjo no. 200 卯 [1603].3.10

Memo
<1> 252 *koku,* 4 *to,* 6 *shō:* Chikubushima *ryō.*
This [amount] is the portion as from before.
<2> 47 *koku,* 5 *to,* 4 *shō:* from within the village of Hayasaki.
I have explained this to Tsuzuki Dono 都築殿, so you will receive it.
Total of 300 *koku.*
The end.

[To] Chikubushima Sōchū 竹生嶋惣中

From [the office of] Katō Kiza 加[藤]喜左
Ogawa Ichizaemon 小川市左衛門
(cipher)

DOCUMENT 32

Higashi Asai Gun shi, Chikubushima monjo no. 202 — Keichō 8 [1603].5.15

The matter of the rice to be passed over.
Total of 16 *koku,* 6 *shō:*
The above portion, the supplementary part of the Hayasaki Village Chikubushima *ryō* of 300 *koku,* is passed over. Regarding the lacking portion of 47 *koku,* 5, *to,* 4 *shō,* it should be divided from that year's *mononari* 物成 [tax] and presented [to Chikubushima]. Without fail, the above portion shall be passed over. Regarding the matter of the *shitaji* [下地 farm land], Yoshinaga 吉長 holds [the relevant records]. When [Yoshinaga] returns from Fushimi, I will borrow [the records], write down [the information] and present it [to you]. You are thus informed. The end.

[To]: Hori[e] Gohyōe Dono 堀[江]五兵衛殿
Kan[be] Kuzaemon Dono 神[邊]九左衛門殿
mairu 参

[From] Tsu[zuki] Ukon 都[築]右近

DOCUMENT 33

Higashi Asai Gun shi, Chikubushima monjo no. 204 — Keichō 8 [1603].10.16

The matter of receipt of storage rice [*onkuramai* 御藏米]
Total of 16 *koku,* 6 *shō;* note *Kyōmasu* 京升.
The above is received as part of the Chikubushima total of 300 *koku.* The end.

[To]: Hori[e] Gohyōe Dono 堀江五兵衛殿
Kan[be] Kuzaemon Dono 神邊九左衛門殿
mairu 参

[From] Chikubushima Sōchū 竹生嶋惣中
Hōorin'in 法輪院
Kinchikubō 金竹坊

DOCUMENT 34

Higashi Asai Gun shi, Chikubushima monjo no. 201 — 5.15

Regarding the portion of the Chikubushima *ryō* of 300 *koku* that was determined during the *onawa* 御縄 [i.e., Ieyasu's 1602 survey] to be lacking, according to the wishes of Katō Kizaemon Dono 加藤喜左衛門殿, he signed 47 *koku,* 5 *to,* 4 *shō* over to the *goryōsho* 御領所, and it was passed over, so Ogawa Ichizaemon Dono 小川市左衛門殿's document is added and last year's portion passed over [to Chikubushima]. Regarding the matter of *shitaji* [下地 farm land], Yoshinaga 吉長 has the record book, and I will get it from him, write down the relevant passages and give it to you. [In other words] Yoshinaga is in Fushimi and, once he returns, I will receive the record book without fail and give to you [an account of the relevant materials]. Anyway, I have returned to the Kantō, but two days ago when I went to [Chikubushima] I received *sake.* This was greatly appreciated. At any rate, when I next make a visit [to Chikubushima], I look forward to meeting you.

[To] Chikubushima 竹生嶋
Sōchū 惣中

[From] Tsu[zuki] Ukon 都[築]右近
Furunaga 古長 (cipher)

DOCUMENT 35

Higashi Asai Gun shi, Chikubushima monjo no. 209 — Keichō 18 [1613].4.10

Regarding the matter of 300 *koku* from within Hayasaki in Asai County in Ōmi Province. Following precedent, it should all be donated. It is so commanded.

[From Tokugawa Ieyasu vermilion seal]

DOCUMENT 36
Higashi Asai Gun shi, Chikubushima monjo no. 210 Genna 3 [1617].7.21

Regarding the matter of 300 *koku* from within the Chikubushima *ryō* of Hayasaki in Asai County in Ōmi Province. Following the precedent of Keichō 18 [1613].4.10, it should all be donated; there shall be no negligence. It is so commanded.

[From Tokugawa Hidetada vermilion seal]

DOCUMENT 37
Higashi Asai Gun shi, Chikubushima monjo no. 211 Kan'ei 13 [1636].11.9

Regarding the matter of 300 *koku* from within the Chikubushima *ryō* of Hayasaki in Asai County in Ōmi Province. Following the precedents of Keichō 18 [1613].4.10 and Genna 3 [1617].7.21, it should all be donated; there shall be no negligence. It is so commanded.

[From Tokugawa Iemitsu vermilion seal]

DOCUMENT 38 ?.20
Higashi Asai Gun shi, Chikubushima monjo no. 198

Thank you for your troubles. You promptly sent in gratitude to Hideyori 秀頼 records of rituals as well as [other gifts]. Already, Katagiri Ichinokami Dono 片桐東市正殿 has presented them [to Hideyori]. [Hideyori] felt very fortunate and has examined these valuable things. [Hideyori] indicated that the Sutra Hall [Kyōdō きやうだう] of your place should also be constructed. Discussion with Katagiri Ichinokami Dono—.[9] Respectfully conveyed.

[To] Chikubushima Sōzan 竹生嶋惣山 [From] Amenomori Chōsuke 雨森長介
Nao 直 (cipher)

DOCUMENT 39
1603.6 ridgepole placard

With reverence: Lotus-Law Solitary-Ruler Dragon-Treasure-Deity-on-Head Most-Excellent-Eloquence-Talent-Deity Wish-Granting-Jewel Ruler 法華獨王頂上龍寶神最勝辯才天如意寶珠王,
[she] was endowed with [her] true form at the great beginning of the opening of heaven and earth;
[she] revealed [her] divine spirit at the start of the transformation of darkness *[yin]* and light *[yang]*.
As such,
[Benzaiten] already achieved the truth of original enlightenment and true suchness [*hongaku shinnyo* 本覺眞如], and immersed [her] body in the vow-ocean [*gankai* 願海] of the salvation of all living things;
[Benzaiten] truly attained the spirit of eternal tranquillity and the real suchness [*jōjaku hōni* 常寂法爾], and gave [her] heart to the obligation-mountain [*onzan* 恩山] to the benefit of the multitudinous beings.
Furthermore,
[Benzaiten] acts only with mercy;
[she] offers sincere pity.
Earlier, it is said, during the forming of [her] natural disposition [*hinshitsu* 禀質],
[Benzaiten] embraced more than the hardships of the Eight Kinds of Suffering so as to torture her sagely body;

9. Most of this sentence is illegible.

[she] sustained the severe misfortunes of the Seven Disasters in order to lose her divine life.

Furthermore,

[Benzaiten] deeply grieved the committing of evil;

[she] humbly lamented the doing of wickedness.

Directly,

[Benzaiten] made vows and practiced the rituals, and quickly gained the wish-fulfilling gem [*nyoi hōju* 如意寶珠], and settled in the house of prosperity and longevity;

[she] accumulated merit and built up virtue, and so administered the seal and key of self-cultivation [*shūshin inyaku* 修身印鎰, and reached the source of wealth and honor.

Accordingly [Benzaiten] bestowed compassion;

[she] gave sympathy to the impoverished people;

[she] had mercy on the lowborn people.

They humbly expect the benevolent shelter of [Benzaiten];

with the Buddha-state that has no beginning and no end, [Benzaiten] shows [her] holy form, and emits the fine light of the great mercy and great compassion and great joy and great charity;

with the divine spirit that is difficult to understand and difficult to attain, [she] reaches the Buddha-mind and celebrates the long life of ten thousand joys and ten thousand virtues and ten thousand congratulations and ten thousand years.

Long ago [Benzaiten] knotted her fortuitous karma with Japan, and [she] came riding on the clouds and borne by the mist;

[Benzaiten] settled on this distant Chikubushima and sang of the misty scenes of the several thousand *kei* 頃 of the lake of Ōmi;

[Benzaiten] moved to this far-off Mount Hōrai 蓬来 and gazed over the gentle waves of the thirty thousand *ri* 里 of wind-swept water;

[Benzaiten] long dwelled on this island but the people did not know it. At this time Amaterasu Ōmikami 天照皇太神 appeared in a vision to the Emperor Shōmu 聖武 and said, "On the lake of Ōmi there is an island, and it is the place where the Tennyo 天女 has long lived. Quickly, religious buildings [*dōkaku* 堂閣] should be constructed and the Tennyo worshipped." The emperor thought it an astonishing oracle and sent Gyōki 行基 and the vassal Miyako no Yoshika 都良香 [to Chikubushima] and a building was established as a sacred place; soon thereafter official rank was bestowed, fortune was bestowed, and pleasure was bestowed, and accordingly the rich and poor who made the pilgrimage were not deterred by the one thousand *ri* of the steep path, they arrived one after another. However, dust gradually accumulated and over time the beams and pillars of the buildings decayed and passed the point of just bending. Naidaijin Toyotomi Ason Hideyori Kō 内大臣豐臣朝臣秀頼公, thankfully, [gave] an order for restoration, and Katagiri Higashi Ichinokami 片桐東市正 respectfully carried it out,

[Katagiri Katsumoto] notified the official granaries and used gold and silver without restraint;

[he] opened the government storehouses and carried out millet.

The reconstruction work on the buildings of the whole island was completed in a short time. Accordingly,

the Blue Dragon emerged in celebration,

the White Snake arose in joy.

This numinous deity [i.e., Benzaiten]

[the people] pointed at and said, "Shutsu Garashin 酒津迦羅神", [the people] called and said, "Hanshin Garashin 飯神迦羅神", and much *sake* and rice were provided, saving the people of the Seven Paths;

[the people] named and said, "Fukuhō Kōmyōnyo 福寶光明女", [the people] declared and said, "Tokuhō Kōmyōnyo 徳寶光明女", and much fortune and goodness were bestowed, bathing the people of the Four Seas.

Moreover,

[Benzaiten] holds [her] bow and arrows; [she] subjugates the demons and hindrances from outside the heavens and proffers the benefit [*rishō* 利生] of long life;

[she] tempers [her] sword [*muken* 鉾劒]; [she] repels the bandits and enemies in the sea and is devoted to the arts of military victory.

Thus,

[Benzaiten] churns the waves of benevolence in the vast ocean; sometimes [she] transforms the Eight Dragon Kings [*dairyūō* 大龍王] and makes followers of the Seven Thousand Yaksha [*yasha* 夜叉];

[Benzaiten] directs the light of virtue on all the paths of the world; sometimes [she] makes appear the Three Kōtenshi 光天子 and employs the Fifteen Attendants [Jūgo Dōji 十五童子].

From now, for hereafter,

East of the sun will not encounter a disastrous situation;
West of the castle will not experience the grief of decline.[10]

This prosperity, from thousands of years ago and for tens of thousands of years, the old men of the countryside sing of Gyōshun 堯舜;[11] [Benzaiten] of the heavens and the land will live in the firm castle.

Katagiri Higashi Ichinokami
Katsumoto 且元 (cipher)

Keichō 8 [1603].6. *Nyoiju no hi* 如意珠日

Daiku Ken no Kami 大工権守
Shoku Tajima no Kami 小工但馬守
Bugyō 奉行 Amenomori Chōsuke 雨森長介 (cipher)

10. These references are obscure. Perhaps they refer to Japan.
11. This refers to two sage rulers of China in ancient times, Yao and Shun.

Bibliography

Adolphson, Mikael S. *The Gates of Power: Monks, Courtiers, and Warriors in Premodern Japan.* Honolulu: University of Hawai'i Press, 2000.

Akita Hiroki. *Oda Nobunaga to Azuchijō.* Osaka: Sōgensha, 1990.

Akiyama Terukazu, Ōta Hirotarō, Nishikawa Shinji, and Fukuyama Toshio, eds. *Byōdōin taikan.* 3 vols. Tokyo: Iwanami Shoten, 1987–1992.

Asao Naohiro. "Bakuhansei to tennō." In *Kinsei,* pp. 187–222. Vol. 3 of *Taikei Nihon kokka shi,* ed. Hara Hidesaburō, Minegishi Sumio, Sasaki Junnosuke, and Nakamura Masanori. Tokyo: Tōkyō Daigaku Shuppankai, 1975.

———. "'Shōgun kenryoku' no sōshutsu." Pts. 1–3. *Rekishi hyōron,* no. 241 (August 1970), pp. 70–78; no. 266 (August 1972), pp. 46–59; no. 293 (September 1974), pp. 20–36.

———. "Toyotomi seiken ron." In *Kinsei 1,* pp. 159–210. Vol. 9 of *Iwanami kōza Nihon rekishi.* Tokyo: Iwanami Shoten, 1963.

Asao, Naohiro, and Marius B. Jansen. "Shogun and Tennō." In *Japan before Tokugawa: Political Consolidation and Economic Growth, 1500–1650,* ed. John Whitney Hall, Nagahara Keiji, and Kozo Yamamura, pp. 248–70. Princeton: Princeton University Press, 1981.

Asaoka Okisada (1800–1856). *Koga bikō.* Revised and enlarged by Ōta Kin as *Zōtei koga bikō.* 3 vols. plus separate index vol. 1904–1905; reprint, Kyoto: Shibunkaku, 1970.

Bagley, Robert W. "Meaning and Explanation." *Archives of Asian Art* 46 (1993), pp. 6–26.

Berry, Mary Elizabeth. *The Culture of Civil War in Kyoto.* Berkeley, Los Angeles, London: University of California Press, 1994.

———. *Hideyoshi.* Harvard East Asian Series, no. 97. Cambridge, Mass. Harvard University Press, 1982.

Bielefeldt, Carl. "Dōgen's Shōbōgenzō Sansuikyo." In *The Mountain Spirit,* ed. Michael Charles Tobias and Harold Drasdo, pp. 37–49. Woodstock, N.Y.: Overlook Press, 1979.

Bijutsu Kenkyūjo, ed. *Momoyama jidai kinpeki shōhekiga.* Tokyo: Ōtsuka Kōgeisha, 1937.

Bock, Felicia Gressitt, trans. *Engi-shiki: Procedures of the Engi Era.* 2 vols. Tokyo: Sophia University, 1970–1972.

Bodiford, William M. *Sōtō Zen in Medieval Japan.* Kuroda Institute: Studies in East Asian Buddhism 8. Honolulu: University of Hawaii Press, 1993.

Bolitho, Harold. *Treasures among Men: The Fudai Daimyo in Tokugawa Japan.* New Haven and London: Yale University Press, 1974.

Bonshun (1553–1632). *Shunkyū ki.* Ed. Kamata Jun'ichi. 5 vols. *Shiryō sanshū kokiroku hen.* Tokyo: Zoku Gunsho Ruijū Kanseikai, 1970–1983.

Boot, W. J. "The Death of a Shogun: Deification in Early Modern Japan." In *Shinto in History: Ways of the Kami,* ed. John Breen and Mark Teeuwen, pp. 144–66. Honolulu: University of Hawai'i Press, 2000.

———. "The Deification of Tokugawa Ieyasu." *Japan Foundation Newsletter* 14, no. 5 (February 1987), pp. 10–13.

Boscaro, Adriana, ed. and trans. *101 Letters of Hideyoshi.* Monumenta Nipponica monograph 54. Tokyo: Sophia University, 1975.

Boxer, C. R. "Padre João Rodrigues Tçuzu S. J. and his Japanese Grammars of 1604 and 1620." In *Portuguese Merchants and Missionaries in Feudal Japan, 1543–1640,* pp. 338–63. London: Variorum Reprints, 1986.

Breen, John, and Mark Teeuwen, eds. *Shinto in History: Ways of the Kami.* Honolulu: University of Hawai'i Press, 2000.

Brinker, Helmut, and Hiroshi Kanazawa. *Zen Masters of Meditation in Images and Writings.* Trans. Andreas Leisinger. Zürich: Artibus Asiae, 1996.

Brock, Karen. "The Making and Remaking of *Miraculous Origins of Mt. Shigi.*" *Archives of Asian Art* 45 (1992), pp. 42–71.

Brommell, N. S., and Perry Smith, eds. *Urushi: Proceedings of the Urushi Study Group, June 10–27, 1985, Tokyo.* Marina del Rey, California: Getty Conservation Institute, 1988.

Brown, Kendall H. *The Politics of Reclusion: Painting and Power in Momoyama Japan.* Honolulu: University of Hawai'i Press, 1997.

Chanoyu Konwakai, ed. *Yamanoue no Sōji ki no kenkyū.* 3 vols. Tokyo: Santokuan, 1993–1997.

Chidester, David, and Edward T. Linenthal, eds. *American Sacred Space.* Bloomington and Indianapolis: Indiana University Press, 1995.

Chikubushima monjo. Original documents in the Nagahama Castle Historical Museum.

Chin Shunshin and Mine Kakukai. *Chikubushima Hōgonji.* Vol. 3 of *Koji junrei: Ōmi.* Kyoto: Tankōsha, 1980.

Chino Kaori and Nishi Kazuo. *Fikushon toshite no kaiga: Bijutsushi no me, kenchikushi no me.* Tokyo: Perikansha, 1991.

Chmielewski, Janusz. "The Problem of Early Loan-words in Chinese as Illustrated by the Word *p'u-t'ao.*" *Rocznik orientalistyczny* 22, no. 2 (1958), pp. 7–45.

———. "Two Early Loan-words in Chinese." *Rocznik orientalistyczny* 24, no. 2 (1961), pp. 65–86.

Cleary, Thomas, trans. *The Flower Ornament Scripture: A Translation of the Avatamsaka Sutra.* Boulder and London: Shambhala, 1993.

CM. See *Chikubushima monjo.*

Coaldrake, William H. *Architecture and Authority in Japan.* The Nissan Institute/Routledge Japanese Studies Series. London and New York: Routledge, 1996.

———. "Edo Architecture and Tokugawa Law." *Monumenta Nipponica* 36, no. 3 (Autumn 1981), pp. 235–84.

———. "Gateways of Power: Edo Architecture and Tokugawa Authority 1603–1651." Ph.D. diss., Harvard University, 1983.

———. *The Way of the Carpenter: Tools and Japanese Architecture.* New York, Tokyo: Weatherhill, 1990.

Coats, Bruce Arthur. "The Architecture of Zen-sect Buddhist Monasteries in Japan, 1200–1500." Ph.D. diss., Harvard University, 1985.

Collcutt, Martin. "Buddhism: The Threat of Eradication." In *Japan in Transition: From Tokugawa to Meiji,* ed. Marius B. Jansen and Gilbert Rozman, pp. 143–67. Princeton: Princeton University Press, 1988.

"Competition and Collaboration: Hereditary Schools in Japanese Culture." *Fenway Court.* Boston: Trustees of the Isabella Stewart Gardner Museum, 1993.

Confucius. *The Analects (Lun yü).* Trans. D. C. Lau. Penguin Classics. London and New York: Penguin Books, 1979.

Cooper, Michael. "The Early Jesuits in Japan and Buddhism." In *Portuguese Voyages to Asia and Japan in the Renaissance Period,* ed. Peter Milward, pp. 43–57. Tokyo: Renaissance Institute, Sophia University, 1994.

———. *Rodrigues the Interpreter: An Early Jesuit in Japan and China.* New York and Tokyo: Weatherhill, 1974.

———. *The Southern Barbarians: The First Europeans in Japan.* Tokyo and Palo Alto: Kodansha International, 1971.

———, ed. *João Rodrigues's Account of Sixteenth-Century Japan.* Ser. 3, vol. 7. London: Hakluyt Society, 2001.

———, comp. and ann. *They Came to Japan: An Anthology of European Reports on Japan, 1543–1640.* Berkeley and Los Angeles: University of California Press, 1965.

———, trans. and ed. *This Island of Japon: João Rodrigues' Account of 16th-century Japan.* Tokyo and New York: Kodansha International Ltd., 1973.

Cort, Louise Allison. "The Great Kitano Tea Gathering." *Chanoyu Quarterly,* no. 31 (1982), pp. 15–20.

Cunningham, Michael R. *Buddhist Treasures from Nara.* Cleveland: Cleveland Museum of Art, 1998.

———. *The Triumph of Japanese Style: Sixteenth Century Art in Japan.* Cleveland: Cleveland Museum of Art, 1991.

Dai Nihon shiryō. Ed. Tōkyō Daigaku. Tokyo: Tōkyō Daigaku, 1901–.

de Visser, Marinus Willem. *Ancient Buddhism in Japan, Sutras and Ceremonies in Use in the Seventh and Eighth Centuries A.D. and their History in Later Times.* Leiden: E. J. Brill, 1935.

Diary of Richard Cocks: Cape-merchant in the English Factory in Japan, 1615–1622, with Correspondence. Ed. Edward Maunde Thompson. 2 vols. Hakluyt Society, First Series, no. 66, 1883; reprint, New York: Burt Franklin, n.d.

DNS. See *Dai Nihon shiryō.*

Doi Tadao, ed. *Vocabvlario da Lingoa de Iapam, Nippo jisho.* Tokyo: Iwanami Shoten, 1960.

Doi Tadao, Morita Takeshi, and Chōnan Minoru, eds. and trans. *Hōyaku Nippo jisho.* Tokyo: Iwanami Shoten, 1980.

Doi Tsugiyoshi. *Kano Eitoku, Mitsunobu.* Vol. 9 of *Nihon bijutsu kaiga zenshū.* Tokyo: Shūeisha, 1978.

———. *Kinsei Nihon kaiga no kenkyū.* Tokyo: Bijutsu Shuppansha, 1970.

———. *Momoyama no shōhekiga.* Vol. 14 of *Nihon no bijutsu.* Tokyo: Heibonsha, 1964.

———. "Tsukubusuma Jinja no tenjōga." *Kyōto,* no. 20 (June 1952), pp. 27–29.

ELIADE, MIRCEA, ed. *The Encyclopedia of Religion.* New York: Macmillan Publishing Company, 1987. S.v. "The Sacred and the Profane," by Carsten Colpe.

ELISON, GEORGE. "The Cross and the Sword: Patterns of Momoyama History." In *Warlords, Artists, and Commoners: Japan in the Sixteenth Century,* ed. George Elison and Bardwell L. Smith, pp. 55–85. Honolulu: University of Hawaii Press, 1981.

———. "Hideyoshi, the Bountiful Minister." In *Warlords, Artists, and Commoners: Japan in the Sixteenth Century,* ed. George Elison and Bardwell L. Smith, pp. 223–44. Honolulu: University of Hawaii Press, 1981.

ENDERS, SIEGFRIED RCT, and NIELS GUTSCHOW, eds. *Hozon: Architectural and Urban Conservation in Japan.* Stuttgart and London: Edition Axel Menges, 1998.

Engi shiki. In vol. 26 of *Shintei zōho kokushi taikei,* ed. Kuroita Katsumi. Tokyo: Kokushi Taikei Kankōkai, 1937.

FOARD, JAMES H. "The Boundaries of Compassion: Buddhism and National Tradition in Japanese Pilgrimage." *Journal of Asian Studies* 41, no. 2. (February 1982), pp. 231–51.

FOWLER, SHERRY. "In Search of the Dragon: Mount Murō's Sacred Topography." *Japanese Journal of Religious Studies* 24, nos. 1–2 (Spring 1997), pp. 145–61.

FROIS, LUIS, S. J. (1532–1597). *Nihon shi.* Trans. Matsuda Kiichi and Kawasaki Momota. 12 vols. Tokyo: Chūō Kōronsha, 1977–1980.

FUJII KEISUKE. "Daigoji: Sanjō, sanka no garan to rekishi." In *Daigoji,* pp. 89–130. Vol. 9 of *Nihon meikenchiku shashin senshū.* Tokyo: Shinchōsha, 1992.

FUJII NAOMASA. "Toyotomi Hideyori no shaji zōei to sono ikō." *Ōtemae Joshi Daigaku ronshū,* no. 17 (1983), pp. 48–72.

FUJINO TAMOTSU. *Shintei bakuhan taisei shi no kenkyū.* Tokyo: Yoshikawa Kōbunkan, 1975.

FUJIOKA MICHIO. *Kinsei no kenchiku.* Tokyo: Chūō Kōron Bijutsu Shuppan, 1971.

FUJITA TSUNEHARU. "Keichō nana nen Ōmi no kuni kenchi o megutte." *Hisutoria,* no. 129 (December 1990), pp. 157–84.

FUJIWARA GIICHI. "Momoyama jidai no kenchiku chōkoku." Pts. 1–2. *Sōbi,* no. 7 (1954), pp. 12–13; no. 8, pp. 13–14.

———. *Zōho Nihon ko kenchiku zuroku.* 1948; reprint, Kyoto: Kyōto Shoin, 1962.

FUKUYAMA TOSHIO. *Jiin kenchiku no kenkyū.* 3 vols. *Fukuyama Toshio chosakushū.* Tokyo: Chūō Kōron Bijutsu Shuppan, 1982–1983.

———. "Munafuda kō." In vol. 3 of *Jiin kenchiku no kenkyū,* pp. 243–62. *Fukuyama Toshio chosakushū.* Tokyo: Chūō Kōron Bijutsu Shuppan, 1983.

FUNABASHI HIDEKATA (1575–1614). *Keichō nikken roku.* Ed. Yamamoto Takeo. *Shiryō sanshū kokiroku hen.* Tokyo: Zoku Gunsho Ruijū Kanseikai, 1981–.

GERHART, KAREN M. *The Eyes of Power: Art and Early Tokugawa Authority.* Honolulu: University of Hawai'i Press, 1999.

GIEN (1558–1626). *Daigoji shin yōroku.* Ed. Daigoji Bunkazai Kenkyūjo. 2 vols. Tokyo: Hōzōkan, 1991.

———. *Gien Jugō nikki.* Ed. Iyanaga Teizō et al. 3 vols. *Shiryō sanshū kokiroku hen.* Tokyo: Zoku Gunsho Ruijū Kanseikai, 1976–.

GJN. See Gien. *Gien Jugō nikki.*

GÓMEZ, LUIS O. *The Land of Bliss: The Paradise of the Buddha of Measureless Light, Sanskrit and Chinese Versions of the Sukhāvatīvyūha Sutras.* Studies in the Buddhist Traditions. Honolulu: University of Hawai'i Press; Kyoto: Higashi Honganji Shinshū Ōtani-ha, 1996.

GOODWIN, JANET R. *Alms and Vagabonds: Buddhist Temples and Popular Patronage in Medieval Japan.* Honolulu: University of Hawaii Press, 1994.

GOTŌ BIJUTSUKAN GAKUGEIBU, ed. *Yamanoue no Sōji ki: Tenshō jūyon nen no me.* Tokyo: Gotoh Museum, 1995.

GRAPARD, ALLAN G. "Flying Mountains and Walkers of Emptiness: Toward a Definition of Sacred Space in Japanese Religions." *History of Religions* 21, no. 3 (February 1982), pp. 195–221.

———. "Japan's Ignored Cultural Revolution: The Separation of Shinto and Buddhist Divinities in Meiji *(shimbutsu bunri)* and a Case Study: Tonomine." *History of Religions* 23, no. 3 (February 1984), pp. 240–65.

———. "*Keiranshūyōshū:* A Different Perspective on Mt. Hiei in the Medieval Period." In *Re-Visioning "Kamakura" Buddhism,* ed. Richard K. Payne, pp. 55–69. Kuroda Institute: Studies in East Asian Buddhism 11. Honolulu: University of Hawai'i Press, 1998.

———. "On Kūkai's Stone Inscription for Shōdō." In *The Mountain Spirit,* ed. Michael Charles Tobias and Harold Drasdo, pp. 51–59. Woodstock, N.Y.: Overlook Press, 1979.

HAGA KŌSHIRŌ. *Azuchi Momoyama jidai no bunka.* Nihon rekishi shinsho. Tokyo: Shibundō, 1964.

HAGS. See *Higashi Asai Gun shi.*

HAINO AKIO. "Raiun makie kodō." *Gakusō,* no. 5 (March 1983), pp. 121–28.

———. "Tsukubusuma Jinja Honden no makie sōshoku." *Gakusō,* no. 3 (March 1981), pp. 53–86.

HALL, JOHN WHITNEY, ed. *Early Modern Japan.* Vol. 4 of *The Cambridge History of Japan,* ed. John Whitney Hall, Marius B. Jansen, Madoka Kanai, and Denis Twitchett. Cambridge: Cambridge University Press, 1991.

HALL, JOHN WHITNEY, NAGAHARA KEIJI, and KOZO YAMAMURA, eds. *Japan before Tokugawa: Political Consolidation and Economic Growth, 1500–1650.* Princeton: Princeton University Press, 1981.

HALL, JOHN WHITNEY, and TAKESHI TOYODA, eds. *Japan in the Muromachi Age.* Berkeley and Los Angeles: University of California Press, 1977.

HASEGAWA, YOSHIO. "Urushi Coating and Color Painting Applied to Japanese Architectural Cultural Monuments." In *Urushi: Proceedings of the Urushi Study Group, June 10–27, 1985, Tokyo,* ed. N. S. Brommell and Perry Smith, pp. 57–65. Marina del Rey, Calif. Getty Conservation Institute, 1988.

HAYASHIDA KŌZEN. *Chishakuin shi.* Kyoto: Sōhonzan Chishakuin, 1915.

HAYAZAKI KAN'EN, ed. *Kami o itsuku shima no memorii: Chikubushima.* Shiga Ken Biwachō Kankōkai.

Heike monogatari. Ann. Kajihara Masaaki and Yamashita Hiroaki. 2 vols. Tokyo: Iwanami Shoten, 1991–93.

HICKMAN, MONEY L., et al. *Japan's Golden Age: Momoyama.* New Haven and London: Yale University Press, 1996.

Higashi Asai Gun shi. 4 vols. 1927; reprint, Nagaokakyō: Nihon Shiryō Kankōkai, 1975.

HIRAI KIYOSHI. "Reibyō kenchiku." In *Kinsei bushō no bijutsu: Himejijō to Nijōjō,* ed. Takeda Tsuneo and Hirai Kiyoshi, pp. 178–90. Vol. 18 of *Nihon bijutsu zenshū.* Tokyo: Gakushū Kenkyūsha, 1979.

———, ed. *Momoyama kenchiku. Nihon no bijutsu,* no. 200. Tokyo: Shibundō, 1983.

HŌGONJI, ed. *Chikubushima no kinenchō.* 1929.

IMAI SŌKYŪ (1520–1593). *Imai Sōkyū chanoyu nikki nukigaki.* Ed. Nagashima Fukutarō. In vol. 10 of *Chadō koten zenshū,* ed. Sen Sōshitsu, pp. 3–64. Kyoto: Tankō Shinsha, 1961.

INAGAKI EIZŌ. *Jinja to reibyō.* Vol. 16 of *Genshoku Nihon no bijutsu.* Tokyo: Shōgakukan, 1968.

INAGAKI HISAO in collaboration with HAROLD STEWART. *The Three Pure Land Sutras: The Larger Sutra on Amitāyus (The Sutra on the Buddha of Infinite Life) (Taishō, Volume 12, Number 360), The Sutra on Contemplation of Amitāyus (The Sutra on Visualization of the Buddha of Infinite Life) (Taishō, Volume 12, Number 365), The Smaller Sutra on Amitāyus (The Sutra on Amitāyus Buddha) (Taishō, Volume 12, Number 366).* BDK English Tripitaka 12-II, III, IV. Berkeley: Numata Center for Buddhist Translation and Research, 1995.

INOUE YASUYO. *Toyotomi Hideyori.* Tokyo: Inoue Yasuyo, 1992.

IRITA SEIZŌ. "Maeda Kikuhime no gazō." *Bijutsu kenkyū,* no. 38 (February 1935), pp. 12–13.

ISHIMARU SHŌUN and ISO HIROSHI. *Ōmi no shōhekiga.* Kyoto: Kyōto Shoin, 1981.

ITŌ FUTOSHI. "Chūsei kōki ni okeru Ōmi Chikubushima no jiji to shakai." M.A. thesis, Kokugakuin Daigaku, 1990.

ITŌ NOBUO. "Momoyama jidai o chūshin toshita kenchiku no shosō." *Museum,* no. 34 (January 1954), pp. 19–21.

———, ed. *Daiku chōkoku.* Inax Booklet, vol. 6, no. 3. Tokyo: Inax, 1988.

———, ed. *Zuihōden: Date Masamune no haka to sono ihin.* Sendai: Zuihōden Saikon Kiseikai, 1979.

ITŌ SHINSHŌ. "Keichōki ni okeru Tokugawa Ieyasu to Kinai jisha: 'Seishō Oshō bun'an' no bunseki o tōshite." *Machikaneyama ronsō,* no. 28 (1994), pp. 57–82.

Iwanami kōza Nihon rekishi. 23 vols. Tokyo: Iwanami Shoten, 1962–1964.

IWASHIMIZU HACHIMANGŪ, ed. *Iwashimizu Hachimangū shi.* Tokyo: Zoku Gunsho Ruijū Kanseikai, 1932.

IZUMI TAKEO. "Chikubushima Benzaiten zō." *Kokka,* no. 1247 (September 1999), pp. 20–23.

IZUMIYA YASUO. *Kōfukuji.* Tokyo: Yoshikawa Kōbunkan, 1997.

JEKK. See Nanka Genkō. *Jōe Enmyō Kokushi kyohakuroku.*

JŪYŌ BUNKAZAI HENSAN IINKAI, ed. *Shin shitei jūyō bunkazai: Kaisetsuban.* 13 vols. Tokyo: Mainichi Shinbunsha, 1980–1984.

'KADOKAWA NIHON CHIMEI DAIJITEN' HENSAN IINKAI, ed. *Kadokawa Nihon chimei daijiten.* 49 vols. Tokyo: Kadokawa Shoten, 1978–1990.

KAEMPFER, ENGELBERT (1651–1716). *The History of Japan, Together with a Description of the Kingdom of Siam, 1690–92.* 3 vols. Translated by J. G. Scheuchzer. Glasgow: James MacLehose and Sons, 1906.

KAGEYAMA HARUKI. "Chikubushima saireizu." *Yamato bunka,* no. 27 (September 1958), pp. 39–47.

KAJŪJI HARETOYO (1544–1602). *Haretoyo ki.* Ed. Takeuchi Rizō. In vol. 9 of *Zoku shiryō taisei,* pp. 109–380 Kyoto: Rinsen Shoten, 1967.

KAMIYA SŌTAN (1553–1635). *Sōtan nikki.* Ed. Haga Kōshirō. In vol. 6 of *Chadō koten zenshū,* pp. 131–403. Kyoto: Tankō Shinsha, 1958.

KANAGAWA PREFECTURAL MUSEUM, ed. *Tokiwayama Bunko meihin ten.* Yokohama: Kanagawa Prefectural Museum, 1983.

KAN'EIJI, ed. *Jigen Daishi zenshū.* 2 vols. 1916; reprint, Tokyo: Kokusho Kankōkai, 1976.

KANO EINŌ (1631–1697). *Honchō gashi.* In vol. 2 of *Nihon garon taikan,* ed. Sakazaki Shizuka, pp. 951–1054. Tokyo: Arusu, 1929.

KASAI MASAAKI, SASAKI SUSUMU, and TAKEI AKIO, ann. *Yakuchū Honchō gashi.* Kyoto: Dōhōsha Shuppan, 1985.

KATAOKA HAJIME, ed. *Hideyoshi to Kyōto—Hōkoku Jinja shahō ten: Hōtaikō botsugo yonhyaku nen kinen.* Kyoto: Hōkoku Jinja, 1998.

KATŌ HIROSHI. "Kodō no kōzō to sōshoku." *Museum,* no. 449 (August 1988), pp. 4–17.

———. *Umi o watatta nihon shikki III (gihō to hyōgen). Nihon no bijutsu,* no. 428. Tokyo: Shibundō, 2002.

KAWADA SADAMU. *Busshari to kyō no shōgon. Nihon no bijutsu,* no. 280. Tokyo: Shibundō, 1989.

KAWAI MASATOMO and WAKISAKA ATSUSHI, eds. *Momoyama no shōheiga: Eitoku, Tōhaku, Yūshō.* Vol. 17 of *Nihon bijutsu zenshū.* Tokyo: Gakushū Kenkyūsha, 1978.

KAWAKAMI KOZAN and OGISU JUNDŌ. *Zōho Myōshinji shi.* Kyoto: Shibunkaku, 1975.

KAWAKAMI MITSUGU. "Myōshinji no jiiki keikan to kenchiku." In *Myōshinji.* Vol. 24 of *Nihon koji bijutsu zenshū,* ed. Miya Tsugio, pp. 90–98. Tokyo: Shūeisha, 1982.

———. *Zen'in no kenchiku: Zensō no sumai to saikyō.* Kyoto: Kawara Shoten, 1968.

KAWAKATSU MASATARŌ. "Hideyori no shaji kenchiku saiko." *Shiseki to bijutsu,* no. 71 (October 1936), pp. 589–600.

KAWAKATSU MASATARŌ and SASAKI RIZŌ. *Kyōto komei shuki.* Kyoto: Suzukake Shuppanbu, 1941.

KAWAMURA YOSHIZŌ. *Chikubushima yōran.* Tokyo: Kawamura Yoshizō, 1900.

KAWAUCHI MASAYOSHI. "Hōkokusha no seiritsu katei ni tsuite: Hideyoshi shinkakuka o megutte." *Hisutoria,* no. 164 (April 1999), pp. 56–70.

———. "Kyōto Higashiyama Daibutsu Sensōe ni tsuite: Chūkinsei ikōki ni okeru kenryoku to shūkyō." *Nihonshi kenkyū,* no. 425 (January 1998), pp. 1–25.

Kazarishi no waza. Inax Booklet, vol. 9, no. 2. Tokyo: Inax, 1989.

Kegon kyō (Dai hōkōbutsu Kegon kyō). T. 278.9; T. 279.10.

Keichō nikken roku. See Funabashi Hidekata. *Keichō nikken roku.*

KETELAAR, JAMES. *Of Heretics and Martyrs in Meiji Japan: Buddhism and Its Persecution.* Princeton: Princeton University Press, 1990.

KII GUN YAKUSHO and FUSHIMI CHŌ YAKUBA, eds. *Kyōto Fu Kii Gun shi, Fushimi Chō shi.* 1915, 1929; reprint, Kyoto: Rinsen Shoten, 1972.

KIMURA NOBUKO. "Toyotomi Hideyori no jisha zōei ni tsuite." *Nihon kenchiku gakkai keikakukei ronbunshū,* no. 499 (September 1997), pp. 171–77.

———. "Toyotomi Hideyori no sakuji taisei ni tsuite." *Nihon kenchiku gakkai keikakukei ronbunshū,* no. 511 (September 1998), pp. 185–92.

KIMURA YOSHIHIRO, ERYŪ YOSHIYUKI, and NISHIKAWA TAKEO. *Ōmi jinbutsu den.* Ōtsu: Kōbundō Shoten, 1976.

KITA, SANDY. *The Last Tosa: Iwasa Katsumochi Matabei, Bridge to Ukiyo-e.* Honolulu: University of Hawai'i Press, 1999.

KITAGAWA, ANNE ROSE. "Substance Beneath the Symbols: Lacquer in Japanese Culture." *Oriental Art* 45, no. 3 (Autumn 1999), pp. 2–15.

KITAGAWA HIROSHI. "Hōkōji Daibutsuden ni matsurareta Zenkōji Nyorai." *Kankō no Ōsaka,* no. 458 (July 1989), pp. 8–9; no. 459 (August 1989), pp. 8–9.

———. "Kami ni matsurareta Hideyoshi to Ieyasu: Hōkokusha, Tōshōgū." In *Yomigaeru chūsei 2: Honganji kara tenka ichi e Ōsaka,* ed. Sakuma Takashi, pp. 220–25. Tokyo: Heibonsha, 1989.

———. "Ōsaka fuyu no jin zu byōbu, natsu no jin zu byōbu ni egakareta Ōsakajō: Gokurakubashi no kentō." In *Sengoku gassen zu byōbu no sekai,* ed. Wakayama Prefectural Museum, pp. 13–17. Wakayama: Wakayama Prefectural Museum, 1997.

———. "Ōsaka no jin saikō." Unpublished lecture notes and handout, Osaka, 1999.

———. "Toyotomi Hideyoshi zō to Hōkokusha." In *Shōzōga o yomu,* ed. Kuroda Hideo, pp. 199–238. Tokyo: Kadokawa Shoten, 1998.

KITAMURA SHIRŌ, TSUKAMOTO YŌTARŌ, and KONOSHIMA MASAO. *Honzō zufu sōgō kaisetsu.* 3 vols. Kyoto: Dōhōsha Shuppan, 1986–1990.

KIYOHARA SADAO. "Shintō shijō ni okeru Benzaiten." *Rekishi chiri* 27, no. 3 (March 1916), pp. 247–57.

KLEIN, BETTINA; adapted and expanded by CAROLYN WHEELWRIGHT. "Japanese *Kinbyōbu:* The Gold-leafed Folding Screens of the Muromachi Period (1333–1573)." Pts. 1–2. *Artibus Asiae,* vol. 45, no. 1 (1984), pp. 5–34; vol. 45, nos. 2–3 (1984), pp. 101–74.

"Ko kenchiku meibun shū." Pts. 1–6. *Kōkan bijutsu shiryō,* nos. 88–93, 1957. TMs [photocopy].

KOBAYASHI NORIKO. "Botan mon makie taiko." *Kokka,* no. 1156 (March 1992), pp. 35–39.

Kobori Kōsen. "Benzaiten no shinkō to shūhō: Chie, fukutoku no sonten." *Tendai,* no. 6 (November 1982), pp. 32–40.

Kōgei Bijutsu Shūei Kankōkai, ed. *Kōgei bijutsu shūei,* 3 vols. Kyoto: Kōgei Bijutsu Shūei Kankōkai, 1925–1926.

Kokuhō Tsukubusuma Jinja Keidai Shuppansho, ed. *Kokuhō Tsukubusuma Jinja Honden shūri kōji hōkokusho.* Shiga Prefecture: Kokuhō Tsukubusuma Jinja Keidai Shuppansho, 1937.

Kokuhō Zuiganji Dainiki Shūri Iinkai, ed. *Kokuhō, jūyō bunkazai Zuiganji shūri kōji hōkokusho.* Miyagi Prefecture: Kokuhō Zuiganji Dainiki Shuri Iinkai, 1958.

Kokuritsu Gekijō Nōgakudō ChōsaYōseika, ed. *Momoyama jidai to nōgaku.* Tokyo: Kokuritsu Gekijō, 1988.

Kokushi Daijiten Henshū Iinkai, ed. *Kokushi daijiten.* 15 vols. Tokyo: Yoshikawa Kōbunkan, 1979–1997.

Komatsu Shigemi. "Tokubetsuten: '*Nihon no sho*' e no tebiki." In *Tokubetsuten: Nihon no sho,* pp. 8–31. Tokyo: Tokyo National Museum, 1978.

Komatsu Taishū and Katō Hiroshi. *Shitsugeihin no kanshō kiso chishiki.* Tokyo: Shibundō, 1997.

Kondō Yoshihiro. "Toyokuni daimyōjin no bunshi ni tsuite." In *Ueki Hakase Kanreki kinen kokushigaku ronshū,* pp. 357–77. Ueki Hakase Kanreki Kinen Shuku Gakkai, 1938.

Konkōmyō saishōō kyō. T. 665.16.

Konoe Nobutada (1565–1614). *Sanmyakuin ki.* Ed. Konoe Michitaka, Nawa Osamu, and Hashimoto Masanobu. *Shiryō sanshū kokiroku hen.* Tokyo: Zoku Gunsho Ruijū Kanseikai, 1975.

Kōshū (1276–1350). *Keiran shūyōshū.* In T. 2410.76.503–888.

Koyama Hiroshi, Satō Kikuo, and Satō Ken'ichirō, eds. *Yōkyokushū l.* Vol. 33 of *Nihon koten bungaku zenshū.* Tokyo: Shōgakukan, 1973.

KTJHSKH. See Kokuhō Tsukubusuma Jinja Keidai Shuppansho, ed., *Kokuhō Tsukubusuma Jinja Honden shūri kōji hōkokusho.*

Kuck, Loraine. *The World of the Japanese Garden, from Chinese Origins to Modern Landscape Art.* Repr. with corrections; New York, Tokyo: Weatherhill, 1980.

Kuroda Toshio. *Jisha seiryoku: Mō hitotsu no chūsei shakai.* Iwanami shinsho, no. 117. Tokyo: Iwanami Shoten, 1980.

———. *Nihon chūsei no kokka to shūkyō.* Tokyo: Iwanami Shoten, 1975.

———. "Shinto in the History of Japanese Religion." *Journal of Japanese Studies* 7, no. 1 (Winter 1981), pp. 1–21.

Kuroda, Taizō, Melinda Takeuchi, and Yūzō Yamane. *Worlds Seen and Imagined: Japanese Screens from The Idemitsu Museum of Arts.* New York: Asia Society Galleries and Abbeville Press, 1995.

Kuwata Tadachika. *Taikō Hideyoshi no tegami.* Kadokawa bunko, no. 2349. Tokyo: Kadokawa Shoten, 1965.

———. *Taikō kashindan.* Tokyo: Shin Jinbutsu Ōraisha, 1971.

———. *Toyotomi Hideyoshi.* Kuwata Tadachika chōsakushū, no. 5. Tokyo: Akita Shoten, 1979.

———. *Toyotomi Hideyoshi kenkyū.* Tokyo: Kadokawa Shoten, 1975.

———. *Yamanoue Sōji ki no kenkyū.* Kyoto: Kawara Shoten, 1957.

———. *Yodogimi.* Jinbutsu sōsho, no. 7. Tokyo: Yoshikawa Kōbunkan, 1958.

———, ed. *Taikō shiryō shū.* Vol. 1 of *Sengoku shiryō sōsho.* Tokyo: Jinbutsu Ōraisha, 1965.

———, ed. *Toyotomi Hideyoshi no subete.* Tokyo: Shin Jinbutsu Ōraisha, 1981.

Kyōto Fu Kyōiku Chō Bunkazai Hogoka Jūyō Bunkazai Myōshinji Daihōjō Shūri Jimusho, ed. *Jūyō bunkazai Myōshinji Daihōjō shūri kōji hōkokusho.* 1959.

Kyōto Fu Kyōiku Iinkai Jimukyoku Shidōbu Bunkazai Hogoka Jūyō Bunkazai Kōdaiji Kaisandō Shūri Jimusho, ed. *Jūyō bunkazai Kōdaiji Kaisandō shūri kōji hōkokusho.* 1951.

Kyoto National Museum. *Kōdaiji makie.* Kyoto: Kyoto National Museum, 1971.

———, ed. *Hideyoshi to Nene no tera: Kōdaiji no meihō.* Kyoto National Museum, 1995.

———, ed. *Kōdaiji makie to Nanban shikki.* Kyoto: Kyoto National Museum, 1987.

———, ed. *Tokubetsu tenrankai: Makie—shikkoku to ōgon no Nihonbi.* Kyoto: Kyoto National Museum, 1995.

Kyōto Shi. *Kyōto no rekishi.* 10 vols. Tokyo: Gakugei Shorin, 1968–1976.

———. *Shiryō Kyōto no rekishi.* 16 vols. Tokyo: Heibonsha, 1979–1991.

Kyōto Shi Maizō Bunkazai Chōsa Sentaa, ed. *Sōhonzan Chishakuin keidai: Shōunji Kyakuden ato no hakkutsu chōsa: Chishakuin Kōdō shinchiku keikaku yoteichi no maizō bunkazai hakkutsu chōsa hōkoku.* Kyoto: Sōhonzan Chishakuin, 1995.

Kyōtobō mokushi, Shimogyō ken. Vol. 17 of *Shinshū Kyōto sōsho.* Kyoto: Kōsaisha, 1969.

LARSEN, KNUT EINAR. *Architectural Preservation in Japan.* Trondheim, Norway: Tapir Publishers, 1994.

LAVIN, IRVING. *Bernini and the Unity of the Visual Arts.* New York and London: Pierpont Morgan Library and Oxford University Press, 1980.

LEIRIA, LEONOR. "The Art of Lacquering According to the Namban-Jin Written Sources." *Bulletin of Portuguese/Japanese Studies* 3 (December 2001), pp. 9–26.

LEVINE, GREGORY P. A. "Jukōin: Art, Architecture, and Mortuary Culture at a Japanese Zen Buddhist Temple." Ph.D. diss., Princeton University, 1997.

———. "Switching Sites and Identities: The Founder's Statue at the Buddhist Temple Kōrin'in." *The Art Bulletin* 83, no. 1 (March 2001), pp. 72–104.

LI SHIZHEN (1518–1593). *Bencao gangmu.* 2 vols. Beijing: Renmin Weisheng Chubanshe, 1982.

LUDVIK, CATHERINE. "From Sarasvatī to Benzaiten (India, China, Japan)." Ph.D. diss., University of Toronto, 2001.

———. "La Benzaiten à huit bras: Durgā déesse guerrière sous l'apparence de Sarasvatī." *Cahiers d'Extrême-Asie,* no. 11 (1999–2000), pp. 292–338.

MACWILLIAMS, MARK WHEELER. "Kannon *Engi:* Strategies of Indigenization in Kannon Temple Myths of the *Saikoku sanjūsansho Kannon reijōki* and the *Sanjūsansho bandō Kannon reijōki.*" Ph.D. diss., University of Chicago, 1990.

MAEDA TAIJI, NISHI DAIYU, MATSUYAMA TETSUO, TOTSU KEINOSUKE, and HIRAKAWA SHINGO. *Tōdaiji Daibutsu no kenkyū: Rekishi to chūzō gijutsu.* 2 vols. Tokyo: Iwanami Shoten, 1997.

MASS, JEFFREY P. *The Kamakura Bakufu: A Study in Documents.* Stanford: Stanford University Press, 1976.

MASS, JEFFREY P., and WILLIAM B. HAUSER, eds. *The Bakufu in Japanese History.* Stanford: Stanford University Press, 1985.

MATSUDA KIICHI, trans. *Jūroku, shichi seiki Iezusukai Nihon hōkokushū.* Kyoto: Dōhōsha Shuppan, 1987–.

MATSUOKA TOSHIRŌ. *Ōsakajō no rekishi to kōzō.* Tokyo: Meicho Shuppan, 1988.

MCCALLUM, DONALD F. *Zenkōji and Its Icon: A Study in Medieval Japanese Religious Art.* Princeton: Princeton University Press, 1994.

MCCLAIN, JAMES L., and WAKITA OSAMU, eds. *Osaka, the Merchant's Capital of Early Modern Japan.* Ithaca, N.Y.: Cornell University Press, 1999.

MCKELWAY, MATTHEW PHILIP. "Capitalscapes: Painting and Politics in 16th–17th Century Japan." Ph.D diss., Columbia University, 1999.

———. "In or Our of the Capital? Reading Point of View in *Rakuchū Rakugai Zu:* The Case of the Sanjō Version." *Transactions of the International Conference of Eastern Studies,* no. 40 (1995), pp. 100–118.

———. "The Partisan View: Rakuchū Rakugai Screens in the Mary and Jackson Burke Collection." *Orientations* 28, no. 40 (February 1997), pp. 48–57.

MCMULLIN, NEIL. *Buddhism and the State in Sixteenth-Century Japan.* Princeton: Princeton University Press, 1984.

———. "Historical and Historiographical Issues in the Study of Pre-Modern Japanese Religions." *Japanese Journal of Religious Studies* 16, no. 1 (March 1989), pp. 3–40.

———. "The *Lotus Sutra* and Politics in the Mid-Heian Period." In *The Lotus Sutra in Japanese Cuture,* ed. George J. Tanabe, Jr. and Willa Jane Tanabe, pp. 119–41. Honolulu: University of Hawaii Press, 1989.

Meishō shiseki: Chikubushima hozon kanri keikaku. Shiga: Shiga Ken Kyōiku Iinkai, 1979.

MIKI SEIICHIRŌ. "Hōkōji Daibutsuden no zōei ni kansuru ichikōsatsu." In *Chūsei, kinsei no kokka to shakai,* ed. Nagahara Keiji, Inagaki Yasuhiko, and Yamaguchi Keiji, pp. 185–213. Tokyo: Tōkyō Daigaku Shuppankai, 1986.

———. "Hokokusha no zōei ni kansuru ichikōsatsu." *Nagoya Daigaku Bungakubu kenkyū ronshū* 98, *Shigaku* 33 (1987), pp. 195–209.

———, ed. *Oda, Toyotomi seiken: Kenkyū bunken mokuroku (1998 nen 3 gatsu genzai).* Nagoya: Miki Seiichirō, Nagoya Daigaku Bungakubu Nihonshi Kenkyūshitsu, 1999.

———, ed. *Toyotomi Hideyoshi monjo mokuroku.* Nagoya: Nagoya Daigaku Bungakubu Kokushigaku Kenkyūshitsu, 1989.

Minamoto no Yoritomo Kō happyaku nensai kinen: Minamoto no Yoritomo Kō ten. Kamakura: Tsurugaoka Hachimangū, 1999.

MINER, EARL, HIROKO ODAGIRI, and ROBERT E. MORRELL. *The Princeton Companion to Classical Japanese Literature.* Princeton: Princeton University Press, 1985.

MIYA TSUGIO, ed. *Myōshinji.* Vol. 24 of *Nihon koji bijutsu zenshū.* Tokyo: Shūeisha, 1982.

MIYACHI NAOKAZU. "Hōtaikō to Toyokuni Daimyōjin." In *Jingi to kokushi,* pp. 310–82. Tokyo: Kokin Shoin, 1926.

Miyahata Mineo. *Ōmi no matsuri to minzoku.* Kyoto: Nakanishiya Shuppan, 1988.

Miyajima Keiichi. "Asai shi kenryoku no keisei: Chikubushima shihai o chūshin ni shite." In *Daimyō ryōgoku o aruku,* ed. Nagahara Keiji, pp. 175–99. Tokyo: Yoshikawa Kōbunkan, 1993.

Miyakami Shigetaka. "Azuchijō tenshu no fukugen to sono shiryō ni tsuite: Naitō Akira shi 'Azuchijō no kenkyū' ni taisuru gimon." *Kokka,* no. 998 (March 1977), pp. 7–26; no. 999 (April 1977), pp. 5–27.

Miyata Noboru. "Benten shinkō." In vol. 2 of *Nihon shūkyō shi no nazo,* ed. Wakamori Tarō, pp. 265–73, Tokyo: Kōsei Shuppansha, 1976.

———. *Ikigami shinkō: Hito o kami ni matsuru shūzoku.* Hanawa shinsho, no. 35. Tokyo: Hanawa Shobō, 1970.

Mizuo Hiroshi. "Chikubushima fūzoku zu." *Kokka,* no. 990 (May 1976), pp. 27–28.

MOA Museum of Art, ed. *Ōgon no chashitsu, chadōgu.* Shizuoka: MOA Museum of Art, 1998.

Mochimaru Kazuo. "Toyotomi Hideyoshi gazō to hissha Kano Mitsunobu ni tsuite." *Bijutsu kenkyū,* no. 153 (March 1949), pp. 90–98.

Moku Masao. "Katagiri Katsumoto to Keichō no shūri." *Gekkan bunkazai,* no. 151 (April 1976), pp. 4–15.

Mori Masato. "Chikubushima." *Kokubungaku kaishaku to kanshō* 47, no. 3 (March 1982), pp. 120–21.

Morioka Eiichi. "Katagiri Katsumoto no Kita Ōmi ni okeru jisha fukkō." *Shiritsu Nagahamajō Rekishi Hakubutsukan nenpō,* no. 7 (April 1998), pp. 69–75.

Morioka Eiichi and Ōta Hiroshi. "Shiryō shōkai: *Chikubushima hōgachō.*" *Shiritsu Nagahamajō Rekishi Hakubutsukan nenpō,* no. 1 (March 1987), pp. 79–88.

Morita Takeshi, ed. *Hōyaku Nippo jisho sakuin.* Tokyo: Iwanami Shoten, 1989.

Moriya Katsuhisa. "Toyotomi Hideyoshi no toshi kaizō." In *Hideyoshi to Kyōto—Hōkoku Jinja shahō ten: Hōtaikō botsugo yonhyaku nen kinen,* ed. Kataoka Hajime, pp. 5–9. Kyoto: Hōkoku Jinja, 1998.

Morohashi Tetsuji, ed. *Dai kanwa jiten.* 13 vols. Tokyo: Taishūkan Shoten, 1955–1960.

Morse, Anne Nishimura, and Samuel Crowell Morse. *Object as Insight: Japanese Buddhist Art and Ritual.* Katonah, N.Y.: Katonah Museum of Art, 1996.

Munakata Kiyohiko. *Sacred Mountains in Chinese Art.* Champaign, Ill.: Krannert Art Museum, University of Illinois at Urbana-Champaign; Urbana: University of Illinois Press, 1991.

Murakami Jin'ichi. *Reibyō kenchiku. Nihon no bijutsu,* no. 295. Tokyo: Shibundō, 1990.

Murakami Naojirō, trans. *Iezusukai Nihon nenpō.* Tokyo: Yūshōdō Shoten, 1969.

Murasaki Shikibu. *The Tale of Genji.* Translated by Royall Tyler. New York: Viking Penguin, 2001.

Murayama Shōei. *Chishakuin shi.* Kyoto: Kōbō Daishi Onki Jimukyoku, 1934.

Muryōju kyō. T. 360.12.

Museum of Modern Art, Shiga and Kyōto Shinbunsha, eds. *Tokubetsuten: Ōmi hakkei: Kokoku fūkeiga no seiritsu to tenkai.* Ōtsu: Museum of Modern Art, Shiga and Kyōto Shinbunsha, 1988.

Museum Yamato Bunkakan, ed. *Nihon no shōzōga.* Nara: Museum Yamato Bunkakan, 1991.

Nagahama Castle Historical Museum, ed. *Botsugo yonhyaku nen tokubetsu tenrankai: Ishida Mitsunari—Hideyoshi o sasaeta chi no sanbō.* Nagahama: Nagahama Castle Historical Museum, 1999.

———, ed. *Kaikan go shūnen kinen tokubetsuten: Hashiba Hideyoshi to kohoku, Nagahama.* Nagahama: Nagahama Castle Historical Museum, 1988.

———, ed. *Tokubetsu tenrankai: Ishida Mitsunari, dai ni shō—Sengoku o shissō shita Hideyoshi bugyō.* Nagahama: Nagahama Castle Historical Museum, 2000.

———, ed. *Tokubetsuten: Chikubushima Hōgonji.* Nagahama: Nagahama Castle Historical Museum, 1992.

Naitō Akira. "Azuchijō no kenkyū." *Kokka,* no. 987 (February 1976), pp. 7–117; no. 988 (March 1976), pp. 7–63.

———. *Fukugen Azuchijō: Nobunaga no risō to ōgon no tenshu.* Tokyo: Kōdansha, 1994.

Nakai Nobuhiko and Takahashi Masahiko. "Daikugashira Nakaike monjo." Pts. 1–2. *Shigaku* 37, no. 1 (June 1964), pp. 97–108; 37, no. 2 (August 1964), pp. 225–38.

Nakajima Seiichi. "Chikubushima rengee." In *Bukkyō gyōji saiji ki: Hachigatsu mandō,* ed. Setouchi Jakuchō, Fujii Masao, and Miyata Noboru, pp. 175–84. Tokyo: Nihon Aato Sentaa, 1989.

Nakamura Kōya. *Tokugawa Ieyasu monjo no kenkyū.* 4 vols. Tokyo: Nihon Gakujutsu Shinkōkai, 1958–1971.

———. *Yododono to Hideyori.* Tokyo: Kokumin Bunka Kenkyūkai, 1966.

NAKASATO TOSHIKATSU. *Chūsonji no shitsugei. Nihon no bijutsu,* no. 318. Tokyo: Shibundō, 1992.

NAMIKI SEISHI. "Kōdaiji mitamaya zushi makie kō: 'Kōdaiji makie' shiron 1." *Uryū: Kyōto Geijutsu Tanki Daigaki kenkyū kiyō,* no. 12 (December 1989), pp. 1–10.

NANIWADA TŌRU. "Chikubushima shinkō to ezu." *Nihon bijutsu kōgei,* no. 381 (June 1970), pp. 78–82.

NANKA GENKŌ (1538–1604). *Jōe Enmyō Kokushi kyohakuroku.* 3 vols. Woodblock edition published in 1753.

NARA KEN BUNKAZAI HOZON JIMUSHO, ed. *Jūyō bunkazai Yoshino Mikumari Jinja Haiden, Heiden shūri kōji hōkokusho.* Nara Ken Kyōiku Iinkai, 1976.

NARAZAKI MUNESHIGE. "Hizen Nagoyajō zu to Kano Mitsunobu." *Kokka,* no. 915 (June 1968), pp. 51–60.

NARUMI YOSHIHIRO. "Chōkoku no jiko shuchō: Kishū ni okeru tenkai o miru." In *Daiku chōkoku,* ed. Itō Nobuo, pp. 47–53. Inax Booklet, vol. 6, no. 3. Tokyo: Inax, 1988.

NATIONAL MUSEUM OF JAPANESE HISTORY, ed. *Egakareta Edo.* Sakura: National Museum of Japanese History, 1991.

———, ed. *"Hibunken shiryō no kisoteki kenkyū (munafuda)" hōkokusho: Shaji no kokuhō, jūbun kenzōbutsu nado: Munafuda meibun shūsei.* 6 vols. Sakura: National Museum of Japanese History, 1993–1997.

———, ed. *Nihon kenchiku no sōshoku saishiki.* Sakura: Kokuritsu Rekishi Minzoku Hakubutsukan Shinkōkai, 1990.

NEDACHI KENSUKE. *Kichijō, Benzaiten zō, Nihon no bijutsu,* no. 317. Tokyo: Shibundō, 1992.

NEZU INSTITUTE OF FINE ARTS, ed. *Nachi no taki: Kumano no shizen to shinkō no zōkei.* Tokyo: Nezu Institute of Fine Arts, 1991.

Nihon meisho fūzoku zue. 19 vols. Tokyo: Kadokawa Shoten, 1979–1988.

Nihon no mon'yō. 33 vols. Kyoto: Kōrinsha, 1970–1988.

NIHON REKISHI CHIRI GAKKAI, ed. *Azuchi Momoyama jidai shiron.* 1915; reprint, Tokyo: Nihon Tosho Sentaa, 1981.

NISHI KAZUO. *Kenchikushi kenkyū no shinshiten 1: Kenchiku to shōhekiga.* Tokyo: Chūō Kōron Bijutsu Shuppan, 1999.

NISHIGORI RYŌSUKE. *Tenbu no Butsuzō jiten.* Tokyo: Tōkyō Bijutsu, 1983.

NISHIYAMA MASARU. "Toyotomi 'shiso' shinwa no fūkei." *Shisō,* no. 829 (July 1993), pp. 83–100.

Nō no tomechō. 1588–1615. Handwritten copy in the Library of Kyoto University.

NOSCO, PETER. "Keeping the Faith: *Bakuhan* Policy towards Religions in Seventeenth-century Japan." In *Religion in Japan: Arrows to Heaven and Earth,* ed. P. F. Kornicki and I. J. McMullen, pp. 135–55. Cambridge: Cambridge University Press, 1991.

NUMATA RAISUKE. *Nihon monshō gaku.* Rev. ed. Tokyo: Shin Jinbutsu Ōraisha, 1972.

ŌBUCHI TAKEMI, ed. *Momoyama no mon'yō.* Tokyo: Mainichi Shinbunsha, 1976.

OKADA JŌ, MATSUDA GONROKU, and ARAKAWA HIROKAZU, eds. *Nihon no shitsugei: Fukyūban.* 6 vols. Tokyo: Chūō Kōronsha, 1991.

OKUDAIRA SHUNROKU. *Rakuchū rakugaizu, Funakibon: Machi no nigiwai ga kikoeru.* Tokyo: Shōgakukan, 2001.

OKUNO TAKAHIRO. *Zōtei Oda Nobunaga monjo no kenkyū.* 3 vols. Tokyo: Yoshikawa Kōbunkan, 1988.

ŌKUWA HITOSHI. "Tenshōji no sōken, chūzetsu kara Daibutsu zōei e: Tenshōki Toyotomi seiken to Bukkyō." *Ōtani gakuhō* 63, no. 2 (September 1983), pp. 29–42.

ŌMI KOBIJUTSU TAIKAN KANKŌKAI, ed. *Ōmi kobijutsu taikan.* 10 portfolios. Kyoto: Yamamoto Koshū, 1955–1959.

ŌMURA SEIGAI. "Benzaiten." Pts. 1–2. *Mikkyō* 1, no. 1 (February 1911), pp. 84–105; no. 2 (May 1911), pp. 1–22.

ONO RANZAN (1729–1810). *Honzō kōmoku keimō.* Ed. Sugimoto Tsutomu. Tokyo: Waseda Daigaku Shuppanbu, 1974.

OOMS, HERMAN. "Neo-Confucianism and the Formation of Early Tokugawa Ideology: Contours of a Problem." In *Confucianism and Tokugawa Culture,* ed. Peter Nosco, pp. 27–61. Princeton: Princeton University Press, 1984.

———. *Tokugawa Ideology: Early Constructs, 1570–1680.* Princeton: Princeton University Press, 1985.

OSAKA CASTLE, ed. *Hideyoshi to Momoyama bunka: Ōsakajō Tenshukaku meihin ten.* Osaka: Mainichi Shinbun, 1996.

———, ed. *Seitan yonhyaku nen kinen tokubetsuten: Toyotomi Hideyori ten.* Osaka: Ōsakajō Tenshukaku Tokubetsu Jigyō Iinkai, 1993.

———, ed. *Tenshukaku fukkō rokujusshūnen kinen tokubetsuten: Toyotomi Hideyoshi ten.* Osaka: Osaka Castle, 1991.

———, ed. *Yodogimi to Hideyori ten.* Osaka: Ōsakajō Tenshukaku Tokubetsu Jigyō Iinkai, 1975.

OSAKA CITY MUSEUM, ed. *Shaji sankei mandara.* Tokyo: Heibonsha, 1987.

Osaka City Museum and Suntory Museum of Art, et al., eds. *Ōgon to wabi: Hideyoshi ten.* Osaka: NHK Ōsaka Hōsōkyoku, 1996.

Ōsaka Fu Shi Senmon Iinkai, ed. *Ōsaka Fu shi.* 8 vols. Osaka: Ōsaka Fu, 1978–1991.

Ōta Gyūichi (b. 1527). *Shinchō Kō ki.* Ann. Okuno Takahiro and Iwasawa Yoshihiko. Tokyo: Kadokawa Shoten, 1969.

———. *Toyokuni daimyōjin sairei ki.* In *Zoku gunsho ruijū,* ed. Hanawa Hokiichi, ser. 3, vol. 63, pp. 223–31. Tokyo: Zoku Gunsho Ruijū Kanseikai, 1924.

Ōta Hirotarō. *Nihon kenchiku no tokushitsu.* Vol. 1 of *Nihon kenchiku shi ronshū.* Tokyo: Iwanami Shoten, 1983.

———. *Nihon kenchiku shi josetsu: Zōho dai ni han.* Tokyo: Shōkokusha, 1989.

Oyudono no Ue no nikki. 11 vols. Ed. Wada Masao and Saiki Kazuma. *Zoku Gunsho Ruijū, hoi.* Tokyo: Zoku Gunsho Ruijū Kanseikai, 1964–1966.

Oze Hoan (1564–1640). *Taikōki.* Ann. Hinotani Teruhiko and Emoto Hiroshi. Shin Nihon koten bungaku taikei, no. 60. Tokyo: Iwanami Shoten, 1996.

Pekarik, Andrew J. *Japanese Lacquer, 1600–1900: Selections from the Charles A. Greenfield Collection.* New York: Metropolitan Museum of Art, 1980.

Phillips, Quitman E. "*Honchō gashi* and the Kano Myth." *Archives of Asian Art* 47 (1994), pp. 46–57.

———. *The Practices of Painting in Japan, 1475–1500.* Stanford: Stanford University Press, 2000.

Richard, Naomi Noble, ed. *The Great Eastern Temple: Treasures of Japanese Buddhist Art from Tōdai-ji.* Chicago: Art Institute of Chicago, 1986.

RN. See *Rokuon nichiroku.*

Rokuon nichiroku. Ed. Tsuji Zennosuke. 6 vols. 1934–1937; reprint, Tokyo: Zoku Gunsho Ruijū Kanseikai, 1961–1962. Separate index vol. ed. Tsuji Zennosuke and Nomura Tsuneshige. Tokyo: Zoku Gunsho Ruijū Kanseikai, 1962.

Rosenfield, John M., in collaboration with Fumiko E. Cranston. *Extraordinary Persons: Works by Eccentric, Nonconformist Japanese Artists of the Early Modern Era (1580–1868) in the Collection of Kimiko and John Powers.* Ed. Naomi Noble Richard. 3 vols. Cambridge, Mass.: Harvard University Art Museums, 1999.

Saiki Kazuma. "Momoyama jidai to iu koshō." *Nihon rekishi,* no. 209 (October 1965), pp. 84–85.

———, ed. *Ko kiroku gaku gairon.* Tokyo: Yoshikawa Kōbunkan, 1990.

Sakai City Museum, ed. *Sakai shū: Chanoyu o tsukutta hitobito.* Sakai: Sakai City Museum, 1989.

Sakurai Narihiro. *Toyotomi Hideyoshi no kyojō.* Tokyo: Nihon Jōkaku Shiryōkan Shuppankai, 1970.

Sakurai Toshio. "Tsukubusuma Jinja Honden." In *Shaden 3.* Vol. 3 of *Nihon kenchiku shi kiso shiryō shūsei,* ed. Ōta Hirotarō, pp. 40–47. Tokyo: Chūō Kōron Bijutsu Shuppan, 1981.

———. "Yoshino Mikumari Jinja Honden." In *Shaden 3.* Vol. 3 of *Nihon kenchiku shi kiso shiryō shūsei,* ed. Ōta Hirotarō, pp. 48–55. Tokyo: Chūō Kōron Bijutsu Shuppan, 1981.

Sakurai Toshio and Tada Shinji. *Ōsaka Fu jinja honden ikō shūsei.* Tokyo: Hōsei Daigaku Shuppankyoku, 1983.

Samonides, William Harry. "The Kōami Family of Maki-e Lacquerers." Ph.D. diss., Harvard University, 1991.

———. "Patronizing Images: Kōdai-in and Toyotomi Hideyoshi at Kōdaiji." *Nichibunken Japan Review* 7 (1996), pp. 99–125.

Sandler, Mark H. "Water Dragons: Sacred Cataracts in Japanese Art." *Asian Art and Culture* 8 (Spring/Summer 1995), pp. 74–91.

Sanford, James H., William R. LaFleur, and Masatoshi Nagatomi, eds. *Flowing Traces: Buddhism in the Literary and Visual Arts of Japan.* Princeton: Princeton University Press, 1992.

Sangawa Tatsukiyo (1697–1739), ed. *Ōmi yochi shi ryaku.* Ann. Kojima Suteichi as *Kōtei tōchū Ōmi yochi shi ryaku.* Tokyo: Rekishi Toshosha, 1968.

Sankeien Hoshōkai, ed. *Sankeien.* Yokohama: Sankeien Hoshōkai, 1992.

San'yō Shinbunsha, ed. *Nene to Kinoshita ke monjo.* Okayama Shi: San'yō Shinbunsha, 1982.

Sasaki Takamasa. "Chikubushima ni okeru shinbutsu bunri ni tsuite." *Ōtani gakuhō* 55, no. 2 (September 1975), pp. 1–13.

Sasama Yoshihiko. *Benzaiten shinkō to zokushin.* Tokyo: Yūzankaku, 1991.

Satō Dōshin. *<Nihon bijutsu> tanjō: Kindai Nihon no "kotoba" to senryaku.* Kodansha sensho métier 92. Tokyo: Kōdansha, 1996.

Satō Masahiko. *Tenjōura no bunkashi: Munafuda wa kataru.* Tokyo: Kōdansha, 1995.

Sawa Jitsuei. *Chikubushima shi.* Chikubushima: Hōgonji Jimusho, 1975.

Sawamura Masashi. "Hōryūji Tōin Denpōdō." In *Butsudō 1.* Vol. 4 of *Nihon kenchiku shi kiso shiryō shūsei,* ed. Ōta Hirotarō, pp. 43–51. Tokyo: Chūō Kōron Bijutsu Shuppan, 1981.

SEKINE SHUN'ICHI. *Hotoke, bosatsu to dōnai no shōgon. Nihon no bijutsu*, no. 281. Tokyo: Shibundō, 1989.

SEZON MUSEUM OF ART and SHIZUOKA PREFECTURAL MUSEUM OF ART, eds. *Via Orientalis: Porutogaru to Nanban bunka ten.* Tokyo: Nihon Hōsō Kyōkai, 1993.

SHIGA KEN, ed. *Shiga Ken shi.* 6 vols. 1927–1928.

Shiga Ken hōmotsu mokuroku. 1888. Original in the Shiryōkan, Tokyo National Museum.

SHIGA KEN KYŌIKU IINKAI JIMUKYOKU BUNKABU BUNKAZAI HOGOKA, ed. *Chikubushima Hōgonji monjo mokuroku.* Shiga: Shiga Ken Kyōiku Iinkai Jimukyoku Bunkabu Bunkazai Hogoka, 1992.

SHIMADA SHŪJIRŌ. "Jikkan to boku budō." In *Chūgoku kaigashi kenkyū*, pp. 136–51. Vol. 2 of *Shimada Shūjirō chosakushū.* Tokyo: Chūō Kōron Bijutsu Shuppan, 1993. (First published in *Bijutsu kenkyū*, no. 337 [February 1987], pp. 102–12.)

SHIMADA SHŪJIRŌ and IRIYA YOSHITAKA, eds. *Zenrin gasan: Chūsei suibokuga o yomu.* Tokyo: Mainichi Shinbunsha, 1987.

SHIMIZU MASUMI. "*Heike monogatari* no juyō, kinsei (chūshaku shi o fukumu)." In *Heike monogatari: Hihyō to bunkashi*, ed. Yamashita Hiroaki, pp. 135–57. Tokyo: Kyūko Shoin, 1997.

SHIMIZU, YOSHIAKI. "Multiple Connections: *The Vegetable Nehan* of Itō Jakuchū." In *Flowing Traces: Buddhism in the Literary and Visual Arts of Japan*, ed. James H. Sanford, William R. LaFleur, and Masatoshi Nagatomi, pp. 201–33. Princeton: Princeton University Press, 1992.

———. "Problems of Moku'an Rei'en (?–1323–1345)." Ph.D. diss., Princeton University, 1974.

———. "The Shigisan-engi Scrolls, c. 1175." In *Pictorial Narrative in Antiquity and the Middle Ages*, ed. Herbert L. Kessler and Marianna Shreve Simpson, pp. 115–29. Studies in the History of Art, vol. 16. Washington: National Gallery of Art, 1985.

———. "Workshop Management of the Early Kano Painters, ca. A.D. 1530–1600." *Archives of Asian Art* 34 (1981), pp. 32–47.

———, ed. *Japan: The Shaping of Daimyo Culture, 1185–1868.* Washington, D.C.: National Gallery of Art, 1988.

SHIMOMURA NOBUHIRO. "Aru Toyotomi Hideyori no monjo." *Nagoyashi Hakubutsukan dayori*, no. 110 (June 1996), p. 878.

SHIMONAKA YASABURŌ, ed. *Daijiten.* 26 vols. Tokyo: Heibonsha, 1934–1936.

Shiryō sōran. Ed. Tōkyō Daigaku Shiryō Hensanjo. 17 vols. Tokyo: Tōkyō Daigaku Shuppankai, 1923–1963.

SHIZUOKA PREFECTURAL MUSEUM OF ART, ed. *Kaikan sanshūnen kinen ten: Kanoha no kyoshōtachi.* Shizuoka: Kanoha no Kyoshōtachi Ten Jikkō Iinkai, 1989.

Shōmei. Ed. Ōta Hirotarō and Itō Yōtarō. Tokyo: Kajima Kenkyūjo Shuppankai, 1971.

SK. See Bonshun. *Shunkyū ki.*

SMITH, HENRY D., II. "Five Myths about Early Modern Japan." In *Asia in Western and World History: A Guide for Teaching*, ed. Ainslie T. Embree and Carol Gluck, pp. 514–22. Armonk, N.Y. and London: M.E. Sharpe, 1997.

———. *Taizansō and the One-Mat Room (Taizansō: Matsuura Takeshirō no ichijōjiki no sekai).* Tokyo: Hachiro Yuasa Memorial Museum, International Christian University, 1993.

SMITH, JONATHAN Z. "The Bare Facts of Ritual." In *Imagining Religion: From Babylon to Jonestown*, pp. 53–65. Chicago and London: University of Chicago Press, 1982.

———. "The Wobbling Pivot." In *To Take Place: Toward Theory in Ritual*, pp. 88–103. Chicago and London: University of Chicago Press, 1987.

SŌHONZAN DAIGOJI and NIHON KEIZAI SHINBUN, eds. *Inori to bi no denshō: Daigojiten: Hideyoshi, Daigo no hanami yonhyaku nen.* Nihon Keizai Shinbun, 1998.

SONE YŪJI. "Keichō yon nen no Tokugawa Ieyasu to Katagiri Katsumoto." *Nihon rekishi*, no. 454 (March 1986), pp. 44–52.

STALKER, JOHN, and GEORGE PARKER. *A Treatise of Japanning and Varnishing 1688.* Chicago, Quadrangle Books, 1960.

SUGIYAMA HIROSHI, WATANABE TAKERU, FUTAKI KEN'ICHI, and OWADA TETSUO, eds. *Toyotomi Hideyoshi jiten.* Tokyo: Shin Jinbutsu Ōraisha, 1990.

SUNTORY MUSEUM OF ART, ed. *Megamitachi no Nihon.* Tokyo: Suntory Museum of Art, 1994.

SUWA HARUO and NAITŌ AKIRA, eds. *Edozu byōbu.* Tokyo: Mainichi Shinbunsha, 1972.

SUZUKI HIROYUKI. "Byōbue ni okeru shajitsu: Naizenbon Hōkoku saireizu to chūkū no shikaku." In *Tōyō bijutsu ni okeru shajitsu: Kokusai kōryū bijutsushi kenkyūkai dai 12 kai shinpojiamu*, pp. 71–79. Osaka: Kokusai Kōryū Bijutsushi Kenkyūkai, 1994.

———. *Kano Hideyori hitsu, Takao kanpūzu byōbu: Kioku no katachi.* E wa kataru, vol. 8. Tokyo: Heibonsha, 1994.

———. "The Reconstruction of the Body and the Inauguration of 'Bijutsu (Fine Arts)' in the

Meiji Period." 1997 TMs [photocopy] prepared for College Art Association Conference.

T. See *Taishō shinshū Daizōkyō.*

Taishō shinshū Daizōkyō. Ed. Takakusu Junjirō, Watanabe Kaigyoku, et al. 85 vols. Tokyo: Taishō Issaikyō Kankōkai, 1924–1934.

Takayanagi Mitsutoshi. "Toyotomi Hideyoshi no Ōsakajō ni tsuite." *Kokushigaku,* no. 9 (December 1931), pp. 1–30.

Takayanagi, Shun'chi. "The Glory That Was Azuchi." *Monumenta Nipponica* 32, no. 4 (Winter 1977), pp. 515–24.

Takeda Tsuneo. "Kinsei shoki josei shōzōga ni kansuru ichikōsatsu." *Yamato bunka,* no. 56 (September 1972), pp. 12–22.

———. *Kinsei shoki shōheiga no kenkyū.* 2 vols. Tokyo: Yoshikawa Kōbunkan, 1983.

———. *Shōheiga.* Vol. 13 of *Genshoku Nihon no bijutsu.* Tokyo: Shōgakukan, 1967.

———. "Tenzuiji Kyakuden gakō: Eitoku taiga o megutte." In *Bijutsushi no danmen,* pp. 317–33. Osaka: Seibundō, 1995.

———. "Toyokuni sairei zu no tokushitsu to tenkai." In *Fūzokuga: Sairei, kabuki,* ed. Takeda Tsuneo, pp. 111–23. Vol. 13 of *Nihon byōbue shūsei.* Tokyo: Kōdansha, 1978.

———, ed. *Fūzokuga: Rakuchū rakugai.* Vol. 11 of *Nihon byōbue shūsei.* Tokyo: Kōdansha, 1978.

———, ed. *Fūzokuga: Sairei, kabuki.* Vol. 13 of *Nihon byōbue shūsei.* Tokyo: Kōdansha, 1978.

———, ed. *Kano Eitoku. Nihon no bijutsu,* no. 94. Tokyo: Shibundō, 1974.

———, ed. *Momoyama kaiga. Nihon no bijutsu,* no. 208. Tokyo: Shibundō, 1983.

Takeda Tsuneo and Kano Hiroyuki, eds. *Kenrantaru taiga 1: Momoyama zenki no kachō.* Vol. 3 of *Kachōga no sekai.* Tokyo: Gakushū Kenkyūsha, 1982.

Takeuchi, Melinda. "The Golden Link: Place, Poetry, and Paradise in a Medieval Japanese Design." In *Worlds Seen and Imagined: Japanese Screens from The Idemitsu Museum of Art,* Taizō Kuroda, Melinda Takeuchi, and Yūzō Yamane, pp. 30–53. New York: Asia Society Galleries, 1995.

Takeuchi Naoji. *Kōgetsu Sōgan: Bokuseki no utsushi—Zenrin bokuseki kantei nichiroku—no kenkyū.* Tokyo: Kokusho Kankōkai, 1976–.

The Tale of the Heike. Trans. Helen Craig McCullough. Stanford: Stanford University Press, 1988.

Tamamuro Fumio. *Nihon bukkyō shi: Kinsei.* Tokyo: Yoshikawa Kōbunkan, 1987.

Tamon'in nikki. Ed. Tsuji Zennosuke. 5 vols. Tokyo: Sankyō Shoin, 1935–1939.

Tanaka Hiromi, ed., "Honkoku *Yamanoue no Sōji ki* Takeda ke otsubon." In *Yamanoue no Sōji ki kenkyū,* ed. Chanoyu Konwakai, vol. 2, pp. 83–128. Tokyo: Santokuan, 1994.

Tanaka Hisao. "Ōta Gyūichi *Shinchō Kō ki* seiritsu kō." *Teikoku Gakushiin kiji* 5, nos. 2–3 (November 1947), pp. 137–57.

Tanaka Tomohiko. "Ishiyama yori gyakuuchi to tōgoku no junreisha: Saigoku junreiro no fukugen." *Kōbe Daigaku Bungakubu kiyō,* no. 15 (March 1988), pp. 1–23.

Tanaka Toyozō. "Hōkokusai no byōbu ni tsuite." *Kokka,* no. 352 (September 1919), pp. 90–102.

Tanomura Tadao. "Hōkokusai zu byōbu." *Kokka,* no. 805 (April 1959), pp. 119–25.

Taylor, Mark C., ed. *Critical Terms for Religious Studies.* Chicago and London: University of Chicago Press, 1998.

TCH. See Nagahama Castle Historical Museum, *Tokubetsuten: Chikubushima Hōgonji.*

ten Grotenhuis, Elizabeth. *Japanese Mandalas: Representations of Sacred Geography.* Honolulu: University of Hawai'i Press, 1999.

Tendaishū Jimonha Goonki Jimukyoku, ed. *Onjōji no kenkyū.* Ōtsu: Tendaishū Jimonha Goonki Jimukyoku, 1931; reprint, Kyoto: Shibunkaku Shuppan, 1978.

Tennōjiya kaiki. Ed. Nagashima Fukutarō. Vols. 7–8 of *Chado koten zenshū,* ed. Sen Sōshitsu. Kyoto: Tankōsha, 1959.

Teramura Keiji, ed. *Tsukubusuma Jinja shaki.* 1892.

TN. See *Tamon'in nikki.*

Toda Teisuke, Kawakami Mitsugu, Nagai Norio, and Yabe Yoshiaki, eds. *Zenshū jiin to teien: Nanbokuchō, Muromachi no kenchiku, chōkoku, kōgei.* Vol. 11 of *Nihon bijutsu zenshū.* Tokyo: Kōdansha, 1993.

Tōdaiki. In vol. 2 of *Shiseki zassan,* ed. Hayakawa Junzaburō, pp. 1–214. Tokyo: Kokusho Kankōkai, 1911.

Tōji (Kyōō Gokokuji) Hōmotsukan, ed. *Tōji no Tenbuzō.* Kyoto: Tōji (Kyōō Gokokuji) Hōmotsukan, 1993.

Tokitsune Kyō ki. See Yamashina Tokitsune. *Tokitsune Kyō ki.*

Tokuda Kōen, Yoshimura Motoo, and Haino Akio. *Kōdaiji makie.* Tokyo: Benridō, 1981.

Tokugawa Art Museum, ed. *Shōgun no goten: Edojō shōhekiga no shitae.* Nagoya: Tokugawa Art Museum, 1988.

———, ed. *Tokugawa Ieyasu tanjō yonhyaku gojū nen kinen: Ieyasu no isan—Sunpu onbunbutsu.* Nagoya: Tokugawa Art Museum; Mito: Tokugawa Museum, 1992.

Tokugawa Yoshinobu. *Shinshū Tokugawa Ieyasu*

monjo no kenkyū. Tokyo: Tokugawa Reimeikai, 1983.

TOKUNAGA SHIN'ICHIRŌ. *Shiga kenjin*. Tokyo: Shin Jinbutsu Ōraisha, 1976.

TOKYO METROPOLITAN EDO-TOKYO MUSEUM, ed. *Edo Tōkyō Hakubutsukan: Sōgō annai*. Tokyo: Edo Tōkyō Rekishi Zaidan, 1993.

TOKYO NATIONAL MUSEUM, ed. *Sōgen no kaiga*. Kyoto: Benridō, 1962.

TOKYO NATIONAL MUSEUM, et al., ed. *Tōdaijiten*. Asahi Shinbunsha, 1980.

TŌKYŌ TEIKOKU DAIGAKU, ed. *Dai Nihon komonjo, iewake*. Tokyo: Tōkyō Teikoku Daigaku, 1904–.

TŌKYŌ TO DAITŌ KUYAKUSHO. *Daitō Ku shi: Enkakuhen*. Tokyo: Tōkyō To Daitō Kuyakusho, 1966.

TOTMAN, CONRAD. *The Green Archipelago: Forestry in Preindustrial Japan*. Berkeley, Los Angeles, London: University of California Press, 1989.

TSUDA SABURŌ. *Hideyoshi, hideo densetsu no kiseki: Shirarezaru uramenshi*. Tokyo: Rokkō Shuppan, 1991.

———. *Hideyoshi, hideo densetsu no nazo: Hiyoshimaru kara Hōtaikō e*. Chūkō bunko, no. 800. Tokyo: Chūō Kōronsha, 1997.

———. *Hideyoshi no higeki: Massatsu sareta Toyotomi ke no eika*. PHP Bunko. Tokyo: PHP Kenkyūjo, 1989.

TSUJI NOBUO. "Funaki ke kyūzōbon rakuchū rakugai zu byōbu no kentō." In *Fūzokuga: Rakuchū rakugai*, ed. Takeda Tsuneo, pp. 122–29. Vol. 11 of *Nihon byōbue shūsei*. Tokyo: Kōdansha, 1978.

———. "Kano Motonobu." Pts. 1–5. *Bijutsu kenkyū*, no. 246 (May 1966), pp. 10–29; no. 249 (November 1966), pp. 129–59; no. 270 (July 1970), pp. 41–78; no. 271 (September 1970), pp. 85–125; no. 272 (November 1970), pp. 150–67.

———. *Kisō no zufu: Karakuri, Jakuchū, kazari*. Tokyo: Heibonsha, 1989.

———. "Momoyama no ishō." In *Eitoku to shōheiga: Momoyama no kaiga, kōgei 2*, ed. Tsuji Nobuo, Kōno Motoaki, and Yabe Yoshiaki, pp. 156–63. Vol. 15 of *Nihon bijutsu zenshū*. Tokyo: Kōdansha, 1991.

———. "Ornament (Kazari)—An Approach to Japanese Culture." *Archives of Asian Art* 47 (1994), pp. 35–45.

———. *Sengoku jidai Kanoha no kenkyū: Kano Motonobu o chūshin to shite*. Tokyo: Yoshikawa Kōbunkan, 1994.

———. "Toyokuni matsurie byōbu." *Kokka*, no. 924 (July 1970), pp. 23–31.

TSUJI NOBUO, HIRAI KIYOSHI, and YABE YOSHIAKI, eds. *Shiro to chashitsu: Momoyama no kenchiku, kōgei 1*. Vol. 14 of *Nihon bijutsu zenshū*. Tokyo: Kōdansha, 1992.

TSUJI NOBUO, KŌNO MOTOAKI, and YABE YOSHIAKI, eds. *Eitoku to shōheiga: Momoyama no kaiga, kōgei 2*. Vol. 15 of *Nihon bijutsu zenshū*. Tokyo: Kōdansha, 1991.

TSUJI ZENNOSUKE. *Nihon Bukkyō shi*. 10 vols. Tokyo: Iwanami Shoten, 1944–1955.

TSUNODA, RYUSAKU, et al., eds. *Sources of Japanese Tradition*. 2 vols. Paperback ed. New York: Columbia University Press, 1964.

TYLER, ROYALL. "'The Path of My Mountain': Buddhism in Nō." In *Flowing Traces: Buddhism in the Literary and Visual Arts of Japan*, ed. James H. Sanford, William R. LaFleur, and Masatoshi Nagatomi, pp. 149–79. Princeton: Princeton University Press, 1992.

TYLER, ROYALL, ed. and trans. *Japanese Nō Dramas*. New York: Penguin Books, 1992.

TYLER, SUSAN. "Honji suijaki Faith." *Japanese Journal of Religious Studies* 16, nos. 2–3 (June/September 1989), pp. 227–50.

UCHIDA KUSUO. "Toyotomi Hideyoshi no Ōsakajō kensetsu." In *Yomigaeru chūsei 2: Honganji kara tenka ichi e Ōsaka*, ed. Sakuma Takashi, pp. 34–55. Tokyo: Heibonsha, 1989.

UEYAMA SHUNPEI, ed. *Kenkyū happyō to zadankai: Bukkyō bijutsu in okeru "shōgon"*. Bukkyō Bijutsu Kenkyū Ueno Kinen Zaidan Josei Kenkyūkai, report no. 15. Kyoto: Bukkyō Bijutsu Kenkyū Ueno Kinen Zaidan Josei Kenkyūkai, 1987.

USAMI TATSUO. "Keichō jishin ni koto yosete." *Nihon rekishi*, no 590 (July 1997), pp. 67–69.

WAKISAKA ATSUSHI. "Ōsaka o egaku shobyōbu no myakuryaku." *Ōsaka Shiritsu Bijutsukan kiyō*, no. 6 (1986), pp. 5–32.

WAKISAKA ATSUSHI and TANAKA TOSHIO, eds. *Kenrantaru taiga 2: Momoyama kōki no kachō*. Vol. 4 of *Kachōga no sekai*. Tokyo: Gakushū Kenkyūsha, 1982.

WAKITA OSAMU. "The Emergence of the State in Sixteenth Century Japan: From Oda to Tokugawa." *Journal of Japanese Studies* 8, no. 2 (Summer 1982), pp. 343–67.

———. *Ōsaka jidai to Hideyoshi*. Shōgakukan Raiburari 127. Tokyo: Shōgakukan, 1999.

WANG QI [WANG CH'I] (act. 1565–1614). *Sancai tuhui [San-ts'ai t'u-hui]*. Taibei: Chengwen Chubanshe [Taipei: Ch'eng-wen Ch'u-pan-she, 1970].

WATANABE YOSUKE. *Hōtaikō no shiteki seikatsu*. Nihon bunka meicho sen. Osaka: Sōgensha, 1939.

WATSKY, ANDREW M. "The Art of the Ensemble: The Tsukubusuma Sanctuary, 1570–1615." Ph.D. diss., Princeton University, 1994.

———. "Commerce, Politics, and Tea: The Career of Imai Sōkyū." *Monumenta Nipponica* 50, no. 1 (Spring 1995), pp. 47–65.

———. "Floral Motifs and Mortality: Restoring Numinous Meaning to a Momoyama Building." *Archives of Asian Art* 50 (1997–1998), pp. 62–92.

———. "Sutemaru no gen'ei: Tsukubusuma Jinja Honden moya o megutte." *Bijutsu kenkyū,* no. 366 (February 1997), pp. 51–76.

WATT, JAMES C. Y., and BARBARA BRENNAN FORD. *East Asian Lacquer: The Florence and Herbert Irving Collection.* New York: Metropolitan Museum of Art, 1991.

WHEELWRIGHT, CAROLYN K. "Kano Painters of the Sixteenth Century A.D.: The Development of Motonobu's Daisen-in Style." *Archives of Asian Art* 34 (1981), pp. 6–31.

———. "Kano Shōei." Ph.D. diss., Princeton University, 1981.

———. "A Visualization of Eitoku's Lost Paintings at Azuchi Castle." In *Warlords, Artists, and Commoners: Japan in the Sixteenth Century,* ed. George Elison and Bardwell L. Smith, pp. 87–111. Honolulu: University of Hawaii Press, 1981.

YABU KEIZŌ. *Toyotomi Hideyori.* Tokyo: Shin Jinbutsu Ōraisha, 1987.

YAMAGISHI MOTOO. *Nihon katchū ronshū.* Tokyo: Nihon Katchū Ronshū Kankōkai, 1991.

YAMAMOTO HIKARI, ed. *Oda Nobunaga: Tenka fubu e no michi.* Bessatsu rekishi dokuhon, vol. 14, no. 6. Tokyo: Shin Jinbutsu Ōraisha, 1989.

YAMAMOTO SHINJI and MIZUNO KATSUHIKO. *Kyō, Fushimi rekishi no tabi.* Tokyo: Yamakawa Shuppansha, 1991.

YAMAMURO KYŌKO. *Ōgon Taikō.* Chūkō shinsho, no. 1105. Tokyo: Chūō Kōronsha, 1993.

YAMASHINA TOKITSUNE (1543–1611). *Tokitsune Kyō ki.* Ed. Tōkyō Daigaku Shiryō Hensanjo. 14 vols. *Dai Nihon kokiroku.* Tokyo: Iwanami Shoten, 1959–1991.

YAMASHITA HIROAKI, ed. *Heike monogatari: Hihyō to bunkashi.* Tokyo: Kyūko Shoin, 1997.

YIENGPRUKSAWAN, MIMI HALL. *Hiraizumi: Buddhist Art and Regional Politics in Twelfth-Century Japan.* Harvard East Asian Monographs, no. 171. Cambridge, Mass.: Harvard University Asia Center, 1998.

———. "The House of Gold: Fujiwara Kiyohira's Konjikidō." *Monumenta Nipponica* 48, no. 1 (Spring 1993), pp. 33–52.

———. "The Legacy of Buddhist Art at Nara." In *Buddhist Treasures from Nara,* ed. Michael R. Cunningham, pp. 1–34. Cleveland: Cleveland Museum of Art, 1998.

YOKOHAMA HISTORY MUSEUM. *Tokubetsuten: Hideyoshi shūrai: Kinsei Kantō no makuake.* Yokohama: Yokohama History Museum, 1999.

YOKOTA FUYUHIKO. "Kinsei toshi to shokunin shūdan." In vol. 3 of *Nihon toshi shi nyūmon,* ed. Takahashi Yasuo and Yoshida Nobuyuki, pp. 37–60. Tokyo: Tōkyō Daigaku Shuppankai, 1990.

YONEMOTO, MARCIA. "The 'Spatial Vernacular' in Tokugawa Maps." *The Journal of Asian Studies* 59, no. 3 (August 2000), pp. 647–66.

YONEMURA, ANN. "Decoration and Representation in Japanese Lacquer." *Oriental Art* 45, no. 3 (Autumn 1999), pp. 16–22.

———. *Japanese Lacquer.* Washington, D.C.: Freer Gallery of Art, Smithsonian Institution, 1979.

YOSHIDA KANEMI (1535–1610). *Kanemi Kyō ki.* Ed. Saiki Kazuma and Someya Mitsuhiro. *Shiryō sanshū dai ikki.* Tokyo: Zoku Gunsho Ruijū Kanseikai, 1971–.

YOSHIMURA, MOTOO. "Innovations in Kodaiji Makie." In *Urushi: Proceedings of the Urushi Study Group, June 10–27, 1985, Tokyo,* ed. N. S. Brommell and Perry Smith, pp. 7–12. Marina del Rey, Calif.: Getty Conservation Institute, 1988.

YOSHINO CHŌ SHI HENSHŪ IINKAI, ed. *Yoshino Chō shi.* 2 vols. Nara: Yoshino Machiyakuba, 1972.

YOSHINO TOMIO. "Kōdaiji makie ni tsuite." *Gasetsu* (January 1941), pp. 76–83.

YOSHIOKA YUKIO, ed. *Nihon no ishō.* 16 vols. Kyoto: Kyōto Shoin, 1983–1987.

ZAIDANHŌJIN BUNKAZAI KENZŌBUTSU HOZON GIJUTSU GYŌKAI, ed. *Shiryō kyūkokuhō kenzōbutsu shitei setsumei.* Tokyo: Zaidanhōjin Bunkazai Kenzōbutsu Hozon Gijutsu Gyōkai, 1982.

ZHU XI (1130–1200). *Sishu jizhu,* commentary on *Analects* 3:25 (Sibu beiyao ed.).

Zōgyoku wakashū. In vol. 16 of *Gunsho ruijū,* pp. 271–84. 1934; rev. ed., Tokyo: Zoku Gunsho Ruijū Kanseikai Yōsha, 1939.

Illustration Credits

The photographs of the Tsukubusuma Main Hall used in this book, unless otherwise noted, were made as part of an extensive photography project of the site that the author conducted in 1993 with Fukushima Tsuneo and the photographers Morishita Tadao and Hashimoto Hirobumi of the publishing firm Kōrinsha (no longer in existence). This project was supported by the Tsukubusuma Jinja and a Spears grant from the Department of Art and Archaeology of Princeton University. Permission to use these and other photographs of the Tsukubusuma Main Hall was granted by the Tsukubusuma Jinja.

Other photographs were provided by present owners, except where otherwise noted in the captions. Permission to use these photographs was generously granted courtesy of the following: Byōdōin, Uji: *Fig. 89;* Chishakuin, Kyoto: *Figs. 44, 45;* Chōkokuji, Nagano Prefecture: *Figs. 65, 66;* Chūsonji, Iwate Prefecture: *Figs. 90, 91;* Daigoji, Kyoto: *Figs. 47, 103, 130, 140, 141;* Gotoh Museum, Tokyo: *Fig. 143;* Gyokuhōin, Myōshinji, Kyoto: *Fig. 46;* Hōgonji, Chikubushima, Shiga Prefecture: *Figs. 101, 102, 137, 138;* Hōjuin, Hyōgo Prefecture: *Figs. 112, 113;* Hōkōji, Kyoto: *Fig. 129;* Itabashi Art Museum, Tokyo: *Fig. 155;* Jōshinji, Kinomoto, Shiga Prefecture: *Fig. 139;* Jōtokuji, Fukui Prefecture: *Figs. 28, 29;* Kawakami collection, Tokyo: *Fig. 42;* Keiunji, Hyōgo Prefecture: *Fig. 76;* Kōdaiji, Kyoto: *Figs. 62, 106, 146;* Kongōbuji, Wakayama Prefecture: *Figs. 96, 97;* Kumano Hayatama Taisha, Wakayama Prefecture: *Fig. 111;* Masaki Museum of Art, Wakayama Prefecture: *Fig. 79;* Mitsui Bunko Foundation, Tokyo: *Fig. 43;* MOA Museum of Art, Shizuoka Prefecture: *Fig. 31;* Myōhōji, Ishikawa Prefecture: *Fig. 77;* Myōkian, Kyoto: *Fig. 32;* Myōshinji, Kyoto: *Figs. 87, 88;* Nagoya City Museum: *Fig. 107;* Nara Prefectural Museum of Art: *Fig. 25;* National Museum of Japanese History, Chiba Prefecture: *Fig. 48;* Nikkō Tōshōgū, Tochigi Prefecture: *Fig. 158;* Onjōji, Ōtsu: *Figs. 92–94, 142;* Osaka Castle: *Fig. 116;* Ōsasahara Jinja, Shiga Prefecture: *Figs. 98, 99;* Rinkain, Kyoto: *Fig. 23;* Saikyōji, Shiga Prefecture: *Figs. 22, 78;* Sankōji, Aomori Prefecture: *Figs. 63, 64;* Sunritz Hattori Museum of Arts, Nagano Prefecture: *Fig. 73;* Tokugawa Art Museum, Nagoya: *Figs. 144, 145;* Tokyo Metropolitan Central Library: *Figs. 156, 157;* Tokyo National Museum: *Figs. 26, 27, 30, 33, 74, 95, 100, 108–10, 121;* Tokyo National University of Fine Arts and Music: *Fig. 24;* Toyokuni Jinja, Kyoto: *Figs. 131–36;* Tsukubusuma Jinja: *Fig. 1;* Tsurugaoka Hachimangū, Kanagawa Prefecture: *Fig. 120.*

Index

Aikyōgen 間狂言, 304n.35
Akechi Mitsuhide 明智光秀, 68, 99
Aki Province 安芸国, 55
Almeida, Luis de, 77
Amaterasu Ōmikami 天照大神, Chikubushima and, 242, 243
Amenomori Chōsuke 雨森長介, 240, 245
Amidanotake あみだのたけ, 205
Analects of Confucius, 189
Anashi Jinja 穴師神社, 221
Annyō 安養. *See* Realm of Peace and Sustenance
Annyōkai 安養界. *See* Realm of Peace and Sustenance
Aoba 青葉, Nō flute named, 64–65
Appropriation and assemblage: of architecture, 245–52; in *chanoyu*, 252–57
Architectural coloring, 108, 112, 113, 150, 188, 196, 213, 265. *See also* Ensemble; Tsukubusuma Main Hall
Architecture: as emblem of Momoyama stability, 31–32; Momoyama restorations of, 252; mortuary, 92, 111–13, 116–17, 121, 141–42, 143, 231; moving of, 245–52; new forms of, 36–38; prefabrication of, 246; and unsubstantiated Hideyoshi provenance, 246. *See also* Ensemble; Tsukubusuma Main Hall
Aristocrat-abbot, 98, 99, 205
Asai 浅井 (house), 53, 59, 62–63, 66, 235
Asai County 浅井郡, 42
Asai Hisamasa 浅井久政, 62, 63
Asai Nagamasa 浅井長政, 62, 63, 66, 200, 244
Asakura 朝倉 (house), 59
Asano Nagayoshi (Nagamasa) 浅野長吉 (長政), 98, 99
Ashikaga 足利 (shoguns), 58
Ashikaga Yoshimitsu 足利義満, 173, 302n.108
Ashikaga Yoshimochi 足利義持, 81
Ashikaga Yoshinori 足利義教, 65, 302n.108
Atago Shrine 愛宕神社, 36, 85
Azaihime no Mikoto 浅井姫命: in *Chikubushima engi*, 51, 52; as manifestation of Benzaiten, 40; as manifestation of Shaka, 52; worshipped on Chikubushima, 42
Azuchi Castle 安土城, 28, 150, 195, 232, 233, 252; compared to Osaka Castle, 70; Confucian imagery at, 190; incorporation of sacred into, 60; paintings at, 151, 152–53; secondary literature on, 281n.53
Azuchi-Momoyama period 安土桃山時代, 28

Bakudenshō 莫伝抄, 290n.36
Bakuhan 幕藩, 297n.1
Bencao gangmu 本草綱目, 134
Benten sanbukyō 辯天三部経, 233, 243
Benzaiten 辯才天 (first character is sometimes written as 辨 or 弁; middle character is sometimes written as 財): and Chikubushima, 32, 40–41, 42, 53, 54, 55–57, 65, 67, 87, 232, 233, 235–39, 240–44, 272, 273–74; and Durgā, 303n.16; and Edo, 270–72, 272–74; and Fifteen Attendants, 233, 243, 266; as goddess of music, 232–33; and Japan, 55–56, 232–35; manifested as Blue Dragon and White Snake, 242; manifested as Dragon God, 237; manifested as White Dragon, 55; Minamoto no Yoritomo and, 233; Nobunaga and worship of, at Sōkenji, 60, 233; as protector deity, 40–41, 232–33, 243, 274; referred to as Benzai Tennyo, 56, 238; referred to as Tennyo, 55, 62, 65, 237; sculptures of, on Chikubushima, 41, 233, 235, 265–66, *Fig. 137*; worship of, beyond Chikubushima, 233–35
Benzaiten Hall on Chikubushima. *See under* Tsukubusuma Main Hall
Benzai Tennyo 弁才天女. *See* Benzaiten
Benzaitensha 弁財天社. *See* Benzaiten Hall on Chikubushima
Bessho Magoemon 別所孫右衛門. *See* Bessho Shigemune
Bessho Shigemune 別所重宗, 284n.18
Besson zakki 別尊雑記, 302n.5
Bianji 遍吉, 123
Bijutsu 美術, 292–93n.1
Bishamonten 毘沙門天, 238, 265
Bitchū Province 備中国, 201
Biwa 琵琶, as attribute of Benzaiten, 233
Biwa, Lake 琵琶湖, 32, 40, 54, 60, 66, 199, 231, 237, 270
Biwa hōshi 琵琶法師, 55, 80
Blanquez, S. Pedro Bautista, 72
Bokuseki no utsushi 墨蹟之写, 123, 290n.28
Bokushinsai Nobusada 卜真斎信貞, 66, 67, 74–75, 239
Bonshun 梵舜: on conflagration at Great Buddha Hall, Kyoto, 217; on earthquake of 1596, 92; on Hideyoshi's death, 100, 204–5; on Hōgonji gate, 239; on painting of Toyokuni Special Festival of 1604, 210; and pilgrimage to Chikubushima, 235; on Toyokuni Festivals, 208; on Toyokuni Special Festival of 1604, 209, 213, 215, 220. *See also Shunkyū ki*
Bosatsubon 井品, 238
Bugaku 舞楽, 209, 235
Bugyō 奉行, 294n.20
Bumon chōkyū 武門長久, 222
Bunroku 文禄, 28
Byōbu 屏風, 153
Byōdōin 平等院, 146, *Fig. 89*

Caron, François, on interiors of Japanese architecture, 150
Chacha 茶々, 86. *See also* Yododono
Chanoyu 茶の湯, 36, 64, 68, 69–70, 144, 145; appropriation and assemblage in, 252–57
Cheng 程, Master, 296n.64
Chikubushima 竹生嶋 or 竹生島, xi, 100, 202, *Fig. 1*; and annual income, 66, 74, 75, 239–40; and annual income deficit, 75, 239–40; as center of Benzaiten worship, 32, 40–41, 42, 53–57, 65, 67, 87, 232, 233, 235–39, 240–44, 272, 273–74; and cormorants, 278n.4; description of, 40; in Edo period, 267–68, 272; fire in 1558 on, 42, 49, 57, 62, 281n.65; and Hideyori, 240–44; and Hideyoshi, 42, 61–63, 65–67, 73–75, 232, 244, 272; and Ieyasu, 239–40, 245, 272, 304n.26; and *Keiran shūyōshū*, 50, 55–57, 238; lumber on, 62–63, 65–66; and Nobunaga, 60, 61–67, 272; Nobunaga's pilgrimage to, 232; origin of, according to *Chikubushima engi*, 51; origin of name of, according to *Chikubushima engi*, 51–52; possibility of Hideyoshi promise to construct Hondō on, 75; replication of, in Edo, 269–72; ridgepole placards for buildings on, 49–50, 197, 240–44, 266, 274, *Fig. 138*; and ridgepole placard text of 1603, 240–44, 266, 274, *Fig. 138*; as sacred place, 32, 33, 40, 42, 51, 54–55, 57, 67, 232, 237–38, 240–43, 267–68, 272, 273–74; and Sensōe, 83; and Sutemaru, 86–87; and *Tale of the Heike*, 54–55, 236, 243; and text transcribed by Gien, 238–39; and Tokugawa, 239–40; and Toyotomi after Hideyoshi's death, 75, 239, 240–44, 266; typhoon damage to, in 1934, 279n.15. *See also Chikubushima,* Nō drama entitled; Lotus Festival on Chikubushima; Tsukubusuma Main Hall
Chikubushima 竹生嶋, Nō drama entitled, 50, 236–38; locations of performances of, 208, 236–37; synopsis of, 237
Chikubushima engi 竹生嶋縁起, 50–54, 55, 56, 243
Chikubushima hōgachō 竹生嶋奉加帳, 67, 74
Chikushū 筑州. *See* Toyotomi Hideyoshi
Chingo kokka 鎮護国家, 227
Chinju 鎮守, 204, 205
Chion'in 知恩院, 229
Chishakuin 智積院, 89, 90, 100, 229, 286n.83
Chōgen 重源, 80
Chōjuin 長寿院, Benzaiten Hall at, 233
Chōnahajime 釿始: on Chikubushima, 279n.19; at Great Buddha Hall, Kyoto, 218
Chrysanthemum, 103, 108, 117, 126, 164–65; iconography of, in Momoyama period, 128–31; as *katamigusa*, 128, 131, 263
Chrysanthemum Princess. *See* Kikuhime
Chūsonji 中尊寺. *See* Konjikidō
Cocks, Richard: on Great Buddha Hall, Kyoto, 218; on Toyokuni Shrine, 206, 214
Confucius, 190
Coppindall, Ralph, 159
Cormorants, and Chikubushima, 278n.4
Crane-and-pine motif. *See* Tsurumatsu
Crests, chrysanthemum and paulownia, 110–11, 128, 163, 175, 176, 194, 213, 250, 266
Cypress Tree, attributed to Kano Eitoku, 157, *Fig. 95*

Daibutsu 大仏, lacquer workshop near, 49
Daibutsu *banshō* 大仏番匠, 94
Daibutsuden 大仏殿. *See* Great Buddha Hall, Kyoto; Tōdaiji
Daigo, Emperor 醍醐天皇, 237
Daigoji 醍醐寺, 25, 72, 73, 81, 99, 100, 205, 206, 302n.5; Benzaiten at, 233; and earthquake of 1596, 94; Hideyori's restoration of Golden Hall and other buildings at, 222–23, 246; Hideyoshi and blossom viewing at, 94–97, 250, *Fig. 48*; Hideyoshi's promised restoration of buildings at, 96–97, 222; Hideyoshi's restoration of pagoda at, 30, 94–96, 196, 222, *Fig. 47*; lacquered gate at, 175; Mieidō of, 223, 251; Niō Gate at, 96; ridgepole placard of Golden Hall at, 222–23; as site of Toyokuni Shrine branch, 208. *See also* Gien; Sanbōin
Daigoji shin'yōroku 醍醐寺新要録, 306n.71
Daihannya kyō 大般若経, 203, 226
Daikakuji 大覚寺, 292n.69
Daikoku 大黒, 214
Daikokuten 大黒天, 265
Daishō 大聖. *See* Shōtoku Taishi
Daishōkoku Denka 大相国殿下. *See* Toyotomi Hideyoshi
Daitokuji 大徳寺, 60, 76, 77, 85, 89, 90, 123
Dankafu 断家譜, 297n.8
Date Masamune 伊達政宗, 99, 199–200, 292n.67
Dengaku 田楽, 209
Denka 殿下. *See* Toyotomi Hideyoshi
Denpōdō 伝法堂. *See* Hōryūji
Durgā, and Benzaiten, 303n.16

Earthquake of 1596, 92–94, 99, 216, 222, 246, 252
Ebikōryō 海老虹梁 of Benzaiten Hall on Chikubushima, 46, 231, 260
Ebisu エビス, 214
Edo 江戸, city of, 204, 268–73
Edo Castle 江戸城, 229, 269; Nō play *Chikubushima* performed at, 236; representation of Chikubushima in, 307n.7
Edo zukan kōmoku, kon 江戸図鑑綱目坤, 271, *Figs. 156, 157*
Eishun 英俊. *See* Tamon'in Eishun
Emperor. *See* Imperial Court
Engi 縁起, 50–51. *See also Chikubushima engi*
Engi shiki 延喜式, 278n.11
Enkeizan Sōkenji Zenji kōkatsuchō 遠景山總見寺禅寺校割帳, 281n.54. *See also* Sōkenji
En'nin 円仁, 53
Enoshima 江ノ島, 40, 56, 233
Enryakuji 延暦寺, 53, 57–58, 62, 63, 76, 204, 269; destruction of, by Nobunaga, 59; reconstruction of, 73, 222; and Sensōe, 83, 84–85. *See also* Hiei, Mount
Ensemble, 33, 108, 144, 252; architecture and, 188; component parts of, 150–51; creating Sutemaru's, 190–96; definition of, 146; early Japanese examples of, 146–49; evaluating the, 188–90; Momoyama examples of, 150, 188–89; Tōshōgū as, 273.

See also Tsukubusuma Main Hall
Enshun 演俊, 251
Enza 円座, tea caddy named, *Fig. 143*

Flor aßischanada, 134
Flowers, Birds, and Insects of the Four Seasons, painting of, owned by Agency for Cultural Affairs, 113–16
Frois, Luis: on Azuchi Castle, 60, 152; on Gifu Castle, 153; on Great Buddha, Kyoto, 76–77; on Nobunaga's destruction of Enryakuji, 59; on Osaka Castle, 70, 153
Fugen Bosatsu 普賢菩薩, 290n.30
Fuji, Mount 富士山, 32, 39
Fujito 藤戸, 246, *Fig. 140*. *See also* Sanbōin
Fujiwara no Kiyohira 藤原清衡, 293n.9
Fukushima Masanori 福島正則, 297n.4
Fumon 普文, 51–54
Funabashi Hidekata 舟橋秀賢, 188; and pilgrimage to Take no Benzaiten, 233; on Toyokuni Special Festival of 1604, 214. *See also Keichō nikken roku*
Funaki screens 舟木家本. *See Sights in and around the Capital*
Furong 芙蓉, 133. *See also Fuyō*
Fūryū odori 風流踊, 214–15
Fusai 婦齋, 49
Fusai Uchishōzaemon 婦齋内小左衛門, 279n.21
Fushimi Castle 伏見城, 28, 99, 203, 205, 220, 229, 306n.67; and earthquake of 1596, 92; transfer of buildings to or from, 246, 250–51; transfer of gate from, to Nishi Honganji, 246; transfer of Niō gate from, to Onjōji, 250–51, 252
Fusuma 襖, 106–7
Futara 二荒, 39
Fuyō 芙蓉, 103 , 108, 126, 131–33, 155, 164–65, 191; as *Hibiscus mutabilis*, 288n.1; painting of, in Masaki Museum of Art, 133, 134, *Fig. 79*; and Sutemaru, 133–36

Gangōji 元興寺, 302n.4
Geishū 芸州, 294n.20
Gien 義演 25, 26, 206, 232; and appropriation of buildings, 250–51; on Benzaiten at Daigoji, 233; on earthquake of 1596, 92–94; and ensembles, 188–90; and final illness and death of Hideyoshi, 205; on Hōkōji, 82; on Jurakutei site, 246; on lacquered gate at Daigoji, 175–76; on lacquered gate at Toyokuni Shrine, 188, 217, 245–46; and pilgrimage to Chikubushima, 235; and restoration of Golden Hall at Daigoji, 222–23; on restoration of Great Buddha and Great Buddha Hall, Kyoto, 216–17, 218, 227; on restoration of pagoda at Daigoji, 94–96, 196; on ridgepole placard for Golden Hall, 222–23; and ridgepole placards, 225; and rituals for Tokugawa, 203; and rituals for Toyotomi, 203–4; on Sensōe, 83; and term *jinzen jinbi*, 189–90, 196, 227; and Tōdaiji, 81; on Toyokuni Shrine, 204–5; and Toyokuni Shrine at Daigoji, 208; on Toyokuni Special Festival of 1604, 210, 213, 214; transcribes reference to Chikubushima, 238–39. *See also* Daigoji; *Gien Jugō nikki*; Sanbōin
Gien Jugō nikki 義演准后日記 285n.39. *See also* Gien
Gifu 岐阜, 67
Gifu Castle 岐阜城, 153
Gion Festival 祇園祭, 30, 219
Gion Shōja 祇園精舎, 217
Gion Shrine 祇園社, 85
Gobugyō 五奉行, 199
Godaidō 五大堂, of Daigoji, 223
Gokuraku Bridge 極楽橋. *See* Osaka Castle
Gokuraku Gate 極楽門, 304n.38. *See also* Toyokuni Shrine, gates at
Gold Layer: in *Chikubushima engi*, 51, 52; in *Tale of the Heike*, 55
Gold Tea Room, 36, 231, *Fig. 31*
Golfao, 134
Gongen zukuri 権現造, 298n.29
Goryūganmai 御立願米, 87
Gosha Jinja 五社神社, 245
Goshirakawa, Emperor 後白河天皇, 80–81
Gōshū 江州, 55
Gotairō 五大老, 199
Goten 御殿. *See* Benzaiten Hall on Chikubushima
Gotō Harumasa 五嶋玄雅, inkstone case received from Hideyoshi by, 177–79, *Fig. 116*
Gotō Heishirō 後藤平四郎, 150
Gotō kafu 後藤家譜, 195
Gotō Kōjō 後藤光乗, 195
Gotō Yūjō 後藤祐乗, 195
Goyōzei, Emperor 後陽成天皇: receiving of, by Hideyoshi, 71, 302n.108; and Toyokuni Daimyōjin, 205; and Toyokuni Shrine in Nagahama, 208
Grapevine, iconography of, 121–26
Great Buddha, Kyoto, 198, 204, 205, 206; compared with Great Buddha in Nara, 76, 77, 82–83; construction of, by Hideyoshi, 76, 82–83; damage to, by earthquake of 1596, 92–94; destruction of, by fire, 217; restorations of, by Toyotomi after Hideyoshi's death, 216–18; restoration of, by Hideyoshi, 98; Richard Cocks on, 218; as Vairocana, 24. *See also* Great Buddha Hall, Kyoto; Hōkōji
Great Buddha, Nara. *See* Tōdaiji
Great Buddha Hall, Kyoto, 24, 88–89, 90, 101, 141, 146, 205, 229, 252; bell of, 31, 218, *Fig. 129*; compared with Great Buddha Hall in Nara, 72, 82–83; construction of, by Hideyoshi, 76–77, 82–83, 217; damage to, by earthquake of 1596, 92; depicted in Funaki screens, 31–32; depicted in Toyokuni Special Festival of 1604 painting, 211, 214–16, 219; destruction of, by fire, 217; lacquer workshop near, 49, 246; restorations of, by Toyotomi after Hideyoshi's death, 216–19, 227; as site of Toyokuni Special Festival of 1604, 209, 211, 214–16, 219; and Zenkōji Amida triad, 98–100. *See also* Great Buddha, Kyoto; Hōkōji
Great Buddha Hall, Nara. *See* Tōdaiji
Gregory XIII, Pope, 276n.13
Gukei Yūe 愚溪右慧, 121
Gyōki 行基: and Chikubushima, 242, 243; in *Chikubushima engi*, 51–52, 53; at Tōdaiji, 79
Gyokuhōin 玉鳳院, Sutemaru *tamaya* in, 92, 289n.14, *Fig. 46*

Haizetsuroku 廃絶録, 297n.8
Haretoyo ki 晴豊記, 88. *See also* Kajūji Haretoyo
Harigaki 針描, 179, 183

Hasegawa 長谷川 (workshop): *Maple Tree and Autumn Plants* by, *Fig. 44*; paintings by, 89, 100
Hasegawa Kyūzō 長谷川久蔵, 287n.87
Hasegawa Tōhaku 長谷川等伯, 287n.87
Hashiba Chikuzen 羽柴筑前. *See* Toyotomi Hideyoshi
Hasu 蓮, 134–35
Hatsugan 発願, 226
Hayasaki 早崎, 61, 63, 65, 66, 240
Hayashi Razan 林羅山, 134
Heiguri County 平群郡, 224
Heike 平家, 50, 54
Heike nōkyō 平家納経, 190
Hibiscus mutabilis. See Fuyō
Hiei, Mount 比叡山, 39, 51, 53, 59, 73; replication of, in Edo, 269. *See also* Enryakuji
Higuchi Naofusa 樋口直房, 63
Hijiri Jinja 聖神社, 221
Hirado 平戸, 206
Hiraizumi Fujiwara 平泉藤原, 233
Hiramakie 平蒔絵, 179, 182, 183, 184. *See also Makie* lacquer
Hisashi 庇. *See* Benzaiten Hall on Chikubushima
Histoire de l'Eglise du Japon, by R. P. Crasset, 297n.6
History of the Church of Japan, The, 23, 25, 151, 166. *See also* Rodrigues, João
Hiunkaku 飛雲閣, 246
Hōden 宝殿 278n.12
Hōgen 法眼, 82
Hōgonji 宝厳寺, 41; Karamon gate at, 163, 191, 239, 245, 246, 288–89n.7, 304n.38, *Figs. 101, 102*
Hōin 法印, 82
Hōjō 北条 (house), 86
Hōju 宝珠, 233, 243
Hōjuin 宝樹院: Benzaiten as central deity of, 235; *zushi* containing sculpture of Hideyoshi at, 175, *Figs. 112, 113*
Hokke 法華, 53, 58
Hokkeji 法華寺, 301n.92
Hokke Zanmaidō 法華三昧堂, 53
Hōkōji 方広寺, 72, 82, 101, 188, 206, 214, 243; bell of, 202, *Fig. 129*; construction of, by Hideyoshi, 49, 76–77, 82–83; damage to, by earthquake of 1596, 92–94; restoration of, by Toyotomi after Hideyoshi's death, 198, 216, 219, 222; ridgepole placard of, 225; and Zenkōji Amida triad, 98–99, 198. *See also* Great Buddha, Kyoto; Great Buddha Hall, Kyoto
Hōkokusai 豊国祭. *See* Toyokuni Festival
Hōkoku Shrine 豊国神社. *See* Toyokuni Shrine
Hōmotsu 宝物, 74
Honchō gashi 本朝画史, 195
Hondō 本堂, of Chikubushima, 75
Honganji 本願寺, 58, 59, 60, 70, 72, 204; Nō play *Chikubushima* performed at, 236
Honnōji 本能寺, 68
Honzanji 本山寺, 221
Honzō kōmoku keimō 本草綱目啓蒙, 291n.53
Hōrai, Mount 蓬莱山, Chikubushima as, 54, 242, 243
Horikawa, Emperor 堀河天皇, 84
Hōryū Gakumonji 法隆学問寺, 224
Hōryūji 法隆寺, 30, 60; Hideyori's restoration of, 224–25; ridgepole placard of Denpōdō at, 224–25
Hōshō 宝生, 209
Hōshōin 宝性院, 86
Hosshōji 法勝寺, 84–85
Hōteki 法敵, 60

Ibukio no Mikoto 気吹雄命, 51
Ichinokami 市正. *See* Katagiri Katsumoto
Ichinotani 一の谷, 55
Ido 井戸, teabowl, 255
Ifufura Jinja 意冨布良神社, 245
Ikkō 一向, 84, 226
Ima Hachimangū 今八幡宮, 301n.99
Imahama 今浜, 66
Imai Sōkyū 今井宗久, 254
Imazu 今津, 235
Imperial Court, 30, 36, 68, 70, 71, 80, 110, 199, 200; and deification of Hideyoshi, 205; Nō play *Chikubushima* performed at, 236; and rituals for Hideyoshi, 99; and Sensōe, 84–85; and Toyokuni Shrine Festivals, 208, 209
Inoue 井上 collection, Riguan painting formerly in, 123–26, *Fig. 73*
Ise Province 伊勢国, 201
Ise Shrine 伊勢神宮, 72, 85, 221, 224, 229; Hideyori and Yododono repair of Uji Bridge at, 223–24; Hideyoshi and, 223
Ishida Masazumi 石田正澄, 88
Ishida Mitsunari 石田三成, 199
Ishikawa Mitsumasa 石川光政, 66
Ishikawa Mitsushige 石川光重, 87, 88
Ishikawa Ryūsen 石川流宣, 307n.8
Ishiyama 石山, 58
Isono Kazumasa 磯野員昌, 64
Isono Tanba no Kami 磯野丹波守. *See* Isono Kazumasa
Isuzu River 五十鈴川, 223
Itō Hidemori 伊藤秀盛, 74–75
Itsukushima 厳島, 55
Iwashimizu Hachimangū 岩清水八幡宮, building sponsored by Hideyori at, 189–90
Iyo Province 伊予国, 201
Izumi Province 和泉国, 199, 221
Izumo Shrine 出雲大社, Hideyori's restoration of, 221, 224

Jesuits in Japan, 23, 60. *See also* Almeida, Luis de; Frois, Luis; Rodrigues, João; Valignano, Alessandro; Vilela, Gaspar; *Vocabvlario da Lingoa de Iapam*
Ji 時, 84
Jie 桀, [Tyrant], 296n.64
Jie Daishi Sōjō shūiden 慈恵大師僧正拾遺伝, 303n.20
Jingoji 神護寺, 36
Jinja 神社, 43
Jinoko 地の粉, 180, 185
Jinzen jinbi 尽善尽美, 189–90, 196, 204, 227, 301n.89
Jizō 地蔵, Sutemaru and, of Jōshinji, 87
Jō 丈, 82
Jōdo 浄土, 84, 116
Jōdo Shin 浄土真, 58, 72, 73
Jōe Enmyō Kokushi kyohakuroku 定慧圓明國師虛白録, 286n.81. *See also* Nanka Genkō
Jōō Imogashira 紹鴎芋頭, freshwater container named, 253–57, *Fig. 144*
Jōrakuji 常楽寺, 251
Jōshinji 浄信寺: commemorative lantern at, 245, *Fig. 139*; and Hideyori, 244–45; and Hideyoshi, 245; and Sutemaru, 87
Jōtokuji 浄得寺, map of Japan at, 32, 271, *Figs. 28, 29*
Juggling, 213
Jūji Bosatsubon 十地菩薩品, 56

Jurakutei 聚楽第, 70–71, 101, 150, 157, 246, *Fig. 43*; Hideyoshi's dismantling of, 246

Kaempfer, Engelbert, 267–68, 287n.100
Kaerumata 蟇股, 159, 265
Kaga Province 加賀国, 131
Kagura 神楽, 85, 208, 209
Kai Province 甲斐国, 98
Kajūji Haretoyo 勧修寺晴豊, 88. *See also Haretoyo ki*
Kakiwari 描割, 183, 184
Kakurinji 鶴林寺, 302n.7
Kamakura 鎌倉, 183
Kami 神, 42, 72–73, 208
Kamiya Sōtan 神屋宗湛, 303n.14
Kamo River 賀茂川, 30
Kangakuin 勧学院. *See* Kano Mitsunobu
Kanjinchō 勧進帳. *See* Temple solicitation register
Kanju 巻数, 74, 203
Kanmei nikki 寛明日記, entry on Chikubushima in, 269–70
Kanmu, Emperor 桓武天皇, 53
Kannon 観音, 39, 60, 217, 238; and Chikubushima, 40, 54; images of, on Chikubushima, 52; pilgrimage route devoted to, 54, 268
Kannondō 観音堂, on Chikubushima, 43, 75
Kano 狩野 (workshop), 71, 150, 157, 195, 211; and copy of painting by Riguan, 123, *Fig. 74*
Kano Eitoku 狩野永徳, 89, 157, 195; at Azuchi Castle, 150, 152, 195; *Cypress Tree* attributed to, *Fig. 95*; at Jurakutei, 71, 157; at Osaka Castle, 157; at Tenzuiji, 89–90
Kano Hideyori 狩野秀頼, *Maple Viewing at Mount Takao* by, 34–36, 110, 172, *Figs. 30, 108*
Kano Mitsunobu 狩野光信: attribution of Tsukubusuma Main Hall paintings to, 154–58; at Azuchi Castle, 150; at Fushimi Castle, 158; at Jurakutei, 157; at Kangakuin, 154–57, 194, 294n.20, *Figs. 92–94*; at Nagoya Castle in Kyushu, 157; at Osaka Castle, 157; at Shōkokuji Dharma Hall, 158; portraits of Hideyoshi attributed to, 294n.27; as supervisor of Sutemaru's ensemble, 191–95
Kano Motonobu 狩野元信, 195
Kano Naizen 狩野内膳: painting of *Tale of the Heike* by, 284n.30; painting of Toyokuni Special Festival of 1604 by, 211–16, 218–19, 219–20, *Figs. 131–36*
Kano Nakanobu 狩野中信, 290n.32
Kano Ryūsetsu 狩野柳雪, 290n.32
Kano Sanraku 狩野山楽: at Fushimi Castle, 158; at Jurakutei, 71
Kano Sokuyo 狩野即誉, *Pilgrimage to Kan'eiji* by, 270–71, *Fig. 155*
Kano Tan'yū 狩野探幽, 290n.32; at Nijō Castle, 195
Kano Tōsen 狩野董川, 290n.32
Kanpaku 関白: Hideyori as, 201; Hideyoshi as, 68
Kanpaku Dono 関白殿. *See* Toyotomi Hideyoshi
Kanpaku Sashōfu 関白左相府. *See* Toyotomi Hideyoshi
Kanshinji 観心寺, 221
Kanze 観世, 209
Karahafu 唐破風, 278n.14
Karamon 唐門. *See* Hōgonji; Sanbōin
Kasuga Shrine 春日大社, 85
Katagiri Higashi Ichinokami 片桐東市正. *See* Katagiri Katsumoto
Katagiri Katsumoto 片桐且元, 220; as administrator of Toyotomi construction projects, 49–50, 198, 221, 224, 225, 240–44, 245; holdings of, increased by Hideyori, 201; as possible traitor to Toyotomi, 198; referred to as Ichinokami, 223; referred to as Katagiri Higashi Ichinokami, 224
Katagiri Sadataka 片桐貞隆, 188, 201
Katami 形見, 128
Katamigusa 形見草, 128; chysanthemum as, 128, 131, 263
Katano Jinja 片埜神社, 221
Katō Kiyomasa 加藤清正, 207
Kawachi Province 河内国, 199, 201, 221
Kegon Sutra 華厳経: possible reference to, in *Tale of the Heike*, 55; reference to, in *Chikubushima engi*, 52; reference to, in Chikubushima temple solicitation register, 56–57, 238; reference to, in *Keiran shūyōshū*, 56–57, 238; reference to, in text transcribed by Gien, 238–39
Kei 頃, 242
Keichō 慶長, 28
Keichō nikken roku 慶長日件録, 284n.30. *See also* Funabashi Hidekata
Keikōin Shuyō 慶光院周養, 223
Keiran shūyōshū 渓嵐拾葉集, references to Chikubushima in, 50, 55–57, 236, 238
Keiunji 慶雲寺, portrait of young boy in, 128, 131, 133, 135, *Fig. 76*
Kekkō kyōmokuji 結構驚目耳, 188
Keman 華鬘, 83
Kenninji 建仁寺, 72
Kesa 袈裟, 83
Keyaki 欅, 49
Kikuhime 菊姫, 131
Kimon 鬼門 (demon's gate, northeast), 53, 54, 271–72
Kinbyōbu 金屏風, 113–16
Kinichi 忌日, 205
Kinki 近畿, 279n.15
Kinomoto 木之本, 245. *See also* Jōshinji
Kinoshita Tōkichirō Hideyoshi 木下藤吉郎秀吉. *See* Toyotomi Hideyoshi
Kinoshita Yoshitaka 木下吉隆, 283n.14
Kinpusenji 金峰山寺, 222
Kirei kyōmoku 奇麗驚目, 188
Kita no Mandokoro 北政所, 86, 176; and restoration of Tōji, 94, 222; and rituals for Hideyoshi, 99; and Toyokuni Festivals, 208; visit to Daigoji by, 96
Kitano Shrine 北野神社, 85; Hideyoshi's *chanoyu* gathering at, 222, 293n.4; as model of Toyokuni Shrine, 204; reconstruction of, by Toyotomi, 226
Kiyomizudera 清水寺, 85, 229, 238
Kiyotaki River 清滝川, 36
Klein, Bettina, 113–16
Kō 公, 189, 226
Kobayakawa Takakage 小早川隆景, 233
Kōdaiji 高台寺, 190, 229; decoration of, 112; *makie*-lacquered chest in, 169, 177, *Fig. 106*; *makie*-lacquered *tamaya* at, 112, 176, 182, 184, 257, *Figs. 62, 146*;

Kōdaiji *(continued)*
as mortuary building, 111–12, 116–17
Kōdaiji *makie* 高台寺蒔絵, 183–84
Kōfukuji 興福寺, 85; Sutemaru and, 87
Kōfu Zenkōji 甲府善光寺, 98
Kōgetsu Sōgan 江月宗玩, 123, 126
Kōhai 向拝, 277n.17
Kojiki 古事記, 205
Kojima 小嶋, 42
Kokei Sōchin 古渓宗陳, 76, 245
Komatsu 小松, 235
Kōmon Denka 黄門殿下. *See* Toyotomi Hideyori
Kōmyō, Empress 光明皇后, 77
Konda Hachimangū 誉田八幡宮, 221
Kongō 金剛, 209
Kongōbuji 金剛峰寺, 57, 158. *See also* Kōya, Mount
Konjikidō 金色堂, 146–49, 175, 184, 293n.9, *Figs. 90, 91*
Konkōmyō kyō 金光明経. *See Sutra of Golden Light*
Konkōmyō Shitennō Gokokuji 金光明四天王護国寺. *See* Tōdaiji
Konoe Nobutada 近衛信尹, 301n.102
Konparu 金春, 209
Konrinzai 金輪際. *See* Gold Layer
Korea and China, invasions of, 69, 76, 157–58; as response to Sutemaru's death, 88
Kōrei, Emperor 孝霊天皇, 51
Kōshō 康正, 82
Kōshū 光宗, 55
Kōya, Mount 高野山, 39, 73, 85, 238; and Sutemaru, 86. *See also* Kongōbuji
Kōyashū 高野衆, 217
Kōzan Shōnin Ōgo 興山上人応其. *See* Ōgo, Monk
Kuden 口伝, 145
Kujō Dono 九条殿, 210
Kūkai 空海, 238
Kumano 熊野, 39, 221
Kumano Hayatama Taisha 熊野速玉大社, lacquer box donated to, 173, 179, *Fig. 111*
Kunōzan 久能山, 230
Kuramadera 鞍馬寺, 85, 238; lacquered building at, 175
Kuroda Nagamasa 黒田長政, 297n.4
Kuwayama Shigeharu 桑山重晴, 175, 235
Kuwayama Shigekatsu 桑山重勝, 67
Kyakuden 客殿, inscription regarding, of Kangakuin, 294n.20
Kyō 卿, 226
Kyoto 京都, 24, 31–32, 38, 49, 59, 81, 82, 133, 161, 188, 198, 200, 220, 229, 231, 268–69; and earthquake of 1596, 92–94, 99, 216, 222, 246, 252; rebuilding of, by Hideyoshi, 69–72, 92, 94–100, 101, 204; religious construction in, by Toyotomi, 30, 76–77, 204, 216–19, 222; as site of Toyokuni Festivals, 208–16. *See also Sights in and around the Capital*
Kyōtobō mokushi, Shimogyō, ken 京都坊目誌下京乾 305n.62

Lacquer, 143; on architecture, 146–49, 150, 175–76, 189, 206; definition of, 166–67; in sacred contexts, 173–76; shell (or mother-of-pearl)-inlaid, 146–49, 169; workshop near Great Buddha Hall, Kyoto, 49, 185, 246. *See also Makie* lacquer
Li Shizhen 李時珍, 134
Lotus, 134–35
Lotus Festival on Chikubushima, 41, 54, 235–36, 268; Asai and, 62, 244; Benzaiten sculptures made for, 41, 233, 235, *Fig. 137*; depiction of, 41–42, 219, *Fig. 33*; Hideyoshi and, 67, 75; referred to as *sairei*, 67; referred to as *shinji*, 236; referred to as *tennyo* ritual, 62

Maeda Gen'i 前田玄以, 84, 87, 99; and Daigoji, 94, 222–23; referred to as Tokuzen'in Gon no Sōjō Gen'i, 222; and Shōunji, 90; and Toyokuni Shrine, 204, 205
Maeda Kikuhime 前田菊姫, portrait of, 131, *Fig. 78*
Maeda Toshiie 前田利家, 131
Mairado 舞良戸, 106
Makie 蒔絵 lacquer, 108, 150, 166–88, 196, 213, 227, 265; on architecture, 149, 188–89, 217, 245–46; drum body dated to 1566 decorated with, 183–84, *Fig. 121*; drum body owned by Shizuka decorated with, 64–65; in sacred contexts, 173–76; Tsurugaoka Hachimangū sword sheaths decorated with, 183, *Fig. 120*. *See also* Ensemble; Kōdaiji; Lacquer; Tsukubusuma Main Hall
Map, of Japan, *Fig. 29*
Maple Tree and Autumn Plants, by Hasegawa workshop, 89, 100, *Fig. 44*
Maple Viewing at Mount Takao, by Kano Hideyori, 34–36, 110, *Figs. 30, 108*; lacquer represented in, 172, *Fig. 108*
Masaki Museum of Art 正木美術館, painting of *fuyō* in, 133, 134, *Fig. 79*
Mashita Nagamori 増田長盛, 87, 99
Matsudaira 松平, 113
Matsunaga Hisahide 松永久秀, 81
Matsushima 松島, relief wood carvings at Godaidō in, 296n.70
Matsuura Takeshirō 松浦武四郎, 307n.84
Meibutsu 名物, 64, 145
Meiji period 明治時代, and Western conceptions of art, 143, 292–93n.1
Metalwork, 108, 112, 149, 150, 195, 196, 213, 265. *See also* Ensemble; Tsukubusuma Main Hall
Mieidō 御影堂, of Daigoji, 223, 251
Miidera 三井寺. *See* Onjōji
Mikasa 三笠, 39
Mikumari Jinja 水分神社, 222, 296n.69
Minamoto 源 (house), 50, 54, 79–80
Minamoto no Yoritomo 源頼朝, 229; and Benzaiten, 233; as patron of Tōdaiji, 80–81
Minamoto no Yoshitsune 源義経, 65
Minbukyō Dono 民部卿殿, 63
Minoo 箕面, 56
Mino Province 美濃国, 98, 201
Miraculous Origins of Mount Shigi, 79
Misu Jinja 三栖神社, Benzaiten Hall at, 233
Mitarashi みたらし reeds for Chikubushima Benzaiten, 74
Mitsuden 密伝, 145
Miyajima 宮島, 39–40
Miyako no Yoshika 都良香, 242
Miyoshi 三好 (house), 58

Mizusashi 水指, 253
Mochinobu 持信, 65
Momoyama period 桃山時代, discussion of term, 28
Monju Rōin 文殊楼院, 53
Monzeki 門跡. *See* Aristocrat-abbot
Monzenmachi 門前町, 63
Mōri Terumoto 毛利輝元, 76
Moya 母屋. *See* Tsukubusuma Main Hall
Munafuda 棟札. *See* Ridgepole placards
Munein 宗印, 82
Munesada 宗貞, 82
Murō, Mount 室生山, 39
Muryōjuin 無量寿院, 86
Muryōju kyō 無量寿経, 120, 121
Mutsu Province 陸奥国, 112, 278n.5
Myōhōin 妙法院, 72, 285n.49
Myōhōji 妙法寺, 291n.39
Myōjin 明神, 51
Myōkakuin 妙覚院, on Chikubushima, 235
Myōren 命蓮, 79
Myōshinji 妙心寺, 60, 89, 90, 92; Sutemaru's armor preserved at, 139–40, *Figs. 87, 88*; Sutemaru's funeral at, 88, 140

Nachi 那智, 39
Nagahama 長浜: as Hideyoshi's seat of power, 66, 67, 68, 74, 232, 244; Toyokuni Shrine branch at, 208
Nagasaki 長崎, 134
Nagoya Castle 名護屋城, in Kyushu, 157, 200
Naidaijin 内大臣. *See* Toyotomi Hideyori
Naifu 内府. *See* Tokugawa Ieyasu
Najima 名嶋, 233
Nanban lacquer 南蛮漆器, 169; portable altar as example of, *Fig. 107*
Nanbu Toshinao 南部利直, *tamaya* of, 289n.14
Nanbu Toshiyasu 南部利康, *tamaya* of, 112, 116, 289n.14, *Figs. 63, 64*
Nandaimon 南大門, 301n.95
Nanka Genkō 南化玄興: biography of, 287n.89; as Chief Abbot of Shōunji, 88, 133; as eulogist of Sutemaru, 133–36; as inscriber of portrait, 128–31. *See also Jōe Enmyō Kokushi kyohakuroku*
Nanzenji 南禅寺, 72, 222, 229
Nara 奈良, 77, 221, 222. *See also* Hōryūji; Kōfukuji; Tōdaiji
Negoroji 根来寺, 57, 286n.83; destruction of, by Hideyoshi, 73; hall moved from, 76, 245
Neo-Confucianism, 190
Nichiren 日蓮, 57–58, 68, 84
Nihon shoki 日本書紀, 205
Nijō Castle 二条城, 195, 201, 204, 229, 289n.20; depicted in Funaki screens, 31; Nō play *Chikubushima* performed at, 236. *See also* Tokugawa (house); Tokugawa Ieyasu
Nikkō 日光, 166, 230, 273. *See also* Tōshōgū
Ninnōgyō 仁王経, 298n.27
Niō Gate 仁王門. *See* Daigoji; Fushimi Castle; Onjōji
Nishi Honganji 西本願寺, 246, 289n.20
Nishimura Kiyoemon 西村清右衛門, 240
Nō 能, 222, 236; at Toyokuni Shrine, 208, 209, 210, 213. *See also Chikubushima*, Nō drama entitled
Nō no tomechō 能之留帳, 236
Nusa 幣, 209
Nushi 塗師, 49
Nyoirindō 如意輪堂, of Daigoji, 223
Nyoishu 如意珠, 243

Odani Castle 小谷城, 63
Oda Nobukatsu 織田信雄, 98
Oda Nobunaga 織田信長, 26, 28, 58, 72, 76, 85, 98, 99, 145, 150, 152, 246; and *chanoyu*, 64, 68; and Chikubushima, 60, 61–67, 272; death of, 68; and defeat of Asai, 63, 200; deification of, 60–61; and destruction of Enryakuji, 59, 63; and Honganji, 58, 59, 60, 72, 226; and pilgrimage to Chikubushima, 232; and policies towards religious establishments, 58–60, 66–67, 73; power of, defined in sacred terms, 60, 72, 223; referred to as Tonosama, 65; secondary literature on deification of, 281n.57; and Tōdaiji, 81. *See also* Azuchi Castle
Oda Nobutada 織田信忠, 98
Odawara 小田原, 200
Ogawa Ichizaemon 小川市左衛門, 239
Ōgo 応其, Monk, 73; and Daigoji, 222–23, 225; referred to as Kōzan Shōnin Ōgo, 222; on Sutemaru, 86; and Toyokuni Shrine, 204
Ōhara 大原, 157
Oi ヲイ, 214
Okishima 沖島, 32
Ōmandokoro 大政所, 85, 87, 291nn.46, 60
Ōmi Province 近江国, 38, 40, 55, 63, 66, 67, 68, 75, 87, 200, 201, 233, 235, 236, 237, 239, 245, 273
Onbyō 御廟, 278n.12
Ōne Ichizaemon 大音市左衛門. *See* Ōne Takanori
Ōne Takanori 大音孝則, 240, 245
Onjōji 園城寺, 154; Niō Gate at, 250–51, *Fig. 142*
Ōnoki Gorōzaemon 大野木五郎左衛門, 240
Onsho 御書, 75
Osaka 大坂, 32, 38, 68, 74, 166, 221; bridges at, 159–61. *See also* Osaka Castle
Ōsaka Asahi shinbun 大阪朝日新聞, 279n.15
Osaka Campaigns of 1614–1615 大坂の陣, 28, 31, 70, 89, 202, 208, 219, 225, 229, 267
Osaka Castle 大坂城, 28, 68, 69–70, 100, 150, 157, 199, 200, 203, *Fig. 42*; compared with Azuchi Castle, 70; Gokuraku Bridge of, 246; site of Ishiyama Honganji taken for, 70; Toyokuni Shrine branch at, 208
Ōsaka Mainichi shinbun 大阪毎日新聞, 279n.15
Ōsaki Hachiman Jinja 大崎八幡神社, 289n.20
Ōsasahara Jinja Honden 大笹原神社本殿, relief wood carvings on, 159, *Figs. 98, 99*
Ōshū 奥州, 293n.9
Ōta Gyūichi 太田牛一: as Nobunaga's biographer, 232; on paintings at Azuchi Castle, 152; on Toyokuni Special Festival of 1604, 210
Ōtani Yoshitsugu 大谷吉継, 297n.4
Otogoze 乙コせ, 254
Otokoyama 男山. *See* Iwashimizu Hachimangū
Ōtsu 大津, 98, 99
Ōtsuzumi 大鼓, 214
Owari Ke Bon *Sunpu onbunbutsu*

ondōguchō 尾張家本「駿府御分物御道具帳」, 306n.74
Owari Province 尾張国, 98
Oze Hoan 小瀬甫庵, on Nobunaga's destruction of Enryakuji, 59

Painting, 113–17, 128–31, 150, 151–58, 265. *See also* Ensemble; Hasegawa (workshop); Kano Eitoku; Kano Hideyori; Kano Mitsunobu; Kano Naizen; Riguan; *Sights in and around the Capital*; Tsukubusuma Main Hall
Peng Lai 蓬莱, 54
Phoenix Hall. *See* Byōdōin
Pingshi Ruzhi 平石如砥, 290n.33
Portraiture, mortuary, 36, 128–31
Pure Land, 23, 110, 120–23, 126, 146, 176; Realm of Peace and Sustenance as, 123; represented in gold-leafed folding screens, 116–17
Putao 葡萄, 290n.25. *See also* Grapevine

Rakuchū rakugai zu 洛中洛外図. See *Sights in and around the Capital*
Rakuyō meisho shū 洛陽名所集, 302n.114
Realm of Peace and Sustenance, 123, 290n.31
Reii 霊異, 52
Rengee 蓮華会. *See* Lotus Festival on Chikubushima
Rengee tōyaku kadofumi roku 蓮華会頭役門文録, 303n.23
Rhus verniciflua, 167. *See also* Lacquer
Ri 里, 121, 232
Ridgepole placards, 225, 233; for Chikubushima buildings, 49–50, 197, 240–44, 266, *Fig. 138*; for Denpōdō of Hōryūji, 224–25; Gien and, 222–23, 225; for Golden Hall at Daigoji, 222–23; for Hōkōji, 225; placement of, 225, 301n.99
Riguan 日観: grape paintings by, 121–26, *Fig. 73*; Kano copy of painting by, 123, *Fig. 74*
Ritsu 律, 84
Rodrigues, João: on Japanese religion, 23–25; on Jurakutei, 71; on lacquer, 166–72; on painting, 151–52; on Toyokuni Special Festival of 1604, 220. *See also History of the Church of Japan, The*
Rokkaku 六角 (house), 58
Rōkō 労功, 217
Rokuhara Mitsuji 六波羅蜜寺, 72
Rokuon'in 鹿苑院, 98
Rokuon nichiroku 鹿苑日録, 279n.31; on Chikubushima, 54, 282n.74, 305n.52; on conflagration at Great Buddha Hall, Kyoto, 217; on ridgepole placard, 225; on Zenkōji Amida triad and Great Buddha Hall, Kyoto, 98–99
Rumor and hearsay, 59, 77, 88, 94, 99, 202, 216–18, 225, 226–28
Ryūgan 立願, 226

Sacred, the, 38, 50, 60, 85, 121, 202, 223, 269–72, 274; definition of, 24–25, 275n.2; in Momoyama period, 23–26, 228–29; and Momoyama visual arts, 24, 34–38, 110; and protection of Japan, 25, 52, 53, 61, 72, 73, 76, 77–79, 81, 84–85, 203, 206, 223, 226, 229, 242–43, 266, 271–72, 274
Sacred places, 32, 39–40, 50, 161, 220, 232, 238, 269, 272
Sagara 相良 (house), 88
Saichō 最澄, 53
Saidaiji 西大寺, 302n.4
Saiga 雑賀, 73
Sairei 祭礼. *See* Lotus Festival
Sakai 堺, 245; and earthquake of 1596, 94
Sakaki 榊, 209
Sanada Nobuyuki 真田信之, *tamaya* of, 113, 116, 121, *Figs. 65, 66*
Sanbōin 三宝院, 97, 100; garden of, 246, 250, *Figs. 140, 141*; Karamon of, 163, *Fig. 103*; referred to as *monzeki*, 250. *See also* Daigoji
Sanbōin monjo 三宝院文書, 301n.105
Sancai tuhui 三才図絵, 133
Sanjūsangendō 三十三間堂, 76, 77, 217
Sankei 参詣, 235
Sankyōin 三経院, 301n.95
Sannōin 山王院, relief wood carvings on, 158–59, *Figs. 96, 97*
Sanuki Province 讃岐国, 201
Satomura Jōha 里村紹巴, 222
Sefurisan 背振山, 56
Seiami 盛阿彌, 49
Seiami Yōzaemon 盛阿彌與左衛門, 279n.21
Seiitaishōgun 征夷大将軍, 200
Seiryōji 清涼寺, 222, 302n.7
Sekigahara, Battle of 関ケ原の戦, 40, 198, 199, 200, 202, 203, 207, 236, 239, 250; painting of, 220
Sengoku 戦国. *See* Warring States
Sen Hime 千姫, 199
Sen no Rikyū 千利休, 36, 254
Sensōe 千僧会, 83–85, 99; different Buddhist sects involved in, 84
Setsu 説, 52
Settsu Province 摂津国, 199, 201, 221
Seventh Avenue Atelier, 83
Shaka Nyorai 釈迦如来, and Chikubushima, 52, 53
Shao 韶, 189
Shengrong 聲容, 190
Shibata Katsuie 柴田勝家, 68, 200
Shichijō Bussho 七条仏所. *See* Seventh Avenue Atelier
Shiga County 志賀郡, 235
Shigi, Mount 信貴山. *See Miraculous Origins of Mount Shigi*
Shimazu 島津 (house), 58
Shinano Province 信濃国, 98, 99
Shinbutsu shūgō 神仏習合. *See* Shinto and Buddhism, amalgam of
Shinden 寝殿, 97
Shingon 真言, 57, 72, 73, 84, 86, 98
Shinji 神事. *See* Lotus Festival on Chikubushima
Shinobazu Pond 不忍池, 269–71, *Fig. 159*
Shinohara Kazutaka 篠原一孝, portrait of wife of, 131, *Fig. 77*
Shinryūin 神竜院, 287n.93
Shinto and Buddhism: amalgam of, 25, 40, 52, 275n.5; separation of, 42, 278n.9
Shirahige Jinja 白鬚神社, 245
Shishi 獅子, 108
Shitennō 四天王, 214
Shitennōji 四天王寺: Hideyori's restoration of, 221, 226; and Hideyoshi, 85
Shizuka 静, drum owned by, 64

Sho 疏, 52
Shōchū Gōka okibumi 正仲剛可置文, 281n.54
Shōgon 荘厳, 36, 53, 83, 150, 173, 196, 232, 263–66, 273
Shōka 松花, large tea jar named, 255, *Fig. 145*
Shōkōin 照光院, 250
Shōkokuji 相国寺, 72, 98, 222, 229
Shokuhō 織豊, 276n.9
Shōmei 匠明, 299n.46
Shōmu, Emperor 聖武天皇: and Chikubushima, 242, 243; and Tōdaiji, 77–79, 81, 83, 243, 252
Shonanoka 初七日, of Sutemaru, 133
Shōtoku Taishi 聖徳太子: and Hōryūji, 224–25; referred to as Daishō, 224; and Shitennōji, 226
Shōunji 祥雲寺, 100, 101, 133, 195; construction of, 88–92; depicted in Funaki screens, 32; as original site of Sutemaru's memorial structure in Kyoto, 141–42. *See also* Nanka Genkō; Toyotomi Sutemaru
Shun 舜, King, 189–90
Shunkyū ki 舜旧記, 287n.93. *See also* Bonshun
Sights in and around the Capital, 30, 219, 269; depiction of relief wood carvings in Funaki screens of, 161, *Fig. 100*; depiction of Shōunji/Chishakuin in Funaki screens of, 32, 90, 276n.14, *Fig. 45*; Funaki screens of, 30–32, *Figs. 26, 27, 45, 100*
Sōhei 僧兵, 57
Sōjiji 総持寺, 221
Sōken'in 総見院, 76
Sōkenji 總見寺, 60, 61, 233
Sugi 杉, 49
Sunpu 駿府. *See* Tokugawa Ieyasu
Sutoku, Emperor 崇徳天皇, 85
Sutra of Golden Light, 77–78; Benzaiten in, 232

Tabasami 手挟み, 159
Taian 待庵, 38, 231, *Fig. 32*
Taiheizan Tenshōji 太平山天正寺, 76
Taikō 太閤. *See* Toyotomi Hideyoshi
Taikōki 太閤記, on Great Buddha Hall, Kyoto, 82–83
Taira 平 (house), 50, 54, 79–80
Taira no Kiyomori 平清盛, 190
Taira no Tsunemasa 平経正, 54–55
Tairei 台霊. *See* Toyotomi Sutemaru
Taizōkai 胎蔵界, 302n.5
Takamakie 高蒔絵, 179–80. *See also Makie* lacquer
Takao 高雄. *See Maple Viewing at Mount Takao*
Takeda Shingen 武田信玄, 58; and Zenkōji, 98
Take no Benzaiten 嶽之弁才天, 233
Takeno Jōō 武野紹鴎, 253, 254
Tale of the Heike, 50, 217; Chikubushima in, 54–55, 236, 243; destruction of Tōdaiji in, 79–80
Tamaya 霊屋. *See* Architecture, mortuary
Tamon'in Eishun 多聞院英俊: on Hōkōji, 82; on Sutemaru, 86–88. *See also Tamon'in nikki*
Tamon'in nikki 多聞院日記, 285n.41. *See also* Tamon'in Eishun
Tanaka Yoshimasa 田中吉政, and Lotus Festival on Chikubushima, 236
Tanba Province 丹波国, 201
Tang 湯, King, 296n.64
Temple solicitation register, 56–57, 238, 278n.12
Tenbun Hokke Disturbance 天文法華の乱, 57–58
Tendai 天台, 53, 57, 83, 84, 98
Tengu 天狗, 214
Tenka fubu 天下布武, 63
Tenkai 天海, 270, 272
Tenka ichi 天下一, 145, 253
Tennōji 天王寺. *See* Shitennōji
Tennokawa 天川, 55, 233
Tennyo 天女. *See* Benzaiten
Tenshō 天正, 28, 76, 88
Tenshōji 天正寺, 75–76, 245
Tenzuiji 天瑞寺, 85, 89–90, 100
Toba, Emperor 鳥羽天皇, 85
Tōdaiji 東大寺, 72, 77–82, 243, 302n.4; and Sensōe, 84–85; and Tokugawa Ieyasu, 229
Tōdaiki 当代記: on Hideyori-sponsored religious construction, 226–27; on restoration of Great Buddha and Great Buddha Hall, Kyoto, 217–18; on restoration of Kuramadera building, 175; on rumors of Toyotomi economic ruin, 218, 227–28
Tōeizan 東叡山, 269
Tōfukuji 東福寺, 72, 76, 88
Tōji 東寺, 72, 85, 238, 302n.7; and earthquake of 1596, 92; restoration of, by Hideyori, 222; restoration of, promised by Kita no Mandokoro, 94; ridgepole placard for Golden Hall of, 225
Tōkaidō 東海道, 98
Tokitsugu Kyō ki 言継卿記, 280n.48. *See also* Yamashina Tokitsugu
Tokitsune Kyō ki 言経卿記, 284n.30. *See also* Yamashina Tokitsune
Toko 床, 294n.20
Tokugawa 徳川 (house), 31, 166, 197, 204, 220, 268, 273; ascent of, 198–202, 228; and Chikubushima, 239–40; and replication of Chikubushima in Edo, 269–72
Tokugawa Hidetada 徳川秀忠, 199, 240; as Seiitaishōgun, 200
Tokugawa Iemitsu 徳川家光, 240, 273
Tokugawa Ieyasu 徳川家康, 28, 68, 89, 94, 166, 199–202; and *chanoyu* objects, 253; and Chikubushima, 239–40, 245, 272, 304n.26; deification of, 61, 230, 272; and Hōgonji gate, 239, 245; and land rights, 239; referred to as Naifu, 239, 250; and religious construction, 229; and religious rituals, 203; and restoration of Great Buddha and Great Buddha Hall, Kyoto, 217, 227; and restoration of Tōdaiji, 229; and ridgepole placard for Hōkōji, 225; as Seiitaishōgun, 200; and Sunpu, 200, 229; and Toyokuni Shrine, 205, 208; and Toyokuni Special Festival of 1604, 220, 228; and Zenkōji Amida triad, 98. *See also* Tōshōgū
Tokugawa Yoshinao 徳川義直, 306n.74
Tokuzen'in Gon no Sōjō Gen'i 徳善院権僧正玄以. *See* Maeda Gen'i
Tonda Kyūzaemon 富田久左衛門, 236
Tōnin 頭人, 62, 235
Tonosama 殿様. *See* Oda Nobunaga
Toriawase 取合せ, 257

Tōshō Daigongen 東照大権現, 230, 272–73
Tōshōgū 東照宮, 166, 230, 272–73, *Fig. 158*. *See also* Nikkō
Toyokuni 豊国, 161
Toyokuni Daimyōjin 豊国大明神, 205, 206, 208, 214, 219, 227, 229
Toyokuni Festival, 208; Nō play *Chikubushima* performed at, 208, 236
Toyokuni Rinjisai 豊国臨時祭. *See* Toyokuni Special Festival of 1604
Toyokuni Rinjisairei 豊国臨時祭礼. *See* Toyokuni Special Festival of 1604
Toyokuni Shrine 豊国神社, 198, 209, 210, 216, 220, 236, 238; branches of, 207–8; creation of, 204–7; depicted in Funaki screens, 32, 161; depicted in painting of Toyokuni Special Festival of 1604, 211–14; dismantling of, 229–30; gates at, 163, 188, 217, 239, 245–46, 288n.7, 304n.38; Richard Cocks on, 206. *See also* Toyokuni Festival; Toyokuni Special Festival of 1604
Toyokuni Special Festival of 1604, 209–16; 228; interpretation of, 219–20; painting of, 210–11; painting of, by Kano Naizen, 211–16, 218–19, 219–20, *Figs. 131–36*; secondary literature on painting of, by Kano Naizen, 299n.58; Tokugawa and, 220. *See also* Toyokuni Shrine
Toyotomi 豊臣 (house), 26–30, 31, 33, 36, 42, 72, 99–100, 110, 202–4
Toyotomi (house), after Hideyoshi's death, 28, 166, 197; and Chikubushima, 75, 239, 240–44, 266; destruction of, 28, 31, 70, 89, 202, 208, 219, 225, 229, 267; domain and political authority of, 198–201, 297n.8; and Great Buddha Hall, Kyoto, 216–19; and religious ritual, 202–4; and rumors of economic ruin, 218, 227–28; and the sacred, 202–4, 228–29, 232; secondary literature on, and sponsorship of religious construction, 300nn.79, 80; and sponsorship of religious construction, 198, 203, 204–8, 216–19, 220–29, 240–45, 266; and Toyokuni Festivals, 208–20; and Toyokuni Shrine, 204–8. *See also* Toyotomi Hideyori; Yodudono
Toyotomi Ason Udaijin Hideyori Kō 豊臣朝臣右大臣秀頼公. *See* Toyotomi Hideyori
Toyotomi Hidetsugu 豊臣秀次, 246
Toyotomi Hideyori 豊臣秀頼, 28, 228, *Fig. 24*; birth of, 200, 246; and calligraphy, 206, *Fig. 130*; and Emperor Shōmu, 243; as Hideyoshi's heir, 199–200, 206, 223, 225; as *kanpaku*, 201; and motivations behind religious construction, 226, 252; as Naidaijin, 200, 242; pact made to, by senior Hideyoshi vassals, 99, 198, 199; as patron of Chikubushima, 240–44; as patron of religious construction, 189, 197, 204, 220–27, 266; as patron of religious sites near Chikubushima, 244–45; and promised construction of Sutra Hall on Chikubushima, 240; referred to as Kōmon Denka, 222; referred to as Toyotomi Ason Udaijin Hideyori Kō, 224; referred to as Udaijin Toyotomi Ason Hideyori Kō, 189; and restoration of Daigoji, 222–23, 246; and restoration of Hōryūji, 224–25; and restoration of Ise, 223–24; and restoration of Shitennōji, 226; and rumors of survival after 1615, 202; and Shōtoku Taishi, 224–25, 243; and Toyokuni Shrine, 205, 208; and Toyokuni Shrine gate, 239; and Toyokuni Special Festival of 1604, 209; and visit to Daigoji with Hideyoshi, 96. *See also* Toyotomi (house), after Hideyoshi's death; Yodudono
Toyotomi Hideyoshi 豊臣秀吉, 26, 110, 111, *Fig. 22*; and Benzaiten, 233; and blossom viewing at Daigoji, 94–97, 250; and *chanoyu*, 36, 69–70, 253–57; and Chikubushima, 42, 61–63, 65–67, 73–75, 232, 244, 272; and construction of Great Buddha and Great Buddha Hall, Kyoto, 49, 76–77, 82–83, 217; cult of, 223; and Daigoji, 94–97, 163, 196; deification of, 36, 61, 73, 204–6, 228; and Emperor Shōmu, 81–82, 243; final illness and death of, 99–100, 198, 199; and invasions of Korea and China, 69, 76, 88, 157–58; and Jurakutei, 70–71, 101, 150, 246; as *kanpaku*, 68, 201; lacquered saddle owned by, 173, 180, *Figs. 109, 110*; and Nagahama, 66, 67, 68, 74, 244; and pact by his senior vassals, 99, 198, 199; and policies towards religious establishments, 73; portraits of, attributed to Kano Mitsunobu, 294n.27; and possibility of children in Nagahama, 285–86n.62; and rebuilding of Kyoto, 69–72, 92, 94–100, 101, 204; receiving of Emperor Goyōzei by, 71, 302n.108; referred to as Chikushū, 65–67; referred to as Daishōkoku Denka, 222; referred to as Denka, 88; referred to as Hashiba Chikuzen, 232; referred to as Kanpaku Dono, 87; referred to as Kanpaku Sashōfu, 88; referred to as Kinoshita Tōkichirō Hideyoshi, 61; referred to as Taikō, 217, 220, 227, 250; and religious construction, 33, 72, 75–77, 85, 100, 141–42, 145, 222; and religious ritual, 72, 83–88, 142; and restoration of Great Buddha and Great Buddha Hall, 98–100; and the sacred, 72–73, 75, 76, 223; secondary literature on deification of, 298n.28; and Sutemaru, 86–92, 128, 133, 141–42; and Tōdaiji, 81–82; and Yoshino, 222; and Zenkōji Amida triad, 98–100. *See also* Osaka Castle; Tenshōji; Toyokuni Daimyōjin; Toyokuni Festival; Toyokuni Shrine; Toyokuni Special Festival of 1604; Yodudono
Toyotomi Sutemaru 豊臣棄丸, 28, 32, 33, 128, 200, *Fig. 23*; armor associated with, 139–40, *Figs. 87, 88*; birth and death of, 86–88, 133; and Chikubushima, 86–87; and crane and pine motif, 136–40; eulogies written for, 133–34; and *fuyō*, 133–36; and nickname Tsurumatsu, 140; referred to as Tairei, 88; referred to as Wakagimi, 86; rituals in response to illness of, 86–88. *See also* Nanka Genkō; Shōunji; Tsukubusuma Main Hall

Tsuda Sōgyū 津田宗及, 306n.75
Tsugawa Jinja 積川神社, 221
Tsukubusuma Jinja 都久夫須麻神社, 274; origin of name, 42–43
Tsukubusuma Jinja Honden 都久夫須麻神社本殿, 32–33, 42. *See also* Tsukubusuma Main Hall
Tsukubusuma Main Hall (also referred to as Tsukubusuma Jinja Honden), 75, *Figs. 2–21, 34–41, 49–61, 67–72, 75, 80–86, 104, 105, 114, 115, 117–19, 122–28, 147–54*; as composite architecture, 33, 43–50, 231; conservation of, in 1936–1937, 46–50, 102–7, 257–60, 266; designation of, as National Treasure, 276–77n.17; as seemingly typical example of Buddhist architecture, 43; transformation of, from Buddhist to Shinto building in 1871, 42–43, 265, 266. *See also* Chikubushima
—*Formerly* Benzaiten Hall on Chikubushima, 32–33, 75, 202, 235; as composite architecture, 33, 43, 197, 231, 257–66; configuration of, 101–3, 106–7, 257–66; decoration of, 38, 107, 260–66; *hisashi* of, 33, 43–50; iconography of, 263–66; *moya* of, 33, 43–50; rebuilding of, after fire in 1558, 49; referred to as Benzaitensha, 42; referred to as Goten, 62; ridgepole placards for, 49–50, 197, 240–44, 266, *Fig. 138*
—*Formerly, in part*, building in Kyoto (also referred to as *moya*): architectural coloring on, 108; art historians and study of, 142; as building moved from Kyoto, 33, 49–50, 100, 101–7; configuration of, 102, 104–7; decoration of, 108; as ensemble, 33, 108; iconography of chrysanthemum in, 128–31; iconography of chrysanthemum and paulownia crests in, 110–11, 128; iconography of coffered ceiling of, 120–21; iconography of crane-and-pine motif in, 136–40; iconography of exterior of, 126–40; iconography of *fuyō* in, 131–36; iconography of grapevine in, 121–26; iconography of interior of, 110–21; iconography of phoenix and paulownia in, 289n.18; *makie* lacquer on, 49, 108, 120, 121, 141, 142; metalwork on, 108; paintings in, 107, 108, 117–21, 128, 135; reconfiguration of crane-and-pine motif in, 136–39; relief wood carvings on, 108, 126, 128, 131–33, 135, 141; secondary literature on lacquer and paintings in, 292n.69; Shōunji as original Kyoto location of, 141–42
—*Formerly, in part*, building in Kyoto (identified as Sutemaru's memorial structure), 33, 141–42, 143; architectural coloring on, 150, 194, 195, 196; construction of, 246; as ensemble, 150, 190–96, 197; iconographic changes of, with move to Chikubushima, 263–66; *makie* lacquer on, 150, 166, 176–82, 184–88, 194–96; metalwork on, 150, 195; move of, to Chikubushima, 197, 231; paintings in, 150, 153–58, 191–96; paintings in, attributed to Kano Mitsunobu, 154–58; pictorial space in, 191–96; relief wood carvings on, 150, 164–66, 191–96
Tsurugaoka Hachimangū 鶴岡八幡宮, sword sheaths at, 183, *Fig. 120*
Tsurumatsu 鶴松: crane-and-pine motif, 136–40; as nickname of Sutemaru, 140
Tsuzumi 鼓, 214

Uda, Emperor 宇多天皇, 53
Udaijin Toyotomi Ason Hideyori Kō 右大臣豊臣朝臣秀頼公. *See* Toyotomi Hideyori
Uesugi Kenshin 上杉謙信, 58
Uga Benzaiten 宇賀辯才天, 233, 235, 243
Ugajin 宇賀神, 233
Uji Bridge 宇治橋. *See* Ise Shrine
Urushi 漆, 166, 167, 259n.39. *See also* Lacquer; *Makie* lacquer
Uruxar, 166–67

Vairocana Buddha, 24, 78, 80
Valignano, Alessandro, 144–45, 257, 276n.13
Vermilion-seal document, 64, 73, 74, 75, 95, 240
Vilela, Gaspar, 284n.24, 293n.12
Vocabvlario da Lingoa de Iapam, 24, 36, 134, 257, 290n.31, 290n.34, 295n.39

Wakagimi 若君. *See* Toyotomi Sutemaru
Wakakusadera 若草寺, 224
Wakishōji 脇障子, 159
Wang Qi 王圻, 133
Warring States, 58, 61, 63, 72
Wood carvings, relief, 108, 113, 146, 150, 158–66, 196, 221, 263–65. *See also* Ensemble; Tsukubusuma Main Hall
Wu 武, King, 189–90

Xutang Zhiyu 虚堂智愚, 255

Yakata 館, 189
Yakushi 薬師, 53, 86
Yamagami Morishita 山神森下, Daigoji tea house at, 250, 252
Yamanoue no Sōji 山上宗二, 306n.75
Yamanoue no Sōji ki 山上宗二記, 145, 253, 254, 282n.86, 293n.3
Yamashina Tokitsugu 山科言継: on Nobunaga's destruction of Enryakuji, 59. *See also Tokitsugu Kyō ki*
Yamashina Tokitsune 山科言経: on conflagration at Great Buddha Hall, Kyoto, 217; on earthquake of 1596, 92; and painting of Benzaiten and Fifteen Attendants, 233; and *Tale of the Heike*, 80; on Toyokuni Special Festival of 1604, 210; on Zenkōji Amida triad, 98. *See also Tokitsune Kyō ki*
Yamashiro Province 山城国, 201
Yamato Province 大和国, 201, 224
Yao 堯, 296n.64
Yasaka Jinja 八坂神社, 229
Yatsumune zukuri 八棟作, Toyokuni Shrine as, 204
Yodo Castle 淀城, 86
Yododono 淀殿, 28, 86, 203, 209, 228, *Fig. 25*; biography of, 200; and Chikubushima, 244; and Toyokuni Shrine, 205, 208; and Toyotomi religious construction, 223–24, 226–27, 301n.106. *See also* Toyotomi Hideyori; Toyotomi (house), after Hideyoshi's death
Yōmeimon 陽明門, 273
Yoshida Kanemi 吉田兼見: on Great Buddha, 76; on Sute-

Yoshida Kanemi *(continued)*
maru, 86, 88; and Toyokuni Shrine, 205, 211
Yoshida Nagayoshi 吉田良義, 211
Yoshida Shrine 吉田神社, 203, 230
Yoshino 吉野: restoration projects at, by Hideyoshi and Hideyori, 222; as site of Benzaiten worship, 55
Yoshino mōde 吉野詣, 222
Yoshizō 吉藏, 279n.21
Yudate no shinji 湯立の神事, 209
Yuigon 遺言, 205

Zaō Gongen 蔵王権現, 222
Zashiki 座敷, 153
Zen 禅, 72, 84, 89, 90, 116, 128; and grapes, 121–23
Zenkōji 善光寺, Amida triad of, 98–100, 198
Zenkōji Nyorai 善光寺如来. *See* Zenkōji, Amida triad of
Zhou 紂, [Tyrant], 296n.64
Zhu Xi 朱熹, 189–90
Zōgyoku wakashū 蔵玉和歌集, 290n.34
Zushi 厨子, 175, 257, 259, 265